The System of Antichrist:

Truth & Falsehood
in Postmodernism
and the New Age

CHARLES UPTON

THE SYSTEM
OF ANTICHRIST

TRUTH & FALSEHOOD
IN POSTMODERNISM
AND THE NEW AGE

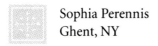

Sophia Perennis
Ghent, NY

First published in the USA
by Sophia Perennis, Ghent, NY 2001
Series editor: James R. Wetmore
© copyright 2001

For information, address:
Sophia Perennis, 343 Rte 21C
Ghent NY 12075
Printed in the United States of America

Library of Congress Cataloging-in-Publication Data

Upton, Charles, 1948–
The system of Antichrist : truth and falsehood in postmodernism and
the New Age / Charles Upton

p.   cm.
Includes index
ISBN 0 900588 30 6 (pbk : alk. paper)
ISBN 0 900588 38 1 (cloth : alk. paper)
1. New Age movement. 2. Tradition (Philosophy). 3.
Antichrist—Miscellanea. 4. Postmodernism—Religious aspects. I. Title
BP605.N48 U68 2001
299'.93—dc21   2001000394

By the same author:

Hammering Hot Iron: A Spiritual Critique of Bly's Iron John
Doorkeepers of the Heart: Versions of Rabi'a
The Wars of Love (in press)

Contents

Nasir [Sherif of Medina] *rolled over on his back, with my glasses, and begin to study the stars, counting aloud first one group and then another; crying out with surprise at discovering little lights not noticed by his unaided eye. Auda set us on to talk of telescopes — of the great ones — and of how man in three hundred years had so far advanced from his first essay that now he built glasses as long as a tent, through which he counted thousands of unknown stars. We slipped into talk of suns beyond suns, sizes and distances beyond wit. 'What will now happen with this knowledge?' asked Mohammed. 'We shall set to, and many learned and some clever men together will make glasses as more powerful than ours, as ours than Galileo's; and yet more hundreds of astronomers will distinguish and reckon yet more thousands of now unseen stars, mapping them, and giving each one its name. When we see them all, there will be no night in heaven.' 'Why are the Westerners always wanting all?' provokingly said Auda. 'Behind our few stars we can see God, who is not behind your millions.' 'We want the world's end, Auda.' 'But that is God's,' complained Zaal. . . .*

〜 T. E. Lawrence, from *Seven Pillars of Wisdom*

A body of my people will not cease to fight for the truth until the coming forth of the Antichris . . . but God will slay him at the hand of Jesus, who will show them his blood upon the lance.

〜 Hadith

Preface

IN THIS BOOK I WILL ESSAY TEN THINGS:

✳ To take soundings in the present religious and cultural scene from the standpoint of traditional metaphysics.

✳ To introduce to a wider reading public the doctrines of the 'Traditionalist School': René Guénon, Ananda Coomaraswamy, Frithjof Schuon, Martin Lings, Titus Burckhardt, Seyyed Hossein Nasr, Huston Smith et. al., and in the process give the reader a glimpse into the city of Traditionalism, and the field of spiritual battle presently surrounding it.

✳ On the basis of traditional metaphysics, to critique the doctrines of the New Age spiritualities within the context of postmodernism, of which they are one expression.

✳ To demonstrate, in the course of this critique, that metaphysics, mysticism and esoterism are fundamentally different from, and often radically opposed to, magical practices, the pursuit of psychic powers, and the channeling of 'spirit entities'.

✳ To demonstrate to my Christian friends that they are not the only ones who see in Neo-Paganism and the New Age a decline in our culture's understanding of both God and man.

✳ To present lore and prophecy relating to the 'latter days' of the present cycle from the standpoint of comparative religion, drawing upon relevant doctrines from Buddhism, Hinduism, Judaism, Christianity, Islam, Zoroastrianism and the Native Americans.

✳ To publish the signs and speculate upon the social, psychic and spiritual nature of that being known to Christianity, Judaism and Islam as the Antichrist; to present him as both an individual and a system; to warn those willing to be warned against the spiritual seduction and terror he represents, and against the regime which will be—and is—the social expression of that seduction and that terror.

✳ To trace the roots of Antichrist in the forgetful and/or fallen nature of man.

✳ To begin to define the particular quality of spirituality proper to apocalyptic times, the dangers it faces, the unique opportunities open to it.

✳ To trace my own course from the 'spiritual revolution' of the 1960s, through the world of the New Age spiritualities, to the threshold of traditional esoterism and metaphysics.

If I mean to hit these ten targets, I cannot make conformity with contemporary belief-systems my central aim, since it is my intent precisely to criticize these belief-systems. I can write neither as a modernist-materialist, whose unifying paradigm is history, nor as a postmodern juggler of alternate realities, who claims to need no such paradigm. The point from which I hope to write, subject to my limitations, is the *sophia perennis*, the Always So.

The modernist-materialist worldview, according to which historical dynamics and supernatural interventions cannot both be credited as explanations for the daily news, still has power. And postmodernism, now clearly the dominant view, while it may be closer to validating both these realities, only admits them as closed worlds of meaning united by no 'overarching paradigm'. Consequently I have been forced—not against my will, but rather in line with my delight—to return to traditional metaphysics (which, though profoundly consistent, cannot be a closed system since it opens on the Infinite) as the only worldview which can make unified sense of postmodern experience, as postmodern ideology clearly and admittedly cannot. Sometimes I write as a scholar, sometimes as a speculative 'theosopher', sometimes as a popularizer of basic metaphysical principles for the general reader, sometimes as a social critic, sometimes as an autobiographer, sometimes as a poet. I cross these forbidden borders deliberately. So shrunken and fragmented is the consciousness of 'latter day' humanity—partly as an automatic reflection of the quality of the time, partly as the result of a deliberate program of mass social hypnosis—that only the stress of the encounter with a socially-prohibited breadth and depth of significance can shake it awake, now that repeated shocks, and the subsequent anaesthesia, have beaten it senseless. The specific medicine for the shock of despair is the deeper shock of meaning. Where time and history have crushed us under their 'unbearable lightness', nothing but the weight of eternity, breaking through the thin, brittle shell of the postmodern sky, can set us on our feet. This is one of the several meanings of the word 'apocalypse'.

Introduction

At the beginning of the third millennium, the human race is in the process of forgetting what it means to be human. We don't know who or what we are; we don't know what we are supposed to be doing here, in a cosmos rapidly becoming nothing to us but a screen for the projection of random and increasingly demonic fantasies. Human life is no longer felt to be valuable in the face of eternity simply because it is a creation of God, nor is it as easy as it once was for us to see the human enterprise as worth something because of our collective achievements or the historical momentum which produced them, since without a scale of values rooted in eternity, achievement cannot be measured, and without an eternal goal toward which time is necessarily tending (in the spiritual not the material sense, given that eternity cannot lie at the end of an accelerating linear momentum which is precisely a flight from all that is eternal), history is a road leading nowhere. The name we've given to this state of affairs is 'postmodernism'.

We all, somehow, know this. We feel it in our bones. But we can't encompass it; we can't define the scale of what we face or what we've lost, because we no longer possess the true scale of what we are. We assume the name postmodern, but it would be closer to the truth to say that we are *posthuman*—not in essence, but in effect, since any concept of human nature adequate to the human essence has been discarded as *passé*.

Humanism is not enough to tell us what it is to be human. Science is even less capable of shouldering this burden, which is why it has mostly given up trying. Only religion, understood in its deepest sense, can ask this question and answer it. And only a thorough understanding of the social and psychic forces that hide the face of the Absolute and Infinite Reality we call 'God' can show us the true scale of what menaces the human form in these 'latter days', when the present cycle of biological and human time is drawing to a close. If the name 'God' denotes the eternal truth of things, and the name 'Man' the central mirror of this Truth in terrestrial space and time, then the name of those forces of obscurity and denial which are opposed to 'Man', in their fully revealed and terminal form, is 'Antichrist'.

✳ The Latter Days

It is common nowadays for many to imagine that the universe, in line with progressive and evolutionary ideas, must somehow be advancing spiritually. If we come to the conclusion that the spiritual evolution of the macrocosm is not possible, we may even wonder what is the worth or profit in material existence. What good is it? What is it for? For fear of becoming 'Gnostics' who deny the value of terrestrial life, we end by denying the *eternal* significance of this very life.

The problem with the concept that the universe evolves to higher levels of organization, which is basic to the doctrines of Teilhard de Chardin, Rudolf Steiner, and many other New Age teachers (as well as to the attempt within Judaism to apply Lurianic Kabbalah—and within Ismailism, the idea of a mass 'unveiling' of spiritual realities—to historical evolution) is the Second Law of Thermodynamics. This law states that, via entropy, the overall order of matter/energy in the universe is always decreasing, a decrease which is inseparable in principle from the expansion of the universe, starting at the Big Bang. At one point scientists posited the existence of large amounts of 'dark matter' which would allow the universe to contract again, via gravitation, after the momentum of the Big Bang is spent. As of this writing, however, scientific opinion is tending away from this hypothesis. So it would seem that the material universe must continue expanding, and its disorder increasing, forever.

This is strictly in line with traditional metaphysics. 'This whole world is on fire,' said the Buddha. 'All is perishing,' says the Koran, 'except His Face.' Creation, in the traditional view, is a successive 'stepping down' of higher orders of reality to lower ones. God, who in His Essence is totally beyond form, number, matter, energy, space and time, must—as Frithjof Schuon never tired of pointing out—'overflow' into these dimensions of existence because He is Infinite; no barrier exists in His Nature which would prevent the radiation of His superabundant Being.

Traditional eschatologies, by and large, are in line with the Second Law of Thermodynamics. In the place of progress—a myth no older than, perhaps, the 17th century, at least in its present form—they posit a spiritual, social and cultural 'entropy'. This is certainly true of Hinduism and classical Greco-Roman mythology, with their idea that a given cycle of manifestation emerges fully formed from the Creator in the form of a Golden Age, to be succeeded by a Silver Age, a Bronze Age, and finally by the present Iron Age, which ends in an eschatological cataclysm, a Purification Day, after which the Golden Age of the next cycle commences. This scheme is more or less accepted, through different mythological languages, by traditional Jews, Christians and Hindus, and even Lakota (Sioux) Indians, and other 'primal' peoples. (The Buddhists, though their doctrine of cycles tends to deny the possibility of an abrupt renewal, also accepts that the present era will end in cataclysm.) Those doctrines within traditional revealed religions which seem to speak of the spiritual progress of the manifest world itself, such as the concept in Lurianic Kabbalah of the *tikkun* or universal restoration, are either a mis-application of the lore of individual spiritual development to collective history, usually in line with 18th century Enlightenment ideas of progress and their Renaissance precursors; or of the doctrine that God continually creates and holds in existence this manifest world, and may therefore give an individual, religious dispensation or particular nation a special role in renewing the Divine Image for a given human time and place, within the larger context of overall spiritual degeneration; or of the eschatological return of all manifestation to God at the 'end of time'. Whatever is created must leave the House of the Creator in order to come into existence; whatever has emerged into cosmic manifestation has already begun to die.

Believers periodically predict the final (though temporary) triumph of evil in the latter days, the end of the world and the coming of the Messiah. Non-believers routinely scoff when such predictions seemingly fail to materialize. They will have the opportunity to continue scoffing until the world really does end, after which neither believers nor non-believers will, in worldly terms at least, have either the opportunity or the impulse to say 'I told you so.' At that ultimate moment of truth they will find themselves face-to-face with a Reality so profound, so rigorously demanding, that their opinions—right or wrong—along with all the psychological reasons they had for holding them, will dwindle into insignificance. Only their essential motive for holding to Truth or sinking into error will remain to them, as the sign of their eternal destiny before the face of God.

Non-believers say, 'some people in every generation have always thought they were living through the darkest times in history; all this whining about the degeneration of humanity in the "latter days" is nothing new.' And believers, at least traditional believers, agree with them. According to a *hadith* of the Prophet Muhammad (peace and blessings be upon him), 'no generation will come upon you that is not followed by a worse.' The course of history is not uniformly downward, in the traditional view—there are peaks and troughs, religious revivals, 'redresses', partial renewals of a given spiritual tradition leading to small and short-lived 'golden ages', heroic struggles of succeeding generations to cut their losses and re-stabilize society on lower levels, delirious renaissances based on the sudden impulse to squander the cultural and spiritual capital inherited from earlier ages—but the basic drift is always away from order and in the direction of chaos. The ability of the race to see, understand, draw its life from, and base its social and cultural forms on higher spiritual realities inevitably diminishes; as it speeds ever farther from the spiritual Sun, the light of Truth fades into the surrounding darkness; and the warmth of Life fades along with it. The final result of this inevitable process is the end of a particular world or world-age. This world may never end according to the time-table of those simple-minded people who take eschatological predictions literally, but it will have to end some time. And given that we presently have more ways at our disposal than ever before in human history of bringing this world to an end in concrete terms, through nuclear or chemical or biological warfare, or environmental degradation—or the deconstruction of the human form itself through a genetic engineering driven by blind economic forces, by the whims emotionally imbalanced or demonically inspired fools, and certainly by primal human fear and desire untempered by even the shadow of wisdom—a meditation on the End Times is timely, to say the least.

And, in sober fact, it is always timely. Every day a new generation passes into oblivion. It is always the worst of times: one day farther from the Garden of Eden, when the world, fresh from the Creator's hand, was young— and always the best of times: one day nearer to the inevitable Moment when contingency and illusion must crumble, and Absolute Reality dawn, definitively, upon this dying world, this moving image of Eternity.

✳ The Antichrist

The spiritual degeneration of humanity cannot go on forever; it must reach a terminal point, beyond which the human form itself, at least in its earthly incarnation, could not survive. And in line with the principle of *corruptio optimi pessima*—'the corruption of the best is the worst'—the nadir of human spiritual receptivity must, according to the doctrine of many spiritual traditions, manifest not simply as the disappearance of spirituality, but as the satanic counterfeit of it. This is the origin of the myth of the Antichrist, which few in the West realize is as important in Islam as it is to Christianity, given that Muslims believe that the prophet Jesus will return to earth at the end of the age to give battle to that Adversary, and slay him in battle.

Just as the ego is the shadow of the Divine Self within us, so the Antichrist is the shadow of the Messiah, of the eschatological savior who represents the complete unveiling of the Divine Self at the end of this cycle. The ego will often reach a climax of despair, delusion and violence just when a spiritual breakthrough is imminent; in the same way the Antichrist will gather to himself all the social and psychic forces which have willed to resist God at the very moment the Face of the Absolute is about to dawn upon the world. The words of Meister Eckhart might well have been said of the Antichrist, as they were most certainly said of the human ego: 'The more he blasphemes, the more he praises God.'

✳ The Messiah

Throughout history, religions which look for a Messiah have always tended to concretize him. This or that Mahdi rises within Islam, only to be either co-opted or defeated. Sabbatai Zevi, the false Messiah, profoundly moves the whole Jewish world in the 17th century, and then converts, under threat of death by the Turkish Sultan, to Islam. And Christianity is certainly not without its false Christs and false prophets. So who is the real Messiah? How can we recognize him?

The real Messiah is eternally arriving in this world, eternally shattering its spatio-temporal dimensions, and eternally drawing his followers into the fellowship of His kingdom. To the degree that 'false' messiahs are receptive to this truth, they are actually in some sense partial messiahs, imperfect reflections of the Messiah himself. But to the degree that they identify with their messianic role on the level of the ego, thereby pandering to the collective ego of their followers — and they always do — they are antichrists. Humanity, sunk in materialism, cannot be awakened from 'the nightmare of history' without some form of historical hope. Yet this hope is always dashed. The revolution is co-opted. The renaissance fades. The spiritual renewal inevitably becomes food for the literalization of the doctrine and hardening of social and cultural lines. The Spirit is always giving life; the letter is always dragging that life into the tomb of contingency, into time and history. Those who, responding to messianic hope, pass from the turmoil of time to the vision of Eternity, have met the real Messiah. Those who fail to break their pact with time, either because they hope for something from fate and contingency, or foolishly believe they can manipulate them for their own ends, have fallen into the snare of the Antichrist.

So when will the real Messiah come? The answer is always two-fold: he will come Now; he will come at the End. If we stand in the Now, we stand in wait for him; if we fail to occupy the Now, we will miss him when he comes. We have already missed him, times without number. But when Now and the End come together—the end of this ego, the end of this world—then we are standing in the presence of the Messiah.

History is always carrying us away from the day of the messianic advent, the door of the Now—and yet history must end some day; this endless departure must, in one mysterious moment, be changed into an arrival. What we receive in the secrecy of our hearts and what dawns on the 'horizons' of outer reality, must one day come together. In the words of the Koran, 'I will show them My signs on the horizons and in themselves, until they know that it is the Truth. Is this not enough for you, since I am over all things the Witness?'

✴ The Prophecy of René Guénon

My basic approach to the material presented in this book is that of traditional metaphysics, as presented by the writers of the Traditionalist School. For 'pure' metaphysics I have mostly followed Frithjof Schuon. For eschatology itself—the science of the 'last things'—I have relied on Martin Lings, particularly his book *The Eleventh Hour*, and even more so on the founder of the Traditionalists, René Guénon, whose prophetic masterpiece, *The Reign of Quantity and the Signs of the Times*, first published in 1945, grows more relevant with every passing year. But though it was the Traditionalists who pointed me in the direction of the scriptures of the world religions, the writings of the great sages and the legends of the primal peoples, I have not strictly limited myself in every case to their doctrines or perspectives, but have in many cases consulted the primary documents themselves. To paraphrase Blake, I have looked through their eyes, not with them.

In *The Reign of Quantity*, Guénon saw history in terms of the Hindu concept of the *manvantara*, the cycle of manifestation composed of Golden, Silver, Bronze, and Iron ages. He saw this cycle as an inevitable descent from the pole of Essence, or *forma*,—the Hindu *Purusha*—toward the pole of Substance, or *materia*—the Hindu *Prakriti*. Essence is qualitative, while actually lying above quality. Substance is quantitative, while in reality situated below quantity.

As the cycle progresses, or rather descends, the very nature of time and space changes. In earlier ages, space dominates; the forms of things are more important, more real, than the changes they undergo; time is 'relatively eternal'. As the cycle moves on, however, time begins to take over, melting down space and the forms within it until everything is an accelerating flow of change.

Maybe we can better understand what Guénon was talking about if we notice that when we are a state of deep calm, space is more real than time; when we are agitated, time becomes more real than space. And it shouldn't be too hard to see how faster modes of travel, and especially the electronic media, which disturb and agitate consciousness, also annihilate space; cyberspace, in particular, is the annihilation of all spacial dimension. In these latter days, nothing has a stable form. Everything moves faster and faster, until all form—including the Human Form itself—becomes a shapeless blur.

But this constant acceleration of time can't go on forever. At one point it will have to stop. 'Time the devourer,' quotes Guénon, 'ends by devouring itself.' At the end of time, time will instantaneously be changed into space again. This ultimate, timeless point is simultaneously the end of this cycle of manifestation and the beginning of the 'next'.

But before this ultimate transformation, in the latter days of the present cycle, certain final developments must take place. Since quantity has particularly to do with matter, the 'reign of quantity' must also be the reign of materialism—and where materialistic ideas dominate, the very cosmic environment becomes in a sense more material. The 'age of miracles' ceases; the world becomes less permeable to the influences of higher planes of reality; the very belief in such planes, as well as in an eternal and transcendent God, becomes harder to maintain.

The very heaviness of materialism, however, ultimately results in a sort of 'brittleness'. The cosmic environment, having lost much of the flexibility which allowed it to be moved by the Divine Spirit, begins to crack, like an old tree that can no longer bend to the wind, and ends by being uprooted in the storm. But these cracks in the cosmic environment, in the 'Great Wall' separating the material world from the realm of subtle energies, first happen in the 'downward' rather than the 'upward' direction, letting in a flood of 'infra-psychic' forces, either neutral or actively demonic. In the general 'volatilization' of the sense-world produced by the electronic media and our 'information culture', perhaps also by the prevalence of electromagnetic pollution and the release of nuclear energy; by the contemporary interest in psychedelic drugs, magic and psychic powers; and most obviously by what we've come to call the 'UFO phenomenon' which has had an incalculable effect upon our common view of reality, we can see the direct effects of these forces on the quality of our consciousness, the structure of our society, our cultural forms and our economic priorities.

Nor do these infra-psychic forces operate alone. Cultural trends develop around the infra-psychic *zeitgeist*, and within the context of these trends, organized groups grow up in response to the forces which have brought them into being. In some cases these groups are simply made up of people who espouse the modernist or postmodernist myths determined by the 'spirit of the times'. Other groups, however, will openly worship the forces which have inspired them, not understanding that they have in fact taken a stand against the perennial wisdom, the metaphysical truths of the ages. These Guénon terms 'anti-traditional' or 'pseudo-initiatic'. Most New Age organizations would fall under this definition. And lastly, there are other groups whose goal is to deliberately undermine revealed religion and traditional metaphysics, so as to bring in the reign of the Antichrist; these, in Guénon's terms, are the agents of 'counter-tradition' and the 'counter-initiation'; they are 'Satan's contemplatives', whose role is to subvert, not simply exoteric religion, but esoteric spirituality as well.

However depressing this may sound, the truth is that such developments are entirely lawful, given the lateness of the hour. The lowest possibilities of manifestation must also have their day in the course of the cycle; fortunately, since they are inherently unstable, being based not upon Truth but solely upon power, that day will be short. 'There needs be evil,' said Jesus, 'but woe to him through whom evil comes.' And there are certain spiritual possibilities of the highest order which could never be realized except in the face of this most demonic of challenges to the integrity of the human spirit.

✳ My Worthy Opponents

In this book I will try, among other things, to expose the errors of postmodernism by criticizing some of the central doctrines of what has come to be called 'New Age spirituality', the contemporary name for a strand of extra-Christian and sometimes anti-Christian occultism which can be traced back at least as far as the Renaissance. If postmodernism is the ultimate philosophical denial of metaphysics, then an analysis of the false metaphysics of the New Age is one avenue by which postmodernism can be critiqued—not necessarily the best one, but without doubt the one I am best fitted to pursue, given my background.

Let me make four things clear before I go any further: First, the world of New Age spiritualities is not in itself the system of Antichrist. Every spirituality on Earth will ultimately contribute something to that regime—the false spiritualities by their very existence, the true ones according to the principle of *corruptio optimi pessima*, 'the worst is the corruption of the best'. This is why the Muslims, for example, believe that the Antichrist will be Muslim, and the Orthodox Christians that he will arise within Eastern Orthodoxy.

Second, not everyone involved with New Age spiritualities is necessarily a lost soul. For all I know, some may even be saints—but God knows best. Despite the commercialism of the New Age, many of its practitioners are sincere. And since the Spirit of God 'bloweth where it listeth,' some are necessarily on the long and thorny road to the fullness of divine Truth, though I would never direct a traveler to Truth via that particular road. This is not to say that sincerity is enough to protect a person from being intellectually and spiritually damaged by doctrines which are objectively false, only that the sincere person is capable of repenting of his or her error in the face of doctrines which are objectively true, while the hypocrite cannot.

Third, I do not mean to father the errors of every New Age teacher or postmodern ideologue I criticize on all the others. Most of my adversaries deplore many of the same modern evils that I do. I am not implying that they are all parts of some vast and unified conspiracy. I only take them as signposts on the many separate tributaries flowing into the center of the contemporary darkness.

Fourth, not all New Age practices are necessarily destructive. Some of them, particularly various forms of holistic healing, are only good. I myself have gotten real benefit from them.

Having said this, however, I need to make it crystal clear that, in my educated opinion, the general motion of New Age belief is toward an extremely sinister and dangerous point of the compass. Furthermore, I will take it as axiomatic in this book that whenever New Age doctrine contradicts what has come to be called the 'perennial philosophy', those core metaphysical principles which are shared by all the world's major religions and wisdom-traditions, then it is the New Age, not the wisdom of the ages, which is in error.

✳ My History

I was raised a Catholic—a more or less traditional one, since most of my Catholic life, until I was about sixteen years old, was lived in an essentially pre-Vatican II Church. I like to say that I am of the last Catholic generation (the Baby Boomers) who could fully identify with James Joyce's *A Portrait of the Artist as a Young Man*. As a member of the Baby Boom living in the San Francisco Bay Area, I passed through hippydom, protested the Vietnam War—I was present on street level at the Chicago Democratic Convention in 1968—experimented with psychedelic drugs, felt an attraction to Hinduism and Buddhism, and went through a largely self-taught flirtation with shamanism and kundalini yoga. I was also a poet (secretly I still am) and a protégé of Beat Generation poet Lew Welch, who introduced me to my first real Sufi initiate, Samuel Lewis (known affectionately, in hippy style, as Sufi Sam), as well as to Carlos Castaneda—writer on, and practitioner of, some form of Native American sorcery—before he became too well-known to risk appearance at hippy beach parties featuring the Grateful Dead. ('I lay before you death and life: therefore choose life.')

In the first half of the '80s I went through a second period of political activism in opposition to U.S. intervention in Nicaragua and El Salvador, when my wife and I joined a local Presbyterian church in order to participate in the Sanctuary movement for Central American refugees, and worship God (possibly in that order). We were immersed during that period in the worldview of Liberation Theology, which I now characterize as the most generous and compassionate way still open to the Christian tradition if it wants to destroy itself. Nonetheless I remain convinced that if it were not for the efforts of the North American churches, we would have been faced with a second Vietnam in Central America and southern Mexico, vastly more destructive to U.S. culture and political stability than a distant war in Asia.

In the second half of the '80s I took a pass through the New Age, not because I felt any deep identification with it—though for all my grain-of-salt attitude, somewhere I must have believed in it—but because I wanted to see if there was still anything left of the 'spiritual revolution' of the 1960s, and because socializing with people less responsible than I was made me seem that much wiser and more mature in my own eyes. I found a few upwardly-mobile 'Yuppies' leading a larger mass of downwardly-mobile semi- or ex-hippies toward a hoped-for, vaguely-Messianic 'paradigm-shift' which turned out, in my estimation, to be nothing but the tender-minded advance guard action for today's tough-minded economic globalism. The New Agers of the '80s were adept at global networking, including 'citizen diplomacy' to the Soviet Union, even before the birth of the World Wide Web, though there were also plenty of personal computer pioneers among them. Through Global Family and other networks we organized several yearly World Peace Prayer days, culminating in August '87 in Harmonic Convergence, brainchild of visionary artist and symbol-manipulator Jose Arguelles. Harmonic Convergence was the first, and possibly the last, true international folkevent. Based on Arguelles' interpretation of the Mayan calendar, August 16 and 17, 1987 were supposed to herald a major shift in the Earth's energy-balance and the quality of global consciousness.

The Convergence brought together as never before New Agers, liberal Christians, Hindus, Buddhists, and primal peoples from around the world. American Indians from both continents, British Wiccans, and even Australian Aborigines participated, enacting simultaneous rituals for enlightenment and Earth-healing of the most varied and ambiguous nature.

In a small way, I was one of the organizers of the Convergence. I led a retreat on Mt. Tamalpias in Marin County, California. I collected dreams from all over the world dreamt on or near the Convergence, and bound them into a manuscript I called *The Harmonic Convergence Book of Dreams*. Before and after the Convergence, I explored and practiced various forms of shamanic dreaming—at least that's what I called it.

Then, it was over. Either nothing, or something, happened. What happened to me was that I realized, in the very center of my being, that I was headed way too far in too many unguided and uncharted directions. Chaos loomed. What if we didn't save the Earth? What if the spiritual revolution did not unfold as planned? What if most or all of what we were involved with were nothing but childish fantasy, or perhaps the first few notes of some rising symphony of darkness?

By God's grace I turned, one-hundred and eighty degrees, and sought guidance from a traditional source, Islamic esoterism. After twelve years I can look back, and see how narrowly I escaped destruction.

✳ My Confession

I would love to be able to write this book in the style of most authors of the Traditionalist school, simply letting the Truth speak for itself without autobiographical or confessional intrusions on the writer's part. But I can't do it.

This book *is* autobiographical and confessional, because, being a book about the Antichrist, the subject matter is my ego. If I didn't admit this fact, *The System of Antichrist* would lead my readers astray; it would be an act of dishonesty.

Many spiritual teachers say that whatever evil you see in the world, know that you are the ultimate source of it. All that happens is God's will, and God wills only the good; the vision of evil is nothing but the vision of one's own ego; the Antichrist is, precisely, the ego. The keynote of my ego is 'fear of matter' or 'fear of the world'—a fact that explains, incidentally, my earlier attraction to Gnosticism, which wove an entire heretical but very plausible worldview around the identical fear. That is my essential trauma, my major blind spot, my central attachment. I even invented a joke which goes: 'Have you heard the news? Scientists have discovered that matter itself is toxic.' The interesting thing is that when I tell this joke, about seven out of ten listeners don't see the humor of it: '*Really? They did?*' I take this to mean that my style of ego, though entirely my own responsibility and certainly no one else's fault, is actually fairly common to our time, a fact which should come as no surprise given the present state of the world. And so the story of my ego, reflected not in the mirror of its own subjectivity, but as far as possible in the Divine Objectivity, the Mirror of God, may—God willing—be of help to others living through the same latter days of this present cycle.

To say that 'all evil is in the ego' is not, however, to deny the universal human experience of the existence of a world, one that is often filled with delusion and suffering; anything else would violate the virtue of compassion. Divine Manifestation is broadcasting on all channels; the sin of the ego is simply to keep the attention tuned to fewer and narrower bands. The ego does not create, in other words; it only edits. The evil it sees is an edited version of a real objective situation, which is, ultimately, God Himself. My ego has not invented the evils and falsehoods revealed in this book; it has simply paid attention to them. But if something is attended to by the ego alone, it falls into the ego's blind spot (which, of course, is all the ego really is); it drops out of sight. Whatever the ego pays attention to it identifies with, and whatever it identifies with it can no longer see. In the reverse process, spiritual purification or *catharsis*, what has been hidden by the ego begins to appear, first as a series of evils to be combatted, then as a cluster of sins to be repented of, next as a spectrum of illusions to be seen through, and finally as a constellation of acts of God, perfect in essence, whether expressing the merciful Divine delight which comes of willing conformation to the law of the human form as God has created it, or the wrathful Divine justice which compensates for, and ultimately heals, our violations of that form.

The oblivious ego happily at one with its blindness and with a naive belief in its own desire is what Sufism calls the 'commanding self', the self which incites to evil. The evil-combatting ego is the 'accusing self', described it as 'evil' (because it witnesses evil) 'but not inciting to evil.' (As a correspondent covering the Vietnam War once wrote, 'I learned that you are as responsible for what you see as for what you do.') The war of the embryonic accusing self against outer evils is the 'lesser *jihad*', usually translated as 'holy war', and the struggle of the fully-grown accusing self against its own sins is the 'greater *jihad*'. The psyche purified of egotism, which sees all events as perfect acts of God, without thereby becoming blind or cold to the sufferings of others, is called the 'self at peace'.

The Orthodox Christian classic the *Philokalia* comments in the following terms on the point of transition from commanding to accusing self which I have defined as 'the lesser *jihad*':

> Spiritual knowledge teaches us that, at the outset, the soul in pursuit of theology [which in Eastern Orthodoxy denotes spiritual realization, not simply theory] is troubled by many passions, above all by anger and hatred. This happens to it not so much because the demons are arousing these passions, as because it is making progress. So long as the soul is worldly-minded, it remains unmoved and untroubled no matter how much it sees people trampling justice under foot. Preoccupied with its own desires, it pays no attention to the justice of God. When, however, because of its disdain for this world and its love for God, it begins to rise above its passions, it cannot bear, even in its dreams, to see justice set at nought. It becomes infuriated with evil-doers and remains angry until it sees the violators of justice forced to make amends.
>
> This, then, is why it hates the unjust and loves the just. The eye of the soul cannot be led astray when its veil, by which I mean the body, is refined to near-transparency through self-control. Nevertheless, it is much better to lament the insensitivity of the unjust than to hate them; for even should they deserve our hatred, it is senseless for a soul which loves God to be disturbed by hatred, since when hatred is present in the soul spiritual knowledge is paralyzed.

Without a passage through the wilderness of spiritual combat, both outer and inner, there is no arrival at the Abode of Peace. Some, however, remain too long in that wilderness, struggling to repent, but unable to 'repent of repentance'. In the words of Omar Khayyam,

Come, fill the Cup, and in the Fire of Spring
The Winter Garment of Repentance fling:
The Bird of Time has but a little way
To fly—and Lo! The Bird is on the Wing.

This book is partly in the form of a Jeremiad, a denunciation of the evils and
falsehoods of the postmodern world, and the realm of New Age spiritualities. This dimension of *The System of Antichrist* is written out of the first stirrings of the accusing self, which must be tempered on the field of the lesser
jihad, the world of social struggle. But in the course of the writing, I began
to realize that every error I saw and denounced in others, I myself had once
believed in, often quite recently. In some cases the act of writing itself ran up
against living residues of errors I still didn't want to let go of, and cast them
out. This dimension of the book constitutes a 'Confessions'; it is written out
of the accusing self proper, whose field is the greater *jihad*, where whatever
was once attack and defense is now self-examination and repentance. And
what else but a partly confessional approach could give me the right to
brand evils and expose errors in others who, for all I know, may be closer to
God than I am? Neo-Paganism (of the Celtic brand), sorcery and New Age
ideas were once living realities to me. I took the *Seth* material, the deification
of the psychic dimension, as Gospel for years, and even experimented with
channeling. As in *The Course in Miracles*, I longed to deny the limitations of
the contingent world we live in, to pretend that the conditions of discarnate
reality could be realized here and now without sacrifice or suffering. I dabbled in sorcery like *Carlos Castaneda*, via some of his methods, and others I
intuited and/or invented, during a dark and traumatized period of my life. I
arrived at the edge of the world he offered, which was characterized by inexplicable events of deep weirdness, and a few instances of actual 'action-at-a-
distance' (*whose* action, I now wonder), but I proceeded no further along
that road simply because I saw no reason to do so. (I thank God for sending
the angel, invisible to me then, who barred my way.) Like *Deepak Chopra*, I
hoped that a technical understanding and operative use of spiritual Truth
would automatically produce physical and material well-being. As in *The
Celestine Prophecy*, I envisioned myself as a member of an enlightened spiritual vanguard who could change the downward course of history by trusting
and acting on our intuitions, with no guidance from either a revealed tradition or a spiritual Master. Like *John Mack*, I allowed my mind to dwell upon
sinister realities, and called them good. Like *William Quinn*, I hoped that my
understanding of metaphysics would place me among the pioneers of a new
World Order, and grant me membership in a group whose influence would

outlast the coming holocaust. By means of a Blakean/Gnostic epic poem I even hoped, like *Benjamin Creme*, to herald a Messiah designed largely by myself, and magically compel his appearance to save the world. Consequently I am now compelled to chew nails writing about the Antichrist — because once without knowing it, or at least without admitting it, I was among his servants.

Each of these dabblings, these false starts, these unguided or misguided excursions left its mark upon my soul, which is why the spiritual Path, for me, has sometimes resembled the untangling of a bale of rusty barbed-wire. Based on my own past mistakes, I now can warn others. It is my hope that, in doing so, it will turn out that my mistakes were not entirely in vain, and that William Blake was not simply making excuses when he said, 'If the Fool would persist in his folly, he would become wise.'

✳ My Apologia

This book represents a struggle for me between two apparently opposed ideas of the nature of existence and the spiritual life. These contending conceptions take the field as the champions of two sides of my soul — or perhaps the 'two souls' which 'dwell in my breast apart' (in Goethe's words) are really the champions of those conceptions. I take it on faith — which, in St Paul's words, is 'the evidence of things not seen' — that these two views of reality are fundamentally not opposed, because Being is One. Like the knightly combat between Balin and Balan in Mallory's *Morte d'Arthur*, the brothers are fighting only because they do not recognize each other; their faces are masked. But the level on which their apparent opposition is resolved lies so deep in the nature of God that I have only rarely seen it, and have barely begun to learn how to live it. On the one hand, my tradition and my spiritual Master teach me that if I see anything wrong in God's creation, this wrong is really in me; that all events are acts of God, and that everything God does is good. I deeply believe this to be true; sometimes I have even known it. On the other hand, God has imposed upon me, as an essential part of my character, the need to say No to 'the World', to refuse in the core of my spiritual will to 'buy' what that World has to offer and what it claims to be true. The imperative for this refusal is to be found in every spiritual tradition, where the knowledge that the world reported by senses is in fact a veiled manifestation of the Absolute Truth is always balanced by the command to reject, at least for oneself, the beliefs and agendas of those who don't realize this.

'The World' is the collective conception of things based on the human ego. What is good from the spiritual point of view 'the World' calls evil, or foolish; what is fundamentally destructive to any possibility of spiritual liberation and self-transcendence 'the World' calls wise and good. My Sufism teaches me that this 'World' is, in essence, nothing but my ego, and that the best way of overcoming this ego is to strive to see how all things are acts, or faces, or words of God—except *me*. In the words of Lao Tzu, 'all things are clear, I alone am clouded.' And this is profoundly true: nothing veils the face of God in all things but this little, fundamentally non-existent 'me'. But the spiritual practice of seeing all things except 'me' as manifestations of God, like any other spiritual practice, can go wrong. And the point where a practice based on deep spiritual truth becomes twisted is inevitably the breeding-ground for a deep spiritual error.

Islam is considered a militant religion. It is not any more militant in theory than Hinduism, with its conception of divinely-ordained combat in *The Bhagavad-Gita*, or, in practice, than Christianity with its Crusades. Even Buddhism, the religion most committed to non-violence, absorbed the Samurai creed, and supported the Japanese war effort in World War II. But Islam, like Judaism in some ways, grew up in war; within a few years of the Prophet's death, *dar-al-Islam* was a world empire built by the sword. This militancy the Sufis have by-and-large sublimated, following the well-known *hadith* of the Prophet, according to which, while returning home with his followers after a military campaign, he said to them: 'Now we return from the lesser *jihad* to the greater one.' 'And what is the greater *jihad*?' 'The war against the [passional] soul'—the commanding self. (The Russian word *podvig*, from the Eastern Orthodox tradition, often translated as 'ascetic exploit', represents a similar concept.) But this does not mean that Sufis totally rejected the lesser *jihad*. Many a Sufi, like some Christian saints, participated in war. Ali ibn abi-Talib was both the great military hero of the first generation of Islam, and the first spiritual master, after the Prophet himself, claimed by most living Sufi orders. Both Christian and Muslim chivalry recognized that the agony, exaltation and self-sacrifice of battle could be dedicated to a spiritual end; the lesser *jihad* could, God willing, be made to serve the greater.

But *jihad* does not simply mean 'holy war'; it is better translated as 'striving in the way of God.' This striving can be for social justice, for the alleviation of human suffering, or for the preservation of one's spiritual tradition. There is, of course, no question that such struggle can sometimes increase one's egotism instead of overcoming it—especially one's *collective* egotism. To worship one's nation or even one's religion in place of God is one of the worst forms of idolatry, and the hardest to recognize, since a person can show great self-sacrifice in the cause of national and religious idols, even unto death. However, one can equally sacrifice one's life to an idol like alcohol; and there is a danger of idolatry in the greater *jihad* as well, since to take pride in one's spiritual achievements is to turn one's whole treasure over to Iblis (the Muslim Satan), who is adept at disguising spiritual pride as the deepest humility and self-sacrifice.

This book is conceived as a struggle, a *jihad* against the spiritual errors of postmodernism and the New Age. These errors exist in the World; they are as objectively real, and even more destructive spiritually, than any material army of barbarians or totalitarians or terrorists. They are like a fifth column; they destroy religion from within; they corrupt the human soul. As idols, they leave their imprints on the souls of all who worship them. Because I myself have worshipped these idols, I must now take upon myself part of the responsibility of overturning them. And just as I can point to definite spiritual doctrines, beginning with the poetry of William Blake, and presently including the writings of Frithjof Schuon, the other writers of the Traditionalist school, and my own spiritual Master, which have literally saved my spiritual life (though in the case of my Master, I was saved not so much by his writings as by his Presence), so I now hope, God willing, to extend that spiritual help—not in my own name, but in that of my teachers—to all who may be able to profit from it.

But in so doing, I must contradict and criticize the words of others. I hope to be able to do this chivalrously, without unnecessarily hurting the feelings or staining the character of my opponents. But this is an ideal which cannot, in practice, be fully attained. Of course feelings will be hurt. If one cannot wield the material sword without dealing and receiving wounds, just as little can one wield the intellectual one. I am told by my Master that it is not Sufi-like to criticize the religious beliefs of others. And it has always been my practice to gladly extend, not merely tolerance, but real veneration and support, to all true faiths, a practice which is generally in line with the teaching of the Koran. Yet Muhammad cast the Pagan idols out of the Kaaba. Was he, then, an enemy of religion? No, because those idols did not represent religion, but rather the corruption of it. The writers I criticize by name in this book are all either openly opposed to the traditional religions, most often Christianity, or else have published mis-representations, open or covert, of the doctrines of these religions. In criticizing them, therefore, I am defending all that has traditionally been known as 'religion'.

But don't the purveyors of New Age and Neo-Pagan doctrines have a 'right' to worship as they see fit? Who am I to deny the rights of others? And what right has any religion to claim superiority over any other? Is this not the road to fanaticism, the Inquisition, to 'holy war' in its most perverted sense?

Certainly it can be. On the other hand, if we take religious freedom as an absolute, then we must permit, for example, the practice of human sacrifice, which formed an integral part of certain religions of Pagan antiquity. So religious freedom, precious as it is, cannot be an absolute. As Frithjof Schuon repeats, quoting the Hindu *rishis*, 'there is no right superior to that of Truth.' Postmodern culture, of course, does not believe in Truth. It holds no absolutes, because it sees questions of truth only in terms of power. What is called truth, historically, is viewed as nothing but the triumph of this or that power bloc. If 'there is no god but God,' this is because Islam triumphed politically and militarily over Paganism on the Arabian peninsula; it is certainly not because Truth is One, because Being, in actual fact, is a transcendent Unity. But if this statement about the nature of Being is not true *intrinsically*, then no religious doctrine or metaphysical statement is true. And if no religious doctrine is true, then all religions are denied, and ultimately destroyed. Is this, then, freedom of religion?

For myself, I fundamentally oppose physical coercion in religious matters. In the words of the Prophet, 'there is no compulsion in religion.' True, in an Islamic or other traditional society based on a divinely-instituted religious law, social cohesion is based on upholding and obeying that law. And no one who neglects a universally-available avenue of salvation like the Muslim *shari'ah* can be considered truly dedicated to that salvation. But in a pluralistic society such as ours, where separation of church and state is fundamental, any attempt to legislate religious doctrine or practice is destructive, except where the 'religion' in question overtly and profoundly violates the mores, as in the case of human sacrifice mentioned above. (I hasten to add that though such sacrifice has undoubtedly occurred among Satanist groups, it is vigorously disavowed and opposed by Neo-Pagans as a whole.) On the other hand, I have always felt justified in criticizing spiritual error. To the degree that the sword of the material lesser *jihad* is denied me, and rightly so, I have taken up the sword of the intellectual lesser *jihad*. Where there is freedom of religion, there is necessarily also freedom of speech in religious matters.

But in all this eminently well-justified criticism of other people's ideas, where is the understanding that all things, all people and even all ideas are manifestations of God, that the only thing which does not manifest Him is this clenched, crabby little 'me' who is always finding fault with God's creation? Did not Jesus advise his followers to remove the beam from their own eyes before they tried to remove the mote from the eye of another? Did not Ibn al-'Arabi teach that God accepts every conception of Him, no matter how limited, as a valid form of worship? Did he not fault even the prophet Noah, up to a point, for denouncing the Paganism of his time, since all Pagan idols, if their worshippers had only known it—and if Noah had only known it—were really forms of the One God? Yet God saved Noah the transcendentalist and swept the idol-worshippers away in the flood, while Ibn al-'Arabi himself advised the ruler of Konya to prohibit public worship on the part of Christians—just as medieval Christendom did in the case of non-Christian religions—because the unity and Islamic character of *dar al-Islam* needed to be maintained.

Once upon a time, says Rumi, Moses encountered a shepherd, whose idea of worshipping God was to comb His hair, wash His feet and give Him milk to drink. The prophet thundered against the shepherd for dragging God down to the human level: 'Far be it from Him to need His hair combed! God is Lord of the Worlds; He is infinitely beyond your paltry conception of His Majesty. Rectify your practice, then. Worship Him in Spirit, not in form.' But as Moses traveled on, God came to him in a vision and chastised him: 'My servant the shepherd worshipped me according to his conception—as do you. You have misjudged him; his sincerity is perfect in My sight.' Distraught and repentant, Moses ran back to the shepherd to ask his forgiveness. 'I beg your pardon, shepherd, for God has revealed to me that I had seriously misjudged you. Please continue to worship Him as seems right to you.' 'But I was about to thank you for your instruction!' the shepherd answered. 'The shock you administered opened my eyes to a vastly greater conception of God than the one I had previously held. After what I have seen, I can never return to my former practice.' So both Moses and the shepherd learned something. Once Moses had judged in God's name, the enlightening judgement of God fell on all parties, Moses included. The shepherd overcame his attachment to form, based on the pride of his ignorance, while Moses overcame his attachment to transcendence, based on the pride of his knowledge.

According to William Blake, the only way to forgive one's enemy is to separate the individual from his state. This is fairly easy for me to do, except when it appears to me that my opponent is being devious and dishonest; at this point, righteous (or self-righteous) anger becomes a temptation. And to

someone such as myself who believes in objective Truth, most manifestations of the postmodern mindset will tend to appear as dishonesty—which
is not necessarily the same thing as insincerity, I must remind myself, but is
rather an *objective dishonesty* enforced by prevailing intellectual conditions,
just as criminal activity is enforced (if it really is) upon those inner city
youth who have found no other way of making a living. And the correct use
of such anger—the specific approach that, God willing, will make it righteous instead of self-righteous—is not to fix my opponent in his error so
that I can judge him as damned (the state of another's soul before God being
both beyond my ken and none of my business), but to separate him from it,
as with a cutting torch, in my consciousness as hopefully also in his, and
turn the flame upon the error alone. At this point I have a chance to see that
the error in question is mine as well, that it is part of that little 'me' which
veils the face of God, since if it didn't have a foothold in my nature I would
never have crossed swords with it.

Given creation there will necessarily be error, and given error there will
necessarily be monsters. When monsters threaten human life, we must go to
war with them—yet the real monster is in us, in 'me'. The monstrousness of
error is also part of God's will, since there is nothing that is not. But what is
error's function? How can that which denies God be in some sense a part of
Him? In the words of the *Tao Te Ching*, 'The foolish student hears of the Tao
and laughs aloud. If there were no laughter, the Tao would not be what it is.'
As Rumi said, 'things are defined by their opposites.' If we did not know
what to avoid, we could not clearly see what to embrace. Human will is free,
and the field of this freedom is the choice between self-annihilating Truth as
presented by the spiritual Intellect, and self-serving error as purveyed by the
ego. Without this choice, the love of God, archetype of all other love, would
be impossible. Therefore error, even though it is a manifestation of God's
wrath, is ultimately and in a deeper sense a manifestation of His Mercy,
since 'My mercy precedeth My wrath'; in the words of William Blake, 'to be
in error and to be cast out is part of God's plan.' We come into the field of
this Mercy, on one level, by exposing a given error, and thereby invoking the
Truth hidden behind it—but I could expose spiritual error until Doomsday,
and never really know, in the marrow of my bones, that God holds the universe in the palm of His hand, that all acts are God's acts, and all God does
is good. Only if I make every criticism of another's ideas an occasion of
death to self can I move toward this knowledge.

But how can scoring points on one's opponent with the sword of the dis-
cursive intellect be a death to self? If I win, I feel good about myself; I feel

powerful; my ego gets fat and sleek. The only way I know to dedicate intellectual *jihad* to the spiritual Path is to admit that criticizing other people's ideas causes pain to both self and other; and then to feel that pain completely; and finally to let it burn out those places in one's soul where the errors in question, and consequently the need to criticize those errors, had taken root. It is to interpret esoterically, and in line with the rules of the greater *jihad*, the doctrine of Jesus that 'he who lives by the sword shall die by the sword.'

Perhaps some people are able, from the start, to completely avoid criticizing whatever appears in manifest being. Others may be exempted from criticizing evil simply because they don't possess the talent for it. And then there are those who really do accept the most horrendous manifestations—not just of suffering, but of falsehood and delusion—as God's perfect will, because they have attained the spiritual station where nothing appears to them in the realm of events but the direct action of God. These people are closer to God than I am; their level of surrender, of *Islam*, is beyond my present capacity. Their station is that of Rabi'a when she said, 'I love God: I have no time left in which to hate the devil.'

These are the ones who have awakened from the dream of evil. But there are others—many others—who have not yet fully awakened *to* the dream of evil. Their conscience is asleep, or half-asleep Many people fear the evil around them because they see how it is destroying humanity and ruining the earth. Yet they cannot morally and spiritually reject the things they hate and fear because they see no objective ground of good to stand on from which those things could be called 'evil'. They end by resignedly accepting forces and conditions which are destroying their souls. And many others, either out of naive acceptance of the abnormal, or deeply repressed despair, uncritically accept as good—or at least as inevitable and therefore 'good' in effect—the most satanic distortions of human life. They do not say: 'If I die after eating poisoned food I will be grateful, because that is God's will'; they say instead: 'This food is not really poisoned; if I eat it I will become healthy and strong, and if I feed it to others I am doing them a service.' So if I tell them 'Avoid that dish, it is full of poison,' that is an act of friendship—if, that is, I can sincerely offer that warning in the spirit of friendship. If I castigate the World, it is only to throw a rope to those who are drowning in that World, whose consciences have been systematically perverted, so much so that if they begin to suspect that a given action or belief may seriously damage their souls and violate their human integrity, they have no way to present this intuition to themselves, no language to say it in. People in this condition—

and there are many of them — will routinely experience feelings of guilt before the judgement of the World for the crime of wanting to do good; they are ashamed of their highest and noblest impulses; they are ashamed of God. They have been taught to accept all things, with a complacency indistinguishable from total despair, not as the will of God but as the decree of the World, whose goal is to crush out anything in their souls which might remind them that God is real. Rather than transcending evil, they have not yet reached the point where the word 'evil' means anything to them outside of their own personal discomfort. This is how nihilism masquerades as spiritual detachment. And if I myself were not tempted to the same nihilism then I would not have been required to wrestle with it, and this book would never have been written. Perhaps only psychopaths — there are many eminently 'well-adjusted' psychopaths in today's society — are completely taken over by the nihilism of the World. But the World and its nihilism have at least a toe-hold in all of us, unless we are actually saints, and that toe-hold is becoming more toxic and virulent by the hour. In the words of Rabi'a,

> Where a part of you goes
> The rest will follow—given time.
> You call yourself a teacher:
> Therefore learn.

If a Jew accepts the holocaust because it was God's will, that is true piety, true *Islam*. If another Jew accepts it because it was Hitler's will, then goes on to secretly envy Hitler, then that is idolatry and blasphemy. 'There needs be evil,' said Jesus, 'but woe to him through whom evil comes.' Those who have invested their hopes and fears, their fundamental sense of reality in the world desperately need help from a Reality which transcends that world. This book is written to remind them that such help exists. On the other hand, the essence of 'investing' in something is the act of paying attention to it. If I saw no world but only God, I would be a source of light and help to all who were drowning in the sea of the world; but this is beyond my power — though not beyond God's. My station is more like that of Rabi'a's 'holy friends' in the following poem:

> One day Rabi'a was sick,
> And so her holy friends came to visit her, sat by her bedside,
> And began putting down the world.
> 'You must be pretty interested in this "world",' said Rabi'a,
> 'Otherwise you wouldn't talk about it so much:
> Whoever breaks the merchandise
> Has to have bought it first.'

It is easy to see God in the petals of the rose or in the form of a beautiful woman. It is harder t o see Him, not only His Majesty and Wrath but even His Beauty and His Mercy, in the horrors of today's world. But if God can be seen *there*, then no trace of reproach against His creation or His sovereign decrees can remain in the Heart. And this is the self at peace.

✳ My Hope

The Antichrist may or may not be an individual, though many traditional authorities, both exoteric and esoteric, including orthodox Muslims and Christians, and writers like Martin Lings and René Guénon, say he will be, and I am inclined to agree. (1 John 2:18 speaks of several antichrists.) But whether or not he will be a single individual, he is already a *system*. This is why I am not interested in speculating as to who in my own or somebody else's rogues' gallery might secretly be the Antichrist, any more than I think it either worthwhile or possible (at least for me) to date his rise. The relationship of apocalyptic symbology to historical time is oblique, not direct. If Antichrist is known as a *principle*, however, then the beliefs, trends and individuals in the outer world which manifest this principle, to one degree or another, can be recognized. But unless the greater system of that principle is understood—at least as far as the inherent absurdity of evil will allow—then if and when the individual appears in whom this system is destined to reach its most complete and terminal form, we may find ourselves unable to recognize him. I hope, in this book, to help the reader make sense out of the chaos and darkness of these latter days, avoid unconscious participation in soul-destroying evil, and intuit the Divine Mercy which is always there, hidden in even the most dire conditions, as a clear sign of that higher Reality, mysteriously present behind the mask of this one, where Truth is synonymous with Goodness, and evil only another name for illusion: 'All is perishing,' says the Koran, 'except His Face.'

Part One:
Tradition vs. The New Age

Foreword

THERE is currently considerable confusion between 'religion' and 'belief systems'. Indeed, certain academics attempt to reduce all religions to 'belief systems' that have somehow 'caught on'. But there is a distinction to be made between them, for genuine religions are based on Revelation, which provides them a fixed creed, code, and cult independent of any individual thought or feeling, while belief systems not based on Revelation are inevitably subject to human opinion. Of course, many founders of sects base themselves partially on Revelation—accepting what they like and rejecting what they don't—and most such sects claim inspiration by the Holy Spirit. But the fact remains that they are all based at least in part on the thinking and feeling that resides in the psyche and is subject to illusion, a problem that can only be avoided by adhering to a fixed external source. Unfortunately, many religious representatives currently attack the revealed basis of their faiths in an attempt to accommodate them to the values of the modern world, which in effect reduces them to the same level as other belief systems.

Once it is recognized that most of our belief systems are based on feelings and thoughts—all properties that lie within the realm of the psyche—it follows that it becomes impossible to criticize any given belief system. All religions and belief systems are equivalent because everyone's truth or beliefs—providing they do not create a problem for others—are of equal value. For one to say that any given cult or religion is false is an act of presumption which no one dares to express. Moreover, it is thought that it is this kind of exclusive outlook that has led to conflict and war—all in the name of God—and hence such attitudes must be eschewed. (It should be noted however that it is, as St. Paul said, 'our lusts and our greeds' that are the root cause of conflicts.) In the practical order, whatever works for an individual is considered acceptable. And indeed, psychiatrists are now recognizing that 'religion' has its use in that it helps people face problems in life, and a belief in the afterlife makes death easier to deal with.

Most of modern religion is rooted and centered in the psyche, so that by the very nature of things people can state that what is true for them is true. The psyche has no absolutes, and hence the individual has no real commitments. What is more dangerous is that by attempting to find some measure of truth in this nebulous realm, one opens one's soul to influences of a possibly nefarious nature. Many, like Jung himself, have let 'spirit guides' instruct them in how to live and act, spirit guides who describe themselves as 'angels', which indeed they are, for as an earlier age believed, there are spirits abroad who are 'fallen angels' only too ready to invade our psyches when opportunity avails. And so it is that 'channeling' has become the rage, with a host of 'guides' ranging from Ramtha to Seth, supposedly providing us access to some form of superconsciousness or 'god consciousness' which is the evolutionary result of repeated births within the framework of this universe. It is but a short step from this to involvement in the occult. Traditional societies have always forbidden intercourse with such spirits, not only because of the spiritual dangers involved, but also because such contacts can lead to psychiatric aberrations, as is well illustrated in the biblical story of Saul.

The new age movement has been well characterized as the secularization of religion and the spiritualization of psychology. Those who easily see through the insipid nature of materialism seek for something 'spiritual' to satisfy the cravings of their heart. Limited by the Cartesian outlook, which denies the truly spiritual nature of man, they make idols of music and the arts, love and nature—all circumscribed by their psychic ramifications. This leads them, and indeed many in religions life, to turn to the psyche for fulfillment.

Those 'trapped' in the psyche, who center their lives in feelings or in the conviction that their private and individual thoughts are absolute, are said by medieval authors to be 'in love with themselves'. This 'self-love', as opposed to 'Self-love', is seen as a defect to be corrected. Immediately one hears the protest of those who declare that no one is going to tell them how to think or behave. They insist on the freedom to decide these things for themselves. And this is quite understandable in one whose whole outlook is based on the Cartesian principle that we consist exclusively of body and mind. If that is all we are, then indeed they have a right to such a stand, for your mind and body have no more authority than mine. Recognizing the tripartite nature of man, however—which in no way denies the psyche—orients one toward the reestablishment of a hierarchy of order in which the Spirit directs the psyche, just as the psyche directs, or should direct, the body.

But the Spirit is not just within us; it is also above and outside us. And ultimately, it *is* us: our faculties are rooted in the Lord, and 'in His Light we we see Light.'

✳

Charles Upton's book is a remarkable exposition of what results from the acceptance of Cartesian dualism, the idea that our totality consists of body and mind alone. In one sense it demonstrates the innumerable forms that pseudo-religious cults can take when they base truth on feelings and private opinions, rather than revelation. And perhaps even more importantly, it shows how all these sects are fundamentally similar both in origin and in outlook. For someone seeking the truth, this book provides an excellent guide through the maze of modern religious 'offerings'.

⌒Rama P. Coomaraswamy, MD, FACS, Clinical Assistant Professor of Psychiatry, Albert Einstein College of Medicine, New York, NY

1

Postmodernism, Globalism, & the New Age

At the beginning of the Third Millennium, our space is dominated by the globalization of the earth, the 'melting pot' of all national, tribal and religious cultures, and our time by 'postmodernism', in which we seemingly approach an impossible condition where all the ages of the past, by virtue of the information culture, are equally available, equally valid, equally falsified, and equally corrupt. This age, the terminal one for the present cycle of manifestation, presents us with unparalleled spiritual dangers, as well as unique spiritual opportunities. In this chapter are explored many of the dangers and a few of the opportunities—social, philosophical, religious and metaphysical—which lie under the sign of the End.

❋ What is Postmodernism?

The times we live in have been called 'postmodern'. What exactly does this mean? What could possibly come *after* being 'up to date'? And if something really might come after, how could we possibly be contemporary with it? Does 'postmodern' mean 'after history'? Could it, perhaps, have something to do with the 'end of time'?

Postmodernism, or postmodernity, is a name for the general quality of our time. But it also refers to certain trends in philosophy, art and literary criticism. The following is a short overview of postmodern philosophy; after I've made some of its basic concepts as clear as possible, I'll do what I can to show how these concepts, or assumptions, or prejudices, apply to other areas of contemporary life.

According to Huston Smith in *Beyond the Post-Modern Mind*, 'modernism' was (and is) based on the belief that '(a) nothing that lacks a material component exists, and (b) in what does exist the physical component has the final say.' So modernism is essentially naturalism, or materialism. This naturalism took over, beginning with the Renaissance and accelerating during the scientific revolution of the 17th century, as metaphysics and revealed religion began to be marginalized. The unified worldview presented by theology was replaced by a new unity—or rather a new belief that unity could finally be achieved—founded on the study of nature and human history. The more facts we discovered in these areas, the more material would be available for the construction of the Grand Design.

But according to postmodernism, there is no Grand Design. Truth is plural, and ultimately subjective. Reality *is* only as it is configured: by a given historical period, or society, or language, or individual. There is nothing really out there but a mass of chaotic potential waiting to be pulled into some arbitrary shape. Huston Smith names Kant, Kierkegaard, Nietzsche, Heidegger, Wittgenstein, and the deconstructionist Jacques Derrida as among the witting or unwitting architects of the movement, which began to overtake modernism, at least in Western societies, in the first half of the 20th century.

Kant taught that the human being can never experience transcendent Truth, or the objective reality (*noumenon*) of anything at all, but only the world of *phenomena* as presented to us by our fixed and inborn patterns of perception. And Nietzsche, with his 'death of God', announced the end of metaphysics, a terrifying but historically inevitable development, while doing all he could to further it by attacking Christianity and substituting the Stoic doctrine of the endless circular return of all things for the metaphysical notion of changeless eternal principles within the mind of God. (What could be more nihilistic than to work for a result you believe is terrible simply because you think it's inevitable?) According to Prof. Smith, Kierkegaard also played a part through his notion that objective truth dehumanizes. This belief is held today by millions of people, who apply it not to Hegelian philosophy as Kierkegaard did, however, but to science. Then came Heidegger, who said that there is no objective truth beyond what a particular historical period defines as real; Wittgenstein, who maintained that there is no objective truth beyond that defined by cultures and mediated by language; and Derrida, who tells us that any attempt to define an objective truth must necessarily exclude, and therefore marginalize, and therefore oppress other possible versions of what is true. Cultural and philosophical diversity should be celebrated because unity tyrannizes. To believe that a society, or a language, or even a text, has some inherent structure is oppressive. Consequently anyone who thinks that he or she has grasped the real meaning of a text, including the person who wrote it, is deluded—except for Derrida and the deconstructionists, apparently. Jacques Derrida might have had a brilliant career as a devastating satirist of postmodernism, except for the fact that humor can only exist on the border between the real and the absurd, and the deconstructionists, humorless as they are, have removed the first of these two terms from consideration.

Here is postmodernism in a nutshell: (1) There is no objective truth, therefore, (2) reality is not perceived but rather constructed, by inherent patterns of perception, or by history, or by society and language, or by the individual, thus (3) all attempts to create comprehensive worldviews that transcend history, or society, or even (ultimately) the individual are oppressive, therefore (4) all such arbitrarily constructed worldviews should be deconstructed in order to celebrate diversity and preserve the rights of marginalized minority constructions of reality (which, of course, since they too are constructions, must also be deconstructed; so much for the preservation of minority rights). So postmodernism ends in deconstructionism, and deconstructionism ends (or hopefully will) in the deconstruction of deconstructionism: if the constructed view of the majority oppresses minorities, so do minority views oppress individuals . . . and individual views (why not?) the views of the subpersonalities within the individual, as those subpersonalities oppress the experience of split seconds of consciousness, etc., etc., etc. Does anyone not recognize here the familiar quality of our daily life, the progressive pulverizing of reality? It's as if the deconstructionists were total creatures of the electronic media, people who consider it a crime to possess an attention-span because that would impose arbitrary and oppressive form upon 'pure' experience; at least that's the terminal phase toward which they appear to be headed. If we take them seriously, will we have to conclude that to exist at all is to oppress and be oppressed? That the end of oppression must be the end of existence? That the final goal of postmodern nihilism is and should be annihilation? Maybe the word 'postmodernism' really does refer to the termination of history, the end of time. Obviously, it's a house founded upon sand.

Modernism and postmodernism are entirely capable of working together in the contemporary mind, and even in the mind of a single individual, to neutralize the traditional or metaphysical view of reality. To take only one example, if I point out to such an individual that certain social trends fit the traditional definition of demonism precisely, and have consequences that no one in his right mind would deliberately pursue, his chaotic postmodern side will validate these trends as part of the universal 'celebration of diversity', while his materialistic modern side will deny that such a thing as demonism can exist. In doing this, he has of course denied part of the diversity he has just finished validating; but because these two sides of his consciousness never meet, the contradiction between them is 'no problem', and it would continue to be 'no problem' even if they did meet, since postmodernism sees inconsistency as a kind of 'richness', and consistency, even logical consistency, as a form of oppression. Here we can see how postmodernism really is the dominant view, of which modernism has become nothing more than a sub-set, one more disrelated item in the postmodern spectrum of 'diversity'. And both the postmodern celebration and the modern denial act together to support rather than oppose the trends in question — trends which the very same individual, with still another disrelated facet of his fragmented consciousness, may sincerely deplore.

✳ The Truth Hidden in Postmodernism

But is there anything good in postmodernism? Huston Smith mentions the deconstructionists' useful warning that absolutist claims, including metaphysical claims, *can* tyrannize, and their admirable championing of the Other, both in terms of outcast minorities and of marginalized ideas. If postmodernism sees all worldviews as constructed—as a function of power, that is, rather than truth—then deconstructionism must arise as a defender of the many diverse views which command less power than the view which happens to be dominant in a particular place and time. He cautions us, however, against the absolutizing of this very diversity, since 'we would not honor the otherness of the Other if we did not also recognize her identity with us.'

Smith sees deconstructionism, the most radical of postmodern trends, as a kind of Gödel's Theorem in the realm of philosophy. The mathematician Kurt Gödel proved that no system can be both complete and consistent. It must leave things out to be consistent; to be complete, it must include contradictions. 'Since there can be no system that is complete and consistent,' Smith reminds us, 'it is impossible that any one system has all the truth. Other voices should be listened to.' It is equally impossible, however, that all the truth could be known by adding system to system. Information, quantitative truth, can be amassed; transcendent, spiritual Truth cannot.

But what, exactly, is a *system*? Existence itself, on its own level, is complete, though we can never experience all it contains. It is also mysteriously consistent, impressing those who deeply contemplate it as a *universe*, an ordered cosmos, an expression of the Tao. Yet it is never perfectly predictable. A system, then, is an attempt to synthesize, through a construction of the human mind, the completeness and consistency we can only intuit in primordial existence itself.

In any traditional society based on a religious revelation, little if any dissonance is apparent, to most of the people most of the time, between the sacred system of myth, theology and ritual, and existence itself. It is only in this age of enforced pluralism, when all surviving religious revelations, the mythological 'universes' of many primitive tribes, diverse philosophical systems and distinct artistic universes-of-sensibility, the historicity and naturalism of the modernist worldview, the paradigms of science and scientism, and the anti-worldview worldview of postmodernism meet head-on, that a sociological 'Gödel's Theorem' has become necessary.

In earlier times, such as late antiquity, or during much of the history of India, when many religions and philosophies met and cross-pollinated, *syncretism*, for good or ill, was still possible. There remained enough of the primordial sense of the unity of existence for philosophers to be able to paint a more-or-less unified picture of the cosmos which embraced the plurality of religious forms, and for the common people to accept religious pluralism as more or less in the natural course of things, as part of the 'ecology' of the spirit—though such syncretism was always on a lower level than any single traditional form, and often inimical to the higher sense of the sacred mediated by these forms. But we have largely lost even that vague, intuitive sense of unity. The worldviews of science and revelation, materialism and transcendentalism are too radically opposed to be reconciled. This is not to say that there isn't plenty of syncretism in today's world; in a way this is syncretism's 'golden age'. It's simply that syncretism no longer has the power to overcome, even partially and relatively (which is all it was ever capable of), our existential anxiety and cognitive fragmentation. When we try to embrace completeness, in these times, we are immediately faced with agonizing contradiction. When we opt for consistency we are left with something isolating, constricting, and radically incomplete.

The terms 'complete' and 'consistent' are both horizontal in a sense. If the table-top is of infinite extent, it will include 'everything'—everything on the plane of the table, that is—but the small part we can see will not make sense. If the table is finite, small enough to take in at one glance, it will be consistent, but it will leave a lot out; if we look beyond its borders we will see many other tables. Neither the word 'complete' nor the word 'consistent', however, can carry the full weight of the metaphysical terms Reality and Truth, both of which are names of God. Only God, let us say, is both totally complete and perfectly consistent—and God is not a system. His completeness cannot be encompassed or exhausted because it is Infinite; His consistency cannot be defined or rationalized because it is Absolute. Gödel's Theorem, then, is the mathematical expression God's transcendence of the cosmos, of the relative poverty of the cosmos when considered apart from God. But given that we have largely lost the immediate sense of higher unseen worlds, more real than this one, and of a Divine and Transcendent Absolute, Gödel's Theorem becomes merely ironic, the mathematical expression of the postmodern despair of objective truth.

When the north is frozen, the west flooded, the south on fire and the east blocked by a landslide, the only way out is Up. A given philosophical system is not required to be either totally consistent or totally complete to do its work. It does not have to be God, any more than an elevator needs to be the size of the whole building. This is so because God Himself is *already* God; consistency and completeness are already taken care of. All a philosophy (or, to be strictly accurate, a *theosophy*) really needs is to be open, in the vertical dimension, to transcendent Truth, the sense of the Absolute, and to conform its formulations, imperfect as they must be, to that sense. And as long as we realize that religion, unlike philosophy, is addressed to man's whole being, not simply his mind, the same can be said of any viable religious form. It does not need to be absolutely consistent or complete; only God can be that. All it needs is to have preserved, operatively intact, in its dogma, ritual, morality and contemplative practice, the living ray of God by which it came into the world, and along which the human souls within it can return to the Source Who sent it.

To understand this is to overcome doctrinal idolatry, which can be defined as the worship of a system of belief, heterodox or orthodox, in place of God. Don't misunderstand me: doctrinal orthodoxy is necessary if we are to have a living relationship with the Absolute. It is the furthest thing from utilitarianism or pragmatism. It is not arbitrary, but rather integral and necessary to the revelation it expresses. In Frithjof Schuon's terms, it is 'relatively absolute'. Religious doctrines possessing true orthodoxy are providential. They are operatively effective not because they are complex enough or simple enough or fascinating enough to spiritually motivate us, but because they are objectively true: not totally complete and consistent, but still the highest possible expressions (though not always the only ones) of God's Reality and His relationship with His creation for a given religious universe. They are like elevators which go all the way to the Top Floor. Other elevators may take you part of the way, but if your goal is the Top Floor, you will first have to return to the ground floor before catching the elevator you need. And although more than one elevator, more than one revealed tradition, may ascend to the Top Floor, it is not possible to take two at once.

Doctrinal idolatry is one form of the more universal *idolatry of views*, the inevitable human tendency to mistake one's view of reality for reality itself. Postmodernism at its best, since it denies the completeness and consistency of any one view of things, should be able to work against this idolatry of views, and give its adherents some sense of the transcendent incomparability of the unique 'forms of life', as well as unique individuals and unique moments—a level of understanding permanently attained only by the greatest mystics, such as the Sufi Ibn al-'Arabi, who see all events as acts or symbolic aspects of God—'He (Allah) is every day at some new work' says the Koran—by those who have cleanly transcended systematic dogma while in no way denying it. As William Blake teaches, the concrete uniqueness of 'minute particulars' is closer than the abstract idea of transcendence to the true revelation of God. In practice, however, postmodernism seems to be having the opposite effect. Though Prof. Smith speaks of Jacques Derrida's grudging and intermittent respect for metaphysics, and of certain metaphysical intuitions in Heidegger, for the most part postmodernism is even more anti-metaphysical than modernism is. And without the vertical dimension, without a concrete sense of the Absolute, the celebration of diversity as *opposed* to unity can only be an ironic comment on the impossibility of arriving at objective truth, coupled with a nihilistic denial that such truth is even desirable.

Our views are not reality; they are, however, views *of* reality, though varying widely in capacity and accuracy. Even the paranoid builds his delusion on some trace or aspect of truth. But if we deny that there is any objective truth beyond our views, does this prevent us from idolizing them, since we understand that they aren't 'real'? Or does it rather force us to idolize them, since they are now the only 'reality' there is? And is a world inhabited by solipsists, which postmodernism via the electronic media is in the process of creating, really a tolerant world? If I accept you only because you are a part of me (rather than *me being a part of you*, a blasphemy against solipsism), have I really accepted you?

In a way, contemplative practice can be defined as work to overcome the idolatry of views. Concentration on the Absolute entails the progressive realization, moment by moment, that our views of God's Reality are not God. As we come to understand, and accept, that no conception of ours can contain the Absolute, we learn to let our conceptions go. In the technical terminology of mysticism, this is the 'apophatic' contemplation of God's transcendence.

But that's only half of the picture. As we let go of our conceptions, greater conceptions are born, which we must also let go of, thus making room for conceptions which are greater still. And as the process continues, we come to realize that these conceptions are not our feeble attempts to understand God, but God's generous and merciful Self-revelations to us. Because we are finite, we can never contain His total Self-revelation, except by the annihilation of our separate and self-defined existence, which is ultimately reborn as one of the infinite Self-revelations of God carried within His greater existence. But we can accept God's self-revelations to us as free gifts by which aspects of His inconceivable Essence can become known to us, according to our capacity. This is the 'cataphatic' contemplation of God's immanence.

Like contemplative practice, postmodern philosophy works against the 'naive realism' which makes us believe that objective reality is limited to what we see, that things are simply what they seem. But it also teaches us, paradoxically, that things are *only* what we see, that nothing, or nothing intelligible, is really out there. And instead of placing these two truths in relation to each other, as in traditional metaphysics, it sets them at each other's throats. Rather than positing a Reality which transcends all our views, it denies that such a Reality could be; in place of the Divine Emptiness beyond all conception, we are left with a literal hollowness, a dead lack. And instead of positing our conceptions of things as Self-manifestations of that Inconceivable Reality, it sees them as the ultimately arbitrary productions of a blind material substratum lacking all unity, productions which are formed and mediated, all but unconsciously, only by the 'egos' of history, society, language, and the isolated individual. So instead of Inaccessibility married to Manifestation, we have the inadequacy of all conception married to its blind and endless proliferation. Postmodern nihilism, then, is a kind of counterfeit mysticism, a distorted shadow of the Absolute itself. And when the shadow of the Absolute, the one that Muslims call 'Iblis', becomes the guiding principle of an entire historical epoch, then we must conclude that the end of the cycle is near.

✳ Postmodernism and the New Age

New Age spiritualities seem opposed in many ways to postmodernism. They believe in the objective truth of transcendent realities. They are not interested in limiting that truth to what can be seen through the lens of this or that language or society or historical epoch. Rather than deconstructing scriptures and mythologies, they search the scriptures and mythologies of the whole world and all human history for clues to some hidden truth. They believe in 'deep structure'. The secret of metaphysics and prophecy is hidden in the dimensions of the Great Pyramid; Madame Blavatsky's 'Book of Dzyan' is the oldest scripture in the world and the key to all the others; the teachings of Seth or *A Course in Miracles* or *The Celestine Prophecy* reveal the destined shape of human history and the actual, objective structure of the universe. They may be heterodox from the standpoint of the traditional orthodoxies, but they are not postmodern.

Or are they? The first similarity between the New Age and postmodernism is that both are pluralistic; both like to 'celebrate diversity'. The New Age may have inherited the residue of Christendom's belief in objective, metaphysical truth; yet the word 'objectivity' is not congenial to New Agers. To them, as to postmoderns in general, it tends to be synonymous with 'orthodoxy', 'dogmatism', and 'hierarchy', which are in turn synonymous with 'oppression'.

The plurality of New Age spiritualities is not divisiveness; it is not sectarian. Transcendence is sought, but it is essentially a subjective transcendence—which is a contradiction in terms, since it is precisely our subjectivity, our limited egotistical standpoint, which must be transcended. And as transcendence and subjectivity are both embraced as values, spiritual authority is simultaneously sought and distrusted. Gurus amass followings, but it is concurrently believed, even by many of the followers themselves, that 'you are your own guru'. More and more New Agers channel psychic entities in an attempt to sidestep the spiritual authority of human mentors, valid or otherwise; but then they give the 'entity' in question absolute authority over their view of reality—an authority which can be 'massaged' when necessary, however, since there is nothing easier than operating one's 'entity' like a ventriloquist's dummy so it will tell us what we want to hear. The New Age shares with postmodernism a distrust of authority, while at the same time possessing its own authorities, just as postmodernism does.

It is common practice for many New Agers not to remain loyal to a single teacher or single view, but to deliberately multiply them. The more teachers and teachings one can collect—and in terms of the Neo-Pagan end of the spectrum, the more gods and goddesses—the wider one's area of consciousness is thought to be. This tendency might be defined as 'the reign of quantity' in the religious field, and it is indistinguishable from postmodern pluralism, since if there is no objective reality, 'expansion of consciousness' can only be horizontal and quantitative. In the same way, the belief that everyone is his own guru, or can channel his own entity, or should construct his own 'personal myth' is nothing but a folk rendition of the doctrine of postmodern philosophy that 'reality is, only as it is configured.'

The plurality and diversity of New Age doctrine guarantee that it can never transcend the psychic level. The domain of Spirit is objective and unitary; that of the psyche is necessarily multiple, since it is based on the subjective points-of-view of its many inhabitants, human and otherwise. Objective, archetypal, spiritual Truth may be reflected there, but it is also refracted, broken up, like the image of the Sun in a windswept bay. No single fragment of the Sun's image in the shifting waves is the whole Sun; here postmodernism's caution against the absolutization of subjective views is well taken. But neither can the Sun be seen whole by adding fragmentary image to fragmentary image; a million snapshots of the Sun sparkling on the water will never add up to the image of the whole Sun. And only such a unitary image can demonstrate that there is such a thing as the Sun itself, a reality in its own right, standing on a higher plane than its reflection.

New Age religious subjectivism is basically an attempt to take refuge in the subjective psyche against the terror of the world, against materialism and scientism, understanding the psyche as in some sense transcendent of material conditions, but ignoring the fact that if the psyche is not grounded in Spirit, in something higher than itself, it becomes a mere appendage of material conditions, as Karl Marx so clearly demonstrated. A subjective transcendence is a fragmented transcendence, and a fragmented transcendence cannot be truly transcendent.

✳ Globalism and Antichrist

Globalism and One World Government, in my opinion, are not the system of Antichrist, though they are among the factors which will make that regime possible.

I believe the system of Antichrist will emerge—is in fact emerging—out of the conflict between the New World Order and the spectrum of militant reactions against it.

In Jesus' time, the One World Government was the Roman Empire. The Zealots were the anti-Roman revolutionaries and/or militias. Jesus was careful not to be drawn into making statements which would compromise the Zealot cause and make him appear as a Roman collaborator. But he also related to Roman military officers, and toadies of Rome like the Jewish tax collectors, in ways that scandalized many Jewish nationalist patriots. He emerged from the common people oppressed both by Rome and by the colonial Jewish ruling classes who did Rome's dirty work, and he denounced those sectors of the ruling class—the Scribes, Pharisees, Sadducees and Herodians—who made common cause with the Empire, while speaking no word against the Zealots and Essenes, who did not. But he did not identify with the violent 'vanguard' who acted in the people's name. So we can say that if Christ worked to avoid being identified either with the Roman Empire or with its militant opponents, by the same token we should be careful not to strictly identify Antichrist either with One World Government or with anti-globalist terrorism. Together they will provide the milieu out of which he will emerge; but just as Christ avoided being claimed by either party because it was his mission to redeem not the Jews alone but all humanity, so Antichrist will 'play both sides against the middle' in the latter days to build his power over all aspects of the human soul. Antichrist is not primarily the enemy of democracy or national autonomy, in other words, but of Humanity itself, considered as made in the image and likeness of God. In its deepest essence, the battle between Christ and Antichrist is not between freedom and tyranny (though where true freedom is, the Antichrist cannot come), nor between traditional religious bodies and secular society (though the field of this conflict may, at least in some cases, be closer to the real war), but that between the sacred presence of God in the human heart, and the sacrilegious violation of that presence: 'When ye therefore shall see the Abomination of Desolation, spoken of by Daniel the prophet, stand in the holy place (whoso readeth, let him understand), then let them which be in Judea flee into the mountains' (Matt. 24:15–16).

Globalism is in the process of destroying all traditional and national cultures, undermining and compromising all traditional religious forms. But to simply oppose all planning and action on a global scale is also problematic. The ironic truth is that given globalism, we need globalism. If business is international, unions must be international too, or wages might eventually be driven below the subsistence level everywhere. If epidemics are global, public health efforts must cross national boundaries. If pollution is global, efforts to limit it must be global. If crime is global, the police must be also. If 'emerging' nations and terrorist gangs develop weapons of mass destruction, efforts must be made to limit their spread. We have no choice but to try and manage the earth on a planetary level. But the struggle to accomplish this is itself producing ambiguous results. If the powers that be can use environmentalism, public health efforts, armed peacemaking and the war against international crime, terrorism and the drug trade to further consolidate their power, they will. Or rather, they are. Anyone who opposes the effort to save the environment or cut into the international drug trade or limit the possibility of nuclear terrorism is working against the best interests of humanity and the earth. But anyone who identifies with these efforts or places his or her hopes in them is deluded. The earth cannot be managed on a planetary level because the forces of globalism which aspire to do the managing—global business and finance in other words, followed and not led by the trend toward political unification—are the same forces which are creating these problems in the first place. The global spread of industry and exploitation of resources—originated and presently driven, despite the communist interlude, by trans-national capitalism—are the origin of environmental degradation. By destroying traditional subsistence economies and proletarianizing labor—helped greatly in this by the brutal collectivization of agriculture, at the expense of tens of millions of lives, in communist Russia and China—by exploiting cheap labor and threatening national and religious cultural identities, the forces of global capitalism have themselves created the global underground trade in drugs, weapons, endangered animal species, slaves... all monuments to the entrepreneurial spirit. Only a One World Government could possibly limit the destructive power of these international economic forces. But when and if such a government emerges, even though it may have some mitigating influence on global disasters, it will be the agent of these forces, not their adversary.

Politics is the art of the ephemeral. Whatever of human value is gained through political action is temporary, ambiguous and corruptible. This is the nature of time and history—of matter itself. Action for social justice, action to save the environment are laudable. Every person who can avoid being crushed by circumstances without becoming an exploiter and oppressor of others is a blessing to the race. Every species which can be saved from extinction remains as an incomparable mirror of one unique aspect of the Divine nature, and may (or may not) add to the biodiversity available in the next cycle of terrestrial manifestation, since we can't absolutely know whether or not the end of this *aeon* must entail the total destruction of all life on earth, or even all human life; all we know is that it will be the end for 'us'.

But the battle against Antichrist is on a different level. Though for some it may include a political expression, it is essentially spiritual. 'My kingdom is not of this world.' It is a struggle to save, not the world, but the human soul—starting, and finishing if necessary, with one's own.

✻ Vectors of Antichrist in the Three Religious 'Estates'

Huston Smith divides all religious manifestations into three basic levels: church religion, folk religion, and mystical religion. There is a great deal of crossover among these domains, yet the division remains fundamentally sound. Much is clarified if we realize that not everything that passes for 'religion' has the same orientation, the same field of activity, the same ultimate goal.

As I see it, the primary goal of church religion is salvation for the individual in an after-death state. The primary goal of folk religion is the fulfillment of human desire and the protection of human life from harm. The primary goal of mystical religion is the realization of God, the final liberation from contingent existence, in this very life. Folk religion, therefore, can be designated as the religion of this world; church religion, of the next world; and mystical religion, of the Absolute, beyond both this world and the next. This scheme is obviously far from perfect, but despite the many exceptions to it, I still feel it's a useful way of making sense out of the diverse tendencies that fall under the word 'religion'.

Certainly church religion has as one of its secondary goals the protection of the individual and the community from harm and the attainment of morally acceptable goals in this life. And every religion based on revelation has at least one door within it, whether widely recognized or half-forgotten, which opens onto the mystical Path. Nor is folk religion entirely without elements which bear upon the destiny of the soul in the afterlife—as, for example, the veneration of ancestors—and many folk religions contain remnants of mystical doctrines expressed in terms of myth and folklore. Furthermore, while mystical religion renounces the attachment to worldly success and security, and considers personal immortality in a blissful afterlife to be either a severely limited goal ('paradise is the prison of the gnostics') or a veiled metaphor for mystical Union itself, the blessing of a realized saint or sage has always been recognized as helpful to the salvation of one's soul, as a source of protection, and even in some cases as a talisman for worldly success, depending upon the intent and capacity of the recipient. Nonetheless, the three goals of power (via magic), salvation (via obedience), and liberation (via realization) characterize the essence of folk religion, church religion and mystical religion respectively.

Judaism, Christianity and Islam are church religions which contain mystical elements—Kabbalah, Hesychasm, and Sufism—and have included a certain amount of folk religion as well. Buddhism is primarily a mystical religion, though in its Pure Land or Amidist forms it tends to become a religion of salvation, while still considering the attainment of a blissful afterlife as only the first step toward final Enlightenment. In China and elsewhere Buddhism incorporated a number of folk elements, and the Nichiren Shoshu sect and others like it, with their emphasis on worldly success, though still oriented toward final Enlightenment, shares the fundamental goal of folk religion.

Confucianism, in its avoidance (though not denial) of supernaturalism, is more a system of social wisdom and morality, though a profound and providential one, than what we would think of as a religion. Taoism, the other major Chinese tradition, takes three forms, according to Huston Smith: philosophical Taoism, yogic-hygienic Taoism, and established church Taoism. Philosophical and yogic-hygienic Taoism are primarily mystical, roughly corresponding to *jñana*-yoga and *raja*-yoga within Hinduism (though yogic-hygienic Taoism, with its emphasis on health and longevity, incorporates folk elements), while church Taoism might be described as a magical folk religion become an organized church. Taoism shares with shamanism, one of its distant ancestors, a closer union of magic and mysticism than has been the case in the Abrahamic religions, in Buddhism (outside of the Vajrayana sects), and perhaps even in Hinduism; and yet the two tendencies remain distinct.

As for Hinduism, it encompasses all three elements: every conceivable form of magical and/or polytheistic folk religion; a higher 'church' polytheism, based on the cults of the major gods and goddesses; and a rich mystical spirituality, largely derived from the transcendental teachings of the Vedanta, and including the cults of Kali, Shiva, and the avatars of Vishnu reinterpreted as forms of the unitary Absolute.

The dominant form in Europe the United States has traditionally been church religion; and since North American Christianity has been predominantly Protestant, both mystical and folk spiritualities have been largely excluded—though some brands of charismatic Protestantism have partially filled the gap, not by incorporating folk religion, but by nearly turning

Christianity into a magical folk religion itself. This was not quite the case in the traditional Catholicism of Latin America, which embraced many more folk elements, and preserved to some degree the mystical dimension, at least within the context of monasticism. Mysticism lived on in North American Catholicism as well—as witness such figures as Thomas Merton—but a narrow, though often extremely deep, church Protestantism, and church Catholicism, remained the reality denoted by the word 'religion' in the minds of the majority of Americans until perhaps the late '60s.

The suppression of both folk religion and mystical religion in the North American context made possible a fundamental error which gained great cultural power in the 1960s and '70s, and has continued to spread to the present day: namely, that folk religion is in fact mystical. As has so often been the case throughout history, in politics as well as religion, essentially incompatible ideas became linked in the popular mind by virtue of their common exclusion from the official view of reality. Even though folk religion's pursuit of worldly safety and success is at the opposite pole from mystical religion's goal of renunciation and liberation, the prevailing historical dynamic insured that many people who professed an interest in mysticism would be interested in magic as well; the felt need to 'drop out' of narrow church religiosity meant that one was very likely to 'drop in' to everything which church religion had left out, whether exalted, simply vulgar, or actively sinister.

Evangelical Protestantism continues, not surprisingly, to propagate the error that metaphysics and mysticism (at one pole) and magic and psychic phenomena (at the other) are really the same thing, while Liberal Protestantism and Catholicism have fallen into the same error from the opposite direction: many Liberals believe that the lost mystical dimension of Christianity—or *their* Christianity—can be resurrected by including more folk elements, through an interest in world mythology, Pagan religion, shamanism, and even witchcraft. And Charismatic Protestantism (and Catholicism) have done what they can to turn Christianity into a magical or folk religion.

The suppression of mystical religion in North American Christianity led even such contemplatives as Thomas Merton to seek the lost mystical dimension in non-Christian traditions. This has had the ambiguous effect of awakening Christianity to its own mystical aspects at the expense of polluting it with heterogeneous elements which, though undoubtedly of profound truth and spiritual efficacy within their own traditional contexts, have tended to cast a distorting shadow on traditional Christian metaphysical

philosophy and mystical spirituality. And the inability of American Protestantism to sanctify, insofar as possible, the folk dimension—something both
Catholicism and Russian Orthodoxy were better able to do, though not
without tolerating from time to time certain ambiguous elements—coupled
with the creeping apostasy of Roman Catholicism itself, opened American
Christianity to subversion by both Neo-Paganism, whether in the form of
Afro-American religions like Santerría or mass-marketed 'Pagan' revivals
like the Wicca of Starhawk, and various New Age and/or neo-spiritualist
ideas. Nor can the great and destructive influence of Jungianism—a psychology having many valid insights on its own level, but taking the unfortunate form of a pseudo-mysticism incorporating many folk elements—be
discounted, especially within liberal Protestantism and the Catholic
Church.

Given that mystical religion is the core, either intrinsic or recognized, of
every true spirituality, and that the magical element, the desire to pursue
worldly success and avoid worldly harm by subtle means, will always present
itself at the door of our religious life, demanding to be recognized, we must
take both into account. If we fail to do so, the result will be pseudo-mysticism on the one hand, and sorcery on the other. The danger of sorcery is
only overcome by incorporating powerful and spiritually effective petitionary prayer into our religious life, while realizing at the same time that we
must 'seek first the kingdom of God and His righteousness' which is 'not of
this world'; to the degree that the miraculous power of theurgy withdraws
from our spiritual life, at least within a Christian context, the subversive
power of magic will take its place. And the danger of pseudo-mysticism can
only be overcome through real mysticism, the metaphysical and operative
aspects of which, in terms of Christianity, are fully presented in the patristic
tradition and the writings of the mystical saints of both the Eastern and
Western churches. Without a comprehensive understanding and a living
practice of its own mystical tradition, the Christian churches leave themselves open to invasion by a false metaphysics and a false contemplative
practice—the religion of Antichrist.

Certain aspects of folk religion are clearly poised to pay tribute to the
Antichrist's regime, not because folk religion (in a contemporary North
American context, primarily Neo-Paganism) is always evil in itself—it is
capable, at its best, of giving people a viable way of dealing with each other
and the world around them, and awakening them, at least up to a point, to
the sacred significance of the natural world—but because satanic forces can
use it to subvert both church religion and mystical religion. And mystical

religion can faithfully serve the Antichrist all by itself, if it begins to see itself as a rival to church religion, and thus as an alternative 'church' rather than as the mystical depth of a given tradition, of which its 'church' is the necessary and providential outer form. If it takes this road, it will finally both undermine that 'church' and betray its own essence. And church religion itself, if it degenerates into a narrow legalism on the one hand or an anti-intellectual fideism on the other, necessarily opens its door to the twin subversions of pseudo-mysticism and sorcery.

In the world of the New Age, sorcery and pseudo-mysticism have come together. Yet New Age spirituality cannot really be called 'folk religion', since it is being mass-marketed, in a very sophisticated way, to a 'mass' that is no longer really a 'folk'. And it draws as much on, say, advanced brain research and the speculations of post-Einsteinian physics as it does on ancient traditions like shamanism. Spiritual liberation is preached, and mystical techniques which claim to be able to produce it are taught. Yet the New Age cannot be characterized as mystical religion either, since the liberation in question is approached either through a false metaphysics, through true metaphysical principles taken out of context, or through purely psychic means, which are insufficient by definition for spiritual liberation, since it is the dominance of the psyche—the universe, whether subtle or gross, defined by the human ego—from which the spiritual Path exists to liberate us. And spiritual liberation is presented by the New Age not as the fruit of the renunciation of the world, but as fully compatible with the magical pursuit of worldly goals, if not in itself the most powerful magic of all. The central New Age tenet seems to be, 'you *can* serve God and Mammon.' Furthermore, the techniques being widely disseminated are either meaningless fantasies, useful psychological tools which have nothing spiritual about them, dangerous magical techniques, or, again, true mystical practices which, however, can be reliably effective only within a living spiritual tradition possessing an orthodox doctrine and a 'hands-on' understanding of how contemplative spirituality is to be practiced, within both the doctrinal and the moral contexts. But if anything characterizes New Age spirituality, it is the reduction of the doctrinal or metaphysical understanding of the universe, its relationship to its divine Principle, and the essential nature of that Principle to a set of technical rules, coupled with the tendency to take methods of contemplative or yogic or magical practice out of any *moral* context, as well as out of a sufficient doctrinal one. If it requires no moral commitment to operate a personal computer, neither is any required for the magical operation of the human nervous system, and the manipulation of the subtle forces which that nervous system may, under certain circumstances, tap into. To any person with an understanding of true spirituality, either devotional or contemplative, the inevitable outcome of such an approach is painfully obvious. It is not so obvious, unfortunately, to the New Age practitioners themselves, who think that their dangerous and chaotic experimentation with human consciousness is mystical spirituality, and have been carefully trained to prejudge as 'prejudice' any warnings or expressions of concern on the part of those better informed than they are. A lack of listeners, however, in no way absolves the better-informed from their duty to speak.

In books such as *Theosophy: History of a Pseudo-Religion*, *The Spiritist Fallacy*, and *The Reign of Quantity and the Signs of the Times*, the metaphysical philosopher René Guénon preached not against magical folk-religion *per se* (unless spiritualism can be considered an a-typical modern folk-religion) but specifically against certain more sophisticated movements of the modern era—Theosophy, occultism and others—which go beyond 'traditional' folk practices. These movements represented to him not merely a 'worldly' religion of the common folk, whether effectively magical or merely superstitious, but, at least in some cases, a deliberate and conscious attempt to subvert both church religion and mystical spirituality through a chaotic mixture of folk elements, misunderstood or misrepresented mystical spiritualities, heretical doctrines, and even forms of outright satanism. He considered the growth of such movements as one of the first clear signs of the advent of Antichrist, and therefore as heralds of the apocalyptic end of the present cycle, after which a new cycle will be initiated by a new *avatara*—an event called, in Christian terms, the *parousia*, the second coming of Christ.

✳ The World Wide Web

One of the clearest expressions of postmodernism is the 'information culture', whose 'mystical body' is the internet. There is no question but that the World Wide Web is useful. It makes researching huge masses of data much easier, and facilitates certain forms of creative communication which were never before possible. The price of this undeniable example of 'progress' is nonetheless higher than can be paid by even the best use of it. (As a friend of mine once said, when I asked him what computers are good for, 'they are good for dealing with the information explosion created by computers.') It is not always a sin to use the internet, but it *is* always a spiritual danger, whose scope and depth cannot be defined simply in terms of the kind of information we choose to access by means of it. (According to a recent study, internet use produces symptoms of depression and loneliness. A slight but statistically significant increase in these symptoms can develop from as little as one hour per week on-line.)

The internet is the perfect socio-technological symbol of postmodernism. There is no 'over-arching paradigm' to give order and coherence to the view of reality it presents. 'Reality' is simply what is configured by the individual according to his needs, his interests, his fears and his desires. Like Jung's 'collective unconscious', the Web represents not an objective reality, either material or metaphysical, but rather a mass subjectivity with objective consequences. It might be characterized as a form of mass training in solipsism or autistic introversion, whence the proverbial social retardation of the 'computer nerd'. Nothing exists but the 'me' and its global tendrils. I am the thinker; you are my thought. The world is my nervous system.

The megalomania potentially generated by the web-induced fantasy that I am speaking to the 'whole world' from behind a screen of electronic anonymity, coupled with the lack of any touchstone for objective reality which could cut that megalomania down to size, guarantees that the less objective and therefore more extreme and unbalanced visions of 'reality' proffered on the internet will gain a power out of all proportion to their intrinsic worth, especially given the extreme passivity which, side-by-side with ego-inflation, is an inevitable consequence of the suppression of any sense of reality outside the 'me'. Experience, without a living relationship with objective truth to replenish it, enters a state of accelerating entropy. Such entropy began in the West with the marginalization of religion and the death of metaphysics, and presently seems headed, on the analogy of the second law of thermodynamics, toward a kind of 'heat-death' of meaning, where even the relative objectivity represented by a common world of sense-experience is marginalized by the dominance of the electronic media. If the theoretical end of an exploding universe is the stagnation of a uniform temperature, the corresponding end of the information explosion seems destined to be a kind of 'uniform temperature of meaning,' where rumor is elevated to the status of fact and fact degraded to the level of arbitrary opinion, where no datum will be any more significant or meaningful than any other. But fortunately—or unfortunately—such a theoretical limit of meaninglessness cannot in fact be reached. In the words of René Guénon from *The Reign of Quantity and the Signs of the Times*, 'After the egalitarianism of our times'—the information culture being a kind of egalitarianism of meaning—'there will again be a visible established hierarchy, but an inverted hierarchy, indeed a real "counter-hierarchy", the summit of which will be occupied by the being who will in reality be situated nearer than any other being to the very bottom of the "pit of Hell".

The internet, on the metaphysical level, is in some ways a satanic inversion of the immanence of God. Nicholas of Cusa, in an attempt to represent this immanence, characterized God as 'an infinite sphere whose center is everywhere and whose circumference is nowhere.' This is an apt description of the internet. It is the first utility apparently run by no one, or everyone. (*Apparently* so, because although no one runs it, people like Bill Gates who have the economic and technical power to exploit it are using our on-line experience that 'intent configures reality' to hide the fact that they are feeding us, as if it were primordial nature itself, the very terms, methods and systems by which we are 'free' to configure it.) According to the mythology of New Age spiritual populism—which was a big influence, via Peter Russell (*The Global Brain*), Barbara Marx Hubbard, and others, on the development of the internet—each of us, *on the plane of manifestation*, is equally divine. How reality is configured by me is therefore no more or less valid than how it is configured by you. We believed that if the truth that 'the center is everywhere' could be effectively realized globally, then God would be incarnate on a mass level and the Earth would be saved. But when Nicholas of Cusa said 'the center is everywhere,' he did not mean that the worldviews of a pedophile or a paranoid schizophrenic were of equal value to those of a dedicated social critic like Noam Chomsky or a spiritual philosopher like Huston Smith. He meant that the *atman*, the Divine Witness, is immanent in all beings, including all human beings. Although the degree to which it is realized, or betrayed, differs radically from case to case, it is still the transcendent core of every person. The Divine Witness is not the *subjectivity* of each of us, however, but precisely what transcends this subjectivity, and in so doing presents us with things as they are. As the *Absolute* Subject, the *atman* is not this or that subjective ego with its eccentric configuration of experience; it is That which witnesses nothing but Absolute Objective Truth. Only God's 'configuration' of reality, that formless Essence which is the Form of every form, is absolutely true. His act of configuring embraces all of ours, from that of the criminal to that of the saint; the saint is a saint, however, precisely because his configuration approximates most nearly to God's, the criminal a criminal because his departs most radically from it.

To place the truth that 'the center is everywhere' on the plane of manifest conditions, not on the plane of a transcendent, Absolute Reality which is nonetheless immanent in all things, is to transform the vision of God in all things into an 'absolutization of the relative', a deification of illusion. It is to worship *avidya-maya*, the universe of conditions insofar as it veils rather than reveals the Absolute. And one of the universal symbols for this *maya*, from many cultures and traditions, is the spiderweb. Thus the World Wide Web, in its main drift though not according to its undeniably valuable uses, is an expression of *avidya-maya*, the power of ignorance. And as Marshall McLuhan taught us, the main drift is what counts: The medium is the message. The essential form of a medium—or of a technology, such as nuclear power or genetic engineering—is of greater overall effect on consciousness and society than the things we decide to use it for. The essential form of the World Wide Web, with its flood of subjectively-configured information (much of it indistinguishable from simple lying), its denial of objectivity, and its consequent suppression of both detachment and intellectual scope, is well expressed in Nietzsche's declaration: 'Nothing is true; everything is permitted'—the battle-cry of postmodernism in six words.

In the Golden Age, perception conforms, insofar as possible, to Reality. In the Kali Age, perception departs from Reality, insofar as possible, and ultimately goes to war with it—a war the Bible calls 'Armageddon'. When perception-become-virtual-illusion goes to war with Truth, Truth must take the wrathful form of Kali, whose non-manifest essence is Shiva: Absolute Reality as destroyer of the world-illusion.

Before this ultimate battle, however, suppressed objectivity, now degraded from the level of intelligence to the level of power alone, will return in negative and counterfeit form. Where nothing is true and everything permitted, those who seize power can configure reality as if they were God Himself—but configure it *according to what?* With objective truth suppressed and power absolutized, what reality can the powerful turn to for a design according to which that power could be expressed? No reality but power itself, which means: no truth but chaos. Therefore, after the powerful have finished seizing their power, the Antichrist will seize them. Antichrist, that towering instability, that center of mass subjectivity rising up against objective truth through power alone, will be the universal, devastating, and final expression of postmodernism. And the Web will be his Whore. What is a prostitute, after all, but an expression of the human desire that objective reality conform to subjective fantasy? And what does the experience of frequenting prostitutes teach us—if objectivity can ever free us from that experience so we can learn from it—but that those who desire power over their fantasies are simply giving their fantasies power over them?

This is the Web: watch and learn.

✳ Postmodernism and Globalism

Postmodernism is the religious, philosophical and cultural ideology of globalism. But how can this be? How can an economic and political world unification rise out of a worldview — or an anti-worldview — which exalts diversity and defines all unity, including political unity, as oppression?

The ironic answer is that Unity, which postmodernism denies, is implied in every statement it makes, for the simple reason that every assertion that the whole of reality is this or that way — even the assertion that it is multiple, diverse, and without objective referent — is an example of it. The doctrine that there is no over-arching paradigm is itself an over-arching paradigm. So even though Unity is denied, it is perpetually invoked; but to invoke something which is both intellectually denied and emotionally feared is to make sure that it will present its most negative face.

Unity *is*. If we don't take cognizance of it, then it will not express itself in terms of cognizance, but by power. In other words, the denial of all unities, of which metaphysical Unity is the root principle, makes it certain that no view can stand as a rival to the 'unity' of naked power. Postmodernism melts down traditional religions, cultures and forms-of-life, and power takes over. Thus postmodernism paves the way for globalism, first by destroying any view which could rival it, and secondly by creating a level of chaos which calls for repressive measures — in the mistaken belief that chaos is freedom (see *Chapter Six*). Unity is a metaphysical truth. If denied, it will reassert itself not so much against as *by means of* this denial: and this is the system of Antichrist. In René Guénon's terms from *The Reign of Quantity*, out of the modernist-materialist Reign of Quantity, whose terminal phase is postmodernism, is ultimately born the Reign of Inverted Quality, where democratic egalitarianism is destroyed not in the name of aristocracy but of chaos, to the benefit of those globalist socio-economic wizards to whom cultural chaos is natural, and the high road to power. Diversity, for them, entails accepting the existence a multi-ethnic global ruling class, since no one who can't work with Limeys, Frogs, Camel Jockies, Japs, Gooks, and Niggers can be effectively cosmopolitan according to today's model. Like the good communist, the good globalist learns that race doesn't matter, culture is an impediment which can and should be overcome, and all that really counts is class. Furthermore, no one is more helpful in legitimizing such 'world-class' mores than the white (or black) supremacist bigots and ethnic separatist/terrorists who represent their reverse mirror image. World cultural fusion is also a way for the ruling elite to globalize markets, standardize both consumers and the workforce, and permanently mesmerize the masses, not simply by throwing a temporary cloak of secrecy around their actions, but by destroying even the normal human desire to know what's really going on, by means of an ideology which preaches that nothing in fact *is* going on, outside of the subjective fantasies of the isolated individual. And the horrors of social chaos, weapons of mass destruction and environmental degradation make such an insane ideology very attractive as an escape—to those, that is, who have not yet decided on the assisted suicide which Jack Kavorkian, that perfectly contemporary and highly relevant postmodern satanist, will gladly provide for them, with the increasingly open blessing of the world as it is, and as it is destined to become.

One of the 'prophets' of this solipsistic dementia based on fear and denial, interestingly enough, was LSD pioneer Timothy Leary. Toward the end of his life, when he was dying of cancer, he made statements like the following: Since the earth is dying, our best recourse is to travel *en masse* into cyberspace, into virtual reality, and leave the earth behind; that's the technological and cultural 'new frontier'. He forgot only one thing: that virtual reality still requires both the human nervous system to experience it and a source of energy to power our computers. Food, water, shelter and air will still be needed, along with power plants and an 'extended service contract' in case our computers break down. Other 'less imbalanced' minds, however, have apparently thought of a way around these limitations: We will simply upload our consciousness directly into computers which will be serviced by robots who do not need food, water, shelter and air.

Ah well... to each his own. But back to postmodernism on a slightly more human level: In all this 'celebration of diversity', just who is it doing the real celebrating? Not the declassé 'locals' mired in marginalized worldviews which were once cultures, religions, civilizations. Not the obsolete modernists celebrating defunct 'literary' unities. Only those can truly celebrate the diversity of worldviews who are heir to them: the global elite. Certainly a kind of diversity is necessarily part of postmodern mass culture, a diversity portrayed as 'richness'—but the narrowed attention-span and tunnel vision which its quality of supersonic jagged disjuncture creates in most people cannot reach the level of 'overview' where this 'diversity' can even be *perceived* in order to be 'celebrated'. And the quantitative multiplication of such 'diversity', to the detriment of those qualitative elements without which the concept of diversity is meaningless, renders postmodern experience, for all its kaleidoscopic 'richness', strangely uniform and dead. The consciousness of the masses tends to be stuck, more hopelessly every day, in the split second of reaction-to-stimulus, devoid of both a wisely contemplated past and a reasonably projected future—a mode of 'consciousness' which is precisely the ego's version, the satanic counterfeit, of that Eternal Present through which God, as the Absolute Witness within us, views the world. Only those with the cultural, economic and technological *power* to command the simultaneous presence of many views of reality can place a significant percentage of the whole postmodern diversity on the same banquet table at the same time—but never all of it, and never for long: because the change unleashed by global information technology is too chaotic and rapid for anyone to really keep up with; because the rate of attrition and turnover of the ones who administer the global marketplace is also speeding up; and because the postmodern destruction of human consciousness must eventually affect those who hope to profit from it—perhaps more rapidly, and certainly more deeply, than it affects even its most willing puppets and most vulnerable dupes. Those who poison the well will ultimately be forced to drink from it.

A multiplicity of views can only be perceived from the point-of-view of an all-embracing Unity. But the ability to perceive any view other than one's own is also denied—implicitly if not openly—by the most extreme forms of postmodernism, according to the doctrine that there is no perception of objective reality but only the construction of it. If reality is based only on constructed views, the same is true of any view we can have of the view of another—and how can we celebrate the diversity of views if we deny our ability to objectively perceive any view other than our own? Postmodernism takes from phenomenology the imperative to see through others' eyes, to walk a mile in their shoes. But it also takes the denial of a single objective truth, which leads to an absolutization of the subjective, necessarily implying an absolutization of *my* subjectivity, which of course makes it impossible for me to see through other people's eyes. Postmodernism, then, is the despairing gesture of one solipsist (*me*, of course) in the direction of other conjectural solipsists whose existence he must deny even as he signals to them through the smoke.

But even this is not the bottom of the postmodern swamp. Without the liberating and stabilizing presence of objective reality outside the 'me' where all subjective standpoints converge, everything is ego—and the ego is defined not by truth but by power. This ego, however, having no intrinsic reality, is in fact the weakest of all imaginable pseudo-realities. As such, its solipsism is destined to be devoured by a larger solipsism, a greater unreality, a more powerful weakness—by the regime of those who, in the name of power, have most completely emptied themselves of reality, in the service of

that greatest unreality, that most powerful weakness of all—the Antichrist.
In Guénon's words:

> The Antichrist must evidently be as near as it is possible to be to 'disintegra-
> tion', so that one could say that his individuality, while it is developed in a
> monstrous fashion, is nevertheless at the same time almost annihilated, thus
> realizing the inverse of the effacement of the 'ego' before the 'Self', or in other
> words, realizing confusion in 'chaos' as against fusion in principial Unity ...
> ⌐THE REIGN OF QUANTITY, p 327).

The deliberately sought and meticulously engineered unreality of the postmodern world is also, in the same way, a satanic counterfeit of the Buddhist
doctrine of the 'voidness' of phenomena. To the Buddhists, the phenomenal
world in its essential reality—to the eyes of one fully awakened—is void of
self-nature, of any relative or contingent limitation. The voidness of things is
one with their 'suchness', which is another way of saying that things are free
of all limiting definitions because they are, in essence, incomparable. All
forms are manifestations of their absolute Principle, which is not however a
separate cognitive object; sangsara itself is Nirvana. To the postmodernist,
on the other hand, forms are 'absolutely' relative. There is nothing in them
but their self-nature, relative and indefinable as it is, and this is their 'voidness'. In their impermanent and contingent limitation, 'as such', they are all
that exists; they are opaque and manifest nothing; there is no Nirvana, no
Buddha-nature in them, only a sangsara which can never be seen as it is—as
a world of illusion based on craving and ignorance—because no liberating
Truth exists beyond it in light of which its illusory nature might be grasped.
There is no exit.

✳ Postmodernism and Paranoia

Michael Kelley, in an article entitled 'The Road to Paranoia' (*The New
Yorker*, June 19, 1995) coined the term 'fusion paranoia' to describe the coming
together of the lunatic fringes of both left and right, plus the purveyors of
specialized paranoias from all points of the compass, in a general anti-government, anti-globalist stew seasoned with plenty of racism and incipient
domestic terrorism. He also points out how paranoia has become much
more acceptable in the 'mainstream' of American political life. 'In an age of
fusion paranoia,' Kelley writes, 'there is no longer any distinction made
between credible charges and utterly unfounded slanders. Any suggestion of

conspiratorial evil against a prominent politician, no matter how extreme the charge or how scanty the evidence, glides from the margins of politics to the center, on a sort of media conveyor belt that carries it from the rantings of fringe groups of the right and the left into the respectable zone of public discourse.'

Such established paranoia is integral to the postmodern ethos. If there is no objective truth, there is no way to distinguish between credible charges and wild rumors. If there is no objective truth, any established view of reality is automatically suspect; it can only be understood as a conspiracy of the powerful against the weak (which, of course, it sometimes is). If there is no objective truth, anyone who can launch a rumor which can't be definitively disproved—a process the internet seems to have been specifically designed to encourage—can feel that he, like Almighty God, has created 'reality' out of nothing.

What exactly is paranoia? It is the attempt of the human mind to reach cognitive closure in a situation that does not allow for it, either because there is too little information to warrant that closure, or—as with the paranoid schizophrenic—too much information to make sense of, except through delusion.

Our postmodern information culture is perfectly designed to create paranoia. We are forced by it to process too much information; and this too much is, in another sense, also too little, since as the quantity of facts (or conjectures, or fantasies) increases, our certainty as to the truth of any single fact decreases. As an attempt to reach cognitive closure, however, paranoia is nothing but a normal and necessary human faculty which has taken a distorted and pathological form: the ability to create a stable outlook, a consistent and unified worldview. In a world which denies that there is such a thing as objective truth, this normal faculty is forced to work itself into a state of insanity, like the daughters of Danaos in hell trying to draw water with a sieve.

The prevalence of paranoia in our culture is proof that we are not at ease with postmodernism, that the willingness to permanently defer cognitive closure, which postmodernism demands, runs counter to human nature. It's good evidence that we will never be comfortable with the idea that there is no objective truth. And this is postmodernism's greatest danger: In its understandable attempt to avoid totalitarian ideologies, it is storing up in the collective unconscious, through its own 'totalitarian relativism', a deep desire for the lost Unity which was once provided by religion, metaphysics and the intellectual intuition of God. When our exhaustion with chaos and relativism reaches the breaking-point—which will also be the point when our ability to recognize true, objective, metaphysical Unity is most deeply eroded—then our unconscious desire for that Unity will explosively emerge. And the one who can best fulfill this desire, on a global level—no matter how unrealistic his promises are, since our collective sense of reality will then be at its lowest ebb—will step into the role of Antichrist.

✳ The Globalist Religions

It stands to reason that somewhere in the councils of the great, ideas and proposals such as the following are being seriously discussed:

'Every stable civilization known to history has been based in one way or another upon religion. The traditional religions are divisive, the cause of wars and social instability, because no single one of them is destined to ultimately triumph on a global level; they will always be at odds. The global New World Order therefore needs a religion of its own.

'No religion really comes from 'God'; all are creations of the human mind. Essentially, they are expressions of our human potential. The greatest social engineers of human history have been the priests, who by laborious trial and error have discovered the laws of establishing social stability and orienting all the human resources of a given civilization toward the central goals of that civilization. Once the global civilization of the New World Order becomes a reality, there is a real danger that it will be destroyed by, among other factors, inter-religious wars. Therefore we must create a new religion which will supersede all the others, taking what is best from each of them, but leaving their divisiveness and opposition to progress behind. We owe it to the peace and security of the world to establish such a religion.

'This new religion must combine the deepest mythic 'archetypes' of the human past with an exaltation of technology and world unity. Exactly what form it will take is not yet known; we are still in the phase of research and development. We will give our patronage to various experimental religions, watch how they operate and observe their effects upon national and global societies, as well as their interactions with the traditional religions. What fails, we will discard; what works, we will incorporate.

Various 'new religions' have already gotten wind of our plans in this regard, at least in their general outline. They are beginning to show up on our doorstep, petitioning our patronage. Some of them we will reject, others we will adopt as pilot programs. A fruitful interchange is thus growing up between religious trends arising from the mass level, and the results of our own propaganda and social engineering experiments. The Church of Scientology, Benjamin Creme's 'Maitreya' cult, EST and its successors, the Avatar training seminars, the various UFO cults, Sun Myung Moon's Unification Church . . . all have something to teach us. We will take from each what seems useful, and discard whatever does not prove itself in the field.

Exactly who the 'we' in this scenario are is unclear. Are the planners of the global religion a single 'steering committee', the sort of simplistic idea immediately attractive to paranoids everywhere? Do they merely represent the half-conscious 'culture' of the multinational corporations? Or does the truth lie somewhere in between?

At Ted Turner's 'Millennium Summit' in 2000, there was a resounding call to quash religious proselytism; similar sentiments have been expressed in other sectors of liberal ecumenism. It appears that the global elites want to use the legitimate concern about the excesses of Western missionaries in the East to limit the right of all religions to make converts. If every religion points to the same Reality, the reasoning goes, then religious differences are mere turf-wars. Religions are nothing but 'cultural expressions' mediated either by the accidents of birth or by 'lifestyle choices'; to claim that a religion is in any sense true is like claiming that only one brand of soap or make of automobile is valid. Let them keep to their own territory, like the picturesque tourist attractions they are. And let them make no claims to ownership of that territory; all ground belongs to the elites. Under globalism, religion is to be 'federal', with the rights of individual religions severely limited, as were states' rights after the American Civil War.

George Bush, past U.S. President and C.I.A. director, spoke in the late '90s to a convention of the Unification Church, which at that time was planning to set up a 'world fusion' community, possibly in Brazil, in the form of a cluster of smaller communities, each representing one member nation of the U.N. Why would a 'statesman' of Bush's stature be interested in the Moonies, which in the public mind are nothing but a discredited cult of brainwashed flower-vendors?

The World Parliament of Religions, which still meets on a regular basis, represents an early attempt at this kind of quasi-political ecumenism. At the date of this writing, The United Religions Initiative, which in part grew out of the Parliament, is striving to organize the world's religions into a permanent council on the order of the U.N.; they have solid financial backing, and are already organized in 58 countries. And we are sure to see many similar attempts in the future. Such forays into global ecumenism have heretofore been mostly the province of impractical idealists, remote from the centers of international power. The emergence of a global 'New World Order', however, may have changed everything. Given that global economic and cultural imperialism has re-ignited 'tribalist' separatist movements the world over, many of which are religiously motivated—the Iranian Revolution being only the biggest and most obvious example—a push to homogenize the world's religions in the name of political and economic stability is rising ever higher on the agendas of the globalist power elite.

The idea that ancient spiritual wisdom and new religious 'technologies' (in the jargon of the corporate culture) are of great interest to the global elite is strange only to those who have never investigated that possibility. I recall a day in the 1980s when I sat, in the role of a friend of a friend, within the grounds of a hillside palace in Hillsboro, California, with executives from Hewlett-Packard and their spiritual training consultants—New Age in all but name. Depending on the view of reality the reader subscribes to, I was either privy to a dark yuppie conspiracy, or privileged to sit in on a convocation of pure idealists. And idealists they were. They sincerely wanted healthy and happy workers, creative interchange between labor and management, protection of the environment (bottom line permitting), a vision of the social role of the corporate sector based on the highest spiritual principles, as they understood them—a win/win situation all around. Certainly they were inventing the new global religion as they went along; what's wrong with that? They were the cutting edge of global progress, of the new information culture which was transforming the world. What better place for spiritual values and high ethical ideals?

The only problem was, they didn't believe in God—at least not in a God who, in relation to us if not in His own Essence, is capable of conscious intent and independent action. Spirituality was their experiment, their product, their property. Obedience to transpersonal norms established by the Creator through revelation of His Will to avatars, saints and prophets was not in their vocabulary of ideas. I remember joking to the friend who invited me to that gathering, imagining a magazine ad which ran:

INFORMATION.

THE HIGHEST GOOD.

'Of course,' he said. 'What's funny about that?'

✳ Liberal vs. United Front Ecumenism

Conservative Christians tend to think of themselves as the only ones who see any danger in postmodernism and the New Age. And they lump New Age spiritualities together with all Eastern religions and Native American spiritualities as part of what Fr. Seraphim Rose called 'the religion of the future'—the regime of the Antichrist. Unfortunately, they have real reasons for seeing things this way.

Hinduism and Buddhism entered American culture largely through the counter-culture of the '60s (and earlier), which also embraced, or misappropriated, Native American religious ideas and practices. (*Black Elk Speaks*, and of course *The Tibetan Book of the Dead*, were a common sight on hippy bookshelves.) Many Tibetan Buddhist teachers in this country seem still to have ties with the counterculture; a generally Neo-Pagan 'alternative' culture eagerly embraces the lamas, most of whom see no reason to separate themselves from it. (This cannot be said of all Tibetan teachers, however; I am told that the brother of the Dalai Lama, Dr Thubten Jigme Norbu, has real problems with the New Age.) So the 'world fusion spirituality' which includes ultra-Liberal Christianity, Western Buddhism, Westernized Hinduism, various commercialized Native American spiritualities (from the semi-traditional to the totally spurious), Neo-Paganism, the New Age, and certain strands of so-called Sufism, is a reality in this country. Its existence seems to prove the conservative Christians right in their belief that only Christianity can stand against 'the world', against postmodernism, against the 'false prophets' of the New Age who herald the advent of Antichrist.

The doctrines of the Traditionalist School, however, demonstrate that the great revealed religions of the world—Hinduism, Buddhism, Judaism, Christianity, and Islam—have more intrinsic affinity with each other, infinitely more, than any one of them has with Neo-Paganism or the New Age—certain more or less ironic social trends notwithstanding. A liberal ecumenism which ignores or compromises doctrine is only destructive to the cause of religion. A united front ecumenism, which would work toward a common understanding among the revealed religions of the spiritual, cultural and intellectual forces which menace all of them—not least of which are postmodernism, globalism, militant ethnic and religious separatism, Neo-Pagan and New Age doctrines—and do so without empty fraternization or limp doctrinal compromise, is a much more fruitful possibility. Such an inter-religious understanding would include not merely a respect for theological differences but a mutual will to accentuate doctrinal particularities: let the Jews be more Jewish, the Christians more Christian, the Hindus more Hindu, the Buddhists more Buddhist, the Muslims more Muslim, in the realization that the One Truth can be approached only through the particular forms of Divine revelation, not through whatever lowest ethical or doctrinal common denominator all the religions might be able to agree upon—and whatever quasi-political 'oversight committee' might emerge, via the United Religions Initiative or some similar attempt, in the name of it. The basis of such an understanding would be the principle that Frithjof Schuon called The Transcendent Unity of Religions, according to which the paths represented by the various orthodox revelations can finally meet only on the plane of the Transcendent, only in God Himself.

This doctrine, unfortunately, is highly susceptible to misinterpretation, that being one of its eschatological features: it must be announced, and it must—at least by some—be misinterpreted. To take only one example, William E. Swing, the Episcopalian Bishop of California, who presents a version of the Transcendent Unity of Religions in his *The Coming United Religions*—handbook of the United Religions Initiative—based on an inaccurate reading of Huston Smith's introduction to Schuon's *The Transcendent Unity of Religions*, says that 'The important distinction is not between religions but between people within each religion'—the exoterists and the esoterists. The esoterists 'intuit that they are ultimately in unity with people of other religions because all come together at the apex, in the Divine,' while the exoterists 'would wed the form of faith to the content or final truth of their own faith' (p 59). The exoterists are exclusivists, in other words, while the esoterists are universalists. According to Schuon, however, the fact that more than one religion is necessary in this manifest world is also an esoteric truth, which is why he characterizes the various Divine revelations as 'relatively Absolute'. In *Christianity/Islam: Essays in Esoteric Ecumenism*, he says:

> Every religion by definition wants to be the best, and 'must want' to be the best, as a whole and also as regards its constitutive elements; this is only natural, so to speak, or rather 'supernaturally natural' . . . religious oppositions cannot but be, not only because forms exclude one another . . . but because, in the case of religions, each form vehicles an element of absoluteness that constitutes the justification for its existence; now the absolute does not tolerate otherness nor, with all the more reason, plurality. . . . To say form is to say exclusion of possibilities, whence the necessity for those excluded to become realized in other forms. . . . (p 151)

The primary purpose of a united front ecumenism would be to oppose both globalist syncretism and militant ethnic/religious separatism, not necessarily in any high-profile way—unless God wills otherwise, and who is to say He won't?—in order to help the traditional religions purify their doctrines from the influence of them. Little can perhaps be done to reverse the degeneration of religion on a collective level, but it is still possible, and certainly worthwhile, to more clearly define the real parting of the ways between the Transcendent Unity of Religions and a globalist syncretism which is emphatically not an expression of the unity-in-multiplicity of God's self-revelation, but the mere ape of it—a counterfeit contrived in the cleverness of the human mind attempting to operate beyond the bounds of that revelation, in the darkness outside.

2

Who are the Traditionalists?

In this chapter I give a short overview of the doctrines of the Traditionalist School, based on the works of the founder of the school, René Guénon, and even more so upon those of the recently deceased master of the school, Frithjof Schuon, applying them to present social conditions and contrasting them with the false and self-destructive ideas on which the postmodern world is based. The central metaphysical doctrines I derive mostly from Schuon, the prophetic critique of the modern world more from Guénon.

True ideas are living things. Every mind that is host to them and every situation we apply them to brings out new facets of their unified and changeless meaning.

✳ Who are the Traditionalists?

The Traditionalist writers deal primarily with traditional metaphysics, which has little or nothing to do with most of what you'll find in the 'metaphysics' section of your local bookstore: books on magic, psychic powers and UFO encounters. Metaphysics is mystical theology and/or philosophy; it has more to do with Plato and St Augustine than with Aliester Crowley or Terry Cole Whitaker.

Most people investigating religion and spirituality these days will tend to get the impression that there are only two basic choices: the fundamentalist Christian Right, or the world which includes liberal Judeo-Christianity, Eastern religions, Neo-Paganism and the New Age. This is of course an over-simplification, since there are plenty of liberal Christians and members of Eastern religions who don't identify with the New Age, as well as non-Christian forms of 'fundamentalism' such as that of some Muslims (though by no means all), Jews, or even Hindus. But broadly viewed, the person interested in religion but as yet without a solid commitment will tend to be pulled in one of these two directions. And if he or she can't identify with either of them, then the prospect for serious religious commitment will look pretty bleak, and cynicism in religious matters seem the only mature response.

This is where the Traditionalists come in. Like some of the Liberals, they recognize the validity of all the world's major religions; but where the Liberals will often pay lip service to mysticism, while taking it out of its true context, the Traditionalists recognize in mysticism and metaphysics the true center and depth of every religious tradition, the depth at which we can truly say that every religion, from its necessarily unique perspective, is talking about the same Divine Reality.

On the other hand, like the conservative Christians, they understand that a religious tradition is something sacred that can't be changed at the whim of fashion without destroying it, and that to chaotically mix elements from different religions, trying to create some kind of ecumenical mishmash, is to desecrate religion itself, since it's as necessary for God to reveal Himself in different unique religious forms as it is for there to be different and unique human beings. The Liberals are wrong when they think that the only valid kind of ecumenism is *syncretism*, the mixing of religions. And the Conservatives are wrong too, not only because they can't see the Divine operating in other religions than their own, but also because they don't know how to distinguish the heights of mysticism and metaphysical philosophy from the most frivolous and dangerous search for magical and psychic powers, and consequently tend to cut out vast areas of their own tradition. The Fathers of the Church who were great metaphysicians, like Clement of Alexandria or Gregory of Nyssa, are not to be compared with Elron Hubbard; the great Christian mystics, like Meister Eckhart or St John of the Cross, are not to be confused with Carlos Castaneda. As far as I can tell, only the Traditionalists really understand these principles. Since they are neither chaotic Liberals not exclusivist Conservatives, they represent a real 'third force' in religion today.

✳ Who is the Sage?

We have some idea of what a 'saint' is. When we hear the word we think of someone like Mother Theresa, or of an almost mythological figure like St Peter or St Francis who lived a long time ago. But what is a 'sage'? If a saint is an example of sanctity, of a deep and often heroically self-sacrificing good-ness, what quality does a sage exemplify?

The quality in question is 'knowledge'. Today we are taught by social con-ditioning to think of knowledge as information, and of information almost exclusively in terms of 'hard data': technical information and well-established facts. As the poet T. S. Eliot said, 'Where is the wisdom lost in knowledge? Where is the knowledge lost in information?' We define a mass of digi-talized factual blips as 'information', forgetting that the word originally meant 'that which *forms* us *within*.' This belief, that only factual or technical knowledge is objectively valid, is so pervasive that I was not as shocked as I should have been recently to hear a woman on a Christian radio station say that you 'didn't have to be a rocket scientist' to understand a particular doctrine—implying, to me, the idea that there might be more difficult doc-trines that maybe only a rocket scientist *could* understand, that metaphysical wisdom is only a kind of technical expertise. On the other hand, one of the traditionalist writers, Wolfgang Smith, *is* a rocket scientist; he developed the equations which allow spaceships to reenter the Earth's atmosphere without incinerating. So the objectivity of the great scientist and that of the meta-physical sage are not entirely unrelated. Nonetheless, it is still true that we falsely believe that all objective knowledge must be scientific or technical in nature; the idea that there could be a higher level of objectivity that deals with spiritual things is completely foreign to us.

The contemporary mind is divided into two main compartments: scien-tific or practical knowledge is considered 'objective', while 'spiritual' knowl-edge, to the degree that we admit that there is such a thing, is seen as 'subjective', which means that we tend to take our impressions of things as absolutes in this realm; since spiritual knowledge is subjective by definition, what other person or dogmatic creed or traditional authority has the right to question *my* impressions? Let them be satisfied with their own im-pressions—that's their 'right'—and leave me to mine, since for them to attempt to convert me to their way of thinking, using the impossible and unfair argument that their beliefs are somehow 'objectively true', is really nothing but a vampire-like attempt on their part to transform *me* into *them*.

This is how most of us react nowadays when confronted with religious doctrines and philosophical ideas, which is one reason why, at least in 'lib-eral' circles, psychology is replacing theology. Ever since Descartes made the radical split between body and mind, 'objective' has progressively come to mean *material* and 'subjective' *psychological*; consequently the notion that there is an objective realm of spiritual truth has gradually disappeared, with the result that everything spiritual, since it is considered essentially subjective, has been reduced to the psychological, to the productions of the isolated individual mind, feeding on its own impressions. And Carl Jung's concept of a *mass* subjectivity—the 'collective unconscious'—while true and useful on its own level has in no way restored the vision of an objective spiritual order, only replaced it with a parody of the truth, at least in the minds of those who confuse psychology with metaphysics, making it that much harder for the real metaphysical truth to be understood.

It is this state of affairs Frithjof Schuon spent his life trying to remedy; and this is a work that only a *sage* can do. It is the role of saints to overcome pride, vice and selfishness, first in themselves, and then, as far as possible, in the society around them. The role of the sage, on the contrary, is to overcome illusion and untruth, first in his or her own soul and then in the society that he or she confronts. We need to remember however—and Schuon continually reminds us of this—that sanctity and sagacity are intimately related. no one with a vicious soul can attain a deep and stable knowledge of God and His relationship with the universe which is His manifestation; intelligence as we usually understand it, coupled with an interest in metaphysical ideas, plus access to the writings of the great metaphysicians of history, is not enough to make a sage. The other requirement is purity-of-heart, since one must be purely, or let us say 'virginally' receptive to Divine Truth if this Truth is to become a 'realization' and not simply an intellectual object which we possess as we would a house or a car. Perfection is not required; both saints and sages are tempted, and sometimes fall. What is required is a lack of fundamental resistance to the perfection God holds in store for us—an essence which is open to Knowledge by means of Goodness, since it knows that the Absolute Truth is also the Sovereign Good.

Few people have heard of Frithjof Schuon, though the handful who have heard him in depth include people of the stature of poet T.S. Eliot, who said of Schuon's first major book, *The Transcendent Unity of Religions*, 'I have met with no more impressive work in the comparative study of Oriental and Occidental religion,' and Professor Huston Smith, who has written of Schuon, 'In depth and breadth a paragon of our time. I know of no living thinker who begins to rival him.' And this tendency to appeal to the few, and find few ways of access to the popular mind, or even to the world of academia, if not exactly as it should be, is nonetheless as it must be. 'The secret protects itself.' And in a contemporary world awash in poisonous illusions, a voice sharing none of the assumptions on which the whole modern mindset is based, and speaking uncompromisingly from the standpoint of objective truth, will necessarily fall mostly on deaf ears. As in the Gospel parable, even if the seed is fertile, if it falls on stony ground, nothing will grow. And yet it is also true, especially of our times but to a degree true of all times, that it's hard to predict where fertile soil may turn up.

True metaphysical intellectuals have great difficult in finding each other these days. On the one hand, the world of academia has largely lost any love of wisdom for its own sake, and the 'intellectuals' society favors are essentially propagandists in the pay of big business and big government. On the other hand, the world of occultism, psychology, 'alternative' religions and 'New Age' spirituality is no more interested in traditional metaphysics than the 'intelligentsia' are. Though it may pay lip service to some of the great figures in the history of metaphysics and mysticism, it takes them out of their traditional context, and either empties them of all meaning or perverts them to the point where they are made to represent ideas that are diametrically opposed to their actual doctrines. To Conservative Christianity, mysticism is a dirty word. Liberal Christianity sometimes seems to value mysticism and metaphysics, but in reality it sees things much more in terms of sociology, history, psychology, and the physical sciences. And the various Eastern religions in the West are either making common cause—often merely by default—with New Age and/or various anti-traditional attitudes, or else are sealed within the veneration of their own masters and gurus, who may or may not be true saints or sages representing the living essence of their respective traditions, but in any case usually cannot effectively criticize the attitudes of the modern world, nor always preserve the fullness of their own traditional doctrines in the face of it. Given this state of things, Frithjof Schuon and the other writers of his school, both living and dead, represent a metaphysical alternative to the narrow, reactionary religion of the fundamentalists and the formless and chaotic religion, if we can still use that name for it, of liberals and the New Age. At their best, they represent a way beyond both fanatical religious exclusivism, and the formless syncretism of 'world fusion spirituality' which in so many ways represents the first stirrings of the global regime of the Antichrist.

✻ What is Metaphysics?

The English language is filled with 'fallen words', words which used to carry a full load of meaning, but have now been reduced to shadows of their former selves. What were once precisely accurate terms understood by all educated people are now mere clichés, if their meanings have not actually been inverted. Words once filled with allusion and resonance and depth-of-implication have gone flat.

Such a word is 'metaphysics'. The 'metaphysical' section of your local bookstore will likely contain books that have nothing whatever to do with what the word 'metaphysics' has meant from Aristotle down to the last half-century. It's true that the word literally means 'beyond physics', but it has always been used to denote what we can loosely call mystical philosophy: the study of 'first principles'. These principles are permanent truths, statements about eternal realities. They have to do with Being, and with the relationship of Being to the universe—spiritual, psychic and material—which allows It to appear. They even touch upon what is beyond Being. To use religious language, metaphysics has to do with the nature of God, and the relationship of God to the cosmos, and to humankind. Metaphysics is therefore the natural partner of theology; the only difference is that theology studies 'revelation', what God has revealed to us on His own initiative, and metaphysics studies God and His manifestation starting from our God-given ability to know Him simply because He is our Creator, and therefore something of Him remains within our nature. This does not mean, however, that theology and metaphysics make up two distinct worlds, since it is primarily God's Self-revelation in the great religious traditions which awakens, from the sleep of our fallen (or forgetful) nature, our 'supernaturally natural' ability to know Him, and it is specifically through *Intellection*—metaphysical intuition—perfectly married to Divine Love, that this Self-revelation comes to be perfected in the human soul. [NOTE: In Eastern Orthodox Christianity, the word 'theology' covers much more than it does in the West, since it incorporates an operative or contemplative dimension. It denotes not theory alone but also realization, making it roughly synonymous with the Islamic term *ma'rifah*.]

During most of Christian history up to the end of the Middle Ages, theology and metaphysical philosophy were either the same thing or closely related, though the temptation to separate them was certainly always there, since some metaphysicians tended to see scripture-studying theologians as people mechanically working with 'second-hand' material, while some theologians habitually viewed metaphysicians as potential heretics, arrogantly prying into divine mysteries on their own initiative without the sanction of scripture and tradition. Each saw the 'shadow' of the other, not the essence. Both were right about how metaphysics or theology can go wrong, but not about what these two ways of knowing God actually are in themselves. It was only in the 18th century, however, during the period for some reason called the 'Enlightenment', that theology and philosophy really started to diverge, though the seeds of this divergence were planted as early as the Renaissance. But philosophy was still basically metaphysics; philosophers were still asking the ultimate questions: What is the nature of Being? How can we know It? And how does Being-in-itself relate to the universe of nature and human experience? It remained for the modern period, with pragmatism, logical positivism, phenomenology, and post-modern decon-structionism, to finally separate 'philosophy' from metaphysics. Ultimate questions were not considered to mean anything; they were no longer 'hip'. Philosophy was reduced to secondary reflections on the findings of the social and physical sciences. And finally even theology began to follow phi-losophy down this long and narrowing road. The very concept of First Prin-ciples went out of style, with the result that time and change were believed to be more real than eternal truth; in fact the very existence of eternal truth was denied. It was looked upon as a kind of medieval superstition, to be studied only as part of the 'history of ideas'. It's as if a beautiful woman with a courageous character and a lovely soul were to come up to me and say 'I've always loved you,' and I were to respond by saying to myself 'I find her phys-ically attractive because of an inborn genetic propensity directing me to breed with a healthy member of the species, coupled with a culturally-con-ditioned sensitivity to the Western European/North American standard of physical beauty, and am attracted to her personality due to a culturally-inherited appreciation for specific character-types, including certain hold-overs from pre-post-modern Judeo-Christian morality. She is possibly attracted to me for some of the same reasons; however, it is possible that she is projecting on me qualities I do not possess, due to a faulty critical capacity on her part; it is also possible that she is deliberately mis-representing her feelings in order to gain advantage.' Now it's obvious that such thoughts would not be *entirely* void of meaning, but its equally obvious that they com-pletely miss the main point. In other words, the possibility that I might actually be in the presence of true love, and that this love might really have something eternal about it, despite the fact that beautiful personalities can fade and beautiful bodies must become old and die, is entirely cut out.

So it is with contemporary philosophy separated from metaphysics. It can come up with a lot of interesting details and useful perspectives, but it misses the main point, which is that the word 'philosophy' means 'love of wisdom'. The true philosopher must be a metaphysician, and the true meta-physician will know wisdom as eminently lovable. The central symbol of this love of wisdom in the Judeo-Christian world is the figure of Holy Wisdom, *Hagia Sophia*. As she says in the book of *Proverbs* (8:17), 'I love them that love me; and those that seek me early shall find me.'

✳ Why is it Important?

That we even have to ask a question like this shows just how dark the times have become. And in one sense it is an exercise in futility, since those born with a potential ability to understand metaphysics most likely already know the answer, while those without this potential can never be 'convinced'. Metaphysics is the world of certainty, not the world of opinions. Still, we really do have to ask it, because in a society no longer based on spiritual principles, metaphysics can seem meaningless, or at best a mere 'interest', like white water rafting or gourmet cooking.

Society's challenge to *all* intellectual interests is, 'if you're so smart, why aren't you rich?' which may tempt some people who have a natural affinity for metaphysics to 'talk back' to society, perhaps by trying to prove that metaphysical 'truth principles' can help you make money, or at least by claiming that the value of metaphysics lies somewhere else than in the fact that it is true. The idea that it is valuable because it can help build psychological stability, or improve society, or make people more sensitive to the environment is the death of metaphysics, just as the idea that you can love someone because they fulfill this or that physical or psychological or social need is the death of true love. Now true metaphysics and true love *do* have a positive effect on other levels of existence; they do fulfil real needs, though we can neither predict nor control how this influence will materialize. But if we go after these things for their 'cash value' and not because they are beautiful and true in themselves, then we are nothing but thieves. As it says in the Gospels, 'seek ye *first* the Kingdom of Heaven, and all these things shall be added unto you,' and 'whoever seeks to keep his life shall lose it, but whoever loses his life, for My sake, shall find it.' C. S. Lewis in *The Screwtape Letters* (pp 108–109) puts it like this, through the mouth of his demon Screwtape:

> Certainly we do not want men to allow their Christianity to flow over into their political life, for the establishment of anything like a just society would be a major disaster. On the other hand, we do want, and want very much, to make men treat Christianity as a means. . . . The thing to do is to get a man at first to value social justice as a thing which the Enemy demands, and then work him to the stage at which he values Christianity because it may

produce social justice. . . . 'Believe this, not because it is true, but for some other reason.' That's the game.

And what Lewis says of faith here goes double for spiritual intuition, since to sell out faith for its cash value produces only hypocrisy or fanaticism, whereas to sell out spiritual intuition produces black magic.

So one answer to the question 'Why is metaphysics important?' is: 'So that we don't lose the very concept of objective Truth.' Metaphysics deals in absolutes, in the necessary implications of Absolute Truth. If we no longer believe in Absolute Truth, then everything becomes relative. If everything becomes relative, then Truth is replaced by *power*; it is reduced to whatever this or that powerful individual or government or special interest has the *power to say* is true. And this is exactly how we look at questions of truth today: we believe that they are nothing but masks for questions of power. Have you ever tried to hold a conversation with a convinced partisan of this or that position? It can be very difficult to sit down with him or her and 'reason together' about the truth or falsity of that position, partly because the partisan is already convinced, but also partly because he or she is busy trying to analyze your motives, to discover which side you're on and exactly what you're trying to pull. Everything the partisan says is said 'for effect', and has been for quite some time, and so it's very hard for him or her to believe that you are raising an issue or asking a question simply because you want to know what is true; the *disinterested* quest for truth has long since been dropped from the partisan's repertoire. He or she has sacrificed truth to power, and assumes that everyone else has done the same thing. And the belief that truth is always necessarily sacrificed to power becomes a self-fulfilling prophecy; once partisanship is assumed to be universal, nothing outside partisanship is either recognized or allowed. Religions become not visions of Divine Truth but socio-historical entities with this or that agenda. The study of history is considered to have nothing to do with an impartial attempt to discover what really happened, and why, but is assumed to be part of the program of this or that power-bloc. The same goes for ethics; good and evil have nothing universal about them, but are only the expression of the vested interest of this or that religion or class or culture. Sociological findings and economic data are likewise pressed into the service of special interests; finally even scientific data—as, for example, those which might prove or disprove the Darwinian theory of evolution—are not immune. And if the assumption that truth must serve power is pushed far enough, it infects the world of human relations: what I say to another is not based on truth, but only on advantage. Walking the streets of any major American city, you will soon discover, if you haven't already, that eye-contact has nothing to do with a desire to *see* another person simply because you want to get an impression of who they are, but is limited to questions of power: can I get sex, or drugs, or money from that person? Do they want the same from me? Is this someone I can victimize, or someone who may hurt me? Those who are not interested in these things will quickly develop the ability not to attract attention to themselves; they will learn not to make eye-contact if they can possibly help it. (In rural areas, people will sometimes still say hello to strangers for 'no reason'; to those who've lived their lives in cities, it can come as quite a shock.)

This is the ultimate result of the growth of the kind of society in which metaphysics has no place. Without a sense of absolute, objective Truth, everything becomes subjectivized, which is why psychology is now replacing both theology and philosophy. And when spiritual Truth is hidden, not even psychology can maintain its own level, but is pushed in a materialistic direction, till all that's left of it is behaviorism, and finally psychopharmacology. Furthermore, when the Absolute is replaced by the subjective, all subjectivities are 'absolutized'. My individual experience is just as 'absolute' as yours, and yours as mine; this is called 'tolerance'. But if there is no objective Reality which includes both of us because it is bigger than us, if we are nothing but separate and hermetically-sealed universes of experience, how can we relate to each other? Only (as in C.S. Lewis' vision of Hell in *The Screwtape Letters*) by *eating* each other. If all is subjective, if there is no objective truth, then either you must become part of me, or I will end up becoming a part of you, the only other option being to devour each other equally (if only that were possible), and call it 'love'. And so the whole complex of what is called 'co-dependency' can ultimately be put down to the suppression of the sense of objective Truth, the highest and most complete form of which is metaphysics.

Given that truth *is* often sacrificed to power in this world, we must keep our critical edge; otherwise we will not be able to find our way through the desert where power is the chief, and arrive at the oasis where Truth is King. But if we become so suspicious and cynical that we no longer believe that there *is* such a thing as the truth, we have obviously gone too far... or not far enough. If the police want to find out who committed a murder, they must question the truth of the stories they hear; they can't simply take them at face value. But if they become so cynical listening to lies and half-truths year after year that they no longer believe that such a thing as objective truth actually exists, that somebody really did commit that murder, which means that the other suspects in question did not, then they can no longer fulfill their proper function, as when a police force is tempted to round up 'the usual suspects' to satisfy public pressure. Likewise postmodern criticism, which is as opposed to metaphysics as any view of things I can possibly imagine, may become so involved in questioning the motives of those making statements about what is true that they forget, and finally consciously deny, that *anything* is true—except as a statement with no objective point of reference, which has a 'right' to exist equal to that of any other statement, just as a species of plant or animal has a right to be saved from extinction because it is unique and irreplaceable. But doctrines are not animals. No animal or race of human beings can be 'wrong', but doctrines *can* be wrong. If I teach that a diet high in cholesterol is good for your heart, and somebody else teaches the opposite, these statements do not have an equal right to exist as manifestations of cultural belief or personal self-expression; one is right and the other is wrong.

Postmodernists use the same argument when it comes to human cultures: each has an equal right to exist as a unique expression of the human spirit. But here the question becomes ambiguous, because, whereas each expression of integral human culture, whether 'primal' like that of the Australians or Hopis or 'developed' like North African Islamic or Greek Orthodox culture, is part of the irreplaceable heritage of the race, still, a culture like that of the Thai Buddhists and the 'culture' of a drug cartel, or the world technocratic 'culture' that is presently destroying the whole Earth both culturally and environmentally (itself included), do not have an equal right to exist. But in a world where metaphysical knowledge is suppressed, everything is placed on the same level of value; the most wholesome and the most destructive beliefs or cultural manifestations have an equal right to exist, simply because they are there. The only thing the postmodernists seem to fear is the tyranny of uniformity, where one dominant culture takes over everything, and suppresses all minority folkways and beliefs. This, of course, is exactly what is happening in the world today, and it is profoundly destructive. But to place a culture like that of the Hopi, which fosters virtues such as politeness, self-effacement, friendliness and a profound ritual seriousness dedicated to maintaining balance between the needs of the people and the powers of the spiritual world, on the same level as that of the island of Dobu, based on black magic, where the admired 'virtues' (at least as of the 1930s when anthropologist Ruth Benedict wrote about them) are the ability to betray one's friends and fellow villagers, cause their crops to fail, and strike them with disease, is not impartial; it is slanderously destructive to Hopi culture while leaving Dobu culture unscathed. Only an understanding of integral metaphysics derived from the study of the pinnacles of the human spirit as expressed in the world's great religions and wisdom traditions can give us the objective standards against which we can judge whether a given culture is healthy, tired, degenerate, or actively subversive of the truth. Nor is the postmodern 'celebration of diversity' necessarily healthy for the primal and marginalized cultures it seeks to protect, since to deny the validity of an absolute hierarchy-of-values is finally to deny the hierarchy-of-values of each individual culture, which, insofar as that culture is concerned, is absolute. If no cultural manifestation is more or less valid than another, then if the younger generation of Hopis become socialized around, say, the 'culture' of drug use and heavy metal music, with the result that Hopi culture dies, who can complain? Furthermore, it turns out that the partisans of the emerging global technocratic culture and those who talk about the need to celebrate diversity are very often the same people; they want to celebrate cultural diversity because, as global economic technocrats, they have no local culture of their own. They have to exploit local cultures on a global scale to fill their spiritual needs, just as they exploit cheap labor to satisfy their economic ones. When I stated, above, that 'world fusion spirituality' is the religion of the Antichrist, this is part of what I meant.

So a society's relationship to metaphysical truth has everything to do with the essential nature of that society. But social value of metaphysics is only a reflection of much deeper levels of truth, one of which has to do with the fact that some people absolutely need metaphysical knowledge if they are to have a living relationship with God. These people are not 'believers'; they are 'knowers'. Faith is not enough for them, not because they scorn faith but because they are capable of knowledge, and will not be allowed to 'bury their talent' without serious consequences. But in a society like ours which both fundamentally denies objective metaphysical truth, and at the same time provides a vast spectrum of false doctrines, either foolish, unconsciously sinister or deliberately subversive, which masquerade as metaphysics, the person with the potential to be a 'knower' is misdirected at every turn, and is in danger of becoming either a religious skeptic, since the religious doctrines he is exposed to seem childish to him (ignorant as he is of their deeper meaning), or an apologist for seemingly more sophisticated doctrines which, unknown to him, are radically opposed to traditional metaphysics.

The temptations, tests, and pitfalls facing the 'knowers' are formidable; they have a much longer and harder road to travel than the believers. They will be moving through areas of knowledge which, though not opposed to orthodox religious doctrine, cannot in the nature of things be made explicit to every normally intelligent adult. Consequently they will be exposed to false ideas of every kind, some of which are extremely subtle and fascinating. Navigation across such a sea requires both a keen intellectual vigilance and a firm and constant responsiveness to the will of God. And they will also have to confront, at one point, the demon of Intellectual Pride, especially if they feel misunderstood or persecuted by the believers. The only things that can save them are a radical humility before God, and a clear understanding that just because they possess sophisticated metaphysical knowledge doesn't mean that they can't also be damned, while the simplest believer, if sincerely following a true doctrine, is saved even if he or she has never heard of such knowledge. As it says in the Gospels, 'to whom much is given, much will be required.' This is why it is traditionally understood that the path of sacred knowledge cannot be safely traveled, except in rare and unpredictable instances, without both an orthodox doctrinal framework and the guidance of a spiritual master.

Metaphysics is also important because 'simple' faith is becoming rarer all the time. In the days when most people lived within closed religious universes there was little question about what to believe, since there were few or no 'alternatives'. One was a believer, a libertine, a scoundrel, or maybe a secret atheist, but one was not confused and uncertain about what to believe, at least not to the degree that so many are today. To be confronted by hundreds of cults and religions, and therapies masquerading as religions, to be asked to choose from among them the one which represents Divine Truth with no tradition of Divine Truth to tell you how, and then, exhausted by the struggle, to give up the quest for objectivity and opt for the one (or the ten) systems which seem most compatible with your personal style—which means that instead of worshipping God you are actually worshipping yourself—this was not among the pitfalls facing a member of any traditional culture.

In an emerging global society where the doctrines and practices of every world religion, and every mystical path within these religions, plus dozens of forms of traditional shamanism, are becoming available everywhere to serious seekers, and also to frivolous curiosity-seekers and budding magicians on the trail of psychic power, religion becomes relativized. If more than one religion is true, then no religion can be absolute—but the essential rationale for any religion is just this: that it gives access to Absolute Truth. So religious 'believers' have no recourse but to either violently denounce other religions—this is the origin of the Christian and Muslim and Jewish and Hindu 'fundamentalism' we see today—or else to 'relax', to become 'promiscuous ecumenists', spiritual dabblers, and wine-tasters, like today's religious 'liberals', who deny that there can be such a thing as Absolute Truth, except that kind of 'truth' which, as we saw above, is considered to be nothing but a mask of power. It is here that Frithjof Schuon's concept of the 'relative absoluteness' of any traditional religion is so important; it is, in fact, the only way out of this dichotomy. Only metaphysics can demonstrate both that there is an Absolute Truth common to all true religions (remembering that not everything which calls itself a 'religion' actually is), but that this Truth cannot be reached by *combining* them, since the existence of different religious revelations, like that of different races or different individuals, is metaphysically necessary. As it says in the Koran, 'Allah, if He had willed, could have made you one people.'

Any intelligent and spiritually sensitive individual, with or without a religious background, must pass through the fires of religious skepticism in today's world. Simple belief, unless one is fortunate enough to retain a real simplicity of soul, to be among those we call 'the salt of the earth', is no longer possible for many today. The sophisticated ability to see the depth and value in religious traditions other than one's own will almost inevitably erode one's faith, at least to begin with. For such a person there is no way 'back' to simple religious faith; the only way is 'forward', to an understanding that there *is* an Absolute Truth behind all the religions, which, however, can only be reached by following one of the religions all the way to that Truth. The only remedy for the disease of sophistication is a greater sophistication, which finally returns to simplicity. Where religious relativism has destroyed faith, nothing but metaphysical understanding can restore it.

But it is unfair and unrealistic to demand metaphysical understanding of everyone. A world in which everyone was a metaphysician or a mystic would be an extremely unbalanced place. This is why metaphysicians, in today's world, must struggle to find their niche in society, from which they can make their contribution to the whole. And in a society as anti-traditional and anti-metaphysical as the emerging global New Order, this is not an easy job, particularly because it has to include an understanding that both fundamentalism and promiscuous ecumenism are part of the quality of the times. Metaphysicians may criticize them, but they can't make them go away. Still, to be under the curse of being able to understand people who will never understand you has always been the metaphysician's fate, and this is as it should be, because unless a spiritual gift is also a burden, the gifted one will become inflated with spiritual pride, and fall, like Icarus did when he flew too near the Sun. Furthermore, without the surrounding darkness of spiritual ignorance to hold it down, the light of spiritual understanding would leave this world entirely—and, according to traditional doctrine, if this were to happen the world would be destroyed. As Rumi says,

> If there were no heedlessness, this world would cease to be. Desire for God, memory of the other world, 'inebriation', and ecstasy are the architects of the other world. If everyone were attuned to that world, we would all abandon this world and go there. God, however, wants us to be here that there may be two worlds. To that end He has stationed two headmen, heedlessness and heedfulness, so that both worlds will flourish.
> ∼SIGNS OF THE UNSEEN [*Fihi ma-Fihi*], p 114

In the last analysis, however, all these reasons why metaphysics is important are only side issues. The real reason why metaphysics is important is because it is true, and whatever is true is also good. God Himself, since He is Absolute Truth, is also the Sovereign Good. In a proverb of the Hindu rishis, which Schuon so often quotes: 'There is no right superior to that of Truth.'

✳ What is Tradition? What is Man?

Nowadays when we talk about 'tradition', we tend to mean any custom or belief that has lasted for more than one generation—or even for a shorter period, as when a place of business will advertise itself as 'a tradition since 1979.' In Catholicism, Eastern Orthodoxy and the Hebrew Kabbalah, 'tradition' refers to doctrines which are passed down either by word of mouth, or in such forms as liturgy and iconography. 'Tradition' can sometimes also refer to the writings of the Fathers of the Church, the Jewish rabbis, and (within Islam) the Sufis, which will include, among other things, the traditional sciences of scriptural hermeneutics. Tradition, then, is not opposed to scripture; it is a way of transmitting the same doctrines that scripture transmits by different means. When the Protestant reformers adopted the doctrine of *sola scriptura*, the Christian tradition in the West was radically impoverished. However, since they were reacting to an impoverishment that already existed, given that lines of traditional transmission within Catholicism were already dying out, the Protestants cannot be entirely blamed for this degeneration.

The Traditionalist School uses the word 'Tradition' in a specific sense. To them, it means 'the sum total of the transmission of Divine Truth by human means from the beginning of time until now,' via scripture, commentary, oral teaching, sacred art, or in any other way. As such, it is the partner of Revelation. According to an image used by traditionalist James Cutsinger, Revealed Truth descends 'vertically'; it enters time directly from Eternity, like a stone dropped into a still pool. If the stone is Revelation, the ripples which spread horizontally from the point where the stone hits the water are Tradition. Each of the major world religions represents an instance of Revelation, and thus a renewal of Tradition. The original Revelation, however, was the creation of the universe, which is why nature is often called 'God's first scripture'. And the sum total and synthesis of this universal Divine manifestation is the Human Form, which is why, in Islamic doctrine (as well as in the Jewish historian Josephus) Adam is seen as the first prophet, the recipient of God's primordial Self-revelation. In both Genesis and the Koran, it is said that Adam, while still in the Garden of Eden, named the animals. Esoterically, this means that he knew them as projections of the eternal archetypes within the Divine Nature. He didn't *invent* their names, in other words, but looked within his own heart, his spiritual Intellect, and there understood the Attributes or Names of God which were represented by the forms of the natural world around him.

Tradition, then, is not just anything that comes to us from the remote past; plenty of philosophical errors and religious heresies are of ancient pedigree. It is specifically the transmission of Absolute Truth via the human form and human consciousness—a transmission which is so crucial that, according to many authorities, if it were absolutely to cease the world would be destroyed. It is the 'stem' of creation, the vital connection between the flower of the visible universe and its Divine Ground. Cut the stem, and the flower withers.

✳ What is the Intellect?

Another one of the 'fallen words' is *intellect*. To most of us, it means logic, rationality, or even the ability to manipulate and remember large amounts of information. Not so to the scholastic philosophers of the Middle Ages. To them, *intellectus* (the Latin translation of the Greek *nous*) meant the faculty by which we can understand spiritual or metaphysical Truth directly, just as the human eye 'understands' light. They distinguished it from *ratio*, the rational or logical mind. Given a premise, ratio can reach a conclusion, but it does not thereby reach an entirely 'new' truth. It has no power to apprehend Truth on its own, only to demonstrate the logical implications of an already given truth, a truth 'given' to it by *intellectus*. Intellect is the source of all *axioms*—of truths which cannot be demonstrated, only intuitively known.

According to almost all ancient traditions, including traditional Christianity and Platonic philosophy, the human being is composed of three levels of being: Spirit, soul and body—in Greek, *Pneuma* (or *Nous*), *psyche* and *soma*; in Latin, *Spiritus* (or *Intellectus*), *anima*, and *corpus*. In the modern era, however, the distinction between Spirit and soul has been lost, with disastrous consequences. We now tend to believe, unless we are complete materialists, that anything which isn't material must be spiritual, which often means to us that whatever we encounter through dreams or psychological introspection or psychic experiences must be 'true', and by implication 'good'—or at least not to be criticized, even if we hate or fear it… even less so, of course, if it is pleasant or fascinating. And it is precisely this metaphysical error—that there is no distinction between psyche and Spirit—which is at this moment opening whole masses of people to demonic influences, and which will make it possible for Antichrist to concoct a plausible *psychic* counterfeit of the eternal *Spiritual* Reality.

If we knew psyche and Spirit as two different things (or, rather, two different levels of being) we would not, for example, patronize the many 'psychic hotlines' now advertised on TV and elsewhere, because we would know that just because someone can tell you the color of your underwear or what you did last Tuesday, it doesn't mean her or she is necessarily either wise or good. And the fact is that many psychics (though certainly not all) often have imbalanced personalities, and will tend to use their psychic powers dishonestly, since those powers have given them a certain ability to 'live by their wits'.

I once worked with a woman who was extremely psychic. She picked up that a murder had been committed in a storefront we were planning to rent, a fact which was later confirmed by the real estate agent. During a phone conversation with me she was able to find objects hidden in an apartment where I was staying, which she had never visited, when I myself didn't know where the objects were. But the main way she used her powers was to swindle people out of money and avoid prosecution.

Psychics often have 'boundary' problems. They are so open to other people's subtle energies that the line between themselves and others tends to blur. Many schizophrenics have the same difficulty, and often a certain degree of psychic sensitivity as well. This excessively permeable 'ego-boundary' can also result in various forms of radical discourtesy, 'co-dependency', and a dissipation of the person's psychic energy into the surrounding environment, making him or her into a sort of 'vampire' who must drain other people's vitality simply to replace what is constantly being lost. It can also open such a person to demonic possession.

In a conversation with a Buddhist of the Gelugpa lineage (the school of Tibetan Vajrayana Buddhism to which the Dalai Lama belongs), I was told that there are two kinds of clairvoyance: the legitimate kind, that of the advanced Buddhist sage, which develops directly from the virtues of compassion and concentration (a rare but not *abnormal* deepening of care and attentiveness which is primarily used in the context of spiritual direction), and what is called 'contaminated' clairvoyance, which is one of the karmic consequences of an interrupted course of spiritual development, and is considered to be a major obstacle to Enlightenment.

So 'psychic' is not synonymous with 'Spiritual'. The psyche is a level of being based on the subject/object polarity, where 'objective' experience is conditioned by the 'subjectivity' of the experiencer. Spirit or Intellect transcends this polarity. We can describe it as perfectly Objective, since it is what it is whether or not I am aware of it, and with equal validity as the Absolute Subject (or at least a 'ray' of this Divine Subject intersecting the human soul), since it is the ultimate Witness of all that is happening, either on the plane of the spiritual archetypes, or within my psyche, or in the material world. In either case, It transcends my individual subjectivity. It is not, as some imagine, my ego blasphemously absolutized; it is not the big 'Me'. Rather, it is God saying 'I Am' within me, whether or not I am aware of it, whether or not I am faithful to the implications of it. 'It is not I who live,' said St Paul, 'but Christ lives in me.' Or in the words of Meister Eckhart, 'There is Something within the soul which is uncreated and uncreatable.'

This 'Something' is the Intellect. In a way, it is our inborn ability to know God directly. In another way, it is God's own Self-knowledge, which we may or may not consciously participate in, but which in any case is the Source of our life. Seen from the standpoint of our psychic subjectivity, such knowledge is ultimately impossible, since no limited individual consciousness can encompass the Absolute: 'The light shineth in the darkness, but the darkness comprehendeth it not.' Seen from the standpoint of the Intellect, however, such knowledge is not only possible, but necessary, since complete Knowledge of the Truth is an integral part of the Truth itself. This is why one of the names for God in Hinduism is *Satchitananda*—Being or Truth

(*Sat*), Consciousness of that Truth (*Chit*) and the Bliss of the union between Truth and Consciousness (*Ananda*). It is also one meaning of the first verse of the Gospel of St John: 'In the beginning was the Word, and the Word was with God, and the Word was God.'

✳ Faith, Belief, and Knowledge

Faith and knowledge are sometimes seen as opposed, especially in the Christian world. Those who think they can reach God through knowledge rather than faith are often labeled 'Gnostics'—a term which really does mean something, even though it is so often applied as kind generic slander to whatever the speaker or writer is suspicious of in the area of religion, much as the words 'commie' or 'fascist' have been used in the area of politics. The Traditionalists themselves are sometimes branded as Gnostics, by those who do not fully understand their doctrines.

The Gnostics were an extremely heterogeneous group of religious sects in late antiquity, who nonetheless tended to share certain doctrines: that the psychic and material universes are the product of a 'fall' within the Godhead rather than a manifestation of that Godhead in space, time, and human consciousness; that matter itself is evil; that God is consequently 'alien' to the creation; that the cosmos is created and ruled instead by evil and/or deluded false Gods, often headed by an evil Demiurge, who are usually identified with the concentric planetary spheres of the Ptolemaic (geocentric) cosmology, considered as a kind of cosmic prison; that the sin of Adam was a heroic, Promethean revolt against this evil Demiurge; that the way out of the cosmic prison is through knowledge *as opposed to* faith—specifically, knowledge of how the fallen world was created and how and by whom it is ruled; that faith is really nothing but a blind belief in the false, oppressive system of things which is the universe; that the savior, often but not always identified with Christ, slips into this false world in disguise so as to fool the cosmic rulers, and brings salvation to the spiritual elite in the form of a secret knowledge or *gnosis*; that this Savior does not really incarnate in the material world but is a kind of apparition (as in the Docetist heresy), who never actually suffered on the cross, or died, or rose from the dead, and who (as in the Arian heresy) is not divine, but rather one of the eternal Aeons, a kind of archangel; that, since the cosmos is false and ruled by false gods, the appropriate 'morality' is either to opt out of it entirely, through an extreme asceticism that sometimes led, in certain Gnostic sects, to suicide by starvation, or else to openly flaunt the false morality of the world rulers through libertinism and rebellious self-indulgence. In some ways Gnosticism was a Christian heresy, in some ways a spectrum of independent religious movements.

It ought to be fairly obvious that Gnosticism, like all heresies, contains a grain of truth, though placed in a false context. The truth in this case is that humanity is somehow fallen, whether through ignorance or transgression or a combination of the two, and that consequently the world we inhabit has radical limitations which in the unfallen state of 'Eden' did not exist. According to Christian doctrine, even death itself is a product of the fall of man; it is not really 'natural'. The error of the Gnostics was to become so obsessed with the consequences of the fall that they forgot that 'the heavens declare the glory of God, and the earth shows forth His handiwork'; in theological terms, they denied the immanence of God in His creation, making him totally transcendent, and therefore 'alien'. And so, for all their supposed esoteric intellectual sophistication, they in some ways took the fall of man too literally. Obsessed with falsity and error, they forgot that error, though it produces real effects, is not real in itself. They *concretized* it; consequently their 'gnosis' was not the pure ability to see through error in contemplation of Divine Truth, but became an attempt to 'outwit' the world rulers by means of a special, occult knowledge. This is not to say that there was no true metaphysical understanding among the Gnostics, only that the errors of the movement placed that knowledge in a false, distorted context. And, as the Sufis say, 'it only takes one dog to spoil a whole pool of rosewater.'

The struggle of the early Christians against the sectarian Gnostics—as well as the similar struggle going on today with various Neo-Gnostics—have tended to obscure the truth that faith and knowledge are not opposed, but in fact intimately related. Those Christians who take the position that all metaphysics is a kind of Gnosticism—or those Muslims and orientalists who look on Sufi metaphysics as a kind of Neo-Platonism, or shamanism, or Buddhism, rather that as the quintessence of Islam, based on an understanding of the Koranic revelation deep enough to penetrate not only the mind and the will but the spiritual Heart—and who therefore think that we should not try to know the truths of God directly, since the human intellect is incapable of this, but simply take them on 'blind faith', are mistaken. They have in fact fallen into a kind of Gnostic heresy of their own by repeating the radical Gnostic opposition between faith and knowledge. On the other hand, their belief that the human mind is incapable of acquiring divine Wisdom is also true, in two specific senses: first, because Wisdom is a gift, not an acquisition; second, because only God can know God. They are unaware, however, that the human being, and his Archetype in the Divine Nature which Sufis call *al-insan-al-kamil*, 'the perfect man', and Christians 'God the Son' (not to deny, of course, the irreducible differences between these two doctrines) is the very form of this divine Self-knowledge.

Faith cannot be limited to belief (though belief is a necessary part of it) but is rather the beginning of direct and objective knowledge. *Crede ut intellegas*: 'believe that you might understand.' It is true that the attempt to access Divine Knowledge while ignoring revealed doctrine is a form of spiritual pride, doomed to disaster. But to struggle to believe religious doctrine on will-power alone, while denying that such belief can ever flower into true understanding, is to hold the gifts of the Spirit in contempt. In the words of St Paul, faith is 'the presence of things hoped for, the evidence of things not seen.' In other words, faith is *virtual intellection* — and one synonym for intellection is *gnosis*.

Many Fathers of the Church, such as Clement of Alexandria, Maximos the Confessor and Dionysius the Areopagite, were metaphysicians and 'gnostics' in just this sense — which does *not* mean that they espoused the heresy of Gnosticism. According to Clement, 'We may gain some inkling of what God is if we attempt by means of every sensation to reach the reality of each creature, not giving up until we are alive to what transcends it.' In the words of Dionysius, 'It is . . . false to repeat the commonplace that it is in matter as such that evil resides. For to speak truly, matter itself also participates in the order, the beauty, the form. . . .' And Maximos declares that

> [God] shows himself to our minds to the extent of our ability to understand, through visible objects which act like letters of the alphabet. . . . He, the undifferentiated, is seen in differentiated things, the simple in the compound. He who has no beginning is seen in things that must have a beginning; the invisible in the visible; the intangible in the tangible. Thus he gathers us together in himself, through every object. . . .

no one who teaches such doctrines, who believes that the heavens declare the glory of God as these church fathers clearly do, can be called a heretical or sectarian Gnostic.

Faith is 'the presence of things hoped for' in the sense that *gnosis* is virtual within the human soul. It is 'the evidence of things not seen' in the sense that through faith — which is greater than belief though less than direct knowledge, since it may be defined as the *receptivity to intellection*, the readiness to know — invisible realities can appear to the mind as symbols, and to the senses as material objects symbolically understood. In the words of Frithjof Schuon, 'Sensible forms correspond with exactness to intellections' (*The Transcendent Unity of Religions*, p 62).

✳ What is Esoterism?

In popular usage, the word 'esoteric' means something like 'unnecessarily obscure and complicated,' as when we are asked not to get 'too esoteric' but 'keep it simple'. Those with a superficial interest in mystical spirituality often tend to define esoterism, in effect, as 'special secrets for special people,' while those who distrust mysticism, partly in reaction to this 'elitist' attitude, will see it as a secret, heretical doctrine, opposed to revelation and tradition.

According to the doctrines of some of the Sufis (the 'organized' mystics within Islam), as well as to the Shïite sect (the partisans of the Prophet's cousin and son-in-law Ali, who was both the fourth Sunni caliph and first Shïite Imam), there is a 'balance' in all things, and particularly in religion, between inner and outer. Within every form is essence, and essence is always manifesting as form. Seen in this way, mystical spirituality is the inner essence of religion, while religion is the outer form of mysticism. But it is not 'merely' the outer form; inner and outer are equally necessary. As the Sufis say, without the shell, the kernel will rot. In the Koran, for example, God is named both 'the Inner' (*al-Batin*) and 'the Outer' (*al-Zahir*), terms which could also be translated as 'the esoteric' and 'the *exoteric*'. In Islamic history, those exoteric clergy who periodically persecuted the Sufis gave rise to various forms of Muslim 'fundamentalism', which threatened to cut the Heart out of Islam, while those Sufis who went too far in the other direction, in an attempt to become pure *batinis*, often developed heretical tendencies which threatened the tradition in another way; they tried, as it were, to live as a Heart without a body.

Any spiritual tradition needs both inner and outer expressions. Even Buddhism, which is perhaps closer than any other tradition to a pure esoterism, requires morality (*sila*) as a complementary balance to wisdom (*prajña*) and concentration (*dhyana*). And the same is true of scripture. If the Bible or the Koran is limited to the socio-historical and moral levels of meaning—or even the psychological level—then its *essential* meaning is denied; it is reduced to the stature of something any moral philosopher could have produced on the basis of an enlightened common sense. But if an esoteric hermeneutics is used to deny the socio-historical, moral and psychological levels of meaning, then the scripture in question is not being understood in a complete or balanced way, with the result that the esoteric or metaphysical level suffers too, since to emphasize the inner 'spiritual' meaning of scripture and discard the outer 'physical' meaning implies that Spirit is not the Source of the life of soul and body, but something outside them, something without any 'organic' connection to our lives, an 'alien God' like that of the Gnostics, a sort of phantom or ghost: and this is a metaphysical error.

Religious exoterics often believe that esoterism is nothing but a kind of alternative doctrine, and thus necessarily a heresy—a misconception which is daily reinforced by those thousands of self-styled pseudo-esoterics, or occultists, who believe the same thing. These people are proud to call themselves 'heretics', as if this word denoted a kind of heroic rebelliousness based on a deeper understanding of spiritual things than that of the simpleminded, superficial 'orthodox', whereas it is really nothing but an admission that their own understanding is superficial, that they are in a state of metaphysical error. The tragedy of exoteric religion is that it possesses the 'pearl of great price', the 'one thing needful', but in so many cases has misplaced it. The tragedy of those who initially possess a certain amount of esoteric spiritual understanding is that they often succumb to the temptation to falsely equate 'orthodoxy' with 'exoterism', and then go on to repeat the error of many exoterics by falsely identifying 'esoterism' with 'heresy', forgetting that if their esoteric understanding were true, then they would necessarily be of the essence of orthodoxy, and in some ways—or on some occasions—potentially even more orthodox than the exoterics themselves.

The sin of the exoterics is militant stupidity which crushes all doctrinal subtlety. The sin of the esoterics is intellectual pride, leading in some cases to a frivolous trifling with the doctrine. Orthodox religious doctrine can only be entirely safeguarded through a balance between the two, which will sometimes be out in the open, and sometimes hidden away for safekeeping.

Esoterism, then, is not an alternate doctrine, though the writings of certain esoterics, like Meister Eckhart within Christianity, for example, or Ibn al-'Arabi within Islam, may make it seem so in the eyes of those with less subtlety and depth of understanding. Esoterism is *gnosis*, a present witnessing of the truths of God emanating from the depths of the Divine nature. It is ultimately not doctrine, but realization.

Those who are available to this realization will necessarily constitute a kind of elite. Nowadays there is no more unpopular, in fact despised, ideal than that of a spiritual or political elite—and with good reason. History is full of object-lessons on the damage which self-styled and self-interested elites can do—like, for example, the Ismaili 'Assassins' within Islam, that brotherhood of esoteric terrorists—but if I have a brain tumor, and need an operation, I hope to God the doctor who performs it is as 'elite' as he or she can get! Likewise there are certain deep spiritual functions which only a rare few can fulfill; we call them 'saints'. Not all saints are intellectuals, though *gnosis* must be virtually present in them, since sanctity is based upon the submission of the will to God, and the face of God presented to the will, which carries the precise shape of the Divine Truth which much be submitted to, is the Intellect. Nor are all intellectual saints esoterics: Thomas Aquinas is a good example of the 'non-esoteric metaphysician'. It is only in the rarest saints, like Maximos the Confessor and possibly St Bernard, the spiritual patron of the Templars, that sanctity and *gnosis* are combined. There are also those who fall short of realized sainthood but still possess a degree of *gnosis*, though not the highest degree, and it is from these that many of the problems associated with self-styled esoterics originate, especially if they fail to realize their limitations, but idolize the Intellect instead of worshipping God by means of it. There are even those who possess a certain degree of actual esoteric insight—though in this case it can't really be called spiritual, but is rather a high-level psychic counterfeit of spiritual knowledge—who are in league with Satan, unknowingly, and sometimes knowingly: and these are the most dangerous people on earth, since from among them, 'Satan's contemplatives' (*awliya al-Shaytan*), will be chosen the 'elite guard' of the Antichrist.

When spiritual elites take organized form in the outer world, we are in the presence of both the highest potential for the spiritual transformation of society, and the most satanic temptation to titanic spiritual pride. This is why, according to the opinion of some, a true spiritual elite, as in the legend of the Knights of the Round Table, never lasts long in historical terms: it is either destroyed by the sin of pride, or else dissolved, deliberately by its enlightened masters or providentially by God Himself, before it can become totally corrupt. Within Islam, many Sufi circles lasted as living manifestations only as long as the life of their teacher, and then either broke up or lived on as empty husks—though this is certainly not true of the major surviving Sufi orders, where the transmission of true spiritual *baraka* (grace) has in some cases gone on for many centuries. Within Christianity, the clearest example of a visible spiritual elite was, according to some, the Templars, whose brutal suppression by the French monarchy, abetted by the papacy, was either the tragic destruction of a deeply esoteric spirituality by jealous and stupid exoterics, or the necessary termination of a heretical and corrupt international brotherhood with too much wealth, power and independence, or maybe a little of both.

It is true that 'esoteric' knowledge used to be imparted only to members of the spiritual elite, firstly because only they were interested, and secondly because an esoteric interpretation of the doctrine can unbalance the minds of those who are attracted to it but can't fully understand it. But in our own times, all the esoteric secrets that can be told have been or are being told, so there's nothing more to lose on that score; this is why Traditionalists often quote the proverb of the Kabbalists, 'it is better for the doctrine to be misunderstood than for it to be forgotten.' The fact is that not everyone can understand metaphysics—which is what is meant by the phrase 'the secret protects itself'—and not everyone who can understand it mentally is capable of being transformed by it spiritually. But the quality of the time now demands that the whole truth be told, sink or swim, since the 'cat is out of the bag', and it is vital that this truth reach those comparative few who, dispersed throughout the population of the world, can profit from the full expression of it.

Nor is the question about whether to reveal or conceal esoteric doctrines really a new one. Guénon searched for a secret esoteric potential within Catholicism, possibly a survival of Templarism, but he didn't find it. And many people today are still trying to discover, or invent, an esoteric Christianity. But according to Schuon, Christianity itself *is* esoteric Christianity. The Christian revelation is a kind of 'eso-exoterism', an esoteric initiation made available to all; the initiatory rites are baptism and confirmation. In Islam, the esoteric lore is guarded the Sufis, the organized mystics. In Christianity, at least pre-Reformation Christianity, it was dispersed throughout the whole tradition, 'hidden in plain sight'. Catholicism possessed it, but, in the absence of an organized esoteric tradition comparable to Sufism, it didn't understand the value of the treasure intrusted to it, which is why it is today in the process of 'throwing out the baby with the bath water'. Only within Eastern Orthodoxy, largely due to the presence of Hesychasm, has it remained relatively intact—which is not to say that the fullness of Christ's salvation, and thus the potentiality of esoterism, is not also present in some Protestant churches, and in Catholicism too, as witness the great esoterists like Jacob Boehme within Lutheranism.

Schuon's view of Christianity is partly confirmed by an interesting historical sidelight: Among the Mandaeans, an ancient Gnostic sect of southern Iraq, who claim to have been founded by John the Baptist, and who, according to some scholars, may be descended from the Essenes, Jesus is looked on as a kind of renegade who revealed their esoteric doctrines to the public. This demonstrates, to my mind, that the fertile spiritual potential in Jesus' ministry lay in manifesting the inner depth of the doctrine, not concealing it, and that the roots of the Gnostic heresy may lie in the attempt of various

esoteric circles to develop their own *exoterism*, their own 'alternative' doctrine, rather than remaining as a 'leaven' or 'mustard seed' within Christianity as a whole. On the other hand, Jesus well knew that not everyone would
be capable of understanding the revealed depth of the doctrine, which is
why in the Gospels he is continually saying things like 'he who has ears to
hear, let him hear,' and why he spoke to the people in parables, but to his
chosen disciples directly and openly. The central image of this 'eso-exoteric'
quality of Christianity is the Transfiguration of Christ, where the inner light
of the tradition was openly revealed. But the fact remains that not everyone
has eyes to see that light: even Peter, one of the chosen twelve, didn't entirely
understand what was happening. So the secret protects itself.

According to the wisdom inherent in the Divine economy, membership
in a true spiritual elite, organized or not, is necessarily the heaviest burden
that can be borne by the human soul, though Intellection itself can be seen
as a compensatory grace, since, as Jesus said, 'my yoke is easy and my burden
light.' And this is only right: 'To whom much is given, much will be
required.' There is no greater foolishness than for someone to believe that
his or her esoteric insight is a kind of advantage, a 'plum'. To understand
things that people with greater sanctity, and even greater mental intelligence, will never understand—things which, if you fail in your spiritual life,
will only damn you that much deeper—is a hard destiny, just as to return
from heroic battle with an arm missing may be a badge of honor, but it is
not a case of good fortune as the term is usually understood. As traditionalist writer Rama Coomaraswamy pointed out to me, in the traditional
Hindu caste system, the *dharma* (sacred duty) of the two higher castes, the
Brahmins (priests and spiritual intellectuals) and the Kshatriyas (warriors
and administrators) included built-in safeguards against the pride of their
high position. The Brahmins, who were forbidden to work for a living, had
to beg for their daily bread from door-to-door among the third caste, the
Vaishyas, the hard-working solid citizens; this is a humiliation which intellectuals who are not good at making money, such as myself, know only too
well. And the heroic pride of the Kshatriyas was tempered by the ever-
present possibility of injury, mutilation and death in battle.

So an integral part of the practice of a member of the spiritual elite is: not
to identify one's ego with one's function—to remember God, as the Sufis
say, and forget oneself. In other words, the humility required of the esoteric
is much more radical than that which is sufficient for the exoteric, amount-
ing to actual self-annihilation. As Groucho Marx said (undoubtedly repeating, in the form of a one-line 'Nasruddin' joke, a real piece of esoteric lore,

probably transmitted through the Hasidim), 'I would never join a club that would have me as a member.'

Frithjof Schuon was perhaps one of the dozen greatest metaphysicians of known history, comparable in many ways to the Hindu sage Shankaracharya, the Christian *jñani* Meister Eckhart, or the neo-Platonic philosopher Plotinus. However, the comparison of the Traditionalist School with Neo-Platonism is meaningful in another way. Platonic and Neo-Platonic philosophy was only able to survive by attaching itself to one of the great revealed religions, primarily Christianity and Islam. The Neo-Platonic tradition profoundly illumined these religious universes, revealing in explicit philosophical language much that would have remained implicit in the densely-symbolic and mythopoetic language of the Bible and the Koran. But neither Christianity nor Islam could have 'taken up residence' within Neo-Platonism, which in itself could not provide a fertile matrix. Without the framework of revealed religion, it slowly but surely died out. Not even the Roman emperor Julian the Apostate could re-establish philosophical Paganism in any viable form. And although part of the reason for the disappearance of the philosophic schools can be put down to Christian persecution, the fact remains that late Platonism was not sufficiently broad-based, or in touch with God's grace, to survive on its own. The gulf between its exalted conceptions and the degenerate Paganism which surrounded it, and which would have had to have provided its popular base, was too great. This may have been one of the reasons why it began, under Iamblichus, to descend into quasi-magical theurgy, and why, according to some speculation, it could even have become the ancestor of certain forms of Western ceremonial magic.

The Traditionalist School faces a similar dilemma. The profound and inspired teachings of Schuon and his colleagues can only serve to re-awaken the world religions to the metaphysical depth of their own orthodox traditions. Up to a point, within both Christianity and Islam, this process has already begun. But to the degree that Traditionalism becomes so enamored of 'pure' metaphysics that it forgets that all metaphysical knowledge, to be spiritually operative, needs a living matrix within one of the great revealed traditions—and, further, that one cannot simply relate to these traditions as if they represented no more than a minimum requirement, a kind of exoteric membership card which, after validating one's esoteric pursuits as orthodox, can then be placed in one's wallet and largely ignored—it is in danger of turning into an 'alternate exoterism': in other words, a cult. According to Ibn al-'Arabi, one of the very greatest Islamic esoterics, the spiritual works which are obligatory for all believers—prayer, fasting, pilgrimage, almsgiving, and testimony of faith—are greater than the 'supererogatory' works, including those performed only by the Sufis. He cautions the Sufi esoterics against becoming deluded by the revelations or 'unveilings' which come to them from God such that they depart from these obligatory works:

> We have come across sincere people among the Folk of Allah who have been duped by this station. They prefer their own unveiling and that which becomes manifest to them in their understanding such that it nullifies the established ruling. They depend upon this in their own case, and they let other people observe the established ruling in its outward significance. But ... anyone who relies upon it is totally confused and has left his affiliation with the Folk of Allah.... It may [even] happen that the possessor of such an unveiling continues to practice the outward sense of that ruling, while he does not believe it in respect of himself. He practices it by stipulating the outward situation (*zahir*), saying to himself, 'To this commandment of the Law I only give the outward dimension (*zahir*) of myself, for I have gained knowledge of its secret (*sirr*). Hence its property in my inmost consciousness (*sirr*) is different from its property in my outward dimension.' Hence he does not believe it in his inmost consciousness while practicing it. If someone practices it like this ...'his practice has failed, and in the world to come he shall be among the losers' (Koran 5:5).
> ⌒ Futuhat al-Makkiyya II 233–34]

One must approach spiritual traditions whole-heartedly, with no secret reservations. Only then will one realize that true esoterism is to be found nowhere but in the rarely-plumbed depths of the orthodox doctrines necessarily accepted by all believers. And this, precisely, is what the Traditionalist School preaches. May they continue to practice what they preach.

✳ The Absolute and the Infinite

According to Frithjof Schuon, God is both Absolute and Infinite:

In metaphysics it is necessary to start from the idea that the Supreme Reality is absolute, and that being absolute it is infinite. That is absolute which allows of no augmentation or diminution, or of no repetition or division; it is therefore that which is at once solely itself and totally itself. And that is infinite which is not determined by any limiting factor and therefore does not end at any boundary....

The Infinite is so to speak the intrinsic dimension of the Absolute; to say Absolute is to say Infinite, the one being inconceivable without the other. The distinction between the Absolute and the Infinite expresses the two fundamental aspects of the Real, that of essentiality and that of potentiality; this is the highest principial prefiguration of the masculine and feminine poles. Universal Radiation, and thus Maya both divine and cosmic, springs from the second aspect, the Infinite, which coincides with All-Possibility.

⁓SURVEY OF METAPHYSICS AND ESOTERISM, pp 15–16

✳ The Sovereign Good

God is not only Absolute and Infinite; He is also Good. The idea of Absoluteness without that of Infinity influences us to picture God as a remote, inaccessible object Who has no need to communicate Himself, a Being Who, rather than creating or emanating all things, excludes and negates all things. The idea of Infinity without Absoluteness communicates a sense of endless, wearying proliferation with no intrinsic center of meaning or reality. The idea of an Absolute and Infinite Reality Who is not at the same time the Sovereign Good posits a God Who is omnipresent and all-powerful, but Who has no intrinsic solidarity with His creation, a God Who, for all his Absoluteness and Infinity, might still be fundamentally cruel in relationship to us. And the concept of a God who is Good alone, being neither Absolute nor Infinite, is nothing but the 'liberal' God, a powerless moral ideal Who wishes us well, but is neither very effective nor very credible when confronted with 'hard reality'. According to Schuon:

The 'Sovereign Good' is the First Cause inasmuch as it is revealed by phenomena that we term 'good', precisely, which is to say that the real and the good coincide. Indeed, it is positive phenomena which attest to the Supreme Reality and not negative, privative or subversive phenomena; the latter would manifest nothingness 'if it existed,' and do so in a certain indirect and paradoxical respect, in the sense that nothing corresponds to an end that is unrealizable but nevertheless tends toward realization.

Therefore, if we call the Supreme Principle the Good, *Agathón*, or if we say that it is the Sovereign Good that is the Absolute and hence the Infinite, it is not because we paradoxically limit the Real, but because we know that every good stems from it and manifests it essentially, and thus reveals its Nature. Assuredly it can be said that the Divinity is 'beyond good and evil', but on condition of adding that this 'beyond' is in its turn a 'good' in the sense that it testifies to an Essence in which there could be no shadow of limitation or privation, and which consequently cannot but be the absolute Good or absolute Plenitude....

⌒Survey of Metaphysics and Esoterism, p16

✳ Transcendence and Immanence

Every valid religious tradition, in one form or another, testifies to the fact that Absolute Reality is both transcendent and immanent. What do these words mean?

To say that God is transcendent means that he is beyond all things and all conceptions. To say that He is immanent means that all forms and conceptions are manifestations of Him. And how could it be otherwise? Imagine an infinite white field with many circles, and circles-within-circles, of vastly different sizes inscribed upon it. Let the infinite field stand for God. The white field is infinitely larger than a circle an inch in diameter; it is also infinitely larger than a circle a mile in diameter. It transcends them both. Yet there is nothing inside either the inch-sized circle or the mile-sized circle but that infinite white field; it is immanent within both of them. Schuon, however, more accurately expresses the meaning of transcendence and immanence, avoiding the pitfalls of my simplistic illustration, when he says:

> in connection with the ... aspects or modes of the Sovereign Good, we also have to consider the relationships of Transcendence and Immanence, the first being connected more to the aspect of Absoluteness, the second to that of Infinitude. According to the first relationship, God alone is the Good; He alone possesses, for example, the quality of beauty; compared to the divine Beauty, the beauty of a creature is nothing, just as existence itself is nothing next to the Divine Being; all this from the point of view of Transcendence. The perspective of Immanence also starts from the axiom that God alone possesses both the qualities and reality; but its conclusion is positive and participative, and thus it will be said that the beauty of a creature—being beauty and not its contrary—is necessarily that of God, since there is no other; and the same is true of all other qualities, without forgetting, at their basis, the miracle of existence. The perspective of Immanence does not nullify creaturely qualities, as does that of Transcendence, but on the contrary makes them divine, if one may so express it.

⌒Survey of Metaphysics and Esoterism, p17

✳ Hierarchy

There is no more unpopular concept today than hierarchy. In most people's vocabulary it means no more or less than 'established, therefore arbitrary, power.'

Liberal modernism rebelled against the old hierarchies of church and state, distributing to 'the people' (in reality, the bourgeoisie), the prerogatives which once belonged to King and Pope. Interpretation of scripture became solely a matter of individual inspiration; a man's home was his castle. The result was the rule of 'predatory capitalism' in which powerful individuals, with no organic or 'corporate' relationship with the masses, seized power, largely by economic means. Marxism grew up in reaction to this. In Communist nations, power was theoretically distributed to the largest and lowest class, the workers, but in reality it was held by a small party oligarchy.

This rebellion against social hierarchies hid the truth that such hierarchies originally existed to provide a concrete image and reminder of the true ontological hierarchy, the Great Chain of Being. An individual king or pope would be despised by the people if he betrayed his archetype, if he did not live up to his function, but the Throne and the Papal See, the archetypes themselves, remained sacrosanct. The priesthood represented God in heaven, and in the next world; the monarchy represented God's active power in this world.

Of course this 'hieratic' social structure was always imperfect. And when in a particular place and time it became degenerate, it stood as the worst form of idolatry. Instead of functioning as a transparent symbol of the Hierarchy of Being, it became a counterfeit of that Hierarchy, a veil over the face of spiritual realities.

In both the Old Testament and the Koran, the prime symbol of such falsification of spiritual hierarchy is the Pharaoh of Egypt. According to the Koran, the Pharaoh literally believed he was God—and this is exactly what happens when an elaborate royal or ecclesiastical structure begins to worship its own knowledge and magnificence instead of the God it exists to serve. True hierarchy, like the ladder in Jacob's dream upon which angels were constantly ascending and descending, is there to provide an ongoing 'two-way communication', so to speak, between manifest existence and its transcendent Source. The universe itself is just such a hierarchy. But when the human concept of hierarchy degenerates and petrifies, the idea of the Divine transcendence becomes nothing but a false image of God's inaccessibility and indifference. At this point when, through God's mercy, the Divine immanence often comes into play in the collective mind. Moses and the Israelites, as slaves of the Egyptians, obviously could not relate to God through the crushing 'pyramid' of the Egyptian religious system (which is not to say that they took nothing from it; at least one of the Psalms was originally an ancient Egyptian hymn). It was to Moses, a fugitive wanted for murder, hiding out in the desert, that God spoke through the burning bush. When hierarchical religion becomes a haven for 'blind guides who keep others out but will not go in themselves,' then the vision of the Divine immanence, of God's merciful availability to the poor and oppressed—to those with real simplicity of soul, innocent of oppressing others, innocent of barren mental and organizational complexities—is unveiled. In light of this, the Exodus can perhaps be seen as a kind of Protestant Reformation against an Egyptian religion become petrified and spiritually dead.

Nonetheless, hierarchy is. It is integral to the nature of Being. Moses, by God's grace and power, was called to ascend Mt. Sinai, symbol of the Hierarchy of Being, to receive the Torah. Those who denied the reality of that Hierarchy, who wanted to relate to God through His Immanence alone while denying His Transcendence, remained below to worship the Golden Calf.

✳ Modes and Hierarchical Levels

The account of the levels of Being which separate the Creator from material universe, while at the same time uniting them, is similar in all the revealed traditions and in the works of many mystical philosophers. But it is never identical, since whatever can be made explicit has already entered the world of relativity. True metaphysical doctrines are vastly more stable, articulate, intelligible and concrete than anything in the material or psychic worlds. But even though the Absolute emanates them, they cannot contain the Absolute; they can only indicate it.

Being is manifested on different levels, but it also appears in terms of different qualities occupying the same level. Levels are vertical; each higher level is the cause of the levels below it, and contains all that is in these lower levels in a higher form. Likewise each lower level is a manifestation or expression—a symbol—of all that is above it; in René Guénon's words, 'the effect is a symbol of the cause.' Modes of Being, on the other hand, are horizontal; they differ in quality and function, but not in degree of reality; they are mutually-defining, polarized manifestations of a single level of Being.

The distinction between modes and levels can be illustrated in the realm of gender. In vertical terms, man, considered as a reflection of the creative Logos, is higher than woman, considered as a reflection of universal receptive Substance. Viewed from the opposite perspective, however, woman, when taken as a symbol of the Divine Essence or Beyond Being, is higher than man, when seen as a symbol of the particularizing thrust of the Logos whose ontological limit is the material world as perceived by the human ego. But in horizontal terms, man and woman are polarized as complementary opposites, on the same level of Being. The right hand is not more real than the left hand; because they are complementary, they are equal. But equality in this sense has nothing to do with sameness or identity. The right hand still maintains its symbolic connection with the higher realms of Being, with truth and the 'right', while the left or 'sinister' hand retains its affinity with the lower realms. On the other hand — pun deliberately intended — the right hand is also connected with the outer conscious ego and the left hand with inner Truth, as Jesus implied when he recommended that, in practicing charity, one should not let his right hand (conscious ego) know what his left hand (inner spiritual impulse) is doing. [NOTE: Whoever meditates on the famous Yin/Yang sign will see in it a visual representation of this paragraph.]

According to Schuon, the Supreme Principle possesses dimensions, modes and degrees or levels. Its dimensions are Absoluteness and Infinity — as well as, in relation to Its *Maya*, to its inherent potentiality for Self-manifestation, Perfection. 'Absoluteness of the Real, Infinitude of the Possible, Perfection of the Good.' Its modes are Wisdom, Power and Goodness, each of which, in turn, is Absolute, Infinite and Perfect. Its degrees or levels are 'the divine Essence, the divine Potentiality and the divine Manifestation; or Beyond-Being, creative Being, and the Spirit or the extentiating Logos which constitutes the divine Center of the total cosmos' (*Survey of Metaphysics and Esoterism*, pp 25–26). Schuon and other metaphysicians — Plotinus, for example, or Dionysius the Areopagite, or Ibn al-'Arabi — multiply these dimensions, modes and degrees of Reality in many different ways, only to return them once more to the absolute simplicity of their Principle. The above rendition is only to give the reader a preliminary idea of some of the more essential principles of Schuon's pure metaphysics.

❋ Love and Knowledge

The writers of the Traditionalist School place the path of *gnosis* or *jñana*, the way of union with God by means of knowledge, higher than the path of devotion or *bhakti*, which is based on love. On the other hand, true knowledge is never separate from love. 'There is a *bhakti* without *jñana*,' Schuon maintains, 'but there is no *jñana* without *bhakti*.'

'In principle, knowledge is greater than love. . . .' Schuon says. However, he goes on to say, '. . . but in fact, in the world, the relationship is inverse, and love, will, individual tendency is in practice more important. . . .' (*Spiritual Perspectives and Human Facts*, p148) So a dynamic love of God is greater in actual effect than a mental or 'worldly' knowledge of metaphysics, because it leads to a still higher knowledge which is true realization. Elsewhere in the same chapter Schuon writes: 'A cult of the intelligence and mental passion take man further from truth. Intelligence withdraws as soon as man puts his trust in it alone. Mental passion pursuing intellectual intuition is like the wind which blows out the light of a candle' (ibid., p132), and: 'All St Paul says of charity concerns effective knowledge, for the latter is love. . . .' (ibid., p138).

So Schuon in one sense defines love as the energy that leads to the Goal, and as in another as an aspect of the Goal itself. As he says in another place, 'The way of love—methodical *bhakti*—presupposes that through it we can go toward God; whereas love as such—intrinsic *bhakti*—accompanies the way of knowledge, *jñana*, and is based essentially on our sensitivity to the divine Beauty' (*Roots of the Human Condition*, p118).

According to Schuon, 'Perfect love is "luminous" and perfect knowledge is "hot". . . . In God Love is Light and Light is Love.' (*Spiritual Perspectives and Human Facts*, p148) 'It is necessary to dig deep into the soil of the soul,' he says, 'through layers of aridity and bitterness, in order to find love and live from it' (*The Essential Writings of Frithjof Schuon*, p451). Nonetheless, Schuon most often writes from a perspective which places knowledge above love. He says:

> For love man is subject and God Object. For knowledge it is God who is Subject and man object. . . . For the spiritual man of emotional temperament to love is to be and to know is to think and the heart represents totality, the very basis of being, and the brain the fragment, the surface. For the spiritual man of intellectual temperament knowledge on the contrary is to be and love is to want or to feel and the heart represents universality or the Self and the

brain individuality or the 'I'. Knowledge starts from the Universal, and love from the individual; it is the absolute Knower who knows, whereas it is the human subject, the creature, who is called upon to love.

⌒SPIRITUAL PERSPECTIVES AND HUMAN FACTS, pp144–145

Four pages later, however, Schuon takes a different tack. After asserting that from the perspective of Knowledge God is the Knower and the human subject the lover, he now says: 'The love of the affective man is that he loves God. The love of the intellectual man is that God loves him; that is to say, he realizes intellectually—but not simply in a theoretical way—that God is Love' (ibid., p149). So here, even for the intellectual man—as for Dante in the *Paradiso*—God loves, and is Love Itself. As Schuon says elsewhere in the same book, '[God] is Love, not because he loves, but he loves because he is Love' (ibid., p107). The acting, personal God is the 'Lover', the Divine Essence is 'Love', and this is true even from the perspective of knowledge. Nonetheless, Schuon's standpoint remains essentially *jñanic* rather than *bhaktic*. In *The Essential Writings of Frithjof Schuon*, pp39–40, he says:

> When we place the emphasis on objective Reality—which then takes precedence in the relation between the subject and the object—the subject becomes object in the sense that, being determined entirely by the object, it forgets the element consciousness; in this case the subject, inasmuch as it is a fragment, is absorbed by the Object inasmuch as it is a totality, as the accident is reintegrated into the Substance.

This is the perspective of *bhakti*, where the lover of God is ecstatically annihilated in his Beloved. But the perspective of *jñana*, where God is not the Absolute Object but rather the *Atman*, the Divine Witness, is higher still:

> But the other manner of seeing things, which reduces everything to the Subject, takes precedence over the point of view that grants primacy to the Object: if we adore God, it is not for the simple reason that He presents Himself to us as an objective reality of a dizzying and crushing immensity—otherwise we would adore the stars and nebulae—but it is above all because this reality, a priori objective, is the greatest of subjects; because He is the absolute Subject of our contingent subjectivity; because He is at once all-powerful, omniscient and benefic Consciousness.

✳ The Problem of Evil

One of the perennial problems in theology is the following: If God is all-powerful, in the sense that He is ultimately responsible for all that occurs, then He must be the author of evil as well. How then can He be the Sovereign Good? And if He is all-good, doesn't there need to be a second principle different from and opposed to Him in order to explain the existence of evil? If so, how can He be all-powerful?

The dualistic Manichaeans adopted the latter position. Judaism and Islam lean more toward the former, while still dogmatically asserting the goodness and mercy of God, in ways that can be fully reconciled with God's omnipotence, however, only from an esoteric perspective. Christianity seemingly tends toward the more dualistic position; its dualism, however, is not primarily that between God and the Devil, but rather between divine goodness and human and angelic free will. God does not will evil, but 'allows' it, though why a good and all-powerful God would allow evil just to give us a chance to struggle against it remains a puzzle to many—at least to those who fail to see that free will is a free gift to us, from God, of an aspect of His own Nature.

If God is good He cannot be all-powerful, and if He is all-powerful He cannot be good—or so it seems. For Schuon, however, this contradiction is easily resolved. Given that God is Infinite, He must radiate the possibilities inherent in His nature, manifesting them as the Hierarchy of Being; and as creation descends this Hierarchy, becoming progressively less real and less alive as it does so, the possibility of evil—which is not a principle in itself but 'merely' a condition of relative unreality or non-entity, just as starvation is not a thing in itself but 'merely' a lack of food—comes into play. (To say that 'He must' radiate His Being does not mean, however, that He is has no choice when it comes to creating the universe, only that this choice is made in eternity, not in time. For us, what we necessarily are by nature and what we freely choose to do are two different things; for God, they are the same.) In Schuon's words

> Evil is the 'possibility of the impossible', lacking which the Infinite would not be the Infinite; to ask why All-Possibility includes the possibility of its own negation—a possibility always reinitiated but never fully actualized—is like asking why Existence is Existence, or why Being is Being'
> ⌇Survey of Metaphysics and Esoterism, p16

✳ Primordiality

To the Traditionalists, religion is primordial. When St Augustine said that Christianity has always existed, but was only called by that name after the coming of Jesus Christ, he was positing this primordiality. Jews and Muslims touch on the same truth when they teach that Adam was the first prophet.

All true religions have a single origin, which in macrocosmic terms is the universe itself, where 'the heavens declare the glory of God and the earth shows forth His handiwork,' and in microcosmic terms the 'theomorphic' nature of Man, 'fearfully and wonderfully made' in the image and likeness of God.

In the Golden Age of this cycle, all religions were one. What the human heart knew of the Creator by direct intellection, the human eye saw, by contemplation, in the objects of the natural world and the form of the human body. Even today some of the 'primal peoples' retain traces of this primordial vision of the cosmos as a manifestation of the Great Spirit. (In recognition of his appreciation of the primal spiritualities, Frithjof Schuon was admitted to tribal membership of both the Crow and the Lakota [Sioux], and counted several traditional medicine men among his spiritual friends.)

Primordiality, however, does not mean that a simple aesthetic or sentimental appreciation of nature can amount to a spiritually effective religious orientation. We are no longer in the Golden Age; the Tree of Religion, whose roots are in eternity, in the unitary Absolute, has branched many times since then. In these latter days, except for unpredictable instances based on individual spiritual destiny, true religion is only found in one of the revealed traditions. The trunk of the tree may be one, but nourishing fruit grows only on the branches.

Revealed religions, however, are not innovations. For all their necessary and providential dissimilarities, due to their place in cosmic time and the nature of the human collectivities to which they were and are addressed, each revelation in a deeper sense is a recollection of the One Primordial Revelation, God's creation of the cosmos, whose conscious and self-transcending center is Man — insofar as, through his indwelling Intellect, he contemplates his Divine Origin by means of it.

✳ The Transcendent Unity of Religions

So all true and revealed religions are branches of the One Truth. They meet not only in the depths of time, but in the depths of the Divine Nature. Outside these depths, however, they necessarily diverge. It is possible, therefore, to see vistas of revealed Truth through many traditions, but it is not possible to practice more than one religion at a time as a means of salvation, any more that one can simultaneously walk down two or three roads. The essence of spiritual truth, like that of human love, is not in the abstract similarities which can be drawn between various religious traditions, but in the particularity of a single tradition, fully conformed to and fully lived. As the Sufis say, better dig one well a hundred feet deep than ten wells ten feet deep if you want to strike water. In Rumi's words,

> When has religion ever been one? It has always been two or three, and war has always raged among coreligionists. How are you going to unify religion? On the Day of Resurrection it will be unified, but here in this world that is impossible because everybody has a different desire and want. Unification is not possible here. At the Resurrection, however, when all will be united, everyone will look to one thing, everyone will hear and speak one thing.
> ⌒ SIGNS OF THE UNSEEN [*Fihi ma-Fihi*] p29

'At the Resurrection' is also 'before the Fall' and 'in the depths of the Divine Nature.'

✳ The Spiritual Path

James S. Cutsinger, in *Advice to the Serious Seeker: Meditations on the Teaching of Frithjof Schuon*, speaks of four aspects of the spiritual Path: Truth, Virtue, Beauty and Prayer.

Truth is metaphysical doctrine, which, with God's grace, can open us to an intuition of the transcendent Intellect at the center of the human soul. But for the soul to become permanently conformed to that Intellect, Virtue is necessary. The three primary virtues here are humility, charity and veracity, which relate to the three major faculties of the soul. Humility conforms the human *will* to the transcendent Intellect, charity conforms the *feelings*, and veracity conforms the thinking *mind*. Or, from another perspective, we can say that each virtue leads the soul into deeper relation with its own Divine archetype: humility opens the soul to the Virtue of God, and thus to a humble appreciation of virtue wherever it may appear; charity to the

Beauty of God, and thus to all Beauty everywhere, including the moral beauty of one who is not physically beautiful, or the virtual beauty of the human state itself in one who lacks even moral beauty; and Veracity to the Truth of God, and thus to Truth in all its forms, including the truth of contingent situations, and even of simple facts. In the Divine Nature, however, these three archetypes are not separate, which is why each of them affects each of the three faculties of the human soul in its own way. Virtue is truth in action, one of whose fruits is moral beauty. Beauty can nourish and strengthen the will, besides being a way of knowing in its own right. And Truth in itself is uniquely strong and incomparably beautiful; it makes possible both emotional honesty and an objective assessment of one's progress in virtue.

In Plato's words, 'Beauty is the splendor of the true.' According to Schuon, 'Beauty, with its breadth of infinity and generosity, breaks down the fixed attitudes and closed systems of . . . spiritual egoism' (*Spiritual Perspectives and Human Facts*, p164). Beautiful things, however, are not without their ambiguities:

> Every Beauty is both a closed door and an open door . . . an obstacle and a vehicle: either Beauty separates us from God because it is entirely identified in our mind with its earthly support, which then assumes the role of idol, or Beauty brings us close to God because we perceive in it the vibrations of Beatitude and Infinity, which emanate from Divine Beauty.
> ⁓ESOTERISM AS PRINCIPLE AND AS WAY, p182

Even in an unworthy object, or in an object made unworthy in relation to us because of our idolatry, Beauty is still a ray of the Divine Nature.

'Virtue is Beauty of the soul, as Beauty is the Virtue of forms' (*Logic and Transcendence*, p246). It is Beauty which allows us to contemplate the forms around us in their 'metaphysical transparency':

> If gold is not lead, that is because it 'knows' the Divine better. It's 'knowledge' is in its very form . . . the rose differs from the water lily by its intellectual particularity, by its 'way of knowing'. . . . A noble animal or a lovely flower is intellectually superior to a base man.
> ⁓SPIRITUAL PERSPECTIVES AND HUMAN FACTS, p121.

The fourth aspect of the spiritual Path, Prayer, is the essence of the other three. Far from being a mere technique for the fulfillment of wishes or the alteration of consciousness, it is essential Beauty, essential Virtue and essential Truth; as one rabbi said, 'prayer itself is the Divine.'

Prayer takes three complementary forms: Canonical prayer, which connects us organically with our chosen spiritual community and tradition; personal prayer, which connects us in our own particularity with the specific face of the Divine which is turned toward that particularity in eternity; and invocatory prayer, which transcends both. Invocatory prayer means the (ideally) perpetual invocation of the Divine Name, a practice which is called *dhikr* in Sufism, the Jesus Prayer or the Prayer of the Heart in Orthodox Christian Hesychasm, and *japam* in Hinduism. Through Invocation, virtually if not actually, we are annihilated in our separate selfhood and divinized through the activity of the Name, since 'God and His Name are one.' In Sufism this is called *fana* and *baqa*, 'annihilation and subsistence-in-God'; in Orthodoxy it is called *theosis* or deification. It is the station St Paul was referring to when he said 'it is not I who live, but Christ lives in me.' When Jesus told his disciples to 'pray without ceasing', he was likely referring to the practice of invocatory prayer. According to Dr Cutsinger, invocation of the Divine Name is of such depth and power that it should never be undertaken on one's own initiative, but only with the permission of a spiritual master — or, lacking access to such a master, on the basis of a solemn vow before God and under the guidance of a spiritual director. Lastly, there is no such thing as a 'generic' Invocation; the Divine Names which carry the power to beget God in the human soul are those which God Himself has revealed to us, in the languages of the Paths which He Himself has founded.

✳ Simplicity of Soul

Metaphysics is complex; its Object is simple. It is complex precisely because its Object is of such simplicity that all conceivable and even inconceivable complexity can exist within It, with no chaos, no mutual obscuration, in a burning and a thundering peace.

Frithjof Schuon assigned a very high place to simplicity of soul. While his books were addressed to 'intellectuals', he also attracted many who had no interest in complex theories. Gnosis, he reminds us, is not a mental acquisition, but rather a gazing, in complete and virginal simplicity, upon the naked Truth, till the Object seen is transformed into the One Who sees. In *Light on the Ancient Worlds* (p109) he writes:

> If the Bible is naive, it is an honor to be naive. If the philosophies that deny the Spirit are intelligent, there is no such thing as intelligence. A humble belief in a Paradise situated among the clouds has at least a background of

inalienable Truth, but it has also and above all the background of a merciful reality in which is no deceit, and that is something beyond price.

✳ Critique of the Modern World

Truth casts a long shadow. If some things are necessarily true, then others are necessarily false. The love of Truth must therefore include a hatred of error, just as the love of one's human beloved must include the will to defend her from whatever would injure or degrade her, even to the point of sacrificing one's life. Anything less is not true love—or true love of wisdom. And yet criticism and defense will always be on a lower level than the assertion of Truth, which itself is lower than Truth's pure contemplation. Every rose has its thorn; roses, nonetheless, are not cultivated for the sake of their thorns, but for their form, their color and their fragrance. Truth, though it has a hard edge to it, is essentially merciful and redeeming; in the words of Allah, one of Whose Names is *al-Haqq*, (the Truth), 'my Mercy precedeth my wrath.' But what of *al-Haqq* in its own Essence, what of Absolute Truth, given that (according to Schuon) the Absolute has no opposite? How can negation of any kind exist within the depths of the Divine Nature? Perhaps the best way to answer this is with two apparently paradoxical proverbs of William Blake, which certainly refer to the level of cosmic manifestation, and perhaps even to that of *maya-in-divinis*: 'Everything possible to be believed is an image of Truth,' and, 'To be in error and to be cast out is part of God's plan.'

The writers of the Traditionalist school have carried on perhaps the most telling critique of the modern and postmodern world we possess. Representative books are *The Bugbear of Literacy* by Ananda K. Coomaraswamy, *The Destruction of the Christian Tradition* by Rama P. Coomaraswamy, *King of the Castle* by Charles LeGai Eaton, *The Crisis of the Modern World* and *The Reign of Quantity and the Signs of the Times* by René Guénon, *Ancient Beliefs and Modern Superstitions* by Martin Lings, sections of *The Transcendent Unity of Religions, Spiritual Perspectives and Human Facts, Light on the Ancient Worlds*, and other works by Frithjof Schuon, and *Beyond the Post-modern Mind* by Huston Smith. The present book was written, in part, to expand and update certain aspects of this critique.

To put the Traditionalist critique of the modern world in a phrase, they don't buy it. How to live within it if you don't buy it, and avail yourself of the unique spiritual opportunities provided by times of collective spiritual darkness, is one of the central questions the Traditionalists attempt to answer.

According to the view of most traditional religions, time is cyclical, and it is entropic. A Divine Self-revelation inaugurates a world-age, which descends from an original Golden Age to a terminal Iron Age, and is finally destroyed, after which a new cycle-of-manifestation descends from the higher worlds. According to this view, *progress* can only be an illusion; for every good that is gained through man's increasing knowledge of and control over nature, a greater cultural and spiritual good is lost. The cycle cannot be reversed. The perversions of the modern world, its destruction of metaphysics, its assaults upon religion and its violations of the natural world and the human form are evil, but they are not unlawful in the highest sense of that word, since the dire consequences of the human violation of divine and natural justice are themselves just. 'There needs be evil, but woe to him through whom evil comes.' Collective humanity in a sense can be forgiven; it is no crime simply to grow old. But the 'old age of the macrocosm' does not absolve individuals from their duty to discern and choose the Truth. And when Truth and deception are so radically polarized, as they must be in these latter days, the choice confronting each individual is more momentous than at any other point in the entire cycle.

The projection of this false myth of progress on biology results in the ideology known as *evolutionism*, the doctrine that the less is the causal origin of the greater, that higher and more complex life forms, including man, have developed incrementally from simpler forms. The Traditionalists, on the other hand, teach that the advent of new life-forms, which the fossil record shows to be more discontinuous than continuous—thus calling Darwin's 'natural selection of random mutations' into serious question—actually represents the descent of matter-organizing spiritual archetypes from the higher planes of Being, in response to God's creative word. These 'Platonic Ideas' of species then draw to themselves the matter they need in order to construct physical vehicles for their life in space and time.

Progressivism and evolutionism are aspects of the wider ideology known as *scientism*, the belief that nothing beyond the material world exists, and therefore that man's purpose and destiny lies in conquering and controlling matter, in the course of which campaign he must learn to define himself as matter and nothing else.

The Traditionalists also have something worthwhile to say against the excesses of *democracy*, which has an intimate historical connection with progressivism, scientism and evolutionism. When truth is degraded to majority opinion, and when the individual consequently attempts to depend for his moral choices upon the mass subjectivity of the collective society around him instead of on objective principles, the result is chaos. (I would only add one caution: According to Plato, democracy always degenerates into tyranny; it therefore behooves us to hold the line at democracy for as long as we can. The danger looming on the postmodern horizon is not democracy, but rather a kind of satanic neo-aristocracy, named by Guénon the 'inverted hierarchy', and identified by him with the regime of Antichrist.)

✳ Guénon vs. The Occultists

The founder of the Traditionalist School, René Guénon (1886–1951), was one of the two or three greatest exponents of 'pure metaphysics' in modern times. In books such as *Introduction to the Study of the Hindu Doctrines*, *Man and His Becoming according to the Vedanta*, *The Symbolism of the Cross*, and *Multiple States of Being*, he reintroduced traditional metaphysics and esoterism, both Oriental and Occidental, to the Western world. But there was another side to his genius. Before his encounter with what he came to call Tradition with a capital 'T', he had deeply and extensively explored the underworld of Western occultism—Rosicrucianism, Masonry, Martinism, Templarism, Neo-Gnosticism, Theosophy, Spiritualism, and other sects—from about 1905 until the early 1920s. He emerged from this period convinced not only of the doctrinal falsity of occultism, especially when compared to the common metaphysical heritage of the great world religions, but also of its profound spiritual danger. He attributed the death of his first wife to dark influences emanating from that quarter, and stated that he felt himself unqualified, even after becoming an orthodox Muslim and Sufi initiate, of assuming the role of spiritual master, since his soul had been marked by a too-intimate contact with evil psychic forces in his earlier years. In an attempt to warn others of this danger, and undoubtedly also as a way of purging himself, he published his second book (in 1921, when his first book, *Introduction to the Study of the Hindu Doctrines*, also appeared) under the title of *Le Théosophisme, histoire d'une pseudo-religion* (*Theosophy: History of a Pseudo-Religion*), an exposé of Madame Blavatsky's Theosophical Society, as well as of the Anthroposophy of Rudolf Steiner. (In the course of the present book, modern Theosophy will crop up several times as the continuing 'shadow' of Traditionalism.) In *Le Théosophisme*, he announced some of the themes to which he would return in several other works, including *L'Erreur Spirite* (*The Spiritist Fallacy*) in 1923, and his prophetic masterpiece *The Reign of Quantity and the Signs of the Times*, 1948, where he applies pure metaphysics to 'social criticism' on the most universal level imaginable, namely the inevitable downward course and apocalyptic end of the present cycle of manifestation on earth. Included among these themes is one which would appear in several places in his work, including *Le Roi du Monde* (*The King of the World*), 1927, and reach its culmination in *The Reign of Quantity*: that of the Antichrist.

In *Theosophy: History of a Pseudo-Religion*, he writes:

The false Messiahs we have seen so far have only performed very inferior miracles, and their disciples were probably not difficult to convert. But who knows what the future has in store? When you reflect that these false Messiahs have never been anything but the more or less unconscious tools of those who conjured them up, and when one thinks more particularly of the series of attempts made in succession by the theosophists [the most famous being their promotion of Krishnamurti as the Messiah; contemporary efforts seem limited to Benjamin Creme's 'Maitreya'], one is forced to the conclusion that they were only trials, experiments as it were, which will be renewed in various forms until success is achieved, and which in the meantime invariably produce a somewhat disquieting effect. Not that we believe that the theosophists, any more than the occultists and the spiritualists, are strong enough by themselves to carry out successfully an enterprise of this nature. But might there not be, behind all these movements, something far more dangerous which their leaders perhaps know nothing about, being themselves in turn the unconscious tools of a higher power?
⁓Quoted in The Morning of the Magicians, Louis Pauwels and Jacques Bergier; Avon Books, 1960, pp 219–220

[Note: The Theosophical Society—or, in contemporary terms, 'Societies'— obviously cannot be blamed for the actions or statements of every one of their members, particularly since they are without official dogma. They undoubtedly embrace many sincere seekers, and their Theosophical Publishing House, under the Quest Books imprint, has even published some of the Traditionalist writers: Frithjof Schuon, Huston Smith—and myself. Yet what Guénon would call 'anti-traditional action' continues to emanate, at least unofficially, from many in that quarter, as we will see in Chapter Eight and Chapter Nine.]

René Guénon was clearly a major figure in the 20th century critique of 'New Age' religions, whatever they happen to call themselves at a given period. What makes him and his followers unique is that they base this critique not on confessional dogmatism, but on universal metaphysics. What other approach could be capable of demonstrating that occultism and New Age doctrine are neither legitimately metaphysical nor really esoteric?

✻ The Spiritist Fallacy: A Synopsis

The following is a synopsis of Guénon's *The Spiritist Fallacy*, based on a manuscript translation by Dr Rama Coomaraswamy. It is highly illuminating in that it exposes many so-called 'cutting-edge' New Age doctrines as often more than a century old, and provides a valuable historical background to today's New Age movement.

Guénon defines spiritualism not simply as the belief that it is possible to communicate with the dead, but that such communication can take place by material means—'spirit' rapping, telekinesis, materializations, etc.. He denies neither the power of spiritualist mediums to produce such phenomena, nor the possibility of a 'mental, intuitive or inspired' communication with the departed—though he does little to define exactly what this form of communication might entail. But he repudiates the idea that such communication is possible by the methods of the spiritualists, and concludes therefore that spiritualist phenomena represent something else entirely.

He sees in spiritualism a kind of expanded materialism. Descartes posited a radical split between 'body' and 'spirit', thus both denying and culturally suppressing the traditional doctrine which, in its simplest form, states that the human form is tri-partite, being composed of body, soul and Spirit. The spiritualists, Theosophists and occultists, in a misguided attempt to restore a more comprehensive and accurate conception, posited a 'peri-spirit' (spiritualism) or 'astral body' (Theosophy) as a bridge between body and spirit. But they saw it, erroneously, as a kind of subtle material body capable of acting upon matter. In reality, however, since body and spirit are not, as Descartes believed, completely isolated from each other, it is unnecessary to posit, as a substitute for the traditional doctrine of soul, a quasi-material reality to bridge the non-existent gap between them.

One difficulty with the conception of the soul as a 'subtle' body is that it makes it seem as if death were nothing more than a discarding of the material body, after which the 'life' of the individual goes on with little fundamental change. (According to Orthodox Christian priest Seraphim Rose in his book *The Soul After Death*, doctrines like this remove the sense of death as a confrontation between the human soul and God, effectively eliminating all idea of divine judgement and destroying one of the fundamental points of orientation for the spiritual life.) Furthermore, if 'peri-spirit', being quasi-material, can act directly upon matter, why is mediumship required for its manifestation, as spiritualists universally claim? Spiritualism teaches that a subtle fluid or energy emanating from the medium, called 'odic force', 'ectenic', 'neuritic force', 'ectoplasm', etc., is a necessary ingredient in spirit manifestation. Why, then, is it necessary to posit the existence of a peri-spirit or astral body in the first place?

(The existence of a subtle body is in fact not as untraditional as Guénon, in his reaction against the clearly anti-traditional doctrines of the spiritualists, and against Descartes, seems to claim in *The Spiritist Fallacy*—an apparent lapse he more than makes up for in other works, notably *Man and His Becoming according to the Vedanta*. Vedanta itself speaks of a subtle body, the *suksma sarira*, which, according to the *Brahma Sutras*, survives until the final Liberation. Jesus, after his resurrection, appeared in a palpable though 'glorified' body, and both Mulla Sadra and Ibn al-'Arabi, Muslim esoterists, hold that a body is necessary to the soul at every stage of existence. An individual being can be defined as a polar relationship between its spiritual source and its formal manifestation, neither of which can exist alone, because they are complementary manifestations of a single Reality. The spiritual pole has precedence over the formal, since Spirit in fact represents this absolute Reality in the mode of polarity with its own manifestation, yet one pole never exists without the other. And in view of this doctrine, Guénon is right to criticize the Spiritualists for viewing death as nothing more than the disappearance of the material body, leaving the subtle body exactly as it was before, because this very disappearance necessitates a 're-polarization' between Spirit and its manifestation on an entirely different level, thus situating the individual being on a new ontological plane. But insofar as he opposes the spiritualist tendency to conceive of the material body as a kind of model for the subtle one, rather than understanding the subtle body as the model for the material one, Guénon is right on the mark.)

Guénon gives a short history of spiritualism, which originated in Hydesville, New York due to a manifestation of 'spirit-rapping' at the house of a German family named Fox (an anglicized form of Voss) in 1847. The 'spirit' produced knocking noises, which are among the phenomena reported throughout history in relation to so-called 'haunted houses'. The 'spirit' was asked various questions, and responded correctly by means of the knocks. What was significant, according to Guénon, was not the phenomenon itself but the unique set of conclusions drawn from it: specifically, that human society was to be advanced and perfected by the establishment of a widespread and ongoing communication between the living and the dead. A Quaker named Isaac Post appeared, who—in the true spirit of Yankee tinkering—designed a 'spirit telegraph', a kind of ouija board, so the 'spirit' could communicate more easily. (Guénon remarks on the similarities between the Quaker form of worship and the practices of spirit mediums.) It was then discovered that the phenomenon became more pronounced when the Fox sisters were in the room, and this, according to Guénon, was the precise moment when the modern world discovered mediumship. The 'spirit' claimed to be that of a peddler who had been murdered and buried in the cellar of the Fox home. Subsequently the cellar was dug up and a skeleton discovered. The interest in these happenings rapidly grew until it became the highly-influential international movement known as Spiritualism. The first national Spiritualist convention took place in 1852 in Cleveland, Ohio, only five years after the original manifestations.

The 'spirits' swarming around Hydesville claimed they were led by Benjamin Franklin, the archetype of all Yankee tinkerers. They also maintained that modern researches into electricity had paved the way for communication with them, and that 'Franklin' was being guided in ways to improve this communication. The author also mentions, in another context, the case of Thomas Edison, Yankee tinkerer become captain of industry, who seriously attempted to construct a 'radio' for communication with the dead!

Guénon asks why a phenomenon which, since antiquity, had been associated with haunted houses would suddenly, in the middle of the 19th century, spawn an international pseudo-religious movement. While admitting that the climate of the times made this development possible, he also notes as significant the fact that Madame Emma Hardinge-Britten, a member of the secret society known as the Hermetic Brotherhood of Luxor which Guénon had investigated earlier, associated herself with the spiritualist movement from the start, and wrote a book entitled *History of Modern American Spiritualism* (1870). The significance lies in the fact that the Brotherhood had always *opposed* spiritualist theories, and had furthermore claimed that the first spiritualist phenomena had actually been produced by *living individuals acting at a distance*—in other words, through sorcery. Apparently Annie Besant of the Theosophical Society on one occasion made a similar claim. Given the suspect nature of these sources, Guénon does not necessarily accept their assertions, but he does allow for the possibility that they might be right. In view of the fact that the Hermetic Brotherhood of Luxor had affinities with various earlier secret societies in Germany, some of them

Masonic, who practiced magic and 'evocations' in the late 18th and early 19th centuries, he speculates that certain 'adepts' associated with the Brotherhood or other groups may have produced the phenomena in Hydesville, possibly taking advantage of the 'psychic residues' clinging to a house in which a violent death had occurred—residues which, he insists, are in no way the 'spirit of the departed.' The aim of these 'adepts', according to Guénon, may have been to produce certain high-profile psychic phenomena in order to combat the philosophy of materialism in the mind of the public, influencing them to believe in the Spiritualist doctrine while themselves knowing better. (I am immediately reminded of the various hoaxes, some of them ingenious enough to require a high level of organization, that continue to turn up around the UFO phenomenon.) As a minimum hypothesis, he thinks it likely that agents of such groups influenced the population of Hydesville through covert propaganda, taking advantage, according to this scenario, of an already-existing situation. But to oppose Materialism with Spiritualism, Guénon makes clear, is simply to combat one error with another—a truth which daily becomes more obvious, as a fascination with various arcane technologies, and psychic or quasi-psychic phenomena like telepathy and UFO encounters, continue to merge in the collective mind.

Next Guénon introduces us to Allan Kardec, the most influential of French Spiritualists, who produced a number of 'channeled' books of 'spirit-philosophy'. He then quotes Daniel Dunglas Home, the most phenomenal 'materialization medium' ever investigated, and reputedly among the most reliable, who claimed that Kardec was really kind of hypnotist who surrounded himself with impressionable mediums whom he treated as hypnotic subjects, with the result that the philosophy they 'channeled' was composed entirely of Kardec's pre-conceived ideas transmitted via suggestion. Guénon accepts this evaluation, except that he attributes the suggestion not to Kardec alone, but to the 'group mind' he shared with certain colleagues.

The author remarks on the fact that modern spiritualism was propagated in America especially in socialist journals and shows how, in France, it assumed the progressive, anti-clerical and 'scientistic' character of the 18th and 19th century revolutionary 'enlightenment'. (Also of interest, incidentally, is the fact that Robert Dale Owen [1801–1877], U.S. Congressman and son of the famous Welsh socialist Robert Owen, was an enthusiastic spiritualist. As a conservative, Guénon was naturally more interested in the ties of spiritualism to the Left, but it is well known that Hitler's National Socialist Party of the extreme Right drew upon many similar influences.)

Guénon shows how the teachings of 'spirits' tend to reflect the ideas of the social milieu in which they appear, since the power of suggestion operates in the collective mind just as it does in the shared mentality of smaller groups. Thus French spiritualism made a dogma out of reincarnation, interpreting it as a form of spiritual progress and 'evolution', while reincarnation was denied in the spirit messages channeled to the more conservative society of England. Socialism and spiritualism became deeply intertwined in France, where the 'spirits' tended to espouse the ideology of the revolution of 1848.

Next Guénon refutes those who claim that spiritualism is a kind of 'esoteric Brahmanism'—there being no such thing—or a Western 'fakirism'. The Arabic word 'fakir', like the Persian 'dervish'—both sometimes used as synonyms for 'Sufi'—means 'poor man' or 'mendicant'. Those people called 'fakirs' by European travelers are (whether fakirs or not) actually magicians. The author makes clear how magic, though a valid 'experimental science' capable of producing real phenomena, is extremely dangerous, which is why it is discouraged by traditional authorities throughout Asia, just as it was in classical antiquity. Magic and spiritualism are radically opposed, since the magician, like the hypnotist, is an active agent with a set goal, while the medium, like the hypnotic subject, is passively open to any and all influences. Nonetheless neither magic nor mediumship can be explained by simple hypnotism. In traditional societies, mediumship is looked on as a calamity, being considered an instance of demonic possession; the idea of exalting such possession to the position of a spiritual gift is an entirely modern and Western development. And as for the deliberate 'evocation' of 'spirits', it has traditionally been considered a serious crime, the crime of necromancy. The forces evoked, however, are not 'souls of the dead' but dangerous psychic residues clinging to the corpse, which explains why black magicians like to frequent graveyards. These residues, which the Hebrews called 'ob', are identical to the Roman 'manes'.

Guénon's assertion that traditional societies took a negative attitude toward magic needs to be clarified. This is certainly true of those societies founded on Judaism, Christianity, Islam, Vedantic Hinduism (though not Hindu society as a whole, which embraces many forms of folk religion where magic, for better or worse, plays a role) and most forms of Buddhism. Magic, especially sorcery and witchcraft, was also largely frowned upon in the pre-Christian Paganism of Europe and the Near East, even though the official cults of these societies might contain what we would think of as magical elements. According to *The Golden Bough* of Sir James Frazer, even the Celtic Druids burned witches. When we consider the great north/central Asian culture area that gave birth to shamanism, however, Guénon's stance needs to be modified. And though Confucius once said, 'I believe in supernatural beings, but I keep them at a distance,' Taoism and Shinto clearly incorporated shamanic elements, through which the beneficent forces of the cosmos were invoked for the general good of the people, while in the unique case of the Vajrayana Buddhism of Tibet and the T'ien-tai Buddhism of China—or some forms of them—similar forces were pressed into the service of Perfect Total Enlightenment. And although the East Asian traditions, alone among the 'world' religions, seem to have maintained an unbroken connection with shamanism (unless we consider Indian yoga and certain practices of Central Asian Sufism as in some ways shamanic), the function of invoking spiritual forces for the protection of society and the healing of disease has been an integral part of every society based on religion—in other words, of every traditional society. The question is, from what ontological level is such power drawn? Is the society in question the direct recipient, via revelation, of a ray of the Absolute? Does it invoke angelic forces for healing, fertility and protection against more demonic forces? At which point, having lost direct touch with the angelic worlds, does it begin to propitiate these demonic forces to keep them satisfied? And when does such propitiation of evil become transformed into the direct service of it? Such questions, especially when we are dealing with 'primitive' societies, have to be answered on a case-by-case basis.

At this point it is necessary to say something about shamanism. Interest in shamanism outside traditional tribal societies was not as prevalent in 1921 as it is today, though Guénon dealt with it briefly in *The Reign of Quantity*, where he admitted that it probably represents a valid spiritual tradition, though in a seriously degenerated condition. In view of this, can Guénon's negative assessment of magic be applied to shamanism as well? The answer depends upon many factors. At its best, shamanism is a kind of 'Hyperborean theurgy' whereby the shaman, through voluntary ascetic suffering, consciously places himself under the guidance of his 'daimon' or 'genius' or 'guardian angel', the specific archetype or 'Name of God' with which he has an intrinsic 'pre-eternal' affinity. But the *loas* or *mysteres* of Voudoo are, in their origin, precisely such Names of God—and Voudoo (like Obeah and Santerría), though it exhibits signs of derivation from an ancient, probably syncretic 'esoterism' where tropical African, Egyptian, Hebrew, and even Christian and Hellenistic elements came together, is clearly a degenerate and contaminated tradition, involved with, though not to be strictly identified with, demonic black magic. Furthermore, even the high 'theurgy' of the Neo-Platonists fell in the direction of magic as the tradition which gave rise to it weakened. So all one can say about shamanism is that, while some of it represents a true traditional spirituality, revealed by God to the Siberians and Native Americans every bit as much as the Torah to the Hebrews or the Koran to the Arabs, much of what passes for shamanism in New Age and Neo-Pagan circles, and among some Native Americans as well, is degenerate, a great deal of it is spurious, and some of it is evil.

Guénon makes a distinction between magic and theurgy, which are situated on vastly different levels, theurgy representing the intervention of celestial powers. The numinous power of the Ark of the Covenant and the Temple of Jerusalem, of holy icons and sacred places, of the tombs of saints, and of the 'overshadowing' of various Sufi orders by the *barakah* (grace) of their founding Shayhks, who may have been dead for centuries, are examples of theurgy, not of magic. This distinction of levels, however, is precisely what the post-modern mind can no longer discern. Contemporary magicians will routinely portray the distinction between the 'magical' and the 'miraculous' solely in terms of political and social power. 'If someone in the Church performs wonders,' they complain, 'it's called a miracle; if we do the same thing, it's branded as magic.' In reality the two are not the same, but the magicians, and in some cases the churchmen themselves, can no longer tell the difference.

Guénon traces the relationship between spiritualism and occultism. He defines as 'occultism' the movement deriving from Eliphas Levi (real name Alphonse-Louis Constant, d. 1875) and further popularized by Papus (Gerard Encausse) who broke with the Theosophical Society in 1890. (Madame Blavatsky used 'occultism' as a synonym for her 'Theosophy', but Guénon makes a distinction between the two movements, though they are obviously close cousins.) Occultism is the result of a misguided attempt to re-discover, or re-invent, initiatory esoterism. It tends to be more centrally-organized, more intellectual or at least elaborately pseudo-intellectual, and more elitist than spiritualism, which resists centralization and gravitates toward pluralism, sentimentality and democracy. Occultism is also imbued with the spirit of 'scientism', which caused it to seek to produce experimentally verifiable phenomena, totally disqualifying it as even an approach to traditional esoterism. French occultists usually opposed spiritualism; nonetheless their own eclecticism sometimes led to attempts at rapprochement. And both occultism and Theosophy, without admitting it, borrowed many doctrines from spiritualism, including that of reincarnation. In this polarization between occultism and spiritualism we can see the roots of the present-day divergence between semi- or pseudo-traditional 'literary' occultism, like that of Jocelyn Godwin and others, and the New Age proper — represented, for example, by Shirley McClaine — with its loose 'you can too' populism and deliberate mass-market appeal. Literary occultism presently seems to be gaining ground against the New Age, at least from my vantage point, since it gives the illusion of substance when contrasted to the airy ephemerality of New Age ideas. If Deepak Chopra represents the marketing of pseudo-Hindu ideas to a New Age audience (in *The Seven Spiritual Laws of Success*), and James Redfield (in *The Celestine Prophecy*) a specifically New Age ideology, one among many, William Quinn (in *The Only Tradition*) is an example of literary occultism attempting to gain academic legitimacy, and to a degree succeeding (see Chapters Four and Eight).

Guénon admits that many 'psychic phenomena', including those produced by mediums, are real. But this fact alone in no way validates the spiritualist explanation of such phenomena, which can be due to many different causes. Mediumship, even when the phenomena produced are genuine, remains a form of mental illness. Some 'spirit obsessions' are simply cases of multiple personality. Furthermore, even genuine mediums may practice fraud, especially the 'professionals'. Given that their powers are not under their own control, they need to supplement them by other means from time to time, since 'the show must go on'. Mediums are sometimes pathological liars as well.

The attempt by scientists to empirically investigate psychic phenomena is compromised from the start, since many investigators are ignorant of the psychological dynamics operating in unstable personalities, and virtually none of them understand metaphysical principles, specifically the ontological distinction between the psychic plane and the spiritual one. One result is that highly psychic and suggestible mediums may channel 'spirits' who, to the delight of the investigator, resoundingly confirm all his pet theories — which, or course, the medium is really tapping directly from the investigator's mind. Competency in one branch of physical science is no guarantee of an investigator's objectivity in the face of such things as personality disorders and psychic phenomena (or, I would add, stage magic).

Spiritualists, like occultists, tend toward an ideology that is humanistic and anti-Catholic, something which has remained true to the present day, at least in terms of anti-Catholicism. Both Jane Roberts of the Seth material, and Helen Schucman, channeler of *A Course in Miracles*, were ex-Catholics with a grudge against the Church; the same can probably be said for Carlos

Castaneda. And James Redfield's *The Celestine Prophecy* is a direct attack on traditional Catholicism. Guénon quotes a passage from the early French spiritualist Charles Fauvety where he declares that morality will one day be a branch of science, not religion, that a mystical faith in Science with a capital 'S' will overturn the authority of all priesthoods. (I am reminded here of the interesting fact that it was U.S. Congressman and Spiritualist Robert Dale Owen who first introduced the legislation through which the Smithsonian Institution, the American Temple of Scientism, was founded, where devotees of the American god of Technique may daily worship the 'Spirit' of St Louis, and other idols.)

Guénon characterizes philosophies such as the spiritualism of psychologist William James which he espoused late in life (though James' father had been a follower of Swedenborg), as well as the spiritualist tendencies of philosopher Henri Bergson, as 'unconscious satanism'. James promised to do everything in his power to communicate with the living after his death; nor does it surprise the author that a host of American mediums dutifully received 'messages' from him—among the most recent being Jane Roberts, who published a book entitled *The Afterdeath Journal of an American Philosopher: The World View of William James* in 1978.

The following represents my own commentary on the validity of 'channelled material':

As I see it, such material can be placed in five categories: (1) banal nonsense; (2) psychotic fantasies; (3) prognostications or clairvoyant perceptions which turn out to be accurate; (4) false philosophies; and (5) philosophies containing elements of truth. Categories 1, 2, and 4 can be explained in terms of mental illness and/or demonic obsession, though it is not always easy to tell these two apart, especially since both may be present in the same soul. Categories 3 and 5 are harder to characterize. An accurate psychic vision of a physical condition, past, present or future (category 3) can simply be an instance of a natural though comparatively rare talent; it may be the sign of an angelic intervention, especially when it results in healing, protection from danger, or enlightenment as to a moral dilemma; it may also, in any given case, be an example of demonic delusion. As for category 5, 'channeled' philosophies containing elements of truth *may* represent an attempt on the part of celestial powers to resurrect certain aspects of traditional wisdom which people in a given region and historical period have lost, but there is no guarantee that this is the case in any given instance. The doctrines of Emmanuel Swedenborg, for example—multi-talented physical scientist turned spiritual visionary—represent perhaps the highest category of 'spirit philosophy'. His *Divine Love and Wisdom* contains elements resembling the esoteric Aristotelianism which developed within Islamic tradition. His doctrine of angels is similar in some ways to the Orthodox Christian doctrine of Dionysius the Areopagite, and his image of the Universal Man to analogous doctrines which can be found in the Church fathers, the Kabbalah, and the Sufis and theosophers of Islam. We can speculate that since such doctrines were not available to a Swedish Lutheran of the 18th century, it was necessary to reintroduce them via direct inspiration. On the other hand, this may not be accurate. Seyyed Hossein Nasr, in *Knowledge and the Sacred*, points out that Lutheranism embraced a theosophical, alchemical and mystical tradition, represented by such figures as Sebastian Franck, Paracelsus, V. Weigel, Jacob Boehme, G. Arnold, G. Gichtel, C. F. Oetinger and others. And physical scientists before and during Swedenborg's time were much more likely to have preserved an interest in 'esoteric' sciences; even Isaac Newton wrote on alchemy. So whether Swedenborg derived his doctrines entirely from direct inspiration or partly through human transmission (he could certainly have gotten his esoteric Aristotelianism from the alchemical tradition, for example) remains debatable. In any case, his doctrines of the structure of the spiritual world all seem transposed to a more literalistic level than that found in many traditional sources, a quality which, as Guénon points out, is common to many 'spirit' teachings. He seems unsure whether that world is a realm of living and embodied symbols of invisible realities, as in Ibn al-'Arabi's doctrine of the *'alam al-mithal*, the 'imaginal plane', or simply a kind of higher material nature. And interspersed with his undeniably lofty doctrines are others of the more fantastic or even psychotic variety, as when, in *Earths in the Universe*, he says that Martians have faces that are half black and half tawny, live on fruit and dress in fibres made of tree bark, or that the atmosphere of the Moon is so different from the earthly one that the inhabitants speak from their stomachs instead of their lungs, with an effect like belching.

In the case of Swedenborg—and the same can perhaps even be said for less reliable 'channeled' teachings such as the *Seth* material and *A Course in Miracles*—it is difficult to determine whether the mixture of sophisticated doctrine and suspect material can simply be put down to imperfect communication, or whether it represents, in some cases at least, a satanic attempt to pervert deep theological, philosophical and esoteric doctrines by associating them with trash. What we can say with greater assurance is that only those who have no access to reliable sources of nourishment will be forced to take their meals mixed with garbage. That a great deal of profound doctrine can be found in Swedenborg's writings is undeniable. But now that the scriptures and classics of the world religions and the writings of history's greatest sages are readily available, we no longer need to take him, and others like him, as uniquely inspired authorities, since we can judge them in the light of their orthodox 'originals'. As Guénon makes clear, there is no longer any reason to rely upon suspect sources, no matter what grains of truth they may contain.

Guénon presents in great detail various fantastic spiritualistic ideas of the 'survival' of the human personality, allowing their absurdity to speak for itself. He deals at length with the theory of reincarnation—reminding us, for example, that the earliest forms of modern spiritualism, the English and American, denied it, and that notable spiritualists like Daniel Dunglas Home violently opposed it—and traces the doctrine to French spiritualism, especially that of Allan Kardec, from which it spread to Theosophy and occultism. He makes a clear distinction between reincarnation, transmigration and metempsychosis, on the basis of which he denies that Hinduism ever taught the reincarnational doctrines later cooked up by the spiritualists. (For a fuller treatment of Guénon's ideas on the impossibility of reincarnation and time-travel, see *Chapter Seven*.)

He shows how spiritualism, based on the 19th century *zeitgeist*, adopted evolutionary theory, reinterpreted it in 'spiritual' terms (as did the Mormons), and identified it with reincarnation. We can still see this influence in the Seth material of Jane Roberts, where the entity 'Seth' is sometimes defined as a 'future portion' of Jane, just as the more sublime, distant and ethereal 'Seth II' is a 'future portion' of Seth—'future', here, taking the place of 'ontologically higher'. By the time the Seth material made its debut in 1963, however, the unquestioned confidence in progress proper to the 19th and the first half of the 20th centuries had begun to falter, due partly to nuclear weapons, partly also to a 'social Einsteinianism' based on a popularized version of the theory of relativity. This erosion of the myth of progress, as well as various theories of multidimensional spacetime, are probably what led Seth, still in many ways a 'macrocosmic progressivist', to speak of biological evolution as a very narrow and simplistic concept, and of reincarnational lifetimes as fundamentally simultaneous rather than successive.

Guénon then deals with the relationship between spiritualism and satanism, characterizing as unconscious satanism any doctrine subversive to traditional metaphysics. He recounts a number of stories suggestive of demonic influence in spiritualist circles, or at least of toxic emanations from the subconscious which, he says, are no less demonic in effect. These include sexual scandals of a sadistic nature as well as stories of intercourse with incubi, like those which often crop up in contemporary UFO lore. He details the repeated attempts of French spiritualists to pervert and misrepresent Catholic doctrine, mentioning a scurrilous brochure on the Eucharist which claimed that 'Jesus was not entirely proud of the clerical role that He played,' in terms highly reminiscent of the Seth material. He mentions groups such as Mental Science and Christian Science which (like *A Course in Miracles*) deny the reality of evil, thereby strengthening the hand of demonic forces. He goes on to speak of spiritualism as a quasi-political movement with great resources for propaganda, characterizing it as a serious danger to public safety.

He admits the validity, in certain cases, of clairvoyance and psychic healing, though such phenomena remain highly ambiguous. But such psychic powers in no way prove that spiritualists can have ongoing intercourse with the souls of the dead, even if this is how the practitioners themselves explain their abilities. Phenomena, says Guénon, can never prove the truth or falsity of doctrine. Finally, he speaks of the dangers of spiritualism for the practitioners themselves, recounting many cases of mental, emotional and physical breakdown, epilepsy, etc.

The Spiritist Fallacy is also valuable for the historical light it throws on the belief in 'aliens' and UFOs. Many spiritualists, according to Guénon, believe that discarnate spirits occupy space. He quotes one Ernest Bosc as calling them 'our friends in Space,' in response to an article in the spiritualist magazine *Fraternist* published in 1913. It may be significant that, fifty-five years later, the hippies were calling extraterrestrials 'space brothers', and the New Age movement since the '70s has all but erased the distinction between space aliens and discarnate spirits.

Guénon mentions, as an example of the inflated pretensions of American spiritualists, a group calling itself the 'Ancient Order of Melchizedek'. He also speaks of an 'Esoteric Fraternity' in Boston led by the blind Hiram Butler. Interestingly enough, this same Order of Melchizedek, as well as Hiram Butler—who also, as it turns out, established a group by the same name in California in 1889, on a communal farm in the foothills of the Sierras—make their appearance in *Messengers of Deception* (1979), by UFO researcher Jacques Vallee. Vallee investigated several groups, both in France and in the United States, calling themselves the Order of Melchizedek, and described the figure of Melchizedek, Abraham's master from the book of *Genesis* who had neither father or mother, as 'a symbol and a rallying point for saucer contactees' (see Chapter Seven). So it seems possible that the widespread belief in UFOs, if not the proliferation of the phenomenon itself, are among the social and psychological fruits of the Spiritualist movement of the late 19th and early 20th centuries, which is in so many ways the direct ancestor of the New Age movement of today.

In *The Spiritist Fallacy*, Guénon has this to say:

What we see . . . in spiritualism and other similar movements are the influences which incontestably come from what some have called the 'Kingdom of Antichrist'. This designation can be taken symbolically, but that changes nothing with regard to reality and doesn't make the influences any less evil. Assuredly those who participate in such movements, and even those who think they direct them, may know nothing of these things. It is this that makes all this so dangerous, for many of them would most certainly flee with horror if they recognized that they were servants of the 'powers of darkness'. But their blindness is often incurable, and their good faith even contributes to their attracting other victims. Does this not allow us to say that the supreme talent of the devil, regardless of how he is conceived, is to make us deny his existence?

3

What is the New Age?

The pseudo-traditional counterfeits, to which belong all the dena-
turings of the ideas of tradition . . . take their most dangerous form
in 'pseudo-initiation', first because in it they are translated into effective action instead of remaining in the form of more or less vague
conceptions, and secondly because they make their attack on tradition from the inside, on what is its very spirit, namely, the esoteric
and initiatic domain.
~RENÉ GUÉNON, *The Reign of Quantity and the Signs of the Times*

THE central error of the New Age is the belief that spiritual
Truth can be new. Certainly raw information can be new. Knowledge of the
material world is necessarily always changing, but Truth itself cannot
change. It has nothing to do with the material world, ruled by events, nor
the psychic world, ruled by beliefs. It is the Rock of Ages, the Always So.

If you believe that the world as a whole can spiritually evolve or progress,
you must believe that Truth can be new. All traditional metaphysics, however, denies this. The Always So is revealed in a single flash; this is the
Word, the Logos, the eternal Beginning. Whatever reflections of this Beginning have come into matter, energy, space and time, and in so doing created
them, have already begun to die. 'All matter is subject to entropy,' says the
Second Law of Thermodynamics. 'This whole world is on fire,' said the
Buddha. 'All is perishing' says the Holy Koran, 'except His Face.'

The doctrines of the New Age are, on one level, an attempt to connect
poorly-understood traditional metaphysics with progressive and evolutionary ideas which are totally incompatible with them. For this reason, it cannot function as a complete spiritual Path. All the sincerity, self-sacrifice,
psychic sensitivity and spiritual ambition in the world cannot make falsehood, or half-truth, into the Always So.

The proponents of New Age ideas thought they were discovering, or re-
inventing, the Truths of the Ages. They were merely distorting them. The

Truth has always been known by the human race, at the conscious core of the race if not in the mind of every member, because the Human Form is the mirror of that Truth in this world. And ever since the first unity of the human race grew old, the deepest channels of this Truth have been the great God-revealed religions. On the level of first principles, which every religion enshrines in its own unique and providential language, nothing need be invented, or re-constructed, or improved. And nothing can be. Certainly the truths of the ages must be expressed differently in different times in places, but such changes in expression are nothing but translations. They are not, and cannot be, revisions.

I. A Short History of the 'Spiritual Revolution' and the New Age Movement

Those of us who remember the 'spiritual revolution' of the Sixties, and the New Age movement which took up the slack, some time in the Seventies, after that revolution died, will have either passively witnessed or actively participated in an orgy of idealism. Psychedelics, meditation, Eastern religions, and psychic or occult knowledge had so deeply transformed those attracted to them—for both better and worse, as it turned out—that all we needed to do, we thought, was spread them further. As the early and mid-20th Century had called for education and culture for the masses, we called for mass enlightenment. What seemed good for us in the inner world of our souls, we believed, had to be good for society as a whole. The legacy of old fashioned American revivalism abruptly encountered psychedelic drugs, exotic religions, 20th Century ideas of evolution and progress, and the shock of the war in Vietnam to produce a 'go for broke' attitude: 'give me Enlightenment or give me Death; *Apocalypse Now*.'

As the mania of the '60s subsided into the introversion of the '70s, the spirit of American populist revivalism was replaced by the equally American spirit of the religious and psychological and psychic hucksterism. The odd Sixties mixture of traditional mysticism and Eastern religion with magic, occultism, mediumship, psychic powers, leftist politics and the first stirrings of magical scientism, underwent a shift; the entrepreneurial, *petite bourgeois* spirit had entered the arena of 'alternative' spiritualities. And with this shift in emphasis, what came to be called the New Age replaced (in part) the 'hippy' ethos. Innumerable new approaches to spirituality and psychotherapy and psychic development took their place alongside the survivals of an older world of spiritualism and Theosophy, Rosicrucianism and literary occultism, which thereby gained a new lease on life.

The New Age still gave lip service to mysticism, self-transcendence and the Eastern idea of enlightenment or liberation. Yet the real center had shifted to the attempt to fulfill the tried-and-true desires for security, pleasure and power through subtle or magical means—an inevitable development, since the '60s ethos was only able to popularize mysticism on the mass level by associating it, through psychedelic drugs, with unbridled self-indulgence. Whether as Neo-Paganism, as the drive to develop psychic powers according to the New Age model, as the attraction to shamanism, or as the infinitely darker attraction to Satanic practices, magic had effectively replaced enlightenment as the dominant paradigm of the world of alternative spiritualities by the beginning of the 1980s.

Unfortunately, both in the public mind, and to a certain extent in actual reality, psychic and magical practices on the one hand, and traditional mysticism and metaphysics on the other, have been lumped together. It is time to separate them. Up till now the New Age has been criticized mostly by materialists—cynical debunkers—and conservative Christians, who give the impression (to the uninformed) that they are simply acting out of a threatened self-interest, like a candidate slinging mud at his opponent. The present critique is among the very few based not on a militant religious exclusivism, or on a modernist defense of 'ordinary reality', but on comparative religion and traditional metaphysics.

The 'New Age' could not exist as a movement without anticipating a mass spiritual and cultural transformation in the (perpetually) immediate future; such anticipation, however, has been around for quite a while. So when did the New Age, as a movement, begin? The Gurdjieffian A. R. Orage edited a very influential journal before WWI called *The New Age*; Swedenborg spoke of a new age dawning, and similar ideas go back at least as far as Joachim da Fiore in medieval Christendom, and include such groups as the Illuminati, who flourished around the time of the French Revolution, as well as the Masons and the Rosicrucians. There is good reason, however, to trace its main roots back to the Renaissance, when the revival of classical learning spawned a mass of 'esoteric' speculation. (I once heard Peter Caddy [of Findhorn] claim at a lecture that the New Age began with the late Renaissance English philosopher, Francis Bacon.) Though some of it was traditionally valid and most of it at least nominally Christian, such speculation could not be fully contained within Catholic orthodoxy. This was undoubtedly in part a compensation for the solidifying of the Christian

mind under scholasticism, and the out-and-out betrayal of Christian metaphysics by scholastic nominalism. The nominalists believed that all distinctions between things are only linguistic, and denied that anything higher
than sense experience could be known by the mind, thus making nominalism the true first ancestor of both modernist naturalism and postmodern
relativism.

The United States has always had a New Age sector. Many of the founding fathers were Masons, which is why we have a pyramid surmounted with
a glowing eye on the back of our dollar bills. The New England Transcen-
dentalists and their ilk were in many ways the direct ancestors of both the
hippy communes of the '60s and today's New Age. And the Shakers, a pure
American product though founded by an Englishwoman, began as a kind of
lay monastic order within Protestantism, became pioneers of 'appropriate
technology', went on to channel spirit entities, and finally became advocates
of a One World Government in the Teddy Roosevelt years.

A complete study of even the American roots of the New Age movement
would take up a whole book; for myself, I can only speak with any authority
for the period stretching from the 'spiritual revolution' of the '60s to about
1988. And while I was in many ways in the thick of things here in Marin
County, California, the reader should understand that any number of other
perspectives on that time period, and other reading lists, might be just as
accurate, if not more so.

A good historical overview of the psychic paradigm on which the New
Age is largely based is *The Occult* by Colin Wilson (Vintage Books, 1973). It's
written in a racy journalistic style, and covers a vast amount of ground.
Although he includes material from all historical periods, his basic history
covers occultism from the 18th century through Blavatsky and Gurdjieff
(and he is certainly not adverse to recounting scandals associated with these
two figures, since they make 'good copy'), though he does bring some of his
lines of inquiry up into the 1950s and '60s, touching among other things
upon the UFO phenomenon. And he is valuable in that he shows many of
the connections between occultism and both primitive shamanism and
modern science.

Another important book was *The Morning of the Magicians* (Avon Books,
1968; earlier English title *The Dawn of Magic*) by Louis Pauwels and Jacques
Bergier, which deals at length with occultism among the Nazis (whom the
authors of course deplore, but also seem to envy), and announces the coming World Magical Technocracy. Bergier is a renegade Guénoniste who
became a convert to technocratic futurism. Another important book on the

interface between technology and psychic powers was *Psychic Discoveries Behind the Iron Curtain*, by Sheila Ostrander and Lynn Schroeder, which came out in the '70s; the 'remote viewers' who came forward in 1997, apparently participants in a U.S. Government-sponsored program to train psychics for espionage, were undoubtedly part of the 'psychic arms race' announced in this book.

One of the major differences between post-war and pre-war occultism is the UFO phenomenon prevalent since the late '40s. The UFO myth was part of the ethos of the Psychedelic Era—many hippies spoke of the 'Mothership' which was supposed to be overshadowing the Earth—but it was in no way dominant. The psychedelic experience was the major paradigm from, say, '65 to maybe '72 or '74; the main proponents of psychedelic spirituality were Ralph Metzner, Timothy Leary, Richard Alpert (Ram Dass), R.E.L. Masters & Jean Houston (*The Varieties of the Psychedelic Experience*) and John Lilly (*The Center of the Cyclone*, which features a psychedelic approach to 'spirit guides'). Leary was the PR showman of the movement, and a true crank; two representative books are *The Psychedelic Experience*, where he applied the paradigm of the *Tibetan Books of the Dead* to the LSD experience, and *The Politics of Ecstasy*.

The most genuine figure among all of these was and is Ram Dass. He might be called the latest, if not last, in the line of the semi- or non-traditional perennialists, stretching through Aldous Huxley and Alan Watts. He introduced a great deal of traditional material from the world's religions into the hippy world; without him, I might never have found Schuon and the Traditionalist School. His books include *Be Here Now*, *Grist for the Mill*, *The Only Dance there Is*, and later books on social service as karma-yoga, such as *How Can I Help?* His 'consciousness' books mix traditional metaphysics, psychic and psychedelic experience, and more-or-less traditional Hinduism (Hinduism for the West, that is, which ignores the traditional requirement of birth in one of the *varnas*, the castes). It was largely through him that the traditional doctrine that the quest for psychic powers will block one's spiritual development entered the hippy world and became, at least for a short time, a cliché. He has also been willing to admit that the Indian gurus who came West by and large did not represent the best Hinduism had to offer. And if there's one thing that separates Ram Dass from the New Age as a whole, it's that he's not an evolutionist, spiritual or otherwise.

As the psychedelic ethos started to wane in the mid-'70s, the New Age paradigm took over, based on channeling 'entities', developing one's psychic powers according to the 'human potential' model (emanating in part from

Esalen Institute and including the Transpersonal Psychology movement featuring Stanislas Grof and others, who also has a background in psychedelic research), the belief in UFOs, and the idea that the evolution of the Earth is about to take a 'quantum leap', moving us through a paradigm shift which we must aid through mass alignment of consciousness.

The work of Ram Dass and Timothy Leary stretches into the early post-'60s New Age era. Ram Dass became involved with channeling through his sponsorship of the *Emmanuel* books [by Pat Rodegast], and Leary, abreast of the times, began to pick up on the technocratic/UFO paradigm. 'Channeling' is central to the New Age, but before I deal with it, I need to mention another seminal figure in the psychedelic movement, Carlos Castaneda, who almost single-handedly re-connected the psychedelic experience with the paradigm of shamanism—at least on the literary level; plenty of hippies were fanning out over the world looking for new psychedelics, searching for medicine men in the American Southwest and the jungles of Africa and Latin America, and bringing to our attention such agents as morning glory seeds, San Pedro cactus, magic mushrooms, yage or ayahuasca (all from Latin America, the discovery of yage by the North American counterculture having been pioneered by Beat Generation writers William Burroughs and Allen Ginsberg in their travels to the Amazon), and ibogaine (from Africa). Peyote, through the Native American Church and Aldous Huxley's *The Doors of Perception*, was probably known a little earlier, as was nitrous oxide via William James' *The Varieties of the Religious Experience*; Beat Generation poet Michael McClure, among others, wrote of his peyote experiences. But it was Castaneda who brought a great deal of this interest together, and connected it with shamanism and especially sorcery. His books are well-written pseudo-documentary accounts of his interactions with Yaqui sorcerer Don Juan Matus, his colleagues and apprentices, in Mexico. They include *The Teachings of Don Juan*; *A Separate Reality*; *Journey to Ixtlan*; *Tales of Power*; *The Second Ring of Power*; *The Eagle's Gift*; *The Fire from Within*; *The Power of Silence*; *The Art of Dreaming*; *Magical Passes*; and *The Wheel of Time*.

The other major Native American influence on the hippy movement was John G. Neihardt's beautiful and deeply spiritual *Black Elk Speaks*, but Castaneda's influence was greater, and not only diverted the hippy interest in Native Americans away from religious piety and toward magic, but also created a 'market' among white folks for every sort of American Indian medicine man or woman, from the genuine through the sinister to the out-and-out charlatan—producing, for example, such light-weight Caucasian spinoffs as Lynn Andrews.

One of the clearest divergences in the world of 'alternative' spiritualities is that between the New Age and Neo-Paganism. The Neo-Pagans who stemmed from the hippy era were led by the psychedelic experience and the spirit of the times in the direction of Gardnerian and other forms of Wicca, or Celtic romanticism, or various forms of Goddess-worship (especially that promoted by Robert Graves) or toward influences, at least literary ones, emanating from the Order of the Golden Dawn. I myself was moved deeply by the powerful echoes of the Celtic Revival which wound themselves like a magic thread through the spiritual revolution of the '60s. They promised a 're-enchantment of the world' in the face of our technological wasteland, a collective re-discovery of the sacredness of nature. And they seemed to have the power to cast a magical glamour over the realm of heterosexual love, reminding us of its transpersonal depth and nobility. Unfortunately, however, the magical paradigm on which this Neo-Pagan revival was based had secret affinities with that other form of magic, human technology; this was one of the greatest and most heartbreaking ironies of my generation's desperate struggle to regain the sacred. Not for nothing is '(Neo-Pagan) Fantasy and Science Fiction' a single literary genre.

At one end of the spectrum, Neo-Pagans will be found keeping company with well-educated literary occultists, like many who published in *Gnosis* magazine, for example, but they also number in their ranks psychedelic-drug-taking magic-dabblers as well as 'serious' practitioners of the craft, at the other. The name of black magician Aliester Crowley is well-known in this realm, if not respected.

Neo-Paganism, pop shamanism and Goddess-worship tend to form a single sub-culture, and all three usually share a background interest in mythology and mythopoeia, often mediated by the psychological theories of Carl Jung. The most 'mainstream' aspect of this ethos is, or was, represented by Joseph Campbell; another tributary was the experimental Findhorn community in Scotland, as presented in the books of Peter and Eileen Caddy (*The Magic of Findhorn*) and others, where human interaction with elemental spirits apparently produced seemingly impossible manifestations of vegetable fertility. To my sensibilities, the Findhorn experiments transmit a *fey* feeling similar to that surrounding other 'horticultural magicians' like George Washington Carver and Luther Burbank (the aura of whose work is still detectable at his home in Santa Rosa), if not Rudolf Steiner. In the 1970s the occultism of horticulture, which includes both magic and 'fringe' technology, was catalogued in a book entitled *The Secret Life of Plants* by Peter Tompkins. Horticultural magic as a whole owes much to the German

Naturphilosophie movement, in which Goethe, a seminal influence on both Jung and Steiner, was a major figure.

Through figures such as ex-Catholic priest Matthew Fox, and his colleague, the witch Starhawk, Neo-Paganism (and this goes double for Jungianism) has made vast inroads into American Christianity, particularly via liberal seminaries such as the Union Theological Seminary and GTU. As opposed to the Neo-Pagans, the New Age practitioners tend to be more fascinated by advanced technology, more into 'channeling' and generally less literary, though often more professionally successful or 'yuppified', than the Neo-Pagans. Still, there is a great deal of crossover between the two groups. Jose Arguelles, for example, who created, through his book *The Mayan Factor*, one of the first international religious folk-events, Harmonic Convergence, on August 16–17, 1987 (claimed as key date for the New Age paradigm-shift, supposedly based on the Mayan Calendar), represents (or did) a bridge between these two tendencies.

Whoever follows the history of channeling will find most of the history of the New Age since the '60s. Both spiritualism and New Age channeling concentrate on the reception of new philosophies, which are often nothing but folk-renditions of poorly-understood science, particularly Einsteinian and post-Einsteinian physics and modern genetics, on the acquisition of psychic powers, including healing, and on the attempt to pierce the veil of the future. Allan Kardec and Stainton Moses, for example—like Swedenborg before them—channeled entire philosophies of the Spirit World in the early 20th century, and Madame Blavatsky was certainly deeply influenced by the 'philosophical' as well as the magical side of spiritualism. The earlier spiritualism perhaps tended to concentrate more than today's channeling on the attempt to prove that the human personality survives death, and on making contact with deceased loved ones on behalf of the living, largely due to the traumatic effect of the First World War; but such concerns have certainly not disappeared.

The major bridge-figure between these two waves of spiritualism is probably trance-physician, historical clairvoyant and prognosticator Edgar Cayce (1877–1945) whose organization, The Association for Research and Enlightenment, is still quite active in Virginia Beach, VA. His record as a healer is astounding, but his other work—including a series of failed attempts to find oil or buried treasure by psychic means—was not up to par. His ministry was limited to medical clairvoyance, a gift he received through a vision at the age of thirteen, until he crossed paths with Theosophist Arthur Lammers, after which his 'readings' began to deal with occult subjects such as astrology,

Atlantis, reincarnation etc., apparently under the influence of questions which Lammers put to him in the trance state. As a devout Christian he was disturbed to realize that he had been channeling ideas which seemed to contradict the Bible, but he finally accepted them. (One is reminded of Guénon's belief that magicians and occultists will often deliberately influence mediums by suggestion, telepathic or otherwise, to make it appear that their own doctrines are also taught by the 'spirits'.) An authorized biography of Cayce, *There Is a River* by Thomas Sugrue, came out in 1973.

The two most influential masses of channeled material behind a great deal of New Age mythology are the 'Seth' material, channeled by Jane Roberts (*The Seth Material; Seth Speaks; The Nature of Personal Reality* and others), and *A Course in Miracles*, where the speaker is supposedly Jesus. Another central book is *Opening to Channel* by Roman and Packer, written on the assumption that everyone can, and should, channel psychic entities. Since then the number of channelers and channeled entities has become so vast that they are almost impossible to track. There is the entity *Ramtha* channeled by J. Z. Knight; and, since the '70s, various new entities have made their appearance, such as *Michael* or *Hilarion*, who may be channeled by more than one medium. The source of this development may be the desire of certain writers or workshop-leaders to ride the coattails of more successful ones, but it has resulted in something on the order of 'psychic fan clubs' following this or that spook—possibly religious sects in embryonic form.

One of the latest and most disturbing developments in New Age channeling is the 'channeling' of aliens, or rather the almost complete confusion of psychic entities and technologically-advanced alien astronauts in the public mind. 'Aliens' may walk through walls, appear and disappear at will, stimulate out-of-body experiences, and even have sex with us in our dreams—still they are looked at as beings from other planets possessing technologies advanced enough to allow them to do these things, although this strict identification of aliens with astronauts is beginning to change. It is here that Fr Seraphim Rose's writing on UFOs is of central importance, as is Guénon's prediction in *The Reign of Quantity* that the world, under the influence of materialism, will reach such a nadir of solidification that the 'great wall' between the material and subtle planes will begin to crack, letting in 'infra-psychic' forces, which partly explains why so many believers must interpret obviously psychic manifestations (with some actual physical effects) in strictly material terms. The contemporary groups, followers of Barbara Hand Clow, who channel the *Pleiadians* (aliens from the Pleiades) may be taken as representative of this development.

Perhaps the most important early announcement of the hopes and goals of the New Age movement was *The Aquarian Conspiracy* by Marilyn Ferguson. An influential attack on the New Age from an evangelical Christian standpoint is *The Hidden Dangers of the Rainbow*, by Constance Cumby. The books of David Spangler (*The Call; Everyday Miracles; Re-Imagining the World*) and *The Global Brain* by Peter Russell have also been extremely influential.

Five other strands in the fabric of the New Age deserve mention. The first is *dream-work*, which is a bridge from Jungian and transpersonal psychology to the world of the occult, largely through the teaching of various techniques of dream-control, and through drawing an equation between *out-of-body experiences* (the central name here being Robert Monroe, who wrote *Journeys Out of Body* and other books, and founded various schools to teach the common man how to astral project) with *lucid dreaming*—the experience of awakening to the fact that you're dreaming while you're still dreaming. Lucid dreaming is a major element in Castaneda's shamanic sorcery. The scientific study of it is associated with Dr Stanley Krippner of the Saybrook Institute and Dr Stephen LeBerge at Stanford, as recounted in his book *Lucid Dreaming*, both of whom have conducted well-designed and funded research on lucid dreaming and dream-control. Dreamwork is also highly influenced, if not largely inspired, by the channeled Seth material.

The *second* strand is the contemporary interest in *angels*, which has produced a number of books. It may represent, up to a point, a form of spirit channeling which is more acceptable to some Christians, being less threatening to them than a connection with 'psychic entities'; but it is also a sign that the sense of transcendence on which monotheism is based is fading from the Western psyche, as happened in the distant past with much of African religion, leaving a multiplicity of subtle 'entities' to fill the widening gap, which are beginning to seem more plausible to many people than some distant Father God. Contemporary interactions with angels include both uninvited interventions and deliberate human attempts to communicate.

To me, this attraction to angels transmits the kind of light, airy feeling I associate with the Unity Church, and seems related in a vague way to contemporary apparitions of the Virgin Mary, which range from those likely to be veridical, through various partial and suspect appearances or 'channelings' within a Catholic framework, to 100% New Age channelings of 'Mother Mary', a name given to the Virgin by Paul McCartney of the Beatles! The Catholic manifestations include ones like those in Scottsdale, Arizona and Emmetsburg, PA, both of which were and are mediated by a woman who (if I've got the story right) was 'inspired' by a priest upon his return from

Medugorje, and then began receiving messages from the Virgin, first in Arizona and later in Pennsylvania. Many Catholic churches apparently have 'Medugorje clubs', started by people who've traveled there, including one in San Bruno just south of San Francisco where children have supposedly been spoken to by Mary; this has led to a highly dubious but still possibly valid vogue in Marian messages.

The *third* strand is the study of *near-death experiences* as a way of trying to understand the afterlife; the major names in the field are Elizabeth Kubler-Ross (*On Death and Dying*, and others) and Raymond A. Moody (*Life after Life*). Moody's book and its sequels by himself and others have acted to 'standardize' the popular conception of the after-death experience to the point where it has become a media cliché: the dark tunnel with a light at the end, the meeting with departed relatives, etc. Fr Seraphim Rose, in *The Soul After Death*, does a good critique of this easy-going and 'non-judgmental' idea of the afterlife.

The *fourth* strand is, as I touched upon above, is *management training*. A friend of mine—former friend, I should say, since his life has become so involved with spiritual darkness that I can no longer relate to him—is a world-class management training consultant, who has worked with major multinational corporations, both in the U.S. and on the Pacific Rim. Through him I learned that, as I put it, 'every management trainer must start his own religion before he can market his services.'

The esoteric truths of the ages, as well as various psychic practices, are being digested and packaged as 'training paradigms' for upper and middle management of the world's largest corporations, often in connection with Chinese and Japanese martial arts—or this was true, at least, when we envied the Japanese economy and wanted to imitate the Japanese management style! Some years ago there was even a scandal at Pacific Telephone when management training consultants employing Gurdjieff techniques went a little overboard, and appeared to be recruiting (which they probably were). A more recent manifestation of this trend was the tempest-in-a-teapot around Jean Houston's work with President and Mrs Clinton, where she would lead them in 'guided visualizations' so they could imagine they were talking with people like Lincoln and FDR (Jean Houston was one of the original LSD researchers, you'll remember). The media people were all set to break the story of 'Seances in the White House!'—but then undoubtedly some of them began to remember that they'd done something very similar in last week's training seminar, and to realize that such 'intuitive problem-solving techniques' like Houston's are now common in large corporations. They are the successors to the techniques of Dale Carnegie and Norman Vincent Peale. So that's just how mainstream the New Age has become.

The *fifth* strand is the *mainstream media*, among which I will mention only the many TV programs based on non-ordinary reality, such as The *X-Files*, and the 'psychic hotlines' where, for several dollars a minute, you can talk to a 'real psychic' who will solve all your problems and tell you how to run your life. Complaints have surfaced that these hotlines are addicting, something like compulsive gambling with the added danger of demonic possession. One hotline has been advertised on TV by Nichele Nichols, an actress who played in the original *Star Trek* series and movies, and whose brother, a member of the Heaven's Gate UFO cult, died in their mass suicide in March of '97.

New Age culture embraces certain traditional or semi-traditional elements. Many Tibetan lamas, for example, (including the Dalai Lama) advertise in New Age circles and are respected there, though I am told that certain other lamas deplore this development. Other traditional Buddhists such as Thich Nhat Hanh, and those with at least a traditional background like Jack Kornfield (though the Buddhism he preaches often seems more like group psychotherapy than the quest for Perfect Total Enlightenment) are also at home in that world. Until recently, Sufism was represented in the New Age world, at least in California, largely by the followers of Samuel Lewis ('Sufi Sam') and Pir Vilayat Khan of the Chishti Order, and Jellaluddin Loras (son of Sulieman Dede) of the Mevlevis, who teaches Mevlevi 'turning' to Americans. Samuel Lewis, who grew up in Fairfax, California, near my home town of San Rafael, and who passed away in 1971, though non-traditional and eclectic, was an actual Sufi initiate, originator of the 'Sufi dancing' that passed for Sufism in most people's minds in California until a few years ago.

Both Pir Vilayat Khan and Samuel Lewis, and Jellaluddin Loras as well, represent an attempt to make Sufism 'universal' by separating it, to one degree or another, from Islam. Though certain more traditional orders such as the Naqshbandis and the Helveti-Jerrahis have been active for decades, the 'hippy-universalist' Chishtis and Mevlevis have represented the main public expression of 'Sufism' in the San Francisco Bay Area until a few years ago, when Ali Kianfar, an Iranian 'uwaysi' or 'disciple of Khidr', and his wife Nahid Angha, began to emerge, organizing large Sufism Conferences in New Age workshop style and manifesting a 'Sufi ecumenism' by including psychologists, a few members of other religious traditions, etc. Even some of the old hippy Sufis, however, are becoming slowly more Islamic, perhaps in response to the excesses of the New Age; the same slow distancing from that world seems true of certain Hindu teachers.

Semi-traditional Hinduism (if there is such a thing) was represented in the counterculture of the '60s and '70s, and partly continues to be, by Ram Dass, Swami Satchidananda, Sri Chinmoy, Swami Muktananda, Da Free John, the followers of Paramhamsa Yogananda and others, including a steady stream of 'Holy Mothers' based in India; Sikkhism by Yogi Bhajan, Kirpal Singh, his son Sant Darshan Singh, and presently by his follower Sant Thakar Singh; and more-or-less traditional Christianity by the ongoing interest in Thomas Merton, whose cultural slot has in some ways been inherited by the Benedictine monk, Brother David Steindl-Rast. But because these figures and their successors are juxtaposed in the minds of New Agers with channeling, shamanism, Neo-Paganism and ecofeminist Goddess-worship, any traditional doctrines they teach tend to disappear into an anti-traditional mindset which denies those doctrines in every particular, without their students or possibly even themselves quite realizing it. Jack Kornfield, for example, did a study of the extremely high percentage of Hindu and Buddhist teachers who have become involved in sexual escapades with their students after coming to the West; but this led him to conclude not that their problems are based on a betrayal or watering-down of their respective traditions—the relaxation of traditional Buddhist monastic vows, for example—but that the traditions themselves are deficient in psychological insight, and therefore need to be supplemented with Western psychological methods.

This mixing of traditional doctrines with the Western social sciences, and elements that might be called 'New Age', is well represented by Naropa Institute in Boulder, Colorado, founded by Chögyam Trungpa, a *tulku* (recognized incarnation of a past teacher) and holder of the Kargüpa Lineage stretching back to Naropa, Marpa, and Milarepa—a fully-empowered traditional exemplar and brilliant writer on Tibetan Buddhism, who became the chosen teacher of the best educated among two generations of the U.S. counterculture (Beat and Hippy) as the wild party of the '60s descended into the deep spiritual depression of the '70s; who Westernized and modernized the tradition, in a radical departure from the practice of most of his co-religionists; who relaxed the traditional monastic vows; and who died, hounded by scandals, of acute alcoholism in 1987.

Here, fortunately, my experience of the world of 'alternative spiritualities' ends. I only want to add that the nationally syndicated radio commentator Hank Hanegraff, of the evangelical Christian Research Institute, has opened my eyes to just how far New Age ideas and psychic practices have come now to penetrate Protestant Christianity, particularly through the charismatic movement.

Without traditional metaphysics, theology declines. Without theology, religion and spirituality are judged only by their power to produce experience. When experience is the only criterion of spirituality, intensity becomes its only measure. When intensity alone becomes the goal, love and truth are excluded, and darkness fills the gap.

II. The Dangers of the Occult

What is 'the Occult'?

God's creation is hierarchical, and the simplest division of this hierarchy is into three levels: material, psychic and Spiritual. Each level is subtler and more alive than the level below it, and contains all that is below it, though in a higher form.

The psychic plane is the natural 'environment' of the human psyche, just as the earth and the material universe are the environment of the human body. It is not purely evil, as some Christians believe, but it is certainly dangerous, since if we break into it either accidentally or on our own initiative, we have lost the protection of the material realm before having necessarily gained the protection of the spiritual realm, and are therefore extremely vulnerable not only to the scattering of our psychic and vital energy, but to obsession or possession by the powers of evil.

Nonetheless, the psychic plane is not exclusively demonic, otherwise we could not receive divine guidance in dreams, nor could physical miracles occur, since every influence from the spiritual realm must pass through the psychic realm before it can come into material reality. But because this is so, it is very difficult to tell whether a psychic or anomalous physical manifestation originates on the psychic or the Spiritual plane. Nonetheless there is a profound difference in level between an act of magic (whether for the purpose of healing or harming) which emanates from the psychic plane, and a miracle originating on the Spiritual plane. Psychic or magical or shamanic practices are 'technologies', instances of wilful intervention by human beings or psychic entities. Miracles are manifestations of the Spirit, the eternal truth and love of God, on the psychic and material levels. They accomplish many different things at once, effortlessly, by the 'unveiling' of a small part of God's infinite Truth and Love.

The psychic plane is a multiple world made up of many subjective 'points of view'. The Spiritual plane is the radiation of objective Divine Reality; they are not the same thing, which is why we can encounter people who are extremely psychic but not spiritual at all. On the material level, we seem to be products of our material environment, through biochemistry, cultural influences, history and evolution. On the psychic level, our environment seems to be the product of our state of consciousness, since as we 'tune in' to different realities, the environment changes. On the spiritual level, we know ourselves to be absolutely dependent upon, created by, and also in some ways symbols of, the Divine Reality of God. Only insofar as we are open to the Spirit can we know who we really are, and what is eternally true; only through the realization of the Spiritual level do we *become* who we really are. Our humanity was designed by God for this realization. If we fail to attain it (the Sufis say) then we are not yet, or only virtually, human beings.

Psychic knowledge is just another kind of knowledge; there is nothing necessarily demonic about it, or necessarily spiritual. Still, a little knowledge is a dangerous thing, and psychic knowledge is definitely very 'little' when compared to spiritual wisdom.

Psychic powers can come to us in five different ways: (1) by birth; (2) through accident, illness or other trauma; (3) as an unexpected gift; (4) through seeking them directly; and, (5) as a by-product of spiritual development. The first two, at least initially, are morally neutral. If someone is born with psychic abilities, or acquires them after a traumatic shock or injury, it is both unwise and unfair to assume that the individual in question is demonically possessed, just as it is unwarranted to assume that their psychic sensitivity is a sign of spiritual wisdom. On the other hand, if someone with psychic abilities remains ignorant of spiritual realities, but bases his or her worldview on psychic information alone, that person is deluded, and is therefore open, potentially but not necessarily, to the influence of deluding demons.

In the case of a 'gift' of psychic powers, their un-sought breakthrough from some invisible source, it is our duty to ask the nature of this source, through consultation with someone affiliated with a traditional spirituality who is knowledgeable in these areas — assuming we can find such a person — and in any case through prayer. It is necessary, in other words, to find out if this gift represents a duty laid upon us by God, or a seductive curse laid upon us by the powers of darkness.

If someone actively seeks and obtains psychic powers, the situation is more serious, though this is a hard principle for many people to understand.

After all, aren't psychic powers simply part of our 'human potential'? And isn't it natural to explore and develop our God-given talents? We learn to walk, to talk, to drive, to make love, to make a living, to swim, to play basketball, to sing, to write, to gain a certain amount of psychological insight into ourselves and others, even to understand philosophy and metaphysics without necessarily becoming demonically possessed. Why should psychic abilities be any different? There is a limit, however, beyond which the self-willed development of our human potential begins to trespass on ground where our right to do whatever we want with our talents is no longer a given. We transgress the same limit every day, in one way or another, by our technological 'progress'. What's wrong with technology? Simply that if we develop it in an excessive or unbalanced way, we will destroy the earth and the human form. What's wrong with psychic powers? Simply that if we develop them in an excessive or unbalanced way, we will destroy our souls.

Occultism is the practice of making contact with the psychic plane on our own initiative, or in response to an invitation coming from that plane alone. Our goal may be to 'access' Spirit through the psyche, but more often it will simply be an attempt to extend the area of our own ego, to pursue in subtler worlds the basic ego-goals of security, pleasure and power. This seems to be, and up to a point actually is, a simple extension of our own psychological self-understanding, a kind of adolescent exploration of our psychic potential. But unless we realize that it is the Spirit of God which is really summoning us to this exploration, and that our true goal must be to come into conscious relationship with Spirit in knowledge and love, and submit to It's guidance, our exploration of the psychic plane will quickly become a worship of our own ego, and will attract those powers of evil whose goal is to eternally separate us from our Creator. This is why to seek psychic powers for the purpose of increasing our security, pleasure and power, or even to 'take heaven by storm'—to 'reach' God through our own self-will—is a profoundly destructive course. If psychic powers appear as a result of our submission to the Will of God, then they are an expression of that Will in our lives, consequently we will not attribute their operation to ourselves, but to our Creator. But even then they may be a 'test' sent by God, to see if we care more for His gifts than we care for Him.

Since the '60s, as I pointed out before, the prevailing paradigm in the world of 'alternative' spirituality has shifted from mysticism to magic. The magical motive was always there; still, the belief that seeking psychic powers can interfere with spiritual development was part of the received wisdom of the time. But nowadays, except in conservative religious circles, and among the Traditionalists, it is rarely heard. With athletic coaches teaching psychic and magical techniques to their teams, and management training consultants to their corporate executives, the idea of using psychic powers of one kind or another to expand 'human potential' has become mainstream, a fact reflected in the content of a high percentage of contemporary TV shows where psychic powers and magical events are becoming commonplace elements in the plots even of programs based ostensibly on 'ordinary, everyday reality', not to mention psychic/science fiction programs like *The X-Files*.

We can't simply say that anyone involved with the psychic realm is seriously damaging his or her psyche, or is destined for damnation. Some natural or even highly trained psychics are consciously practicing their art in the service of humanity and for the greater glory of God. But the whole *drift* of the contemporary interest in psychic realities is profoundly sinister, since the more the paradigm of 'expand your human potential in the search for security, pleasure and power' grows, the more it tends to supplant the paradigm of 'follow the Will of God, even if you have to sacrifice security, pleasure and power to do it.' So magic replaces religion, and the magical worldview is so abysmally inferior to the sublime conceptions of Divine Reality and human destiny preserved by the major world religions that there is simply no comparison. Furthermore, in a world of magic, those without some claim to psychic power will start to feel disenfranchised and vulnerable. I'm reminded of the story told by an anthropologist, who asked a Native American shaman why he became interested in shamanism. His answer was, 'because I was afraid of shamans.' If most people in your environment carry guns or belong to gangs, you'll be tempted to do the same simply to protect yourself. It's the same with magic. Again, this is not to deny that there are service-oriented psychics and 'white' magicians, who are willing to suffer personally to serve God and their community. But unless they are practicing their arts within the safety of a viable spiritual tradition with long experience of their uses and dangers, they are inevitably exposed to those forces who are doing all in their power to prove that 'the road to Hell is paved with good intentions.'

This again brings us the question of *shamanism*, an archaic religious form that is still practiced by several hundred million people in Africa, Asia, the Pacific islands, the Americas, and elsewhere, where religion and magic seem to form a single whole. Any tradition which can produce real holy men like the Lakota Black Elk can't simply be dismissed as paganism or sorcery; nonetheless, practices which fall under the general term 'shamanism' can stretch from the highest mystical theurgy to the most poisonous sorcery to simple charlatanism. René Guénon saw shamanism as possessing 'a highly developed cosmology . . . that might suggest concordances with other traditions in many respects,' including 'rites comparable to some that belong to traditions of the highest order.' On the other hand, the shamanic emphasis on 'inferior traditional sciences, such as magic and divination' means that 'a very real degeneration must be suspected, such as may sometimes amount to a real deviation, as can happen all too easily to such sciences whenever they become over-developed' (*The Reign of Quantity and the Signs of the Times*, pp 217–218). Michael F. Steltenkamp, in *Black Elk, Holy Man of the Oglalla Sioux* (University of Oklahoma Press, 1993) repeats some of Black Elk's own criticisms of shamanism, made after he had converted to Catholicism. He did not entirely reject traditional shamanism, allowing one of his medicine-man friends to conduct a healing ritual for him, with some success, when he was suffering from paralysis in his old age, but he required that Catholic ritual objects such as holy cards be substituted for Oglalla fetishes. And he certainly recognized in Christian humility a virtue higher than the arrogance of many shamans. Furthermore, there is a world of difference between the function of a shaman in a tribal setting, where he or she will represent a large percentage of the survival-technology of the tribe, including the ability to find and attract game, provide rain for agriculture, heal disease, perform psychotherapy, conduct criminal investigations and carry on military intelligence, and the role of these same powers in today's society, where there is greater scope for degeneration and self-aggrandizement than ever before. (As evidence that more primitive peoples view shamanism in much the same was as we view technology, Jean Cocteau repeats a story told by a traveler in Haiti, where trees are apparently sometimes used as supports for telepathy. When a woman wants her distant husband to bring back something from town, for example, she will talk to a tree which somehow relays the message. When asked why her people talked to trees, one woman answered: 'Because we are poor. If we were rich we would have the telephone.')

The wide diffusion of shamanic techniques separated from their traditional context, such as can be picked up at a weekend seminar, is definitely destructive as a general tendency, no matter how 'useful' these practices may be in a given situation. When you can walk into any general interest bookstore, even in the Bible belt, and find books which include among their hodge-podge of psychic technologies recipes on how to cast spells and lay curses, it's pretty clear that things have gotten out of hand. If we lament the easy accessibility of guns and information on how to make bombs, including nuclear weapons, why can't we take the same attitude toward black magic?

Perhaps it's because we legitimately fear the erosion of our constitutional safeguards for freedom of religion, just as opponents of gun control fear the destruction of their constitutional right to 'keep and bear arms'. But it may also be due to the fact that we have a kind of 'selective disbelief' in the powers of evil. I remember an ad I saw in a local free newspaper, where you could pay to have a curse put on someone. I phoned the paper up, and made the point that if they didn't believe in curses they were participating in false advertising, whereas if they did, they were conspiring to commit assault. They didn't listen to me of course, and my impression was that when confronted with the possibility that they might be helping to actually harm people, they repressed any misgivings by denying to themselves that black magic is real, and then countered my accusation of false advertising by telling themselves that it actually *is* real—unconsciously, of course, and all in a split second. This is precisely the kind of mental gymnastics that George Orwell analyzed in 1984 as 'doublethink'—the ability to hold two contradictory beliefs at the same time with no anxiety whatsoever. We are lunatic believers and/or cynical debunkers whenever it suites our need to avoid the confrontation with objective truth. As C.S. Lewis said in *The Screwtape Letters*, p 32, through the mouth of his demon Screwtape,

> When the humans disbelieve in our existence we lose all the pleasing results of direct terrorism, and we make no magicians. On the other hand, when they believe in us, we cannot make them materialists and skeptics. At least, not yet. I have great hopes that we shall learn in due time how to emotionalize and mythologize their science to such an extent that what is, in effect, a belief in us (though not under that name) will creep in . . . if once we can produce our perfect work—the Materialist Magician . . . then the end of the war will be in sight.

But, of course, the Materialist Magician has been with us for some time now; he is the keynote of the present historical period. The idolatry of advanced technology, real or imagined, is our dominant contemporary superstition. I only need remind us that the word we now use for what have always been called 'demons' is now 'aliens'. Aliens abduct us, transport us through the air, probe us, have sex with us, walk through walls into our houses, and appear in our dreams. Over a million Americans claim to have had these experiences, so many in fact that support groups and even large conferences for 'abductees' now represent an independent industry. We can't bring ourselves to call them 'demons', for fear that we might become 'religious fanatics' and thus lose our membership in materialist/technocratic society. But we have to believe every story we hear about them, including the baldly engineered propaganda about the recovery of alien corpses in Roswell, New Mexico (which remains unconvincing to well-known UFO researcher Jacques Vallee), and admit that they possess all the physical and psychic powers common to the kingdom of Satan, otherwise we might be seen as 'narrow-minded sceptics,' rationalistic old fogies with nothing interesting to say at social gatherings. We are in the grip of doublethink.

All these developments were predicted, in their major outlines if not in detail, by René Guénon in *The Reign of Quantity and the Signs of the Times*, published in 1945. According to Guénon, over the past few centuries the world has become less defined by the qualities of things, and more by pure quantity, where the 'success' of a nation (for example) is not measured by depth of culture, height of spiritual understanding, or quality of life, but by gross national product. The 'information culture' is only the latest incarnation of this tendency to quantify everything. But the 'reign of quantity', though it continues to gain power, in one sense peaked in the late 19th and early 20th centuries when materialism as a way of looking at the world was at its height, in the days when it was possible to complacently believe in something called 'ordinary life'. As I pointed out above, such materialism actually resulted, according to Guénon, in a kind of 'solidification of the world'. Back, say, in the 1950s, the report of a supernatural occurrence, or the belief that such things were possible, was often greeted with, 'How can you believe that? This is the 20th century!' But now, at the beginning of the 21st century, the weird seems normal, if not inevitable. In terms of the sounds, images and beliefs produced by popular mass culture, we are living in a kind of permanent Halloween.

As you'll remember, Guénon's explanation for this is as follows: as materialism solidified the world, the sense of the reality of spiritual things, of a world higher than the psychic, the Divine Realm, the Kingdom of God, became harder to maintain. It's as if a kind of psychic smog were spreading over the world, dimming the light of the stars. But already by 1945 (after the first nuclear weapons were detonated, though Guénon makes no mention of this) this heavy, solid materiality—the bleakness of, say, Stalinism or bourgeois capitalism—was already beginning to crack. It had become so hard that it began to get 'brittle', just as atoms of the elements uranium and plutonium, which are even heavier than those of lead, are unstable and radioactive. But these cracks were not in the upward direction, open to the descent of Divine grace; they were in the lower one, on the interface between this world and the 'infrapsychic' or demonic realm. And anyone who is able to look objectively and dispassionately at our present information culture, at the lurid, seductively glamorous and sinister imagery prevalent on television, video games and the internet, will be compelled to agree.

According to Guénon, the only possible outcome of this development is the dissolution of the present world. He and the majority of Traditionalists agree with conservative Christians that we live in the latter days, the Time of the End. This 'End' may entail the destruction of all life on Earth—or it may not. In any case, it cannot be seen exclusively in earthly terms, since the End of the World is an Apocalypse, a 'revelation' of the Eternal Reality of God, as well as the beginning of the next cycle of existence, the 'New Heaven' and the 'New Earth'. So Guénon and other Traditionalists, notably Martin Lings in his book *The Eleventh Hour*, are deliberately ambiguous on this point, as when Guénon says that the present world will dissolve, but this does not mean the end of terrestrial existence, or that we are facing the end of Time, but not the end of Space. Exactly what these oracular statements mean must remain a question for our faculty of spiritual intuition, and the truths this faculty discovers can never be fully translated into terms of space, time, matter and history. But nearly all world religions, including Hinduism, Buddhism, Judaism, Christianity, Islam and certain Native American traditions, all speak of the end of the present world or cycle. And Christianity and Islam in particular emphasize that on the eve of this end, all the psychic powers and psycho-social tendencies that want to deny the reality of God and the dignity of humanity will coalesce into what these two traditions call the reign of the Antichrist, who, whether or not he will be an individual, will certainly be the principle behind the worst inhumanity that the human race can think of to impose on itself, and the Earth. The Traditionalists tend to say that this development cannot be stopped by any form of enlightened social action; on the other hand, they bring forward the myth of the final battle between good and evil at the end of the cycle, the one called Armageddon in the Bible, and which in Islamic doctrine is announced by the Mahdi and concluded by the second coming of Jesus, whom Muslims as well as Christians believe to be the Messiah, who will kill the Antichrist in the final battle. And the tenth avatar of Vishnu in Hinduism, the Kalki avatara, is also pictured as a warrior, wielding a sword and riding a white horse, like the Word of God in the 19th chapter of *Apocalypse*.

But Armageddon cannot simply be something like a total thermonuclear war, because it is a battle in which all the enemies of the restoration of the Divine Order on earth are destroyed. As such it is a manifestation of the battle which goes on in the soul of every one of us, as reflected in the 'real' events of the outer world. But since, as Jesus said, 'ye know not the day nor the hour,' I deliberately want to steer clear of historical prognostication, and concentrate on this 'unseen warfare' within the human soul. As I said above, it is the inborn duty of every human being to realize the truth of God, of the Absolute Reality, as far as one's capacity allows, and to put oneself unreservedly under the guidance and direction of That One. Once this duty is recognized and embraced, however, all the powers of the psychic realm that deny the Absolute will swing into action. The war against these lower forces of the soul is called in Islam 'the greater *jihad*', the greater holy war; it is a human duty more universal, more formidable, and with much more riding on the outcome, than any war on the field of material battle.

According to one possible view, Armageddon is a war between love and power for the prize of knowledge. Even Carl Jung (whom the Traditionalists hate, and with good reason) once said that wherever the power complex is, love becomes impossible. And really the whole question of the dangers of the occult comes down to this: Is our spiritual knowledge going to take love as its bride, or power? Love is a great power in its own right, but wherever subtle knowledge unites with power in order to violate love, we are in the presence of the religion of Antichrist.

✳ Wisdom, Morality, and Technique

In the '60s it looked to many of my generation as if 'organized religion', by which we meant Judaism and church Christianity, was limited to morality, and that morality was completely arbitrary. It was nothing but a set of 'oughts' — still a dirty word in some circles — imposed by 'society' or 'the establishment' or 'the church hierarchy' for no valid reason. On the other hand, there was such a thing as penetrating insight and spiritual wisdom; we felt this 'instinctively'. Religion seemed to bear some relationship to this unknown wisdom — certainly the Bible was full of mystical allusions, if only somebody could understand them — but our priests and ministers didn't seem to possess the key to it. All they were telling us, or all we heard, was 'be good because God says so.' And when we asked '*why* be good, what does it mean, what's behind it all?' all we got from them was the brush-off. The distinct impression was that there really was something there to be known, but our teachers no longer knew it. So of course we looked for it elsewhere: in Eastern religions, in Native American spirituality, in Western spiritualism and occultism. As the poet Allen Ginsberg wrote about the similar experience of the Beat Generation, who were old enough to be our fathers, in his famous poem *Howl*, we were those 'who studied Plotinus Poe St John of the Cross telepathy and bop kabbalah because the cosmos instinctively vibrated at their feet in Kansas.' In the process we discovered that there really was such a thing as Wisdom — though the exact shape and implications of it continued to elude us — and that it was not only something to be believed in, but something that could be realized. You could actually experience it; it was *real*. Not only that, but there had always existed spiritual techniques, like yoga, meditation, shamanism or theurgy, which could turn theoretical knowledge or vague spiritual intimations into real, concrete experience. Of course it was much easier just to take LSD or peyote or magic mushrooms, and be treated to amazing visions and insights which stretched from the horrifying through the ridiculous all the way to the sublime. But the more serious souls among us soon realized that you couldn't take psychedelics forever, that there had to be a more stable and responsible way to pursue enlightenment. This, we felt, was to be provided by more traditional forms of *sadhana* (spiritual practice) like meditation, or more 'advanced' types of psychic gymnastics such as the ones being developed at the Esalen Institute, including encounter groups, sensory deprivation, biofeedback and God knows what else. And so, in reaction to the shallowness we perceived in the Christian or Jewish traditions in which we'd been raised, which could give us nothing besides moral rules without any convincing rationale to back them up, and which were either unwilling or unable to provide the deep explanations of the meaning of life we craved, or give us access to the concrete spiritual practices we felt we needed in order to realize that meaning in depth, we created for ourselves a religious ethos where wisdom was pursued and spiritual technique employed *at the expense of morality*. No one told us that the mystical truths and the deep meaning we needed were at the heart of Christianity and Judaism; that techniques existed within these traditions, and always had — such as the Jesus Prayer within Eastern Orthodoxy — to serve the realization of these truths; and that one of the fundamental mystical techniques, without which no deep meaning could be understood or spiritual wisdom realized, was *morality itself*. We had read, and believed, that mystical understanding came from ego-transcendence; what we were never told was that morality is a necessary element in the science of this transcendence. So we tried to blow our egos away with massive doses of psychedelic drugs, which we thought would make unnecessary the boring work of overcoming simple selfishness in our day-to-day lives. It was the best of both worlds, we thought — mystical illumination via the cheap grace of psychedelics or breathing exercises or strobe lights tuned to the alpha rhythm of the brain, and then, the rest of the time, total self-indulgence. We believed we could have our cake and eat it too… but our cake ate us instead. If our Judaism had been able to provide real tzaddiks, masters of the kabbalah or of merkabah mysticism, along with deep exegesis of the Torah; if our Catholicism had been able to answer our mystical and philosophical longings by dipping into the profound mystical teachings of the Church Fathers, and if there had been something like a monastic third order available to youth which could have given us a mystical orientation and a daily spiritual practice; if our Protestantism had been able to feed us from the mystical well of 'spirituals' like Franz Von Baader and Jacob Boehme, then things might have been very different. But for that 'if' to have been realized, Judeo-Christianity would have had to have been in a very different state: faithful to the depth of its traditions, willing and able to resist every compromise with secularism, confident of its theological orthodoxy, its philosophical understanding and its mystical wisdom. But instead of inviting those from the highways and the byways to the Wedding Feast, the door was closed by those 'blind guides who prevent others from entering, but won't go in themselves.' So we set up a wedding feast of our own in the highways and the byways, which degenerated into an orgy, and finally a riot. Nonetheless, out of that riot came true insights into 'the deep things of God'—which we had no reliable way of distinguishing from the spiritual darkness surrounding them—along with valid elements of traditional esoterism and metaphysics hidden among the rest of the flotsam, which led a minority of us, finally, to stable and living mysticisms rooted in the traditional orthodoxies. Perhaps the memory of the much greater number who were destroyed so that we few might arrive, half-dead, at the door of revealed religion, is part of the motivation behind this book. The name for it 'survivor's guilt'.

✳ Altered States of Consciousness: Grace or Manipulation?

To many Evangelical Christians the terms 'mysticism' and 'altered states of consciousness' can refer to nothing but a dangerous delusion. According to well-known radio teacher Hank Hanegraff, whose insistence upon sound doctrine is deeply refreshing to me, and whose exposures of the false doctrines and dangerous practices now growing up within 'charismatic' Protestantism should be heeded by all, such realities, if realities they be, have no place in Christianity. At best they are self-delusions or the product of hypnotic suggestion; at worst, demonic deceptions.

Is this really true? Let us see.

First, the word 'mysticism' needs to be defined. There is a class of saints in every tradition, the contemplative saints, who are called by God to the kind of a direct experience of Him which most of the saved will experience only after death. Catholic Saints such as John of the Cross or Theresa of Avila dedicated much of their spiritual life to cultivating a readiness for such Union with God, which in the case of most mystics is rare and brief (though in another sense, eternal), a ravishment by the Spirit in which all sense of the existence of the soul as something separate from God is wiped out.

Eastern Orthodox Christianity goes beyond even this sense of Union by describing the successful outcome of the *normal* spiritual life as *theosis*, or deification, which is not simply a rare and isolated experience but a permanent realization of one's indwelling Divinity, according to the doctrine that 'God becomes man so that man might become God.' Sufism likewise speaks of *fana*, annihilation of the human self in its separateness, insofar as we are self-defined and therefore implicitly believe that we are self-created, and *baqa*, eternal subsistence within the Nature of God. Hinduism speaks of the *jivanmukta*, the soul who is perfectly Liberated in this life, and Buddhism of the one who has attained Perfect Total Enlightenment, and so become a Buddha, an 'Awakened' one, who recognizes that all beings in their original nature, in they only knew it, are Awake already.

Mysticism, then, can be defined either as the temporary experience of Union with God, an 'altered state of consciousness' either sought or unsought, produced by God's direct action (called in Sufism *hal*, and in Christianity 'infused contemplation'), or else as a permanent awakening to the reality of God, as in the case of an enlightened saint. It is mysticism in its first definition, that of a rare or unusual experience of God, an 'altered state' in which the individual self is set aside in contemplation of the Divine, which seems to bother many Evangelical Christians.

The New Testament, of course, is filled with stories of 'altered states of consciousness': the Transfiguration of Christ; the descent of the Holy Spirit upon the apostles and the Virgin Mary on Pentecost; the experience of St Paul on the road to Damascus. 'But wait!' says the Evangelical Christian. 'These were not 'altered states of consciousness' because they were not subjective experiences. They were produced by the action of God's grace, operating upon Jesus's disciples from the outside. They were not merely happening within the minds of those who experienced them; they were objectively real.' I fully grant this. But to say that the objective action of God's grace did not in fact profoundly alter the consciousness of the ones who received it is absurd. The real question is: do we believe that the altered states in question were encounters with God *initiated by His action in the human soul*, or do we believe that these encounters were *produced by the altered states themselves*, which were in turn wilfully created by the people experiencing them? God can and does alter human consciousness for the purpose of making it more receptive to Him, but no amount of *self-induced* consciousness-alteration can 'reach' God. As to whether events such as the Transfiguration were objective in the sense that they could have been photographed by satellite, for example, I reserve judgement. I only wish to point out that just because something is a vision, that doesn't mean that it isn't real. Some visions are fantasies or demonic delusions; others are witnessings of objective realities which are higher and more real than the material world.

According to Sufi doctrine, spiritual states are gifts of God, not acquisitions. We can in no way produce them, nor should we even pray for them. Our business is, simply, to remember God and forget ourselves. On the other hand, if we spend every waking hour remembering God, and ultimately every sleeping hour too, spiritual or mystical states may well arrive. To seek them is spiritual greed, but to reject them when they occur may be spiritual ingratitude. To demand gifts from one's Benefactor and to reject them when they are offered are both breaches of courtesy; and in the words of a Sufi proverb, 'Sufism is all courtesy.' The reception of such states says nothing definitive about the degree of spiritual advancement of the recipient, since, according to the Koran, 'God guides aright whom He will and leads astray whom He will.' In other words, God may sometimes punish a person's egotistical greed for spiritual experience and authority by sending him pseudo-mystical states, or rather allowing demonic forces to do so, the ultimate consequences of which will demonstrate to him his own spiritual pride, if he is willing to listen. A similar doctrine is implied by the words of the Lord's Prayer, 'lead us not into temptation,' which have been so puzzling to some Christians that they have altered them to read 'don't put us to the test'—as if God isn't putting us to the test every moment of our lives in one way or another. Furthermore, according to both Sufi and Hindu doctrine, mystical states are sent not because of our spiritual advancement, but because of our impurities. Imagine the rays of the Sun focussed through a magnifying glass on a slab of white marble. If there is sawdust on the marble, it will burst into flames; if the marble is clean, there will be nothing but illumination. The sawdust is our mass of spiritual impurities; the flames are the spiritual states which burn them away; the illumination of the clean stone is Wisdom; the light is the Divine Intellect.

But what about systems of spiritual development like yoga, as practiced by both Hindus and Vajrayana Buddhists, where, far from waiting for God to freely grant the yogi a spiritual state, he actively pursues it through a sophisticated manipulation of the psycho-physical nervous system based on bodily postures (*asanas*), breath-control (*pranayama*), verbal invocation (*mantra*), meditation upon symbolic diagrams (*mandalas* or *yantras*), and symbolic gestures (*mudras*)? Here the question becomes more complicated, and there is no question in my mind that any heavily technique-laden spiritual practice is always in danger of turning into a Promethean struggle to 'take heaven by storm', since the yogi may experience himself as practicing the method not as an obedient response to Divine grace, but on his own initiative, as an independent self-directed ego — and no independent self-directed ego practicing sophisticated psycho-physical techniques on its own initiative will arrive anywhere but at the gates of Hell. Nonetheless the pursuit of spiritual states, if carried on within the context of a tradition which defines this pursuit in terms of obedience to God's Will and labor in His service, can be spiritually effective, and ultimately produce saints. '*Seek* and ye shall find; *ask* and it shall be given; *knock* and it shall be opened unto you.'

Tranquility, vigilance, confidence in God, love of God, love of one's neighbor, consciousness of the Presence of God are 'altered states of consciousness': Tranquility is a different state of mind than agitation, grateful joy than sullen meanness, vigilance than sleepiness, confidence than anxiety, love than hate, consciousness of the Presence of God than the vision of existential absurdity, or everyday boredom. And while we can't simply produce these altered states through willpower, by the same token their advent does require a responsible, 'a response-able' attitude on our part. If someone is lecturing, you don't simply wait in a condition of dull, sleepy boredom until the speaker says something so earthshaking that your fuzzy mind is seized and overpowered by it — no. You sit up and pay attention. And you will never 'hear' what God is saying to you until you are willing to listen for it. Listening is an 'altered' state of consciousness; it's something different than heedlessness. This does not mean that God is not an objective Reality; quite the contrary. The very existence of that objective Reality demands that our state of consciousness be altered so as to come to an understanding of It which is adequate, certainly not to the infinite Reality of God, but at least to the fullness of our God-given human capacity to know Him. And what that Reality demands, it also makes possible. Furthermore, if that Reality overpowers our minds from time to time, so that we enter 'altered states' of spiritual drunkenness or ecstasy, this is not inappropriate, unless we deliberately try to produce such states so we can indulge in them. States like this teach us, in concrete experiential terms, that the human mind cannot encompass God, while at the same time 'widening the borders of our tent,' burning away spiritual impurities and increasing our capacity to understand and obey a Divine Reality we can never fully encompass. And somewhere in our struggle to understand God, or to give up trying to understand Him, we may suddenly come to the realization that we *are understood*. As the Prophet Muhammad said (upon whom be peace), 'pray to God as if you saw Him, because even if you don't see Him, He sees you.' God's perfect understanding of us is the Divine Self, the *atman* within us, which is the meaning of the words of Muhammad, 'he who knows himself knows his Lord.' And that Divine Self within us is just as objective, just as 'absolutely other' from all I can ever experience as my little individual self, as any Almighty Father enthroned in heaven. Whether we view the Absolute as the Noumenon behind all phenomena or as the Self within our psychic subjectivity, the Reality is the same: within subject, or within subjectively-perceived object— yet infinitely beyond both—the One Truth.

Remembering that one is in the presence of God is the central spiritual practice in Eastern Orthodox Christian Hesychasm (the Jesus prayer or the prayer of the heart), Islamic Sufism (*dhikr*), and is also important in Hinduism (as *japam*). All three traditions continue to produce saints, who are the proof of any religion. The majority of Orthodox, Muslim and Hindu saints have practiced this kind of remembering. Not that this or any other spiritual practice can turn one into a saint, or even save one's soul. But if by the grace of God the presence of That One is deeply real to a person, he or she will naturally be moved, in simple gratitude, to work to remove the impediments to this sense of presence, just as a person will naturally pay deep attention to someone he or she loves, or will not want to act foolishly or appear unwashed in the presence of the King. Meditation is not sorcery; it is simply attention. Deep silence is not magic; it is simply respect for the One we hope will speak to us—the One who is speaking even now, if only we were quiet enough to hear Him.

As for more complex spiritual practices, such as postures, visualizations, breathing exercises etc., their goal is no different than simple remembrance: to remove all impediments to a deeper sense of the presence of God. And while their more elaborate nature may make them susceptible to perversion by the promethean self-will, which always wants to believe that it can reach God on its own efforts, in the ambience of grace which is an intact spiritual tradition, such practices will rarely degenerate into magic, but preserve the essence of pure worship.

III. New Age Doctrines Refuted

The New Age contains many sincere seekers, and, for all I know, possibly even some hidden saints (but God knows best). God obviously has both the power and the right to reward those who seek Him sincerely with the gift of His grace, expressed in terms of love, knowledge and power, despite the inadequacy and even the danger of the doctrines a given seeker might hold. But this fact does not render those doctrines any more adequate or less dangerous. Likewise the acceptance of orthodox revealed doctrine does not obviate the dangers of hypocrisy, spiritual pride and the other vices; such doctrine, however, is no less an effective protection and support for the spiritual life, and no less intrinsically true, simply because some of those identified with it are corrupt. I do not intend this refutation of New Age doctrines as in any way a judgement upon the sincerity or spiritual attainments of those who believe in them; since the state of someone's soul is a matter between the individual and God, I have neither the right nor the power to look into it. Christ's parable of the Good Samaritan was not intended to invalidate doctrinal orthodoxy, since 'I come not to destroy the law but to fulfill it.' But it was intended to present the state and destiny of the human soul first of all in terms of 'by their fruits ye shall know them.'

✳ Channeling 'Entities'

The world of alternative spiritualities, and in many ways our society as a whole, has entered a period where the paradigm of magic—which includes both technological magic as well as 'traditional' magical forms—is replacing that of religion, both exoteric and esoteric. Too many people in the New Age, inheritors of hippy spiritual populism, are presently teaching that 'everybody can be a shaman, everybody can channel "entities".' Certainly not all beings on the psychic plane or the world of the Jinn are evil or deluded—according to Islamic doctrine, some of the Jinn are Muslim and some are not—but this doesn't mean that a frivolous opening to that world isn't exposing society to the danger of mass demonic possession, and proving Guénon entirely right in his prediction that human life in the closing days of the cycle would be subject to incursions of the 'infra-psychic'.

The channeling of 'spirit guides' is perhaps the most central manifestation of the New Age spiritualities. It's a practice which, while not always strictly evil, is profoundly dangerous; the majority of these 'entities', when they are not simply figments of the individual imagination, are at best ambiguous, and are in many cases actual demons, whose demonic nature is more clearly revealed with each passing year. And by no means the least destructive aspect of this channeling is that it represents not a simple delusion, but a counterfeit of traditional doctrine. The *daimon* of Socrates, the *genius* or *juno* of the Romans, possibly certain aspects of Neo-Platonic theurgy, the guardian angel in Christianity, the *fravashi* in Zoroastrianism, the spirits of the prophets with whom Ibn al-'Arabi was in contact within Islam, the *yidam* or tutelary deity in Tibetan Buddhism—all these represent, in strictly traditional form, the reality of which spirit channeling is, by and large, the counterfeit. Perhaps the safest approach is to simply call the whole 'intermediate plane' or *'alam al-mithal* demonic, as many Christians have. But if 'there is no right superior to that of truth,' then someone has to admit that the intermediate plane is not strictly demonic, but rather dangerous and ambiguous. Not every fish in the sea is a shark—but beware of sharks. Frithjof Schuon and Seyyed Hossein Nasr speak of magic, for example, as a traditional science, and Schuon will allow that there is such a thing as white magic, which is interaction with 'those Jinn who are Muslim' for the purpose of doing good, though he also cautions against becoming involved with it. But I must admit that telling this truth makes me profoundly nervous, because it may tempt the frivolous to say, 'very well, I'll simply practice white magic and stay away from the black,' a thing which is infinitely easier said than done. Traditional practices such as exorcism do show certain affinities with white magic. True exorcism, however, applies Spiritual power to the psychic plane, whereas white magic pits beneficent psychic powers against evil ones— something which should never be attempted outside a traditional context such as veridical shamanism, supposing that any of us possess the criteria by which true shamanism could be distinguished from its degenerate or counterfeit rivals. I remember a phone conversation I had with a self-taught 'spiritual healer' who performed exorcisms partly through visualization. 'I just explain to the obsessing entity that it doesn't have to act in such an evil manner, that it has other options for spiritual progress open to it. This usually depotentiates it, and allows it to pass on to higher planes.' I wish I had said to him: 'Impressive! If even fallen angels are that easy for you to convert, why don't you go to work on serial killers? They ought to be a piece of cake.'

On the level of metaphysical principles, what separates the Socrates' *daimon* from an 'entity' like Ramtha? How can one tell a guardian angel from a deceptive demon? I believe the answer has to do not solely with the gift of discernment of spirits, which is of course invaluable, but also with one's basic orientation. To the degree that one relates to such beings in terms of will, seeking or coercing them or demanding knowledge from them, then they are nothing but familiar spirits. To the degree that one relates to them in terms of the Intellect, not seeking them but accepting them when they appear, as gifts of wisdom and counsel and knowledge rather than gifts of power, then they are more likely to be angels. Deceptive spirits can approach even the sincere, however, and may take a special interest in perverting the spiritual lives of those who are making real progress in love and knowledge.

Angels are 'messengers'. They are sent by God. Therefore, if one concentrates upon God, not the messenger (and this concentration can only remain stable within the confines of a revealed tradition, though God can always make exceptions) then the messenger will tend to be angelic, whereas if one concentrates on the messenger rather than God, then the messenger probably is, or will become, demonic. When the mailman brings you a letter from your Beloved you don't go to bed with the mailman, nor do you make love to the letter; you remember the One you love, and look forward to meeting That One in the flesh. When the inhabitants of Sodom wanted to *possess* the angels of God—sexual lust being only one form of this possessiveness, which implicitly stands for all the others, particularly spiritual greed— this is exactly what they were doing. And this is what makes me suspicious of the present vogue in 'angels'; it seems to be a sign that the Transcendent God is becoming less real to many people. The sense of a living and ongoing communion with God is a part of normal piety. The apparition of an angel is, normally, a rare occurrence. But when visions of angels become more common than a sense of the reality of God, then the situation is obviously abnormal, and God is on His way, in the collective mind, to becoming a *deus otiosus* like the High God in many (not all) African tribes. North American religion, in this sense, is actually becoming more like the non-Christian and non-Muslim religions of tropical Africa; though we may still admit the existence of the High God who created the world, He is no longer accessible, while various psychic entities, far from being inaccessible, are becoming harder and harder to avoid. To speak in terms of traditional African and Chinese religions, and of Japanese Shinto, these entities *may* represent the Deified Ancestors who in turn symbolize the permanent spiritual archetypes, or divine hypostases, or Names of God; they may also be ghosts and demons. And as the sense of the Transcendent God weakens, we are much more likely to encounter ghosts and demons than archangels.

So in terms of spirit channeling—which in its popular form clearly must be rejected—I believe the right approach is to admit the existence of angels as well as demons, to allow that angelic influences are within the realm of possibility, but to emphasize that, although God may send his angels to communicate with us, the *desire* to encounter an angel is almost always destructive. 'Seek ye first the Kingdom of God and His righteousness, and all these things will be added unto you'—including angels if God so chooses, even though conscious experience of the angelic plane is in no way necessary to the spiritual life. I believe that it is best to admit the possibility of angelic intervention, because if we say that it is possible and even likely that we will encounter demons, but extremely unlikely if not effectively impossible to encounter angels, we may find ourselves preaching the rejection of God's messengers, thus giving further aid and comfort to the powers of darkness.

We shouldn't assume, however, that just because demons and angels are real, 'channeled' figures are always psychic entities. During my 2-year tour through the New Age, I heard a story about channeling that had nothing to do with the supernatural, but a great deal to do with psychology. A woman who had been raised by adoptive parents had been channeling an 'entity' while concurrently seeking her biological parents. Lo and behold, when she found them she discovered that her original given name, which she had no conscious memory of, was the name of her 'entity'! Also during that time I formed the impression that some channeling has to do with both the breakdown of traditional social authority, and a profound lack of intellectual self-confidence on the part of those involved. If one possesses no accepted social wisdom to apply in different circumstances, and does not trust one's own ability to make sense of things, one may psychologically manufacture an infallible 'entity' to fulfill these functions. It's as if, when society does not support an identification of the faculties of rational thought and sound judgement with one's conscious personality, these faculties may become 'autonomous complexes'. If you can't believe in your own ability to think, you can always attribute that ability to your familiar spirit, who will not necessarily be *able* to think, but may at least represent a pathetically hopeful gesture in that direction.

✳ Neo-Pagan Misconceptions

The New Age/Neo-Pagan world fervently believes that its knowledge is esoteric. But since the distinction between psyche and Spirit is rarely made in that world—a distinction which years ago I heard termed 'patriarchal' by members of a 'feminist spirituality collective'—the term 'esoterism' cannot legitimately be applied to it. It is believed in many Neo-Pagan circles that to imagine a level of reality higher than the psychic is to support political tyranny, cooperate with the oppression of women, destroy the natural environment, and God knows what else. Consequently knowledge among Neo-Pagans remains mostly on the psychic level—which, as we have said, is a real level of being which it would do us well to know something about, particularly since, in these times, psychic experiences are becoming harder than ever to avoid. But unless the psyche is guided and protected by the Spirit, such knowledge rapidly becomes delusive, and often demonic.

Many people (and not just the Neo-Pagans), thanks to writers like Sir James Frazer, Robert Graves and their successors, presently believe that the secret, esoteric core of the Judeo-Christian-Islamic tradition is really Paganism. This misconception is on an entirely different level from the 'esoteric ecumenism' (Schuon's term) that allows us to see real affinities between the Abrahamic religions and certain 'high' Paganisms such as Orphism or Neo-Platonism. Writers with a background in Jungian psychology, or an interest in mythographers like Joseph Campbell, will routinely attempt to trace every Biblical passage or Judeo-Christian doctrine back to its supposed 'pagan' root—blindly, automatically, and without letup. Parallels there certainly are, but the rarely-questioned idea, in mythopoetic and Neo-Pagan circles, that Judaism and Christianity are really Paganism in disguise, is simply false. It ignores centuries if not millennia of persecution directed against the Jews by the more powerful Pagan nations of the Near East; it ignores the persecution of the Jewish religion carried on by the Pagan Seleucid Greeks; it ignores the persecution of both Jews and Christians by Greco-Roman Paganism under the Roman Empire; it ignores the later counter-persecution by Christians against Greco-Roman Paganism; it ignores the Muslim destruction of Pagan cults; it ignores centuries of theological polemic by Jews against Pagans, Pagans against Christians and Jews, and Christians and Muslims against Pagans. These persecutions and counter-persecutions were not only political; they also represented real doctrinal disagreements. The Abrahamic religions, whatever differences they may have had among themselves, and whatever lapses in the direction of Paganism they may have fallen into, shared a clear and deliberate opposition to it, just as the Pagans, by and large, opposed the Abrahamic religions. The two different camps believed different things, knew it, and said so. On the other hand, the Abrahamic religions share with the Egyptian religion, and with the archaic Orphic-Pythagorean roots of classical Paganism, a relationship to what Guénon and the Traditionalists call the Primordial Tradition. But this Tradition is not to be strictly identified with either Paganism or Abrahamic monotheism, although the Abrahamic religions did preserve this Primordial Tradition in a purer form than the degenerate Paganism of late antiquity. In any case, the Paganism Frazer and Graves wrote about bore little resemblance to the true Primordial Tradition, though anyone who understands this Tradition can always recognize more or less degenerated remnants of it in the material presented both of these writers, as well as in the Teutonic religion, in Celtic Druidism, in the Babylonian religion, and in the Greek and Roman myths.

✳ Subtle Materialism

Since it lacks a solid and well-articulated doctrine of transcendence, the New Age tends toward a subtle materialism. The Divine and the merely cosmic are often confused. God is conceived of as a form of useful energy which can be tapped and manipulated by human beings, something on the order of 'the Force' from the *Star Wars* movies. The Transpersonal Godhead, of which the Personal God is the first formal manifestation, is envisioned instead as an impersonal power source or set of natural laws, on the order of gravitation or nuclear energy. The human person is subtly devalued; the recognition of the eternal, qualitative value of personhood, since this is falsely identified with an 'all-too-human' egoism, is replaced by a quantitative worship of energy. The secrets of the celestial worlds are to be found in the structure of human DNA. The sense of Eternity is replaced by the space-time paradoxes of post-Einsteinian physics. The words 'God' and 'universe' are used interchangeably; to Deepak Chopra, for example, God is 'the cosmic computer'. And for Jose Arguelles, like Timothy Leary before him, the Center of Being is no longer virtually everywhere — and therefore to be found, from the human standpoint, in the transcendent depths of the spiritual Heart — but is now identified with the center of the *galaxy*. Clearly the whole concept of Being, as compared to that of traditional metaphysics, or even exoteric theology, has taken a quantum slump.

One of the signs of such materialism in the New Age is the idolatry of crystals. I've met New Agers who acted as if they possessed, in crystals of quartz or fluorite or amethyst, actual pieces of God. Such crystallolatry, in our post-Christian culture, is probably based on a decadent understanding of Christ's Incarnation — or possibly on an intuition of the final 'crystallized' form which will be taken by this cycle of manifestation (the Heavenly Jerusalem in the book of *Apocalypse*), mis-interpreted in literalistic terms. According to traditional symbolism, the jewels of which the Heavenly Jerusalem is composed are celestial wisdoms. The use of jewels, crystals and colorful minerals as magical tools — at least outside of traditional shamanism — therefore indicates a degeneration in our collective understanding of Wisdom Itself. Sophia is no longer venerated as a ray of the Divine Nature; matter itself, Sophia's mirror, is worshipped instead. Matter, as Einstein proved, releases immense power — though only at its point of dissolution. Thus our worship of matter is essentially a self-defeating and self-contradictory worship of power.

* The Brighter Side of the New Age: Psychic and Wholistic Healing

The New Age, on one level, represents the re-discovery or re-invention of many of the traditional cosmological sciences, though outside of a religious and metaphysical context which could securely orient them toward the Absolute. For example, many New Age practitioners possess a sophisticated practical knowledge of subtle energies, which, up to a point, can legitimately be used for the purpose of healing. But where, exactly, is that point? It should be obvious that it is an overreaction to call such vaguely New Age physical therapies such as structural integration ('Rolfing') demonic, as some conservative Christians tend to do, who might forbid a Christian to practice, for example, the head-stand from hatha-yoga, as a therapy for chronic sinus infection or to improve the blood-supply to the brain, since it is not Christian, and therefore anti-Christian, and therefore satanic. The fact remains that standing on your head can sometimes heal sinusitis, and that deep-tissue bodywork can improve posture and overcome chronic pain. And to forbid, say, the ecologically-sound practice of biodynamic gardening because it was developed by 'Christian occultist' Rudolf Steiner would be equally foolish.

The practice is one thing, the paradigm which gives rise to it another. One might with equal or even greater justification refuse to have an artificial heart-valve or ocular lens or hip joint surgically implanted because such interventions are based on the paradigm which sees the human body as a biological machine, not the 'image and likeness of God'. On the other hand, the paradigm *does* necessarily influence the practice, in ways which are not always obvious; it takes a degree of spiritual discernment to see where the practice ends and the belief-system of those who developed it begins. Ida Rolf, for example, explained structural integration in terms influenced by modern Theosophy, which is essentially an anti-Christian occultism. But the fact is that Theosophy presents, in distorted form, material stolen from valid traditional teachings, such as the Hindu doctrine of the *koshas*, the various 'sheaths' of the Divine Self within us—intellect, mind, body, etc.—a doctrine which is strictly analogous to teachings of the Christian Fathers on the tripartite nature of man, Spirit, soul, and body, and on the various faculties of the soul. If a family member has been abducted and violated, we don't reject them once they've been returned to us, but work instead to heal them and reintegrate them into the family. The same is true, or should be, of forgotten traditional doctrines taken up in distorted form by occultism. Still, if you can't have your hip replaced without thinking of yourself as a soulless robot, or go through a Rolfing session without buying into distorted occultist ideas, then you'd better not do it.

Nutrition, herbology, various forms of bodywork, acupuncture… all these can be applied, by well-trained practitioners, with good results. Both my wife and myself have greatly benefitted from structural integration, which in her case overcame posture-related problems which she'd suffered from most of her life.

Types of healing which use breathing exercises, such as Rebirthing, are more ambiguous, since to forcibly activate the subtle energy-systems of the body can be physically and psychologically dangerous, particular when practiced outside traditional forms such as yogic *pranayama*, which require a specific diet and lifestyle, the guidance of a teacher, and even a traditional doctrinal framework to be practiced safely. Rebirthing has been very useful to me during times of great stress, but the paradigm it's based upon, which includes in some cases the fantasy of physical immortality, is a definite drawback which needs to be filtered out.

When the form of healing in question deals with even subtler psycho-physical energies than those activated by breath-control, it becomes still more ambiguous. When these energies are conceived of as being altered or enhanced by the intervention of 'healing entities' from the psychic plane, as is traditionally common in shamanism, the situation is even less certain and more open to hidden dangers.

I myself have experienced benefit from some of these practices. For example, the energy channeled by a New Age Japanese church, the Joh-rei Fellowship—which appears to originate on a very high level of the psychic plane—seems entirely benign. The reason I stopped patronizing them, after many years of positive experience, had more to do with the divergence between the worldview of traditional metaphysics which had become central to me, and that of a new Japanese religion dedicated to bringing paradise to earth, even though its doctrine of the coming world 'purification' is not entirely unlike that of the traditional eschatologies, though with a New Age twist. Joh-rei incorporates many traditional Buddhist, Shinto and (ultimately) Taoist/shamanic elements; still, the 'cheap grace' of the experience was perhaps subtly interfering with my willingness to rely upon my own more traditional spiritual practices, and my faith in God.

Joh-rei appears relatively safe in that it does not seem to open up the etheric or subtle-energy body. Various other forms of psychic healing, however, which do intervene powerfully on the subtle-energy level, can inadvertently open one to other influences which are far from healthy.

The most powerful healers of this class are the psychic surgeons of the Philippines. I have experienced that power on a number of occasions, both in the Philippines and here in the U.S. While some charlatans exist, the ones I have encountered are genuine. I am convinced of this, having watched a number of operations and having been operated upon myself. Since there is no way I can prove this, the reader will have to limit him- or herself simply to believing that I believe.

These healers have the power to open parts of the human body with their unaided hands in order to remove foreign matter and diseased tissue, virtually dematerializing specific areas, which then immediately reform, like water in a basin which leaves no gap when an object is taken out of it. There is little or no pain, and no period of convalescence except for a process of 'coming back to normal' on a subtle-energy level, which may take a day or two.

Although the psychic surgeons can approach healing of both serious and simply annoying conditions in ways impossible for modern science, their success-rate, according to their own statistics, is comparable: one third healed, one third helped, and one third unchanged. I was usually in the second third.

While most of the psychic surgeons are Christians, attributing their power to the Holy Spirit — there is no reason to disbelieve them here, necessarily — it's clear that they are using an ancient shamanic technique. Similar powers have been attributed to shamans in many parts of the world, though most early explorers usually explained them as slight-of-hand, another ancient 'spiritual' practice which is still in use by charlatans today.

It's my belief that the psychic surgeons work through the world of the *devas* or the *jinn*, beings resident on the psychic plane who can interact with the material one under certain circumstances. Some of these beings are clearly beneficent, and may indeed be working under the blessing of the Holy Spirit. Still, psychic surgery is not miraculous. It gives the feeling of being an ancient, sophisticated psychic technology developed by cultures who were just as advanced in that regard as we are in our own high-tech brand of magic. It is a well-meaning intervention by highly-trained and service-oriented individuals. It is not a direct act of God.

The genuine psychic surgeons I have encountered are powerful and benevolent. They have helped many. Yet it's true that such surgery, and other forms of psychic healing which deal with the subtle-energy body, carry hidden dangers. One danger is that we may become addicted to the witnessing of wonders and begin to lose our faith, since we are now attempting to base it on demonstration: 'proof' is not faith. 'Because you have seen, Thomas, you believe; blessed are they who have not seen, yet have believed.' And if physical surgery opens one to the risk of post-operative infection, the same may be true of psychic surgery on a more subtle level. If the paradigm of 'getting rid of evil' is not subordinated to the paradigm of 'opening to the truth and love of God,' this merely negative purification may result in the condition spoken of in the parable of Jesus, where the expelled demon wanders in waterless places, remembers his former 'home', returns to find it 'swept and adorned' as if ready to receive him, and brings in with him seven demons more evil than himself. (Ex-New Age healer Clare McGrath-Merkle writes with great insight about this possibility, from hard personal experience, as well as about the psychic, psychological, and physical dangers of subtle energy-work and 'white magic' in general.)

For myself, I can only share two interesting phenomena. Having received definite help from the surgeons for a worrisome health condition, I got into the habit of visiting them whenever they came to my area. Then I noticed an interesting thing: where at first they were helpful, the last two times I saw them my condition returned in a small way just before they arrived, as if it had to be there just so they could heal it. Was their very presence drawing more impurities to the surface? Or had I entered an area of diminishing returns and subtle attachments? Luckily my dilemma was solved by my spiritual director, who, kindly but firmly, asked me to stop seeing them.

The second phenomenon, emotionally comparable to seeing a brick wall collapse on a section of sidewalk one has just been walking on, was that after my last visit to the psychic surgeons, I dreamt of Antichrist. I do not take this to mean, necessarily, that the surgeons are really his servants — though God knows best. But the fact remains that 'psychic religion' relying on signs and wonders will be among the first territories to be conquered and occupied by Antichrist when he comes… and when the landing-craft are launched and the naval bombardment begins, it's not a good idea to stay on the beach.

❋ Nine Principles of the New Age

Dr Rama Coomaraswamy, in an article entitled 'The Desacralization of Hinduism for Western Consumption,' lists nine New Age principles, which he takes from a book by Dr Catheryn Ridall, Ph.D., representing the essence of today's channeled 'spirit teachings'. Below is a summary of them, in which I attempt to disentangle elements of spiritual truth from the matrix of error which is New Age doctrine.

A counterfeit is worse than a simple error. These nine principles are full of errors which, however, are *precisely designed* to obfuscate specific metaphysical truths. And the effect of such counterfeits is that 'you are damned if you do and damned if you don't.' The Devil loves to employ counterfeits, because to accept them is to be led into error, while to reject them without exposing the counterfeit—that is, without bringing forth the true principle which the counterfeit was designed to hide—is to be maneuvered into rejecting the truth that is being counterfeited. I'll attempt to deconstruct the following 'principles', expose the counterfeits they are made of, and present the traditional principles they veil:

1. *Universal evolution of consciousness toward greater love and compassion.*

This is certainly false if applied to the human collectivity or the material universe. The receptivity of incarnate time-conditioned consciousness to Divine Reality waxes and wanes in a cyclical manner, and human receptivity to God on the collective level is now in a steep and irreversible decline. The truth here veiled is that the destiny of the *individual soul on the spiritual path* is to 'evolve' in the sense of 'unwinding what has been wound up,' dissolving the hard kernel of egotism and self-will. This 'evolution' certainly includes the development of compassion—in Mahayana Buddhist terms, 'the realization of emptiness (non-ego) is identical to compassion'—but (and here the principle is deceptive because incomplete) this 'evolution' also results in the development of true, objective knowledge.

2. In the context of universal evolution of consciousness, we can be guided both by beings who are more 'evolved' than us, and by higher parts of ourselves which are themselves evolving.

It is certainly true that persons who are wiser than us, either because they were born wiser, or because they have traveled farther than we have on the spiritual path, can sometimes be delegated by God to guide us, if we fulfill the necessary conditions—as long as we, and they, understand that ultimately God is the only guide.

And in rare instances—such as that of the Sufi guide *Khidr*, who is considered to be an immortal prophet, discarnate, or rather inhabiting a subtle body like the glorified Christ—beings more 'advanced' than us can legitimately guide us in a way we can consciously respond to. But to believe that this rare possibility makes it unnecessary for us to connect ourselves to a revealed tradition, and place ourselves (God willing) under the guidance of a fully-empowered human representative of that tradition, presuming one is available, is false. And to believe that conscious, ongoing contact with a discarnate 'guide' is normal—for anyone but a sorcerer, that is, in communion with his familiar spirit—and that such contact is not an open door to demonic possession, is profoundly deluded. Furthermore, to say we can be guided by our 'higher self' which is *also* evolving, is *false*; to try to spiritually orient oneself to something which is still in the realm of becoming is to reduce the meaning of 'spiritual orientation' to zero. If there is any meaning to the term 'higher self', it can only refer, not to *jiva* (the individual soul) but to *atman*, the level of Spirit within us that Eckhart indicated when he said 'there is Something within the soul which is uncreated and uncreatable.' The *atman* does not guide us in the sense that we can hold a conversation with it, but because, as 'the absolute Subject of our contingent subjectivity' (Schuon), God in the mode of the Witness, it represents virtual *moksha* (the Hindu term for final Liberation) in the sense the Buddha was speaking of when he said 'all beings are enlightened from the beginning,' though he well knew that not all beings within a given time-period would realize this enlightenment. Psychic reflections of the *atman*, suggestive of it though not to be identified with it, may certainly appear in dreams or visions. These reflections will be deceptive, ambiguous, or a vehicle of God's Grace, depending upon God's will for that person and his or her spiritual state. *The Psychology of Sufism* by Dr Javad Nurbakhsh, for example, contains a catalogue of dream-symbols of the spiritual Heart, which Jung would call symbols of the Self archetype. But such symbols only work as reliable psychic signposts within the context of Sufism itself, just as the symbols of the Kabbalah only work for initiated and practicing Kabbalists, etc.

3, 4. The earth is at a critical point in its development; we are witnessing a major shift in values, lifestyles, spiritual orientation; we are moving into greater spiritual maturity; the earth is to undergo a purification of values and social organization; there will be earth-changes such as earthquakes.

It is true that the earth is at a critical point, but the shift in values, lifestyles, spiritual orientation and social organization is *not* toward greater spiritual maturity, but toward chaos and dissolution. It is true that there will be, and already are, earth changes, as were predicted by Jesus for the end of the age, and true that there will be a purification. But the purification will be apocalyptic, not progressive, and will represent the end of the present humanity. The 'new heaven and the new earth' will be for 'another' humanity.

5. Guides are now appearing to help us through this transition to an age of peace; new energies of higher frequency will cause minor disturbances in behavior.

It is *false* that we are transitioning to a time of peace, unless it be a false and temporary peace; therefore the 'guides' who claim to be helping us through this transition are deceptive. Nor are the present disturbances in behavior 'minor', to say the least. It is *true*, in a sense, that we are encountering 'higher energies', but this is because our own level of integration is sinking to the point where the ever-present Grace of God can only be experienced, on the collective level, as wrath, since we are not receptive to it. The 'energy', or ontological level, of the *parousia* so far surpasses what the world can receive that it will shatter the world, making way for 'a new heaven and a new earth'.

6. The human being is one part of a multi-dimensional soul or god-self; we are much more than we think we are.

True and false. As Jesus said, 'ye are all gods, and sons of the Most High.' But he balanced this by saying, 'Why callest thou me good? None is good, save one, that is, God.' It is *true* that humanity exists simultaneously in higher worlds than the material, namely the psychic and the Spiritual. We do not simply ascend to these worlds, or enter them for the first time when we die, because the 'Great Chain of Being' represents the 'ray' whereby God created us, and maintains us in existence, instant-by-instant. If we turn against these higher worlds, however—by giving our allegiance to our ego instead of

God—then they will become our Hell: the psyche, an anguished chaos; the Spirit within us, a cutting, blinding Light which forces us away from the radiant Center of Being, like Michael's legions driving the Devil and his angels into the pit. The central question is this: are these higher aspects of our being claimed by the ego, as if we were self-created, or are they seen as God's gift to us of our very being, which we cannot claim as our own even in material terms? New Age believers like the idea that we exist simultaneously in higher worlds; what they have greater difficulty dealing with is that 'he who tries to preserve his life will lose it, but he who loses his life, for My sake, will find it.' This is because they want to claim these higher worlds for the ego; they teach that we can enter and 'explore' these worlds as a kind of leisure-time activity, by a simple, incremental expansion of our 'human potential', without piety, without sacrifice, without fear of God. Their doctrine is essentially Promethean; they choose to forget that 'twice born needs once dead.'

7. We create our own experience on all levels; there are no victims; we create our own suffering as a learning experience.

It is *false* to say that we create our own experience if the 'we' in question is the individual psyche, because the psyche does not create itself, being wholly contingent on the Spirit of God, and because other individual psyches exist; the solipsism here implied is thus refuted both 'vertically' and 'horizontally'. There is a way, however, in which this is *true*, but only in a negative sense, since we certainly do create some of our own perceptual limitations. Rather than 'we create our own reality,' it would be better to say 'we create our own illusions, which then become our "reality".' The psychology of perception has demonstrated to what degree our view of the world is a learned pattern, determined both by culture and by personal experience, if not by a series of choices based on fear and desire. This means that, to the extent we take the world we perceive as an absolute, we are imprisoned within a subjective pattern, while if we realize that this subjective patterning of experience is relative, that vis-à-vis objective Reality it is nothing but a privation, then we are starting to get free of it, since we have begun to intuit the Absolute Matrix of which it is only an edited version. So when New Age believers say 'we create our own reality,' my reply is 'Yes and no. Our mind and senses do not project this "reality" upon nothing, but rather abstract it out of Infinity, which is the true Reality; the "reality" we create is a limitation imposed on the Infinite.'

To say 'there are no victims' is *true* if by this we mean that everything, in the ultimate sense, is an act of God, and God is just—as Schuon says, even the suffering of the innocent is justified from the point of view which sees cosmic existence itself, while in one sense necessary, as an imbalance in the face of the Absolute. In the words of Rabi'a, 'your existence is a sin with which no other sin can be compared.' The idea that there are no victims is an interpretation of the law of *karma*—but if it is implied in this interpretation that charity toward the suffering is not incumbent upon us, since 'that's just their karma,' or that we can become liberated simply through creating illusions for ourselves and then seeing through them, then it is *false*. *Karma* is not a self-exhausting system; without *dharma*, the operative truth which lifts one above the level of karmic cause-and-effect by positing the reality of self-transcendence, karma can never be 'lived out'; without the Mercy of God's Truth, freely given and freely accepted, along with its 'cross', illusion can never be dispelled. Damnation is the proof that not all suffering has the power to enlighten.

8. *Matter follows thought; our physical reality is created, and can be changed, by our beliefs.*

Matter follows God's thought, not ours; to imply otherwise, to say that we are co-creators in our own right, is *false*. It is *true* that our *experience* can be changed by changing our beliefs, but this change cannot be sovereign, or arbitrary. We can't simply believe whatever we want and think we're thereby controlling the world, because there really is an objective reality, both within us and outside us, something which is exactly the way it is no matter what we happen to believe. And it's also likely that we have as little control over our desires, over what we *want* to believe, as we do over the outside world. To believe that we can change what is through changing what we believe about it is the omnipotence-fantasy of the infantile ego expanded into a false metaphysical principle.

A change in belief can change our experience in two ways only: if we conform our beliefs to objective spiritual Truth, we will see the universe as it really is, as both contingent upon that Truth and a manifestation of it; if our beliefs are determined by our ego, which interprets the world around it only on the basis of its own fears and desires, we will perceive and produce only chaos. Now in a more limited sense, it is *true* that a person in a deep depression, for example, will believe that less is possible vis-à-vis his physical surroundings, while someone in a manic state may temporarily be able to respond to actual physical and psychological possibilities that the depressed one cannot see — but not without dire consequences, since he cannot perceive these possibilities' inherent limitations, which are objectively there, irrespective of belief. It is certainly *true* that a saint can be a vehicle for physical miracles, though this has nothing to do with the manipulation of belief, but is the direct operation of God made possible by faith. A magician may also be able to produce changes in physical matter or situations, and one *could* say that he can do this because he believes he can, but the actual manifestations are produced by psychic forces which exist whether he believes in them or not. The white magician will necessarily understand that he is a vehicle for forces from a subtler plane, but the black magician often believes, *falsely*, that he is *commanding* these forces; he is applying the everyday naive belief that 'I am captain of my fate, I am master of my soul' to subtler planes, not wanting to understand that whoever believes that he with his limited ego is commanding the forces of a subtler realm is actually enslaved by them. The practice of magic is like writing checks on an overdrawn account: though you may be able to 'cash' them, and thereby produce 'phenomena', they will be phenomena of debt, not value. 'And he will not come out again until he has paid the last farthing.' The ego can produce nothing but privation; all power and value are of God.

It is *true* that if we all perfectly conformed our consciousness to objective spiritual Reality, the material world would dissolve and be transformed into Paradise. But this is the farthest thing from the idea that our beliefs *create* reality out of nothing, given that such perfect conformation — which, of course is impossible in practical terms — could not be a function of belief, which sees 'through a glass, darkly,' but only of true objective knowledge. As I pointed out above, the ego does not create; it only edits.

9. *Although our individual expression demonstrates much diversity, we are all ultimately one.*

True. The only question is, in what sense are we one? If this is meant horizontally, on the social level or in terms of sharing in the same subconscious motivations, then the best that can be said is that, for better or worse, we are related, or only 'relatively one'. Our true unity is vertical, by virtue of the *atman* or Divine Self within us; we are all creations, or symbolic manifestations, of the One Divine Self. By virtue of this *atman* we are, at the deepest level of our being, both unique and universal. The Self within us is pure, transpersonal, universal Being, without attributes; in another sense, It is even beyond Being. But since God is unique as well as universal, the Self is also the principle of our unique human integrity, according to which we are not simply humanity in the abstract, but actual human beings, commanded by God to be precisely ourselves, no greater, no less, and no other. And yet this uniqueness is also universal, since it is shared by all human beings, and in fact by all things. Self as the principle of uniqueness is not other than Self as the principle of pure Being, as when God, speaking to Moses in *Exodus*, names Himself 'I Am That I Am', that is to say: 'My unique Essence is not other than My pure Being; it is My unique Essence to *be* pure Being.' And what God can say of Himself, we can also say, virtually at least, of the God, the *atman* within us.

✳ And Two More

To these nine principles, I would like to add two others which I believe are equally integral to New Age belief:

10. *That psyche and Spirit are identical.*

11. *That spirituality is a personal achievement, an exploit, a tour-de-force.*

As I demonstrate in many places throughout this book, both these principles are entirely *false*.

✳ The Christians are Not Alone

Since the New Age is largely a 'post-Christian' phenomenon, and often an overtly anti-Christian one, most of the criticisms of it (if we leave aside the secular humanists who tend to see all religions more-or-less as cults) have come from the Christian camp. Most, but not all. In 'The Desacralization of Hinduism for Western Consumption', Dr Rama Coomaraswamy, a traditional Catholic who lived as an orthodox Hindu for many years as a young man, traces the careers of Sri Aurobindo, Maharishi Mahesh Yogi and Bagwan Shree Rajneesh, presenting them as examples of spurious Hindu teachers whose influence on the New Age has been deep and widespread; such teachers in no way represent normal Hinduism. Coomaraswamy writes: 'What do orthodox exponents of Hinduism think of Mahesh Yogi? The question was put to His Holiness Sri Chandraskharendra Sarasvati, Sri Shankaracharyaswami of the Kamakoti Peetha, 68th Acharya in the line of

Kamakoti Peetha, and one of the highest authorities within the Hindu tradition. His answer was that the man was a fake!'

A second group who have been critical of the New Age, since they have been directly victimized by it, are the traditional Native American spiritual elders. The following excerpts from an article by Gary Knack in the Spring '97 issue of the Native American newspaper *Akwesasne Notes* show how similar the problems with 'New Age med men' are to the more familiar scandals involving Westernized Hindu and Buddhist teachers, Protestant ministers and Catholic priests.

> There are several so-called 'medicine men' out here, of Native descent, who have perverted themselves and cast a disease upon the people. One, as many know, used his respected position to sexually molest children. Upon discovery of this fact, the word was given to keep quiet, as it could hurt the movement. Many of his followers, mostly white, stood by him and they continued working the ignorant white communities in southern California. . . .
> One so-called 'Medicine man' of Lakota descent was promoted locally [in Ashland, Oregon] by a college professor, his agent. He became well known, and still is, for his books and New Age tours . . . we were informed by one of the white women, who regularly sweat with us, that this 'med man' had a local history of sexually probing women in sweats . . . some of the L.A. crowd and child molester followers, approached the New Age 'med man' with cash in hand and wanted to start a multi-racial sundance just outside of Ashland. Done. It started in 1988. We refused to go near it. We started to see the spin-off confusion as the 'med man' ran it for several years. It stoked already swollen egos; families fell apart; one of the Native helpers committed suicide back in South Dakota; another allegedly committed murder; there were armed encounters over drugs; the 'ceremony' was altered to suite white sensibilities, and on and on. Someone else took over after the 'med man' eventually dropped out, but by now the damage was done, and the disease spreading. The want-to-be's were now want-to-be medicine men and women. They are already selling video tapes on the sacred pipe and other ceremonial practices.

Native American spiritual practices, traditional and otherwise, have become highly commercialized in New Age circles. But as Don R. writes in an editorial entitled 'Are Non-Native Americans Meddling in American Indian Ways?' (*New Perspectives, A Journal of Conscious Living*, July 8, 1994):

> Selling or trading sacred objects such as Eagle Feathers or Sacred Pipes is against all Native American Spiritual Teachings and federal law. They are only to be given without attachment for Ceremony only. To break this way

will follow you through eternity in the Afterlife. No money or so-called Medicine Gifts will be taken for teachings, especially Ceremony. Our sacred Ways are a gift from the Grandfathers and the Creator and you do not barter with the Creator.

4

New Age Authorities: A Divided House

Certainly truths are to be found in all the philosophers, and above all half-truths, but these truths are flanked with errors and inconsistencies, and there is moreover no need for them. . . . Truths embedded in errors are fraught indirectly with the venom of their erroneous context. . . .

∽FRITHJOF SCHUON, 'Letter on Existentialism', *The Essential Writings of Frithjof Schuon*

I. The Fallacy of the Psychic Absolute: Truth and Deception in *The Seth Material*

Professor Huston Smith, in *Beyond the Post-Modern Mind*, has traced the development of the postmodern worldview within the formal discipline of philosophy, and academia as a whole. But while the academics were moving away from modernism—which, while it frowned on metaphysics, still believed in a common objective reality based on science, history and psychology—to their present postmodernist denial of any 'overarching paradigm' which might bridge the discrete cultural worldviews we all must deal with in this age of pluralism and globalism, the popular mind, as opaque to academia as academia was to it, was pursuing a parallel course, proving that while there may be no objective reality—a doctrine I enthusiastically deny—there certainly is a common *zeitgeist*. While professors were deconstructing modernism in their departments of literature and philosophy, an upstate New York housewife was doing the same for the mass mind, or at least that segment of it open to 'New Age' ideas.

The most sophisticated and influential 'channeled' philosophy of the post-World War II New Age movement, apart from *A Course in Miracles*, is undoubtedly the *Seth* material, as dictated through Jane Roberts. The representative books are probably *The Seth Material* (Prentice-Hall, 1970; citations from Bantam Books edition, 1970), *Seth Speaks: The Eternal Validity of the Soul* (Prentice-Hall, 1972), and *The Nature of Personal Reality: A Seth Book* (Prentice-Hall, 1974). Mrs Roberts, who died in 1983, was a semi-bohemian ex-Catholic who wrote science fiction before she began to channel Seth, whom she first contacted via the ouija board, and later channeled in the trance state. The above books and others, including her fictional works, almost single-handedly updated spiritualism for a more 'sophisticated' post WW II audience, started the present 'channeling' vogue, and had a powerful effect on contemporary 'dreamwork', including 'lucid dreaming'. The Seth material is in some ways a reinterpretation of spiritualism according to Einsteinian and post-Einsteinian physics, quantum theory, and Jungian psychology. I myself, as a non-traditional 'seeker', was very interested in it at one time.

'Seth' is a lot more sophisticated, witty and apparently more intelligent than the syrupy 'spirit guides' of earlier years. He presents a worldview where each of us lives through many 'reincarnational' lifetimes, except that—from his discarnate point of view—they are simultaneous, not successive, and all of them are facets of a single conscious 'entity', which is in turn only a one aspect of a greater 'entity', and so on in ascending hierarchical order, all the way up to 'All That Is' or 'The Multidimensional God'. Seth also, like many modern physicists, speaks of 'probable realities', and teaches that whenever we choose a course of action from a number of alternatives, other 'probable selves' choose to actualize the alternatives we rejected, so that every possibility of experience is lived out, in one probable world or another. Our various probable selves are also capable, under certain conditions, of communicating with each other, enabling us to choose different and more positive probable futures. And as we simultaneously live many probable lives, so God actualizes Himself in many probable universes, or probable versions of Himself, which is why He is called 'The Multidimensional God'.

Traces of valid esoteric doctrines can be found in the Seth teachings. The idea of God's multidimensionality reminds one of Frithjof Schuon's 'maya-in-divinis', the doctrine that the entire world of manifestation exists as a potential multiplicity within the essentially unitary nature of God, or the Sufi concept of the multiplicity of the Divine Names—analogous to the 'Divine Energies' of St Gregory Palamas—each of which contains all the others. And a doctrine similar to Ibn al-'Arabi's of the primordial longing of the 'permanent archetypes' (*ayan al-thabita*) to be cosmically actualized by the Breath of the Merciful (*nafas-al-Rahman*) via that poignant, nostalgic aspect of the Divine creativity which Henry Corbin, in *Creative Imagination in the Sufism of Ibn 'Arabi*, names 'theopathic', can be found in *The Seth Material*.

Seth teaches that the material world is recreated moment-by-moment, the doctrine called in Islam 'occasionalism'—an ironic slip-of-the-tongue, since he classes Islam as a second-rate religion, far inferior to Christianity, even as both are inferior to Buddhism. And Ibn al-'Arabi's concept of one's 'Lord' as the personal face of the transpersonal Absolute which is turned toward oneself alone is echoed in Seth's statement that '[the] portion of *All That Is* that is aware of itself as you . . . can be called upon for help when necessary. . . . *This portion that knows itself as you, and as more than you, is the personal God, you see*' (*The Seth Material*, p 270). But the whole thing is transposed to a psychic level where the dominant paradigm is 'the adventurous exploration of Being through the development of one's psychic powers,' and is sprinkled with serious errors, such as the idea (from *The Seth Material*, p 267) that if All That Is had not solved the problem of how finite entities could be actualized within the context of the Absolute and Infinite (a question adequately answered in the Kabbalah by the doctrine of *Tsim-Tsum*, God's creative withdrawal into His own Essence to 'make room' for created beings), then the entire universe would have been insane, or that All That Is is eternally in search for a God greater than Himself, Whom He is not sure exists.

This last teaching is none other than a misunderstanding of the traditional doctrine of the relationship between God and Godhead, *Saguna Brahman* and *Nirguna Brahman*, Being, and Beyond-being, which asserts (in the formulation of René Guénon) that Being, far from searching for Beyond-being, is precisely the *affirmation* of Beyond-being. Certain Muslim writers, it is true, speak of the longing of Being for That which is beyond it, deriving the word *Allah* from a root which denotes 'nostalgia'. The nostalgia of Being for Beyond-being is, however, the eternal plunging of the personal God back into His own Essence; it is not a restless uncertainty on His part as to whether this Essence exists. Here we can see how the Seth material draws upon, and distorts, a much deeper stratum of esoteric teaching than the old spirit guides, or even the Theosophists and occultists, were able to get their hands on.

Nonetheless Seth's concept of God, at least according some texts, is enlightening in many ways. On p 241 of *Seth Speaks*, he says:

the term, a supreme being, is in itself distortive, for you naturally project the qualities of human nature upon it. If I told you that God was an idea, you would not understand what I meant, for you do not understand the dimensions in which an idea has its reality, or the energy it can originate and propel. You do not believe in ideas in the same way that you believe in physical objects, so if I tell you that God is an idea, you will misinterpret this to mean that God is less than real—nebulous, without reality, without purpose, and without motive action.

Partly through passages like this in the Seth material, I came to an understanding that objective Ideas are not abstractions but rather densely-packed, conscious realities, in relation to which the psychic and material planes are relatively abstract—which is why Islamic theosophy, like that of Suhrawardi for example, can represent the Platonic Ideas as angels. I am grateful to 'Seth' for helping me toward this perception; I am not grateful for his association of such truths with deceptive falsehoods. If I had not broken that association, I would never have arrived at the doorway of orthodoxy. And the above passage itself is distorted in many ways. Firstly, God in His deepest Reality is 'super-essential', beyond even the 'archangelic' realm of eternal, intelligible, living, conscious and powerful Ideas. And secondly, to divorce Ideas from Personhood, as Seth is doing when he complains about the term 'supreme being', is to push those Ideas in an abstract direction. Personhood, as so many today seem to think, is not the realm of the ego and its banality; ego-consciousness, as an edited version of Personhood conditioned by collective psychic attitudes, is closer to impersonal abstraction than it is to the truth of living persons. Just as the mystery of Ideas or symbols is that they are actually living, conscious entities, so the mystery of persons is that they are also Ideas, symbols, Divine Energies, Names of God. To separate the symbolic from the personal nature of Reality is to render persons banal, and symbols abstract.

Even more accurate than the above passage is this rendition of the Divine Nature from *Seth Speaks*, pp 245–246:

God is more than the sum of all the probable systems of reality He has created, and yet He is within each one of these, without exception. He is therefore within each man and woman. He is also within each spider, shadow, and frog, and this is what man does not like to admit. . . . On the other hand, He is human, in that He is a portion of each individual; and within the vastness of His experience He holds an 'idea-shape' of Himself as human, to which you can relate. He literally was made flesh to dwell amongst you, for He forms your flesh in that He is responsible for the energy that gives vitality and validity to your private multidimensional self, which in turn forms your image in accordance with your own ideas.

It is in passages such as this that Jane/Seth approaches the level of traditional metaphysics, such as that of Ibn al-'Arabi. The traditional doctrine of Transcendence and Immanence is clearly expressed, as well as the esoteric concept of the Archetype of Man *in divinis*. Nonetheless the description of God as a 'portion' of the individual is incorrect; and there is also a danger that the centrality of the human form in terrestrial existence — which includes, as an enacted symbol of this centrality, the uniqueness of Christ's incarnation — may be obscured by Seth's undeniably true description of God's Immanence as a cosmic Incarnation. But the Seth material does not always emanate from so high a level of understanding, and when it falls short of this level it falls pretty far, as we shall see. (For example, on p 280 of *The Nature of Personal Reality*, Seth — like Madame Blavatsky — speaks of times when 'the lines between species were not completely drawn,' when 'men and animals mixed.')

In *The Nature of Personal Reality*, p 480, Seth says that, at least in relation to individuals, that 'Perfection is not being, for all being is in a state of becoming. This does not mean that all being is in a state of becoming perfect, but in a state of becoming more itself.' This is Seth's re-statement of Jung's idea of 'individuation', most likely picked out of Jane's unconscious, which, when applied to the human individual, tends to drive a wedge between self-actualization and self-transcendence. In my opinion, it would be better to say that I become more myself by more deeply realizing the Self within me, by better learning to see my contingent selfhood and the dimensional universe it inhabits from that Absolute perspective. And, in ontological terms (like process theology, and all the other modern errors which subordinate being to becoming) it denies the Perfection of God on the level of pure Being. God's perfection, His 'Self-actualization' insofar as He is 'pure Act', is in danger here of being defined solely in terms of His creativity — as when, on p 241 of *Seth Speaks*, it is said that 'God . . . is first of all a creator. . . .' But He is not, first of all, a creator. First of all, He is Himself, One without a second, with no need to 'exteriorize' Himself as the universe. On the level of pure Being He is the only Reality, beyond 'interior' and 'exterior'; creation, though virtual within Him, is perfectly one with His essential Nature. God does not have to 'prove Himself' through creativity. He emanates the universe simply because there is no barrier in His Nature to prevent this from happening. Nonetheless, on the level where He exists as Creator in relation to this universe, He consciously wills to create, though not as an arbitrary decision. As Einstein said, 'God does not play dice with the universe.' Because God is Act, there is no border in Him between what He Is and what He chooses.

The tendency to exalt becoming over being, like the need to multiply entities and probable universes and spacetime dimensions, is based in part on an inability to conceive of the Eternity of the Divine Nature as anything other than a kind of petrification or stagnation, a dead, static condition that invalidates and freezes all creative motion—whereas, in reality, Eternity is alive with its own stillness, eternally releasing all possibilities into dimensional existence simply by transcending them. In Taoist terms, It accomplishes everything precisely by doing nothing.

Seth/Jane's worship of creativity and becoming at the expense of the limpid peace and radiance of pure Being seems to be based, as it is with most people, on a fear of the loss or invalidation of the self. On p 182 of *Seth Speaks*, Seth warns:

> There is nothing more deadly than nirvana. At least your Christian concepts give you some twilight hopes of a stifling and boring paradise, where your individuality can at least express itself, and nirvana extends no such comfort. Instead it offers you the annihilation of your personality, in a bliss that destroys the integrity of your being. Run from such bliss!

Apart from the misrepresentation of nirvana as literal self-annihilation— Buddhist doctrine considers both the belief in self-annihilation of the Buddha in Nirvana and the belief in his continued self-existence as imbalanced extremes, and therefore errors—and an idea of the Christian paradise that only someone dead to all poetic values could possibly believe in, given the thundering, jeweled, multidimensional and living radiance of the Heavenly Jerusalem in the 21st and 22nd chapters of *Apocalypse*, comparable to Krishna's visionary revelation of his Universal Form in the *Bhagavad-Gita*— this bad spiritual advice simply denotes a fear of 'dying' to a lower and narrower level of being so as to be re-born on a higher and wider one. This is undoubtedly why Jane, under Seth's tutelage, is at such pains to stretch, expand, transform and multiply her psychic self: the same inborn, primary human fear of dying to the subjective psyche so as to be reborn in, and as, the Absolute Objective Spirit. Better reincarnation, simultaneous or otherwise, and a hundred probable universes, than that single death into greater Life. As Seth/Jane says on p 282 of *Seth Speaks*, 'Development unfolds in all directions. The soul is not ascending a series of stairs, each one representing a new and higher point of development.' This *is* literally true of the soul, but it is not true of the *metanoia* by which soul is transcended and Spirit realized. It can be applied to creativity, therefore, but not to contemplation.

On pp 481–482 of *The Nature of Personal Reality*, Seth states the contradiction and the dilemma:

> There is nothing more pompous than false humility. Many people who consider themselves <u>truth seekers</u> and spiritual are filled with it. They often use religious terms to express themselves. They will say, 'I am nothing, but the spirit of God moves through me, and if I do any good it is because of God's spirit and not my own,' or, 'I have no ability of my own. Only the power of God has any ability.'
>
> Now: In those terms you *are* the power of God manifested. You are not pow<u>erless</u>. To the contrary. Through your being the power of God is strengthened, for <u>you are</u> a portion of what He is. You are not simply an insignificant, innocuous lump of clay through which He decides to show Himself.

This is a highly significant passage, both for the truth it expresses and for the error it reveals. If anyone wants to know just how a misunderstanding of Christianity, as well as of the Eastern religions, has spawned the New Age, it's all here.

Certainly people such as Seth describes do exist; it is possible to use the truth that all power and goodness are ascribable to God alone as a way of denying spiritual pride—since one secretly identifies one's *ego* with this all-good and all-powerful Being—as well as of holding on to one's powerlessness and victimhood, as if one were to wait for a God-given miracle of levitation instead of getting out of bed in the morning. But, as should be obvious, this is not what Christ meant when he said, 'Why callest thou me good? None is good, save one, that is, God' (Luke 18:19). It is only a *shadow* of this truth—and to define a truth in terms of its shadow is just as unfair, and as inaccurate, as to define a loving, intelligent and courageous human being in terms of, say, a slight stutter or a facial tic. It's a cheap shot.

As Seth says, I am the power of God manifested. If, however, I ascribe this power to the limited, ego-bound part of myself, I miss the point: that the ego may be the recipient—or perhaps the thief—but God is the Source. To put the ego in the place of God is to block the current of divine vitality and enter the world of shadows. But if I ascribe all goodness and truth and power to God, while realizing that I am nothing in myself but a manifestation of Him, the 'resistance' to this current is overcome. If I am nothing in myself, then I am all God. If, however, I see myself as a *part* of God through whose being 'the power of God is strengthened,' as if I in my minuscule creaturehood could somehow add something to the Infinite, then I am merely partial. And when the consequences of this partiality arrive, when my 'co-creatorship' is revealed as an arrogation to myself of something that is not mine, I will appear as an 'insignificant lump of clay,' a clenched, sullen unresponsiveness to God's grace and power. Ego-identification with God *is* resistance to God; Promethean arrogance is the hidden reverse side of false humility. In William Blake's words, 'Shame is Pride's cloak.' But if I am really nothing in the face of the Glory of God, then the insignificant lump of clay who thinks it can resist that Glory is dissolved.

The dissolution of the ego, however, is not the denial or suppression or invalidation of the human person. In my personhood, I am a living face of God; the ego is simply all that stands between me and this knowledge. My recognized nothingness is nothing but my liberation from the illusory burden of my own self-creation. In Sufi terms, the other side of my annihilation in God—*fana*—is my subsistence in God—*baqa*. Subsisting in Him, I know myself as completely contingent upon Him; I see how I, in my unique personhood, am precisely as God wills me to be. God recognizes a certain aspect of Himself in me alone; no other person, object or entity can fill that role. And the root of my uniqueness is my annihilation. It is in light of this principle that the beautiful passage in *Seth Speaks*, p 384, should be understood: '. . . each man knows within himself that his conscious life is dependent upon a greater dimension of actuality. This greater dimension cannot be actualized in a three-dimensional system, yet the knowledge of this greater dimension floods outward from the innermost heart of being, transforming all it touches.'

Seth is supposed to have the power to survey all space and time, as well as realms beyond them. He speaks on lost civilizations, social and spiritual conditions at the time of Christ, and probable future developments in society and the human psyche. Yet his knowledge of both Christianity and Eastern religions—something which can be checked against actual texts and the knowledge of living teachers—more closely resembles that of an self-educated New Age housewife interested in religion and spirituality. On p 273 of *The Nature of Personal Reality*, Seth claims that 'Many . . . Eastern schools also stress—as do numerous spiritualistic schools—the importance of "the unconscious levels of the self", and teach you to mistrust the conscious mind.' This may or may not be true of spiritualism, particularly as influenced by Jungian psychology, but it is not really characteristic of the 'Eastern schools' of which I am acquainted. The Vedanta stresses the need to become *conscious* of our identity with the indwelling Absolute; it does not teach us to rely on it as an unconscious substratum. The word 'buddha' means *awake*, not asleep; the central practice of Theravadin Buddhism is *mindfulness*, not unconsciousness. Seth, on the other hand, often spoke through Jane Roberts when she was so unconscious that she had no idea what she (or Seth) was saying until she emerged from trance. It would seem that a certain amount of 'projection' is operating here.

On p 400 of *Seth Speaks* the 'Hebrew god' is singled out as a symbol of man's ego in emergence from an earlier archaic identity with nature (reflecting the concepts of anthropologists like Levy-Bruhl, who was an important influence on Carl Jung and his follower Erich Neumann, author of *The Origin and History of Consciousness*); 'God becomes man's ally <u>against</u> nature.' This Hebrew religion of an 'overseer god . . . angry and just and sometimes cruel' is opposed to the ancient polytheisms which recognized the sanctity of nature via the concept of an all-pervading High God of which the various gods are expressions. It would seem that Seth is referring to the pagan fertility religions of Africa and the Near East. Yet the Babylonian god Marduk is a much clearer symbol of the emergent ego than Yahweh, since he heroically slays the archaic female sea-monster Tiamat and creates the celestial and earthly orders out of the fragments of her slaughtered body, though there are some indications in the Old Testament that a similar mythic creation-struggle might at one time have been attributed to Yahweh. And isn't the pagan god Moloch, to whom children were sacrificed by being burned alive, a better symbol of the cruelty of the ego, since Yahweh is also loving and merciful? Perhaps; but since the *zeitgeist*, then and now, favors the re-habilitation of Paganism and the mis-representation of Judeo-Christianity, these facts must be ignored. On p 401, the anti-natural religion of the Hebrews is opposed to those earlier religions where men learned by communicating with a living nature. What, then, are we to make of the rich natural symbolism of the Book of *Job*, or of the Old Testament story of the prophet Elijah being fed by ravens? And how can we interpret the following passage from the Hebrew *Book of Wisdom*?

> It is he [Yahweh] who gave me unerring knowledge of what exists, to know the structure of the world and the activity of the elements, the beginning and middle of the times, the alternation of the solstices and the changes of the seasons, the cycles of the year and the constellations of the stars, the natures of animals and the tempers of wild beasts, the powers of spirits and the reasonings of men, the varieties of plants and the virtues of roots; I

learned both what is secret and what is manifest.

〜 WISDOM 7:17–21

Seth/Jane seems to be a good psychologist, and to know a great deal about how material reality emerges from the psychic domain. I have no doubt that some of what he/she teaches on this level is accurate and useful. He/she has also proved him/herself to be a highly skilled clairvoyant. But given that his/her understanding of what transcends the psychic dimension is radically incomplete and in some cases distorted, it's difficult to separate the wheat from the chaff.

One of the central principles of Seth's teaching, and of many other New Age philosophies, is that *belief creates reality*: 'You make your own reality,' he says; 'There is no other rule. Knowing this is the secret of creativity' (*The Nature of Personal Reality*, p16). But what exactly is a belief? It cannot exist in a vacuum; it must be a belief *about* something, a conviction that something or other is actually the case. But if all reality is created by belief, then nothing objectively exists for a belief to be *about*. And if we become *aware* that reality is created by belief, rather than belief conforming to something which transcends it—namely, reality—then belief, the conviction that something or other is actually the case, cannot exist. To say that belief creates reality, instead of saying that reality is really there, which belief either conforms to or departs from, is to make belief effectively impossible.

On p20 of *The Nature of Personal Reality*, Seth says, 'You take your beliefs about reality as truth. . . .' And, on p26:

> You must realize that any idea you accept as truth is a belief that you hold. You must, then, take the next step and say, "It is not necessarily true, even though I believe it." You will, I hope, learn to discard all beliefs that imply basic limitations.

He is teaching, in other words, that beliefs must be distinguished from reality, and that reality, in essence, is limitless. I certainly have no quarrel with this. But on p24, he asserts, as a fundamental principle, that 'You create your own reality'—by means of belief. Instead of distinguishing reality from belief so that belief can conform more directly to reality, Seth seems to want to distinguish belief from reality so we can change reality to suit our needs. He implies that if we believe something because it is true, we are simply being narrow minded, especially when such a belief limits our options.

To teach both that reality is beyond belief and that it is created by belief is a clear contradiction. The contradiction arises because, according to Seth, 'reality' is neither an objective material world nor an objective metaphysical order, but the 'self'; according to another of his fundamental principles (also p 24), 'The Self Is Not Limited'. But of course our contingent, subjective egos are limited by definition; the only unlimited Self is the indwelling *atman*, God as the Absolute Subject. Is this the 'Self' Seth is referring to? Let us see.

On p 16, right after asserting that 'You make your own reality,' Seth qualifies his statement: 'I have spoken of 'you', yet this must not be confused with the 'you' that you often think you are—the ego alone, for the ego is only a portion of You; it is that expert part of you that deals directly with the contents of your conscious mind, and is concerned most directly with the material portions of your experience.' So an unlimited 'You' is being implied, a You with a capital 'Y', virtually identical with God. But Seth also teaches that each of us creates, via belief, a uniquely personal world. Since God creates *all* worlds, however, this greater You of which the conscious ego is only a portion cannot be God. So we have here, as in a great deal of other New Age doctrine, a confusion between the contingent and Absolute selves. 'Each of you,' says Seth, 'regardless of position, status, circumstances or physical condition, is in control of your own personal experience' (p xxii). In reality, however, only God has absolute control, even over a limited area of existence such as a single individual life. My limited, conditioned selfhood, even if it transcends my day-to-day conscious ego, cannot arrogate to itself that power, as was perhaps demonstrated when Jane Roberts died relatively young of a crippling disease. Only if I have realized the *atman* can 'I' claim that power, because it is now God, not me, who is saying 'I Am' within me.

Here we encounter the inevitable error of psychic philosophies that deny (or, like the Seth doctrines, are uncertain about) the existence of an objective metaphysical order, yet still strive to transcend materialism: they are forced to see the world as a creation of the subjective psyche. Subjective belief must determine material conditions, because the only alternative is that material conditions determine belief, thus making consciousness an epiphenomenon of matter, as in Marxist materialism. But just as consciousness cannot be reduced to matter because, in the words of C.S. Lewis, 'the knowledge of a thing is not one of the thing's parts,' neither can it be defined as the product of arbitrary belief operating in a vacuum, as a projection willed by an incarnate or discarnate entity, or a mass of them. A belief is not a sovereign act of creation, but a more or less accurate image of something which is already there, prior to our belief in it. Insofar as belief conforms to reality, it liberates. Insofar as it departs from reality, it imprisons. Nor is a belief to be considered true only when it denies the limitations of the individual self, and false when it asserts them. Some individual limitations are the product of false and unnecessary beliefs; others represent the necessary limits of all contingent existence. Belief conforms to reality not by denying the limits of the individual self, but by presenting us with a vision of the Absolute Self beyond, and within, all contingent individualities. No amount of honing our creative skills or expanding and multiplying our psychic perceptions can add up to the realization of this Self.

In *The Nature of Personal Reality*, p xxii, Seth says: 'The world as you know it is a picture of your expectations. The world as the race of man knows it is a materialization en masse of your individual expectations.' In a way this is true, though not if we take it to mean that an individual or a race can ever have total and conscious control over events. This 'materialization' is not an act of creation however, but an act of attention. Our individual and mass experience is partly based on what aspects of God's eternal creation we choose to pay attention to; but this field of perceptual choice is also limited—providentially limited—by the human form in which God has created us. That form sets us between a uniquely plastic mode-of-perception which is virtually capable of perceiving anything in earthly experience, as well as in higher planes of reality which constitute the living 'stem' of this experience, and our ability to contemplate the Absolute. Our delegated task, by which we realize in space and time, as well in higher psychic and spiritual planes, our eternal form in the mind of God, is not to pursue all the possibilities inherent in our plastic mode of perception—to do so would be to dissolve in the boundless, and lose the human form—but rather to subordinate this mode of perception, in contemplation, to the Absolute, until the stage is reached where we see, as the universe, precisely what God sees in us, since we see with God's eye.

We don't like being reminded of the truism that our belief only liberates us if it conforms to reality, because the word 'reality' now largely denotes for us 'material reality', and we rebel against the reductionism that our own false definition implies. We rightly feel that there must be something beyond gross material conditions, but see nowhere to turn in search of it but to our own subjectivity. And since we have greater power to control our fantasies— or so it seems—than to affect material reality, we want to believe that we can somehow control material reality *by means of our fantasies*. After all, isn't that what every successful inventor does? The fantasy of flight produced the airplane; the fantasy of remote viewing produced television. We forget that the inventor, to be successful, had to conform his ideas more strictly to the norms of objective material reality than we probably ever will.

Yet there is such a thing as creativity. There is the actualization of possibilities. Such possibilities are not simply arbitrary beliefs made actual in space and time, however, but rather objective realities which exist on a higher plane of the Great Chain of Being than the subjective psyche; this is why creativity can, under the right circumstances, be a part of contemplation—or rather, why contemplation must be at the basis of all true creativity, if it is not to lead us into spiritual darkness. Beyond the subjective psyche with its beliefs lies the objective psychic plane with its living reflections of the eternal archetypes; beyond these reflections lie the archetypes themselves, as revealed in contemplation, which transcend the psychic plane entirely. It is true that the material plane as a whole is a partial manifestation of the psychic plane, which is a partial manifestation of the celestial or archetypal plane, which is a partial manifestation of the Logos, which is a partial manifestation of God. But this does not mean, as Seth asserts, that the conscious beings of the universe create the material plane as a mass materialization of belief. It is God who creates the universe, not us. Since psyche is higher than matter, and therefore functions as its proximate cause, we can say that God creates the material plane *through* us, but only after creating us first. The role of our beliefs is either to lead us further into material reality and the experiences it provides, or else to conform us more closely to the spiritual archetype through which God created us, and ultimately to the Creator Himself. But whether our beliefs draw us to further elaborate the planes of psychic and material manifestation—through art and technology, for example—or to envision, contemplate and unite with our spiritual archetype, they never create anything new. Beliefs undeniably alter experience; on the most fundamental level—a level so deep that it transcends all the vicissitudes of conditional life—they are the only things which can. Whether we are saved or lost, deluded or enlightened has everything to do, at one stage of the game, with belief. But they cannot create; all they can do is condition, limit, modulate. Only if *reality were individual experience*, as the psychic philosophies claim, could beliefs create, and only if there were nothing ontologically higher than the psychic plane would we have to define reality as individual experience, rather than defining individual experience as a more or less accurate vision of reality. We may be 'sub-creators', then, but we are not co-creators. Only God is *Rab el-alamin*, Lord of the Worlds. We may construct, and de-construct; only God creates.

As for Seth's doctrine of a multiplicity of reincarnational lifetimes experienced simultaneously from the standpoint of an inner self, I'm entirely willing to accept the premise that Charles Upton is one facet of a greater 'entity', other facets of whom exist in other places and times, past present and future, an entity which in turn is one facet of an even greater living consciousness. (Seth calls individuals inhabiting my own time who are related to me via a common archetype 'counterparts'.) This is more or less in line with the traditional image of the Great Chain of Being as an inverted tree (cf. the Tree of Life in *Genesis*) whose roots are hidden in the 'sky', in the Formless Absolute. In my own case, such facets *may* include the poet William Blake, the Kabbalist Isaac Luria (or his student Hayyim Vital), and a woman named Theodosia, who seems to have been a Platonist Christian philosopher living in the eastern Mediterranean area in perhaps the 3rd century. As the congregation of a church all share the same patron saint, so I undoubtedly share with many people I will never meet the same 'patron archetype'. (According to the doctrine of Ibn al-'Arabi, every 'friend of God' within Islam is in the family of a certain prophet. Muhammad is the 'trunk' of the Tree of Life for all Muslims, while Ibn al-'Arabi's own particular branch, upon which he was so-to-speak a 'leaf', is the prophet Jesus.) I'm also willing to accept that all the 'lifetimes' united by a common entity are perceived by that entity as simultaneous; such 'relative eternity' is termed 'aeonian time' in Orthodox Christian theology. What I do not accept is that this is a description of reincarnation. Charles Upton is not a reincarnation of Isaac Luria or William Blake, any more than the branch of a tree is actually a twig on some separate branch. We are united not horizontally, branch-to-branch, as if connected by a parasitic vine, but vertically, by virtue of the fact that we spring from the same trunk. Therefore the only *living* way for me to contact the other eternal souls who spring from the same archetype or Name of God as myself is through that archetype itself. To attempt to make contact with them horizontally, as if they were former (or future) lifetimes of Charles Upton, is to solipsistically imprison them within the shell of my ego, violate their integrity and trespass on the ground of their unique personal relationships with our common archetype. It is to relate to them not as complete human souls, but only as ghosts. And once I fully realize our archetype, then such horizontal excursions through multidimensional time to try and contact the lost facets of 'my' being become unnecessary. Such excursions may in some cases represent the early stages of the dawning of that archetype; for me, perhaps they did. But if I had never transcended the reincarnational paradigm, if I had never understood that unity is ontologically higher than multidimensionality, I would have been blown to the four winds.

In *Beyond the Post-modern Mind*, pp 39–40, Huston Smith notes that when postmodernism denies any objective reality outside that 'constructed' by a given culture, this is logically equivalent to the denial of any reality outside that constructed by the individual (and ultimately, I would add, by the complexes, sub-personalities, and disrelated random moments of perception within that individual). 'Self-enclosed, cultural-linguistic, social subjectivities' are nothing more than 'social or collective solipsisms'.

Here is where the Seth mythology reveals itself to be a popular form of postmodern ideology. If every subjective point-of-view is absolute, then there can be no relationship between them. And if there can be no relationship, then all experiences, all objects, and all other people are only aspects of 'me'. So if I need to relate to 'others', and which of us does not, the only possible approach is for me to relate to other 'me's': former lifetimes, future lifetimes, probable versions and present-day counterparts of Charles Upton.

This postmodern narcissism, or solipsism, inseparable from the denial of objective reality, is easily discernible in the Seth's epistemology. On p127 of *The Seth Material*, he uses a wineglass held in Jane's hand, and visible to two other people in the room, to claim that

> None of you sees the glass that the other see. . . . Each of the three of you creates your own glass, in your own personal perspective. Therefore you have three different physical glasses here. . . . Each individual actually creates an entirely different object. . . .'

Immanuel Kant denied, in effect, that the three people in that room could ever experience the wineglass as a 'thing-in-itself'; all they could perceive were three irreducible sets of 'phenomena'. Still the glass-in-itself, the *noumenon*, was real. It remained for postmodern philosophy, and Seth, to deny the reality of the noumenon itself. (When frustrated by such philosophical degeneration, I sometimes relieve myself by imagining that I am in the lobby of a hotel where a conference on postmodernism is going on. A woman attending the conference comes up to me and asks me for directions to the parking garage. 'That's up to you,' I reply. 'Your garage is wherever you construct it to be. Beyond that, I can't help you; I'm parked in a different garage.') And if anyone object that Seth's absolutization of individual points-of-view is not really solipsism, since he grants the same 'absolute' status to the perception of *every* individual, not just Jane Roberts or Charles Upton, I ask that person to consider the following statement from *The Nature of Personal Reality*, p4:

> You project your thoughts, feelings and expectations outward, then you perceive them as the outside reality. When it seems to you that others are

observing you, you are observing yourself from the standpoint of your own projections.

In other words, I can never be a valid experience for others, nor can they be so for me. Objective knowledge of others as persons — in other words, human love — is philosophically ruled out. Perhaps the only exit from Sartre's 'hell is other people,' at least for the full-fledged postmodern solipsist, is, 'but fortunately there *are* no other people. However, to be fair to Seth/Jane, I must also quote an example of the opposite conception:

> The inner world of each man and woman is connected with the inner world of the earth. The spirit becomes flesh. Part of each individual's soul, then, is intimately connected with what we call the world's soul, or the soul of the earth.
> The smallest blade of grass, or flower, is aware of this connection, and without reasoning comprehends its position, its uniqueness and its source of vitality. The atoms and molecules that compose *all* objects, whether it be the body of a person, a table, a stone or a frog, know the great passive thrust of creativity that lies beneath their own existence, and upon which their individuality floats, clear, distinct and unassailable.
> ⌒THE NATURE OF PERSONAL REALITY, p4.)

What is far from certain here is whether or not Seth/Jane realizes that this vision, undeniably beautiful as it is, and true on its own level, contradicts the solipsistic one above. If all objects are sentient, then how can three people observing 'one' wineglass create three different physical wineglasses? Doesn't the wineglass 'know' it is a wineglass, a thing-in-itself, even if no one else is looking at it? And if three observers create three wineglasses, why can't the same three observers create three Charles Uptons, given that both I and the wineglass are sentient beings? If the observer creates the thing observed, then how can it be true to say that 'when it seems to you that others are observing you, you are observing yourself from the standpoint of your own projections'?

At this point we are obviously stuck in a vicious circle of paradox, one which Frithjof Schuon deals with decisively in his essay 'The Enigma of Diversified Subjectivity':

> To speak of a diversified, hence multiple, subjectivity, is no doubt inevitable since the world is what it is, yet it is nonetheless a contradiction in terms because, logically, subjectivity and plurality exclude each other. Indeed, the knowing subject is unique in the face of an indefinite multitude of objects

known or to be known, and this irremovable — though illusory — uniqueness
has about it something absolute from its own vantage point, that of consciousness precisely: no individual can cease being 'I', and empirically there is
no other 'I' than his own.

The problem can be resolved only in a metaphysical reality, the invisible
immanence of which eliminates the apparent absurdity of a subject that is on
the one hand unique by definition and on the other as innumerable as the
objects; the subject paradoxically becomes an object in its turn ... [in the
face of] an absolute Subject that projects contingent subjects in a mysteriously contradictory, yet necessarily homogeneous, fashion.

⁓ROOTS OF THE HUMAN CONDITION, pp 46–47

In other words, as soon as my contingent subjectivity, by virtue of my self-
transcendence on the spiritual Path, becomes merely one more object of the
Divine Witness, to Whom all other subjectivities are objects as well, the
paradox of subjectivity's undeniable plurality vs. its undeniable uniqueness is
also transcended. It is precisely this absolute Subject which I have been calling 'objective reality' since it transcends our contingent, individual subjectivities, and since, in Schuon's wsords (p 46), 'For man, even the Divine Subject
is an object, except at the summit of mystical union.' The 'objective' (because
Absolute) Divine Subject is the indwelling Knower of all that is to be
known. Things can therefore be things-in-themselves, because God knows
them as they are, and in so doing creates them. We witness phenomena; He
gazes, as it were, upon the noumenon, precisely because He witnesses all
things as Himself. And we can mysteriously participate in this witnessing,
not through our contingent subjectivities, but by virtue of the Absolute
Subject, the Divine Witness within us. So the wineglass is indeed a
wineglass — not because, as Seth maintains, the three people viewing it are
telepathically adjusting their subjective perceptions each to the other,
instant-by-instant, but because any material object which can be known,
validly even though not identically, by more than one contingent subject is
thereby a sign of the Absolute Subject within every knower. Matter thus
stands below the contingent subjectivities of the psychic plane as a mirror
and witness to the celestial realities which stand above it. The imperfect but
inexorable convergence of our subjective, phenomenal visions of the material
world testifies to the transcendent reality of the noumenon, which is at once
the hidden Essence of phenomena and the hidden Witness Who realizes
the 'voidness' of phenomena in the act of witnessing that Essence as Himself.
This is precisely why the universe is sacred, and why, incidentally, cyberspace is profane (cyberspace: a way of being of the world while not being in it).

When my contingent subjectivity has become objective to the Absolute Witness, an infinite number of perceptual standpoints becomes virtually available—I say virtually, because when my contingent subjectivity returns in an attempt to access these standpoints in order to make use of them, they disperse.

The dawning of visions of former lifetimes can be a sign of the dissolution of the ego, as when the Buddha, upon enlightenment, remembered all his former lives. The same is true of the vision of probable selves. The same is true of present-time counterparts: when I 'lose my life in order to find it,' then I 'love my neighbor as myself' because I *see* him as myself—or rather, I see both of us as sharing the same Divine Self. If I know that 'it is not I who live, but Christ lives in me,' then I understand precisely how 'ye are all gods, and sons of the Most High.'

The number of former and future lifetimes, present counterparts and probable selves is infinite, since it ultimately includes all sentient beings and all manifest forms. But to the degree that those former lifetimes, counterparts and probable selves are seen as 'mine', the ego has not been transcended. To view them as widening my own area of selfhood, as endowing me with greater knowledge, vitality and creativity is to balk on the threshold of self-transcendence. It is to trade mysticism for magic.

In the Seth doctrines, creativity takes the place of salvation, self-transcendence or enlightenment. It is true that creativity can help us go beyond many of the limiting beliefs which compose our habitual ego-identities, simply because the delivery into the manifest world of a conception greater than we have yet entertained demands that we do so. And if out of laziness, cowardice or an inaccurate self-assessment we 'bury our talent', refusing to engage in the creative struggle demanded by our nature—demanded, in other words, by the God within us—then we will never attain Liberation. But creativity, in itself, is not enough to liberate us. Its energy or *shakti* is directed away from Source towards Its manifestation, while the spiritual Path requires that *shakti* be directed away from manifestation and towards its Source. In other words, contemplation is higher than creativity. And one of the things contemplation teaches us is that only God creates. Contemplation, as it dissolves skin after skin of our ego, may liberate floods of creativity (not all of it, and certainly not the highest types of it, in shapes we can presently understand), since every veil removed from God's face allows more of His Infinite Creative Radiance to shine through. But contemplation of Truth is eternally higher than expression of Truth. Contemplation can exist without expression, but expression cannot exist without contemplation.

According to Seth, there is no such thing as evil. '[A] belief in the good without a belief in the evil may seem highly unrealistic to you. This belief, however, is the best kind of insurance you can have, both during physical life and afterward' (*Seth Speaks*, p192).

> While this may seem like the sheerest Pollyanna, nevertheless there is no evil in basic terms. This does not mean that you do not meet with effects that appear evil, but ... all seeming opposites are other faces of the one supreme drive toward creativity.
> ⁓ THE NATURE OF PERSONAL REALITY, p283

On one level, this is certainly true. Traditional metaphysics teaches that God is both the only Reality and the sovereign Good, whereas evil is a *privatio boni*, a deprivation or diminishment in that Goodness and Reality, a fall in the direction of an unreality which, in its dire effects, is all-too-real. But some of the conclusions drawn by Seth from this principle are far from consistent. On p166 of *The Nature of Personal Reality*, for example, he says:

> Demons of any kind are the result of your beliefs. They are born from a belief in 'unnatural' guilt. You may personify them. You may even meet them in your experience, but if so they are still the product of your immeasurable creativity, though formed by your guilt and your belief in it.

This is like saying 'there are no child molesters or serial killers; these are merely the results of your belief.' On the level of consciousness where God is recognized as the only Reality, there are no demons, no angels, no other people and no 'me', at least as independent realities; there are only the infinite faces of the One God, faces of Mercy and Beauty, of Rigor and Majesty. But if there is a 'me', a conscious being with free will, supposedly capable of creating realities (such as demons) through belief, then there are other beings, both physical and psychic, who also possess free will, and are equally capable of making choices. Demons are simply beings on subtler planes of manifestation who have chosen to rebel against their Creator, just as child molesters are people on the physical plane who have chosen to rebel against the image of God within them. Seth, however, will not admit this possibility:

> As long as you believe in a devil ... you will create one that is real enough for you, and for the others who continue to create him. Because of the energy he is given by others, he will have a certain consciousness of his own, but such a mock devil has no power or reality to those who do not believe in his existence, and who do not give him energy through their belief. He is, in other words, a superlative hallucination.
> ⁓ SETH SPEAKS, pp282–283

This is nonsense. It could certainly be said that, in a way, the German people 'created' Hitler through their beliefs—but did this mean that, once created, he had no objective reality, and no power to hurt those who did not give him their 'energy'? If Tibetan adepts really have the ability to create *tulpus*, visualized mental images become visible and solid on the material plane, then there is nothing to prevent me from being hit over the head by somebody else's 'hallucination'. And Seth does not stop short at discounting the reality of Satan; he also tries to rehabilitate him:

> Satan represents—<u>in terms of the story</u> [of the fall, the rebellious angels]—
> the part of All That Is, or God, who stepped outside of Himself, so to speak,
> and became earthbound with his creatures, offering them free will and choice
> that 'previously' had not been available. Hence you have the majestic ele-
> ments given to Satan, and the power. The earthly characteristics often
> appear as he is depicted in animal form, for he was also of course connected
> with the intuitive terrestrial attributes from which the new human con-
> sciousness would spring.
> ⌒The Nature of Personal Reality, pp 270–271

The Satan here described would seem to be a composite of the Satan of Milton (the majestic elements), the Greek Pan (the earthly, animal characteristics) and the Gnostic version of the serpent in Eden as a liberator and bringer of consciousness, as well as an alternative image of Adam as the first ancestor of man, and even of Christ, that 'portion' of God who incarnates, and offers spiritual freedom to man. All of these attributions may or may not have some symbolic validity in their own widely different contexts—but *not in terms of the story*, which is the Judeo-Christian story. In terms of *that* story, Satan represents the truth that pride and rebelliousness have their roots on an extremely high level of the Hierarchy of Being, the plane where subject/object consciousness first begins to stir. At that point the choice between acknowledging their Divine Source or turning away from It was first presented to the highest spiritual beings, and some of them chose to turn away. But *why does Seth choose to discount this particular story alone*, especially in view of the fact that it is the Judeo-Christian version he is taking off from, not the Gnostic or Pagan Greek or Miltonic one? Why is this the only meaning of the figure of Satan, out of many possible meanings, which he endeavors to hide?

Throughout the books of Jane Roberts, Seth labors to convince Jane that he is real, that he is not simply a figment of her imagination—which of course would not be the case if, as he claims, our experience is created entirely by our beliefs. On pp 15–16 of *Seth Speaks* he says:

Some of my energy is ... projected through Ruburt [Seth's masculine name for Jane], and his energy and mine both activate his physical form during our sessions. ... I am not, therefore, a product of Ruburt's subconscious, any more than he is a product of my subconscious mind. Nor am I a secondary personality, cleverly trying to undermine a precarious ego.

But if, as Seth teaches, we create our own experience, then why is Jane's experience of demons or Satan 'a superlative hallucination', and her experience of Seth a sober, objective reality? Is this glaring inconsistency perhaps based on the assumption that nothing on the psychic plane can be evil, in the sense that a serial killer is evil, because the psychic plane is morally and spiritually higher than the physical one? If so, then we are in the presence of one of the most common, and most dangerous, errors in New Age thinking: that whatever is invisible must be spiritual, and therefore good. We forget that it is the invisible psyche of the serial killer which is the author of his evil, not his physical body. All we can say for dead certain is that deception is operating here.

A further inconsistency appears on pp 284–285 of *The Nature of Personal Reality*:

Your ideas of good and evil as applied to health and illness are highly important ... if you consider illness a kind of moral stigma, then you will simply add an unneeded quality to ill health.
Such judgements are very simplistic, and ignore the great range of human motivation and experience. If you are bound and determined that 'GOD' (in capitals and quotes) creates only 'good', then any physical deficiency, illness or deformity becomes an affront to your belief, threatens it, and makes you angry and resentful. If you become ill you can hate yourself for not being what you should be—a perfect physical image made in the likeness of a perfect God.

This, again, is good psychological criticism, worthy to be applied, say, to Christian Science, or even *A Course in Miracles*. But it contradicts Seth's teaching on p 283 of the same book, that only the good is real. Perhaps Seth is really saying that our ideas of good are too narrow, that the true good of God is not to be identified with our usual sense of what would be pleasant or desirable. If so, then I have no quarrel with him. Still, his inconsistent and illogical unwillingness to admit the reality, on its own plane, of demonic evil makes it difficult for me to entirely trust his motives. Could he, for example, be trying to use the fact that physical reality is necessarily imperfect—despite his teaching that 'each of you ... is in control of your own personal experience'—to deny the *spiritual* truth that man is created in the image and likeness of God?

Seth is hazy on the concept of hierarchy. He often employs it, but in line with the contemporary prejudice against the concept, he also denies it. While asserting, on p 282 of *Seth Speaks*, that 'The soul is not ascending a series of stairs, each one representing a new and higher point of development,' elsewhere he does admit the validity of hierarchy, as in his concept of 'pyramid gestalts', according to which each conscious entity is a facet or aspect of a greater entity, all the way up to All That Is. And on pp 321–328 of *Seth Speaks* he elaborates a hierarchy of his own, composed of states-of-consciousness: state A-1-a, similar to the alpha state, where matter begins to become transparent to consciousness; A-1-b, having to do with 'group presents . . . mass probabilities, racial matters, the movement of civilization'; A-1-c, an extension of the former, where there is more participation in events; A-2, where reincarnational pasts within the present probability line can be investigated; and A-3, having to do with biological, geological and planetary history. Note, however, that all these levels of consciousness represent a deeper penetration into manifest, earthly reality. Traditional renditions of the Hierarchy of Being, on the other hand, are oriented to Absolute Reality; they cover a lot more territory. For example, the five *hadhrat* ('presences') of Sufism, in one rendition, are *jism* (the 'body'), *khayal* (the 'imagination', the psychic domain), *'aql* ('intellect', the angelic world), *Wahidiyah* ('Unity', or Being), and *Ahadiyah* ('Oneness', or Beyond-Being). In terms of this version of the Hierarchy of Being, all the levels listed by Seth have to do exclusively with *jism* as viewed from the standpoint of *khayal*. The hierarchy of Seth, since it is largely psychic and related to creative manifestation, descends to lower ontological levels as it spreads out into dimensional existence. The traditional Hierarchy of Being on the other hand, being in one sense a picture of the individual's self-transcendence on the spiritual Path, rises to higher levels, gathers and synthesizes what was scattered, and ultimately returns to its Divine Source.

The Seth material, like *A Course in Miracles*, also denies the reality of guilt:

> There is no karma to be paid off as punishment unless you believe there are crimes for which you must pay. . . . In larger terms there is no cause and effect either, though these are root assumptions in your reality.
> ⌁THE NATURE OF PERSONAL REALITY, p179

Seth seems to be using the concept of simultaneous time here as a way of sidestepping the idea of retribution, since a past crime (one might think) can only be punished in a future time. The same need to deny the meaning and validity of guilt is undoubtedly behind Seth/Jane's rejection of causality—a denial which is itself denied by the whole burden of the Seth material, which continually hammers into the reader the idea that *belief* (cause) *creates reality* (effect).

Seth's denial of the objective reality of transgression is further contradicted by his whole morality of 'natural guilt' (*The Nature of Personal Reality*, pp 167–168), where 'not going to church on Sunday' and 'having normal aggressive thoughts' are defined as 'not violations', while 'doing violence to your body, or another's' or 'doing violence to the spirit of another' are termed 'violations'. Nor are these acts violations simply because we believe they are, since 'killing while protecting your own body from death at the hands of another through immediate contact is a violation,' even if 'you believe that physical self-defense is the only way to counter such a situation.' Perhaps Seth is actually only denying that guilt can be overcome through punishment. Yet where there is violation, and therefore guilt, there will eventually be a correction, which is precisely what just punishment is. If we flee from the natural and immediate correction provided by 'natural guilt'—which seems to be Seth's term for 'conscience', although it also applies to animals— then correction must take ever more insistent forms until we are finally willing to listen to it: this is 'karmic retribution'.

Like so many other New Age teachers, Jane Roberts and her Seth were openly intolerant of traditional Christianity. According to Seth the 'Christ entity' incarnated in three different human individuals: John the Baptist, Jesus of Nazareth, and St Paul. This idea, which would seem to be a literalistic reading of the doctrine of the Trinity (represented iconically in the Eastern Orthodox tradition by the three travelers, identified as angels, who sojourned with Abraham), has the effect of eroding the central doctrine of Christianity, the Incarnation, by making it quantitative and literalistic, since according to Seth the Christ entity was 'too big to fit' in only one human vehicle. Also, according to Seth, when Christ returns he will be largely unknown—a direct inversion of the traditional doctrine that while Christ in his first advent was lowly and obscure, at least during his earthly life, his second coming will not be in suffering and sacrifice but rather in power and glory.

Seth regales us with tawdry stories of his former lifetime as a degenerate Pope, with a mistress and illegitimate children, who began to lose faith in the Church when he could not explain to himself why God would choose a degenerate like himself as His representative on earth. He claims, coyly, that one of the Gospels, 'not Mark's or John's' is a 'counterfeit' in which 'events [were] twisted to make it appear that some of them happened in a completely different context. . . .' (*The Nature of Personal Reality*, pp 486–487), after which Jane 'intuitively' determines that it is the Gospel according to Matthew—an unlikely story, since Matthew so closely parallels Mark and Luke that the three are termed 'synoptic'. The best we can say about this falsification of Christianity is that a higher spiritual doctrine is being eroded by its own lesser, psychic reflections. The worst interpretation, which seems much more likely in some cases, is that demonic influences are deliberately attacking the Christian faith. Either way the result is subversive, since a more complete and integrated doctrine is being replaced by something less adult in nature, more dissipated and childish.

Seth/Jane goes to great lengths to undermine the central doctrines of Christianity, and in the process uncovers a deep vein of inconsistency and deception. The twelve disciples were not born as men, but created as materializations of the combined energies of Jesus, John the Baptist and St Paul—*tulpus* of the Christ (*Seth Speaks*, p 244). More significantly, as in certain Gnostic heresies, Christ was not physically crucified, thus rendering his resurrection meaningless: without death, there is no triumph over death. A deluded human substitute was crucified in his place. According to *Seth Speaks*, pp 435–436:

> There was a conspiracy in which Judas played a role, in an attempt to make a martyr out of Christ. The man chosen was drugged—hence the necessity of helping him carry the cross (see Luke 23)—and he was told that he was the Christ. . . . Mary came because she was full of sorrow for the man who believed he was her son. . . . The group responsible wanted to make it appear that one particular portion of the Jews had crucified Christ. . . . The tomb was empty because [the conspirators] carted the body away. Mary Magdalene did see Christ, however, immediately after (see Matt. 28). Christ was a great psychic. He caused the wounds to appear then upon His own body, and appeared both physically and in out-of-body states to His followers. He tried, however, to explain what had happened, and His position, but those who were not in on the conspiracy would not understand, and misread his statements. Peter three times denied the Lord (*Matthew 26*), saying he did not know him, because he recognized that that person was not Christ. The plea, 'Peter, why hast thou forsaken me?' came from the man who believed he was Christ—the drugged version. Judas pointed out that man. He knew of the conspiracy, and feared the real Christ would be captured. Therefore he handed over to the authorities a man known to be a self-styled Messiah—to save, not destroy, the life of the historical Christ.

Providentially, this subversive deception breaks down in terms both of fact and of logic. The fact is that Jesus did not say 'Peter, why hast thou forsaken me?' but 'My God, my God, why hast thou forsaken me?' (Mark 15:34). And if Jesus had wanted 'to explain what had happened, and His position'—that He had never been crucified—why would he have caused wounds to appear on his body? And if He chose to go along with the conspiracy after the fact for PR purposes, then Seth is accusing Him of participating in, or at least profiting from, the kidnapping, drugging and murder of an innocent man— as would be implied, if Seth's version of events were true, by John 13:27 (the Gospel of John is accepted by Seth as one of the 'true' Gospels) where Jesus says to Judas at the last supper, 'That thou doest, do quickly'—a statement which is much better interpreted simply as proving that Jesus was not arrested against his will, since he knew Judas' plans. Furthermore, on p 284, Seth contradicts this whole story by saying that 'The Crucifixion ... *arose into the world of physical actuality* [italics mine] out of the inner reality from which your deepest intuitions and insights also spring.' So we are here in the presence of deception, intellectual corruption, and blasphemy—though when I 'bought' the Seth material, I myself couldn't see this obvious fact. Such is the gulf between the illumination of faith and 'the willing suspension of disbelief.'

Not limiting himself to Christianity, Seth also attacks Islam:

Mohammedanism fell far short. In this case the projections were of violence predominating. Love and kinship were secondary to what indeed amounted to baptism and communion through violence and blood.
    ⁓SETH SPEAKS, p 400

While I do not excuse all the excesses of Muslim warriors—or of Christian Crusaders, or of Buddhist Samurai—it is my duty to repeat that the 'five pillars of Islam' are, (1) the testimony of faith, that 'there is no god but God, and Muhammad is the prophet of God'; (2) daily prayer; (3) paying the tax for support of the poor; (4) the fast during Ramadan; and (5) the pilgrimage to Mecca (resources permitting). Jihad, or 'struggling in the way of God', to protect the boundaries of Islam, or for social justice within them, is optional—though the struggle against one's own passions, the 'greater jihad', is not. Islam was born as an epic drama in which over half the known world was conquered in an amazingly short time, and some of that quality has remained imprinted upon it, just as the quality of longsuffering (which Seth also scorns, incidentally) was imprinted on Christianity during its three hundred years of oppression before Constantine lifted the ban. It is partly this history which allowed medieval Islam to raise warfare to a level of honor and chivalry which often put the Christian Crusaders to shame. And anyone who thinks that the saints, mystics, philosophers, poets and architects of Islam fell in any way short of their Christian or Buddhist counterparts is profoundly ignorant. The spiritual arts are evidence of the depth and truth of any religion, as the saints and sages are its proof. By these criteria, Islam is second to none. The Christian philosophy of the Middle Ages was largely influenced by, and created in response to, the philosophy of Islam, which some Christian intellectuals openly admitted was superior to that of Christian Europe. The great Sufi sage Ibn al-'Arabi, whose concepts appear so often in this book, was one of the perhaps five greatest mystical philosophers of all time, if not the very greatest, though many other Sufis rival him. Rumi was, arguably, the greatest mystical poet... but who can forget Jami, Nizami, and the incomparable Hafiz? And towering mystical saints on the order of Junaid, Bayazid, and al-Hallaj, plus so many more that there is no room for all the names of them in this world, burn like stars in the black sky of God. Against this wealth, all Seth/Jane can come up with is a Philistine middle-American prejudice which is, simply, uninformed: Islam, weak in *kinship?* And who else but the Egyptian Mamluks, Muslim warriors, saved Christendom in 1260 from destruction by the Tartars under Hulagu Khan? If it hadn't been for the Mamluk victory under Baybars at Ayn Jalut, there might have been no Christianity left for Seth to falsify. The sword, both physical and intellectual, has its uses—the world being what it is.

Seth/Jane, then, is not only opposed to Christianity but to all the traditional religions, like so many of the New Age leaders who have followed in her footsteps. On p 241 of *Seth Speaks*, he says: 'In a reality that is inconceivably multi-dimensional, the old concepts of god are *relatively* meaningless.' To say this, however, is to deny that the 'deep things of God' have always been known, that they are in fact primordial. It is true that concepts of God are born, live and die with the religions to which they are integral; but this does not mean that knowledge of things Divine can advance or progress or evolve or improve. It cannot do so because its object is eternal. The only change possible is in the receptivity or resistance to that knowledge on the part of human beings; the knowledge itself is immutable. Furthermore, the basic differences between various concepts of God are not differences in fashion but differences in level. There will always be an idea of a Formless Absolute, and of a Personal God, and of the rays or wisdoms or energies by which this God is manifest. There will always be an idea of God's transcendence as well of His immanence, with the emphasis tending to shift from one to the other.

The Divine will always be both illuminated and veiled by its identification with abstract concepts; it will always be both concretely encountered and dragged down to the level of magic through It's identification with miraculous power. It will always be seen as both Unitary and multiple, and its Unity will always be understood either as embracing Its multiple aspects as their essential Principle, or as denying that multiplicity, thereby falling to the level of an abstraction and opening the door to the re-interpretation of Unity as a weak and fading shadow hidden under the riot of that multiplicity. Divine Unity will always be in danger of being interpreted pantheistically, or of sinking in the direction of polytheism, both of which errors end as a fall into materialism. No change of fashion in God-images can alter the basic principles of metaphysics, and the perennial modes in which these principles are expressed, struggled over, and misunderstood.

Given his/her deeply-ingrained opposition to the traditional religions, it is not surprising that Seth/Jane's rendition of the Second Coming of Christ should exhibit many similarities to the traditional image of Antichrist (see Chapter *Nine*). According to Seth, the Christ of the Second Coming will be primarily an incarnation of the Paul portion of the Christ entity:

> He will not come to reward the righteous and send evildoers to eternal doom. He will, however, begin a new religious drama. . . . As happened once before, however, He will not be generally known for who He is. There will be no glorious proclamation to which the whole world will bow. He will return to straighten out Christianity, which will be in a shambles at the time of His arrival, and to set up a new system of thought when the world is sorely in need of one. . . . By this time, all religions will be in severe crisis. He will undermine religious organization—not unite them. His message will be the that of the individual in relation to All That Is. . . . By 2075, all of this will be already accomplished.
>
> You may make note here that Nostradamus saw the dissolution of the Roman Catholic Church as the end of the world. He could not imagine civilization without it, hence many of his later predictions should be read with this in mind.
>
> The third personality of Christ will be known as a great psychic, for it is He who will teach humanity to use those inner senses that alone make true spirituality possible. Slayers and victims will change roles as reincarnational memories rise to the surface of consciousness. Through the development of these abilities, the sacredness of life will be intimately recognized and appreciated.
>
> ⁓SETH SPEAKS, pp389–390

[The] militant quality in man will completely change its nature, and be dispensed with as you know it, when the next Christ personality emerges. . . . In the next century, the inner nature of man, with these developments, will free itself from many constraints that have bound it. A new era will begin—not, now, a heaven on earth, but a far more sane and just world . . . .
⌒SETH SPEAKS, pp 393–394

The metamorphosis . . . will have such strength and power that it will call out from mankind the same qualities from within itself. . . . They will finally break through the veils of physical perception, extending that perception in new ways.
Now, mankind lacks such a focus. The third personality will represent that focus. . . . That personality . . . will not be oriented in terms of one sex, one color, of one race.
For the first time, therefore, it will break through the earthly concepts of personality. It will have the ability to show these diverse effects as it chooses.
⌒SETH SPEAKS, p 397

So this being will 'straighten out Christianity' by undermining all religious organizations, and destroying the Catholic Church, a stated goal of many New Age organizations, including—at least historically—the Theosophical Society. And to say 'Slayers and victims will change roles' can only mean, in this context, that those forces suppressed by Christianity and the other traditional religions will rise and take their vengeance, as is clearly already happening. How, then, will 'the militant nature of man' be 'dispensed with'? And if there will be no 'glorious proclamation' of this 'Christ', how then will he become a 'focus' for all mankind?

A being of no particular sex, race or color is a monster. The erosion of sexual differences—culturally, through sex-change operations, and possibly now through genetic engineering, which may also be able to alter racial characteristics—is the greatest and most dehumanizing evil in the world today. If this being introduces such chaotic alteration and destruction of the human form, then he, she or it is the Antichrist. The 'veils of physical perception' are not transcended by chaotically distorting physical form, but by realizing the Formless, and then by understanding how the Formless symbolically manifests as particular forms. Among of the most central of such symbolic forms is gender, which is one of the deepest emblems of the reality and inner dynamics of the Divine Nature. If we realize the 'metaphysical transparency of phenomena' (in Schuon's phrase), we have transcended the veils of physical perception without altering them, which is why physical forms—particularly those of nature and the human body—can act as symbols of their formless Principle. If, instead, we try to move beyond them by chaotically distorting them, we render them opaque. This is the psychic counterfeit of spiritual transcendence. This distortion of form by which we try to break free from the spacetime conditions of physical existence, from matter considered purely as a veil over higher realities rather than also as a manifestation of them, is based on a mode of demonic deception which is very common in these latter days; it may in fact be the central Satanic temptation of apocalyptic times (see Chapter Seven). If nothing in earthly humanity is sacred to this being, this hoped-for 'third personality', then he is already among the losers.

In *The Further Education of Oversoul Seven* (Prentice-Hall, 1974), one of her fictional books based on the Seth teachings, Jane Roberts gives free rein to her scorn for the traditional religions. In Chapter Seventeen, entitled 'Ram-Ram the Godologist and Case History 9871: J. Christ', the following is to be found:

> Christ lay on a golden couch, spread with royal velvet robes, his eyes closed, his long brown-gray ringlets in disarray about his face, his hands folded upon his chest, and a coverlet pulled up where his johnnie robe left off. He seemed to be asleep or dreaming. . . . Seven leaped back as a gigantic Lucifer appeared in the sky projection. . . .
> 'The original bogeyman,' Ram-Ram said, with great satisfaction. 'Quite effective, don't you think? You might say that Lucifer was Christ's shadow, and represented all the portions of his personality he had to deny: the love of power, the lust for knowledge, and the sheer automatic vitality, or the masculine aspects in earthly terminology. Christ's gentleness, understanding, and so forth, stressed the feminine—'The meek shall inherit the earth' and all that. . . .

(The text, of course, ignores Christ and the moneychangers, as well as his denunciation of the hypocritical Pharisees as 'whited sepulchres'.)

> Seven stepped back ever further as the giant-sized Lucifer changed into a shouting Jehovah, threatening the Israelites and demanding sacrifices . . . delivering the tablets with the Ten Commandments to Moses. But even Moses looked insane, Seven thought unhappily . . . there was fire, brimstone, smoke; there were buildings toppling, stalls squashed, horses and people making agonizing sounds, a donkey with its head just cut off by flying debris. . . .
> 'You'd think Lucifer did all that,' Ram-Ram said. 'But it was Jehovah. You

see? With prenatal memories like that, and a father who wiped out whole populations if they angered him—well, even a divine son would be bound to have problems. To that, add the fact that Christ had a human, not a divine, mother. Jehovah didn't have a divine mate; he was too ill-tempered. No goddess would put up with him. So in a way, Christ was a half-orphan, divinely speaking. He was the son of a father who was basically impotent—hence the *angel* appeared to Mary—a father who took his frustrations out on earth,' and, Ram-Ram added triumphantly, 'on his son.' Why else did he send Christ to be crucified? . . .

(For an answer to this, see the section on *A Course in Miracles*, below.)

The relationship between the twelve men was interesting also. Especially Christ's with John—the tenderness that should have gone to women. . . .' Ram-Ram lifted his shaggy white brows significantly . . .
'But basically, Jehovah and Lucifer are both projections of Christ's mind,' Ram-Ram said.

Jane Roberts reveals herself, in passages like this, as a kind of Salman Rushdie for Christianity, one of all too many over the past hundred and fifty years or so, including Nietzsche, George Bernard Shaw and the writers and producers of 'Jesus Christ, Superstar'. If she were alive today, I would not call for her assassination. I would simply point out to her her destructive childishness, and tell her to grow up. (I would also say the same—I do say the same—to Mr Rushdie.)

In Chapter Eighteen, 'Seven's Disquieting Interview with Christ, a Multidimensional Happening Turns into an Insane Vision, and Jeffy-boy Becomes a Character in a Book', Mrs Roberts presents Christ and Zeus as aging, used-up gods living together in an otherworldly rest home:

now Christ's power seemed to be diminishing to a point where Seven was almost embarrassed for him. Christ was nibbling from the mutton, for example: eating without a knife or fork—he and Zeus both taking very full mouthfuls, with Christ having trouble with the tougher portions. . . . Zeus put his chunk of meat down on the coffee table and said thoughtfully, 'You know, Christ, you could have said that Give-to-Caesar quote, and forgotten. In a lifetime, a person, even a god, speaks so many words…' Christ's eyes blazed dangerously. He spat out a bit of meat into his napkin and said, very emphatically and deliberately, 'I did not say those words. And I didn't curse the poor fig tree either. Being misquoted is one of the worst things that can happen to a god's message. . . .

She goes on:

> Zeus and Christ, all of the inmates of the institution and all the gods in the
> rest home merged into one wildly incoherent supergod, but one so ancient,
> so grandly senile, so sweetly insane that even the grasses trembled at the very
> thought of his approach.... Seven was terrified ... he saw frightened
> pigeons fly to hiding places. He felt the god's breath shake the world to bits
> in endless autumns; leaves committing exultant suicide.... The god's insan-
> ity whispered crookedly through men's chromosomes, tainting them with
> flaws beyond number. The senile god shouted his incoherent truth to multi-
> tudes, who in turn killed their neighbors and rode in bitter triumph through
> endless savage wars. Mad Mohammed flashed his eternal sword; Jehovah in
> fits of holy tremors send down his plagues and flood; Jupiter and Thor threw
> their thunderbolts while Buddha contemplated his divine navel.... Seven
> screamed, 'Stop!'

Finally, in Chapter Nineteen, having dealt with Jehovah, Christ and
Mohammed, she turns her attention to the Virgin Mary. Her 'Mary' says:

> I could never bring myself to discuss ... things of the flesh with my son.... I
> told him, my son, that he came from God.... Without the agency of man. It
> was only a mother's innocent deceit.... My son believed me,' Mary cried in
> an anguished voice. 'He became truly deluded.... It was so bad that Jesus
> finally attempted suicide. They took all the knives and forks and all silver-
> ware away from him at the rest home....

Then, last but not least, the Buddha:

> Will prostrated himself on the ground and said, 'Here I am, Master. I've no
> ego left. I'm done with desire ... please consider me your servant.... I'm fin-
> ished with wants and lusts.' The Buddha lifted his beautiful gelatinous brows
> and said to Oversoul Seven, 'What is he talking about?' 'Excuse me,' Lydia
> interrupted hesitantly. 'Are you an Indian god? If you are, I have some ques-
> tions.' 'I am if it suits your fancy,' Buddha said. 'Now what is that poor fellow
> saying?'...'Om, om, om,' Will chanted, and Buddha snapped: 'Will you shut
> up?' so loudly that Will sprang to his feet. 'Now what's all this nonsense
> about giving up desire? Buddha demanded.

At this point the reader is probably asking him- or herself why I am wast-
ing my time repeating this sort of material. There are three reasons. First,
because the Seth teachings have been immensely influential. Second,
because these passages provide a blindingly clear example of the extremely
common New Age bigotry that is directed not only against Christianity, but

increasingly now against all the world religions. And third, they demonstrate a truth about contemporary American culture: we believe that whatever can be satirized must be satirized, in the name of the freedom of the
personality; that no one but a pompous spoil-sport could fault anyone for
laughing at something held sacred by millions; that laughter is inherently
liberating; that it is incapable of being destructive. We are addicted to a
vicious, disintegrative, childish levity, even if our jokes are no longer funny,
even if the joke is now on us. Like Salman Rushdie, we are possessed by the
archetype of the destructive trickster, well personified by the god Loki, titan
of chaos, who is destined in Nordic mythology to bring about the end of the
world, the Twilight of the Gods. And as Loki was the nemesis of the Norse
sun-hero Baldur, so the Egyptian god Seth, or the Apophis Serpent, was
the nemesis of the Sun. According to Ananda Coomaraswamy, 'there can be
no doubt that for the Egyptians the conflict of the Sun with Apophis-Seth
was one of light against darkness, good against evil' (*The Door in the Sky,
Coomaraswamy on Myth and Meaning*, ed. Rama Coomaraswamy, p III).
Could this Seth-Apophis, perhaps, be the very Seth who spoke through
Jane Roberts?

It is precisely a twilight or senility of the gods that Mrs Roberts depicts in
The Further Education of Oversoul Seven. She does not necessarily do it out of
conscious viciousness; in other books, Seth assigns a very high position to
Christ and the Buddha. Like so many American bohemians, she simply
identifies a traditional sense of the sacred with pompousness, and a trick-
ster-like deflation of that sense with individual liberation.

(To digress for a moment: The attitude of Jane Roberts here resembles
that of the kind of contemporary American Buddhists who can poke fun at
their own tradition, completely without shame. After all, what harm can
come from laughter? If nothing is sacred, nothing can be profaned. And
don't the Zen people say, 'If you see the Buddha, kill him?' Such neo-Bud-
dhists forget that this was said against the backdrop of a profound and courageous seriousness in religious matters—a desperate, all-consuming desire
for liberation from the Wheel of Existence which even led one seeker to
sever his arm just to get his Master's attention. Their attitude is more along
the lines of 'you'd better kill the Buddha now, or some day you might see
him.' And for this murder of holy seriousness, this destruction of all sense of
the sacred, what better and more blameless weapon could there be, than
laughter? I don't mean to imply that a desperate, all-consuming desire for
liberation is always conducive to enlightenment, only that a flip attitude
never is. Healthy laughter, certainly, can help dissolve ego-attachments, but

egotistical levity is nothing but a way of avoiding adult commitment, depth of soul, and loyalty to the truth.)

To be fair to Mrs Roberts, I must add that she does not intend the above passages as a 'serious' attack on the world religions, but rather as a satire of the way in which our images of the divine have degenerated. But like so many satires, they themselves are a perfect example of the attitudes they attempt to deflate.

'Before you say anything [says the Oversoul Seven character later in Chapter Nineteen], I'm terribly disappointed. I thought the gods would have more sense. . . .' 'I took it for granted [says the Cyprus character] that you were perceiving Lydia and Will's *versions* of the gods. . . . The gods as understood by mortals are always conventional personifications. They're like religious psychological statues. . . . Animated superstars; perhaps that term expresses it best of all.' 'But the gods' reality is something else again,' Seven exclaimed. 'How did such a misunderstanding take place? And if there are real gods behind the gods I've met, then how do you find them? If they're always camouflaged by people's beliefs about them, how can anyone find them?'

Well might he ask. If there is no objective truth behind our subjective creations, if there is no real wineglass in the room, only three phantom glasses in three separate worlds, then there is certainly no objectively real God behind our images of Him. Nor does destructive satire directed against images of the sacred in any way help these 'camouflage' realities to become more transparent to the Reality they were designed to represent — quite the reverse. Because the raft is not itself the Opposite Shore, Jane Roberts (like so many people nowadays) feels justified in burning the raft.

God, in His intrinsic Mercy, simply by being the Essence of all things, extends Himself into our conceptions of Him; this, however, is something Mrs Roberts is far from sure of. If she really knew, as Oversoul Seven asserts, that 'All That Is is hidden in us, and in everything else as well,' her imagination would not have produced such vividly degenerate 'God-images' so opaque to the reality of God, without compensating them with images of Majesty and Beauty which are transparent to that Reality. Yet here, as elsewhere, Divine Justice is both intrinsic and immediate: Satirize Christ, Mohammed, Jehovah, Buddha and the Virgin Mary, and all you will be left with is Seth. Wherever the soul of Jane Roberts may now be, I wish her Godspeed, on the wings of that conception, to whatever ultimate goal he may be headed.

II. The Postmodern Traveler: Don Carlos Castaneda

The many books of Carlos Castaneda have, almost single-handedly, introduced sorcery nearly into the mainstream of American society. They have been praised and commented upon by noted anthropologists, psychologists, and exponents of 'human potential'. They have influenced art, entertainment and other areas of culture. They have profoundly altered the way in which whites view Native Americans. They have remained a constant, somber note in the chaotic symphony of 'alternate spiritualities' for over thirty years.

Richard De Mille, son of famous movie producer Cecil B. De Mille, wrote a book in 1976 entitled *Castaneda's Journey*, partly debunking the Don Juan books. He repeats the opinion of psychiatrist Dr Arnold Mandell that 'informant' Don Juan Matus represents a coyote trick played by Castaneda on Dr Harold Garfinkle, his Ph.d supervisor at UCLA. Since Garfinkle, as a good postmodernist, held that all anthropological data is fabricated by anthropologists, Castaneda simply fabricated Don Juan to out-Garfinkle Garfinkle. De Mille traces many of the supposed teachings of the Yaqui sorcerer and his colleagues, and the dramatic magical events recorded in Castaneda's books, to specific occult and literary influences that have nothing to do with native American culture. (I picked out one of these myself: The 'guardian' that appears in *A Separate Reality*, a drooling, airborne monster a hundred feet high, doorkeeper of another dimension, that turns out to be a tiny gnat, is straight out of the story 'The Sphinx' by Edgar Allan Poe.) But even though it can be pretty clearly shown that Castaneda's books are at least partly fictional—in his later ones he himself comes close to dropping the mask of 'reportage'—this only invalidates Castaneda as an anthropologist; it does not invalidate him as a sorcerer.

Carlos Castaneda is, in my opinion, the practitioner of some form of Native American sorcery, perhaps eclectic, perhaps of Toltec origin as he claims at one point, perhaps non-Mexican: a 'neo-shaman' I used to know maintained that 'Don Juan' and his brother sorcerer 'Don Genaro' were actually Navaho Indians; he even told us their names. I know that Castaneda is not a perfect charlatan when it comes to sorcery because, following some of his techniques, and not always with the aid of psychedelic drugs, I came up to the door of the world he proposes—and learned, in the process, that magic is very sad.

Castaneda's books are often written in a striking and powerful style, which can nonetheless become tedious after its initial fascination has worn off. His descriptions of states of 'non-ordinary reality' are precise, vivid, colorful, and sometimes deliberately paradoxical and mind-bending. He is adept at constructing these descriptions so as to appeal to many senses at once, including the visceral one, of which he is a rare and subtle poet. In the character of 'Carlos the Adventurer', which is every bit as much of a literary creation as his Don Juan, may be found the qualities of the confused and terrified sorcerer's apprentice, the priggish academic hobbled by his over-intellectuality, the dedicated researcher reporting on states of 'non-ordinary reality', the impish trickster—though other characters in his books more often assume this role, providing an effective cloak for their author—and the 'man of bone and flesh' stoically encountering a fascinating, hostile and unpredictable world with nothing but his machismo, his 'honor as a man' to back him up. His books are nothing if not poetic, which is why—except for a few places where he trespasses on the ground of religion and so needs to be refuted within the context of the universe of discourse—my answer to him will also be poetic; more so, at least, than the other sections of this chapter.

Whether real, a myth, or something else entirely, Nagual Juan Matus is the picture of a man left alone with his victories. From his perch at the edge of the human world, he views the lives of men, and sees nothing but the passage of phantoms.

Juan is a man who has survived the total destruction of his culture—what, in the terminology of sorcery, he calls the shattering of the *tonal* his people—first by the Conquista, then by the Yaqui Indian Wars. He has survived by learning to live in the world of Power, the world of the *nagual*, which is the world every sorcerer enters in the practice of his craft, whether or not he has a tribe to come back to.

Juan has no tribe to come back to. The only tribe which appears in his books, outside the sorcerers' college itself, is made up of eight Indians drunk on tequila in a small hut. And Juan's only relation to them is that of a thief of souls, who will, if he can, steal a soul here and there, jerk it out of its tiny, sordid life, and plunge with it into the world of Power. Juan Matus is thus the image of the atomic individual, rendered alien by the death of one culture, waiting perhaps for the birth of another, and meanwhile living as an anonymous space-traveler in the deserts of northern Mexico. And Juan's relevance lies in this: that every culture on this planet, from the most primitive to the most industrially-developed, is now losing its *raison d'être*; every *tonal* is being shattered.

But, as Juan says, when the *tonal* dies, the man dies. So how does Juan survive? He survives by the *tonal* of the sorcerer, the 'special consensus', to validate which he needs at least one other — in Juan's case, Genaro. 'The world is only real when I am with this one,' says Juan. So even Don Juan Matus is not self-sufficient. Even Nagual Juan Matus, to survive, needs Man: that is, Love. Victory over fear, clarity, power, old age (the Four Enemies of a Man of Knowledge from *The Teachings of Don Juan*) are not enough.

Also, Juan needs Carlos. Old age is creeping up; Genaro too is old. When Genaro dies, then the world is no longer real. Juan, for all his victories, walks then in the world of phantoms, they who are the dead. So the old man taps his last ally: the young man who will help him continue to validate his world, who will aid him in his battle against the last enemy of a man of knowledge.

Juan Matus is the picture of a man left alone with his victories, that is, a man who has failed: to see other men as phantoms is to be a phantom oneself. His failure, however, is not entirely his own. It is the failure of a culture; it is the failure of the web of human relationships which make up the truth of human life; it is the failure of love.

The books of Carlos Castaneda are, in some ways, a kind of Chicano myth. The coyote Carlos speaks with in *Journey to Ixtlan* is a Chicano coyote, like those traffickers in human desperation who live in the border-country between the U.S. and Mexico. The book itself is one of his many tricks. It may be that Coyote has at least as much place among Chicanos, refugees and migratory workers today as among Native Americans, since his traits of humor, ruthlessness and disguise are particularly useful to a population who must lead double lives.

Folklore has Castaneda sitting in a cafe in Los Angeles and telling one of his friends, 'I'm really in Mexico now.' In this case Carlos, who was born in a number of South American countries, is speaking as a displaced person. He is sitting quietly in a cafe and he is swiftly in transit, like all of us in the post-modern world. He has ten masks, or fifty, which will be enough to carry him to sundown.

One of the main achievements of the sorcerer is the ability to create a 'double', through 'dreaming'. Whatever it may be on the subtle level (presumably valid stories of bi-location have been told of saints), in one sense this double is a myth of the illegal alien or the clandestine revolutionary terrorist: what better way to confuse the FBI or the Immigration and Naturalization Service than by being in two places at once?

And the laughter! Laughter is the leaping skill of the fish in the river of ambiguities; it prevents the identity from solidifying and so becoming a target, for hatred, and for love too.

'You must erase your personal history, you must create a fog around your actions,' Juan tells Carlos; good advice for those whose identity must be unavailable to the police. 'Yes! You are a cluster' says Juan, after he and Genaro have just finished blowing Carlos to smithereens. A cluster: that is, a multiple impersonation, by an alien being, of the culture, the human solidarity, of each separate love that he has lost. 'And they looked like phantoms to me.'

The operative center of the world of sorcery is Power. The sorcerer wields Power, and yet is the slave of it. His encounters with it, conceived as struggles or battles, allow him to store Power in his body—or else they kill him. Once he has stored up enough Power, he can use it to break through into the world of the *nagual*. What happens after that is anybody else's guess, since only Power itself can tell him what Power is to be used for. If his temperament is kind, he will be a kind sorcerer; if cruel, he will be a cruel one. No attempt is made to mold the character; whether the sorcerer ends up as kind or cruel is considered unimportant. The key to the access and control of Power is the Will, defined as one or more cords of energy which spring from the solar plexus, or from a point below the navel.

To say that only Power can tell you what Power is to be used for sounds a little like the principle that higher levels of reality have their own inherent significance, which is why they cannot be used to empower lower-level agendas. Yet Power, pure agency, can never be the owner of meaning, but can only exist as the servant or expression of it—either that, or it is an expression of meaninglessness, a servant of dissipation and chaos, a tool of evil. To say that Power can itself confer meaning is a satanic counterfeit of submission to God's Will: God is not Power alone, but also Goodness and Truth.

The world at large has become a lot more like Castaneda's world since he began publishing in 1968. With consensus as to what constitutes the meaning of human life breaking down everywhere, due to unleashed technology and the clash of cultures in an age of globalist pluralism, there is a great impetus to rely upon self-will alone, to simply seize power—personal, cultural or political—and let *it* tell us what to do with our lives, since nothing else seems to be able to fill this function convincingly. But all power can tell us is, 'get more power'. Without established values based on a stable morality, which is turn is rooted in eternal metaphysical principles, power is without meaning. It is purely nihilistic. Certainly terms like Will and Power have their own specialized meanings within the context of Castaneda's sorcery; nonetheless, both their secular and their magical uses point to a common loss: the loss of our ability to conceive of Absolute Reality as Good. From Nietzsche to Castaneda, the postmodern ethos considers such an identification, which is common to all the traditional religions as well as Platonism, as embarrassingly sentimental, and obviously not the case, since 'real life' is hard and merciless. But life was just as hard in the times of Muhammad, and Jesus, and Socrates, and Lao Tzu; why did they not reach a similar conclusion? Simply because they were on a higher level than either cynical secularism or cynical magic: they knew God.

But even though only Power can define the uses of Power, it becomes progressively clearer, from book to book, that the real purpose of the sorcery of Carlos Castaneda is simply to avoid physical death. His ultimate goal, apparently, is to be able to walk alive into the next world: to imitate, via magic—the gift of a few rare saints, such as the Buddhist Milarepa, and of prophets like Enoch and Elijah, not to mention Jesus Christ, who left no body behind them when they 'died'. Nonetheless, given the far from saintly antics of Castaneda and his colleagues, the real goal would seem to be to transfer consciousness to the subtle etheric 'double' at the point of death—to become a living phantom, a conscious ghost, inhabiting a dimension no less crowded with phantoms than the streets and houses of this world.

Some anthropologists divide magicians or shamans into four categories: the Healer, the Sorcerer, the Wizard and the Witch. The Healer is the well-known tribal shaman who represents the medical and psychotherapeutic expertise of his people, who may locate and attract game, predict or control the weather, carry on criminal investigations, conduct military intelligence, balance the tribal psyche, and generally protect his or her people from psychic and sometimes physical danger.

The Sorcerer is the one who seeks personal power for personal reasons. He is not interested in either helping or dominating other people, being the quintessential loner, the self-directed psychic adventurer.

The Wizard uses his power to dominate others. He is the spiritual tyrant, the architect and agent of a conscious agenda which he labors to impose on the community. The Clingschor figure in the *Parzival* romance was a Wizard, not a Sorcerer.

The Witch, for all his apparent power, is the possessed and helpless pawn of chaos, the one who spreads poison and evil for no conscious reason outside of sheer perversity.

According to this scheme Carlos would be, as he says, a Sorcerer. Now sorcery is prohibited by every major religion because it is defined as black magic, or intercourse with demons. Can such things be attributed to Castaneda? Certainly his sorcery is full of many things usually associated with the black arts: divination, familiar spirits, devastating psychic attacks and counter-attacks (presumably for the purpose of teaching and learning, however), grotesque ghost animals and horrifying humanoid figures that glow in the dark . . . but *all that* aside, isn't little Carlos simply an innocent adventurer with no will to harm but only to explore, to widen the area of his consciousness? Listen:

'What exactly do you want me to do?' I asked in a firm and intimidating tone. 'I told you already!' she said with a yell. 'You and I are the same.' I asked her to explain her meaning. . . . She stood up abruptly and dropped her skirt to the ground. 'This is what I mean!' she yelled, caressing her pubic area. . . . I was dumbfounded. Doña Soledad, the old Indian woman, mother of my friend Pablito, was actually half-naked a few feet away from me, showing me her genitals . . . her body was not the body of an old woman. She had beautifully muscular thighs, dark and hairless. . . .
'You know what to do,' pointing to her pubis. 'We are one here.' She uncovered her robust breasts. 'Doña Soledad, I implore you!' I exclaimed. 'What's come over you? You're Pablito's mother.' 'No, I'm not!' she snapped. 'I'm no one's mother.' (*The Second Ring of Power*, p 21). . . . Her teeth were clenched. Her eyes were fixed on mine. They looked hard and mean. Suddenly she lurched toward me. She stomped with her right foot, like a fencer, and reached out with clawed hands to grab me by my waist as she let out the most chilling shriek. . . . I ran for the car, but with inconceivable agility she rolled to my feet and made me trip over her. I fell face down and she grabbed me by the left foot. I contracted my right leg, and would have kicked her in the face with the sole of my shoe had she not let go of me and rolled. I felt a sharp pain in my right calf. She had grabbed me by the leg . . . she had pinned down both of my legs against the hood. She pulled me toward her and I fell on top of her. . . . I could hardly move under the gigantic pressure of her body. . . . Suddenly I heard a growl and the enormous dog jumped on her back and shoved her away from me. . . . I could hear the furious growling of the dog and the woman's inhuman shrieks. Then suddenly the dog's barking and growling turned into whining and howling as if he were in pain, or as if something were frightening him. I felt a jolt in the pit of my stomach. My ears began to buzz (ibid., p 25). 'The Nagual is not human,' she said. 'What makes you say that?' 'The Nagual is a devil from who knows what time.' Her statements chilled me. I felt my heart pounding. She certainly could not have

found a better audience.... I begged her to explain what she meant by that. 'His touch changed people,' she said, 'He got into your old body. He put something in it. He did the same with me. He left something in me and something took over. Only a devil can do that. Now I am the north wind and I fear nothing, and no one. Before he changed me I was a weak, ugly old woman who would faint at the mere mention of his name.' (ibid., p 37)

Carlos may still be fundamentally innocent, but he definitely keeps bad company. One fears that the people he associated with may not have had the best effect on his character.

If Castaneda had not trespassed on the ground of the Absolute, but limited himself to talking about how to acquire psychic powers, I probably would have left him alone. But he couldn't resist placing certain conceptions derived from sorcery, either traditional or freelance, in place of traditional and orthodox understanding of the nature of God. And God is most certainly behind those conceptions — which is not saying much, since every conception of anything, no matter how limited or distorted, is ultimately an idea of Him. The question is, do these conceptions open on the fullness of His Reality, or do they fix us to a limited view of It which, insofar as it stands as a resistance to that fullness, must endure the blows of that Reality?

Here is the 'God' Castaneda presents us with in *The Second Ring of Power*:

Don Juan ... explained that ... the mold of man was definitely an entity.... He described the mold as being the source, the origin of man, since, without the mold to group together the force of life, there was no way for that force to assemble itself into the shape of man. [La Gorda said:] 'the human mold glows and it is always found in water holes and narrow gullies.... It feeds on water. Without water there is no mold.... The Nagual said that sometimes if we have enough personal power we can catch a glimpse of the mold, even though we are not sorcerers; when that happens, we say that we have seen God. He said that if we call it God it is the truth. The mold is God. (pp 154–155)

Perhaps this is an image of the archetype of Man *in divinis*, as seen by certain schools of Native American sorcerers — but I doubt it, since the pun on 'mold' as *template* and also as *fungus* — 'without water there is no *mold*' — is twisted and demonic.

In *The Eagle's Gift*, pp 176–177, God is presented as the Eagle:

The power that governs the destiny of all living beings is called the Eagle.... The Eagle is devouring the awareness of all creatures that, alive on earth a moment before and now dead, have floated to the Eagle's beak, like a ceaseless swarm of fireflies, to meet their owner, their reason for having had life . . . awareness is the Eagle's food. The Eagle, the power that governs the destinies of all living things, reflects equally and at once all those living things. There is no way, therefore, for man to pray to the Eagle, to ask favors, to hope for grace. The human part of the Eagle is too significant to move the whole. The Eagle, although it is not moved by the circumstances of any living thing, has granted a gift to each of those beings. In its own way and right, any one of them, if it so desires, has the power to keep the flame of awareness, the power to disobey the summons to die and be consumed . . . to seek an opening to freedom and go through it . . . the Eagle has granted that gift in order to perpetuate awareness.

It's always interesting to hear people's ideas of what the Absolute and Infinite Reality is incapable of. According to Frithjof Schuon (himself an Eagle, according to his Native American friends and teachers), God, insofar as he 'governs the destinies of all living beings' — the Personal God, or pure Being — has all power over the universe which is His reflection, except the power to change the essential nature of it as an expanding, and therefore progressively attenuating, image of Him. He can abolish any particular evil, for example, but not evil as such, since what we call evil is precisely a consequence of this attenuation, an inseparable aspect of cosmic manifestation insofar as it both reveals and veils its Principle. Castaneda, however, denies God, as Eagle, the power to grant help. He 'governs the destiny of all living things,' yet he has less concrete power to help us than a policeman on the beat or a directory assistance operator. Some governor. The reason Castaneda gives for this deplorable incapacity is that he 'reflects equally and at once all . . . living things,' and that consequently 'the human part of the Eagle is too insignificant to move the whole.' But who says it has to move the whole? Does the whole Sun have to come through my window for me to catch a ray of it? Does God have to disturb the entire cosmic order just to take care of my little problem? Only if that order is nothing but a machine composed of fixed laws would this be true — rather than the eternal, dynamic Act of a Divine Creator, which is what it actually is. Castaneda's Eagle turns out to be quite a deist here. And yes, in a way, the awareness of creatures is God's food, just as God's Being is the food of creatures. Yet God can live without His creatures, though not as the 'governor of all destinies.' Nor does God 'devour our awareness' only at the moment of our deaths; He sees through our eyes right now, in every instant of our lives simultaneously, because He is in Eternity. We may wait for Him; He does not need to wait for us.

The Eagle's gift, according to Castaneda, is the chance to disobey Him, to escape His clutches. This, of course, is a Satanic distortion of the doctrine of free will, as if the correct use of human will, the one way to freedom, were disobedience to the Principle of Life. As with the Gnostics, this governor of destinies is a kind of Demiurge, an Archon one must bypass or transcend, though He is more generous than his Gnostic equivalent since He Himself has given us the means to do it.

This is nonsense. A level of being is not transcended by flying quickly through a hole in it before it grabs you, but rather by *becoming* it. Awareness transcends lower levels precisely by being 'consumed' by higher ones. Who is devoured by the Eagle is not dissolved in the Eagle's stomach juices; who is devoured by the Eagle becomes the Eagle. The whole sorcerer's cosmology according to Castaneda is here revealed to be a function of the simple fear of identity-loss, the primal fear of death. The sorcerer, as in *Tales of Power*, can leap from a high cliff and not die. Not even the Eagle, not even God can destroy his separate individual awareness, his ego. To make sure that this can never happen, he will even sacrifice his humanity to that tiny, lurid flame. The actual state of affairs, however, is otherwise: 'Who seeks to keep his life will lose it, but who loses his life, for My sake, will find it.'

In *Tales of Power*, Castaneda presents us with what could be construed as another rendition of the Absolute, in his doctrine of the *tonal* and the *nagual*. The *tonal* and *nagual* are the two parts of the human being, as well as the two aspects of being itself. The tonal is everything knowable and intelligible; the tonal of the individual is everything that can be said about or known about him. In a way the tonal is the social self—'person' in the sense of 'mask'—but it is equally the totality of what is knowable about the world around us—which, according to Don Juan, is actually created, or arranged so as to make up a comprehensible order, by that social self. Reality is a learned pattern of perception, a pattern that can be altered.

The *nagual*, on the other hand, is what is beyond definition and ordered knowledge. It is all agency, all power. When the *tonal* is stressed nearly to the point of death, either by the techniques of sorcery or by the blows of life, the *nagual* emerges. Only the sorcerer, however, can survive this emergence, since he has learned both how to deconstruct the *tonal*, and how to use the power of the *nagual* itself to reconstruct it.

This is a very sophisticated concept. The *tonal*—and I certainly could be wrong here—would seem to correspond roughly to the Shakti of Hinduism, the power which creates the world-apparition, and the *nagual* to Shiva, the Formless Absolute, or at least to the psychic extensions of these two, since it is said that the *tonal* begins at birth and ends at death.

Don Juan compares the *tonal* to an island. In *Tales of Power*, he uses a cafe table as a way of illustrating its nature. Carlos asks what the *nagual* is. Is the *nagual* mind? Is it thought, soul, grace, heaven? Is it God? On each occasion, Juan indicates some object on the table—the silverware, or the chili sauce. Everything we attribute to the *nagual*, everything we use to describe it, is only another aspect of the *tonal*. God he compares to the tablecloth, and says:

> I said that the *nagual* was not God, because God is an item of our personal *tonal* and of the *tonal* of the times. The *tonal* is, as I've already said, everything we think the world is composed of, including God, of course. God has no more importance other than being part of the *tonal* of our time.'In my understanding, Don Juan, God is everything. Aren't we talking about the same thing?'No. God is only everything you can think of, therefore, properly speaking, he is only another item on the island. God cannot be witnessed at will, he can only be talked about. The nagual, on the other hand, is at the service of the warrior. It can be witnessed, but it cannot be talked about. (p127)

It's all here: God as a concept with no reality behind it; God as subordinate to history and sociology; God as a powerless phantom, a subject for endless and fruitless discussion. In my opinion, Castaneda didn't learn all this from a mysterious man of knowledge in a cafe in Mexico City; he learned it from his professors at UCLA. It's part and parcel of postmodern academia. God cannot be witnessed? Very well. His effects, however, can be witnessed; in sober fact, there is nothing else but these effects in the all realm of the witnessing. And He also, up to a point, can be talked about—just like the *nagual*, which Don Juan had just been talking about at some length. Nor is God simply 'everything you can think about': in His Essence, according to the Sufis and many others, he is the one 'thing' you cannot think about. Castaneda may know about the *tonal* and the *nagual*, but he knows nothing about what theologians and metaphysicians mean by 'God'.

What the *nagual* actually is according to traditional metaphysics I can't say for sure, since Castaneda presents it in terms of experience rather than concepts, and it is an experience I have not had. If it were the Self of Hinduism, the Formless Absolute—sometimes personified by Shiva as destroyer of the world-illusion—this would explain much, allowing parallels to be drawn between Castaneda's Native American sorcery (if that's what it really is), and Tantric Hinduism. Vajrayana Buddhist teacher Chögyam Trungpa, however, once said that he had hoped to find a sort of Native American Tantra in Castaneda's books, but had given up the search. And on pp140–141 of *Tales of Power*, Castaneda himself put up roadblocks to such an identification:

> [I] contended that in European thought we had accounted for what he called the 'nagual'. I brought in the concept of the Transcendental Ego, or the unobserved observer present in all our thoughts, perceptions and feelings. I explained to Don Juan that the individual could perceive or intuit himself, as a self, through the Transcendental Ego, because this was the only thing capable of judgement, capable of disclosing reality within the realm of its consciousness. Don Juan was unruffled, He laughed. 'Disclosing reality,' he said, mimicking me. 'That's the *tonal*.' I argued that the 'tonal' may be called the Empirical Ego found in one's passing stream of consciousness or experience, while the Transcendental Ego was found behind the stream. 'Watching, I suppose,' he said mockingly. 'That's right. Watching itself,' I said. 'I hear you talking,' he said, 'but you're saying nothing. The *nagual* is not experience or intuition or consciousness. Those terms and everything else you may care to say are only items on the island of the *tonal*.'

Yet on p131, Carlos asks, 'Does the *nagual* have consciousness? Is it aware of things?' And Don Juan answers, 'Of course. It is aware of everything.' But if it is aware of everything, it is none other than the Transcendental Ego—better called, in Hindu terminology, the *atman*, the Self. And even though the *nagual*, if we identify it with the Self, is not an experience—though it most certainly is a realization, one which totally transcends, however, the limited subjectivity of the empirical ego—it is certainly presented as an experience elsewhere in *Tales of Power*. On page 265, speaking of the *nagual*, Don Juan says, 'The *nagual* is unspeakable. All the possible feelings and beings and selves float in it like barges, peaceful, unaltered, forever.' As the eternal reservoir of all forms, it would correspond to the 'intelligible world' of the Neo-Platonic philosopher Iamblichus, which Frithjof Schuon defines as 'Being in so far as it contains the Divine Qualities from which are derived the angelic essences and the existential archetypes' (*Dimensions of Islam*, p148), or possibly to the level of being the Sufis call *Wahidiyah*, 'Unity', defined by Schuon as 'the world of ontological possibilities' (p150). This highest intelligible world is transcended by the *Ahadiyah* or *Dhat* of the Sufis (Beyond-Being or Essence), the *Atman* of the Hindus. The *tonal* would then correspond to the *'aql* or 'intellect' of the Sufis (which is a lower level of being than what Schuon denotes by Intellect with a capital 'I', corresponding to the Sufi *'Ilm*), and all that is below it, in relation to which it stands as the ordering principle, including *khayal*, the imagination or psychic plane, and *jism*, the body.

But in Castaneda's descriptions of *nagual* and *tonal* as experiences, the whole thing is unavoidably presented in much more subjective or psychic terms.

In the world of the *nagual*, Carlos has a sense of falling through the air, his body coming apart and dissolving, till only his head remains:

> All that was left of 'me' was a square centimeter, a nugget, a tiny pebblelike residue. All my feeling was concentrated there; then the nugget seemed to burst and I was in a thousand pieces. I knew, or something somewhere knew, that I was aware of the thousand pieces at once. I was awareness itself. (p 261)

Then, in the world of the *tonal*:

> Then some part of that awareness began to be stirred; it rose, grew. It became localized. And little by little I regained the sense of boundaries, consciousness or whatever, and suddenly the 'me' I knew and was familiar with erupted into the most spectacular view of all the imaginable combinations of 'beautiful' scenes; it was as if I was looking at thousands of pictures of the world, of people, of things. (p 261–262)

Again, *nagual*:

> I exploded. I disintegrated. Something in me gave out; it released something I had kept locked up all my life. I was thoroughly aware that my secret reservoir had been tapped and it poured out unrestrainedly. There was no longer the sweet unity I call 'me'. There was nothing and yet that nothing was filled. It was not light or darkness, hot or cold, pleasant or unpleasant. It was not that I moved or floated or was stationary, neither was I a single unity, a self, as I am accustomed to being. I was a myriad of selves which were all 'me', a colony of separate units that had a special allegiance to one another and would join unavoidably to form a single awareness, my human awareness. It was not that I 'knew' beyond the shadow of a doubt, because there was nothing I could have 'known' with, but all my single awarenesses 'knew' that the 'I', the 'me', of my familiar world was a colony, a conglomerate of separate and independent feelings that has an unbending solidarity to one another. The unbending solidarity of my countless awarenesses, the allegiance that those parts had for one another was my life force (p 262).

And again, *tonal*:

> those nuggets of awareness were scattered. . . .Then something would stir them, and they would join and emerge into an area where all of them had to be pooled in one clump, the 'me' I know. As 'me' 'myself' then I would witness a coherent scene of worldly activity, or a scene that pertained to other worlds

and which I thought must have been pure imagination, or a scene that pertained to 'pure thinking'. that is, I had views of intellectual systems, or of ideas strung together as verbalizations. In some scenes I talked to myself to my heart's content. (p263)

In the world of *nagual*, Carlos comes closer than anywhere else in his books to the classic mystical experience, as in the *tonal* he drinks his fill of mental and imaginative experience. And yet—what invincible narcissism. His identity is blown sky-high, yet all the scattered fragments are still fragments of Carlos. Nowhere in all those unimaginable worlds does he *meet anyone else*— only Carlos, Carlos, Carlos. What clearer illustration could there be of the truth that, without relationship, without love, there is no way out of the ego, unified or pulverized as may be: 'None come to the Father but through Me.' Until the Self, the Formless Absolute is realized, that Self is the Lord above, the Absolutely Other, Personhood Itself, He Who perfectly knows and perfectly loves us, exactly as we are. As Castaneda convincingly demonstrates, in the absence of a conscious and willing relationship to this Personal God, the doorway to the Formless Absolute is closed to us; we 'lose' the ego only to enter the world of the 'life force', the ego's wraith. We become that postmodern hero, the Multiple Man, the man of alternatives. It is true, on the psychic plane, that we are indeed multiple. It is also true that we are born from and destined to Unity, because we are known *by* the One, *as* the One. As medicine for Castaneda's condition, which he shares with so many postmodern travelers through countless alternate worlds, I can only prescribe the *hadith* of Muhammad (upon whom be peace): 'Pray to God as if you saw Him—because even if you don't see Him, He sees you.' Know yourself as known, señor Castaneda, and be at peace.

I was introduced, briefly, to Carlos Castaneda in 1968 by my poetic mentor, Beat Generation poet Lew Welch, at one of his 'Full Moon Mussel Feasts' at Muir Beach, California. Amid the naked and freaking hippies, Castaneda stood out: a short, well-groomed Latino gentleman in a dark suit, a white shirt, and a tie. Not having read any of his books at that time, he was of no interest to me; I fervently hope that I was of as little interest to him. (In later years I realized that Lew had meant this as a kind of initiation for me: not for nothing had he introduced me both to Castaneda and to my first real Sufi teacher. In one way, this book is a response to the choice he laid before me, thirty years ago, in the persons of those two men.)

In the introductory section of *I, Leo*, Lew Welch's unfinished novel, he tells of a vision he once had, in New York City. (Another version of it appears in his collected poems, *Ring of Bone*, in 'Din Poem'.) It was as if he had been given a strange drug by a magician, which would allow him to become a member of the human race. Identical to the inhabitants of earth, he would be able to understand them as if he were one of them, like an anthropologist who lives for years with the tribe he is studying; the report he was pledged to give would therefore be completely accurate. Lew realized this because the drug was beginning to wear off—and as it did, he also realized that everyone else on earth had been given the same drug and the same assignment, and that, more quickly in some cases, more slowly in others, it was losing its power over everyone. He says:

> I have noticed that the anguish, in me, has grown dimmer and dimmer and dimmer. While all the time I keep seeing things clearer and clearer and clearer. And I have also noticed that the more clearly you see things, the more frightened you get. . . . I saw that all these frightened subway rushers were, just like me, having the real (drugged) anguish less and less—and that their present fear was only a withdrawal symptom. Mainly they were realizing that 'love' (one of the drug-caused anguishes) was no longer possible for them. That is what made them afraid. For they are all afraid. I am afraid. However, I think that I am less afraid than they are. I think that what is happening is natural and good, and they, for perhaps they remember the magician less clearly than I, don't think it is natural and good. Therefore they are very terrified. And then, suddenly, I realized that this vision is the vision of all worthwhile books, and men. In Buddhism it is called the void. In Christianity 'the dark night of the soul'. . . . Harte Crane dove to it. Li Po embraced it in his drunken river. . . .
> ⁓I, LEO, pp 7–8

Wrong. The reason that they, and he, were terrified is because when love dies, hell opens. The impossibility of love is not the 'void' of Buddhism; the Buddhists teach that voidness and compassion are two sides of the one thing. And it is not the 'dark night of the soul' of San Juan de la Cruz, because, in Christianity, God is love. On the other hand, it may well have been what Harte Crane and Li Po experienced, two alcoholic poets who committed suicide by drowning, just as Lew Welch, another alcoholic poet, committed suicide by blowing his brains out somewhere in the Sierras— that being the definitive refutation of his argument.

I believe that the above passage shows both the drift of the collective human soul toward the demonic coldness of the latter days, and the area of that soul where Lew Welch and Carlos Castaneda were in accord: the latter, sworn to survive the death of love, and go on; the former, unwilling (at last) to take that oath.

And what does Carlos himself have to say about love? Listen to the words of sorceress doña Soledad:

> Pablito is not my enemy because his eyes were set in the opposite direction, but because he is my son. . . . I have to enter into that other world. Where the Nagual is now. Where Genaro and Eligio are now. Even if I have to destroy Pablito to do that.
> ⁓ THE SECOND RING OF POWER, pp 64–65

Sweet lady. Brave, too! And the sorceress la Gorda, her colleague, is just as sweet:

> to enter into the other world one must be complete. To be a sorcerer one must have all of one's luminosity: no holes, no patches and all the edge of the spirit…''But how did you regain your completeness?' I asked'. . . . I had to refuse those two girls [her daughters],' she said . . . the nagual . . . guided me to do that, and the first thing he made me do was refuse my love for those two children. . . . I had to pat them gently on the head and let my left side snatch the edge out of them.''What happened to them?''Nothing. They never felt a thing. They went home and are now like two grown-up persons. Empty like most people around them. They don't like the company of children because they have no use for them. I would say that they are better of.' (ibid., pp 132–133)

So the destruction of love is part of the program of a sorcerer. It's not done out of meanness; to believe so would be insufferably bourgeois. It's merely a technical requirement.

> Take Soledad. . . . She's the best witch you can find and she's incomplete. She had two children. One of them was a girl. Fortunately for Soledad her daughter died . . . the edge of the spirit of a person who dies goes back to the givers, meaning that that edge goes back to the parents. . . . Soledad's daughter died without leaving any children and Soledad got a boost that closed half her hole [the hole in her spirit]. Now, the only hope she has to close it completely is for Pablito to die. And by the same token, Pablito's great hope for a boost is for Soledad to die. I told her in very strong terms that what she was saying was disgusting and horrifying to me. . . . I explained that I liked children, that I had the most profound respect for them. . . . I could not conceive of hurting a child in any sense, not for any reason.'The Nagual didn't make the rule,' she said. 'The rule is made somewhere out there, and not by a

man. . . . I was a religious woman. I could tell you what I used to repeat not
knowing what it meant. I wanted my soul to enter the kingdom of heaven. I
still want that, except I'm on a different path. The world of the nagual is the
kingdom of heaven (ibid., pp 234–235)

Truer words were never spoken: the rule of that 'different path' was made by
no man, but by an 'angel of light'. Carlos reacts:

I objected to her religious connotation on principle. I had become accustomed by Don Juan never to dwell on that subject. She very calmly explained
that she saw no difference in terms of life-style between us and true nuns
and priests. She pointed out that not only were true nuns and priests complete as a rule, but they did not even weaken themselves with sexual acts.

I will always cheer for the nuns and priests. We are alike. We have given up
the world and yet we are in the midst of it. Priests and nuns would make
great flying sorcerers if someone would tell them that they can do it (ibid.,
p 235)

How refreshingly broad-minded la Gorda is; she allows that nuns and
priests may be good enough to be black magicians! And how postmodern
the whole thing is: the belief that love can be nothing but a terrible, draining
co-dependency, the ultimate threat to one's survival.

Carlos Castaneda has much to say about the warrior and his impeccabil-
ity. To be a true sorcerer, one must be a warrior. From my point of view,
however, a warrior — even if he is unable to live at the center of love — must
pledge his life to defend love up in the border-country, on the guarded
perimeter of the heart. If he fails in this, if he ends by destroying love instead
of defending it, then he is no warrior, but only a bandit.

Clearly Castaneda and I employ the term 'warrior' in two different senses.

But what am I saying? Castaneda is not without love; his beloved is the
Earth herself, as we discover on pp 284–285 of *Tales of Power*:

'Genaro's love is the world' [says Don Juan]. 'He was just now embracing this
enormous earth but since he's so little all he can do is swim in it. . . .' Don
Juan squatted in front of us. He caressed the ground gently. 'This is the pre-
dilection of two warriors,' he said. 'This earth, this world. For a warrior there
can be no greater love. . . . Only if one loves the earth with unbending passion can one release one's sadness. . . . The sadness belongs only to those
who hate the very thing that gives shelter to their beings.' Don Juan again
caressed the ground with tenderness. 'This lovely being, which is alive to its
last recesses and understands every feeling, soothed me, it cured me of my

pains, and finally when I had fully understood my love for it, it taught me freedom.'

Kill your mother, kill your children, then give all your love to the *Earth?* What does she want with the 'love' of psychopaths and polluters? A very pretty concerto Don Juan plays here, on the violin of sentimental nature-worship; however, as Rumi puts it, the world may be as beautiful as a bride, but no one can marry that ravishing one. Most certainly, this lovely Earth is worth many serenades — but only because her beauty and her majesty, her mild, flowering valleys and erupting volcanoes, her Quetzal and her Jaguar, are letters drawn with the Pen of the Beloved. As for herself alone, when considered apart from Him, she is nothing but a planet, an arrangement of material structures and forces. Woe to those who try to swim in that heart of stone, like I did, as if it were the lap of a loving mother! Fools like that will come face to face with the Medusa. They will turn to stone like all these stones around us, who once were men.

Shamanism is profoundly ambiguous in today's world; still, it's not all black magic. It has produced saintly men like Lame Deer and Black Elk, and shamans in the category of the Healers, like the psychic surgeons of the Philippines, are still active. The following story of a 'good sorceress' was told to me by Joan, a Catholic ex-nun who was active in the popular liberation movements of Latin America in the 1980s:

A certain area of Mexico was being terrorized by *brujos* (sorcerers), who constituted a kind of mafia. They were the only physicians in the area, and they used their monopoly over medical care to oppress the populace. Joan was working along side a local *bruja* who opposed the sorcerers; they were training young Catholic catechists as herbal doctors so as to cut into the *brujos'* monopoly. Joan tells of one meeting with the *bruja*, in which her eyes turned entirely sideways, right eye to the right side and left one to the left, after which she clairvoyantly recited Joan's entire life-history. She offered to make Joan her apprentice, and said: 'I will teach you about the powers of the Garlic Flower, the Silver Sword, and the Cross; but the greatest power is Love.' Joan, however, opted to move on to South America instead, to study liberation theology.

So there are still good shamans, true Healers, who would certainly disagree with Carlos Castaneda on the subject of love. Yet the fact that Catholics found it necessary to work with sorcerers, benevolent though they may have been, shows a loss of the theurgic dimension within the Western Church, of powers that are still active within Eastern Orthodoxy, which possesses miraculous icons and continues to produce saintly wonderworkers such as St Seraphim of Sarov and St John Maximovitch of Shanghai and San Francisco, up into contemporary times. And Joan's attraction to liberation theology shows another loss, since it illustrates how Catholicism has been unable to retain an understanding of corporal works of mercy as instances of the eternal mercy of God, and has therefore felt the need to identify them with spurious secular progressivism and false historical hope.

I hope I may be permitted to tell one more shaman-story: When St Innocent, Russian Orthodox apostle to America, traveled to the Aleutian Islands in 1828 he encountered an Aleutian shaman. The shaman was not surprised to see him; he had told the other islanders that a priest would arrive that day. The shaman had been baptized by Orthodox missionaries some time earlier, who, however, had not had time to catechize the natives. But St Innocent, to his amazement, found that the shaman possessed a comprehensive understanding of Christian doctrine. When the saint asked him how this was possible for an illiterate person such as himself, a person without teachers, he replied that 'two companions' had come and taught him everything. According to his description, one of them was the archangel Gabriel, as depicted in Orthodox icons. In other words, he had been catechized by angels. He offered to let St Innocent see these celestial catechists, but the saint finally declined the offer, since the desire to witness wonders may lead to spiritual pride.

A person such as myself, who is not a sorcerer, cannot presume to comment on the validity or spuriousness of a craft into which he has not been initiated. That is a technical matter which can only be competently addressed by the craft's own masters and journeymen. In the same way, not being a swordsman, nor even an aficionado of the martial arts, I can have nothing to say about how a master of *kendo* practices his profession—on the craft level. I can and do have something to say, however, about the value of what he does. I have every right to tell even the greatest swordsman: do not oppress; do not kill the innocent; do not hire yourself out to tyrants; do not take delight in cruelty; do not become corrupted with pride and vanity; do not practice your swordsmanship in such a way that society moves that much closer to being transformed into a mass of warring gangs. This I have a right to say. Likewise I have a right to tell any sorcerer: do not trespass on the integrity of your fellow beings; do not manipulate others; do not cause harm; do not seduce or deceive; do not take the same attitude toward the subtle forces of nature that a logging company does to a stand of ancient redwoods; do not lose your humanity in your other-worldly excursions, so that you become an open wound through which psychic corruption can enter and spread through the human world; do not portray the eternal Fountainhead of all things—Absolute Truth, Absolute Consciousness and Absolute Bliss—as a loveless power-source to be tapped by psychic raiders, like the nuclear industry taps the uranium in the Black Hills; do not act in such a way that you help to kill love between human beings, and the love of God, any faster than it would have been killed anyway, if you had never been born; do not become like Carlos Castaneda, who possesses knowledge, and power, and sensibility, and sentiment, and nostalgia, but not love.

Love seems such a weak word, bloodless somehow, in the face of the wonders and the terrors of sorcery. Yet magic, when investigated directly, is seen to be sad, because its terror and its wonder involve the loss of the human form. In *The Eagle's Gift*, p 308, Don Juan tells Carlos, '. . . warriors have no life of their own. From the moment they understand the nature of awareness, they cease to be persons and the human condition is no longer part of their view.' True, the prophet Muhammad (upon whom be peace) said 'die before you die.' But that death is a death of the ego, not of the person, the latter death being merely the satanic counterfeit of self-transcendence. The human form was created by God to be His representative in this world; since we did not create that form, we have no right to destroy it. The realization that our life is not our own is not the destruction of the human form, but the very principle of it.

Many today, however, do not mourn the progressive loss of that form; they even place their hopes in that loss. If only love were to finally die, finally stop hammering at our conscience, blocking our perceptions, interfering with our efficiency; if only the haunting memory of the wounded trust, the betrayed relationships, the poisoned innocence, were to leave us definitively. Without such ballast holding us down, perhaps we could leap, with superb abandon yet impeccable control, into the world of power! The seething night might close over us. Fainting with fear, and the expectation of things that are coming, we might make that terror our ally. We might face him and salute him with a warrior's honor. In the life-and-death struggle with that adversary, knowledge might be taken as a trophy, and wielded, turning the master key of this world and opening the door of it. Our flight might take us into countless other worlds, universes of exaltation, and abysmal strangeness, and shining wonder. The triumph of the warrior who makes terror his friend even might flower beyond the grave, allowing us to walk alone into that ultimate mystery, that luminous night, with our manhood undiminished. All this might be ours, if only love would lie at peace in its grave. We dug that grave with our own hands, with all the cunning and stoicism we could muster. If only our powerful wings could carry us to the end of the world, where a howling wind might drown out the whispers of it; if only we could find a slab of stone heavy enough to crush and stifle it. The whispers of love, that thin persistent ghost, are like water on a stone. What can the steady drip of water do to solid stone? What power does water have, sweet or salt, to change the face of it? Yet ages pass swiftly under the dry, grassy hill of that other world; the wings of the eagle, his steady strokes, under that separate sky, wave the centuries past—till we come like skeletons, bald and trembling, before the full flesh of our denial. This is the voice of that denial, the very accents of her, caught and recorded by my wife, Jennifer Doane Upton:

> Virgin of Guadalupe, Kali of our continent,
> When I ask you to show me the
> Spiked head of my lover, don't hide it,
> Because I have already seen him
> In your face.
> You have taken his recognition of me
> Away, and in place of my love
> He only feels tremendous pain.
> And even when you smile upon him
> He does not come nearer to you,
> Because he doesn't know that he ever left you.
> Virgin of Guadalupe,
> Do not smile upon me
> In that way
> On the day of my death.

How easy it is to satirize Carlos Castaneda, to unpack all my rhetorical irony against a worthy and vulnerable target on the darker side of things. But, remember, I was there too. I dabbled in the black arts—believing all the time, of course, that there was nothing black about them, that I could love and serve God while playing the 'lyric sorcerer'... a very apt term of Castaneda's, given that poets, especially failed poets, love to think of themselves as magicians. I spent three days and two nights in the cabin of a local witch, a woman to whom men were attracted when they had decided to commit suicide—three deaths I certainly know of. I sat there eating her drugs as a way of doing penance, I suppose, for an overprotected childhood, like so many of my generation, because I felt I needed to acquaint myself with the dark side of things. Well, I did, and soaked up plenty of bitterness in the process, a certain amount of which came out later in the form of this book, as the light and heat of the spiritual Path cooked it out of my bones.

Now there is nothing in these critiques and satires and denunciations that was not first in me. Where else would all that black ink have come from? The darkness in which I dabbled was reflected back to me from the mirror of the world... this mirror having the unique peculiarity that it really does contain portions of all that is reflected in it, truth or falsehood, light or darkness. In the mirror of *Mahamaya* nothing is pure illusion, but nothing is what it seems.

(Now turn away from that dark, smoking mirror, and face the Light.)

III. Transcendence without Immanence: The Neo-Gnosticism of *A Course in Miracles*

(NOTE: *Since* A Course in Miracles *is rather long, I've based most of this critique on two shorter books:* The Most Commonly Asked Questions about A Course in Miracles, *by Gloria and Kenneth Wapnick (1995), and* A Course in Miracles and Christianity: A Dialogue, *by Kenneth Wapnick and Fr W. Norris Clarke, S.J. (1989), both published by The Foundation for a Course in Miracles. Citations from the first appear under the abbreviation MCQCM, and from the second under CMCD. Citations designated 'text', 'workbook' and 'manual' are from the three original volumes of the* Course *itself.*)

The most sophisticated production of the entire New Age culture is *A Course in Miracles*. It represents in many ways the intellectual peak of the movement, and is clearly on a higher level than the fantasies of the psychics and the spiritualists, being a real attempt at metaphysics. Unfortunately, it is built upon a fundamental error, from which many other errors arise.

There is a great deal of profound truth in *A Course in Miracles*: the uncompromising sense of God as Absolute Truth and Love; deep insight into the convoluted games the ego plays to escape this Truth and Love; an understanding that the subject/object mode of consciousness cannot directly witness Absolute Truth; the doctrine of one and only choice which is completely free, that between Truth and illusion; the primacy granted to forgiveness in the process of 'metanoia', that total change of mind by which Truth is chosen and illusion dismissed; the doctrine—entirely true in *one* sense—that humanity never really fell into sin, never entered into the illusion of separation from God. These truths, which the *Course* shares in one way or another with all traditional metaphysics, may even be enough, by God's grace, to make it a true step on the spiritual Path, at least for some. Yet the fundamental error remains. Some, while traveling the way of the *Course*, may overcome this error; but the *Course* itself cannot help them do it. And if this error is not overcome, the way of the *Course* remains like a bridge half-built. The Truth of the Opposite Shore can be seen, but it cannot be reached.

According to the traditional metaphysics of all peoples, the Supreme Principle is both transcendent and immanent. The New Age movement as a whole, given its fascination with the psychic plane and its scientist tendency to glamorize matter, is clearly skewed in the direction of immanence, tending to see any God Who transcends this world as either tyrannical or ineffectual. *A Course in Miracles* however, is skewed in the opposite direction, as if one extreme of error needed to be 'balanced' with the opposite extreme. The God of the *Course* is strictly transcendent. He did not create the world, which is nothing but an illusion of the ego. Since He knows only Truth, He is not even aware that this illusory world 'exists'.

A Course in Miracles is the channeled production of Helen Schucman and her partner Bill Thetford who, like Jane Roberts and her husband Rob, producers of the Seth material, are an example of the classic mediumistic 'triangle' of a female medium who channels a male 'entity' with the help of a male amanuensis—the entity in this case being 'Christ' himself.

According to *Journey Without Distance, The Story Behind A Course in Miracles*, by Robert Skutch (Berkeley, Celestial Arts, 1984), Dr William N. Thetford, Professor of Medical Psychology at Columbia University, met Helen Schucman in the mid 1960s when both were working in Psychology Department of Presbyterian Hospital, of which Dr Thetford was Director. As a child, as well as later in life, Helen was attracted to Catholicism, which she looked to as a possible source of miracles. When such miracles were not forthcoming, or when possibly miraculous events occurred which could be explained away rationally, she became enraged at the Church and turned into a militant atheist. And Bill Thetford, interestingly enough, worked at the University of Chicago during the Second World War on the Manhattan Project, which developed the first atomic bomb.

Shortly before Helen began to channel the *Course*, she had a series of dreams and visions in which she saw herself as a powerful priestess, sometimes helpful, sometimes violent and destructive. One can speculate that her hatred for the Church and her suppressed desire for spiritual authority somehow came together with Bill Thetford's guilt for having helped create nuclear weapons to produce a psychic atmosphere conducive to the birth of the *Course*, filled with new and miraculous teaching capable of saving the world—even though, according to those teachings, the world isn't real, a belief which would certainly absolve the creators of the Bomb from the possible guilt of destroying it.

One of the most puzzling things about Helen Schucman is that *A Course in Miracles* apparently did not 'work' for her. 'Having no belief in God,' she is quoted as saying,

> I resented the material I was taking down, and was strongly impelled to attack it and prove it wrong. On the other hand, I spent considerable time not only in taking it down, but also in dictating it to Bill, so that it was apparent I also took it quite seriously. . . . I was in the impossible position of not believing in my own life's work.
> ⁓JOURNEY WITHOUT DISTANCE, p134

As Willis Harman wrote in the Foreword to the same book:

> I once asked her how it happened that this remarkable document she had been responsible for had brought wisdom and peace to so many, and yet it was seemingly ineffective for her. I will never forget her reply. 'I *know* the Course is true, Bill,' she said—and then after a pause, 'but I don't believe it.'
> ⁓JOURNEY WITHOUT DISTANCE, piv

Clearly the channeler of *A Course in Miracles* was radically divided. This, however, was not simply an ironic psychological quirk: the soul of the channeler of *A Course in Miracles* was necessarily divided because the metaphysics of the *Course* itself is radically dualistic.

This, however, is precisely what the *Course* denies. While other spiritualities, especially biblical Christianity, are branded as dualistic (cf. CMCD, p23), the *Course* is considered to be purely unitarian. *A Course in Miracles* teaches that God did not create the world and knows nothing of it. The world, including our bodies, was created by the ego as an attack upon God; it is an illusion, a dream. This dream, however, has great power: the power to determine every item of our experience, until such time as our belief in it is overcome. So we essentially have two different gods: a totally transcendent God Who is ignorant of the cosmos—similar to the 'Alien God' of the sectarian Gnostics—and the Ego, which (even though it doesn't really exist) is the Creator of the entire universe, and thus analogous to the deluded Gnostic Demiurge, who creates the prison of the physical and psychic cosmos out of the false belief that he is the true God. Simply stated, if the quasi-totality of our experience is different from and opposed to God, then it is effectively a second God. We may claim that it's all illusion; we cannot ignore its effects.

The Supreme Principle is both transcendent and immanent. In one sense it is totally other than the manifest world; in another, it is the Essence of that world. Therefore, according to the unanimous doctrine of traditional metaphysics, the world is both a veil which hides God and a symbolic projection which manifests Him. If it were only a manifestation of God we would take it *as* God, like the Pantheists, and so never rise to the vision of, and Union with, God Himself. And if it were only a veil, the very knowledge of God's existence would be impossible for us, since even His deliberate Self-revelation to us, including the very paper and print of *A Course in Miracles*, would, as soon as it entered this world, become part of the veil, part of the 'attack on God'. And so our relationship to that *Course* could only be (in the *Course's* terminology) a 'special relationship', an ego-identification masquerading as the love of God and the dedication to spiritual enlightenment. If the universe is not a manifestation of God as well as a veil which hides Him, then all our ideas of God, including those presented by the *Course*, are meaningless idols. (According to Dr Wapnick, in *CMCD*, p54, the *Course* teaches that God is neither transcendent nor immanent, since He can be neither *in* nor *beyond* something which does not exist. But the *Course* certainly does teach that He is beyond, not in, this very insistent 'illusion'.)

Dr Wapnick identifies the doctrine of the *Course* that the world is *literally* an illusion with the doctrine of *maya* from the Hindu Vedanta, as well as with the 'highest teaching of Buddhism', and recounts that some involved with the *Course* have termed it 'Christian Vedanta' (*CMCD*, p30). But neither the Hindus nor the Buddhists teach that the world literally isn't real. According to the Vedanta, *maya* does not mean 'illusion'; it means 'apparition'. The *maya* of the Supreme Principle or *Brahman* is not a literal unreality, but a kind of magical image of the Divine which is real in one sense and unreal in another. The thrust of the Vedanta is not to teach us the literal illusoriness of the world, but to overcome *literalism* itself. According to the doctrine of *maya*, the world is not literally an illusion, but if we take it as a literally real object, a thing-in-itself, then we are deluded. It is not a thing-in-itself: it is God's magical Self-manifestation to—and as—His creatures.

Inherent in all apparition, however, is the tendency to take apparition as literally real; the Vedantists term this power of manifestation insofar as it veils its Principle *avidya-maya*. Those under the power of *avidya-maya* need the doctrine of a transcendent Absolute Reality—such as *A Course in Miracles* teaches—which is totally beyond, other than, and greater than this manifest world. But as soon as this transcendent Absolute is realized, then it is known not *exclusively* as Absolute, but also as Infinite. As pure Transcendence, It excludes as unreal all that is other than Itself; as Absoluteness united with Infinity (in terms of Hindu Tantra, *Shiva* united with his *Shakti*), it embraces all things *as* Itself, since if It did not, It would be less than Infinite, and thus not really Absolute.

The recognition that visible and intelligible forms, which veil God if we take them literally, actually manifest Him if we no longer make this mistake, and even constitute a Path back to the full realization of Him, the Vedantists name *vidya-maya*, the fascinating and enlightening power of Absolute Truth. Using the terminology of the *Course*, every time we let go of a 'special relationship' based on ego-identification, the object we release immediately becomes a manifestation of Truth, with which we enter into a 'holy relationship'. And this would not be possible if the world, as the *Course* claims, were literally and absolutely an illusion.

The Buddhists concur in this. Buddhist dialectic, after positing a completely transcendent and indescribable Nirvana, which is 'neither earth, air, fire or water, nor the plane of infinite ether, nor the plane of infinite space, nor the plane of infinite consciousness' etc., etc., finally arrives at (in the *Lankavatara Sutra*): 'But this very *sangsara*, this illusory world created by passion and craving, is itself Nirvana'—the argument being that if there literally were a world of sangsaric illusion outside of and opposed to Nirvana, then Nirvana itself would only be a relative reality, not the Absolute. The Buddhists, at least those of the Mahayana, agree with the *Course* that there is really no independent 'world' based on craving and ignorance, since 'all beings are enlightened from the beginning,' if they only knew it. But if there is no world, they are compelled to ask, what then is this world? They answer this question by saying, not that the world is literally an illusion, but that it is 'void of self-nature'; it has no *literal* existence, no *ego*; consequently they apply to all phenomena the term *shunyata*, 'voidness'. But this voidness, not being literal, cannot be construed as literally denying the reality of the world; such denial would be a false extreme, just as the belief in the literal reality of a world of phenomena possessing their own self-nature is another false extreme. And so Buddhism pairs with *shunyata* a complementary principle, *tathata* or 'suchness'. Precisely *because* all things are void of self-nature (*shunyata*), all things, exactly as they are (in their *tathata*), manifest the Supreme Principle; the Buddha-nature; Nirvana; Enlightenment.

Certainly the *Course* embraces teachings which include elements of immanence; if it did not, if God were absolutely transcendent in every sense, there would be no *Course*, and no students to take it. It teaches that, within this false dream-world, through the merciful action of Christ and the Holy Spirit, a dream of goodness and forgiveness appears. This dream is not real, but it can lead to Reality if we will follow it. What the *Course* denies is that the entire Universe, in one sense, *is* this very liberating and saving dream. Every manifestation, if we relate to it without ego, is a door to the Absolute, because—as the *Course* itself teaches, but doesn't fully understand—in one sense it never left the Absolute; this is Frithjof Schuon's doctrine of 'maya-in-divinis'. (The *Course* too speaks of a perfect and eternal creation within the Divine Nature—analogous to the *aeons* of the Gnostic *pleroma*—but this creation does *not* contain the archetypes of cosmic manifestation.) In terms of cosmogony, this means not only that this illusory Universe, this 'attack on God', can somehow become host to the teachings by which the attack can be undone—according to the *Course*, by realizing that, in Reality, the attack never occurred—but that the initial manifestation of a world seemingly apart from God was not only a veiling of the Absolute Reality which seemed to create a universe of suffering, but also a joyous and liberating manifestation of that Reality. The creation of the Universe was itself a release from prison, a salvation-from-illusion, an act of Divine Mercy. In the *hadith qudsi* of Muhammad (upon whom be peace), God says 'I was a Hidden Treasure and longed to be known, so I created the world that I might be known.' Likewise the answer to the second question, 'Why did God make us?' in the old *Baltimore Catechism* is: 'God made us to show forth His goodness and to share with us His everlasting happiness in heaven.' To understand that the phenomenal world is a prison of suffering requires little insight; that it is also, along with its Genghis Khan, its Auschwitz and its hydrogen bomb, an act of Divine Mercy, is a profoundly esoteric truth—one which I learned in Catholic grammar school.

In Islam there are two Divine Mercies, *al-Rahman* and *al-Rahim*, which are named at the beginning of most *surahs* of the Koran. *Rahman* is God's Universal Mercy, by which He says Yes to all things, thereby creating the Universe; *Rahim* is His particular Mercy, addressed to those who turn to Him in need of salvation, which says Yes to some things—those which help to purify the soul and remind it of His Reality—and No to others, those which veil His Image in the human heart. *Rahim* is the Mercy of redemption; *Rahman* is the Mercy of creation. Before creation, in the depths of the Divine Nature, it is as if all possible beings, who were to become the universe, cried out to be separated from God in order that they might really know Him—something we can begin to understand if we remember that our daily closeness to our human beloved will sometimes hide her from us; 'absence makes the Heart grow fonder.' And God granted them their wish. He sighed a sigh called the *nafas al-Rahman*, the 'breath of the merciful', through which all things came to be. When the Bible says that 'the heavens declare the glory of God,' when the Native American worshipper recognizes the natural world, with all its violence and bloodshed, as his cathedral, and all the living and non-living forms about him as spiritual signs of *Wakan Tanka*, they are relating to God according to His primordial theophany, according to *Rahman*. In the words of *Genesis*, God looked upon the world he had made, and called it good. And insofar as we allow Him to look out through our eyes upon that world, we can too. But the existence of separate sentient beings constituting a Universe was not only a merciful manifestation of God to their living eyes; it was also necessarily a veiling of the fullness of the Divine Nature. And as the cycle of manifestation rolled ahead, this veiling became a source of suffering. That's when the numberless sentient beings lost in the illusion of separation from God cried out to Him to save them; again, God granted their wish. He sent prophets and saviors and avatars to remind us of His Reality, and to establish Paths back to the fullness of that Reality. So all God really does is grant our wishes—the deepest of them, that is; those shallower wishes that He often does not grant, at least in the limited forms according to which we've conceived them, are partial aspects, or poor translations, of our deepest Wish, the one that God wishes for us in Eternity: that we be exactly as we most truly are; that we relate to Him exactly as we alone can.

This is the fable of Allah's creation of all things and the return of all things to Him. It is strictly analogous to the 'outbreathing and inbreathing of Brahman' in Hinduism, and to the Creation, Fall, the Redemption and Restoration in Christianity. And if we understand that it really does not take place in time but rather in Eternity, that these four motions are actually simultaneous, then it is no longer a fable; it is a certain level of *gnosis*.

A Course in Miracles falls short of this gnosis. And the major effect of this shortfall, based on its one-sided metaphysics, is that the relationship between the relative and the Absolute is misunderstood. The truth that relative Being is a necessary sub-set of Absolute Being is not grasped; the Great Chain of Being which unites all things to their transcendent Source, by virtue of the immanence of that Source within them, is therefore broken. And the practical teachings of the *Course*, useful though they may be at a certain stage or for certain people, are not enough to repair it.

In metaphysical terms, then, the error of *A Course in Miracles* is to see the world as *avidya-maya* but not *vidya-maya*, to understand God as transcendent but not immanent, to view phenomena in terms of *shunyata* but not in terms of *tathata*. What are the effects of this error?

To begin with, the role of the ego is misunderstood. It is granted full power to create the universe—though it and the universe are both unreal—as if out of nothing. But in reality, the ego does not create. It does not even create illusion. All it does is edit. The universe is not an illusion created out of nothing, then, but a Reality seen through a distorting mirror. Just as the senses do not report all that exists, even on the material level, but only what they are designed to pick up, so the ego picks and chooses only those aspects of God which it identifies with, and calls this the universe. It may unconsciously believe that it has created this Universe, but—as the *Course* teaches—this is merely a delusion. What it has actually done—and this the *Course* denies—is perceive God according to its own limitations. What else could it perceive, since God is the only Reality? But if it makes up a universe by stringing together limited and fragmented perceptions of God Himself, then that universe cannot, literally and exclusively, be an 'attack on God'. From the standpoint of the subjective ego, though not in its Essence as known by God, it must be an ambiguous attempt both to deny God and to understand Him. Insofar as it is a denial, it must—as the *Course* teaches—be denied. Insofar as it is a partial perception of Absolute Reality, it must—as the *Course* denies—be affirmed.

Dr Wapnick, in *CMCD*, pp 61–62, quotes the following 'affirmation' from the *Course*:

> I am responsible for what I see.
> I choose the feelings I experience, and I decide
> upon the goal I would achieve.
> And everything that seems to happen to me
> I ask for, and receive as I have asked.
> ⁓TEXT, p 418

As it stands, this is not true. The 'I' who sees this and not that, who experiences feelings, decides upon goals, and has things happen to it, is the ego—and the ego is not omnipotent. It is not God. The ego seeks autonomy, and in so doing becomes enslaved by conditions which it can neither choose nor control. Only in the ironic sense has it 'gotten what it asked for'. Wapnick goes on to say that 'this choice simplifies to the decision between the ego or the Holy Spirit as our guide for behavior.' Here I entirely agree: we do not choose our specific experiences; we choose whether to experience them from the ego's standpoint of 'omnipotent victimhood', or in the context of the Holy Spirit, where all events are acts of Divine Mercy and manifestations of Divine Truth. The *Course*, however, denies that God sends experiences—a half-truth, since while God in His Essence is beyond saying Yes to this and No to that, in relation to us, and depending upon our own state, He is truly experienced as laying upon us commands and prohibitions, sending us rewards and tests. If the ego thinks it is controlling its own experience, it is deeply deluded. If it believes that an external God is arbitrarily controlling its experience, it is still partly deluded. But if we can forget the ego in submission to God's Will, operating through apparently external events, we will begin to see that this Will is not arbitrarily imposed, but rather inseparable from the state of its subject. In Sufi terms, this is how *taslim* (submission) leads to the understanding that, in the words of Ibn al-'Arabi, 'the determined (the creature) determines the Determiner (the Lord).'

In *CMCD*, p 63, Dr Wapnick says that 'simply changing or controlling one's behavior—as is the aim of any code of morality—is not enough, since the root cause that is the mind's guilt will still be there.' Agreed. But on p 64, he continues: 'People mistakenly believe that by controlling their behavior they can actually change their thoughts. And then what happens is that the underlying guilt and hatred which have not changed at all become projected out in the form of judgement or persecution, with the person being totally unaware of the true nature of his or her actions because the underlying thought has remained unconscious.' And I agree that this is precisely what *can* happen, and too often has. Yet in traditional Christian asceticism—as represented in the *Philokalia*, for example—a change in behavior is not considered to be the final goal, as the Wapnicks seem to think. It is well understood that the passions which cause sinful behavior live not in the body but in the mind; this is why the struggle against them is sometimes called 'unseen warfare'. It is true that changing our behavior cannot in itself change our thoughts. What it can do however, when practiced in a traditional context where the laws of *askesis* are understood, is to bring these thoughts to the surface. Thoughts which are automatically acted out can never become conscious, but when their outer expression is interrupted they appear in their true form—if, that is, we are taught to watch for them.

The *Course*'s inability to affirm the reality of manifest existence as well as denying it results in several obvious and dangerous errors. To begin with, from the Christian standpoint, it falls into three heresies: Gnosticism, Arianism, and Docetism. (The word 'heresy' suggests to the modern mind nothing beyond an act of rebellion against a dogma arbitrarily imposed by religious authorities for political purposes. What it really is, however, is a mistake, a metaphysical error, usually based on an element of truth taken out of its full and sufficient context.) The Gnostic denial of that God created the world necessarily, but falsely, situates the act of creation—which is an inescapable concept, since it is true—within the Divine Nature itself: Jesus is created, not begotten (Arianism); the Holy Spirit is created as well. The archetype of God's cosmic manifestation, God the Son, is no longer considered divine; therefore the cosmos is no longer real. (The *Course* does speak of the Son and the Holy Spirit as 'created' in eternity not time, and as remaining inseparable from the Father, suggesting in some ways the 'begetting' of the Son and 'procession' of the Spirit in Catholic doctrine; but the word used is still 'creation'.) And when the *Course*, in line with its absolute denial of the world's reality, states that Jesus was never born, never died, and never suffered, this is the error of Docetism.

If the cosmos is unreal, then any distinctions of level within it are meaningless. In the words of the *Course*, 'a hierarchy of illusions is the first law of chaos' (TEXT, p 455). In *MCQCM*, p 24, the Wapnicks elaborate this doctrine as follows:

> 'Beauty is in the eye of the beholder'...is...applicable here, since what one deems as beauty, another may find to be aesthetically displeasing....Similarly, what one society judges as good, another may judge as bad and against the common good. This can be evidenced by a careful study of history, sociology and cultural anthropology...nothing that the world deems beautiful is real, and so it cannot have been created by God...both beauty and goodness are relative concepts and thus are illusory....

But is it really true that goodness and morality are entirely relative? Listen to what C.S. Lewis has to say in his essay 'The Poison of Subjectivism' (*Christian Reflections*, 1967, pp 78–79):

> What of the modern objection—that the ethical standards of different cultures differ so widely that there is no common tradition at all? The answer is that this is a lie—a good, solid, resounding lie. If a man will go into a library and spend a few days with the Encyclopedia of Religion and Ethics he will soon discover the massive unanimity of the practical reason in man. From the Babylonian *Hymn to Samos*, from the Laws of Manu, the [Egyptian] Book of the Dead, the Analects, the Stoics, the Platonists, from Australian aborigines and Redskins, he will collect the same triumphantly monotonous denunciations of oppression, murder, treachery and falsehood, the same

injunctions of kindness to the aged, the young, and the weak, of almsgiving and impartiality and honesty. There are, of course, differences. There are even blindnesses in particular cultures —just as there are savages who cannot count up to twenty. But the pretense that we are presented with a mere chaos —[that] no outline of universally accepted value shows through —is simply false and should be contradicted in season and out of season whenever it is met. Far from finding a chaos, we find exactly what we should expect if good is indeed something objective and reason the organ whereby it is apprehended....

If we once admit that what God means by 'goodness' is sheerly different from what we judge to be good, there is no difference left between pure religion and devil worship.

Perhaps the same cannot be said with quite this level of assurance when it comes to aesthetic taste. Still, in every human culture, flowers are considered beautiful; if you ever encounter someone who is repelled by them (allergies aside), you can be sure that he or she is emotionally ill. There may be no *full* accounting for taste, due to the subjective element. Yet sound taste is still based on objective principles. Aesthetic taste is like taste in food; it can be either healthy or diseased. Someone who finds healthy foods attractive has a healthy sense of taste. But a person who likes junk food or food that has spoiled has a taste that we call 'jaded'. Such a person may derive real pleasure from eating unhealthy food, but that won't prevent it from making him sick.

The denial of the reality of the world tends to reinforce narcissism. The world, including other people, is unreal according to the *Course* —but *since I know this*, I myself must be real. The world is *my* dream; it cannot be God's dream since He doesn't even know about it. This is one of the hidden contradictions in *A Course in Miracles* which undermines its stated aim of overcoming the ego's belief that it is autonomous and self-created. In the Wapnicks' words,

> our world and our lives are our dreams, just as our sleeping dreams —with all their figures and events —are present in our sleeping minds that in a sense are but hallucinations, too ... since the content of the ego's dream is fear, hate, victimization and unforgiveness, all dream figures will have the above themes scripted throughout the dreaming we call 'life' ... there is no one to forgive because, again, all the people in our lives are simply made-up figures in our dreams. Who needs to be forgiven is ourselves —for dreaming in the first place instead of remembering our identity as Christ, awake in God....

Our function of 'releasing our brothers' through forgiveness relates to a function and process that truly occurs only within our minds. . . .
～ MCQCM, pp 78–79

Taking the Wapnicks at their word, based on this passage alone, we might conclude that they subscribe to Jean Paul Sartre's dictum that 'hell is other people.' Clearly I can't forgive others if I don't believe they are real, nor can I love them, respect them or do them justice. They are simply my illusory creations; but unlike God in *Genesis*, I cannot look upon them and call them good. This is solipsism masquerading as enlightenment; to claim that other people do not exist is a form of murder. On p 79, the Wapnicks say that 'By choosing Jesus as our teacher instead of the ego . . . we become reminders to our brothers that they can make the same choice we did. . . .' But, regretfully, 'made-up figures in our dreams' do not have the power of choice. It is admitted on pp 78–79 that my dreaming mind is also a hallucination, but that doesn't prevent it from being more real than its own creations, since it is capable of realizing that these phantoms are indeed phantoms. And if it is itself a hallucination, then who is doing the hallucinating? The *Course* denies that God can be dreaming me, so the only alternative is that I must be dreaming myself. If God is unaware of me as I experience myself in this world, if He did not create me in this dimension, then I must have created myself. If I am my own hallucination, then the ego is indeed self-created, therefore tantamount to God. The *Course* teaches that a portion of the Son, of God's total and perfect creation in eternity, was distracted for a moment, and seemed to fall asleep, thus allowing the 'tiny, mad idea' that we could be separated from God to project the entire illusory universe. But that sleeping, or apparently sleeping, portion of the Son is, precisely, the subtle ego. The only way out of the ego's false belief that it is self-created is for the center of my consciousness to shift from the ego to the *atman*, the Divine Witness — a *metanoia* expressed by St Paul when he said: 'it is not I who live, but Christ lives in me.' If we know ourselves as known by God, then the ego is dissolved. But if God can never witness that ego — as illusion — it can never be dissolved. It remains locked in the illusory dream of its own self-creation. Jesus, according to the *Course*, understands the illusion into which we have fallen; God, identified strictly with the Father, does not; the Holy Spirit is our 'right mind', the thought of God which corrects the false beliefs of the ego. But unless we know ourselves as seen and understood by the Absolute Itself, we can never realize that Absolute as the true Self, the true Seer within us. In the *Course's* terms, we remain caught in the illusion that it is simply our own understanding of the Truth which makes that Truth what it is (cf. Text, p356). In Dr Wapnick's words (MCQCM, p32), 'If students, with Jesus' love beside them, can look without judgement and guilt at their egos in action, then *who* is doing the looking? It cannot be the ego itself, but the mind. . . .' This is accurate, as far as it goes. But this inner Witness which Wapnick calls 'the mind' must ultimately be the Absolute Itself, since if it is anything less, the 'dream of separation' is not transcended; a subtle subject/object mode of perception has not been overcome; the seed of the ego remains. The denial that the mind, on its deepest level, is the Absolute itself, the Divine Witness, is itself an illusion of the ego.

Furthermore, to deny that the universe has even a relative reality is to place an impassable gulf between God and our experience, a gulf which the *Course* then attempts to bridge. But if there is no intrinsic relationship between God and the universe, then the Hierarchy of Being—the only conceivable bridge between them—is invalid. Just as a denial of transcendence collapses this Hierarchy, since it places everything on the same ontological level (ultimately a material one), so the denial of immanence does the same thing, since there is nothing even relatively real outside God with which He could have a hierarchical relationship. In the Wapnicks' words,

> the so-called animal, vegetable and mineral kingdoms are all as much a part of the Sonship [God's eternal creation] as is *homo sapiens*. Distinctions of what is animate and inanimate were arbitrarily introduced by *homo sapiens*, following the ego's teachings, in order to be able to categorize and control an illusory world and to have 'dominion over every living thing' (Gen. 1:26,28). Such a belief is what *A Course in Miracles* refers to as the first law of chaos, that there is a 'hierarchy of illusions' (Text, p455) wherein some aspects of the illusion are considered to be higher, more evolved, or more spiritually inclined than others, as when scientists speak of a 'chain of being', for example, where, by implication, there is a range of life and non-life. In fact, however, all the forms of 'life' are the same, because there are all equal in their being projections of the ego-thought of life-apart-from-God.
> ⁓MCQCM, p34

This is a powerfully destructive half-truth, one which cannot be taken seriously without a certain amount of self-deception, as illustrated by the fact that the *Course* itself posits a spiritual hierarchy when it speaks of 'teachers of God' and the 'teachers of teachers' who are more spiritually enlightened than they; and its hierarchy-collapsing rule that 'there is no order of difficulty in miracles'—in the actions of the Holy Spirit to correct the ego's false ideas—

is belied by such statements as 'the last thing that can help the non-right-minded, or the sick, is an increase in fear. . . . If they are prematurely exposed to a miracle, they may be precipitated into a panic' (TEXT, p 20).

Hierarchy is a reality. If this or any reality is not accepted, it will sneak in through the back door, appearing as a deceptive contradiction rather than a consciously-accepted truth. This is not to say that hierarchy should be absolutized; it remains a relative truth, in one way, since it has to do with the relationship between relative being and Absolute Being. But by virtue of its relation with the Absolute, it partakes of that Absoluteness; in a phrase used by Frithjof Schuon in other contexts, it is 'relatively absolute'. According to traditional metaphysics, the Absolute does not only negate relativity, but also embraces it. In Ibn al-'Arabi's terms, the Absolute is absolutely non-delimited, since It is not delimited by It's own non-delimitation. Limits, possessing their own relative reality, can appear within Reality without that Reality being limited by them; God does not have to take refuge in His own Limitlessness to avoid falling under limitation. He can recklessly pour Himself into relative existence without in any way losing His Absoluteness — which is why relative existence can 'return' to the Absolute through an understanding that its own experienced limitations in no way limit God, but rather express Him.

Hierarchy, then, though it is relative, is also necessary. Reality, not being exclusively transcendent, necessarily manifests Itself in, and as, relative being—simply because, since it is Infinite, there is nothing to prevent it from doing so. If hierarchy were strictly absolute, immanence would be negated. It would be impossible to know the Divine Essence as the essence of all things. God would be fixed at an infinite distance from His creatures, who would be forced either to despair of ever realizing Him, or to attempt to 'take heaven by storm' by climbing the fixed steps of that absolute hierarchy, toward that distant God, by Promethean self-will alone. Conversely, if there were no hierarchy, there could be no spiritual Path, no way to grow in love and knowledge. All experience would be literally defined either as total illusion, or as the Divine Essence. As illusion, it would be without any hope of attaining to Being; as the Divine Essence in a literal sense, it would be without hope in another way, having no possibility of confronting its own limiting illusions and sufferings. If we are all literally God, and something is still radically wrong, then what God can we turn to for help?

Hierarchy, correctly understood, is not oppression; it is mercy, whose servant is justice. Since it is true, it is dealt with in one way or another by any true metaphysical doctrine. Whenever it is excluded, it appears in delusive forms. And the same is true for immanence. *A Course in Miracles*, not surprisingly, also has a doctrine of immanence floating around inside it, but this doctrine is not placed in the right relationship with the *Course's* dominant transcendentalism. It sticks out as a puzzling contradiction, being a sentimental and illogical introduction of love for creatures to compensate for the *Course's* definition of the universe as an attack on God:

> How holy is the smallest grain of sand, when it is realized as being part of the completed picture of God's Son! The forms the broken pieces seem to take mean nothing. For the whole is in each one. And every aspect of the Son of God is just the same as every other part.
> ⁓Text, p 557).

So here, in contradiction to the 'attack on God' definition, the created universe seems to be defined as good, holy, and a part of the 'picture' at least of God's Son, who is God's perfect and eternal creation. But since this doctrine of immanence is not paired with the *Course's* transcendentalism from the start, it is subtly distorted. In line with the denial of hierarchy, the *Course* states, correctly, that 'the whole (of God's Son) is in each one,' each 'broken piece' of him. This is the perspective of immanence. But to say that because the whole is in each form then all forms are the same is an error. God is not only the Universal; He is also the Unique. In terms of *maya-in-divinis*, whose outer expression is cosmic manifestation, this Uniqueness appears in each form through which God manifests. Because God is Universal, the whole of Him appears in every part of his manifestation, though only in Essence, not in form. Because God is Unique, that Uniqueness also appears in every part; no two forms, grains of sand, or human individuals are identical. If this were not true, love would not be possible, since if the whole is present in me in the same way as it is in others, rather than in a way that is unique, just as its manifestation in others is unique, then why do I need others? If 'the forms the broken pieces seem to take mean nothing,' then people in their otherness from me are meaningless, empty forms. Who needs them? If we are only unique, then we are mutually exclusive, and love is denied; if uniqueness is suppressed in the name of the doctrine that the whole is in each, love is denied again. One woman is much like another; if you've seen one redwood tree you've seen them all. But the truth is, we are related to each other by our very otherness, we are akin by our common uniqueness, which is an expression of the Absolute Uniqueness of God. For love to exist, the true relationship between God and the cosmos must be known. For this to be known, we must accept and understand the Great Chain of Being, where the fact that God is the Essence of both me and a rock does not absurdly suppress the truth that I am superior to a rock *since I can know this.*

When *Genesis* speaks of God as giving humanity 'dominion over all living things,' this is a dominion of Intellect, and only secondarily a dominion of will. The idea that it gives us carte blanche to use, alter, distort and destroy all we see is nothing but the ego's misinterpretation of God's commission to us. In Islamic terms, man is God's *khalifa* or vicegerent in material creation because we alone can consciously contemplate this creation as composed of the signs of God (*ayat*), and thus act as the conduit between it and the Spirit that gives it life. This is the meaning of the legend, both Biblical and Koranic, that Adam named the animals: he, as he alone could, recognized them as names or signs of God.

In *CMCD*, p 29, Dr Wapnick speaks of God's nature and uniqueness:

> God is not an individual, with a personal identity or self; that is, He has no form that sets Him off from His creation. He is thoroughly impersonal, as is Plotinus' One. Thus, His uniqueness is not defined by comparing Him with another, but rather God is unique because there *is* no other.

This is less that a millimeter off center — but a miss is as good as a mile. Indeed God is unique; and indeed, in essence, there is no other Reality. But *no* uniqueness, including the uniqueness of the human person, is defined by comparing it with something else; whatever is unique is, by definition, incomparable. The uniqueness of God, then, cannot be used as an argument for His strict impersonality. According to traditional metaphysics, God is both personal and impersonal — in Hindu terminology, both *Saguna Brahman* and *Nirguna Brahman.*

God is impersonal in the sense that He is not limited by form. He is personal in the sense that this limitlessness necessarily appears to us, insofar as we are persons, as Personhood itself. In one way He transcends all the attributes of personality; if He didn't, we could encompass Him; He would be sealed off from Infinity within the boundaries of our limited minds. But in another way, He is the only Person of Whom Reality can be predicated — the single, unique, concrete Reality of which all other forms and beings are relatively abstract 'versions'. From one viewpoint, we can say that the impersonal God, the 'Godhead' of Meister Eckhart, is hierarchically superior to the personal God, Who acts and is only in relation to His Divine and cosmic manifestation. Yet if the Godhead were strictly impersonal in the sense that it lacked or fell short of personhood, the personal God could not be Its first intelligible hypostasis. So it is probably better to call God in His Divine Essence not impersonal, but *transpersonal.* Because after all, what is a person?

Is he limited to what I know of him, to my image of his personality? Is he not just as mysterious in his ultimate depths as God Himself, since those depths in fact open into God Himself? A person is not an impersonal abstraction simply because there is more to him than I can ever know. The depths of Personhood take us far beyond all we can know of persons, yet the pronoun by which we refer to this mystery still is not 'what', but '*Who*'. And this Who, though not limited by form, is not thereby strictly formless either, since 'He is not delimited by His own non-delimitation.' The words of the *Tao Te Ching* are relevant here, though it tends to approach the Absolute through the metaphor of nature rather than of man:

> The Tao is elusive and intangible.
> Oh, it is intangible and elusive, yet within is image.
> Oh, it is intangible and elusive, yet within is form.
> Oh, it is dim and dark, yet within is essence.
> This essence is very real, and therein lies faith.

Being is ranged in ontological ranks; if it weren't, I could not look up to the Truth and ask to be enlightened by it, nor could I be generous and protective to living things below me in the hierarchy. I could neither accept my own creaturely ontological status as being necessarily exalted in some ways and limited on others—subjecting myself, by this refusal, to luciferian arrogance and despair—nor could I aspire to consciously attain that status, if through egotism I had fallen below it, as all of us have in one way or another. And if hierarchy is collapsed, then equality suffers as well. The perspective which allows me to see how I am ontologically inferior to some things and superior to others, though I share with them the identical Divine Essence, also lets me see how I am different from yet related to individuals on the same plane of being as myself. Where hierarchy is squashed, unity can only appear as abstract uniformity, and uniformity destroys both the piety which recognizes higher and lower, and the affection which exists between uniquely different and therefore uniquely related equals. The universe of our experience becomes a flat, barren illusion of the narcissistic ego: an attack upon God.

Nor can *A Course in Miracles* get along without positing the hierarchy it 'officially' denies. In MCQCM, p90, Dr Wapnick says:

> The student is not asked to progress directly from the illusory nightmares of special relationships to the reality of the one relationship with God, but with Jesus as their guide, they first pass through the illusory dreams of forgiveness . . . they first learn that God is a loving Father rather than a

hateful one, and the Holy Spirit a comforting companion to them in the world rather than their enemy. Only then can they learn that there is in fact no world for them to comfort us in. Metaphor has served its purpose.

This is, precisely, a 'hierarchy of illusions'. What is denied, apparently, is that this hierarchy is ontological. It is a hierarchy of experiences, not realities. But according to traditional metaphysics, epistemology and ontology, knowing and being, form an indivisible whole: higher experiences are real experiences of higher worlds. If this were not the case, then all our 'knowing' would be illusory, locked in the circle of the narcissistic ego. Sufis too speak of manifest existence as a metaphor, but they don't deny all reality to it; they simply attribute its reality to God alone, Whom metaphorical existence both manifests and veils. Any experience, therefore, is to some degree an experience of Reality; if it were possible for an experience to lack all reality, we could not experience it. Certainly we can wrongly interpret what we see, as when the Hindus compare *maya* to 'mistaking a rope for a snake.' But it is impossible to see something that is not there, at least on some level. Dr Wapnick speaks of awakening from the belief in the world's reality as like awakening from a dream (*CMCD*, p 19). But who says that dreams are not real? They can give us valid insights, affect our health, even predict the future. They are one level of reality; waking life is another. And God is Reality Itself, beyond sleeping and waking, beyond levels; all sleeping and waking experiences, all ontological levels, are aspects of Him.

The exclusive transcendence of *A Course in Miracles* has one further, chilling consequence: God does not hear our prayers. How could He, if He is totally unaware of this illusory universe of which we are a part? In the words of the workbook, p 335, 'Think not He hears the little prayers of those who call on Him with names of idols cherished by the world. They cannot reach Him thus.' And on pp 69–70, the TEXT says:

> God does not guide, because He can share only perfect knowledge. Guidance
> is evaluative, because it implies that there is a right way and a wrong
> way . . . the Holy Spirit does guide, and provide choice. . . .

This is like saying, 'the Pole Star cannot guide sailors because it does not move; only the astrolabe can guide.' But the motionlessness of the Star, like the perfection of the Divine, *is* guidance. If 'perfection' cannot guide, then it is far from perfect.

The doctrine that God does not hear and answer prayer is an error. According to Ibn al 'Arabi, our image of God, the 'God created in belief' is self-created, and therefore less than God. Yet God, in His intrinsic Mercy, accepts the prayers we address to it, since even though its form is not His, He remains the Essence of it. Our ability to understand His answer may be limited by the form in which we conceive Him, but no form worshipped as God is entirely separate from Him. The Wapnicks, in *MCQCM*, p 120, mention several instances in the *Course* where we are directed to pray to God as if He heard us, especially for forgiveness, but this is explained as a kind of self-re-training, within the context of the illusory dream of the ego, under the tutelage of a Holy Spirit—created, not Divine—who is like the ego's memory of God's Reality.

The reason the *Course* denies that God can hear and respond to our prayers is apparently to emphasize that the Atonement is already complete in Eternity. But since the aspect of us which prays to God in hope of His answer exists in time, we necessarily, and legitimately, experience the Atonement as a process—though if we don't also intuit the eternal reality of the Atonement as underlying this process, the process will never end. But *A Course in Miracles*, like the human ego, seems incapable of imagining that 'time is the moving image of Eternity,' that what is eternal and infinite to God is experienced by the ego-mind as temporal and limited, without any real barrier existing between them, outside of the ego's mis-perception. When the *Course* says that God does not hear our prayers, or that He is unaware of the universe, this is its way of trying to safeguard His Absoluteness and Perfection. Yet in taking this route, it is forced to deny His Infinity. It fails to understand that God, unlike us, can look upon limitation and not be limited by it, just as He can answer our prayers without defining Himself in terms of our needs; He is not 'co-dependent'. His ability to do this is one of the things that makes Him God. God sees all our needs and limitations, but sees them only as His Perfection. How He could witness only His own Perfection and still respond to our needs, how He could be even more deeply aware than we are of the illusions under which we labor and the sufferings we experience, and still know and be nothing but his own Being, Consciousness and Bliss, cannot be understood by the literalistic mind of the *Course*, which is why it must fall into the heresy of Gnosticism to explain the apparently unexplainable. For traditional metaphysics, however—just as for the soul of simple piety, which is so rare in these times—the relationship between the Absolute and the relative, God and the universe, myself and my Lord, is not enigmatic, but transparent.

The text of *A Course in Miracles*, like most channeled material, is extremely uneven. A sophisticated psychology of the ego-in-flight-from-God and a subtle though one-sided metaphysics are mixed in with maudlin devotionalism, simple-minded 'positive thinking' affirmations reminiscent of Christian Science—like the foolish statement on p 42 of the TEXT that 'when you feel tired, it is because you have judged yourself capable of being tired'—deceptive word-play and statements which contradict the main tenets of the *Course*, at least as presented by Dr Wapnick. For example, the following passage appears on p 77: 'Whatever you accept into your mind has reality for you. It is your acceptance of it that makes it real for you ... the mind is capable of creating reality and making illusion. . . .' Certainly whatever you accept as real is real for *you*. But the mind does not *make* reality; it perceives it. Reality, by definition, is what is objectively true and really there, whether or not I perceive or understand it. Elsewhere the *Course* teaches precisely this, as when it defines as an error the belief 'that your understanding is a powerful contribution to the truth, and makes it what it is' (TEXT, p 356). To say that the mind can create reality, but then deny that the act of understanding a truth creates it, is a flat contradiction, one of many which riddle the *Course*.

A paradox is an attempt to put into words a truth that words can only suggest but not define. A contradiction is, simply, a mistake. The *Course* explains its own obvious contradictions as teaching-paradoxes which point to ineffable truths. But at least some of them are simply contradictions, which point to intellectual darkness and chaos. For example, when the TEXT, p 55, claims that 'No force except your own will is strong enough or worthy enough to guide you. In this you are as free as God,' this contradicts the doctrine of the *Course* that while the will is free in Heaven because it is in line with God's will, in the realm of illusion, the world of the 'split mind'—the only place where the concept of 'guidance' has any meaning—the will can do nothing but choose between two guides, the ego and the Holy Spirit; and God does not have to choose who or what will guide Him. In the Wapnicks' words, 'Within the *dream* ... the concept of free will becomes extremely important for it is the mechanism of salvation' (MCQCM, p 70). According to the manual (p 75), 'In this world the only remaining freedom is the freedom of choice; always between two choices or two voices. Will [in Heaven] is not involved in [limited, subject-object] perception at any level, and has nothing to do with choice.' But if one's heavenly will is beyond choice, beyond 'perception', beyond the dream, then—in the *Course*'s terms—it should be too perfect to guide us. This is why—in the *Course*'s terms—Jesus and the Holy Spirit must appear, within the dream, as guides. The will on the level of the dream, within the realm of illusion where guidance is necessary and possible, can only choose (and here I totally agree with the *Course*) between two masters: ego or Spirit. So to say that 'No force except your own will is strong enough or worthy enough to guide you' is untrue, both in reality and according to other tenets of the *Course*. As it stands, it is a call to luciferian self-will, because the human will is not designed to guide, but rather to *follow guidance*. It is the Intellect, the mind of God within us, that guides; power alone is powerless to establish Truth, and meaningless without it. In relation to our will, the Divine Intellect undoubtedly appears as God's Will, since it commands our will's allegiance. It does so, however, not because It overpowers us through force, but because It compels us through Truth. Once a thing is known as true, it masters us; we can only seem to escape the rule of Truth by lying to ourselves. But a known truth covered by a willed lie is a house founded on sand; 'if the Lord does not build the house, they labor in vain who build it.'

The *Course*, however, denies that the Intellect is the Guide of the will; in the words of its 'Jesus', 'We have emphasized that you need understand nothing' (Text, p356). As an excuse for the garbled message of *A Course in Miracles*, these words may have some rationale. As spiritual advice, they are poison. They reduce the meaning of 'guidance' to zero. Willing submission to a truth, spiritual or otherwise, before you fully understand it is the only door to greater understanding; without this submission, no teaching can take place. Yet you have to understand *something* of that truth from the outset even to know that such submission is called for. And after that point, every further submission, every sacrifice of self-will in the presence of a teaching which is objectively true, results in a deepening of that understanding. If it doesn't, you are laboring under a delusion.

Another glaring contradiction in the *Course* is the following: On p30 of the Text, 'Jesus' says that the collective end of the cosmic dream will take place over millions of years. (A similar doctrine can be found, interestingly enough, in the teachings of the Gnostic Valentinus.) But doctrine that the universe is an illusory attack upon God is incompatible with the doctrine of the spiritual evolution of the macrocosm. If, in the *Course's* terms, the misperception of the ego is corrected in a 'holy instant' which is outside time, if time itself is an illusion, then the cosmos cannot be redeemed over time, in one day or in a trillion years. It is true, as the Koran says again and again, that all things return to God—but not through time. The door to God is not in space or duration, but in the depth of the present moment. Certainly the spiritual Path of an individual moves through successive stages and seems to take time. But since the Path is not a line drawn through time, but one which stretches from time to Eternity, those stages are inscribed on the face of Eternity itself. In Sufi terms, the steps of the Path do not lead *to* God, but take place *in* God.

As the *Course* itself teaches, our choice to be guided by the Spirit instead of the ego is a decision to step out of time. Perhaps, one could argue, if all the sentient beings who make up the universe were to make this choice, the dream of the universe would end. But for this to happen the cosmic environment would have to become virtually perfect—an extremely unlikely destiny for an illusory attack upon God. Sentient beings would have to stop being born so they could all make this choice together, since the constant production of ignorant infants would keep renewing the dream. And to make sure that all of them chose rightly they would need an infinite amount of time in which to do so; they would have to stop dying. The dream of the universe, however, is a dream of time; within that dream, time cannot end. And the choice to be guided by Spirit instead of ego, the choice to step out of time, is something only individuals can do. A 'universe' cannot make choices.

Even more disturbing and revealing than the contradictions of the *Course* is its impishly deceptive word-play. On p 71 of the TEXT, for example, the Gospel passage where Jesus says 'my yoke is easy and my burden light' is re-interpreted to mean 'let us join together, for my message is light.' This 'exegesis' is so absurd and in such poor taste that it suggests a demonic will acting to distort the meaning of scripture. 'Light', of course, means both 'easy' and 'radiance' only in English, not in Aramaic. As for 'burden', it may be construed to denote a 'message', since two of its meanings, according to the *American Heritage Dictionary*, are 'A principal or recurring idea; a theme,' and 'The chorus or refrain of a [musical] composition.' This 'burden', however, is derived from the Latin *burda*, 'pipe', while the more familiar 'burden', meaning something hard to carry, is from the Old English *byrthen*. They are two different words. Such childish or elfish games are clearly unworthy of Jesus Christ, though not of the 'Jesus' of the *Course*, who seems to lack the ripeness and humanity, the *salt* of his namesake—not surprisingly, since he was never a born as a man.

One of the most interesting aspects of *A Course in Miracles* is its 'transcendental ego-psychology,' its story of how the ego hides from Divine Truth. This 'myth of the fall' is more-or-less as follows: A portion of the Sonship, God's eternal and perfect creation, fell asleep, or seemed to. In the dream it seemed to be having, it imagined the possibility of separation from God—something which in fact is impossible. This dream resulted in a fundamental mis-perception, an attack upon God which never occurred in reality, since no such attack can occur. But the belief that such an attack occurred resulted in the illusion of a physical universe composed of vast quantities of matter and energy, vast stretches of space and time. The ego believed that it had stolen from God the power to create this universe, and so feared Divine retribution. Consequently it interpreted Jesus' crucifixion not as an act of love on God's part but as the Father's punishment of the Son, as ego, for the sin of trying to exist apart from Him, and thereby creating the universe. Out of fear of this punishment, the ego projected onto Christ what it feared would happen to itself. Christ's vicarious atonement for our sins, through suffering, is therefore not efficacious; it is nothing but a way for the ego to deny its own fear of punishment for a sin it did not really commit. The ego fears to encounter Christ because of the danger that it might realize that no sin ever took place. Since the ego lives on fear and guilt, the realization that the fundamental sin of separation from God never happened would be 'fatal' to it—as illusion. And because no sin was committed, our guilt is unjustified; in a way, guilt itself is the 'sin'.

As a 'shadow' of Christianity, this is a very interesting story. Undoubtedly many people, in these days when the fullness Christian doctrine is rarely taught, experience Christianity in precisely this way, Helen Schucman among them. If so, this variation on the Christian theme might prove useful as a way of understanding how Christian doctrine can become distorted by unconscious ego-beliefs. The *Course's* version of the Christian story could even be called 'Christianity according to the ego.' In this shadow-version, the truth that only God creates the universe is hidden by the error that sees the ego as a rival, though illusory, creator. The *Course* is right when it comes to the error—that the ego could have the power to create a real universe, which in reality it does not—but wrong when is comes to the truth—that the true Creator of the universe is God. (This is the nature of shadow-knowledge; it can criticize error, but it cannot posit Truth.) Likewise when the *Course* criticizes *vicarious atonement*, the dogma that Christ paid the debt of our sin through His suffering and death, it is right about this doctrine's erroneous misinterpretation that would define 'vicariousness' as a kind of scapegoat-function by which our sins are 'taken away' into some wilderness where our responsibility ends. But it is wrong about the truth of the matter: that sinners redeemed by Christ must die with Him in order to rise with Him, that they must 'take up their cross' and follow Him, only to find that His 'yoke is easy' and his 'burden light'. This is not punishment by an angry God; this is victory over death. The *Course* claims that Jesus' disciples believed the crucifixion was the Father's punishment laid on His Son for the sin of man. This is nothing but a foolish slander, since another and greater doctrine was taught openly from the beginning: that the Son's death was the Father's free offering of Himself, as God, in the person of His Son—since Father and Son are 'one substance'—to pay man's debt. And this debt could not have been the 'wounded honor' of the Father which needed to be satisfied, as Anselm claimed—the *Course* seems to rely heavily upon Anselm's theology as its main straw man vis-à-vis the redemption—because the Father's gift of His Son was a sacrifice, not a demand.

The *Course* correctly understands that Jesus's crucifixion and resurrection were for the purpose of demonstrating that no effective attack can really be made upon God, and that His Forgiveness remains available to us despite our guilt if we are only willing to accept it; otherwise it would not be forgiveness. What it fails to understand is that God embraces our suffering and makes it His own, without thereby incurring the slightest damage or diminishment. This is a scandal to the literalistic Gnosticism of *A Course in Miracles*, which is why it must deny that Jesus was ever born, or suffered, or died. But if He did not, then the resurrection was a puny theatrical gesture, and proved nothing. That God could suffer and yet not suffer; that Christ could really be born, really bleed, really die and yet be beyond all that, as the resurrection proved—this is the mystical paradox that the *Course* cannot accept. Normative, orthodox Christianity is far too esoteric for the mind that produced *A Course in Miracles*.

If God is the only Reality, as both the Sufis and *A Course in Miracles* teach, though in radically different senses, then He must be my hidden Essence—a truth expressed by Jesus when he said 'I am in the Father, and the Father in me' (John 14:11), and 'I [am] in them and thou [the Father] in me, that they may be made perfect. . . .' (John 17:23). The implication here is that all my all-too-real suffering is, in Essence, no suffering. When the Hindu saint Ramakrishna was dying of throat cancer, much suffering occurred. We can't say that because Ramakrishna was a saint—or according to some, a minor avatar—he therefore could not have been born in the flesh, and gotten throat cancer, and died of it. It was simply that, to the degree that He was a fully realized being, a *jivanmukhta*, there was no ego there to suffer that suffering. It's not that the suffering never happened; to believe this would be a literalistic superstition. It's simply that the suffering was, in Essence, no suffering, because God, as the indwelling Essence of Ramakrishna, and of you, and of me, does not suffer—which is precisely why He can and does take on all the suffering of the universe.

A Course in Miracles, like Sigmund Freud, claims that not sin but guilt itself is the source of our problems. Since the 'original sin' never took place, guilt is pure illusion, which psychoanalysis and/or the *Course* exist to dispel. We are not forgiven for our sins; we are forgiven for believing that we sinned in the first place. But what could be more guilt-producing than to define the universe as an illusion created by the ego as an attack upon God? As egos, according to this doctrine, we are guilty of the most horrible, cosmic crime imaginable. Of course this crime never really happened—except that every item of our experience, if we believe in the *Course*, shouts to us that it did. So our experience itself becomes the enemy, the pursuing wrathful God; according to the tenets of the *Course*, at least as I read them, *experience is guilt*—except that nothing is really happening. Our experience is unreal.

How, if our will is free to choose between ego and Spirit, can the choice of ego over Spirit not be a sin? And how can we be forgiven for a sin that we never committed? How can we escape a prison we experience an undeniably real if that prison doesn't exist? The *Course*, even as it denies the reality of the universe, takes that universe as a kind of negative absolute, a hopeless situation which contains nothing good, which is precisely why it must be defined as illusion. But if the universe is absolutely unreal—or absolutely real—then we will never find God, either because we will not be able to imagine Him as a Reality which transcends our experience, or we will take all our imagined experiences of Him as meaningless illusions. Likewise the *Course*, even as it denies the reality of guilt, makes guilt into a monster with infinite power to torment, invalidate and imprison us, which is precisely why it must call it unreal. But if guilt is a total illusion—or a total reality—then we will never know forgiveness because we will never seek it; we will either see no need for it, or we will despair of it. And what, after all, is so terrible about guilt, if there is such a thing as forgiveness? Guilt, if we become fully conscious of it by the power of God's grace, leads to that great good fortune known as *remorse*, which is part of the ecstasy of love. We should all be so lucky.

Furthermore, *A Course in Miracles* does not only 're-interpret' Christianity; it also attacks it. On p 4 of *MCQCM*, Dr Wapnick describes 'the biblical God' as 'very much a person who sees sin as real,' and characterizes His relationship with a chosen people and his wrathful and punishing aspect as a 'special love . . . and special hate . . . that are associated with the ego thought system . . . [the section of the *Course* entitled] 'The Laws of Chaos' contains a graphic portrait of this biblical God who has made sin real and thus revealed his ego origins, or better, the egos of the writers of the books of the Bible.' In *CMCD*, p 23, the Bible is described as teaching a 'dualistic' spirituality; in *MCQCM*, p 99, the Wapnicks speak of 'other (non-Christian) spiritualities' as being they whose 'names are legion', using the phrase the possessing demons apply to themselves in Luke 8:30. Deliberately placing itself on a higher plane than the Bible with its 'ego-origins', the *Course* characterizes itself as follows: 'Of all the messages you have received and failed to understand, this course alone is open to your understanding and can be understood. This is *your* language' (Text, p 437); it denies, in other words, that any other spiritual texts or scriptures are even intelligible, while claiming at the same time that 'you need understand nothing.'

Could a kind of psychological projection be operating here? This is certainly one explanation of the *Course's* contradictions, in light of which we can perhaps understand why the Wapnicks, on p 129 of *MCQCM*, actually end up characterizing 'the strong influence of Christianity' under which the Western world has grown up as 'an influence [along with psychoanalysis] that has not been very Christian or spiritual'—as if Christian doctrine could be shown to have been based on a misunderstanding of Christian doctrine.

As is abundantly clear from these quotations, *A Course in Miracles* is considered in some sense to be the exclusive truth; biblical Judaism and Christianity are looked on as illusions of the ego. This intolerance, based on a 'guiltless' willingness—especially in the case of Christianity—to re-write traditional doctrines until they meet the *Course's* criteria of falsity, would seem to be a good example of the tendency the Wapnicks elsewhere try to nip in the bud, when they make the statement that if the *Course's* students were to try to proselytize, they would 'feel drawn to criticize, judge or attack other spiritual paths' (*MCQCM*, p 114).

The *Course's* characterization of Christianity as dualistic is inaccurate because one-sided. It is unaware, for example, that, according to the Bible, the God Who sees sin as real also knows it as unreal: 'Thou art of purer eyes than to behold evil' (Hab. 1:13). Nor is He necessarily a symbol of the ego because He exhibits a wrathful, punishing aspect; His wrath is simply *how the ego must experience Him*, until that ego is sacrificed and released. According to the Bible, the sacrifice acceptable to God is not of the body *per se* but of the ego—not 'the fat of rams' but 'a contrite heart'. Divine wrath is Divine mercy as distorted by the ego, but also *as addressed to the ego*; the only thing which can awaken a deeply self-worshipping ego from the illusion of its own self-creation is the tremendous majesty of God. Certainly if the level of sin and repentance is never transcended, if God's mercy and forgiveness are never intuited behind the face of His justice, the ego must remain sealed in its own narcissism, where it will use masochistic self-torment as an argument in its ongoing attempt to prove that it is self-created. This is why Sufis speak of the need, at one point, to 'repent of repentance'. But if the level of sin and repentance is never reached in the first place, it can never be transcended, since the ego which has trained itself to obey its own impulses as if they were God's will—in Sufi terms, the 'commanding self'—interprets every expression of forgiveness simply as a license to kill.

The *Course* accepts none of this. On p137 of the Text, it says, rightly, that when we choose to be guided by the Spirit, the ego, 'sensing defeat and angered by it . . . regards itself as rejected and becomes retaliative.' This is precisely the meaning of the crucifixion, except that Jesus, since it was His will to give His life for all of us, endured the retaliation not of his individual ego alone, but also of the collective ego of humanity. But *A Course in Miracles*, since it deliberately anti-Christian, cannot see in the crucifixion an obvious illustration of its own doctrine, portraying it instead as a false drama within which the ego believes it must suffer torments to appease an angry God—a distorted half-truth, since the crucifixion is none other than the sacrifice of all that would stand between the Son and the Father's love: *the ego itself.* And it is true, in a way, that the Bible presents God's relationship with His universe in a dualistic light; what else can mythopoetic language do if it wants to tell a story? But the *advaita* aspect of the Bible is there too, not far below the surface: 'I and the Father are one'; 'before Abraham came to be, I am'; 'it is not I who live, but Christ lives in me'; 'the Kingdom of Heaven is within you.' Unfortunately, the mind that produced *A Course in Miracles* is too literalistic to recognize this. And finally, who could seriously believe that the Bible was distorted by the egos of its scribes, many of whom gave their lives as witness to the truth of it, and not allow that the *Course* was just as likely to have been distorted by the ego of Helen Schucman, a lady angry with the Catholic Church, who wasn't even sure that she believed in God?

One of the strangest aspects of *A Course in Miracles*, at least from my perspective, is that it contains a distorted version of Frithjof Schuon's doctrine of the Transcendent Unity of Religions. In its true form, this doctrine states that God has revealed more than one path capable of leading the human soul back to Him; these paths are to be found in the great world religions, as well as in certain 'primordial' spiritualities. Each path is unique, and a person cannot travel on more than one at the same time. On the other hand, the higher metaphysical doctrines of the revealed religions are unanimous, though with many differences in emphasis, in expressing certain universal spiritual principles. But a person's only practical, 'operative' access to these truths remains his allegiance to one religious tradition, both on the level of spiritual practice, and on that of the specific, unique doctrines which provide the necessary context for such practice.

According to the *Course*, 'A universal theology is impossible, but a universal experience is not only possible but necessary' (manual, p 73); and in *MCQCM*, p 113, Dr Wapnick warns students of the *Course* to be 'cautious . . . about attempting to blend together theologies and spiritual approaches that ultimately do not mix.' This seems entirely in line with Schuon's teaching. However, on p 111, Dr Wapnick reveals the real reason for this caution, criticizing the common practice of including *A Course in Miracles* with what Aldous Huxley termed

> the perennial philosophy' [often confused with Schuon's doctrine], a catch-all phrase used to embrace the major mystical traditions of the world . . . this does the Course a profound disservice, because it blurs what is its distinctive contribution to the world's spiritualities: the idea that not only was the physical universe an illusion that God did not create, but that it was also 'made as an attack' on Him. . . . This profound and sophisticated psychological principle, integrated with a pure non-dual metaphysics is what renders *A Course in Miracles* unique among the spiritual and religious thought systems of the world.

So the *Course* is to be held aloof from other metaphysical doctrines not because all valid paths are discrete, but because other paths are less valid. This is nothing less than an exoteric exclusivism, or literalism, masquerading as esotericism. It is accurate on one level to say that 'a universal theology is not possible,' but the reason the *Course* asserts this truth is to obscure another, one which throws *A Course in Miracles* into a less than favorable light: that all theologies, in their metaphysical depths, will be found pointing, from their necessarily unique perspectives, to a single Truth which transcends those perspectives, and yet manifests Itself by means of them. The unity of religions, in other words, is not syncretic or eclectic, but transcendent. The *Course*, however, would deny this unity entirely in the name of its own *exclusive* transcendence. And this is an error. Nor is the *Course* really unique as it claims. Certainly it departs in major respects from the unanimous doctrine of the world's wisdom traditions, particularly in its denial of immanence, but it has a great deal in common with doctrines which those traditions regard, and rightly so, as heresies — most obviously with the Christian heresies of Gnosticism, Arianism and Docetism, since the *Course* is cast in quasi-Christian terms, but also in certain ways with doctrines considered heretical vis-à-vis Buddhism, such as those which asserts the *literal* unreality of phenomena or the *literal* eternal existence of the Buddha. And we have already seen how its doctrine of the literal non-existence of the universe is at odds with the Hindu doctrine of *maya*.

Allowing for the differences between philosophical and mythopoetic language, the doctrine that the universe was created by the ego as an attack upon God is substantially the same as that of the deluded Demiurge in Gnosticism, or the Gnostic Sophia who, like the ego she symbolizes, creates the illusion of matter out of her own auto-erotic self-involvement, without benefit of a consort, this being a mythic representation — true in a sense, if not taken literally — of the ego's illusory belief in its own self-creation. The cosmogony of *A Course in Miracles*, then, is substantially that of the Gnostic heresy; but the 'Jesus' of the *Course* seems ignorant of these affinities.

A Course in Miracles seems to be a kind of over-compensation for the materialism of the modern world (the same may in fact have been true of Gnosticism vis-à-vis late classical Paganism). The heavy, literalistic belief in material reality casts as its shadow the doctrine that the world is pure illusion and God exclusively transcendent. As nuclear fission demonstrated experimentally that the limits of our belief in matter's reality had been reached, so *A Course in Miracles*, demonstrates the same thing metaphysically. The dawning of the doctrine of exclusive transcendence, error though it is, is thus an eschatological sign. Only when the manifest world is almost completely dead to us, only when it has become so opaque to our shrunken spiritual perception that it can no longer be witnessed as a 'sign' of God, does a total denial of even the relative reality of that world begin to look like the only way out.

In my opinion, the heresy known as *A Course in Miracles* is an inevitable consequence of the contemporary suppression of traditional metaphysics within Christianity, particularly the Catholic Church. In MCQCM, p 123, Helen Schucman is quoted as saying of the *Course*, 'Finally, there is a spiritual system for intellectuals.' The hunger for metaphysical depth and intellectual enlightenment is here; it is an inescapable part of the quality of our time. But if the Church can no longer satisfy it, then woe to the Church! It is here that the contemporary Catholic rejection of traditional metaphysics, and the recurring Christian distrust of its own sapiential dimension, even within Orthodoxy, comes home to roost. As if Clement of Alexandria, Dionysius the Areopagite, Maximos the Confessor, Meister Eckhart, Scotus Eriugena — to mention only a few — were not among the greatest spiritual intellectuals of the human race. But, of course, most Christians have never read them, and this is one reason why Helen Schucman, a potential pneumatic intellectual educated by Catholic nuns, was able to bring through her heretical doctrines, which have since taken hold within the Church itself. Doctrine abhors a vacuum; only true, traditional Christian metaphysics can prevent this vacuum in the Church from being filled with dangerous

half-truths like Mrs Schucman's. *A Course in Miracles* was not a bad production, in a certain way, for a non-traditional freelance. But it wasn't enough,
and in the realm of Truth insufficiency is not neutral; it is subversive. A little
metaphysics is a dangerous thing, because once imbalanced ideas have taken
root on a high intellectual level, such as the *Course* attempts to occupy, the
full metaphysical doctrine, which alone is fully efficacious—for those with
the capacity for it—stands little chance of being recognized. Perhaps the real
purpose of *A Course in Miracles* is to attract, and spiritually neutralize, those
with the capacity to understand and profit from metaphysical Truth. If so,
then who is its author?

IV. *The Celestine Prophecy*: A Pre-Columbian Singles Culture

One of the most popular made-up New Age mythologies of recent years is
to be found in *The Celestine Prophecy*, and its sequels, by James Redfield. The
book is clearly fictional, but Mr Redfield's readers usually agree to ignore
this so they can let themselves fall under the spell of a fascinating spiritual
adventure!

The book is an account of the discovery of a mysterious Aramaic manuscript in a Peruvian archaeological site, the Celestine Ruins. The manuscript, dated 600 BC, predicts that *in these very decades*, the human race will
undergo a mass cultural and spiritual transformation, based on an understanding of the Nine Insights contained in the manuscript. The only problem is, the Peruvian authorities, incited by the conservative Catholic bishop
Cardinal Sebastian, are trying to suppress the manuscript by military force.
But an intrepid network of scientists and academics from around the world,
drawn to Peru by their interest in the manuscript, are struggling alongside
local progressive Catholic priests to preserve it from the forces of reaction.

The doctrine of *The Celestine Prophecy* is as follows: Once more and more
of us admit that mysteriously meaningful synchronistic events keep happening (The First Insight), and then develop a sense of historical perspective
which will show us, (1), that the Christian Middle Ages were spiritual in a
way, except that they were controlled by narrow-minded churchmen who
stifled evolution, and (2), that the explorations and scientific advances of the
second millennium, especially since the Renaissance, were an attempt to find
out the purpose of earthly life after the narrow-minded Middle Ages fell
apart, but that, (3), we gave up waiting for the answer to arrive and settled

for material comfort instead (together, the Second Insight), then we can learn to see the energy-auras around plants, rocks and other people, and make them stronger (the Third Insight). Once we can channel energy to plants and to each other, we will be able to stop competing with one another for life-energy (the Fourth Insight) and have cosmic mystical experiences (the Fifth Insight), which will help us to get beyond the four different ways of struggling for attention and power we learned as children (the Sixth Insight), after which we will be able to see how all events, even negative ones, are part of the flow of spiritual evolution, and link up with it (the Seventh Insight). After that we'll be able to raise our children differently by always having one adult giving total attention to one child, and also overcome co-dependence in romantic and other relationships (together, the Eighth Insight), which will allow us to create a new planetary culture where population will be controlled, where energy will be cheap and plentiful, where vast primeval forests will be allowed to grow, where cities will be self-contained, totally automated and run by artificial intelligence, and where our energy-vibrations will reach such a high level that we will de-materialize, one by one, and walk into Heaven without dying!

The Celestine Prophecy is here revealed as a hodge-podge of contemporary psychological and pseudo-esoteric ideas chaotically stitched together with the thread of a literary fantasy. The idea of mysterious prophecies discovered in Latin America at a Mayan/Inca site, and having to do with the last decades of the second millennium and the first decades of the third, most likely derived from Jose Arguelles' claims for the macro-predictive value Mayan calendar. Synchronicity (Insight One) comes from Carl Jung; historical perspective (Insight Two) from an ignorance of history; auras (Insight Three) from psychic research and the reports of clairvoyants; power struggles over energy (Insight Four) from contemporary psychology, modern psychic teachings, and the common experience of people trying to relate when they don't really love each other; a false idea of 'mystical experience' (Insight Five) from evolutionary theory; the analysis of different styles of interpersonal manipulation (Insight Six) from pop psychology, or systems like the enneagram (in Helen Palmer's rendition, not the traditional form of it used by the Naqshbandi Sufis), or direct observation; spiritual evolution (Insight Seven), from Darwinian theory misapplied; a new interpersonal ethic (Insight Eight), from pop psychology; a new planetary culture (Insight Nine), from common futuristic projections; the style of the writing itself, from Carlos Castaneda. Insights One, Three, Four and Six are valid on their own widely separated levels, but they don't line up to make anything approaching an organic whole. Even Insight *Eight* has a little something to recommend it, if it isn't used to justify aloofness and lack of commitment in relationships, which it usually is. The whole mish-mash is neither integrated nor ancient, however—but that's not a problem, apparently, because Redfield makes no hard claims for the authenticity of the manuscript his system is supposedly based upon; and the non-existent manuscript was destroyed by the forces of reaction at the end of the book anyway, so we are left with nothing but the fantasies we project into that void. The fantasies we are *directed* to project.

The Celestine Prophecy is based on the mores of the global New Age singles culture expanded to cosmic proportions. All the protagonists are single, either because they are part of the New Age singles culture, or because they are priests. There are no married Peruvians, either, among the forces of good. The children of light are cautioned against entering into committed relationships until they are highly evolved, and the only family situation presented is among the unenlightened 'locals', given as an illustration of the interpersonal problems that can be overcome by the Fourth Insight. The only child among the forces of spiritual progress is apparently living with a single mother.

The Catholic Church is the enemy. The unenlightened hierarchy fear the manuscript because it will undercut their power if people learn to 'evolve' without their permission. They believe that if people transcend their need for spiritual authority they will run amok.

The persecuted progressive priests of the forces of good are all Chardinians. Instead of salvation, they believe in collective linear spiritual progress toward the Omega Point. They expect no apocalypse. They believe that the Celestine manuscript will at last illuminate the real meaning of the Catholic tradition, even though it denies that tradition in every particular.

Which side do *you* identify with? The old fogies of the Church, with their repressive emphasis on authority and suffering, or the New Age singles culture, which promises a renewed and paradisiacal earth, where all you have to do is learn to notice synchronicities, see the auras around plants, pay attention to children and avoid co-dependent relationships and you can dissolve into pure light? The choice is simple—*and it is yours!*

Perhaps the reader is wondering why I'm taking the time to criticize what is obviously a fantasy. There are a number of reasons.

First, *The Celestine Prophecy* represents part of the 'tender-minded' (or soft-headed) ideology of the coming global civilization. Their enemies are, (1) the Catholic Church, representing a potential rival internationalism as well as a force acting to preserve folkways which stand in globalism's way, and, (2) the Peruvian government, a 'backward' nationalism which globalism, represented here by the International Network of the Academic Art Thieves of the Forces of Light who are trying to steal the manuscript, is everywhere attempting to sweep aside. Second, they are extremely popular, or were until fairly recently. And third, as an attempt to mis-represent, subvert and ultimately replace Christian doctrine, they represent one of the many New Age foreshadowings of the regime of Antichrist.

Let's begin with a few *factual errors*:

(1) On p 8, Aramaic is given as the language much of the Old Testament is written in. But almost all of the Old Testament is actually written in Hebrew. Only parts of the books of Ezra and Daniel, and isolated sentences, are in Aramaic.

(2) On p 22, the following picture is painted of the Christian Middle Ages:

> You find yourself in the class of your father—essentially peasant or aristocrat—and you know that you will always be confined to that class. But regardless of which class you're in . . . you soon realize that social position is secondary to the spiritual reality of life as defined by the churchmen. . . . If you follow their instructions, you are assured that a rewarding afterlife will follow. But if you fail to heed the course they prescribe, then, well . . . there is excommunication and certain damnation.

The implication here is that the Church enforced social immobility while directing all a person's attention to the afterlife. But in actual fact, the Church was for all practical purposes the only avenue of upward social mobility available in the Middle Ages. By means of a clerical career, a peasant could even become Pope. And to say that those who followed the churchmen's instructions would be saved, and those who did not, damned via excommunication, gives a very distorted picture. The 'churchmen's instructions' were not arbitrary decrees imposed by a kind of occupying army—clearly implied by the image of a Peruvian Cardinal secretly directing a regime of military terror—but an expression of the orthodox Christian doctrine which, with a few glaring exceptions, was accepted as natural by all sectors of society. On the political level, you might not like the actions of the local bishop, or even the Pope, but you would take the doctrine they taught, as well as their right to teach it, as a matter of course, in common with most people in most places and times of the Medieval world. And sinners were not routinely damned via excommunication; they were, and are, rendered incapable by their own egotism of withstanding the direct light of God's Love after death, experiencing it instead, because of their resistance to it, as hellfire. God, not man, judges sinners, and He judges them only according to their own intent. Excommunication was not a punishment for sin *per se*, but was reserved for those who openly defied the doctrinal authority of the Church.

(3) On p 29 we read that at

the end of the millennium. . . . A four hundred year old obsession had been completed. We had created the means of material security, and now seemed to be ready—poised, in fact—to find out why we had done it.' The only thing wrong with this statement is that it does not apply to most of the people on Earth.

(4) On p 42 it is stated that

Experiments [in quantum physics] have revealed that when you break apart small aspects of . . . energy, what we call elementary particles, and try to observe how they operate, the act of observation itself alters the results—as if these elementary particles are influenced by what the experimenter expects. . . . In other words, the basic stuff of the universe, at its core, is looking like a kind of pure energy that is malleable to human intention. . . .

This is a total misrepresentation of quantum physics. The fact that observation affects experimental results on the quantum level has nothing to do with the expectations of the experimenter. It is rather an 'exclusion principle' which defines the absolute limits to accuracy in measurement. The expectations of the experimenter do affect results insofar as they determine the working hypothesis on which the experiment is constructed, just as the particular questions I ask you about your life will have an effect upon the responses you give me. But the particular shape of your life is really there, whether or not I question you about it. In the same way, the shape of nature is not determined by the questions we ask it. If it were, scientific experimentation would be meaningless.

The 'didactic' purpose of the doctrine that reality itself, not simply experience, is affected by expectation, is to justify the acceptance of fantasy as real—particularly directed or *suggested* fantasy, since that's the only thing we're left with if there is no reality-check, no extant *manuscript*. With no way to evaluate the objective reality of a given statement, or any motivation to do so, or ultimately—and here's where *The Celestine Prophecy* is purely postmodern—any belief that such a thing as objective reality exists, then the one with the *chutzpa* and the personal power-motive to arbitrarily define reality, the stage magician who says to his clueless audience 'imagine this with me,' is God—at least temporarily. This is the negative side of the 'guided visualizations' so common in New Age workshops: they function as training sessions in uncritical suggestibility.

(5) On p 59: 'The old Newtonian idea is that everything happens by chance . . . that every event has a line of causation independent of our attitude.' But, of course, to say that everything happens by chance is to deny that independent lines of causation can exist. Newton did not say everything happens by chance; he said that everything happens by independent lines of causation. Redfield's thinking is so garbled here, apart from his simple ignorance of the facts, that I'm led to conclude that his denial of independent lines of causation has caused him to deny the validity of logical thinking as well, which is why he's forgotten how to do it. But if objective reality is influenced by one's attitude, independent of the simple consequences of one's actions, then maybe if Redfield adopts the attitude that Newton actually said that everything depends upon chance—even if he actually didn't—then, in a sense, he actually did—if, that is, we *believe* that he did. I *saw* the magician saw that lady in half with my own eyes, and so he really did, because seeing is believing. Or rather, as Redfield and other stage magicians know, *believing is seeing*. It's called 'mis-direction of attention.'

(6) On p 235: 'The ruins where the Ninth [Insight] was found is [*sic*] called the Celestine Temples, the *Heavenly* Temples.' The word 'Celestine', however, actually refers to the Celestine Order of Catholic monks, founded by Pope Celestine V around 1260. The Celestine monasteries were destroyed during and after the French Revolution; consequently much of Western Europe was host to various 'Celestine ruins'. So obsessively does Redfield wish to supplant the Catholic Church that he even appropriates the name of one of its monastic orders.

(7) On p 237, the conservative Cardinal Sebastian is portrayed as living in expectation of 'the rapture'. But conservative and traditional Catholics don't believe in the rapture, which is an Evangelical Christian doctrine of fairly recent origin.

From factual errors, we now move on to *misrepresentations of love*.

On p 116, the 'Father Sanchez' character, like the Deepak Chopra of *The Seven Spiritual Laws of Success*, and in line with the mores of the international singles culture, preaches against the idea that love ever requires sacrifice. How common this belief is, at least in the developed nations of the West. 'I thought it would be wonderful,' we say, 'and for a while it was wonderful, but then it started to be terrible, so I left.' Our preaching, much of it justified, against 'co-dependency', is too often used to hide the fact that we routinely consider that our relationships, like the other things we buy into, should simply be there to fulfill our expectations. If the things we wanted out of the relationship are not immediately forthcoming, we take it back for a refund, exactly as we would a defective product. 'If it doesn't *work*, why *keep* it?' we say to ourselves. 'Why should I be expected to spend my own resources to repair something that should have been better made in the first place? It's not my job to fix it; what I want is a *replacement*.' In the words of 'Father Sanchez':

> The role of love has been misunderstood for a long time. Love is not some-thing we should do to be good or to make the world a better place out of some abstract moral responsibility, or because we should give up our hedo-nism. Connecting with energy feels like excitement, then euphoria, and then love. Finding enough energy to maintain that state of love certainly helps the world, but it most directly helps us. It is the most hedonistic thing we can do.

Love, in other words, is a buzz. It has nothing to do with compassionate ser-vice (*agape*), much less with appreciation of and devotion to the unique per-sonhood of another (*amor*); it is a form or level of *energy*. Here we see again the pantheistic tendency to believe that energy is on a higher level of being than personhood. It is true that if the flow of life-energy is depleted, our own personhood and that of others is suppressed. But this is because *life-energy is the field-expression of personhood*, the *shakti* of it, not a substitute for it. In Hindu terms, there is no *Prakriti* (primal matter/energy) without *Purusha* (the indwelling Divine 'Person'); and our own unique personhood, as well as that of others, is the most direct manifestation of the Divine within us. To substitute feel-good energy for developed personhood, as well as for self-sacrifice, character-development, empathy, and all the other things which serve this personhood, and which alone make the world of mature human love and adult relationships possible, is perilously close to limiting human love to sexual attraction, or to other subtler forms of attraction which are equally impersonal and ephemeral.

Co-dependency is not 'too much relatedness,' but a failure to relate to the other as a real person. My ego sees the other as part of me, and the other does the same, producing a confusion of identities. There is no relationship and no polarity because there is no personal definition, only an impersonal field of psychic energy, filled with half-conscious expectations and desires. Such a field may sometimes feel 'spiritual' because lack of personal definition takes the hard edge off the ego. But the ego is still there, all the more danger-ous for being less focused and less visible.

According to *The Celestine Prophecy*, co-dependency is universal; as the 'Karla' character says, [p195], 'We're all co-dependent, and we're all growing out of it now.' She describes the 'usual' relationship between a man and a woman as 'a power-struggle'. 'We've always wondered,' she says, 'what causes the bliss and euphoria of love to end, to suddenly turn into conflict, and now'—due to the mysterious Manuscript discovered in the Peruvian jungles—'we know.' She goes on:

'when we first begin to evolve, we automatically begin to receive our oppo-site-sex energy ... from ... the universe. But ... if another person comes along who offers this energy directly we can cut ourself off from the true source ... and regress ... until we learn how to avoid this situation, we are walking around like a circle half complete. You know, we look like the letter C. We are very susceptible to a person of the opposite sex, some other circle half complete, coming up and joining us—completing the circle that way— and giving us a burst of euphoria and energy that feels like the wholeness that a full connection with the universe produces. In reality, we have only joined with another person who is looking for their other half on the outside too.

'You see, the problem with this completed person, this O, that both people think they have reached, is that it has taken two people to make this one whole person, one supplying the female energy and the other supplying the male. This one whole person consequently has two heads, or egos. Both peo-ple want to run the whole person they have created and so, just as in child-hood, both people want to command the other, as if the other were themselves. This kind of illusion of completeness always breaks down into a power struggle. In the end, each person must take the other for granted and even invalidate them so they can lead this whole self in the direction they want to go. But of course that doesn't work, at least not any more. Perhaps in the past, one of the partners was willing to submit themselves to the other— usually the woman, sometimes the man. But we are waking up now. No one wants to be subservient to anyone else any longer.'

'.... So much for romance,' I said.

'Oh, we can still have romance,' Karla replied. 'But first we have to complete the circle on our own. We have to stabilize our channel with the universe. That takes time, but afterwards ... we can have what the Manuscript calls a higher-relationship When we connect romantically with another whole per-son after that, we create a super-person. ... But it never pulls us from the path of our individual evolution.' (pp193–195)

There is a lot of truth in this picture of co-dependency, which is one of the psychological diseases particular to our time, when the entire system of The World conspires against anything resembling character-development. There is truth in the diagnosis, as far as it goes, but I do have serious problems with the treatment.

To begin with, the 'universe' through which we receive our 'opposite-sex energy' is filled with other persons, who mediate this energy to us. The child raised by wolves will not be able to relate very well to other human beings, whether or not they are of the opposite sex. The only way to learn relationship is by relating.

To look at the 'universe' as the prime source of sexual relatedness, and actual people of the opposite sex as secondary, is another of the many devastating effects of pantheism, nature-worship and the idolatry of energy. Again, there is no field of 'sexual energy' without actual sexed persons. To separate other persons, whether as individuals or as representatives of their gender, from their trans-personal archetypes in the mind of God is to turn them into idols of one's ego; this Redfield understands. But to relate to transpersonal 'energies' instead of real people is also idolatry — not of individuals, but of the archetypes. The first idolatry produces a contracted, stagnant, 'all-too-human' condition of depleted energy; the second produces an 'all-too-divine' condition of ego-inflation, an explosive scattering of the soul.

'Karla' describes the co-dependent relationship as 'one whole person' with 'two heads'. But, of course, it is not a whole person, but a mass of illusions, identifications, projections, and self-contradictions. And whether such a relationship can eventually mature, or whether it is ultimately better for the partners to dissolve it and enter into other relationships later after they've done some growing up, can only be answered case by case; there is no general rule. But if one thing is certain, it is that a person cannot 'complete the circle' that lets him or her relate to others 'on [his or her] own.' Relationship is only learned by relating. People can wait their whole lives until they are 'complete' enough to have a meaningful relationship and never get there, because they are trying to become perfect hermetically-sealed narcissistic egos with no human needs, and who wants to relate to someone like that? Such a person will also be incapable of submitting to another with dignity, as well as of accepting submission from another with justice and grace, because the weak narcissistic ego can never submit, only identify and manipulate. Certainly the hopelessly co-dependent person would do well to take a sabbatical from intimate relationships, interrupt the cycle of identification, self-desecration and manipulation, and learn that there is more in life than a sexual partner. But if the co-dependent person tries to wait until he has become totally self-sufficient — in other words, until his ego has become God — before entering into a love relationship, then long may he wait.

As incarnate human beings, we live in a relative world, which means that, as creatures though not as Names of God, we are fundamentally incomplete. We need each other, and this is as it should be. Without this need, human society would be impossible. Only a luciferian arrogance would wish to deny the inherent limits of our creaturehood. Such arrogance, however, is a common aspect of the collective human psyche of the latter days, because to the degree that God is no longer real to us, we must project the perfection which belongs to Him alone either upon the universe (in materialistic nature-worship) or human relationships (in co-dependency) or pseudo-self-sufficiency (in narcissism). When Jesus said, 'be ye perfect, even as your Father in Heaven is perfect,' he was not directing us to try and achieve perfection on the psychic level, but rather to recognize that true perfection is 'heavenly' or celestial, that it is a spiritual reality, not a psychic one, since 'who by taking thought can add one inch to his stature?' Recognizing the inherent limits of the psyche, we are led to recognize the 'Father within' Who transcends it, the perfection of God which, though it is other than all we define ourselves to be, is nonetheless our true Being: 'It is not I who live, but Christ lives in me.' And if we realize that completion lies in God alone, we will not put our human relationships under the impossible stress of demanding that they be complete, but will understand them as incomplete by nature, and therefore as opportunities to develop the virtues of patience, compassion, loving kindness, courtesy, courage and self-respect, as channels for the expression of Divine Love in the human world. Through the virtues, the human psyche reaches its highest level of development, and so becomes conformed, up to the limit of its capacity, to its spiritual Source.

There is such a thing as the 'higher-relationship'; Redfield is right about that. There is no greater spiritual alchemy than a loving marriage consciously lived as part of the spiritual path. But this higher romance or spiritual marriage is not a perfect union of two perfectly self-sufficient individuals, but is rather a relationship forged in the fires of *mutual* subservience — as opposed to a fixed pattern of dominance-and-sub-mission — where each partner, often overcoming great resistance, worships God in the person of the other. But as 'Karla' says, 'no one wants to be subservient to anyone else any longer,' and this is why unstable ego-conflicts have replaced stable marriages as the 'norm' in contemporary society.

Spiritual romance is the mutual veneration of the other as a living symbol of the Divine Self—rather than, as in the case of co-dependency, the mutual idolatry of the ego in the person of the other. It is not some kind of glamorous, archetypal sexual fantasy for two, however, as in much of what's come to be called the 'sacred sexuality movement', but a recognition of the transpersonal archetypes of gender in both oneself and the other. And since these archetypes of gender are not something the ego can own, they cannot be embodied through an inflation of the personality to the archetypal level, but only through a humble submission to that which transcends the personality entirely.

Moving beyond misrepresentations of love, we will now take a look at the closely related *misrepresentations of religion and spirituality*.

On p106, Redfield makes it clear that he conceives of God, or rather of the thing he believes in instead of God, as 'energy from another source—a source we will eventually learn to tap at will.' Like Deepak Chopra, James Redfield sees the Divine as a passive and all-but-unconscious energy which can be 'tapped' like any other natural resource. And it is always *me*, always the individual ego, who does the tapping. Any sense that this 'energy', in relation to us, might possess a conscious intent of Its own is looked on as a primitive Christian superstition. That It might decide to tap *us*, instead of we It, is never dreamed of. After all, says the mind of the New Age, no one wants to be subservient to anyone else any longer—and if willing subservience to another human being is such a problem, think how terrible and unnatural it would be to be subservient to the Absolute Itself!

In the fifth chapter of *The Celestine Prophecy*, the narrator has what he identifies as a mystical experience. It is, however, an experience which has almost nothing in common with the universal report of the mystics and contemplatives of the world's religions and wisdom traditions throughout history. Stimulated by his fear of being captured or killed by pursuing soldiers who are trying to suppress the Manuscript, he experiences, (1) that the Earth is actually a sphere, that outer space exists below his feet as well as above his head; (2) an identification of the natural world as part of his body; (3) the panorama of cosmic and biological evolution from the Big Bang to man; and (4) the insight that evolution continues in the consciousness of human beings, and has something to do with synchronistic coincidences.

Genuine mystical experience is timeless. It is based on a profound sense of relationship with, or absorption in, a higher order of Reality. In its introverted form it transcends the material world entirely, while in its extroverted form it transfigures that world, producing a vision of the material dimension as a symbolic manifestation of a higher Reality which transcends space, time, matter and energy. The narrator's vision, however, is simply that of a wider vista of space, time, matter and energy; it is in no way mystical. Furthermore, to see human beings as the flower of an evolutionary process and the vanguard of further evolutionary development is to identify the individual as the highest level of being; but if nothing is considered higher than the individual, then that individual cannot relate to, or be absorbed within, a higher Reality. So again, the narrator's experience cannot be called mystical.

It is certainly true, according to esoteric philosophy, that the created order returns to its Divine Source through the conscious spiritual unfolding of individual sentient beings. But this 'evolution', this unfolding of the individual through a transcendence of the self-identified ego, is not a continuance of the cosmogonic process, but a *reversal* of this process. Rather than a further elaboration of created forms, it is a progressive dissolution of these forms, leading to their reintegration into their respective prototypes on ever higher levels of being. The word 'evolution' means an 'unwinding', a 'turning out' of what has been wound up, or turned in upon itself, to produce the ego-bound consciousness and the world of material forms. Seen from the point-of-view of manifestation, creation is an 'involution', a process of self-involvement, while 'evolution' is the opposite process through which creation is unwound, dissolved, and the original Unity unveiled. Rather than 'carrying forth the universe's evolution toward higher and higher vibrational complexity' (p 117), we are actually *either* carrying it to higher and higher levels of *simplicity*, or helping it *degenerate* into greater and greater complexity and self-involvement.

Man is the most complex life-form on earth, because we are in some sense the synthesis and epitome of all other forms. If, as we are told in the Bible and the Koran, Adam named the animals, it was because he contained within himself all the names of God of which the natural forms of the universe are projections. He could name them because, being Man, he already knew their names. So from the esoteric perspective, the purpose of human complexity is to make it possible for us to return to the simplicity of our Origin in the name of all things.

After a certain line is crossed, the further complexification of human life starts to destroy that life, and the natural world around it; we obviously crossed that line some time ago. When the creation of life arrives at self-conscious sentient being, the return to Source has already begun; as it says in the Koran, 'to Him [Allah] does the whole matter revert.' But though this return is ultimately inevitable, self-conscious being can return to its Source by one of two roads: the road of simplification or 'recollection' leading to the salvation of the soul and its reintegration into its prototype, or the road of further complexification or 'scattering', leading to the fragmentation of the soul, the destruction of life, and the ultimate return to Source, after an aeon of suffering, via the road of penitential fire. The whole purpose of religion, as a projection of God's Mercy into this world, is to define these paths, showing us how to choose the first and avoid the second.

The habit of seeing ever-increasing complexification as an ascension to higher ontological levels—an error that Teilhard de Chardin's whole system is based upon, which is probably where Redfield got it—is inseparable from the worldview of materialism. Seen from the standpoint of matter, greater complexification is higher being. Seen from the standpoint of consciousness, higher being is reached through simplification, through recollection, through gathering together what was scattered. This is what *meditation* is all about. The mind which returns to simplicity, to what the Taoists call the 'uncarved block', is calm enough to witness vast reaches of cosmic complexity; the agitated mind can only witness a few tangled and repetitive obsessions. But the peace which allows the collected mind to witness the complexity of things also lets it know them in their primal simplicity, as faces of the One. This is how all things return to their Source: through purification of consciousness.

On p176, Redfield sets up, as a straw man representing the traditional religious position, a 'Father Costous', who presents the Church's reasons for opposing the Manuscript:

> 'You think that the Manuscript is undermining your religion?' I asked Costous gently. He looked at me with condescension. 'Not just our religion; everyone's religion. Do you think there is no plan for this world? God is in control. He assigns our destiny. Our job is to obey the laws set forth by God. Evolution is a myth. God creates the future the way he wants it. To say humans can make themselves evolve takes the will of God out of the picture. It allows people to be selfish and separate. They think that their evolution is the important thing, not God's plan. They will treat each other even worse than they do now.'

To say 'God . . . assigns our destiny. . . . God creates the future the way he wants it. . . .' is essentially to deny free will. But the Catholic Church teaches that human will *is* free. In the words of St Augustine from the *City of God*, 'we assert both that God knows all things before they happen and that we do by our free will everything that we feel and know would not happen without our volition.' So Redfield is mistaken here.

Furthermore, when he has his 'Father Costous' oppose 'humans making themselves evolve' to 'the will of God', he is letting personal 'evolution' stand for what traditional Catholic theology calls 'good works', and 'the will of God' for Divine grace—as if Catholicism taught that the soul is saved by grace alone, or by faith as a gift of grace. But Catholicism in fact teaches that the soul is saved by faith *and works*, that to labor for our own spiritual 'evolution'—for which read 'sanctification'—on the basis of God-given faith and under the influence of Divine Grace is not only a possibility, but a duty. On the other hand, 'Father Costous' is entirely right when he says that if we believe we can 'make' ourselves develop spiritually outside the context of God's will and God's plan, we will become selfish and separate. This happens to be one of the 'laws of God', which are not arbitrary decrees of some cosmic tyrant as Redfield seems to think, but simply the nature of things. The 'culture of narcissism', to use Christopher Lasch's name for it, is one consequence of the mass ignorance of this particular law.

On pp 235–36, the progressive, pro-Manuscript priest 'Father Sanchez' has the following exchange with the conservative 'Cardinal Sebastian':

[Sebastian]: 'We know what spirituality is, Father Sanchez.'
'Do we? I think not. We've spent centuries talking about it, visualizing it, professing our belief in it. But we've always characterized this connection as something an individual must do to avoid something bad happening, rather than to acquire something good and tremendous. The Manuscript describes the inspiration that comes when we are truly loving others and evolving our lives forward.'

James Redfield apparently believes, judging from this passage, that Christianity has produced no saints, no mystics, no sages, that it has all been an academic exercise or wish-fulfillment fantasy, even though lasting for two millennia. But of course Christianity has taught from the beginning that love is the highest virtue; it has produced both paragons of human love, like St Francis or Mother Theresa, and spent more blood, sweat and treasure on concrete works of mercy than the New Age ever will, even if it were to make service to the poor, the sick and the homeless its first priority, which it shows little sign of doing. And to say that Christianity had no inkling that spirituality could be something 'good and tremendous' until this fictional Manuscript came along is of course absurd. All the testimony of scripture, all the testimony of the saints, the mystics, the spiritual giants of Christianity disproves it absolutely.

On p 236, 'Sanchez' and 'Sebastian' argue about spiritual evolution:

[Sanchez]: 'The Manuscript describes the progress of succeeding generations as an evolution of understanding, an evolution toward higher spirituality and vibration. Each generation incorporates more energy and accumulates more truth and then passes that status on to the people of the next generation, who extend it further.'

'That's nonsense,' Sebastian said. 'There is only one way to become more spiritual, and that is by following the examples in the scriptures.'

'Exactly!' Sanchez said. 'But again, what are the examples? Isn't the story of the scriptures a story of people learning to receive God's energy and will within? Isn't that what the early prophets led the people to do in the Old Testament? And isn't that receptivity to God's energy within what culminated in the life of a carpenter's son, to the extent that we say God, himself, descended to Earth?

'Isn't the story of the New Testament,' he continued, 'the story of a group of people being filled with some kind of energy that transformed them? Didn't Jesus say, himself, that what he did, we could do also, and more? We've never really taken that idea seriously, not until now. We're only now grasping what Jesus was talking about, where he was leading us. The Manuscript identified what he meant! How to do it!'

In other words, we always had the theory; all we were missing was the *instruction manual.* (How else can a technological society view spirituality, except as a process of overcoming technical difficulties?) But are we to believe that where thousands of heroic and saintly lives dedicated to prayer, meditation and service have failed, the overcoming of co-dependency, the appreciation of coincidences and the seeing of auras around plants will succeed? Due to the widespread cultural ignorance of true spirituality, not to mention of our own historical traditions, many apparently do. And certainly the story of the scriptures has to do, on one level, with receiving God's energy and will within. But the idea of collective spiritual progress through the generations is not part of that story, in either the Old Testament or the New. From Eden to human history was a fall. From rule of the chosen people by prophets and judges to rule by kings was another. And the New Testament also, even if we leave aside the book of Apocalypse, and in common with all other traditional scriptures, predicts not evolution but degeneration:

There shall arise false Christs, and false prophets, and shall show great signs
and wonders: insomuch that, if it were possible, they shall deceive the very
elect.

⁓Matt. 24:24

This know also, that in the last days perilous times shall come.
For men shall be lovers of their own selves, covetous, boasters, proud, blas-
phemers, disobedient to parents, unthankful, unholy,
Without natural affection, truce breakers, false accusers, incontinent, fierce,
despisers of those that are good,
Traitors, heady, high-minded, lovers of pleasures more than lovers of God;
Having a form of godliness but denying the power thereof…

⁓ II Tim. 3:1–5

As for Jesus's prediction that his followers would do even greater things than
he, the fact that a small band of the outlawed devotees of an executed
teacher would go on to found a religion which would supplant the most
powerful empire on Earth clearly fulfills that prediction. And whoever has
attained sanctification has, like Jesus, overcome death.

Despite its attempt to create an 'alternative' spiritual worldview, *The Celestine Prophecy* is not so much a book of spiritual teachings as it is a spiritual-
ized ideology designed, either consciously or unconsciously, to justify and
glamorize the emerging global economy. On pp 225–227, the 'Dobson' character says:

> The next cultural shift will be an automation of the production of
> goods … freeing up everyone's time, so that we can pursue other
> endeavors … our gifts … should go to the persons who have given us spiri-
> tual truth. When people come into our lives at just the right time to give us
> the answers we need, we should give them money. This is how we will begin
> to supplement our incomes and ease out of the occupations which limit us.
> As more people engage in this spiritual economy we will begin a real shift
> into the culture of the next millennium. … Paying others for their insights
> will begin the transformation and then as more and more parts of the econ-
> omy are automated, currency will disappear.

So the information age is identified with a new millennial spirituality. Never
mind that globalization continues to widen the rift between rich and poor,
or that many employed by the global information economy are presently
working 60 hours a week and more, or that two salaries are now required to
keep up a middle class lifestyle, thus 'freeing up' our children to be raised by
television and socialized by gangs. And never mind that millions whose time

has been 'freed up' by automation are now homeless. (The unemployment rate, we must remember, is the percentage of recently-employed workers who are presently jobless; it says nothing about the growing numbers of non-workers who haven't had a job in years.) And how is paying people for spiritual truth fundamentally different from the selling of indulgences in pre-Reformation Catholicism? If you pay people for a gift, it is no longer a gift but a product. In the words of Jesus, 'you cannot serve God and Mammon.' The correct way of showing gratitude for a spiritual insight is either to repay the giver with an insight of your own, or pass the original insight on to another who is worthy of it, when the place, time and circumstances are right. And the highest form of gratitude is to recognize that all insight comes from God, and then work to realize that gift of insight in your own life.

Here we can see how the New Age workshop culture, the trade in 'spiritual services' of which *The Celestine Prophecy*, along with its companion audio-tapes, groups, networks and workshops is a prime example, is simply one sector of the emerging service-based information economy in the developed nations. Perhaps this is all the New Age really is. But, if true, what is the significance of this?

René Guénon, in chapter 16 of *The Reign of Quantity* entitled 'The Degeneration of Coinage', shows how money has progressively lost its qualitative or symbolical content, and has degenerated in the direction of pure quantity—a fact only further confirmed by today's electronic fund-transfer system, where 'money' is no longer either coin or paper, but simply a recorded number. Based on this trend, and on the metaphysical principle that such a thing as an absolutely 'pure quantity' cannot exist, he predicts, like 'Dobson', that money will disappear. But in chapter 39, 'The Great Parody or Spirituality Inverted', where he characterizes the reign of Antichrist as 'a false 'spiritual restoration' . . . a sort of reintroduction of quality in all things' (p 326), and goes on to say (p 359, n 2):

> Money itself, or whatever may take its place, will once more possess a qualitative character of this sort, for it is said that 'no man might buy or sell, save that he had the mark, or the name of the beast, or the number of his name' (Rev. 13:17), and this implies the actual use in connection with money of the inverted symbols of the 'counter-tradition. . . .'

It is of course no sin, though it may be an *occasion* of sin, to sell books one has written or objects of art one has produced for the purpose of transmitting spiritual ideas. But the direct monetary quantification of insight itself, such as James Redfield proposes, foreshadows the development that René

Guénon predicts, especially since Redfield too speaks of the disappearance of currency.

Spiritual insight is purely qualitative, being literally 'priceless'. Furthermore, according to traditional teachings, spiritual knowledge may be given, but it cannot be acquired. The attempt to buy sacred things, and by so doing render them quantitative—which is based on the intellectual error that it is *possible* to buy sacred things—is known in Christianity as the sin of 'simony', named after the magician and Gnostic heresiarch Simon Magus, who offered to buy the miraculous power of the Holy Spirit from Simon Peter in Acts 8:9–24, as if it were a kind of professional or technical secret. To the degree that the information culture attempts to quantify spiritual insight on a monetary basis, it is engaging precisely in simony. And since insight is essentially qualitative, not quantitative—a fact which the information culture seems to have been created precisely to deny—its use as a form of currency confirms Guénon's prediction that 'Money . . . or whatever may take its place, will once more possess [an inverted] qualitative character' under the regime of Antichrist.'

In characterizing *The Celestine Prophecy* as a precursor to that regime, I am not asserting that James Redfield is (or is not) the conscious promoter of a spiritually subversive agenda, only that he is the victim, and also the beneficiary, of a false hope.

V. Having It vs. Eating It: The Entrepreneurial Hinduism of Deepak Chopra

In the Kali age wealth alone will be the criterion of pedigree, morality, and merit . . . want of riches will be the sole test of impiety.
⁀ THE BHAGAVATA PURANA

Deepak Chopra, holistic M.D., one-time follower of Maharishi Mahesh Yogi, and CEO of the Chopra Center for Well-being, is perhaps the most successful teacher in the Western world, and beyond it, among those who do not so much preach false metaphysical principles as apply true ones to false objects—in the case of Dr Chopra, worldly success. I do not dispute his expertise as a physician, nor the common New Age truism that a healing of the soul can sometimes heal the body too, up to a point. What I do dispute is the strict identification of salvation or enlightenment with physical or even emotional well-being. God's omnipotence gives Him the power to heal any illness. It also gives Him the right to demand from us all that we possess, including physical health, to require that we place no 'gods' before Him, but choose Him alone. Jesus healed leprosy and congenital blindness; he even raised the dead. But he also called upon his followers to face martyrdom, to sacrifice attachment to well-being in the name of something infinitely higher, to 'take up their cross and follow Him.'

In his *The Seven Spiritual Laws of Success*, Dr Chopra makes the following claim for his method:

> When this knowledge is incorporated in your consciousness, it will give you the ability to create unlimited wealth with effortless ease, and to experience success in every endeavor.... Success is the ability to fulfill your desires with effortless ease.... Material abundance, in all its expressions, happens to be one of those things that makes the journey more enjoyable. But success also includes good health, energy and enthusiasm for life, fulfilling relationships, creative freedom, emotional and psychological stability, a sense of well-being, and peace of mind.

In other words, Dr Chopra strictly identifies God-realization with material well-being.

But this, of course, is idolatry. When the great Indian saint Ramakrishna was dying of throat cancer, his followers begged him to heal himself with his yoga-power. His answer was: 'But this is what the Mother wants. How can *I* want something else?'

Let me deal, one at a time, with Deepak Chopra's seven laws:

1. *The Law of Pure Potentiality*

> The source of all creation is pure consciousness.... Pure potentiality seeking expression from the unmanifest to the manifest. And when we realize that our true Self is one of pure potentiality, we align with the power that manifests everything in the universe.

The first law, for the most part, is true as stated. However, Dr Chopra goes on to say that 'When you discover your essential nature and know who you really are, *in that knowing itself* is the ability to fulfill any dream you have, because you are the eternal possibility, the immeasurable potentiality of all that was, is, and will be' (p10). This can only mean that God, who is your true Self, has the ability to fulfill any dream God has. In order to see the truth of this, one need only point to the universe. But as soon as the word 'you' is defined by its desires, as the one who lacks and therefore desires material abundance, good health, energy and enthusiasm for life, fulfilling relationships, creative freedom, emotional and psychological stability, a sense of well-being and peace of mind, then we are obviously no longer talking about God, but about a being limited by matter, energy, space, time and personality—all parts of that Veil over the face of God created by desire itself. We are in the presence of a contingent being who might never have been born, was born, and will inevitably die. This being does not have unlimited potentiality, just as the Ocean cannot be contained in a cup. It is merely one expression, selected out of infinity potentiality, of the creative power of God.

Dr Chopra claims for that power based on knowledge of the Self that 'It draws people to you, and also draws things that you want to you. It magnetizes people, situations and circumstances to support your desires. This is also called support from the laws of nature. It is the support of divinity; it is the support that comes from being in a state of grace' (p13). Now it is certainly true that the Self draws all things toward it; as the Koran teaches, all things return to Allah. Once a void is created in the field of egotism, which in subjective terms is one's self-concept and in objective ones the world of 'ordinary reality', energy rushes in to fill that void, and unite with the radiant *atman*, the Divine Self within it. If, using Tantric terminology, we call this Divine Self 'Shiva', then the energy attracted to It, which is the universal field of Its own Self-expression, is Its 'Shakti'. *Shakti* is the energy of universal desire, desire on the level of the Divine, as in the *hadith* where Allah says 'I was a hidden treasure and desired to be known, so I created the universe that I might be known.' But the only way to access the level of God's desire is to transcend one's own desires; in the words of Jesus, 'Not my will but Thine be done.' The Divine *Shakti*, in other words, does not support *your* personal desires, but is a manifestation of God's own 'desire', His Infinite Self-manifesting radiance. On the other hand, *our truest desires are part of what God desires for us*, since they are aspects of the unique form in which He has willed to create us. It is this level of desire which is fulfilled when we come into the field of God's Self-manifesting radiance. But the only way to access this level of desire is to give up all that we can imagine desiring *for ourselves*, and rest in what God Himself desires for us. We cannot *use* the Infinite to fulfill the demands of the finite; we cannot have our cake and eat it too. If we attempt this anyway, and it seems to be working, we are actually in the process of 'spending our good karma', cashing in our potential for liberating union with God to buy the material and psychological goods of this world.

Our ego has not been transcended, it has only become more subtle—and the consequences for any ego which believes it can use the Absolute to fulfill its own tiny desires is that it progressively comes to see itself *as* the Absolute, at which point the face of the Absolute becomes veiled. When this happens, the energy of Divine abundance is cut off. In Judeo-Christian terms, this is known as 'the fall of Lucifer'. According to Buddhist doctrine, those souls who, having accumulated a great heap of spiritual merit, decide to spend it on the 'successful' fulfillment of desire instead of final liberation from desire, who squander their good karma on intellectual, emotional and material binges apparently not followed—until much later—by any serious hangover, are said to be in 'Deva-loka', the realm of the long-lived gods who dwell in blissful ignorance. But even if they are able to exist for thousands of aeons in that state, it does finally come to an end; the hell-worlds open their jaws. And these souls, having spent countless aeons letting their spiritual faculties atrophy without the challenge of difficult karma, have no power to escape those jaws—until much, much later. In the words of Jesus, 'they will not come out again until they have paid the last farthing.'

2. The Law of Giving

> The universe operates through dynamic exchange. . . . Giving and receiving are different aspects of the flow of energy in the universe. And in our willing- ness to give that which we seek, we keep the abundance of the universe circu- lating in our lives.

This law also is more or less true. Egotism, in fact, can be defined as what- ever obstructs the flow of life energy. Dr Chopra goes on to say, 'The more you give, the more you will receive, because you will keep the abundance of the universe circulating in your life' (pp 29–30); 'If, through the act of giving, you feel you have lost something, then the gift is not truly given and will not cause increase (p 30); 'If you want joy, give joy to others; if you want love, learn to give love; if you want attention and appreciation, learn to give atten- tion and appreciation; if you want material affluence, help others to become materially affluent' (pp 30–31). All this is true, and definitely worth repeat- ing. Yet it leaves a lot unsaid. To begin with, Dr Chopra, though he rightly recommends that each act of giving be accompanied with a prayer for the happiness of the receiver, tends to keep everything on the level of *material* happiness. This level, however, cannot be maintained. Our giving and receiving must either grow in the direction of seeing that only God is the Giver, and from there to the station of desiring nothing from God but God

Himself, and ultimately to the knowledge that God, in addition to being the only Giver, is the only Receiver as well, or it will decay instead, in the direction of attachment to strictly material benefits, and end by reducing the act of giving to a kind of magical spell for forcing the universe to come across. What is missing, here, is the sense that one is called upon to give not only material goods, attention, love and happiness, but also one's entire sense of identity. This is another way of saying that one must learn to give, not with assurance of return, but completely without hope of return.

Only this is true giving; everything else is just buying and selling. To give without hope of return is to give away a part of one's identity, unconditionally, and forever. But our sense of identity, which doesn't want to die, rarely gives up without a fight, which means that often one *does* have to go through the feeling of having 'lost something' in making a gift; this is what is meant by *sacrifice*. Jesus Christ gave his life freely, but not without suffering: 'If it be possible, let this cup pass from me; yet not my will but Thine be done.' Yet he also forgave his executioners; he held no grudge, but completed his sacrifice, and released it. Only if that feeling of loss-of-identity is not sacrificed in turn, but retained instead as a grievance against fate, is the gift in question 'not truly given'.

Dr Chopra maintains that 'Money is really a symbol of the life energy we exchange and the life energy we use as a result of the service we provide to the universe' (p 28) 'Like a river, money must keep flowing, otherwise it begins to clog, to suffocate and strangle its very own life force' (p 30). This is true on the plane of ideals, and is an expansive and uplifting way to look at money. But we all know how imperfectly it applies on the plane of fact. There are enough exceptions to that rule in this world, even if we leave aside pyramid marketing schemes, to make me think twice about hiring Dr Chopra as my financial adviser. The universe may in a sense be a free market economy, but it is not exempt from boom and bust. Perfect justice is not possible on the plane of manifestation because manifestation itself is the product of a primal imbalance. One of the consequences of this imbalance is that even the intent to pay off one's karmic debts generates more karma. Only in God is justice perfect, and therefore unnecessary. To take less than Him is to remain in debt; to sell all one has and buy Him is to cancel both debt and debtor. 'He who seeks to keep his life shall lose it, but he who loses his life, for My sake, shall find it.'

Dr Chopra's doctrine that money must be kept flowing is based on the Hindu concept of the *vasor dhara*, the 'Stream of Wealth', whose continuance is one of the results of the Vedic Sacrifice. This Stream does not circulate *horizontally,* however, from person to person, but rather *vertically,* rising from the human world to the world of the gods in the smoke of the Sacrifice, and returning from the world of the gods to the world of humanity in the form of rain, which symbolizes all the goods of life conceived of as a 'rain of blessings'. For Deepak Chopra, passing things *around* has clearly replaced giving things *up.* This tendency to interpret horizontally and quantitatively sacred doctrines which were originally conceived in vertical and qualitative terms is inseparable from the modern and post-modern mindsets; it is the origin, for example, of the doctrine of evolution, which replaces ontological hierarchy with historical development.

The Vedic Sacrifice is indeed offered for both the material and the spiritual good of the sacrificer, in both this world and the next. The material fruit of the sacrifice is that neither the sacrificer nor his people shall die of want; the spiritual fruit is the direct knowledge of God. But according to Ananda Coomaraswamy,

> These distinctions of temporal from eternal goods correspond to that which is sharply drawn in the Brahmanas between a mere patronage or performance of the rites and a comprehension of them, the mere participator securing only the immediate, and the Comprehensor . . . both ends of the operation.

He furthermore points out that according to the Brahmanas, 'the victim is a representative of the sacrificer himself, or as the texts express it, *is* the sacrificer himself.' The Vedic Sacrifice is therefore named *atmayajña* or 'self-sacrifice'. It is uncertain whether or not Deepak Chopra really understands this.

3. The Law of 'Karma' or Cause and Effect

Every action generates a force of energy that returns to us in like kind. . . . What we sow is what we reap And when we choose actions that bring happiness and success to others, the fruit of our karma is happiness and success.

True—as long as we remember that not all karmic fruits are harvested in this life, and that the definition of 'good karma' for a person dedicated to the pursuit of happiness is one thing, and for someone else dedicated to the quest for liberation, another. The quality of the first is desirability; the quality of the second is whatever conduces to liberation, be it pain or pleasure, good health or ill health, affluence or poverty. The fruit of the first is intermittent and temporary happiness. The fruit of the second is God, Whose bliss is beyond all limitation; It cannot be defined in terms of the experiencer, the object experienced, or even experience itself. It is called 'Bliss' not because It is an experience, but because the earned and given right to rest in close proximity to It is Paradise.

On p 40, Dr Chopra says,

> We are infinite choice-makers. In every moment of existence, we are in that field of all possibilities where we have access to an infinity of choices . . . the best way to maximize the use of karmic law is to become consciously aware of the choices we make in every moment.

There are a number of things wrong with this statement. To begin with, what is so wonderful about having access to infinite choices in every moment? Aren't three or four alternatives hard enough to choose between without being confronted with millions?

Infinite choice is not the same thing as infinite possibility. Sufi popularizer Idries Shah once pointed out that instead of freedom of choice, we ought to aspire to freedom *from* choice. Rather than applying hundreds of criteria from psychology, sociology, politics, economics, biology, philosophy, theology, etc., to each new choice, wouldn't it be better if we were so sure of the *one* right thing to do at any given moment that choice no longer troubled us? Being 'in the Tao' does not mean coming into a field of infinite choices; it is rather the spontaneous right action springing from 'choiceless awareness'.

The idea of 'an infinity of choices' is essentially meaningless, and arises from a confusion between the human will and the Will of God. Infinity belongs to God alone, Who is beyond all choice, since He wills the simultaneous actualization of every possibility in the depths of His own nature, by His eternal act of Self-understanding—though not, of course, within a limited set of contingent circumstances, such as a human life, an historical era, or a material universe. God does not choose between alternatives, He wills what is—though from our conditioned and limited standpoints, we must experience Him as saying *yes* to some things and *no* to others. As conscious but limited beings, it is we who are confronted with alternatives, and therefore choices. Our point of contact with Infinity is not in the world of alternatives, but in the world of Unity. There is only one infinite choice our will can make: to deny itself, and submit to the Will of God—to allow that One, Who is totally beyond choice, to choose for us. In the way of submitting to God's Will choices must, of course, be made. It remains our responsibility to choose those circumstances in the relative world which best support that Submission, and those actions which best express what God is commanding us to accomplish in this same relative world. These choices are not infinite, however, but limited, and therefore *relative*—necessarily so, since relativity is

274 ✳ THE SYSTEM OF ANTICHRIST

the essence of choice. They are the echoes of the Unity of God's Will in the contingent and multiple realm of our personal will. Without Submission, without the One Infinite Choice, they are nothing but impediments.

On pp 43–44, Dr Chopra gives the criterion according to which choices should be made:

> At the moment you consciously make a choice, pay attention to your body and ask your body, 'If I make this choice, what happens?' If your body sends you a message of comfort, that's the right choice. If your body sends a message of discomfort, that's not the appropriate choice. . . . For some people the message of comfort and discomfort is in the area of the solar plexus, but for most people it's in the area of the heart. . . . Only the heart knows the correct answer. Most people think the heart is mushy and sentimental. But it's not. The heart is intuitive; it's holistic, it taps into the cosmic computer.

Here we have a huge confusion of levels. What the 'body', the 'solar plexus', the 'heart' tells us may be the true voice of *conscience*, of the Divine Intellect within us. It may also be the voice of the unconscious ego, the 'commanding self'. Dr Chopra assumes a level of spiritual development in his readers which would allow them to tell the difference. But such 'discernment of spirits' is in fact quite rare, at least when it comes to any real certainty. The 'no' we often feel in the solar plexus *may* be the voice of God's will; this *chakra*, however, is notoriously vulnerable to the dictates of the commanding self, since it relates to matters of personal power, in particular to the fight-or-flight response. And the intuitive, holistic 'heart' Dr Chopra asks us to rely on is not reliably available to the consciousness of most people, though may unveil itself at unpredictable moments, only to be swiftly hidden again. On its outer layers the 'heart *chakra*' is the site of our 'mammalian' feelings: affection, pride, courage, sadness. Only on the deepest level, which can be reached through radical Submission alone, is the true 'spiritual Heart' available to us. And this Heart is on a vastly higher plane of being than our ability, which must always be imperfect, to manipulate cosmic laws.

On the face of it, Dr Chopra seems to be saying, 'if it feels good, do it.' His idea of what feels good is obviously much more subtle than that of an alcoholic or a drug addict; it is more truly *Epicurean* (in the original sense of the word) since it recognizes that the successful pursuit of joy and well-being requires a degree of wisdom. But to say that any sense of physical distress while contemplating a course of action means that you should reject it is profoundly wrong. For Dr Chopra there are no 'hard choices'; what is right is always what is easy. But this is in any sense true only of those who love God's will more than anything else, more than power, success, material wealth, or physical health, who are willing to sacrifice all the goods of mortal life to follow the Truth. And even for them, choosing the True as opposed to the desirable is not always easy. Jesus had his agony in the garden. Gandhi suffered personally, both physically and emotionally, in his fasts and prison terms, to free his nation; if he had caved in before these 'messages of discomfort,' India might still be a British colony. And I'm sure that Dietrich Bonhoeffer, who risked and finally lost his life by opposing the Nazis, did not embark on his heroic journey without plenty of cold thrills of fear in his solar plexus.

The Hindu spiritual classic *The Bhagavad-Gita*, set against the background of the great war between the closely-related clans of the Pandavas and the Kauravas, begins with a dialogue between Arjuna, hero of the Pandavas, and his charioteer Krishna, who is God Himself. The scene is the battlefield of Kurukshetra; the time is immediately before the battle. Arjuna says:

> Krishna, Krishna,
> Now as I look on
> These my kinsmen
> Arrayed for battle
> My limbs are weakened,
> My mouth is parching,
> My body trembles,
> My hair stands upright,
> My skin seems burning,
> The bow Gandiva
> Slips from my hand,
> My brain is whirling
> Round and round,
> I can stand no longer.
> Krishna, I see such
> Omens of evil!
> What hope can come from
> This killing of kinsmen?

Having spoken thus, Arjuna threw aside his arrows and his bow in the midst of the battlefield. He sat down on the seat of the chariot, and his heart was overcome with sorrow. 'Arjuna' [Krishna replies], 'is this hour of battle the time for scruples and fancies? Are they worthy of you, who seek enlightenment? Any brave man who merely hopes for fame or heaven would despise them . . . shake off this cowardice, Arjuna. Stand up.'

Arjuna is one of the greatest heroes of his time, both physically and spiritually. Yet even he was nearly crushed by the thought of the fratricidal war about to begin. His body refused to stand on its feet; sorrow clouded his heart. If he had listened to the 'wisdom' of his body in that moment, he would have betrayed his destiny. Only Krishna, the voice of Absolute Truth within him, could rouse him. Those who, like Arjuna, have both the capacity for deep inner listening and the courage to follow the inner Voice wherever it leads, can take Dr Chopra's advice. All others are in danger of being led astray by such glib appeals to the 'wisdom of the body'. This is why most traditions speak about the need for a living spiritual Master, or a spiritually viable community based on a true divinely-revealed religion, who can be that Voice for us until we can really hear it, and unquestioningly obey it, without outside help.

4. The Law of Least Effort

> Nature's intelligence functions with effortless ease.... With carefreeness, harmony and love. And when we harness the forces of harmony, joy and love, we create success and good fortune with effortless ease.

Yes—but Love will not be harnessed. Harnessed joy is not free of care. Harmony, in harness, begins to turn into discord. And nature is also home to the tiger, the virus, the earthquake. The action of God, of the Tao, is effortless. To the degree that we make this effortlessness our own, we are no longer attached to success or good fortune. Whatever God sends, health or illness, joy or suffering, wealth or poverty, is good fortune, because it is His will. Resting in God's will, flowing with the Tao, will undoubtedly overcome many self-created problems. Tension and struggle narrow our focus and sap our vital energy. But those who believe that God owes them material good fortune because they have trusted in Him may find themselves confronted with the lesson of Job, and begin to learn something about real trust. 'Though he slay me, yet I will trust in Him.' Love will never submit to being harnessed, because Love is the Driver. May He harness us to *His* chariot; may He do us that honor. As Dr Chopra says on pp 58–59:

> Responsibility means not blaming anyone or anything for your situation, including yourself. Having accepted this circumstance, this event, this problem, responsibility then means the *ability* to have a creative *response* to the situation *as it is now*. All problems contain the seed of opportunity, and this awareness allows you to take the moment and transform it into a better situation or thing. Once you do this, every upsetting situation will

become an opportunity for the creation of something new and beautiful, and every so-called tormentor or tyrant will become your teacher. Reality is an interpretation.

All true—except that it is really God Who takes the moment and transforms it, not me. My job, my precise and ongoing responsibility, is simply to get out of His way. And it is not Reality which is an interpretation, only subjective experience. Reality, *What Is*, is beyond interpretation entirely. In the words of Lew Welch, it is 'what goes on whether I look at it or not.'

5. *The Law of Intention and Desire*

Inherent in every intention and desire is the mechanics for its fulfillment. . . . Intention and desire in the field of pure potentiality have infinite organizing power. And when we introduce an intention in the fertile ground of pure potentiality, we put this infinite organizing power to work for us.

Again, the finite cannot use the Infinite to empower its agendas. It is true that a desire *arising out of* the field of pure potentiality has immense organizing power. The first such 'desire', the one with the greatest possible organizing power, is the Logos, the First Intellect, the seed of universal manifestation. But even its power is not infinite because any desire, even God's desire to be known by His creatures, is a limit established within the field of pure potentiality. And given that this field is the Infinite itself, from what point 'outside' It could a desire be introduced? Infinity has no 'outside'.

Deepak Chopra, and so many others, routinely invert the relationship between creature and Creator because they look on God as totally passive; a kind of infinite natural resource that is there for us to exploit, when and how we will, to get what we want. 'At the level of the quantum field,' says Dr Chopra (p 67), 'there is nothing other than energy and information. The quantum field is just another name for the field of pure consciousness or pure potentiality.' So God, for Chopra, is nothing but a subtle material energy like radio waves or magnetism. This is the error of *pantheism*—which, as we see so clearly in this case, is really another name for subtle materialism.

Pantheism arises when *Nirguna Brahman*, the Impersonal Absolute, 'the Divine without characteristics', is misunderstood, leading to a denial of *Saguna Brahman*, 'the Divine with characteristics', the personal God. *Saguna Brahman* is Being; *Nirguna Brahman* is Beyond Being, or Non-Being. But as Guénon put it, 'Being is the *affirmation* of Non-Being.' The Personal God is the highest possible conception the creatures can have of the Impersonal Absolute. This Absolute is not 'impersonal' because it lacks Personhood—if it were, the Personal God would not be It's highest symbol and It's most concrete manifestation—but because it is absolutely beyond conception. If It were not, then the creatures could comprehend, encompass and possess God—who would, by this fact, no longer be God.

The tendency to use the Impersonal Absolute to deny the Personal God, all-too-common among many people shallowly interested in mysticism and metaphysics, is simply another form of the ego's desire to *be* God. But without the Personal God occupying His proper rung of the hierarchy, *Nirguna Brahman* is subtly falsified. Our sense of Its Absolute Transcendence starts to slip. It begins to be known not as It really is, as the Divine Essence, totally beyond conception, but rather as universal potentiality, Divine power, *Mahashakti*. This is the meaning of the traditional doctrine that Adam fell because he aspired to direct knowledge of the unknowable Godhead, as well as of the saying of Jesus that 'none come to the father but through me,' indicating that none who deny or try to bypass *Saguna Brahman* can come to *Nirguna Brahman*. And when the unknowable, transcendent Godhead is mistaken for His power, His *Shakti*, then the *Shaktiman*, the power-*holder*, the motionless transcendent Act which fertilizes this dynamic potential, is obscured. It is no longer *Shiva*, no longer God who fills this role—it is *me*. Without a *Purusha* ('Person'), an *Ishvara* ('Lord'), a *Saguna Brahman* to complement the *Prakriti* of pure potentiality conceived of as primal matter/energy, without a conscious, willing and acting personal God, infinitely greater than I am (even though His essential Act is simply to Be), who else can fill that role? Me, the little ego, is now the one whose desires the *Mahashakti*, the Great Mother, is there to fulfill. And She will fulfill them, up to a point. Those who intuit Her reality are free to draw on Her power—but not without consequences. The karmic consequence of our belief that we are empowered and entitled to tap Her energy to realize our personal desires, is simply to be freed from this delusion—by *Kali*, the Black One, the Terrible Mother. After suckling at the breast of Beauty, we will slowly, or suddenly, be transferred to the breast of Rigor. This, in fact, is one way of looking at the entire cycle of God's manifestation, whether individual, planetary or cosmic, or even a single moment of spiritual forgetfulness, which begins in the presence of God, falls to the point where we believe that the ego *is* God, and ends by the sacrifice of that ego before the face of God. It also explains why the last of the Four Ages in Hindu cosmology is named the Kali Yuga.

Wizards are those who consort with the Great Mother as individuals, people with personal desires, not as vehicles of the Absolute. The magical recipe of Deepak the Wizard for using God to get what you want has five parts to it:

(1) Unite with essential Being. (2) Release your intentions and desires into the womb of that Being. (3) Maintain your contact with essential Being; protect the seed of your intention from the eyes of the world. (4) Relinquish your attachment to the outcome. (5) Let the universe take care of the details.

There is much wisdom in this recipe. It is a wiser approach than the simple 'power of positive thinking', and makes a nearly perfect diagram of petitionary prayer. Furthermore, it raises the conception of the prayer of petition to a higher level than simply imploring God to help us, as if we were trying to manipulate Him by making Him feel sorry for us. There is only one thing missing from it, and that is the understanding that our deepest desires do not come from ourselves; they come from God. And any desire *from* God is really a desire *for* Him. In the words of a prayer by the Sufi master Bayazid Bistami, 'O God, You know what I want.'

Personal desires are nothing but edited versions of what God Himself wants for us. We want Him to give us a car, a house, a lover, a successful career. He wants to give us Himself. To 'Release your intentions and desires into the womb of Being' (number 2) and to 'relinquish your attachment to the outcome' (number 4) are really ways of saying to God, 'This is what I think I want for myself, but I now sacrifice this desire in favor of what You want for me. Not my will but Thine be done.' It is said that 'man's extremity is God's opportunity.' Where our ability ends, God's begins. And our deepest desires are one avenue to this extremity. If we never admit what we most deeply want in this life, either because it seems unspiritual to have desires, or because we have secretly despaired of their ever being fulfilled (and these are often two sides of the same coin), then we will never arrive at that depth of soul where our desires end, and God's begin. But if we never sacrifice those deepest desires to God once we reach them, we will never see their true shape, never know them as more or less accurate reflections of God's *specific* desires for us.

6. The Law of Detachment

In detachment lies the wisdom of uncertainty. . . . In the wisdom of uncertainty lies the freedom from our past, from the known, which is the prison of past conditioning. And in our willingness to step into the unknown, the field of all possibilities, we surrender ourselves to the creative mind that orchestrates the dance of the universe.

Once again, Dr Chopra tells us that 'in order to acquire anything in the physical universe, you have to relinquish your attachment to it' (p 83). But to relinquish one's attachment to something *in order to acquire it* is not to relinquish one's attachment. You can't have your cake and eat it too. Jesus said 'Seek ye first the Kingdom of Heaven and its righteousness, and all these things [i.e., the basic necessities of life] shall be added unto you.' He did *not* say, 'If you want all these things, simply seek the Kingdom of Heaven and you'll get them.' The difference between Deepak Chopra and Jesus may be subtle, but it is immense. Like a friend of mine said, 'God cannot be used as a means to an end, because He *is* the End.' When Jesus promised that 'all these things shall be added unto you,' he was teaching us not to let our worry about how to maintain our lives distract us from putting God first; he was not giving us a way of operating what Dr Chopra likes to call 'the cosmic computer'. As we have seen, Dr Chopra maintains that 'this knowledge will give you the ability to create unlimited wealth . . . and to experience success in every endeavor.' Lao Tzu, however, is much closer to the truth when he says 'too much success is not an advantage' and 'he who knows that enough is enough will always have enough.'

'Anything you want can be acquired through detachment, because detachment is based on the unquestioning belief in your true Self' (p 84). Would it be unfair of me at this point to ask why Dr Chopra is apparently unwilling to end world hunger, war, and environmental destruction? Does he really not want these things? But more to the point: Deepak Chopra's central error seems to be the belief that his true Self is a kind of infinite Deepak Chopra, though he's decent enough to grant that in my case it will be a kind of infinite Charles Upton. The Vedic sages of India taught the doctrine of *Tat twam asi*, 'That art thou'. But *Tat twam asi* does not mean 'you' (the ego) 'are That' (the Self); it means 'That' (the Self) 'is the real you,' as in Shankaracharya's doctrine that our feeling of being ourselves is a sign of the Absolute and Transcendent Self within us. 'That' is not an extension of 'me'; 'I' am an extension of 'That'.

And, certainly, there is wisdom in uncertainty. Certainly, as Dr Chopra tells us, overcoming our attachment to security, which is really an attachment to the known past, will help us experience 'excitement, adventure, mystery . . . the fun of life . . . the magic, the celebration, the exhilaration and the exultation of your own spirit' (p 87)—plus all the chills and spills that go with it. But when he says 'What is the known? The known is our past' (p 86), he's limiting 'the known' to accumulated knowledge, forgetting that there is also *jñana*, eternal knowledge, the realization of the Self. And that Self expresses itself, on one level, through the eternal metaphysical principles underlying all valid religions, which have the power to open our consciousness to that Self's reality. Wisdom is not attained by giving up knowledge, only our attachment to knowledge. Knowledge must be transcended, but only in the direction of its Source, not in the direction of chaos and ignorance. The wisdom of uncertainty is gained by replacing an illusory certainty on the plane of phenomena with a true certainty of the reality of God. And given the contemporary worship of chaos and ignorance, which has almost reached the stature of a religious belief in these latter days, this point must be emphasized again and again.

Dr Chopra's list of things we need to transcend in order to open to the wisdom of uncertainty includes 'helplessness, hopelessness, mundane needs, trivial concerns, quiet desperation, and seriousness' (p 85). I fully agree that all these things imprison us—all except 'seriousness'. Seriousness is one of the most beautiful things there is, on earth or in Paradise.

7. The Law of 'Dharma' or Purpose in Life

Everyone has a purpose in life. . . . A unique gift or special talent to give others. And when we blend this unique talent with service to others, we experience the ecstasy and exultation of our own spirit, which is the ultimate goal of all goals.

Dr Chopra divides the Law of Dharma into three components: To discover the true Self; to uncover, nurture and express one's specific God-given talents; to dedicate these talents to the service of others. This is wholly admirable. However, I question whether the paradigm 'you can get whatever you want' will lead to this result, in the absence of a sense of *hierarchy* in the realm of desire, an understanding that some desires are higher and less egotistical than others.

Prof. Huston Smith, in *The World's Religions*, makes the following assertion: 'If we were to characterize Hinduism as a whole—its vast literature, its complicated rituals, its sprawling folkways, its opulent art—and compress it into a single affirmation, we would find it saying: You can have what you want.' He goes on to present Hinduism's ascending hierarchy of desires as *pleasure; success; service;* and *Liberation.* Pleasure, as an undeniably natural desire, can be legitimately sought, according to Hindu belief—until the time arrives when we begin to experience its limitations, and come to understand that pleasure is fundamentally inseparable from pain. At this point we will likely feel the attraction of worldly success, another legitimate human goal.

But those who pursue success will ultimately learn that just as pleasure is inseparable from pain, success and gain are inseparable from failure and loss. Even if we still retain our power and possessions, we may lose the sense that they make for a meaningful life. And, of course, 'you can't take it with you.' Those who feel the hollowness of worldly success will next be attracted to a life of duty and service. What could power, wealth, or fame mean to a person like Mother Theresa, except as they might further her goal of service to humanity? But even duty and service are not ultimately satisfying. 'The poor ye have always with you' leads to a realization that 'my kingdom is not of this world.' And in the hearts of those who feel constricted even by the horizon of universal service will be born the longing for *moksha*, union with God, Liberation.

There is a natural progression, then, from the self-involvement of pleasure, through the self-assertion of power and the self-sacrifice of service, to the self-transcendence of Liberation. And 'higher' also means 'wider': each incarnation of desire inhabits a more expansive universe. The world of pleasure is the body. The world of power is the family, the estate, the firm—also the party, the class, the church, the nation. Service too inhabits party, class, church, and nation, but sees them with wider eyes, as opportunities for self-sacrifice rather than the accumulation of personal power. Ultimately it embraces the entire world—and the other world as well, since the fruits of self-sacrifice in this life will be enjoyed in the next. And, finally, the field of Liberation is God Himself. Not many, of course, will live to fully experience all four worlds of desire, but this is not ultimately a problem, since if the course is not completed in this life, it may be finished in the lives to come.

Deepak Chopra seems to lack this sense of the development and refinement of desire, leading to its ultimate transcendence. He retains implicit faith in the absoluteness and universality of the common human aspirations to health and wealth and well-being; he even allows a place for service, as long as it requires no self-sacrifice. But average human desirousness remains his given, his first principle. It's the one thing he never questions. However, as Peter O'Toole said, in his title role in the motion picture *Lawrence of Arabia*, 'You can do whatever you want, but you can't *want* whatever you want.' Desire is not just something to be fulfilled; it is also something to be altered, purified, and sometimes renounced. If there is any one principle of spiritual common sense that the New Age doesn't want to hear, it is this one. 'You can have perfect health and unlimited wealth' doesn't sound bad at all. 'You can have unlimited women and unlimited power,' however, has quite a different ring to it, while 'you can have an unlimited supply of drugs, alcohol and pornography' also comes under the heading of 'getting whatever you want,' if these things are indeed what you want.

No amount of service to others will, in itself, purify lower desires. It *may* do so, if the form of service you offer is part of your God-given *dharma*. But it may also be a way of hiding from the work you need to be doing on yourself, or of compensating for the bad karma you are generating in other parts of your life so you can go on generating it. It is certainly true that all of us are required by the human mandate to be of service to others. The essence of this service, however, does not consist in solving people's problems, but rather in loving them. Those who are incapable of loving others unless they can somehow concretely help them do not know what love is. Closer than problem-solving to true love and service is *empathy*. Problem-solving based on a sincere, objective and detached empathy is less likely than the quantitative, clinical approach to create more problems than it solves.

Empathy, or compassion, often requires suffering. True compassion is a detached 'suffering-with' the one who is in pain. It does not collect the sufferer's pain and then dump it back on him—a condition we call 'pity'. Neither does it poison the helper with the pain he is attempting to relieve, making him a source of further pain to the people around him, and a reproach to the sufferer as well. In spiritual compassion, the ability to sit with another's pain and the ability to release that pain in the presence of God are the same thing.

Suffering, however, is a scandal to the New Age, a morbid medieval obsession, a shameful defeat of the whole program of ecstasy and positive affirmation and unlimited success, not to mention a signal to your social-Darwinian competitors that you are probably not fitted to survive because insufficiently 'evolved'. If our capacity to suffer—to stay with a difficult relationship, for example, or some other life-struggle, in the name of a higher principle—is so much less than that of our grandparents, this may be because we have eliminated love as an acceptable life-purpose, and replaced it with a combination of serving others and getting what we want. How many contemporary couples, for instance, think of their relationship as a sort of negotiated deal where service and selfishness are contractually balanced so both people can *get what they want?* The only thing people really want, however, *is* love, and love is a Reality which already possesses them—a truth which the magical self-gratifying ego, and the world it defines, will never accept.

✳ Addendum

In his later book, *The Path to Love*, Deepak Chopra seems a bit more mature and realistic in some areas—admitting, for example, that money and power are things we must struggle to obtain. He also says two very important things that I entirely agree with: First, that we are taught in this culture that romantic love has nothing to do with spirituality, and second, that romantic love can be part of the spiritual Path, because through this love we may sense the presence of Eternity. (Dante's *Divine Comedy* and *La Vita Nuova* prove this beyond question.)

Contemporary society looks at romantic love not as an intimation of Eternity but as a surrender to time and chaos; only the ego is forever. And we are not simply taught that romantic love can't be spiritual; we are also taught that we *are* in fact being taught that it *is* spiritual. The cynical nihilists who hate romantic love like to pretend that we are still oppressed by and in rebellion against Victorian mores, whereas we are actually being oppressed by nihilist mores, and the rebellion is long overdue.

Part Two:
Spiritual Warfare

5

The Shadows of God

If Gods combine against Man Setting their Dominion above
The Human Form Divine. Thrown down from their high Station
In the Eternal heavens of the Human Imagination: buried beneath
In dark oblivion with incessant pangs ages on ages
In Enmity & war first weakened then in stern repentance
They must renew their brightness & their disorganized functions
Again reorganize till they assume the image of the human
Cooperating in the bliss of Man obeying his Will
Servants to the Infinite and Eternal of the Human form
⌒Williαm Blake, from *The Four Zoas*

In the well-known words of St Paul from the book of *Ephesians*,
'We wrestle not against flesh and blood but against principalities, against
powers, against the rulers of the darkness of this world, against spiritual
wickedness in high places.' These principalities and powers, in my opinion,
can be legitimately seen as elements of the system of the Antichrist, a system
which 'constellates' only at the end of the aeon, but which is virtually present
all throughout 'fallen' human history, as when Paul speaks of 'the god of this
world [who] hath blinded the eyes of them that believe not' (2 Cor. 4:4).
The 'god of this world' is obviously Satan, but Satan in his particular aspect
as the patron of 'worldliness', of the organized social and mass psychological
system created by the human ego in rebellion against God. The Antichrist
per se represents the establishment of this system in its terminal form for
this aeon via the breakthrough of sub-human, 'infra-psychic' forces into
human history, just as Christ—and Muhammad, and the Buddha, and the
Hindu Avatars—represent the breakthrough of Divine Wisdom and Love.

For many of the early Christians, the Roman Empire represented, for
obvious reasons, the system of Antichrist. The Roman Emperor was worshipped as a god at one time, at least in the provinces, and the Number of
the Beast, 666, is often solved as a numerological reference to the emperor

Nero. The central grievance of the Jewish Zealots, the anti-Roman guerrilla terrorists of Jesus' time, was that to require that the Jews pay taxes to Rome was an act of emperor-worship and thus a blasphemy against God, especially since the Roman denarius in which the tax was to be paid bore an image of the emperor, and so was technically an idol in the eyes of many Jews, who, like the Muslims in later centuries, prohibited the making of any image of Yahweh, and considered any deity who could be visually represented as inherently false. That Jesus was on one level sympathetic to the Zealots, though he was certainly not a political revolutionary—any more than he was a collaborator with Rome—is shown by the fact that he criticized every known Jewish sect of his time—Pharisees, Sadducees, Scribes, and Herodians—except the Zealots and the Essenes, and numbered one Simon the Zealot among his disciples, though we can't be sure whether 'Zealot' refers to Simon's affiliation or only his character.

In the *Apocalypse*, the central symbol of the Antichrist is the Beast, who acts as an agent of the Dragon (Satan). Upon the Beast rides the Whore, whose name is Mystery, Babylon the Great. The seven heads of the Beast, which are seven kings, are also seven mountains upon which she sits, like the seven mountains of Rome And so, on one level, the Beast is the Roman Empire, compared by the writer of the book to the Babylonian captivity of the Jews. This identification of the Beast with Rome has led certain Protestant sects to see it as a symbol of the Roman Catholic Church—an attribution which would be partly justified only in the case of the complete apostasy of Catholicism, which, in my opinion, cannot be assumed to have happened even now.

The Dragon of the *Apocalypse*, identified with Satan, represents a perverted *spiritual* order. Based on this Satanic order is the perverted *social* order of the Beast. And the Whore of Babylon, who rides the Beast—that is, who both guides it and is carried along by it—is the perverted *psychic* order of the latter days. The seven heads of the Beast, who are seven kings with whom Babylon consorts and seven mountains upon which she reigns, symbolize—among other things—the seven major faculties of the soul, which in antiquity were represented by the seven planets: the Moon, fertility and sub-conscious emotion; Mercury, thought, cunning and the ability to deal with information; Venus, love, sexuality and relatedness; the Sun, intellect, the spiritual center of the soul and source of its life; Mars, will and aggression; Jupiter, leadership ability and philosophical intelligence; Saturn, long-term planning ability, mystical knowledge and the wisdom of old age. If the Beast and the Whore 'occupy' the seven provinces of the soul, this indicates that the regime of Antichrist has conquered and perverted all these aspects of human life, both socially and psychologically, a perversion which is represented in Catholic theology by the seven deadly sins. According to Martin Lings, in his article 'The Seven Deadly Sins in the Light of the Symbolism of Number', *superbia* (pride) is related to the Sun, *avaritia* (avarice) to Saturn, *luxuria* (lust) to Venus, *invidia* (envy) to Mercury, *gula* (gluttony) to Jupiter, *ira* (anger) to Mars, and *accidia* (sloth) to the Moon.' The power of the Beast over the human soul is symbolized by the 'mark of the Beast' — who in this case is actually, according to the *Apocalypse*, a second Beast, servant of the first, identified as the False Prophet — which is placed either upon the right hand or upon the forehead. The mark upon the right hand symbolizes power over the will, and that upon the forehead power over the intelligence: when the intelligence is darkened, the will is overpowered as well, since it must now follow error instead of Truth.

The regime of Antichrist, then, operates on three levels, which are the three ontological levels of the human being: the material level, including both the socio-historical realm and the human body; the psychic level, embracing both the conscious and the sub-conscious mind; and the spiritual level, which though it cannot ultimately be perverted, since it is Divine, can be obscured by the powers of darkness, and also *counterfeited*, according to the principle that 'Satan is the ape of God'.

The Beast, who is Antichrist, is thus the counterfeit of Christ, a perverse and distorted version of the image of God within us. Under his regime, all the powers and qualities of the human form, considered as God's central act of Self-revelation in this world ('who has seen me has seen the Father' said Jesus, speaking as the Divine Archetype of Humanity) are aped by demonic forces: wisdom, love, miracles of healing and control over natural forces, and even the resurrection of the body, all will be enacted in counterfeit, 'so as to lead astray, if possible, even the elect.'

Evangelical Christians tend to concentrate on predictions relating to how the system of Antichrist will appear in future history and society. This is a valid and important level upon which to view the matter, though we have to be careful not to interpret scripture too narrowly, since an event recounted in a densely-symbolic text like the *Apocalypse* may appear in history as several different events, or trends, happening at various times. My intent, however, is to concentrate more on the psychic and metaphysical aspects of 'the darkness of this world', including that level of things where the unconscious mind interacts with society, the realm where the powers of darkness appear as *unconscious belief-systems and social mores.*

A spiritually degenerate society rules its members not only by police-state tactics, or by influencing them to consciously believe false doctrines, but also by indoctrinating them to adopt certain beliefs *unconsciously*, beliefs that will have all the more power over them by this very unconsciousness, since they are never brought into the light of day where they can be critically evaluated. An evil society will inculcate these beliefs deliberately, through various sorts of propaganda, indoctrination, and mind-control. On the other hand, the rulers of the society in question will in some ways be just as unconscious as the population they indoctrinate. While they may consciously lie to the people on questions of fact, nonetheless they take the *fundamental* beliefs they disseminate absolutely for granted, and are therefore unconscious of them. The deepest lies—the unconscious social mores and the false conceptions of God on which they are based—appear to our rulers simply as the nature of things. Because they believe in them implicitly, they need never become aware of them *as beliefs*. If you want to delude others, it is best to begin by deluding yourself; that way none can question your 'sincerity'.

These beliefs act like possessing demons, controlling the psyche from within, and punishing any move of thought, feeling or intuition which is at odds with their view of reality, most often through feelings of shame, fear, uncontrollable anger, frigid pride, or deep depression, all of which will be temptations to the same fundamental sin, the sin of despair. (This is not to say that all such feelings are demonic attacks. There is also a healthy shame which protects us from shameful acts, a healthy fear which defends us from physical and spiritual danger, a healthy anger at evil or injustice, a healthy 'pride' which takes the form of self-respect or veneration of the worthy, and a healthy sorrow which appears as compassion, or remorse.) Furthermore, what is an unconscious false belief on the psychological level *is precisely a devil* on the psychic or spiritual level. In the parable of Jesus' exorcism of the lone demoniac, the demons which possess him give their name as 'legion', which is an obvious reference not only to the Roman military occupation of Judea, but also to the possession of the Jewish soul, via 'internalized oppression', by the unconscious social mores of the Roman imperium.

The devils who 'administer' the false belief-systems in question are not to be compared with those who tempt us to personal self-indulgence, to lust, for example, or sloth, or anger. They are more on the order of fallen cherubim, great spiritual intelligences who have turned against God. They are demons of the intellect, not demons of the will. When St Paul speaks of 'principalities and powers' who are 'the rulers of the darkness of this world', these are the beings he is referring to.

On a certain level, these fallen cherubim constitute an articulate system of error, a direct counterfeit of the divine or celestial *pleroma* which appears in the *Apocalypse* as the Throne of the Lamb surrounded by the four Living Creatures, the seven Lamps, the twenty-four Elders, etc. The symbolic meaning of these figures may never be precisely known (though it clearly was at one time); it is enough to say, in this context, that they represent God's first, spiritual creation, prior to the material universe, though they are 'prior' more in the spiritual than the temporal sense, since the first creation is eternal in relation to our temporal, material one, not simply 'prior' to it in time.

After meditating for many years on these subjects, I believe I have gained a certain amount of insight into what C. S. Lewis jocularly named, in his *Screwtape Letters*, the 'Lowerarchy' — the system of infernal domination of collective human society, not simply of individual human beings — and most particularly into the level represented by the number *four*, which would appear to be the Satanic counterfeit of the Four Living Creatures. I have been deeply influenced in these meditations by the 'prophetic books' of William Blake, *The Four Zoas, Milton,* and *Jerusalem* — themselves influenced by the Hebrew Kabbalah — where in obscure and flaming visionary language he analyses the Fall and Redemption of Man in terms of the fall of the four central faculties of the human soul, the Four Zoas or Living Creatures, and their redemption by Christ, who is the eternal spiritual Intellect. My intent here is certainly not to create an alternate theology, but merely to throw a poetic and metaphorical light on certain psychic consequences of the fall of man, which, according to traditional authorities, as well as to the fairly obvious meaning of the book of *Genesis*, includes both the perversion of the will and the darkening of the Intellect.

The fall of man, seen in intellectual terms, begins as a primal misunderstanding of the true nature of God. All else follows from this, since a failure to understand Who God really is distorts our picture of every other thing, person, situation, or level of being. Where the intellect is darkened by spiritual ignorance, it can reveal to us only shadows of the Truth, false objects which the will is attracted to because of their partial resemblance to the Truth they hide, in the course of which it becomes weakened and distorted, until it can no longer will the Good — even if, by the Grace of God, the darkness of the Intellect were to be lifted for a moment, and that Good revealed.

A shadow requires three things: a source of light, an opaque object, and a field where the shadow falls. If the light is God, the opaque object, the ego, and the field where the shadow falls, the universe, then the shadows of the ego, projected by the Light of God, are false beliefs, which appear to that ego not as its own shadows, nor even as beliefs, but as the literal nature of reality: the shadows of God.

The ego, by definition, does not know itself. It tries to convince us that we can become unique and original if we submit to its magic. It forgets that egotism actually stereotypes us, makes us drearily predictable, because human egos, at root, are much alike. Our deepest fears and desires, of which the ego is composed, are very few and very common.

God is the only Reality, the sole object, and subject, of all knowledge. But when primal fear and desire, which are the seed-form of the ego, separate subject from object, so that the perceiving subject is apparently no longer God—as in Reality it always is, since only God, in the last analysis, is Witness of His own manifestation—then limited and conditioned views of Reality are born, held within the minds of limited and conditioned subjects. From one point of view, these limited views, and the limited subjects who perceive them, are the creative manifestation of God in space and time; from another, they are God's shadows, His veils. When these shadows become thick, and their darkness intense, it appears as if God were absent from His creation. It is into these places and times of the apparent 'death of God' that God sends the prophets, saviors and avatars who found and renew the great wisdom traditions.

Looked at in one way, false beliefs are nothing but illusions; to take them too seriously is to grant them more reality than they deserve. But to the degree that false beliefs are actually believed, especially on the collective level, they produce real effects, not only on the psychic plane, but on the social, physiological and environmental ones as well. Illusion—whose moral name is evil—is essentially a privation, a lack. One can never make complete sense of it because, as a 'hole' in reality rather than a reality in its own right, it is fundamentally absurd. However, a condition such as starvation is also a 'mere' lack, a lack of food; but its consequences are far from illusory. In the same way, false beliefs, and the demonic powers who administrate them, have real effects, which we ignore at our peril. The 'principalities and powers', then, can be considered as fundamental *misperceptions of the nature of God* by the deepest, most hidden layers of the human ego—which, from another perspective, is entirely composed of these misconceptions. In other words, they are *idols*, false gods like the Golden Calf destroyed by Moses, or the pagan idols swept out of the Kaaba by the Prophet Muhammad (upon whom be peace).

Conceive of the most fundamental and universal idols, the primal shadows of God, as four: the idolatry of *Law*, the idolatry of *Fate*, the idolatry of *Chaos*, and the idolatry of *Self*. These are the primordial elementals of the human ego, the analysis of the darkened order of perception created by the fall of man, the 'rulers of the darkness of this world'. To the darkened perception of the self-worshipping ego they appear as powers in their own right, and also—since they are in perpetual conflict—as real alternatives. But in reality they are in perpetual collusion to prevent us from seeing any light of Truth beyond the tragic and ironic alternatives they propose. And far from being independent self-existing powers, they are nothing at root but the emblems of our fundamental recoil from the incandescent Glory of God, projected, like the shadows in Plato's cave, on the landscape of the psyche, and thence on nature and society. Yet from another perspective, they are, precisely, demons, spiritual powers in rebellion against God. We can solve this apparent paradox if we realize that it is only the ego's alienation from God which opens it to the influence of such demonic forces, who are in a similar state of alienation, and that the origin of such alienation in both cases is ignorance or delusion. The deluded ego worships itself instead of God—whether in arrogance or in despair—and the forms which this self-worship takes are the forms of demonic powers. Practically speaking, we must admit both that these powers are in deliberate, active opposition to God and the spiritual life, and that they themselves are deluded, even as they attempt, with infernal cunning, to delude us. In other words, their power is entirely negative, being based on ignorance alone, which is why they are called 'powers of darkness'. And though it will always be necessary, given our fallen condition, to struggle with them will-against-will, it is only the dispersal of the shadows of ignorance, in the light of the Divine Intellect, which finally breaks their power.

✳ Idolatry of Law

God is a lawgiver. The Torah, the Laws of Manu, the Islamic *shari'at* were given to humanity not as an arbitrary imposition of tyrannical rules, but as mercy—which is why ancient peoples looked on lawgiving kings and sages as among the supreme benefactors of the race. Given that humanity had fallen from Eden, from the direct perception of Divine Reality, law became a necessity. A sacred law is an expression of the true shape of the human culture, and ultimately the Human Form, to which that law applies. By the divine act of lawgiving, God creates a given culture in space and time: not through an arbitrary decree, but through His vision of that culture as an eternal facet of the Divine Humanity within His own nature. To command, 'you shall not kill, you shall not steal, you shall not commit adultery, you shall not forget to acknowledge the Divine Source of your life' is like ordering us not to cut off our arms or put out our eyes. As a safeguard of our integral humanity, the sacred law is beholden to that humanity. It is cut to fit us; we are not, as in the myth of the bed of Procrustes, mutilated to fit it. As Jesus said, 'the Sabbath was made for man, not man for the Sabbath.' Revealed law is necessary because we find ourselves within time, and so need a vehicle whereby eternal principles can be applied to changing situations.

The very sacredness of revealed law, however, makes it vulnerable to the growth of idolatry. We forget that it was given to protect us, and begin to use it as a tool in the service of the collective ego, a weapon against the Image of God within us. God is Absolute, and the eternal principles are absolute relative to cosmic manifestation, but when our sense of absoluteness is displaced by being identified with contingent situations, idolatry is born. And the essence of the *idolatry of Law* is that we impose it blindly, mechanically, without regard for the actual shape of the situations it was created to regulate, or the true nature of the people it was written to protect. Every truly sacred law is not merely a set of duties and prohibitions, but an expression in the moral realm of eternal, metaphysical principles. 'Keep holy the Lord's Day,' for example, refers, on an esoteric level, to the Eternal Present as God's resting-place, and 'Thou shalt not covet thy neighbor's wife' to what the Hindus call *svadharma*, one's unique spiritual duty and destiny—symbolized by a man's wife, the image of his soul—which cannot be exchanged, and which no other can fulfil: 'Better one's own *dharma*, no matter how poorly performed, than the *dharma* of another, no matter how well.' These eternal principles do not exist behind the letter of the law alone, but equally behind the face of the human situation the law must confront and regulate. But when this is forgotten, when law is applied *indiscriminately* rather than impartially, it is transformed into a bloody idol, demanding, like the pagan god Moloch in the Old Testament, the sacrifice of our children (esoterically speaking, our creativity) and, like the Aztec war-god Huitzilopochtli, our still-beating hearts (the Image of God within us). Prescribing the same remedy for all seems impartial, yet nothing is more destructive, precisely as if a physician were to prescribe penicillin or insulin to every patient indiscriminately, to avoid the work of diagnosis and the humbling realization that he or she does not already know the precise nature of the disease. As Blake

said, 'One law for the Lion and the Ox is oppression.' When the certainty
derived from an understanding of eternal principles is used as an excuse for
failing to engage with real people and actual situations in the work of discernment, the *idolatry of Law* is in full force.

The false religion of Law is best represented by the legalism of the Abrahamic religions, when it expands beyond its legitimate bounds and denies
Mercy. A great deal of Jesus' ministry was directed against this idolatry, represented in the Gospels by the Scribes and Pharisees. The idolatry of Law
includes either the false doctrine that God's law is greater than God, that
He is a slave to it rather than its Creator, or the allied error—held by the
more extreme Asharites within Islam—that His Will is arbitrary, and thus
takes precedence over even His Nature, as if God could will to be whatever
he wants, even if it be something other than God. This second error, however, could better be described as a synthesis of the idolatry of Law and the
idolatry of Selfhood (see below) since it sees God as a kind of rebel—a rebel
against Himself. When this spirit of legalism is expressed socially, it
becomes a tyrannical police state, most likely (at least in these days) protecting an economic monopoly which impoverishes the masses and excludes
them from participation in the life of the nation and/or world, and which
protects its own power through various forms of propaganda, mind-control
and state terror. Expressed psychologically, it becomes the rigid, authoritarian character, filled with frigid pride, which represses and dominates its own
thoughts, feelings, sensations and perceptions as brutally as any dictator
dominates the unfortunate populace.

✳ Idolatry of Fate

God is the nature of things. A recognition of the nature of things, which the
Chinese call Tao, the Hindus *rta*, and the ancient Egyptians *maat*, the manifestation of necessary Being in the cosmic order, is the basis of contemplative spirituality. The way things naturally are, the realm of natural law,
manifests as appropriateness, beauty and inevitability; through it we can
contemplate the Divine Names or Platonic Ideas, the eternal archetypes
within the mind of God.

Contemplation is like space. Empty in itself, it shows us the pattern
whereby things are related to one another outside time, *sub specie aeternitatis*.
Law enters time, and so manifests as speech and spoken scripture; contemplation, being of the nature of space, is better symbolized by the Hindu

mandala, the sacred calligraphy of the Koran, or the Eastern Orthodox icon. But when pure contemplation is darkened, when the primordial receptivity of the soul is lost, then *Fate* is born. We can no longer contemplate the eternal pattern of things; consequently the Always So is transformed into the fated, the hopelessly inevitable. The still surface of the lake of contemplation is disturbed by time—not the creative time of sacred law, but time as conditioned by the fear of what might happen in the future now that we can no longer see the shape of what always is. Under the regime of Fate, vertical causality—the sense that everything happens by virtue of God's eternal will for this particular moment—is veiled, and replaced by horizontal causality. Past causes are now seen as the origin of future events, but since the roots of the past are hidden, the shape of the future is hidden as well. Events are unpredictable because their causes are veiled in mystery; by the same token, they are inevitable.

The pre-Socratic philosopher Heraclitus said 'character is fate,' an oracular statement that can be taken in two different ways. In the words of the Prophet Muhammad (upon whom be peace), 'he who knows himself knows his Lord.' This means that if one can see oneself with the perfect objectivity of the Divine Self or Witness within the human soul, one will know that little 'me' out there as a projection into space and time of a specific archetype within the mind of God—and so fate holds no surprises. All happenings are seen as perfectly appropriate to the shape of the self to which they happen; God's will for a particular individual within a particular moment is indistinguishable from that person's will for himself, since the two are one. On the other hand, if character is unconscious—which it usually is, no matter how much psychological introspection we do or how much feedback we get from others, since we can only know who we really are in the objective light of God—then it is projected into the world of events as a mysterious fate which we can't escape, no matter what we do. The same things keep happening, over and over again, and all our attempts to escape them only seem to quicken the pace of their pursuit. The Greek tragedies, with their sense of the 'fatal flaw', are the best illustrations we have in literature of this darker side of Heraclitus' saying.

These obsessively repetitive events continue to happen because of the kind of fundamental forgetfulness which the Greeks called *amnesia*, and the Muslims *ghaflah*—the forgetfulness of the Divine Witness within us, which leads to a general inability to pay attention, as well as to an ignorance of our essential character and real needs. We keep asking for things, forgetting that we've done so, and then reacting with shock when our unconscious wishes come true. If we were aware of the wishes hidden within us, then we could distinguish between *essential* and *imposed* character, between the accidental wishes implanted in us by circumstances or other people's agendas, and the essential wishes that are inseparable from who we are in the mind of God. The first kind of wish can never really be fulfilled; the second kind is fulfilled already, in a higher world — a world which, paradoxically, can only be unveiled to us through our struggle to find and fulfill our true wishes in this imperfect world, where that fulfillment can never be complete, or, even if momentarily it seems complete, can never last.

Until we awaken from our amnesia, we are under the regime of Fate. Every time something 'fatal' happens, we are appalled to realize that we haven't escaped the curse even yet. And as each twist of fate which has sprung at us out of the mysterious future passes into the hidden past, it adds to the store of apparent *karma* by which the mysterious 'past' seems to be the origin of the hidden 'future'. Just as our body can become addicted to certain drugs, our destiny can become addicted to certain events. If an eternal archetype or character in the mind of God is veiled by the darkening of the individual mind, or the mind of society as a whole, it becomes the center of a karmic cycle or 'vicious circle', something which Blake called 'the circle of destiny'. When the Stoic philosophers tried to absolutize natural cycles in the doctrine of the 'eternal return', which maintained that all events endlessly recur in exactly the same way to exactly the same people through vast and unending cycles of time, they were erecting the 'circle of destiny' into an idol, like the Greek Fates, or the Roman goddess Fortuna who used to be worshipped by spinning the familiar 'wheel of fortune'. In so doing they were reacting to an alienation from the sense of eternity which was prevalent in classical antiquity. St Augustine, in *The City of God*, criticizes this doctrine, implying that the belief in a circle of destiny is actually based on a circular argument, since (I would add) if the premises upon which an argument is based are not seen as axiomatic, and thus eternal in relation to the motion of the argument, that motion becomes circular. Those who remember God in eternity know all events as eternally present. Those who forget God become like 'moving white dots' (Blake) between a forgotten past dominated by nostalgia and a mysterious future ruled by fear. They live in a world where forgetfulness of the past is compulsory, and where all who forget the past are condemned to repeat it.

The false religion of Fate manifests either as a cult of the cycles of nature, as in the negative and mechanistic aspects of the Mesopotamian star-worship from which *astrology* is derived (which is not in all cases fatalistic, since it can sometimes approach a vision of the eternal archetypes) or the Calvinist denial of free will based on a false doctrine of predestination, which sees God's eternal will for the individual as something other than the sum total of the individual's own decisions, whereas in reality God's 'foreknowledge' of our decisions does not cause them, but is simply His vision of them *sub specie aeternitatis*. Expressed in psychological and social terms, this Fate-worship becomes a largely-unconscious 'zodiac' of *social typology* — of imposed rather than essential character — where the unconscious social mores determine the individual's fate via society's expectations for him, which progressively become his own expectations for himself. As the idolatry of Law is pride, so the idolatry of Fate is fear. [NOTE: The best concentrated analysis of the Fate Idol I've ever encountered is the story 'The Lottery in Babylon', by Jorge Luis Borges.]

✳ Idolatry of Chaos

God is infinite life. The vast profusion of the 'ten-thousand things' eternally overflows into manifestation out of the Divine Infinity. God sends sacred laws, but He is greater than they. He manifests as the cosmic order, but He is not limited by it. There are no barriers in God to the infinite radiation of His Being, and this is His perfect freedom, a freedom which does not begin to be exhausted by universe after universe, bursting with life.

But we cannot act as God does. We are contingent, He is Absolute. He is beyond form, while we are bound to the forms in which He has created us. He absolutely transcends us. But when we forget this, when His transcendence is veiled and we see only His immanence in the world visible to our senses, and then *identify* with it, we start to believe that the path to freedom lies through formlessness and dissipation. Since we've lost the vision of how form emanates from what is *above* form, we seek the divine Infinity in what is *below* form, in a Dionysian intoxication which ends as it did with King Pentheus in Euripides' *The Bacchae*. Pentheus, king of Thebes, despises the new cult of Dionysus (or Bacchus, god of wine, perhaps also of the psychedelic mushroom *amanita muscaria*) which has invaded Greece, and been taken up by women — the *bacchantes* — who dance ecstatically, and tear living animals apart in their frenzy. Dionysus assumes the guise of a suspicious underworld type, is arrested and brought to the palace. There he offers to tell Pentheus where he can view the Bacchic revelers in their secret forest sanctuary. Pentheus, voyeuristically fascinated, takes him up on his offer, goes out to spy on the *bacchantes*, and is torn limb from limb by his own mother, Agave, who in her frenzy mistakes him for an animal. Euripides is saying here that to seek the divine life in what is below form, by idealizing and worshipping one's animal nature, is to be torn to pieces by our mother, who is material nature; *mater* = matter. This is the idolatry of *Chaos*.

The false religion of Chaos is the Dionysian, which includes various kinds of political, social and moral anarchism; those forms of false mysticism which identify God with formlessness instead of supra-formal Essence, and higher consciousness, in a simple-minded way, with intoxication; and those forms of psychotherapy which make release from constriction, inhibition and character-armor the central factor. Those who, like Pentheus, are narrow-mindedly 'civilized' rather than broadly cultured, will often seek this kind of release in a return to the simplicity of Nature, conceived of as a maternal paradise of safety, self-indulgence, ease and irresponsibility — forgetting that, for example, no African Bushman or Australian Aborigine could survive for a single day without a greater degree of endurance, courage, and vigilance than most city-dwellers will ever possess. If the dominant emotion of Fate is fear, the dominant emotion of Chaos is shame.

✳ Idolatry of Selfhood

God is the Absolute Subject, the *atman*, the transcendent and immanent Self, the *imago dei* within each of us. By virtue of this *atman*, we are, at the deepest level of our being, both unique and universal. The Self within us is pure, impersonal, universal Being, without attributes; according to some metaphysicians, including Frithjof Schuon, it is better described as Beyond Being, given that it can never be an object of consciousness subject to definition, since 'the eye cannot see itself'. But because God is unique as well as universal, this Self is also the principle of our unique human integrity, the way in which we are not simply humanity in the abstract, but actual human beings, commanded by God to be precisely ourselves, no greater, no less, and no other. And yet this uniqueness is also universal, since it is shared by all human beings, and in fact by all things. Self as the principle of uniqueness is not other than Self as the principle of pure Being, as when God, speaking to Moses in *Exodus*, names Himself as 'I Am That I Am': My unique Essence is not other than My pure Being; it is My unique Essence to *be* pure Being.

And what God can say of Himself, we can also say, certainly not of our limited human personalities, but of the God, the *atman*, within us. In St Paul's words: 'It is not I who live, but Christ lives in me.'

But when uniqueness is separated from being, it loses its universality. This is just what happens when we ascribe uniqueness to ourselves alone while denying it to others. This is the *idolatry of Self*. When we worship our own separate selfhood as if it were God, we start to believe that self-willed isolation is the road to integrity, and that, in Sartre's words, 'hell is other people.' Consequently we can only relate comfortably to others if we see them as subordinates—that is, as lesser parts of ourselves. This is the irony of self-worship. Seeking unity and integrity through isolation and dominance, we gradually become filled with the ghosts of all the relationships we have denied and betrayed. Our quest for individuality ('undividedness') at all costs results only in fragmentation. We ourselves become 'the lonely crowd'.

The false religion of Selfhood is Prometheanism, which includes all forms of *hubris*: the solipsistic, New Age belief that 'I create my own reality' (the truth being more on the order of 'I create my own illusion'); the idea that spiritual development is a kind of exploit or heroic achievement to be gloried in; the sense that the individual can only gain integrity and significance by breaking the law and rebelling against the mores; and the driving will of Western, and by now global, society to conquer nature, deny God, and remold human life according to the most demented 'idealism' imaginable, even at the risk of destroying both humanity and the earth. If Law is ruled by pride, Fate by fear, and Chaos by shame, Selfhood is ruled by anger.

These four idols—Law, Fate, Chaos, and Selfhood—are an analysis of the fallen order of perception known in Christian theology as 'this world'. They do not operate in isolation. Tyrannical and mechanistic Law takes on the aspect of mysterious Fate. Ignorance of the law is no excuse, we are told, and yet who can ever know that law in its entirety? And Fate, in reality, is not the operation of being-in-itself, but of an established, though hidden, order of things, an artificial system, an idolatrous Law. Tyrannical Law imposed on the individual produces the self-willed rebel, and so Law reinforces Selfhood. Imposed on society or nature, it produces Chaos. And both Rebellion and Chaos make necessary ever-more tyrannical, blind and mechanistic Law. In the name of the war on drugs, we destroy civil rights. In the name of wildlands management, we burn Yellowstone National Park. But the more blindly we try to impose order on nature and society, the more chaos and rebellion we create.

Fate imposed on the individual promotes Selfhood, since to be self-willed, and suffer the consequences, seems inevitable, while the only way of possessing individual integrity seems to be to submit to one's Fate: 'a man's got to do what a man's got to do,' even if—or *especially if*—the results are fatal. And Fate imposed on society produces Chaos. If a whole generation of adolescents believe that they are fated to fail, drug-taking and dissipation seem the only way out, and society dissolves. So both the self-willed individual fated to die—like the Irish hero Cuchulainn who was chosen, empowered, exalted, and doomed by the Goddess Morrigan—and the chaotic individual destined to degradation and madness, are servants of Fate. The chaotic individual is susceptible to shame in the face of those more fortunate individuals upon whom Fate seems to smile; and these fortunate sons and daughters must maintain their high position in the court of Fate by casting shame upon those who are vulnerable to it, in an attempt to avoid an adverse fate by forcing others to live it out. So while Law manifests as explicit rules, Fate often wears the mask of unconscious social morality. If we are the 'right kind of person', society welcomes us; if we are the 'wrong kind', even though our actions are impeccable, we lose. And if we try to free ourselves from this enforced moral typology, the only alternatives seem to be to violently rebel, or else to embrace the very shame society imposes upon us, and overcome its stigma by reveling in it. But to revel in shame is only to descend into Chaos, while to rebel against Fate is to sacrifice oneself to it. Cuchulainn fought against the Goddess to whom he owed his prowess, and was destroyed: he rebelled against his fate, and therefore met it.

So we can see that both submission to and rebellion against these idols only grants them a reality they do not in fact possess, thereby increasing their power. To submit to false Law is ultimately to be forced to commit the very crimes which that Law punishes, just as to worship a false moral uprightness is to place oneself under a false shame. In the words of Blake, 'Prisons are built with stones of [false] Law / Brothels with bricks of [false] Religion.' And to rebel against Law is to finally *become* it, as in the well-known fate of the successful revolutionary who replaces one tyranny with another. Furthermore, to become Law is to ultimately fall under the power of Fate, as when the established system grows beyond the control of those administering it, and descends into Chaos. To submit to Chaos in a deluded search for peace, as in the case of alcoholism or drug addiction, is to fall under both the shame of Fate and the punishment of Law, and to expose oneself to the wilful impulses of the separate fragments or 'complexes' of one's soul, which are part of Selfhood, thus making that soul vulnerable as well to the violent and wilful Selfhoods of others. A person who is violently out of control attracts the violence of other people; a woman who has been drugged is in danger of being raped. And when the soul makes this wilfulness its own in hopes of defending itself, when it aggressively asserts itself in an attempt to overcome Chaos, or to defend itself against other people's aggression, Law is always there to pass sentence. Likewise those who rebel against the shame of Chaos by trying to be 'the right kind of people' in the eyes of a degenerate society, who seek the moral blessing of the system of 'this world' in an attempt to get Fate on their side, will find themselves shamefully compromised. Passing from Fate to Law, they will become agents of the very system of oppression they once sought to oppose, of that tyrannical establishment whose blind, mechanistic Law created Chaos in the first place.

It should be obvious, then, that 'this world' provides no way out, because no single worldly idol can give us shelter from, or power against, the others. They are in collusion, and their function is to prevent us from glimpsing any Reality outside the hopeless terms they lay down.

But why are the primal idols four in number? Is this just a convenient way of looking at things, or is there a deeper structure underlying this fourness? In a way, both statements are true. The mysteries of the Divine Nature, Its relationship to Its creative manifestation, and Its distortion by the human ego, can never be perfectly defined or systematized, mathematically or otherwise. And yet, in the process of contemplating these mysteries, certain forms arise, which are more suggestive of the 'deep things of God' than anything our material or psychic consciousness can perceive or create. From tradition to tradition, from moment to moment of spiritual insight, the forms which appear are always similar but never identical, thereby demonstrating both that God is perfectly concrete, infinitely real and absolutely unique, and that His ultimate Essence is completely beyond conception.

See it like this: The subject/object mode of perception in which we find ourselves immersed, where 'I' am a human subject, and 'that out there' a world, is a projection, on a lower level, of God's mirror-like Self-understanding within the depths of His own nature. Hidden within my perceiving human subjectivity is the Divine Subject, God as the eternal Witness of all the worlds. Hidden behind the 'world out there' is the Divine Object, the face of God eternally present behind the forms and events of our lives. Thus the dyad 'God and His Self-knowledge' is the archetype of the dyad 'me and my world', making four in all.

When the Divine Subject is veiled, its Divine Object is transformed from a perfect reflection of that Witness into a mysterious world with a 'will of its own'—the world of Fate. Simultaneously, the Subject becomes conditioned by its attempt to make sense of that mysterious world—in other words, to impose Law upon it from without, rather than seeing the harmonious pattern within it—and is finally obscured. All that remains of it is the idol of

Selfhood, an ego-bound, self-identified human subjectivity, attempting to impose its own will upon a 'world out there', which, since it is conditioned and obscured by that very fallen subjectivity, must appear as a meaningless Chaos, as in Heisenberg's view of random indeterminacy as the fundamental principle of the material world. In other words, as consciousness falls from the level of Divine Self-understanding to the level of human egotism, idols are generated, which fill the void left by the (apparent) withdrawal of the Presence of God.

From one point of view, these four idols are the satanic counterfeits—the ego-based distortions—of what in the Hebrew Kabbalah are called 'the four worlds', which are related to the Four Living Creatures (Hebrew *hayoth*) that appear both in the vision of Ezekiel and the *Apocalypse* of St John. From the standpoint of the four worlds, the descent from Divine Subject to human ego is not a 'fall' but a progressive manifestation of God which never fundamentally departs from the Divine Nature. Leo Schaya, in *The Universal Meaning of the Kabbalah*, describes these worlds in the following terms, as the 'esoteric anatomy' of Man considered as 'the image and likeness of God':

> The revelatory, creative and redemptive light of the divine Being is, so to speak, 'refracted' through the causal 'prism' of his aspects, the *Sephiroth*, into the indefinite multitude and variety of universal manifestation. The immense hierarchy of onto-cosmological degrees, with all they contain, is established by this 'refraction' of the divine light; these degrees are recapitulated in the four 'worlds' (*olamim*), namely' *olam ha'atsiluth*, the transcendent 'world of emanation' which is that of the *Sephiroth*; *olam haberiyah*, the ideal or spiritual 'world of creation', filled with the divine immanence (*Shekinah*) alone; *olam ha'yetsirah*, the subtle 'world of formation' inhabited by angels, genii and souls; and *olam ha'asiyah*, the sensory and corporeal 'world made of fact'. (p 26)

> Man is the most perfect image of universal reality in the whole of creation; he is the 'incarnated' recapitulation of all the cosmic degrees and of their divine archetypes . . . he represents the most evident symbol of the ten *Sefiroth*, and his integral personality embraces all the worlds: his pure and uncreated being is identified with the Sephirothic 'world of emanation' . . . his spirit, with the prototypical 'world of creation' . . . his soul with the subtle 'world of formation' . . . his body, with the sensory 'world of fact'. (p 70)

The 'world of emanation' is related to the Divine Subject; it is the archetype of sacred law—the ten *Sephiroth* being the prototypes of the Ten Commandments. The 'world of creation' is related to the Divine Object; it is the archetype of wisdom and contemplation. The 'world of formation' is related to the subtle form of the cosmos as the object of the individual human subject; it is the archetype of universal life-energy, of the perceived world considered as the *shakti,* or radiant self-manifesting energy, of that subject, by virtue of the Divine Subject hidden within it. The 'world of fact' is related to the uniqueness of the human person. It is the archetype of the human subject itself, as represented by the human body, the most concrete fact of our experience. The idolatry of Law is thus the counterfeit of the world of emanation; the idolatry of Fate, of the world of creation; the idolatry of Chaos, of the world of formation; the idolatry of Selfhood, of the world of fact.

But what is the way out of the system of this fallen world? The true and sufficient answer to this question is: to plumb the depth and fulfill the conditions of any one of the great religions or wisdom traditions, which were sent by God to save us from our fallen, or forgetful, or ignorant human condition. And the specifically intellectual or *jñanic* answer—within the context of one of these traditions, sincerely embraced and fully lived—is: not to struggle with the shapes of idolatrous illusion, not to rebel against or seek power from the shadows of God, but simply to *see* them, and, thereby, to see through them. Behind Fate is pure contemplation, whose symbols include the Buddhist Prajnaparamita, the White Buffalo Cow Woman of the Lakota, and the Judeo-Christian Holy Wisdom. Behind Law is the prophetic function which Blake called the Imagination, by which eternal principles forever renew their covenant with the unique moments of our lives. Behind Chaos is *shakti,* the universal power of the Absolute, the 'spirit of God' which 'moved on the face of the waters', and which, in its redemptive mode, is the cosmic attraction of all things back to their single transcendent Source. And behind Selfhood is the unseen Seer, the One Self of All within the human heart. As we awake to these four aspects of the Divine, these 'four living creatures'—by God's grace, and by our own full and willing cooperation with it—the abstract separative ego is dissolved in the light of the One Reality.

But to return to our main subject: how does this system of idolatry, and the fallen world based upon it, relate to the Antichrist? If we take Antichrist to be an individual, we can see the four primal idols as a kind of analysis of his character. In other words, we can expect Antichrist, and the system he administers, to be simultaneously the most authoritarian, the most rebellious, the most chaotic, and the most fatalistic one imaginable. (To the degree that Antichrist is the 'ape of Christ', however, his character as the quintessence of idolatry will be hidden from the people. His fatalism will tend to appear to them as certainty and assurance, his chaos as freedom and

spontaneity, his rebelliousness as courage and integrity, and his authoritarianism as the aura of divine right.)

All four of these elements, in one degree or another, appear in the character of Adolph Hitler, who can certainly be described as a precursor to the
Antichrist. His authoritarianism is obvious, since he created an iron police
state over most of Europe. But he was also a rebel, a 'socialist' revolutionary,
who overturned the hereditary power of the German nobility and the
landowning *junkers*. His appeal to the generation of his time was a call to
'rebellion' against real or imagined authority: the Versailles treaty, the
Weimar Republic, the Jews. And yet his language, and ultimately his
actions, were fatalistic. In *Mein Kampf* he appealed to such 'gods' as 'nature'
and 'destiny' to support the contention that his *Reich* was destined to last a
thousand years (making it, incidentally, a satanic counterfeit of the Christian millennium). He placed great reliance on astrologers and other pro-
gnosticators. And late in the war, with Germany in full retreat, when he
could have cut his losses both militarily and politically in many ways, he
chose to look at Germany's defeat in fatalistic terms. Rather than recognizing it as a serious but not terminal setback for the nation, he saw it as a Göt-
terdammerung, an inevitable and apocalyptic cataclysm. Far from trying to
avoid this fate, he demonstrated the depth of his fate-worship by ultimately
siding with it, and doing all he could to make it as destructive as possible.
He ordered Germany's vital remaining food stores and industrial plants
destroyed, and even flooded the Berlin underground, killing thousands of
German citizens who has taken refuge there against the invading Red Army.
And apart from the chaos created by his authoritarianism, rebelliousness
and fatalism, he also incorporated chaotic self-indulgence into his party program, as in the 'Strength through Joy' movement within the Hitler Youth,
where sexual promiscuity was made nearly compulsory. Furthermore, his
erratic decision-making late in the war, to take only one of many possible
examples, demonstrated the fundamental chaos of his character.

But we don't always need to turn to Hitler to understand the system of
the Antichrist, though he will always be a highly valuable case-in-point.
What about present day global society? Dictatorial regimes, religious and
ethnic terrorism, a multinational economic order which enriches the few
and impoverishes the masses, multinational criminal cartels which mas-
sively profit from this state of affairs, widespread moral degeneracy which
calls into being repressive moral codes and attitudes, the natural environment descending into chaos, threatening our food and oxygen supplies,
spawning new diseases, various proposals to turn the human body, via

genetic engineering, bionics, psychopharmacology and electronic mind-control, into a bio-technological robot in order to control this social and biological chaos, if not the ultimate fantasy of 'up-loading' human consciousness into sophisticated computers and so dispensing with the body entirely—this is the state of the world we live in. And so those who want to pinpoint the exact year and month the Antichrist will appear may be missing the point: in a sense, he is here already. And even if he is destined to appear at one point as a single individual, as evangelical Christians, traditional Muslims, and Traditionalist writers (notably René Guénon and Martin Lings) all predict, nonetheless we can not conveniently isolate him within that individual form and that historical period. He is everywhere and at all times in the fallen order of human history, because, in essence, he is nothing but the human ego in rebellion against God. He has been virtually present in the human soul, and its social expression, ever since Adam and Eve ate the apple.

In the '60s it was generally true that those with a liberal or left-wing background would tend to see political or economic tyranny (Law) and repressive, compulsive morality (Fate) as the ultimate evils, whereas people with a right-wing, conservative background would be more likely to view as absolute the evils of violent revolution and/or criminal activity (Selfhood) and moral degeneracy (Chaos). This assessment is still accurate to a great degree. However, it has been equally true since at least the late '70s—if not the '30s—that 'politically correct' liberals will identify with certain established governmental policies which conservatives view as tyrannical; and now that the radical anti-government torch has been passed from the leftist revolutionaries to the right-wing secessionist militias, many conservatives, both radical and moderate, perceive the government as singling them out for persecution. But in any case, *I cannot stress strongly enough* that these partial views, true as they may be in their own sphere, are totally insufficient to define the social manifestation of the spiritual evil we are here calling the Antichrist. Infernal evil can use *any* set of social mores and any political or economic system to build its power, since one of its ploys is to set up insoluble conflicts based on falsely-defined alternatives. In other words, it draws the sides wrong, so that, for example, 'liberals' who think that they believe in the sanctity of life as an absolute, opposing all war and defending even the worst mass murderer against the death penalty, will find themselves supporting doctor-assisted suicide, deaf to all stories of its abuse (as well as to the understanding that it is an abuse in itself), while 'conservatives' who vociferously oppose the use of illegal drugs will take somebody like Ollie

North as their hero, deaf to all evidence that he may have participated in cocaine smuggling to help fund the secret Contra war. And once the conflict of good against evil is falsely defined, then all the courage and idealism in the world only goes to strengthen the evil and erode the good. Infernal forces set right against left, Jews against Muslims, women against men in such a way that their respective positions become so narrowly conceived that damage is done and darkness spread no matter which side one takes—a situation which led W. B. Yeats, in his poem 'The Second Coming' which prophesies the advent of the Antichrist, to describe the latter days as a time in which 'the best lack all conviction, while the worst are filled with passionate intensity.' This is not to say, of course, that some social systems are not better than others, and that we are not sometimes called upon to take sides in social conflicts. Not all perceived oppositions are demonic delusions; to believe so is a delusion in itself. But unless we have a broad enough view of the nature of collective evil—which is nothing but the outer expression of the power of the human ego, and the infernal forces which that ego invokes, to pervert and appropriate *anything it can imagine*—then we will never understand the system of the Antichrist, and may consequently find ourselves unintentionally paying tribute to it, even (or especially!) in the very act of opposing it. It is true that Jesus said, 'I come not to bring peace but a sword'—but he also said 'resist not evil,' and 'sit thou at my right hand, while I make thine enemy thy footstool.'

The Traditionalist School is nothing if not conservative, since its theory of history is based on the 'entropic' degeneration of man and society from an original Golden Age. But I myself reached its threshold by moving through, and hopefully beyond, the liberal counterculture and the world of leftist politics, and I certainly haven't repudiated all the values I learned in that ambiguous arena. Nonetheless, like Christopher Lasch in *The True and Only Heaven*, I've had (at the very least) to separate the values of 'democracy' from those of 'progress'. According to the story told in Plato's *Republic* of the degeneration of human society over the course of the aeon, first comes 'aristocracy', which Martin Lings identifies with theocracy; this is rule by the 'best', the spiritual intellectuals, in Hindu terms the *Brahmin* caste. Next 'timocracy' appears, rule by those of noble character, the king and his courtiers, the *Kshatriya* caste. Next comes 'oligarchy', rule by an ill-defined class of powerful individuals—perhaps the rich, given that Plato's other name for oligarchy is 'plutocracy'. After oligarchy comes 'democracy', rule by the people. And last comes 'tyranny', rule by dictators and demagogues. Therefore, according to this view, even though we may lament that we are no longer ruled by wise philosophers and kings (to the degree that we ever were)—remembering that the 'throne' itself could be a good thing, in times when the institution was spiritually alive, even if a particular king abused his authority and so was justified in being deposed—the fact that we are now in the phase of democracy means that we must hold the line here as long as possible, whatever democracy's shortcomings, since the only alternative, according to Plato, is tyranny. And this tyranny—authoritarian, rebellious, chaotic and fatalistic—will be the socio-political expression (the Beast) of the mass cultural and psychic disposition of the end times (the Whore), which is the reflection of a counterfeit, and thus satanic, spiritual order (the Dragon). This is one possible rendition, and I believe it is a useful one, of the system of Antichrist.

But we must be careful never to assume that whatever most repels us and seems most evil to us must be the regime of the Antichrist. In worldly terms—and 'the world' has struck its roots deep in the souls of most of us—the Antichrist will look like a good proposition. He will attract us by making a perverted appeal to what is best in us. He will not only seize power; he will also appropriate values. In the Shiïte Muslim account, the Mahdi—the Islamic 'messiah', sometimes identified with Elias, who will appear before the Second Coming of Jesus—will wear a yellow turban, and the servants of the Antichrist green ones. This is strange, since the color yellow in Islam usually symbolizes weakness, as in Western folk-symbolism it stands for either cowardice or infectious disease. But green is the color of Paradise—specifically, in some systems, of the Paradise of the perfection of the Divine Immanence, which comes after the blackness of the transcendent, unknowable Divine Essence, and thus represents the highest stage of realization. So in the regime of Antichrist, as René Guénon predicted, the significance of spiritual symbolism will be inverted. As it says in 2 Cor. 11:14, 'Satan himself is transformed into an angel of light.'

6

The War Against Love

THE modern world does not only pervert our beliefs and our actions, it also devastates our feelings—as witness the violation, by almost every sector of contemporary society, religious, secular and 'esoteric', of the realm of romantic love. We used to say, 'Love conquers all'; but since nothing is left to us now of the word 'love' but dumb sentimentality and the automatic reaction to sexual stimulus, we have forgotten the incomparable power of that Conqueror, forgotten that only Love can press all the human faculties, including courage, self-sacrifice and strategic intelligence, into Her service.

Romantic love has been a buried foundation, and sometimes an acknowledged pillar, of European civilization for almost a thousand years. It reached its highest literary expression in the *Parzival* of Wolfram von Eschenbach, and in Dante's *Divine Comedy*, the greatest single compendium of spiritual knowledge in Western Christendom, where the lore of the troubadours was fully reunited to the Christian tradition, culminating in the figure of Beatrice Portinari as an incarnation of Holy Wisdom. And since, if my family genealogy is accurate, I am 29th in direct (though often female) line from Eleanor of Aquitaine, who presided over the famous Courts of Love, and thus 31st in line from her grandfather Guillaume of Poitiers, the first troubadour, my ancestors now press me to speak for Love again, in the face of the darkness of the latter days, and to refute the slander of 'the World' that Love is blind. On the contrary, it is passion that is blind, but Love's vision penetrates like an arrow, into the depth of the spiritual Heart.

The Antichrist will be the perfect shell. He will be politically, culturally, religiously and even metaphysically 'correct'. Everything he does, according to all explicit criteria, will initially appear to be right. Those who recognize and oppose him will not seem spiritual in the eyes of the world; perhaps not even in their own eyes. They will appear unbalanced, arrogant, reactionary, petty. In the face of the towering emptiness of the Beast, only a healthy emotional nature which has endured the shame of Love, whose feelings are grounded in Love Itself, will have the power to smell the corruption, the 'dead men's bones and all uncleanness,' hidden in that whitewashed tomb.

✳ The Love of Many will Grow Cold

The system of Antichrist will be, and is, an articulated, established regime of emotional coldness. While criticizing corrupt social trends or false metaphysical ideas, we must never forget that the mind cannot be darkened, nor can human society become really monstrous, unless the affections are also polluted with false glamour, numbed and petrified with arrogance and self-loathing, poisoned with unlived sorrow and repressed fear.

The plague of emotional coldness which is now pandemic in the world affects us without our being aware of it. Gross atrocities may temporarily awaken us to our collective condition, but they also numb us. Once our basic trust in God is eroded—assuming we ever possessed it—we fall back for emotional security upon human society, upon a kind of collective mammalian warmth which we hope will protect us from the metaphysical anxiety we feel. And when society becomes insecure, we attempt to fall back even further, upon instinct itself. Just as humanistic sentiment replaces faith in God, so addiction to the energy, glamour and viciousness of sub-human emotional reactions replaces sentiment. But as collective human behavior is beginning to demonstrate, there is even less security in instinct than in society, since for human society to exist at all a certain amount of human responsibility has to be exercised; somebody has to 'mind the store'.

In 2 Tim. 3:3, St Paul says that, as the age draws toward its close, people will be 'without natural affection'. And contemporary American culture—to limit my critique to what I know first-hand—shows every evidence of this. For parents to abuse children is common, and it is not unknown for children to murder parents. An all-pervading lovelessness has led to a general emotional flattening and a weakening of the texture of the soul—as if, in our hunger for security, we unconsciously aspired to be transformed into something on the order of computer-generated images; such images cannot suffer from existential angst, and there is little to mourn if they end by being 'deleted'. This emotional flattening manifests in gross terms as a plague of psychotic violence, as if the perpetrators of monstrous crimes were somehow trying to shock themselves back to three-dimensional reality (while only numbing themselves further), and in a more subtle way as a widespread lack of what used to be called 'common' courtesy, apparently based upon a deep-seated, I might almost say *superstitious* fear of sentiment. Nor are these two poles unrelated, since a collective lack of sensitivity to the feelings of others means that everyone is always being offended, and offended people are always getting angry.

The effects of this freezing of the human soul are nowhere more apparent than in the world of heterosexual relations. Among its consequences are promiscuity, bland serial monogamy, and what I call the 'parallel marriage', derived from the mores of the singles culture and supported by the structure of the two-career family, in which one's spouse is only a kind of roommate, where the practical act of facing the world has almost completely replaced the emotional act of facing each other.

Sociologist Herbert Hendin, writing in 1975 when the present regime of emotional coldness was being established in the comedown from the psychic and social upheavals of the '60s, recorded this impression of the college students he studied:

> Women . . . to shield themselves from male anger . . . attempt to create a life that seems expressly designed to rule out the possibility of being affected by a man. The fear of involvement is profound, pervasive . . . a fear of being totally wiped out, or losing the fight for self-validation . . . most young women avoid real intimacy with a man, feeling that caring itself is self-destructive . . . for both sexes in society, caring for anyone deeply is becoming synonymous with losing. . . . In a culture that institutionalizes lack of commitment, it is very hard to be committed; in a nation that seems determined to strip sex of romance and tenderness, it is very hard to be a tender and faithful lover.

These words in many ways echo those of the medieval German poet, Gottfried Von Strassburg—just to remind us that Love has been under the gun in this world ever since mankind first sought the fruit of a 'knowledge' that Love cannot give:

> I pity love with all my heart; for though almost all today hold and cleave to her, no one concedes her due. We all want our pleasure of her, and to consort with her. But no! Love is not what we, with our deceptions, are now making of her for each other . . . . It is really true, what they say, 'Love is harried and hounded to the ends of the earth.' All that we possess of her is the word, the name alone remains to us; and that, too, we have so bandied about, misused and vulgarized, that the poor thing is ashamed of her name, disgusted with the very sound of it.

Once a person's heart has become cold, he or she has already lost the faculty by which that coldness could be discerned, just as someone whose conscience has died can no longer feel his or her own lack of conscience, or a person whose taste has become jaded can no longer 'taste' his or her own bad taste. There are plenty among us—let us pray that we are not among them—whose hearts are dead already, leaving their rational minds relatively intact, and even more capable in some ways of operating efficiently in a society based on 'spiritual wickedness in high places,' on a psychopathic coldness which is on its way to becoming the norm. As Jesus said, when his disciples asked him what would be the signs of his coming at the end of the present world, 'because iniquity shall abound, the love of many shall wax cold' (Matt. 24:12).

The story of this unconscious freezing of the emotions is told by Hans Christian Andersen in his fairy tale 'The Snow Queen': A demon, who is also a professor or schoolteacher, invents a mirror in which all that is evil grows to monstrous proportions, while good things appear distorted and shrunken. He and his students travel all over the world with the mirror, mocking everything that is good. They even try to fly up to heaven and mock the angels, but the higher they fly the heavier the mirror becomes, till it slips from their grasp and shatters into a million pieces. Some pieces of the mirror are taken and used for windows, through which the world appears ugly and twisted. Tiny slivers get into people's eyes, destroying their ability to see the good in anything, while others work their way into people's hearts, which freeze into blocks of ice.

These developments announce the coming of the Snow Queen, who lives in an ice palace beyond the Arctic Circle, and flies over the world with the snowstorm to destroy warmth and love wherever she finds it. The young hero of the tale is kidnapped and taken to her palace, where he is taught how to play a kind of board-game called 'the ice-pictures of reason'. He is finally rescued by his childhood sweetheart, who must go on a long and dangerous quest to find him and restore his soul.

'The Snow Queen' is undoubtedly an unconscious allegory of the fall of the 'Hyperborean Paradise' spoken of by René Guénon as the original land of the Primordial Tradition—the last folkloric vestige of which, strangely enough, is the myth of Santa Claus. The Snow Queen is a kind of 'Anti-Santa Claus' who replaces warmth and generosity with a frigid possessiveness. The same kind of frigidity can affect those who try to understand metaphysical ideas with the mind alone. In many fairy tales, such as the Spanish tale 'The White Parrot' or the Persian 'The Bath Badgerd', anyone who approaches the sacred Center with the wrong attitude—curiosity, for example, or the hunger for power—is turned, not to ice, but to stone.

'The Snow Queen' is the story of the occupation of the 'pole', the spiritual center of human consciousness, by the regime of materialistic rationalism, which is articulated in higher academia and disseminated to the masses through the public school system, veiling the direct perception of God and destroying the faith by which this perception might be restored. The 'still point of the turning world' symbolized by the Pole Star, the point where Eternity intersects time, is transformed into the regime of Fate, the inexorably circling constellations of the World Clock, expressed in terms of 19th century science as mechanistic determinism, and in theology by the error known as Deism, which denied God's immanence in His creation, reducing it to a soulless mechanism. If, as Schuon says, the Renaissance was the revenge of classical Paganism on Christendom, we can see the figure of Andersen's Snow Queen—who, at the end of the tale, is vanquished by Christian love—as a symbolic union of Neo-Paganism and scientism (both of which ultimately sprang from the Renaissance), something like the Goddess of Reason worshipped in the de-sacralized cathedrals of France during the Revolution.

Andersen's way of opposing the coldness of rationalistic materialism was through sentimentality—which, as Guénon points out, is no more than the affective expression of materialism itself. Since materialism denies the existence of the higher realities available to Intellection, emotion must now root itself not in eternal Truth but in the world of nature and the senses, a world subject to time and decay. This inverted orientation necessarily transforms sound, intelligent human emotion into sentimentality, nostalgia and the attraction to death, as with the English and German Romantic poets who worshipped nature instead of God. To those with a sense of transcendence, the world of nature, like the human form of which it is the living *shakti*, is the locus-of-manifestation for all the Names and Energies of God. For those without this sense, it is a heartless battlefield, a bio-technological mechanism, and ultimately a graveyard, whether or not they are able to throw over it a temporary cloak of lyric fascination.

When Guénon was writing, the regime of bourgeois sentimentalism was in full force; we need only remember the vulgar and cloying veneration of 'the Little Flower', St Theresa of Lisieux, to see what he was up against as an expositor of pure metaphysics—though we must remember, as Thomas Merton points out, that St Theresa was a real saint. Schuon himself had great respect for her, and even thought that some of her writings showed elements of true *gnosis*. This battle against a degenerate emotionalism partly explains why Guénon wrote with his particular brand of *sang froid*, which led some to describe him as 'an eye without a body'. In order to defend himself and his mission against false sentimentalities and enthusiasms of all kinds, he wrote without fervor, protected only by the thorn of an aloof and measured irony.

Sentimentality, however, is no longer our problem. If there is any single sign of the transition from the twilight of the modern age to the dawn of postmodernism, it is the rage of both popular and academic culture to pull down all the idols of sentiment, idols which were well-established as of the late '50s and early '60s. If the officially established emotions of the Victorian era were triumphalism and sentimentality, so our postmodern status quo enforces vulgarity, emotional numbness, terror, sinister fascination, disgust and despair. That postmodernism as a cultural regime could presume to 'establish' itself on such a foundation of sand is a perfect illustration of the principle of 'a house divided against itself'. It will not stand.

✳ How the Denial of Love can Pervert Metaphysics

In these times, when all primary human relationships are being systematically devastated—through the mechanization of reproduction, for example—many of us have tried to take refuge in God from the destruction of human love, both by means of the group identity offered by exoteric religion, and through the mysteries and struggles of the spiritual Path. But since the very state of cultural decay which has brought human love to the brink of extinction has also removed the normal exoteric supports of the esoteric Way—for example, the support of a spiritually-based social morality that both nourishes and protectively conceals the inner Reality—the esoteric enterprise itself is now more exposed to worldliness and 'spiritual materialism' than perhaps at any time in its history. The spiritual Path is more and more being thought of not as the crown of human life but as a substitute for it; we forget that 'none come to the Father'—God's transcendence—'but through Me'—God's humanity. As Schuon has written:

> In the case of some people the intention of loving God brings with it an inability to love men; now the second of these things destroys the former. In a vulgar soul solicitude for spiritual love and for mortification may bring with it an icy self-centeredness....

Regretfully, the same can be said for a spiritual Path which emphasizes Intellection over sentimental devotion — not because this emphasis is not fully justified in the case of the *jñanic* spiritual temperament, but because a certain percentage of those attracted to metaphysics and the *idea* of Intellection will inevitably interpret this to mean that an attachment to spiritual knowledge justifies, or even requires, the abandonment of spiritual and human love. But as Schuon warns us, in *Spiritual Perspectives and Human Facts*:

> A cult of the intelligence and mental passion take man further from truth. Intelligence withdraws as soon as man puts his trust in it alone. Mental passion pursuing intellectual intuition is like the wind which blows out the light of a candle.

My wife, Jennifer Doane Upton, in the essay 'Dante's Vision of Spiritual Love', deals with this error:

> It is habitually assumed in today's world that feeling is strictly subjective. But it is more accurate to say that some feelings are objectively true and others objectively false. If you love a demon, for example, your feelings are not *true*. The modern world revels in the passions, but in many ways it attempts to kill the 'still, small voice' of objective feeling. True feeling can often seem small and unimportant, like alpine flowers, even though these apparently insignificant plants have the power to endure great cold.
> Many people today who have an interest in metaphysics tend to believe that feelings are mere 'accidents'. Yet one can lose one's soul through false feeling, while true feeling can save it, and nothing that has to do with salvation and damnation can be only accidental. In *Paradiso* 26:59–63 [Allen Mandelbaum's translation], Dante says:

> > The Death which He, that I might live, endured
> > And hope, whereto the faithful, as I, cling
> > Joined with that living knowledge [i.e. the 'bitings' of
> > Divine Love in union with human love] have secured
> > That from the sea of the erring love retrieved
> > On the shore of the right love I stand assured.

Given the belief prevailing in metaphysical circles that affections are accidental, some conclude that because the soul is the realm of the affections, it is therefore the principle of the passions and vices, including pride. But feeling is certainly no more *inherently* prideful than thought. True feeling relates to the more spiritual aspects of the soul; only false feeling is involved with the

passions. And Love, which is of divine origin, pertains to more than the feeling soul. But though Love is more than feeling, it never excludes feeling; if
Love is there, feeling is there. The feeling may be there obliquely; sometimes
one may be more objectively loving by acting against certain feelings. Nonetheless, Love is always the crown of true feeling, which means objective feeling. *Paradiso* 26:28–39:

> [The] good, soon as 'tis perceived as good
> Enkindles love and makes it more to live
> The more of good it can itself include.
> Therefore to the Essence, whose prerogative
> Is, that what good outside of it is known
> Is naught else than a light its own beams give
> More than else whither must in love be drawn
> The mind of him whose vision can attain
> The verity the proof is founded on.
> This verity to my intellect is made plain
> By Him who to that prime love testifies
> Which all the eternal substances maintain.

According to Frithjof Schuon, 'there is *bhakti* without *jñana*, but there is no
jñana without *bhakti*'; though knowledge is higher than love, love is more
fundamental than knowledge. On the other hand, Schuon's follower Martin
Lings, whose work and presence are so admirable that I hesitate to criticize
him, speaks in *The Eleventh Hour* of a perspective of knowledge *rather than*
love as proper for our time. In my opinion, this is already at the very least a
radical narrowing-down of Schuon's teaching.

If, as Schuon never tires of repeating, there is no right superior to the
truth, then it must be admitted, because it is true, that it is next to impossible to tell many contemporary Westerners that knowledge is in some sense
higher than love (though, in another way, love is more fundamental than
knowledge) without their *hearing* you say that compassion should therefore
be de-emphasized, feelings distrusted, and the struggle to develop emotional intelligence abandoned. One reason for this is that many people who
are attracted to intellectuality, both spiritual and secular, are simply in flight
from emotional pain. Their attempt to pacify and harmonize emotion by
means of mental discipline therefore often becomes a struggle to repress
feeling, and a denial of the special quality of insight which only feeling can
give. After all, in a world of mass suffering and dehumanization it is infinitely easier—initially—to despair of compassion, to repress emotion, and
to seal oneself off in a shell of ice against the terror outside... and then (of

course) to go on to reproduce that same terror, in a more concentrated, more intimate, and more soul-destroying form, within that very shell; to take it as one's teacher, and end by becoming its agent. In order to work against this seemingly inevitable misunderstanding, I can do nothing better than quote Schuon's doctrine, from *Survey of Metaphysics and Esoterism*, on the place of emotion in the spiritual life:

> Not to be 'emotional': this seems, nowadays, to be the very condition of 'objectivity', whereas in reality objectivity is independent of the presence or absence of the emotional element.... Emotivity manifests and allows one to perceive those aspects of a good or an evil which mere logical definition could not manifest directly and concretely.... If natural dignity requires a certain impassibility—thereby manifesting the 'motionless mover' and the sense of the sacred—it does not, however, exclude the natural impulses of the soul, as is shown by the lives of the sages and saints, and above all by everyday experience.... In a spiritual man there is a continuity between his inward impassibility—resulting from his consciousness of the Immutable—and his emotion.... In the emotion of the spiritual man, the 'motionless mover' always remains present and accessible. As his emotion is linked to knowledge, the truth is never betrayed.... Fundamentally, we would say that where there is Truth, there is also Love. Each *Deva* possesses its *Shakti*; in the human microcosm, the feeling soul is joined to the discerning intellect, as in the Divine Order Mercy is joined to Omniscience; and as, in the final analysis, Infinitude is consubstantial with the Absolute.

This relationship between feeling and spiritual insight is further elaborated by Jennifer Doane Upton:

> There is, in contemporary society, a profound ignorance of true feeling, leading to an emotional coldness which opens the soul to worldliness, even when doctrinal understanding, in its own dimension, had successfully shut that world out.
> Developed feeling is refined and subtle. Far from being merely sentimental or demonstrative, it often withholds its own demonstration when such a manifestation would destroy the context in which it appears; this explains why, while he is in the *Inferno*, Dante never pronounces Beatrice's name. Feeling must be cultivated, both for the sake of the fullness of human life, and because it itself can be a perfect vehicle for union with God, not only due to the psychic energy it releases, but also because of the particular perceptions which only developed feeling can give; this is not *bhakti* as we usually think of it. There are certain avenues to the transcendent Intellect which are only open through feeling. *Paradiso* 28:1–12:

When she who hath imparadised my mind
Hath stript the truth bare, and its contraries
In the present life of wretched mortal-kind,
As one who, looking in the mirror, sees
A torch's flame that is behind him lit
Ere in his sight, or in his thought, it is
And turns to see if the glass opposite
Have told him truth, and findeth it agree
Therewith, as truly note and measure fit;
So is recorded in my memory
That I turned, looking on those eyes of light
Whence love had made the noose to capture me. . . .

Go back to that old melodious phrase 'true love'. It sounds merely sentimental to us now. But 'true' equals 'objective'; true love is objective love. Many a
time a person has reached the Truth by starting from the thinking function,
only to have that Truth destroyed in his life through false feeling. True feeling, on the other hand, can be a 'homing' faculty, drawing us toward the Center almost faster than we could travel on our own initiative. In the words of
St Bernard, symbol of divine contemplation, to Dante in *Paradiso* 32:149–150:
'And do thou with thy feeling [*l'affezione*] follow on/ My words, that close to
them thy heart may cling.' According to Dante, Love is the Supreme Goal of
the spiritual life, not simply the energy driving it. That Supreme, objective
Love is another name for the transcendent Intellect. In *Paradiso* 32:142–144,
St Bernard says:

And turn we to the Primal Love our eyes,
So that, still gazing toward Him, thou may'st pierce
Into His splendour, as far as in thee lies.

And in *Paradiso* 33:85–92, Dante declares:

I beheld leaves within the unfathomed blaze
Into one volume bound by love, the same
That the universe holds scattered through its maze.
Substance and accidents, and their modes, became
As if together fused, all in such wise
That what I speak of is one simple flame.
Verily I think I saw with mine own eyes
The form that knits the whole world. . . .

In *Spiritual Perspectives and Human Facts*, Schuon says: 'What is "love" at the
start [of the spiritual Path] will appear as "Knowledge" in the result, and

what is "knowledge" at the start will appear in the result as "Love"'; and 'The love of the affective man is that he loves God. The love of the intellectual man is that God loves him; that is to say, he realizes intellectually—but not simply in a theoretical way—that God is Love.'

Dante concurs with this view. In *Paradiso* 28:109–111, he places knowledge firmly above love:

[The] celestial bliss
Is founded on the act that seeth God,
Not on that which loves, which cometh after this.

Throughout the *Paradiso*, however, he never tires of repeating that God is Love, calling Him, for example, 'that Primal Love' (32:142). What both Dante and Schuon are saying, in other words, is not that God is Truth rather than Love, but that the full and serene knowledge of God as Love (and thus also as Truth) is greater than the emotional response to Him, no matter how intense and devoted that response may be, and how necessary for the purification of the soul.

The Devil loves to set up false antitheses, so that whichever side one takes, damage is done and darkness spread. And perhaps his favorite of all is the one between love and knowledge. What could better suit his purposes than to pervert affection till it darkens the intellect, thus identifying love with foolishness in the popular mind, so that the most loving among us are continually wounded until their affections freeze? And what better reveals the quality of satanic pride than that knowledge should be identified with emotional coldness, gnosis with social prestige, and intelligence with cunning, till hard-heartedness itself is seen as a virtue, since if the intelligent are cold, then to become cold must be to become intelligent? In terms of the 'unseen warfare' between the order of Divine Reality and the infernal subversion of that Order, some of the most powerful and intelligent of the 'fallen cherubim' would seem to occupy the split between love and knowledge, and war against all who try to bring them closer together, or intuit their intrinsic unity. (One is reminded of the Norse 'rime giants', spirits of abysmal cold, or of the frozen ninth circle of Dante's *Inferno*, reserved for the betrayers of love.) Instead of our being 'wise as serpents and harmless as doves', these forces would rather see us 'harmless as serpents'—brutally cunning—and 'wise as doves'—naive.

And all metaphysics apart, the complementarity of love and knowledge is, or ought to be, a part of simple common sense. If the collective mind were not so smogged by the corruption of the times it would be easy to see that whatever truly serves love equally serves knowledge, while whatever wounds love also darkens the intellect. If we become comfortable with stupidity we will lose our ability to love God and our neighbor, since we can't love what we don't want to know; and if we become comfortable with lovelessness we will inevitably fall into stupidity, since we can't know something if we are laboring to avoid all intimate contact with it. What could be more obvious? And if we have never learned to love others through knowing them, and to know them by means of loving them, then we will not succeed in the Divine realm after having failed in the human.

✳ The Wasteland

Knowledge has two roads open to it: the road of Love, and the road of Power. If Knowledge marries with Love, thus subordinating Power (which is transformed into the servant of that union), it defines the state of Paradise. If it carries on an adulterous affair with Power, and in so doing subordinates Love (making it the victim of that liaison), it defines the state of Hell.

In the Orthodox Christian icon of St George, the saint is shown as a knight mounted on a white horse, in the act of rescuing a princess from a dragon by impaling him with his lance. If St George is Knowledge, then the princess is Love, and the dragon is Power. In the outer world, the dragon manifests as tyranny, oppression, collective vice, and the established regime of heartlessness; in the inner world, he is the *nafs-al-ammara*, the passional soul, the rule of concupiscence over the human heart. The dragon, in other words, is Satan, the spiritual archetype of Antichrist. And the princess is the energy of Eros, who is either a slave to the power-motive, as with the Whore of Babylon 'with whom the kings of the earth have committed fornication' (Rev. 17:2), or the bride of Knowledge, the living body of Truth, as in the case of the Heavenly Jerusalem, described in Rev. 21:2 as 'coming down out of heaven from God, prepared as a bride adorned for her husband.'

The story of Love enslaved to Power due to the immaturity of Knowledge is told in the Grail romance of *Parzival* by Wolfram von Eschenbach. The Grail King Anfortas, while still an adolescent, is wounded in the testicles during a joust, as punishment for foolish pride in love. His wound never heals, though the presence of the Grail, whose guardian he is, keeps him from dying. His kingdom languishes. At the same time the castrated magician Clingschor, in league with the tyrant king Gramoflanz, casts his evil spell over all lovers, and blights their love. (He was castrated by the King of Sicily, who found him in an adulterous affair with his wife, Queen Iblis — 'Iblis' or 'Eblis' being the Muslim name for Satan.) Gawain and Parzival, knights of Arthur's Round Table on quest for adventure, come into the energy-field of this Wasteland, where love is enslaved and destroyed by pride and power. Gawain endures the ordeals of the Castle of Marvels, which is filled with many women bound by Clingschor's spell, rescues them, and is united with Lady Orgeleuse, his beloved. And Parzival, after many struggles with his own spiritual and emotional immaturity, finally redeems and heals Anfortas, the Grail King, simply by asking what ails him, and is reunited with his wife Condwiramurs, whose name, from the French *conduire-amours*, means 'to guide love'. Parzival himself becomes the new guardian of the Grail.

The regime of Clingschor/Gramoflanz, of perverted spirituality allied with political power, is one rendition, or foreshadowing, of the regime of Antichrist. Whatever curses love, whatever distorts or destroys sexuality — such as human genetic engineering — leads directly to that terminal Wasteland ruled by a castrated magician, where the Beast is ridden by the Whore (the Queen Iblis of the *Parzival* romance), who buys and sells all the goods and treasures of the earth, including the souls of men (Rev. 18:13).

✳ Human Love as God's Mercy

The Western Romantic Tradition, from which this story is drawn, has acted as a balance to the ascetical otherworldliness of Western Christendom for nearly a millennium. And despite its early association with heresies such as Catharism, it went on to form an integral part of Christian culture in Western Europe, as the works of Dante and Shakespeare, which draw deeply on the Romantic Tradition, abundantly prove.

The central value celebrated in the Romantic tradition is that union of spiritual love (*agape*) and passionate desire (*eros*) known as *amor*. In the essay 'High Romance and the Spiritual Path', Jennifer Doane Upton has written:

> Human love in some sense meets its death at the birth of divine love. But in another way it lives again through that very death, and becomes a symbol of that higher love. . . . In High Romance, the spirit descends into and fills out the human level. . . . Often, on account of the intensity of emotion this produces, we feel ashamed when we approach romantic material. All this loving of love, and having to do without love even as we love — it blisters our

self-esteem. . . . When we deny romantic states, we distort the very forms the
spirit is trying to ennoble. The spirit hovers above us, with no way to reach
our humanity. We have allowed it to be stranded.

In Amor, the personhood of the beloved is central—just as, in true spiritual
realization, God is not an abstraction or an insubstantial wraith, but the
most concrete Reality imaginable. From the worldly point of view, this is
viewed as mere lower-class sentimentalism, whereas from a standpoint
tinged with spiritual arrogance, love of the human beloved is seen as nothing
but idolatry, the worship of one's own ego in the person of another. In the
face of such worldly cynicism, and a (no less cynical) false spiritual idealism,
we are ashamed of romantic love—forgetting that, as Schuon reminds us in
Understanding Islam, 'the "romantic" worlds are precisely those in which God
is still probable.' Just as the Victorians indulged themselves in sentimental
romance but were ashamed of sexuality, so we indulge in every form of sexual exhibitionism, but are ashamed of love. The passion, tenderness, and
courage of true romantic love, as opposed to mere sentimental romanticism,
are among the few virtues capable of humanizing heterosexual relations.
One might even say that this depth of love almost alone possesses the power
to extend the spiritual grace of the Christian sacrament of matrimony into
the psychic and interpersonal dimensions. Like all such reflections of God's
Unity in the realm of multiplicity, there is always a danger of dissipation and
fall—and, as always, this danger can be overcome in only one way: through
sacrifice. As Schuon says: 'It is necessary to dig deep into the soil of the soul,
through layers of aridity and bitterness in order to find love and live from it.'

The Western Romantic tradition, with its exaltation of a form of ritual
adultery where strict faithfulness (on the man's part), risk of life and limb,
and an element of ascetic rigor were the operative virtues, began as a rebellion against the heartless convention of worldly aristocratic marriage, where
all personal and feeling-centered values were sacrificed to the quest for political power. The heartless convention of the present day, however, is not marriage, but a vicious lovelessness in all areas of life, coupled with an attachment to the most venomous forms of sexual self-indulgence. The ultimate result of this attachment is the devastation of sexuality itself and a general flattening of the soul, which then becomes vulnerable to worldly pride,
as well as to seduction by the various forms of sub-human unreality proposed by technocratic society. Consequently, in the realm of relationships,
the central act of liberating rebellion against the degenerate social mores is
no longer the dangerous, formalized adultery sung by the troubadours, but

loving marriage itself, where the power employed by God to create the universe—the power of polarity—reaches its point of greatest concentration.

In *Esoterism as Principle and as Way*, Schuon enunciates the principle of personal, human love as a way to, as well as an expression of, union with God:

> An indispensable condition for the innocent and natural experience of earthly happiness is the spiritual capacity of finding happiness in God, and the incapacity to enjoy things outside of Him. We cannot validly and persistently love a creature without carrying him within ourselves by virtue of our attachment to the Creator; not that this inward possession must be perfect, but it must at all events be present as an intention which allows us to perfect it. . . . To be at peace with God is to seek and find our happiness in Him; the creature that he has joined to us may and must help us to reach this with greater facility or with less difficulty, in accordance with our gifts and with grace, whether merited or unmerited. In saying this we evoke the paradox— or rather the mystery—of attachment with a view to detachment, or of outwardness with a view to inwardness, or again, of form with a view to essence. True love attaches us to a sacramental form while separating us from the world, and it thus rejoins the mystery of exteriorized revelation with a view to interiorizing Salvation.
>
> ⌒The Essential Writings of Frithjof Schuon, pp 419–420

To love what is passing, ephemeral and destined for the grave, to love it with a love which, like all love, is eternal at the core, is to taste the full poignancy of existence amid 'the red dust of this world.' And to ultimately see the human object of one's love as transparent to Love Itself is, in Yeats' words, to 'break the teeth of time.' By means of a profound sacrifice of attachment leading to an alchemical transmutation of the affections, it is to transform the nostalgia for the past, which is corruption, into the nostalgia for Eternity, which is bliss. To live in the intimate knowledge of the inevitable death of one's human beloved is, paradoxically, to see her or him *sub specie aeternitatis*: no longer as an object of love, but as a vision of Love Itself, in which the separation between this world and the next is overcome.

To love romantically in the face of the coldness of the latter days, without personal idolatry, and in the name of 'the Love that moves the Sun and the other stars,' is to risk all—power, prestige, security, even life itself, the whole spectrum of worldly, ego-based values—for the sake of that Love. The World, the System of Antichrist, the established regime of collective arrogance and despair, is profoundly threatened by this union of heterosexuality, spirituality and personal love which I have called Amor, and subverts it whenever possible: sometimes through puritanism, sometimes through libertinism, and often through an unholy amalgam of the two, like much of what passes for 'tantra' or 'sacred sexuality' in the world of the New Age, where impersonality masquerades as detachment, and subtilized physical sensation replaces both mystical ecstasy and human love. This sense of threat on the part of the kingdom of Antichrist is a sure sign that there is something in the essence of Amor which, if purified of idolatry and dedicated to God, to Love Itself, has the power to sever that kingdom at the root.

7

UFOs & Traditional Metaphysics: A Postmodern Demonology

WHEN asked to define 'reality', William James gave the following answer: 'Anything is real of which we find ourselves obliged to take account of in any way.' According to this broad (though far from deep) definition, UFOs are certainly real. The mass belief in them has had an immense and incalculable effect upon our society. Nor has this belief simply materialized out of nothing; there is method behind this social, psychic, and empirically documented madness.

Friedrich Nietzsche said, 'Be careful: while you are looking into the abyss, the abyss is looking into you.' This is why I caution the reader not to open to this section while in a state of depression, anxiety, or morbid curiosity. Whoever already knows how bad UFOs are, and is not required by his or her duties to investigate them, should skip this chapter. Those who think there may be something 'spiritual' in them, however, and are not afraid of being seriously disillusioned, should read on.

✳ The Place of the UFO Myth in Contemporary Culture

The UFO phenomenon constitutes a true postmodern demonology—though all too many of those who believe that Unidentified Flying Objects are extraterrestrial visitors treat it more as a postmodern religion. And the religious or quasi-religious relationship to the phenomenon is certainly not limited to the UFO cults *per se*. To take only one example: according to

UFO researcher Jacques Vallee, in his *Messengers of Deception*, the pope and founder of the Church of Scientology L. Ron Hubbard—who died in 1986 and who, according to my late '60s correspondence with ex-Scientologist William Burroughs, had a background in Naval Intelligence—'is said to have practiced ritual magic with a rocket expert named Jack Parsons, who met in the Mojave Desert in 1945 a "Spiritual Being" whom he regarded as a Venusian' (p13). According to Vallee, both Hubbard and Parsons had a background in the Ordo Templi Orientis, founded by black magician Aliester Crowley. Parsons, however, went on to become co-founder of both the Aerojet Corporation and the Jet Propulsion Laboratory.

Whether true or false, such assertions are right in line with the contemporary UFO folklore which informs us that our modern technology is either a 'gift' of the saucer people or a product of back-engineering from the saucer which supposedly crashed in Roswell, New Mexico in the 1947. And such beliefs to be found not only among New Age cults or eccentric hermits living in camping trailers; many 'responsible' and well-established computer professionals, and even corporate executives of our 'information culture', also hold them. And at least one U.S. President, Jimmy Carter, admits to having witnessed a UFO; ideas which were once the province of the 'lunatic fringe' are now increasingly acceptable among the political and corporate elite. So at the very least we can say that UFO mythology is on its way to becoming socially dominant, or at least highly significant, in today's global society—something mythographer Joseph Campbell was well aware of when he became 'mythic advisor' to George Lucas for his *Star Wars* trilogy.

The fact that I've had to delve deeply into traditional metaphysics in order to deal with the UFO phenomenon from a stable intellectual standpoint, and to criticize such beliefs as 'physical' time-travel and literal human reincarnation when dealing with the myth of 'aliens', shows the degree to which ideas which René Guénon called 'counter-initiatory' have occupied the centers of human consciousness abandoned over the past couple of centuries by traditional metaphysics and theology. According to Guénon, in his prophetic work *The Reign of Quantity and the Signs of the Times*, as this cycle of manifestation draws to a close, the cosmic environment first solidifies—this being in a way both the result and the cause of modern materialism—after which it simply fractures, because a material reality absolutely cut off from subtler planes of being is metaphysically impossible. These cracks in the 'great wall' separating the physical universe from the subtle or animic plane initially open in a 'downward' direction, toward the 'infra-psychic' or demonic realm (cf. Rev. 9:1–3); 'magical realism' replaces 'ordinary life'. It is only at the final moment that a great crack opens in the 'upward' direction, at the Second Coming of Christ, the advent of that Being whom the Hindus call the Kalki Avatara, who will bring this world to a close and inaugurate the next cycle of manifestation. And yet, for those with faith in God and an intuition of the Absolute, the 'upward crack', since it opens onto Eternity, is here already; though the mass mind is becoming less and less able to see it, the Door of Grace is not closed: 'Behold I am with you all days, even unto the consummation of the age.' As the dark shadow of a greater Light than this world can produce, the UFO phenomenon is truly an eschatological sign.

There is no question that the UFO myth has deeply affected the mass mind. When the Heaven's Gate cult committed group suicide near San Diego in the March of 1997, the question of the place of UFO ideology in contemporary life became, for a short time, the most compelling question confronting the American people. The followers of M.H. Applewhite, avid *Star Trek* fans, apparently believed that their souls would be reunited after death aboard a 'spaceship' which was invisibly following the Hale-Bopp comet. At the autopsy of the cult members, it was discovered that a number of the males had been castrated, an operation which was later claimed to have been voluntary.

There are some truths which it is shameful to know; the truth about UFOs is one of them. Even fifty years ago, such knowledge could only be encountered by someone pathologically attracted to human degeneracy and the dark side of the spiritual world. But today, what used to be the province of a few black magicians cannot be entirely avoided by any of us.

The UFO phenomenon is perhaps the most sinister complex of beliefs and events to be found among those loosely associated with the New Age. It has emerged from the shadows of pop science fiction and fringe occultism to become part of 'mainstream' American culture—as a belief-system or cultural 'archetype' if not a personal experience. The popular *X-Files* TV series, and the flood of 'New Age' books and publications which present teachings supposedly given by 'aliens'—*The Pleiadian Agenda* by Barbara Hand Clow, for example—are proof enough. In order to make sense of the phenomenon, I will waste no time in speculating whether or not it really is, or could be, occurring, but will simply accept the conclusions of reliable researchers in the field, notably Dr Jacques Vallee, and proceed from there. I will also accept, without apology, the existence of invisible worlds, and the ability of such worlds to impinge upon and alter the physical one. As Frithjof Schuon says,

However restricted the experience of modern man may be in things belonging to the psychic or subtle order, there are still phenomena of that kind which are in no way inaccessible to him in principle, but he treats them from the start as 'superstitions' and hands them over to the occultists. Acceptance of the psychic dimension is in any case part of religion: one cannot deny magic without straying from faith.

⁓ Light on the Ancient Worlds, p104)

It is traditional Catholic doctrine, for example, to teach the reality of magic and witchcraft so that the faithful will be sure to avoid them. I would only add that where modern man denies the reality of psychic phenomena, postmodern man accepts them all too easily, and then uses them to rebel against religion, and finally to replace God.

To face the spiritual darkness which the UFO phenomenon represents and not be damaged, a kind of double consciousness is needed. To begin with, we will have to admit that such things as alien 'landings' and human 'abductions' are actually taking place. But we also need to remember that, as James Cutsinger says, 'there is a greater degree of Being in the beautiful than in the ugly' (*Advice to the Serious Seeker: Meditations on the Teachings of Frithjof Schuon*, p34). In the words of Schuon:

> Nothingness 'is' not, but it 'appears' with respect to the real, as the real projects itself toward the finite. To move away from the Divine Principle is to become 'other than He', while remaining of necessity in Him, since He is the sole reality. This means that the world necessarily comprises—in a relative fashion, of course, since nothingness does not exist—that privation of reality or of perfection which we call 'evil'. On the one hand, evil does not come from God, since being negative, it cannot have any positive cause; on the other, evil results from the unfolding of Divine manifestation, but in this respect, precisely, it is not 'evil,' it is simply the shadow of a process which is positive in itself.
>
> Finally, if we consider in *Maya* [i.e., Divine manifestation conceived of as having a partly illusory nature, of not being what it seems] the quality of 'obscurity' or 'ignorance' (*tamas*) as it is manifested in nature in general or man in particular, we are compelled to see in it what might be called the 'mystery of absurdity'; the absurd is that which, in itself and not as regards its metaphysical cause, is deprived of sufficient reason and manifests no more than its own blind accidentality. The genesis of the world in the first place, and the unfolding of human events, appear as a struggle against absurdity; the intelligible is confirmed as a contrast to the unintelligible.
>
> ⁓ Logic and Transcendence, pp154–155

In other words, evil is like a hole in Being. In a sense it actually exists—you'd better not deny this, or you'll fall into the hole. But in another sense, it isn't real, since it is nothing but a lack or diminishment of reality, an empty space. The world of UFOs is like a waking nightmare, a world of dark unrealities made actual. But if we remember that beauty is more real than ugliness, and that Reality is good in essence, then we can—with God's help—look ugliness in the face and not be conquered by it, not finally *convinced*. Because, as Schuon says, even though evil in its own nature is ultimately unreal, we still have to struggle against it. According to Schuon's pure metaphysics, evil is a product of that inevitable motion of being away from its Divine Principle which manifests as the cosmos. Just as light is always leaving the Sun *because* the Sun is radiant, shining ever more dimly into the surrounding darkness, so the very fact that God is not only Absolute but Infinite means that His Being must communicate itself, must eternally radiate in the direction of a non-being which can never be reached because it exists only as a tendency, not as a real part of Being. But the fact that, as Schuon says, we have to struggle against the constant pull of absurdity and non-being means that the doctrine of evil derived from his pure metaphysics must be balanced by the complementary doctrine that evil is always the product of an abuse of free will, by men or by spiritual beings. This apparent contradiction is resolved by the mysterious identity of choice and destiny, without which God's knowledge of our destiny would negate our freedom, rather than being His eternal and present knowledge of how we decide to use that freedom. And the fact that evil is 'unintelligible' does not mean that there is no order or method in it; if it were 'pure' chaos, it would not exist in even a relative sense. So evil cannot be absolutely unintelligible. It is better to describe it as *motion in the direction of* an absolute unintelligibility which, as pure non-being, can never be reached. Therefore, any organization or design which appears within evil is not part of its own nature, but has been stolen by evil from the Good. This is why true evil always exhibits a tell-tale mixture of diabolical cunning and immense stupidity.

In the first half of the 20th century, the dominant image of extraterrestrials was that of horrible monsters from other worlds who arrive on Earth in spaceships to conquer and destroy. The representative book of this phase was H. G. Wells' *War of the Worlds*, published in 1898, which almost might be taken as prophetic of the First World War, when tanks, flame-throwers, poison gas and aerial bombardment first shocked the world with the horror of technological warfare. The power of this myth over the collective mind was amply demonstrated by Orson Welles' 'War of the Worlds' radio hoax in

1938, on the eve of World War II. (I've always been struck by the fact that both men had nearly the same last name; something was definitely 'welling up' from the psychic underworld.)

This image of extraterrestrials as inhuman monsters is still with us. But in the late 1950s it began to be supplemented by a radically different myth, that of the wise and powerful extraterrestrials who come to Earth to save us from nuclear self-destruction. The famous motion picture starring Michael Rennie, *The Day the Earth Stood Still* (1951) is the representative expression of this idea, which was the view of extraterrestrials dominant in the hippy movement. The hippy belief, appearing the second half of the '60s and inherited by the New Age movement some time in the '70s, had to do with the Space Brothers of the Intergalactic Council—in many ways the folk version of the United Federation of Planets from the *Star Trek* television series—who were either here to save the Earth, or to take all the good hippies away with them to a better world, in a counterculture version of the Evangelical Christian doctrine of 'the rapture'. And the 'Mothership' which was supposed to be hovering invisibly overhead, waiting to receive them, was (in my opinion) a distorted version of the Heavenly Jerusalem. The most detailed written expression of this belief-system was and is a massive 'channeled' text, *The Book of Urantia* (1955), and the myth of the benign extraterrestrial was also the basis of motion pictures like *Close Encounters of the Third Kind* (1977) and *ET* (1982)

Things began to change around the time when Whitley Strieber's sinister book *Communion* was published in 1986. With increasing numbers of reported 'alien abductions'—according to a 1991 survey, between several hundred thousand and several *million* Americans presently believe that they've been victims of such events—the concept of the benign Space Brother slowly began to be replaced by that of the demonic kidnapper, just as the cartoon cliché of the little green man with antennae on his head was turning into that of the 'gray', the corpse-colored, hairless being with huge, black, elongated eyes—an image derived directly from Strieber's descriptions, as depicted on the cover of his book. (UFO researcher Jacques Vallee describes this image as 'wise and benign'; to me it is bone-chilling.) I saw Strieber interviewed once on a PBS documentary. He admitted that his encounters with aliens were the most horrible events of his life, but showed absolutely *no desire to break with them* on account of this. The encounters were so strange and compelling that his fascination for them outweighed all other considerations—including, apparently, his own self-respect. I was reminded of the situation of the abused wife or incested child who can't imagine life apart from his or her abuser. It's a psychological truth that any extremely intense experience becomes 'numinous' in a sense. We tend to identify the most powerful things that have ever happened to us with 'reality' itself. The daughter raped by her father will carry this experience in her psyche as an indelible reference point, which in later life may lead her to demonize and/or idealize other men in whom she sees, or upon whom she projects, aspects of her father. The soldier brutalized in war will seek out other violent situations — perhaps even making his living as a mercenary — because even though he knows that 'war is hell', he can't let it alone. 'Normal life' situations seem empty and unreal; nowhere but in the presence of bloody violence is he entirely 'himself'. He left part of his soul back on the battlefield and keeps returning to the place where he lost it. Only at the scene of the original crime does he feel, for a moment at least, complete.

✳ The Place of UFOs in the Hierarchy of Being

According to traditional metaphysics, as we have seen above, Being is arranged hierarchically, in discrete ontological levels. This is the 'Great Chain of Being' of the 18th century, which, when it 'collapsed' — when, that is, we started to see the hierarchy of Being horizontally in terms of time instead of vertically in terms of eternity — was transformed into the myth of progress. When we no longer recognized the Absolute as the eternal crown of the hierarchy of Being, we were forced to imagine that something bigger and better — or at least weirder and more powerful — lay in the Future. 'God *above*' was replaced by 'whatever is going to happen up *ahead*.' All spiritual traditions and traditional philosophies include the Great Chain of Being in one form or another, but since every metaphysician seems to render it a little differently, I'll take the risk of presenting my own version of it, which probably owes more to Sufi theosopher Ibn al-'Arabi and Traditionalist metaphysician Frithjof Schuon than anyone else, but can't strictly be attributed to either of them. It is based on eight levels of Being, in descending order. Each level not only transcends all that is below it, but also contains, in higher form, all that is below it. The first two levels are purely Divine, the second two Spiritual, the third two psychic, and the fourth two physical.

THE DIVINE

The *first* level is Beyond Being (Dionysius the Areopagite), Godhead (Meister Eckhart), the unknowable Divine Essence.

The *second* level is pure Being, Allah ('the Deity'), God Himself—the personal God Who is Creator, Ruler, Judge and Savior of the universe, while transcending these functions absolutely, since He is not limited by any relationship with created being.

THE SPIRIT

The *third* level is the Intellect, God's primal act of Self-understanding in terms of subject and object—in Christian terms, 'God the Father' and 'God the Son'. Intellect is the ray of the Divine within the creatures—the *nous* of the Neo-Platonic philosophers—about which Eckhart said, 'there is Something in the soul which is uncreated and uncreatable.' In terms of its creative function, the Intellect is the *pneuma*, the Holy Spirit of God that 'moved on the face of the waters'.

The *fourth* level is the Archangelic, the realm of the permanent archetypes or Divine Names, perhaps represented by the Seven Lamps and the Four Living Creatures surrounding the Throne of the Lamb in the *Apocalypse*. This is the level of the eternal metaphysical principles or Platonic Ideas, which, far from being abstractions, are in reality more densely concrete—for all their transparency to the Divine Light—and more highly charged with creative and truth-revealing energy than anything below them.

THE PSYCHE

The *fifth* level is the Angelic, the manifestation of the Spirit on the psychic plane, the plane of thought, emotion and intent. Each angel is both a living, conscious individual and the manifestation of a specific Idea.

The *sixth* level is the Imaginal, the 'astral plane' or *'alam al-mithal*, where every thought, feeling or intent, whatever the level of being it essentially corresponds to, appears as a symbolic image which is at the same time a living being. This is the world of dreams and mental images, which is not simply happening inside this or that individual consciousness, but is continuous with an objective psychic 'environment', just as the human body is continuous with the natural world.

THE MATERIAL WORLD

The *seventh* level is the Etheric. This is the realm of the 'soul of matter', the hidden face of nature, the world of the Celtic *Fairies*, the Muslim *Jinn*, the world of 'bioplasma', of auras, of elemental spirits and subtle energies. It is the World Soul, the essential pattern and subtle substance of the material world.

The *eighth* level is the Material, the world reported by our senses.

Science deals almost exclusively with the eighth level, though it must sometimes confront phenomena emanating from the seventh, and theorize about seventh-level realities in order to explain apparent paradoxes appearing on the eighth. And since science has largely replaced religion and metaphysics as our dominant way of looking at the world, we are at a nearly total loss when it comes to explaining, and especially to *evaluating*, the UFO phenomenon. Because we believe in evolution and progress instead of understanding the eternal hierarchical nature of Being, *anything* that pops through from level seven to level eight, as far as we are concerned, might be God, or Merlin the Magician, or a 'highly-evolved technological race', or God knows what. And the reason why so many seventh-level beings are now appearing to us, on a global level, may be *because* we have lost the ability to evaluate them; they can now represent themselves to us as anything they please.

✳ Who the 'Aliens' Are

According to Muslim doctrine, The Jinn—plural of 'Jinni', the well-known spook from the lamp—are beings inhabiting a plane subtler than the Material but grosser than the Imaginal and Angelic: the *seventh* plane in the Great Chain of Being.

'Aliens' are members of the Jinn. According to Jacques Vallee, the most balanced and reliable of UFO researchers, who was invited to present his findings at a closed conference with U.N. General Secretary Kurt Waldheim (his *Messengers of Deception*, And/Or Press, Berkeley, 1969 and 1994, is a must-read), the phenomenon has three aspects. (1) It is a real, and inexplicable, phenomenon which appears on radar and leaves real physical traces. (2) It is a psychic phenomenon which profoundly affects people's perceptions. (3) It is surrounded by deceptions of the 'Mission Impossible' variety produced by actual human groups, apparently for the purpose of affecting mass belief. But how can we possibly put these three facts together? If UFOs are physically real, we say, then they must be spaceships. If they are psychic, then they must either be the product of mass hysteria, or real psychic entities. But if they are 'staged', then how can they be either? The mind grapples for closure. If they are spaceships, then we must turn to astronomy, NASA and the Defense Department for information on them. If they are subtle entities, then the psychics will tell us what they are up to. And if they are staged events, then we must rely on counter-intelligence and investigative reporting. But if they are all three…??? The critical mind tries to make sense of this, fails, and then shuts down. It is meant to.

Father Seraphim Rose, an American-born Eastern Orthodox priest who died in 1982, gives perhaps the best explanation of the UFO phenomenon that we possess: Simply speaking, they are demons. They do what demons have always done. Their 'craft' are products of a demonic 'technology' which begins in the subtle realm and impinges on this one. In *Orthodoxy and the Religion of the Future* (pp 134, 136) he writes:

> The most puzzling aspect of UFO phenomena to most researchers —
> namely, the strange mingling of physical and psychic characteristics in
> them — is no puzzle at all to readers of Orthodox spiritual books, especially
> the Lives of the Saints. Demons also have 'physical bodies', although the
> 'matter' in them is of such subtlety that it cannot be perceived by men unless
> their spiritual 'doors of perception' are opened, whether with God's will (in
> the case of holy men) or against it (in the case of sorcerers and mediums).
> Orthodox literature has many examples of demonic manifestations which fit
> precisely the UFO pattern: apparitions of 'solid' beings and objects (whether
> demons themselves or their illusory creations) which suddenly 'materialize'
> and 'dematerialize', always with the aim of awing and confusing people and
> ultimately leading them to perdition. The Lives of the 4th-century St
> Anthony the Great (Eastern Orthodox Books, 1976) and the 3rd-century St
> Cyprian the Former Sorcerer (*The Orthodox Word*, 1976, no. 5) are filled with
> such incidents. . . .
> It is clear that the manifestations of today's 'flying saucers' are quite within
> the 'technology' of demons; indeed, nothing else can explain them as well.
> The multifarious demonic deceptions of Orthodox literature have been
> adapted to the mythology of outer space, nothing more . . . [their] purpose
> [is] to awe the beholders with a sense of the 'mysterious', and to produce
> 'proof' of the 'higher intelligences' ('angels', if the victim believes in them, or
> 'space visitors' for modern men), and thereby to gain trust for the *message*
> they wish to communicate.

And lest the reader assume that only a traditional Christian monk could gain this impression, Fr Seraphim (p 132) quotes from the introduction to *UFOs and Related Subjects: An Annotated Bibliography* (by Lynn G. Catoe, U.S. Government Printing Office, Washington, D.C., 1969), prepared by the Library of Congress for the United States Air Force Office of Scientific Research:

> Many of the UFO reports now being published in the popular press recount alleged incidents that are strikingly similar to demonic possession and psychic phenomena which have long been known to theologians and parapsychologists.

Fr Seraphim, writing in the 1970s, relates the UFO phenomenon to the attraction of our culture as a whole to science fiction—a point which was driven home in 1997 when the Heaven's Gate cult, after committing mass suicide, were revealed as computer-savvy 'trekkies'. He writes (pp 103–104):

> The future world and humanity are seen by science fiction ostensibly in terms of 'projections' from present-day scientific discoveries; in actuality, however, these 'projections' correspond quite remarkably to the everyday reality of occult and overtly demonic experience throughout the ages. Among the characteristics of the 'highly evolved' creatures of the future are: communication by mental telepathy, ability to fly, materialize and dematerialize, transform the appearances of things or create illusionary scenes and creatures by 'pure thought', travel at speeds far beyond any modern technology, to take possession of the bodies of earthmen; and the expounding of a 'spiritual' philosophy which is 'beyond all religions' and holds promise of a state where 'advanced intelligences' will no longer be dependent upon matter. All these are standard practices and claims of sorcerers and demons. A recent history of science fiction notes that 'a persistent aspect of the vision of science fiction is the desire to transcend normal experience . . . through the presentation of characters and events that transgress the conditions of space and time as we know them' (Robert Scholes and Eric S. Rabkin, *Science Fiction: History, Science, Vision*. Oxford University Press, 1977, p 175). The scripts of *Star Trek* and other science fiction stories, with their futuristic 'scientific' devices, read in parts like excerpts from the lives of the ancient Orthodox Saints, where the actions of sorcerers are described at a time when sorcery was still a strong part of pagan life.

Fr Seraphim Rose repeats Jacques Vallee's hypothesis that UFOs 'are constructed *both as physical craft and as psychic devices*.' He also accepts Vallee's conclusion, based on a statistical analysis of only those sightings that are most convincing, that they can't be interplanetary spaceships because there are simply too many of them; it is not likely, for example, that the possibly two million Americans who have been abducted by aliens were kidnapped by astronauts. (Dr Vallee, as an astronomer, statistician, and computer scientist, is well equipped to carry on this kind of analysis.) But Fr Seraphim doesn't entirely explain Vallee's hard evidence for deception activities traceable to human groups, though his comparison of them to phenomena produced by the sorcerers of antiquity is highly suggestive. My own depressing hypothesis is this: Various groups of occultists or black magicians bent on world domination, some of whom seem to have ties with the intelligence community (see Vallee, *Messengers of Deception*, and *Revelations*, Ballantine, 1991) and who may or may not possess 'inter-dimensional' technologies provided or inspired by the Jinn, are staging deceptions—the obvious propaganda by which the Roswell event has been sold to the public as the crash of an alien spaceship is a good example—for three purposes: (1) *to divert public attention from other activities they wish to hide*; (2) *to influence the mass mind toward a major paradigm-shift, away from religion and objective science, and toward belief in alien visitors*; and (3), *to invoke, by mass suggestion and sympathetic magic, the demons they worship.* The first two hypotheses were put forward by Jacques Vallee, who clearly documents, in *Messengers of Deception* and elsewhere, the existence of just such groups and individuals clustered around the UFO phenomenon. The third hypothesis is my own. It may be that, early in this century, when literature on mass brainwashing first began to be published, books like *Man the Puppet: The Art of Controlling Minds* [Abram Lipsky, 1925] (which would likely have been available to Hitler and Mussolini, though this particular book seems to have been written by a Jew!), and when broadcast radio and early television were making instantaneous influence over the mass mind possible for the first time, certain black magicians realized that if they could invoke demons for themselves through self-suggestion, it might be possible to invoke them on a mass level through mass suggestion. They tried it, and it worked. They are still doing it. As an example of how such mass suggestion might work, psychiatrist John E. Mack, in his book *Abduction*, reports that one of his patients experienced an encounter with aliens soon after viewing a TV program based on Strieber's *Communion*; another recalled an abduction after reading the book itself. (I don't know enough to accuse Strieber of deliberate demonic invocation, or to exonerate him either; I only want to point out that highly-charged demonic images have a potent life of their own.) We should not conclude by this, however, that such wizards are powerful in the sense that they are more capable than the rest of us of autonomous action and choice. A psychotic arsonist or serial rapist may gain a *feeling* of great power, since it seems to him as if he is able to command the attention and vigorous action of the world around him. But it takes no power to roll a boulder down hill, or write a bad check; all it takes is an obsession that you can't control. True spiritual and social power is creative; it labors to build, to refine, to enlighten. But to ignite an entire forest with a single match is only the appearance of power; in reality it is nothing but deficiency of feeling, lack of intelligence, and weakness of will. To employ the metaphor of addiction, we can compare a true believer's or cynical manipulator's fascination with UFOs and psychic entities to the affects of alcohol or methamphetamine on the human system. Alcohol can produce a surge of emotional energy, amphetamines a similar explosion of physical and mental energy—but the reason we experience this energy is not because it is coming to us, but because it is leaving us. It's exactly the same in the case of those who invoke entities who are fundamentally less real—in the spiritual not the material sense—than human beings: the fascination we feel for them is not something they are giving us; it is something we are giving them, something they are stealing from us. If today's 'alien' shows many similarities to the traditional 'vampire', it is because both of them steal our 'blood', our life-energy, which in the most fundamental sense is nothing other than the spiritual attention we owe to God as the source of our life. As the adulterous affair destroys marriage by diverting erotic energy, so the 'alien' and the 'entity' destroy our relationship to God by diverting spiritual energy.

UFOs are 'apports'. Among the powers attributed to magicians and mediums has always been the ability to materialize objects. Such apports, however, tend to be unstable. They seem to exhibit all the characteristics of ordinary matter, yet they will often dematerialize again after a certain period. (Paramhamsa Yogananda's *Autobiography of a Yogi* is full of stories like this.) UFO phenomena exhibit the same property: undeniably real in a physical sense, they are also fleeting, as if the amount of energy required to maintain them on the material plane were too great to let them stay here for long; they are like fish out of water. And this is precisely in line with the folklore of the Jinn from all nations: they can affect the physical plane, but they can't exist here in any stable way. To hazard a wild speculation, I can let myself wonder whether our computer technology, which has always seemed to me partly inspired by the Jinn, may represent an attempt on their part to construct bodies for themselves that *are* stable in this world, particularly in view of the fact that the Jinn and the UFO aliens seem able to interact with electromagnetic energy: automobile engines die in close proximity to flying saucers; 'Raudive voices' appear spontaneously on magnetic tape, etc., etc. If so, it would also mean that—as in the de Maupassant story 'Le Horla'—they want to supplant us. But if they are so bent upon fascinating us poor, weak mortals with their superior powers, then why do they apparently envy our ability to occupy physical bodies? Could it be that they know full well that the Human Form is God's image and vicegerent on Earth—even if we ourselves have forgotten this—and are therefore doing all in their power to replace it, largely by tempting us to psychically and genetically deconstruct it? But if they, with all their 'wild talents', apparently want to be human, just as they seem to want to make us ever more Jinn-like, to turn us into 'changelings', what does this imply about their evaluation of their own state? Perhaps they simply want to get out of the Fire.

The 'aliens' do not require interaction with occultists and black magicians to appear in this world; but such alliances do make it easier for them, as well as providing them with conscious or unconscious agents willing and/or available to do their bidding. And the ability of these magicians to invoke alien entities on a mass level is simply one aspect of the quality of the time. According to René Guénon in *The Reign of Quantity and the Signs of the Times*,

> since all effective action necessarily presupposes agents, anti-traditional action is like all other kinds of action, so that it cannot be a sort of spontaneous or 'fortuitous' production.... The fact that it has conformed to the specific nature of the cyclic period in which it has been working explains why it was possible and why it was successful, but is not enough to explain the manner of its realization, nor to indicate the various measures put into operation to arrive at its result.

✳ Not All the Jinn are Evil

Not all the Jinn are demons. According to Islamic doctrine, for example, some of the Jinn are 'Muslim' and some are not. The same distinction between benevolent and demonic entities can be found in Celtic fairy lore. The *Dakinis* of Tibetan Buddhism, for example—subtle entities in female form who help Tibetan yogis to attain Liberation—travel in a manner similar to UFOs, and are portrayed as entirely benign and helpful. In the story from the *Jetsün Kahbum* of the death of the famous Tibetan saint Milarepa,

> The *Dakinis* conveyed the *Chaitya* [the reliquary containing the saint's cremated remains] through the skies and held it directly above the chief disciples, so that it sent down its rays of light on the head of each of them....

And in the sky their appeared [the Tantric Deities] Gaypa-Dorje, Demchog, Sang-du, and Dorje-Pa-mo, surrounded by innumerable hosts, who, after circumambulating the Chief Deity, merged in him. Finally, the whole conclave resolved itself into an orb of light, and this sped away toward the East. The *Chaitya* . . . was transported eastward, amid a peal of celestial music. . . .

Hindu *puranas* also mention travel in the subtle realm, on vehicles called *vimanas*; and such travel is not limited to demonic beings. Furthermore, the elemental spirits who form the connection between the natural world and its Creator are not evil, though they may be dangerous; the subtle, conscious archetype of a beautiful oak tree, for example, cannot be called a demon. (A friend of mine, incidentally, once saw—without benefit of psychedelics—a huge, brilliant green disc moving through the forest, passing through tree-trunks as if they were made of air: an elf-ship, apparently.) But the Jinn who are staging the present UFO manifestations almost certainly are demons. According to Seraphim Rose, they are here to prepare us for the religion of the Antichrist. I agree—and I would add that anyone who wants to encounter psychic entities—good, evil or neutral—*because God isn't real enough to him* will become the demons' plaything. It may even be true, though I can't prove it, that those in the Neo-Pagan world who are attracted to the worship of elementals and nature spirits instead of the Divine Spirit may actually be seducing and corrupting those spirits, even if, to begin with, they are basically benign, or neutral. If you were being worshipped by thousands of devotees because they were fascinated by you and believed that their contact with you could give them magical powers, wouldn't you be seriously tempted? Wouldn't you be influenced to forget that your only duty is to remember God and obey His will? The nature spirits are also duty-bound to remember and obey the Source of All Life; insofar as they do so, they become conduits which allow the Divine energy of the Holy Spirit to flow into and sustain the natural world. But if they forget that duty in their desire to fascinate and dominate their human worshippers, that flow of vital energy may be cut off. So it may be true that to worship the natural world, instead of contemplating God by means of it, is actually destructive to it, that an egotistical fascination for the nature spirits may in fact be the subtle-plane archetype of the destruction of the natural world by human greed and technology.

✳ Time-Travel & Reincarnation
Related, & Debunked

The contemporary 'science fiction' myths of time-travel and multi-dimensional space, derived from imaginative speculation on Einsteinian and post-Einsteinian physics, and often applied to the UFO phenomenon, are in some ways replacing the world-view of the revealed religions, since they seem to transcend materialism and provide the 'miraculous' possibilities always associated with religious faith and spiritual experience. For God all things are possible—but if all things, or many strange things, are possible to UFOs, and will be possible to human science in the future, then who needs God? If space, time, matter, and even some mental processes can be manipulated by various subtle material energies, then who needs grace? If time-travel is possible, who needs eternity? This is what is believed, and sometimes openly declared, by those who worship elemental energies via the cult of arcane science. But in reality the myth of time-travel, based for the most part on the belief that it might be possible to locally reverse the flow of time and travel 'backward', actually represents the death of the myth of progress. Here is evidence that if all coherent belief-systems are being deconstructed by of post-modernism, not even scientism is immune to the process.

No less a speculative adventurer than Stephen Hawking has admitted his belief that time-travel is possible. But there are irreducible logical contradictions inherent in it, or at least in our usual way of conceiving of it. We imagine that it may be possible to travel in many directions in time instead of only one, just as we can travel in many directions in space. But if time travel will become possible in the future, then—by definition—it has already happened. And if it has already happened, then where are all the travelers from the future, all the historians, the archaeologists and the tourists? They are concealing themselves, we say, because their open appearance would be too shocking for us, and would alter future history. But if they are traveling from 'then' to 'now', they have already altered future history, whether they appear openly or not. And if future history has been altered by their time-travel, then it was 'always' altered. And if it was 'always' altered, then no 'alteration' has in fact taken place.

But others maintain that they *have* shown themselves, that the 'aliens' now appearing are really travelers to 'now' from our own future time. Why have they come back? Perhaps for the very purpose of altering history, of saving the human race from self-destruction. But if they fail in this attempt, then there will be no future human history for them to have traveled back from; and if they are destined to succeed, then they have already succeeded, so they never had to make the trip in the first place. They, and we, can relax.

Some try to solve the paradox of time-travel by claiming that it is possible to travel to an alternate or probable past, though not to the past we remember. But to 'travel' to a 'parallel' universe is not the same thing as to travel to one's own past. It may or may not be possible to separate, via arcane technology, the human body from it's own proper situation in time. But what then? That body would then enter the chaos of all probable realities, with no way to 'home in' on any one of them, since its only way of 'tuning itself' to a particular reality would be based on its entire structure, which is proper to only one region or quality of space-time. We and our lives are not two separate things—a truth that postmodern culture is doing all in its power to make us forget. Whether one is a yuppie who has thrown his or her home away to pursue the life of an itinerant globalist, or a refugee who is driven from his home by the forces of that same globalism, the post-modern human being is led to experience his or her ego as a self-enclosed monad with no organic relationship to its surroundings. And as we shift surroundings with ever-increasing frequency and emotional randomness, we begin to believe we can shift identities in the same way, that we can be whoever we 'play at' being, on a given day, or in a given moment. And so our identity either dissolves into a schizophrenic Robin Williams-like repertoire of 'postures' or 'routines', or else shrinks into a hard little kernel of impersonal, generic selfhood which we believe can be inserted indifferently into *any* situation because no situation is really native to it. Because our psyches are chaotic and fragmented, time-travel begins to seem possible to us, even natural, because we no longer experience our own *lives* as an integral part of our own *selves*.

If we are going to apply the metaphor of travel in space to travel in time, we will have to be thorough about it. And if we are, we will be forced to admit that if it is impossible to travel in space from San Francisco to New York if there is no New York there to go to, then it would be equally impossible for me to travel from now back to the Middle Ages unless there was a 'me' there in the Middle Ages for me to be.

But perhaps there was, we say. Perhaps I did lead a past life in the Middle Ages, and maybe I can travel back to it somehow. Here we can see how speculation on the possibility of time-travel makes it necessary, at one point, to posit the theory of reincarnation. If post-Einsteinian physics becomes our religion, then belief in reincarnation must, at one point, become a dogma of that religion. Now if I succeed in traveling back to the Middle Ages *physically,* then there must already exist, in potential, a record of the fact that I did so, that the 'me back then' appeared out of nowhere, or that a 'second me' appeared and encountered the 'me back then'. But if I were to discover this record, and later decide *not* to travel back in time, then where did the record come from? Where else but from a future time when I changed my mind and decided to go after all? This means that if I know there is a 'me' back there for me to go to, then I cannot decide not to go to him. And another way of saying 'I cannot decide not to go to him' is to say 'I *am* him'. And if I am him, then the concept of 'travel' becomes meaningless. On the other hand, obviously I am not him. I am myself. This self here and now cannot be super-imposed on that self there and then, because all selves, all forms, all moments, are unique, and are in fact the manifestation in the relative world of the Absolute Uniqueness of God. And so to ask if time-travel is physically possible is not like asking 'is it possible for me to travel from Spain to Germany?'; it is much more like asking 'is it possible for Spain itself to travel to Germany?' Who we are physically is inseparable from the time in which we live, because different times have different intrinsic qualities. According to Guénon in *The Reign of Quantity*,

> It is evident that periods of time are qualitatively differentiated by the events unfolding within them ... the situation of a body in space can vary through the occurrence of movement, whereas that of an event in time is rigidly determined and strictly 'unique', so that the essential nature of events seems to be much more rigidly tied to time than that of bodies is to space.

If I exist in a different time, I must exist in a different state. My state as a newborn infant is inseparable from the year 1948; my state as a 48-year-old man is inseparable from the year 1997. The only way I can 'travel' to 1127 is for me to assume one of the states—that is, one of the individuals—available in 1127. So at the very least, time-travel cannot be physical.

But can it be psychic? Can it be reincarnational? Can a former incarnation of myself know me, by clairvoyant anticipation? Can I know him, by clairvoyant memory? Can we communicate with each other across the seas of multi-dimensional time?

Yes and no. That person in the Middle Ages is not me, nor am I him. As Guénon says in *The Spiritist Fallacy*, 'two identical things are inconceivable, because if they are really identical, they are not two things but one and the same thing; Leibniz is quite right on this point.' Still, we may have an eternal affinity for one another, because we are members of the same 'spiritual family', emanations from the same spiritual archetype or Name of God.

This does not mean, however, that information — and, by implication, causality — can travel back through time from me to him. In reality, I simply inherit certain psychic 'material' from him, just as I would inherit the possessions of a deceased relative: psychic traits, unsolved problems, even memories. This is what is called 'metempsychosis', which is *not* the same thing as reincarnation. When inherited memories appear in my life, which can happen at any time from my birth until my death, it will necessarily seem to me as if I have, at least in a limited sense, gone back in time, since I am reliving another's past experiences. But in reality, those experiences have come forward in time to meet me, on the basis of an affinity — not an identity — between that past human being and myself, an affinity which in essence is eternal, not temporal. And he may also intuit my reality on the basis of the same eternal affinity, though in this case metempsychosis, or psychic inheritance, does not operate; if it did, memories of 'future' lifetimes would be just as common as memories of 'past' ones. He and I may discover our inner affinity over the course of our lives, by a seemingly temporal process — I by memory, he by anticipation — but the affinity itself is eternal in the mind of God; it exists beyond the plane of being where time, multi-dimensional or otherwise, has any meaning. So the only possible conclusion is that the myth of time travel, as well as the doctrine of reincarnation as a horizontal travel by the identical individual soul through time from one physical body to the next, is based on an inability to conceive of the real nature of eternity. Therefore, those who become obsessed with these myths are making themselves available to satanic forces whose goal is to hide from us the reality of eternity by means of a counterfeit, to so dazzle us with multidimensional spaces and multidirectional time-travel that we lose the ability to contemplatively imagine how God can see all things, past, present and future, as well as all probably realities, in an eternal present moment, as the 'Second Person of the Blessed Trinity', the total and integral form His Self-manifestation — in essence, not other than Himself — which, when refracted through the space-time matrix, we perceive by means of our physical senses, and name 'the universe'.

The Traditionalists, at least Ananda Coomaraswamy, René Guénon and Whitall Perry, deny the doctrine of reincarnation, and claim that, while it is accepted as true by many Hindus, and something resembling it by virtually all Buddhists, it is not orthodox teaching. They explain apparent references to chains of reincarnational existences as a misunderstanding, or misapplication, of the two distinct doctrines of *metempsychosis* — the teaching that psychic as well as physical material released by the dead (including memories) can be inherited by the living—and *transmigration*—the teaching that the eternal individuality passes through many states of existence by traveling vertically (or, to be strictly accurate, in an ascending or descending spiral) on the Great Chain of Being, never passing twice through any state, including our incarnate human one. According to Guénon in *The Spiritist Fallacy,*

> transmigration . . . is a question of the passing of the being to other states of existence, which are determined . . . by conditions entirely different from those to which the human personality is subjected. . . . This is what all the traditional Eastern doctrines teach . . . the true doctrine of transmigration, understood in the sense imparted to it by pure metaphysics, which permits once and for all the refutation of the idea of reincarnation.

The Traditionalists maintain that not even Hinduism originally taught the doctrine of reincarnation as it is presently understood. Whitall Perry, in 'Reincarnation: New Flesh on Old Bones' [*Studies in Comparative Religion,* vol. 13, nos. 3 and 4, p153], writes:

> the soul engaged in the *pitri-yana* ('Path of the ancestors') does not 'coast horizontally' through an indeterminate series of lives and death[s], once having been 'launched' into the *samsara,* but rather is 'referred back' at the conclusion of each life to its Source; there is a vertical dimension (symbolized in the Upanishads as a return to the 'Sphere of the Moon'—equatable with *Hiranyagarbha*) which means a direct confrontation (but not yet identity) with its primeval point of Origin. Each 'life' can therefore be regarded as *original,* as a *fresh* entrance into existence or 'descent', whether into a splendid or a terrible domain, and as a unique cyclic experience with a return culminating in a *theophany* or 'Judgement', at which moment every soul does precisely—and with devastating clarity—recall its 'former life'. All the while the door of Liberation into the *deva-yana* ('Path of the gods') remains accessible to the 'Knowers of Truth', once the correct responses are given that allow passage out of the *samsara* and union with supra-formal states of being.

In other words, I am not a 'reincarnation' of that man in the Middle Ages; in reality, both of us are unique 'incarnations', or facets, of the same eternal Archetype or 'Name of God'. Some uncertainty remains as to whether 'soul' in the above passage refers to the unique human individuality or the common Archetype of a whole 'family' of such individualities, but this is no more than a reflection of the primal ambiguity, or rather paradox, of the traditional Hindu doctrine of transmigration: that Brahman, the Absolute Itself, is 'the one and only Transmigrant'—a statement which is paradoxical because the Absolute, being beyond all relativity, is in another sense the only

Reality which could not possibly transmigrate. This paradox is solved by the doctrine of *maya*: that *samsara*, though undeniably real from the point of view of the relative beings who experience it, is *illusion* from the point of view of the Absolute. God knows *samsara* as having no separate reality in itself; He sees it not as the joys and sorrows, the struggles and choices of numberless sentient beings—though He knows full well that those sentient beings actually experience it in this way, and knows this even more deeply than they do themselves—but rather as the infinite self-manifesting radiation of Himself Alone. In other words, when I fully realize the truth that 'God is the one and only transmigrant,' transmigration ends. Furthermore, it is also known—because God knows it—that in Reality it never began.

The failure to realize that transmigration never began because 'the one and only Transmigrant' is the Absolute produces the ambiguous experience of transmigration, which, as a mode of *maya*, is 'both real and unreal'. The failure to understand that each transmigrational existence is a fresh creation—as in the Islamic concept of 'occasionalism', the doctrine that God re-creates the entire universe and the human soul in each new instant—produces the belief in reincarnation; vertical, and sovereign, Divine Act becomes horizontal, and contingent, cause-and-effect. The belief in reincarnation of the identical human individuality in a series of different lifetimes— a doctrine which, incidentally, is not taught by the Buddhists, since they do not posit a unique human individuality in the first place—severs the human soul from its transcendent Source, except at the first origin and the ultimate end of every indeterminate 'chain of lifetimes'. It results in a mechanistic and deistic universe where God can have no merciful, enlightening, forgiving and redeeming relationship with the worlds and the souls He has created— a universe where, because there can be no *dharma*, no saving Divine intervention, no religious dispensations, *karma* is absolute. I can neither repent, in such a universe, nor can God forgive. It was this absolutization of *karma* which led Mme Blavatsky (who, as we shall see, did accept reincarnation in her final work, *The Secret Doctrine*, despite denials by some of her followers) to hate and reject the Christian doctrine of the forgiveness of sins as a violation of the law of *karma*, and even to define prayer and sacrifice, conceived of as attempts to alter or circumvent *karma*, as acts of black magic. But to take *karma* as an absolute is absurd and self-contradictory. *Karma*, as the chain of causal actions and reactions in the relative world of *samsara*, is relative in essence; it can never be absolute. Every condition of causal inevitability on the horizontal plane can be compensated for by the operation of human freedom, and Divine Mercy, on the vertical one.

The doctrine of reincarnation is organically related to the belief in the possibility of time-travel. The mind of materialism, bound to space and time, confronts Eternity, but can neither realize nor understand it; materialism can only see 'another mode of existence' as 'another occasion of *material* existence.' The mind which is incapable of transcending time can conceive of such transcendence only as a greatly-enhanced ability to travel backwards, or laterally, across indefinite horizontal dimensions, to other material realities. The sense of what Sufis call the *waqt*, the eternal Divine Presence as manifest in this particular moment, threatens its most fundamental assumptions, and thus its very existence. In flight from this Presence, it takes refuge in multidimensional spaces and parallel times and reincarnational chains-of-lifetimes. Such complex and arcane theories appeal to us because, simply, we are afraid to encounter God. We are reluctant to admit that this unique moment is eternally saved or eternally lost according to the present quality of our love, wisdom and vigilance, or, conversely, our hatred, delusion, and mental chaos. We want a second chance, or an infinite number of second chances, to be who we are in the sight of God. But if we are in flight from our integral identity *sub specie aeternitatis*, then all those second chances, all those future lifetimes or trips back to the past to clean up our act, are only so many new chances to go to Hell. Time is the Mercy of Eternity, said Blake. It is given to us as a precious gift, as part of our God-given human freedom. If we waste it, there is no second chance. The *desire* to travel in time in order to escape or alter the consequences of our actions is identical with the desire not to be here now, not to be who we really are, not to pay our karmic debts by no longer trying to escape our creditors, not to sit in the Spirit and allow our debts to be forgiven by God's Mercy, not to stand in the presence of God. It is, therefore, purely satanic. To sit in contemplation is to release the past to God and receive from Him the future; to 'travel in time' is to reject what God wants to give us and grab after what He wants to take away from us. In the words of the Sufi Shaykh Ibn Abbad of Ronda, 'The fool is one who strives to procure at each instant some result that Allah has not willed.'

Now it is true that, on the psychic plane, we already exist in a more multi-dimensional space-time than we do on the physical plane. If this were not true, visions of past and future realities, or of various 'parallel' realities, would not be possible, as clearly they are. But we can't 'travel' through these realities without transcending the perceptual framework necessary for physical reality, which includes linear, uni-directional time; and to transcend time is to transcend 'travel' itself, and enter simultaneity. To claim that we can transcend time in order to improve it, that we can travel to the past in order to create a better future, is like claiming that we can improve conditions inside our prison cell by being released from it. But who would assert that the best use of freedom, or even a possible use of it, is to ameliorate bondage? Who else but a deluded magician, who believes he can tap a higher level of being to reinforce the agendas of a lower one, that he can use Truth to manipulate his illusions, Desirelessness to fulfill his desires, Detachment to enhance his personal power? If we consciously realize that aspect of us which transcends the space-time limits of physical reality, then the whole field of physical space-time becomes virtually available to us. But it does not become available to that part of us which is still limited to space-time. The material level of our being which, while we live, is always there, and which always retains the potential to regain control of our total perceptual field, if we let it—the part which is always saying 'I'm afraid of getting old, I'm afraid of dying, I'm afraid of the end of the world, I've got to get out of here, I don't want to realize my limits, I don't want to face my end, why can't somebody freeze me so I can be revived in the future? Why can't somebody invent time-travel so I can get away into the past?'—that part of us cannot manipulate trans-material, multidimensional realities. It can never come into contact with them because, precisely, it is in flight from them. The only way for it to contact them would be for it to die to itself, and *that is the very thing it is attempting to establish contact with them in order to prevent.* This is the vicious circle of materialism attempting to access and control the Spirit for materialistic purposes, the contradiction inherent in the magical world-view, the self-defeating idolatry of subtle material forces and dimensions masquerading as the God-given freedom of the Spirit.

The Jinn do not transcend space and time, but rather exist in a different quality of space and time than we do in our day-to-day material lives. How this more multidimensional relation to the space-time matrix allows them to praise God in unique ways may never be known to us. But it is clear that those Jinn who are 'not Muslim' realize that if they can fascinate and/or terrify us with their own multidimensional reality, which we can never fully make our own in this life, it will powerfully distract us from our own proper relationship with space-time, and thus from the unique and specifically human responsibilities God has provided us with as ways to know Him: to be born; to grow 'in wisdom and age and grace'; in adulthood to struggle with the limitations of incarnate existence to protect and carry on life; in old age to acquire wisdom; at death, to meet our Maker. Whoever doesn't want to play by these rules no longer wants to be a human being; in the words of a 1975 speech, recorded by Jacques Vallee in *Messengers of Deception*, by a member of the Heaven's Gate Cult (or Human Individual Metamorphosis as it was then called), 'a lot of people are tired of playing the human game.' But the human game and the human form are the only way we can relate to the Divine Source of our lives; all the powers of the Jinn can't change this simple fact. But they can hide it from us, and that's exactly what they are presently trying to do. It is true that, on the psychic level of our being, we are every bit as multidimensional as the Jinn are. But it is also true that we are here in physical life for a purpose, that we are designed by God for physical experience as well as for psychic knowledge and Spiritual understanding, and that the purpose of physical life and uni-directional time is to continually present us with an eternal choice: to escape from the present moment, and so enter what the East Indian religions call 'Samsara' and the Abrahamic ones 'Hell', or to stand fully within it, and so ascend, by the vertical path which lifts us out of passing time, to 'Heaven', to higher states of reality. Whether the present activity of the Jinn to distract us from this ultimate human choice is better understood as subversion from their side or an abdication of the human mandate from ours need not concern us. But the eternal choice confronting us in this present moment *must* concern us. It is the 'one thing needful'. Religion has no other purpose but to remind us of it. Everything else is 'the outer darkness, where there will be weeping and gnashing of teeth.' It is nothing but a distraction—perhaps a fatal one. In *Messengers of Deception*, Jacques Vallee quotes a member of a UFO cult called The Order of Melchizedek as telling him, 'we must emphasize the fact that we are receiving a new program! *We do not have to go through the old programming of Armageddon.*' But Armageddon is precisely the ultimate battle between truth and falsehood, conceived of as confronting the entire human race at the same crucial moment. To avoid this battle—which the forces of evil would love to make us believe is somehow possible—is not to 'transcend truth and falsehood' (as if to equally mix reality and illusion were a sign of 'balance' and 'objectivity'), but simply to embrace falsehood, and so find ourselves, in the words of the Koran, 'among the losers'. And the attempt to circumvent God's judgement, to prevent the consequences of human action in this world from being fully confronted and penetrated by Divine Truth, is a central agenda of the New Age. To think we can avoid the battle of Armageddon is, however, to end up on the losing side.

✳ UFO Worship as Counter-Initiation

The interest in the figure of *Melchizedek* in the world of UFO cults, which is documented by Vallee in *Messengers of Deception*, is highly significant.

Melchizedek had no father or mother, so he is, in a sense immortal: unborn, thus never to die. This would place him in the same category as the 'immortal prophets' Enoch, Elias and the Sufi Khidr, who is often identified with Elias. (As Melchizedek was Abraham's master in the Old Testament, so Khidr or Khezr is the name given by Sufis to the master encountered by Moses in the Koran.) According to Guénon in his book *The King of the World*, Melchizedek represents the Primordial Tradition, humanity's original and perennial knowledge of eternal Truth, the trunk of that tree whose branches are the major historical religions. *Enoch* is also big in the UFO world, since he—like Elias, and like the Prophet Muhammad, upon whom be peace—traveled to the next world without undergoing physical death. Such 'ascension' is a gift of God to a rare handful of his saints and prophets; UFO cultists, however, like to identify with their own demonic 'abductions'. Contactee Jim Hurtak, for example, was given a text by his alien teachers which he published as *The Keys of Enoch*. UFO believers also regularly reinterpret Elias' 'fiery chariot' as a UFO.

In *The Reign of Quantity*, René Guénon spoke of the 'counter-initiation'—the attempt by demonic forces to subvert not only revealed religion, but also the more esoteric spiritualities, such as the Kabbalah within Judaism, Sufism within Islam, or Hesychasm within Orthodox Christianity—all of which, in their legitimate forms, are strictly traditional and orthodox, despite the heterodox distortions produced by people like Gurdjieff and Dion Fortune. In my opinion, the UFO phenomenon represents the most concentrated and wide-spread manifestation of this counter-initiation yet to appear, and the one most successful on a mass level. In Whitall Perry's *A Treasury of Traditional Wisdom*, we find the following clue to the interest of UFO cultists in Enoch, provided by 13th century German mystic Mechthild of Magdeburg:

> It pleased Anti-Christ
> To discover all the wisdom
> Enoch had learned from God,
> So that Anti-Christ could openly declare it
> Along with his own false teaching:
> For if only he could draw Enoch to himself
> All the world and great honor would be his.

According to the Traditionalist doctrine of The Transcendent Unity of Religions, all true revealed religions are renditions of the one Primordial Tradition which is as old as humankind. This Tradition, however, cannot be accessed directly, but must be approached via one of the major world religions—otherwise one will probably encounter one of the many attempts at a kind of 'generic' metaphysics, drawing upon fragments of many traditions, some system which represents itself as universal but remains cut off from the Wisdom and Grace of God, the only power which can make either a sage or a saint. Although Truth is One, and the esoteric or mystical centers of all true religions point directly to this same Divine Truth, 'primordialism' cannot be a viable form in itself; the nourishing fruit grows on the branches of the tree, not the trunk. And, as the human door to Divine Reality, the Primordial Tradition can only be fully realized in the mystery of the soul's union with God. It would seem, therefore, that the prevalence of the figure of Melchizedek in UFO and Spiritualist lore is evidence of a satanic perversion of the Transcendent Unity of Religions. If the doctrine of the Unity of Truth can be falsely used to deny the providential efficaciousness of the particular Divine revelations which God has given, so as to promote a 'New Age' religious syncretism—as is in fact happening before our very eyes— then great damage will be done to the sacred forms which the Divine has established as paths for our return to the One who created us. And if the wide ways back to God are blocked (a blockage which, in God's mercy, can never be absolute), then the Powers of the Air, the nations of the kafir Jinn, will have carte blanche to misrepresent the subtle, psychic plane as the Kingdom of Heaven, to replace wisdom with clairvoyance and sanctity with magical and psychic powers in the mind of the mass.

Melchizedek had no father or mother. As such, he symbolizes the primordial Unity of Being, ontologically previous to the pairs-of-opposites that determine manifest existence. The Satanic counterfeit of this transcendence-of-polarity, however, is the denial of polarity. Primordial Humanity, before the fall into time and space, was androgynous, as was Adam before Eve was separated. But the satanic counterfeit of the androgyne, was William Blake pointed out, is what he called the hermaphrodite. In Blake's system, Satan is an hermaphrodite in whom all possible states are chaotically mixed together—a perfect counterfeit of the Unity of Being, where all possibilites are embraced and synthesized by That which transcends them. What falls below polarity apes what transcends it. The figure of Melchizedek, as interpreted by the UFO-worshippers, is thus a satanic counterfeit of principial Unity, symbolizing, among other things, the destruction of sexuality, which modern genetics has now made possible. The self-castration of the members of the Heaven's Gate UFO cult was an act of satanic worship: to destroy sexuality is to separate humanity from its archetype, and end its vicegerency.

✳ Religion, Evolution, & UFOs

Jacques Vallee, in his book *Dimensions* (Contemporary Books, 1988) — possibly under the baneful influence of Whitley Strieber — speaks of the UFO phenomenon, inexplicable and numinous, as the likely origin of past, and maybe even future, religions. But in making this claim he exhibits what I can only call a shocking though very common lack of any sense of proportion, since he places in the same category demonic obsession, appearances of fairies, UFO encounters, and the apparition of the Virgin Mary at Fatima! This is like saying that whoever or whatever emerges from the same hotel — a saint, a swarm of flies, an automobile, a guide-dog, a drug-dealer or a can of garbage — must be of the same nature or have the same agenda. He is so mesmerized by the elementary fact, commonly accepted until quite recently by the vast majority of the human race, that measurable physical manifestations can emerge from the unseen, that the *quality* of what emerges entirely escapes him, largely because the *mechanism* of the emergence cannot be explained in present scientific terms — as if the divine miracles which are Christian or Muslim or Buddhist civilizations, lasting for centuries and millennia and representing the pinnacles of the human spirit, each one overflowing with exquisite art, profound philosophy, noble and dignified social mores, courageous heroism and self-sacrifice, and which continue to produce those mirrors of God in human form, our enlightened saints, could have been thrown together by a few spooks doing aerial acrobatics, abducting and brutalizing innocent bystanders, and raping a few women! I have the greatest respect for Dr Vallee as an objective, scientific and largely unprejudiced investigator of the UFO phenomenon, one who is at no pains to conceal his frequent horror and disgust at some of its manifestations; in *Confrontations* (Ballantine, 1990), for example, he has a chapter on the mysterious illnesses and deaths often associated with UFO contact. He seems to feel, however, that for the purposes of 'objectivity' he must be careful not to draw any conclusions from this disgust. But if one's normal disgust at rotten meat represents the 'organic wisdom' of the body, which is telling us that if we eat rotten meat we will get sick, then why can't he credit his emotional disgust at the UFO phenomenon as representing a similar wisdom of a psychic or Spiritual order? It is here that the limits of Vallee's scientific outlook, or rather his scientific ideology, his *scientism*, make themselves apparent. Because, according to the ideology of scientism — Guénon's 'Reign of Quantity' — it is not permitted to ask qualitative questions, or to base one's conclusions on qualitative considerations, *including morality*. To the degree that Dr Vallee is a good humanist, and therefore possesses a conscience and a sense of honor inherited from Christendom, though not credited to it, he is a man of culture. But one can only lament the complete lack of culture, and even of simple humanity, exhibited by those individuals—and that part of Dr Vallee—which can see and investigate nothing beyond the mechanism of things. Such a person must reduce an exalted religious doctrine and the incomparable civilization produced by it to a 'cultural overlay' on a basically material phenomenon. Moses saw a volcano and founded Judaism; the disciples of Jesus saw a UFO and built Christendom. But to someone with the slightest understanding of what a *religion* is, the vulgar and tasteless tricks produced by today's 'aliens', whose spiritual level seems in many cases to be little above that of the neighborhood child molester, when compared with those profoundly wise, good, and beautiful manifestations which are the world's religions and wisdom traditions—as awesome in aspect as they are sublime in conception—will necessarily appear as just so much excrement. And just because a piece of excrement is pulled like a rabbit out of a hat doesn't make it smell any sweeter. It is often said that 'there is no accounting for taste.' I disagree. A sound taste must be based on some appreciation of the true, the good and the beautiful, which are ultimately nothing but the manifestation of God in this world, of which He alone is the Source. A degenerate taste, on the other hand, bespeaks a wounded soul—either traumatized, and so in need of healing, or deliberately depraved, and so headed for the wrath of God. I only pray that my own decision to write on the subject of UFOs does not indicate the beginnings of a similar depravity in me.

Nonetheless, Dr Vallee has done us a service in pointing out that many of the psycho-physical phenomena surrounding the appearance of the Virgin at Fatima are also commonly reported as part of UFO encounters: a perceived lowering of temperature, temporary paralysis, sweet fragrances, musical sounds, rainbow lights, the ambiguous aerial phenomenon known as 'angel hair' or 'the rain of flowers' (the last four being common features of apparitions of *devas* or *dakinis* in Vajrayana Buddhism), the descent of the object—in the case of Fatima, the sun—with a swinging motion, etc. Such similarities have led him to conclude that UFO manifestations and apparitions of the Virgin, or even the miracles and virgin birth of Jesus—since unexplained asexual pregnancies (which are in all likelihood demonic deceptions) are apparently sometimes reported in relation to 'alien' contacts, at least according to Vallee in *Dimensions*—represent the same order of phenomena. But anyone who expects a world-wide spiritual and cultural renewal such as that brought by Jesus of Nazareth to come from 'Rosemary's

Baby' is deeply deluded. And the truth is, our actual expectations relating to such phenomena are often far from hopeful, whether or not we have the courage to admit it. Somewhere in our souls we all know the difference between the Son of God and the offspring of a demonic *incubus*; our horror movies, if nothing else, prove it. As for the psycho-physical phenomena surrounding apparitions both angelic and demonic, these are best understood as simple material or quasi-material reactions to the passage of a manifestation—*any* manifestation—from the psychic to the physical plane, past the energy-border called by some the 'etheric wall', which, when viewed from the material standpoint, seems in some way related to the electromagnetic spectrum, if we don't simply define it as the space-time matrix itself. It might be permissible in this context, at least provisionally, to re-define the classical 'four elements'—which are traditionally seen as the home of the subtle 'elemental spirits', the gnomes, undines, sylphs and salamanders—as *matter* (Earth, that which stabilizes physical manifestation); *energy* (Water, that which reveals waves in motion); *space* (Air, that which represents the subtle environment of all living beings); and *time* (Fire, that which germinates, transforms, and ultimately consumes, all things). Be that as it may, the truth is that we cannot fully evaluate a veridical apparition, in terms of either its original source or its ultimate consequences, simply by cataloguing the immediate psycho-physical reverberations of its breakthrough into our world. Such manifestations may be miracles, by which I mean that they have their source in the world of Spirit; they may be magical phenomena, having their source on the psychic plane alone; and, if magical, they may be either benign or demonic. In the words of Schuon (*Light on the Ancient Worlds*, p104), 'so far as miracles are concerned, their causes surpass the psychic plane, though their effects come by way of it'—which means that all apparitions, though they may come from different points of origin, must enter our world through the same door; if this were not true, 'the discernment of spirits' would not be one of God's gifts, nor would Jesus have had to remind us that 'by their fruits you shall know them.'

Dr Vallee's scientism appears in the concluding chapter of *Dimensions*. The Introduction is written by Whitley Strieber; Vallee echoes him (unless Strieber is actually echoing Vallee) when, on p291, he states that: 'They [the UFO aliens] are . . . part of the control system for human evolution.' It is sad to realize that a dedicated researcher who values objectivity above all things, and has consequently been able to question the dominant myth that UFOs are spaceships, and to credit not only their inexplicable physical reality, but also their undeniable psychic affects and the hard evidence for human deception surrounding them, without using one truth to hide the others, completely loses that admirable objectivity when it comes to the great idol of scientism, *evolution*. I will not recount the many discrepancies and contradictions in Darwin's doctrine, and in other variations of the belief, which an increasing number of scientists from many fields see as rendering the theory untenable, nor will I quote from the works of those Traditionalist metaphysicians, such as Frithjof Schuon, Martin Lings, Seyyed Hossein Nasr, and Huston Smith, who explain why such a conclusion is philosophically necessary. I will only ask Dr Vallee what the abductions, the weird medical experiments, the animal and human mutilations (which he reports in *Messengers of Deception*), the aerial acrobatics designed to awe and confuse, the sexual molestations, and the use of subtle forces, either psychic or psycho-technological, which paralyze the body and darken the mind, have to do with *evolution*? If we accept the theory of biological evolution, do we not understand it as based on physical processes which have no need of UFOs to help them along? And if we are talking about social or spiritual evolution, what do terror, violation and deception have to do with it? Can a monkey be forced to evolve into a man by torturing or hypnotizing him? Can a society be improved by confusing and terrorizing it? Can a man be forced to evolve into an angel by abducting and sexually molesting him? There is no 'material proof' that the UFO phenomenon represents a conflict between Divine and infra-psychic forces for the attention of the human mind and the allegiance of the human soul, a conflict which may well be the very one named 'Armageddon' in the book of the *Apocalypse* — nor will such proof ever be forthcoming. But I will submit that, to anyone surveying the phenomenon with the full range of his or her human faculties, the 'unseen warfare' hypothesis must appear an infinitely better explanation than the 'evolutionary' one.

✳ Mind Control & *Roswell*: The Spielberg Agenda?

The deception and mind-control activities which cluster around the UFO phenomenon are discernible not only in staged manifestations of seemingly extraterrestrial landings or supernatural events, but also in certain media productions, particularly motion pictures like *Close Encounters of the Third Kind*. Anyone who is really interested in this hypothesis should go down to his or her video store and rent *Close Encounters*, the *Star Wars* trilogy (1977; 1980; 1983), *ET*, *A Fire in the Sky* (1993) and *Roswell*. *A Fire in the Sky*, the story of a supposedly true-life alien abduction, is a fairly innocent and straightforward account of a intensely traumatic event. *Star Wars*, though not without sinister elements common to all science fiction, is an old time 'space opera'. The moral it draws may be opposed at many points to traditional spiritual doctrine, but still, for all its use of mythological themes provided by 'mythic advisor' Joseph Campbell, it is essentially an adventure story told for purposes of entertainment; it is not deliberate propaganda. *ET* is extremely suspect, particularly since it features a parody of Michelangelo's image in the Sistine Chapel of God creating Adam by touching his finger — it regularly produced a kind of maudlin, pseudo-religious reaction in people to whom all normal religious emotions were apparently foreign — but there is nothing in it that can't be explained by the generally-accepted anti-clericalism and aesthetic satanism endemic to Hollywood culture. *Close Encounters of the Third Kind*, on the other hand, with its exaltation of the psychopathic tendency prevalent in contemporary culture to cut all one's economic and emotional ties in the pursuit of some fantastic and empty ideal, is another matter; from the time it first came out I have always thought of it as a mind-control job. It is nothing less than a satanic counterfeit of the 'rapture': instead of sound doctrine and religious faith, in the context of the intense psychic and spiritual energies unleashed at the apocalyptic end of the aeon, leading to the ecstatic experience of the presence of God, it presents emotional nihilism, spiritual emptiness and the lack of any stable frame of reference as the prerequisites for a willing capitulation to inhuman forces — and presents this outcome as 'positive'. The 'hero' of the movie throws his entire life away to pursue the source of the sound in his head of a few musical notes and the mental image of a barren desert crag — experiences which various forms of hypnosis and mind-control may well be able to produce with the greatest of ease — and is rewarded by being willingly abducted by an alien spaceship. That many who viewed *Close Encounters* took it as much more than mere entertainment was demonstrated to me in the late '80s, when I attended a party at the house of New Age musician Constance Demby. A few notes of music had appeared mysteriously on one of her audio tapes! Our blithe and enthusiastic hostess played them for us, and interpreted them, not surprisingly, as a personal message from the Space Brothers, on the model of the musical notes in *Close Encounters*. It goes without saying that no one in the room contradicted her; one of the most effective methods of self-induced mind-control, as we all know, is based on fear of the social *faux-pas!* [NOTE: Not being a film buff, it was only after I finished writing this chapter that I realized that the three productions which seemed most like mind-control to me—*Close Encounters, ET,* and *Roswell*—were all produced by Steven Spielberg! No one, of course, should draw any hard conclusions from this; it may be that Mr Spielberg simply has a mind-control-like style of motion picture production.]

The 1994 TV 'docu-drama' *Roswell*, starring Martin Sheen, about the supposed crash of an alien spaceship in New Mexico in 1947, and the recovery both of alien corpses and of surviving aliens who later died, will serve as an even better example. Jacques Vallee, in *Revelations*, tells us why he believes it unlikely that the Roswell incident was the crash of an alien spacecraft. He also gives us an interesting piece of information which contradicts the TV version of the event. According to Vallee, the first people to reach the supposed crash site encountered another group already there, who described themselves as 'archaeologists'. Vallee speculates that their real role may have been to plant the mysterious material which was later claimed to be the debris of the spaceship—a material which, according to him, could easily have been produced by human technology as it existed in 1947. In *Roswell*, however, the statement is made that the object could not have been a crashed experimental aircraft because 'they'd be looking for it' if it were, but no one appeared; the site, when first approached after the incident, was deserted. Obviously these two statements do not add up.

Among the more common mind-control techniques, useful to anyone who wishes to use it and can command sufficient attention via the media or the internet, is the Government Coverup Ploy: if you assert that a given fact is true but that the government is covering it up, a certain percentage of the public will automatically believe you—especially if you can pressure the government to the point where it will start issuing denials. It's a cheap and reliable tool; even the government itself can use it. *Roswell* is based upon the Government Coverup Ploy, as are a number of even more obviously propagandistic 'documentaries' and 'leaks' relating to the Roswell incident which have subsequently appeared. But *Roswell* is also a good specimen of two much more sophisticated mind-control techniques, ones which must be classed as satanic, since they represent perversions of specific metaphysical principles. I have named these techniques *subliminal contradiction* and *deferred closure.*

In the words of Jacques Vallee,

> it is possible to make large sections of any population believe in the existence of supernatural races, in the possibility of flying machines, in the plurality of inhabited worlds, by exposing them to a few carefully engineered scenes, the

details of which are adapted to the culture and superstitions of a particular time and place

⌒Passport to Magonia [Henry Regnery Co., 1969] pp 150–1

Seraphim Rose comments that

> an important clue to the meaning of these 'engineered scenes' may be seen in the observation often made by careful observers of UFO phenomena, especially CE-III ['close encounters of the third kind', i.e., sightings of sentient 'aliens'] and 'contactee' cases: that they are profoundly 'absurd', or contain at least as much absurdity as reality. Individual 'Close Encounters' have absurd details, like the four pancakes given by a UFO occupant to a Wisconsin chicken farmer in 1961; more significantly, the encounters themselves are strangely pointless, without clear purpose or meaning. A Pennsylvania psychiatrist has suggested that the absurdity present in almost all UFO cases is actually a *hypnotic technique.* 'When the person is disturbed by the absurd or the contradictory, and their mind is searching for meaning, they are extremely open to thought transference, to receiving psychic healing, etc. ([Vallee] *The Invisible College* [E. P. Dutton], p 115).

Precisely. In the technique of subliminal contradiction, two mutually incompatible bits of information are simultaneously projected into the perception of the victim without the contradiction being either pointed out or explained. In the technique of deferred closure, inexplicable data are continually fed to the victim or victims over a period of time, data which always suggest the possibility of a rational explanation but never quite allow it. And since the human mind is designed to seek and produce both perceptual and rational closure, the mind subjected to deferred closure will react to the continued frustration of one of its most basic needs either by sinking into stunned exhaustion, or by producing a paranoid, delusional form of closure. Schizophrenia presents the mind with a flood of data which overwhelms the normal processes of emotional, rational and perceptual closure; paranoid schizophrenia represents a more or less successful attempt to reach relative closure by abnormal means. Deferred closure, then, might be defined as an experimental method for producing paranoid schizophrenia (for a fictional account of this technique, I refer the reader to *That Hideous Strength* by C.S. Lewis, pp 297–298).

Subliminal contradiction and deferred closure are not only mind-control techniques, however; they are also essential elements of postmodern 'philosophy', which believes that contradictory statements are not necessarily mutually exclusive, and that any closure as to the true nature of things, any 'overarching paradigm', is impossible. Postmodernism, both as a philosophy and as a name for our contemporary culture, employs subliminal contradiction and deferred closure simply because it can't imagine anything else; it no longer believes in the existence of objective truth. (This, in itself, is enough to explain 'the Spielberg Agenda', though not to absolutely disprove the existence of a more deliberate attempt at 'social engineering'.)

In *Messengers of Deception* we are introduced to UFO contactee Rael (Claude Vorilhon, whose patronymic subsequently appeared on the TV sci-fi series *Babylon 5* as the name of an alien race, the Vorilhons), a robed and bearded false prophet who wears a medallion based on a design supposedly shown him by the aliens. The design—a combination between a swastika and a star of David—is an instance of subliminal contradiction. And since the contradiction is addressed to the 'right brain' in the form of an image, rather than to the 'left brain' in the form of a statement, it is more likely to be accepted uncritically, since the role of the right cerebral hemisphere is to synthesize data, not analyze it. As soon as a subliminal contradiction is accepted into the field of perception without initial resistance, the critical faculty is stunned, and the mind becomes receptive to suggestion.

I wonder if anyone besides myself has seen the subliminal contradiction ploy as it operates in normal social situations. If a person who wishes to influence you can establish a clear image in your mind of who he is and what is to be expected of him, and then, swiftly and nonchalantly, say or do something which totally contradicts this image, without exhibiting the normal mischievousness or social anxiety which such a shift usually entails, you may accept both your image of him and its contrary simultaneously, and subliminally. If you do, he has stunned you into a state where you can easily be manipulated. A subliminal contradiction between speech and body language can have the same effect.

The UFO phenomenon as a whole, and the crop-circle phenomenon as well, is a case of the deferred closure technique. Are UFOs spaceships? Psychic entities? Human deceptions? Are they wise philosophers come to aid us, or sinister invaders here to destroy us? The ambiguity of the phenomenon in itself produces a state of deferred closure, but it is clear from Dr Vallee's researches that this ambiguity is also being deliberately exploited by human groups. If you put a person in a prison cell along with a sledgehammer, a Barbie Doll, a can of olives and a ball of copper wire, and tell him you'll let him out again as soon as he invents a philosophical system based on these four 'principles', he may astound you with his ability to make 'closure' on the intrinsic meanings of and inter-relationships between elements which, in any objective sense, do not allow for it. His 'system' will say much more about his own deepest hopes, fears, beliefs and root assumptions than it will about the data you've provided him. And once you know what his 'system' is, then you can stress him further by feeding him data which again contradict it, ruining his meticulously-constructed pattern. Even better, you can feed him data which triumphantly confirm it—and onto which are grafted other items of information which you want him to accept as implicitly true. And he *will* accept them, because he experiences them not as alien beliefs which are being forced upon him against his will, but as parts of a pattern which *he himself has created*, through his own labor, imagination, sacrifice, and quest for truth.

Roswell is filled with subliminal contradictions, and the entire plot is an example of deferred closure. It is the story of Jesse Marcel, an Air Force officer who visits the crash site and picks up some of the mysterious material of which the craft was supposedly constructed—and later, in the course of a government coverup of the incident, is forced to lie about his experience. Jesse is the archetypal misunderstood paranoid crank, with whom many Americans can identify—but *we* the omniscient observers know he's telling the truth. We see him years later at a reunion of his old outfit, dying of emphysema. He's still determined to expose the coverup and get to the bottom of what really happened. He runs into a few others who had something to do with the incident, and hears the story about the recovery of alien bodies, and one live occupant. As the stories are told, we see flashbacks to 1947, some supposedly authentic, some only dramatizations of rumors. There is no resolution. Finally the mysterious UFO researcher and/or government and/or anti-government agent, Townsend (the Martin Sheen character) approaches Jesse and tells him more about the bizarre intricacies of the UFO phenomenon than he ever knew—referring, in the process, to *Close Encounters of the Third Kind*, the one other UFO film, except possibly *ET*, I picked out as a mind-control experiment—but leaves him as oppressed and puzzled as ever. Townsend has no final conclusions either, but nonetheless remains mysteriously knowledgeable and intimidating; after meeting with him, Jesse sinks into despair.

Whenever the incident is described, contradictory accounts are given. The alien bodies are smooth-skinned/no, their skin is scaly; their heads are egg-shaped/no, they are pear-shaped; the crashed object is flat and crescent-shaped (we see a quick flash of it)/no, it is egg-shaped (we see a quick contradictory flash); the name of the mortician who was contacted by the Air Force is Paul Davis/no, David Paulus. The bodies number five or six/no, three or four; the bodies are human-like/no, child-like (as if children aren't human)/ no, foetus-like; the ship is cylindrical/no, round/no, egg-shaped/ no, dome-shaped: the disorienting patter goes on and on. At one point we are shown a newspaper headline from the *Roswell Daily Record* reporting on the official debunking of the incident as a crashed weather balloon: 'Gen. *Ramey Empties Roswell Saucer.*' This, on the face of it, means little or nothing, unless it is a bad pun on the act of pouring out spilled tea. Subliminally, it means two different and contradictory things: That the general 'empties' the incident of meaning—i.e., calls it unreal—and that he *unloads* the saucer itself, indicating that it is a real object out of which real things can be taken, presumably the alien bodies. Since this is apparently an actual headline of the time, we can't attribute the subliminal contradiction it contains to Steven Spielberg. So how can we explain it? Elaborate conspiracy theories aside—such as the involvement of the intelligence community in all aspects of the Roswell incident from day one—perhaps someone on the staff of the *Roswell Daily Record* who believed in the crash constructed the headline so as to debunk the official debunkers. Or it may simply represent—and this in no way invalidates the above explanations—the intuitive reaction of the human mind, on a deeply unconscious level, to 'archetypal idea' of the UFO as a 'messenger of deception'.

The action is repeatedly intercut with religious imagery. When Jesse first shows the mysterious saucer-material to his family, it appears below a picture of Jesus on the wall of his home. When Townsend makes his mysterious and mystifying revelations to Jesse, the scene begins with a priest giving a memorial service for deceased fliers outside a hangar; Townsend takes Jesse inside the hangar, tells him the UFO secrets, then leaves. At the end, we return to the memorial service and the priest. The scene is designed to give the distinct though subliminal impression that the Catholic service is the outer or exoteric form, *and the UFO-lore the inner or esoteric meaning.* The themes of the sacred *temenos*, temple or mystery-cave, and the initiatory experience as a spiritual death (the memorial service) are also exploited— but not a death and *rebirth*, since Jesse remains inside the hanger and never re-emerges, in that scene, into the sunlight. The suggestion is that the UFO phenomenon is equivalent to, and will replace, revealed religion—a suggestion made more explicit in the scene where the Air Force brass assigned to investigate the incident repeat the belief that 'aliens' have manipulated human genetics and inspired human religious leaders throughout history, and are told by their superior, 'Think of our religious institutions if all of this were to just come out, what are people going to believe in?' and the scene where Jesse's son tells his dying father, who believes he's close to dis-covering the truth, 'You're close to nothing. Face it, Dad, you're never going to find what you're looking for, you just want an answer like there's some proof out there of God, or an afterlife, UFOs, it's all the same thing, some-thing to hang onto when nothing makes sense, this is fantasy, to make you feel better in the night.' So in the face of death, that 'nothing', that 'night', no faith is permitted; knock, and no door will be opened.

But the real goal of *Roswell* and other UFO-related propaganda is revealed in the scene where an officer participating in the investigation is shown in a picture gallery, looking up (briefly, so as to set up a 'waking suggestion') at perhaps an 18th or 19th century portrait of a haloed 'saint', who is gazing upward and to his right at a light-beam suggestive of God's glory—or a beam from a UFO—but holding in his left hand a red object emitting white flames, flames which are actually kindling his halo; the object appears to be the head of a demon. The officer is asking: 'Under what agency will we be operating?' His colleague answers him, 'None, we will have complete con-trol.' Here we can begin to see the meaning of the tradition that Satan has saints and contemplatives of his own, who answer to neither God nor man. On the other hand, the saint is *under* the light-beam in the painting, just as the officer is under the painting itself; word and image and directly contra-dictory on a subliminal level. And the fact that the saint holds the demon's fiery head—if that's what it is—in his hand, shows that he is in control of it, or believes he is, much as the ceremonial magician of the Renaissance would invoke the power of God, or one of His angels, to give him control over the demon he wished to enslave. Here the desire for Promethean spiritual autonomy is used to deny the truth that the sorcerer, even though he clearly worships his own self-will as if it were God, is in fact handing that will over to the control of an infernal will by that very worship. This is the 'denial'—and also the 'co-dependency'—which affects all magicians: self-determina-tion is enslavement, but every worshipper of self-determination must deny this, until it is too late.

Roswell also does what it can to muddle and neutralize the findings of honest researchers like Vallee. When the military big-wigs are discussing how to cover up the Roswell crash, one asks 'what if people think we are not in control of the skies?' and another answers 'they'd be right'—thus setting up another subliminal contradiction to 'we're in complete control.' Then they propose that 'hoaxes' be carried out, and that true information be leaked through unreliable and suspect sources as part of the coverup. But why hoaxes? How can a convincingly staged UFO appearance or landing convince people that there are no such things as UFOs? It can do so only if it is later proved to be a hoax—but that is the one thing which is almost never absolutely provable when UFO deceptions are alleged. All that Vallee has been able to come up with are tantalizing clues that a particular manifestation could have been a deception, and evidence convincing enough to suggest that the phenomenon as a whole includes deception activities by human groups. But if anything is clear in this murky world, it is that whatever deceptions are being carried on are meant to be believed, not to be disproved. As for leaking of true information via untrustworthy sources, that *is* being done, in order to set up a 'feedback loop' between lunatic cranks and cynical debunkers. But the purpose of such a loop, according to Vallee in *Messengers of Deception*, is to discourage objective investigation of the phenomenon, *not* to convince people that there are no such things as UFOs. If that were its purpose, one would have to conclude that it is not a very effective strategy, given that every time someone who has investigated the actual data, or has himself experienced the phenomenon, hears it cynically debunked by the 'authorities', academic or military, those authorities lose more credibility in his eyes—and every time that person or someone like him voices his or her legitimate feeling that the authorities are either deluded or dishonest in regard to the phenomenon, the officials in question become even more cynical and self-defensive, and so lose that much more *authority* over those upon whose trust they depend. And into that vacuum of social and cultural authority come—the UFOs. Jacques Vallee believes that this method of discouraging objective investigation is largely for the purpose of hiding the activities of human groups, possibly allowing them to test new high-tech weapons, or 'psychotronic' devices for the manipulation of human consciousness, without public or political interference. I agree. But there are other reasons for it. This lowering of collective consciousness and diminishment of our sense of reality is being deliberately engineered for two purposes: first, in order to make the public more suggestible and open to a belief in UFOs, and secondly to lull us into a false sense of 'security'—really a psychic numbness based on repressed fear—so that we will not realize that UFOs represent a mass psychic invasion of the most alarming nature, requiring an immediate and militant response on the plane of spiritual warfare. This *abaissement de niveau mental* is served by a number of devices, not the least of which is the tendency to portray aliens in comic mode, which completes the triad of Fear/Worship/Complacency that can be seen around other horrendous possibilities—that of human cloning, for example. We fear them; we laugh at them in order to deny our fear; as soon as our fear is suppressed, we accept them. This engineered unreality is symbolized in *Roswell* by the alcoholic haze in which the stories of the UFO crash are exchanged at the Air Force reunion; one of the informants, sluggish and overweight, appears floating on his back in a swimming pool with a drink on his belly. It's not an image designed to promote either critical awareness or spiritual vigilance.

The central intent of the writers and producers of *Roswell* surfaces in the scene where Townsend is 'educating' Jesse Marcel in the hangar; the following is an excerpt from their dialogue:

> Townsend: One must proceed cautiously here, on guard against one's desire to want it to be true or want it not to be true. One must be, as much as possible, neutral.
> Jesse Marcel: Well, how can you be neutral? A thing is either true or it's not, there is no middle ground.
> T: Alright, alright . . . then none of it is true.
> J: *None* of it?
> T: Well, maybe some of it...
> J: No, no, you're playing with me—why are you playing with me?
> T: Because maybe you wouldn't even know what was true if you'd seen it all for yourself. How's that for an answer?
> J: Alright, then what did I see out there in that field?
> T: That? . . . why, that was a weather balloon.
> J: *No*, it wasn't, I know what I saw, and it was not from this world.
> T: Don't you understand, Jesse, you have *nothing*, just a lot of old memories and second hand recollections. Nobody is going to take you seriously, not without proof, not without hard evidence.

What is being preached here is nothing less that the impossibility of arriving at objective truth, and ultimately the unreality of objective truth itself. Irreducible subjectivities, with no overarching paradigm to unite them into an integrated vision of reality, are all we have—all we are. It is the whole postmodern age and postmodernist agenda in a nutshell; and since objective Truth is ultimately God, what is being preached is also a denial of God, and His replacement by demonic principalities and powers. But without grounding in the Divine objectivity of the Ground of Being, even our ability to draw rational conclusions from empirical data becomes eroded, since rationality is nothing less than a distant mental echo of Intellection, or Divine Gnosis. In the words of C. S. Lewis from *That Hideous Strength* (1946), his science fiction novel about an invasion of Earth by the forces of the Antichrist (which I heard Traditionalist author James Cutsinger describe as 'The Reign of Quantity in fictional form'):

> The physical sciences, good and innocent in themselves, had already . . . begun to be warped, had been subtly maneuvered in a certain direction. Despair of objective truth had been increasingly insinuated into the scientists; indifference to it, and a concentration upon mere power, had been the result. Babble about the *élan vital* and flirtations with panpsychism were bidding fair to restore the *Anima Mundi* of the magicians. . . . The very experiences of the dissecting room and the pathological laboratory were breeding a conviction that a stifling of all deep-set repugnances was the first essential for progress.

The heart of the matter—which appears in the first two passages of the above dialogue—is a *deliberate* and *engineered* attack upon the concept of objective truth; the postmodernist deconstructionism of academia is nothing but the stifling vapor rising up from a much deeper and darker cauldron. When Townsend says that we must be on guard against *wanting* the extraterrestrial hypothesis to be true or not true, he is accurately presenting one of the prerequisites for real objectivity—then, instead of the word 'objective', he uses the word *neutral*. But neutrality is not necessarily objectivity; it can just as easily denote nihilism or indifference. And Jesse senses this nihilism, which is what leads him to reject the stance of neutrality, to protest that 'A thing is either true or it's not, there's no middle ground.' But as Townsend has set things up, Jesse defeats himself by this very protest, since *he has been manoeuvred into defending objectivity by attacking the very criteria of objectivity*, which have falsely been associated with a nihilistic neutrality—a neutrality which, in this context, is really nothing but another name for 'suggestibility'. How ingenious, how cunning the writers and producer (Steven Spielberg) of *Roswell* were, and are. But if they're so smart, one is led to ask, then why can't they be intelligent? Because that would not be in the interest of the forces they consciously or unconsciously serve; all intelligence is of God.

A truly inverted and satanic *metaphysics* is at the origin of *Roswell*. Subliminal contradiction is a satanic counterfeit of the metaphysical principle that the Absolute is beyond the 'symplegades', the pairs-of-opposites. Deferred closure is a satanic counterfeit of the metaphysical principle that the Infinite cannot, by definition, be contained within any system of thought or perception. Absoluteness and Infinity, as we have seen in the metaphysics of Frithjof Schuon, are properly descriptive of the Divine Essence of God, and nothing else. To apply them to anything relative and contingent, anything in the realm of cosmic manifestation, is the highest form of idolatry, perhaps best characterized as a deception of 'Iblis', the Muslim name for Satan, or the satanic principle, in its most metaphysically subtle mode of action. The Absolute, or Necessary Being, is not realized through an amalgamation or confusion of the pairs of opposites, but through transcendence of them, after which it is seen exactly how the Absolute manifests by means of them. And the Infinite, or Possible Being, is not realized through a foredoomed attempt to reduce the Infinite Possibility within the Divine Nature to a closed system, but simply through accepting what comes and letting go of what must go, in the knowledge that all things are a manifestation of God's will, either in terms of what He positively wills—Being, or the good—and what He negatively allows—the privation of Being, or evil—in view of the fact that universe, though it manifests Him, is not He Himself, and is thus necessarily imperfect. Submission to God's will as manifest in the events of our lives—a submission which does not exclude, but actually requires, our creative response to these events, since our innate desire to live shapely and fully-realized lives is also part of God's will—leads to the gnosis of all events as acts of God, which opens in turn on the deeper gnosis of all manifest forms as eternal, archetypal possibilities within the embrace of the Divine Infinity. The realization of God as Infinite is not the desire for an ultimate philosophical or experiential closure but the sacrifice of this desire in the face of the Divine Immanence; the realization of God as Absolute is not the horizontal confusion or neutralization of polarities, but the vertical intuition of their common Principle in the light of the Divine Transcendence.

In the last scene, we see Jesse Marcel hopelessly puttering around the crash site in the dry autumn grass, looking for 'hard evidence'—remnants of the UFO crash debris which were all collected 30 years ago. He is seeking for certainty not where it can really be found, in the objective Ground of Being, but precisely where it can never be found: in memory. Jesse, his wife and his son come together again as a family around a sense of a bleak, nostalgic futility: 'We can never know the truth,' the movie says, 'but at least we can huddle together emotionally on the basis of a common despair of knowing it.' And so *Roswell* ends with one more satanic counterfeit: that of *humility*. Instead of a pious awe in the face of what transcends form, we are left with a stunned, mesmerized hopelessness in the face of what has never reached it, or has fallen below it. Nonetheless, as Rumi says, counterfeit coins only exist because there really is such a thing as true gold; or, in the words of Meister Eckhart, 'The more he blasphemes, the more he praises God.' So the spiritual practice, here, is not to struggle with the shadows of contradiction and uncertainty, but to turn 180 degrees away from them. It is to let the counterfeit remind you of the Truth: to make hopeless contradiction a way of remembering the Absolute Divine Truth which eternally possesses the power to resolve it, and endless uncertainty a way of remembering the Infinite Divine Life which radiates from the core of that Truth, by which we can, in Blake's famous words, 'see the world in a grain of sand / And Heaven in a wild flower /…hold Infinity in the palm of your hand / And Eternity in an hour.' False humility before what is less real than you are makes you arrogant, and destroys your human dignity. True humility before what is infinitely greater than you are blesses and uplifts you, which is why Muslims say that man, *because* he is God's slave, is thereby His vicegerent, His fully-empowered representative in this world.

✳ Abduction: The Ontological Agenda

Alien contact represents an irruption into the material plane of subhuman forces from the subtle realm, whose goal is the dissolution of our world. But though dissolution is the natural end of any cycle of manifestation, we aren't required to capitulate to the forces which produce it, because there is a spark of the Divine Nature within us which is beyond manifestation entirely, which was not veiled by its beginning nor corrupted by its fall, and will not be altered by its end. But if we forget this, if we turn our spiritual attention away from the Spirit of God and toward the forces of chaos and subversion which are It's shadow, then our return to Him — which, according to the Koran, is the destiny of all beings — will be indefinitely delayed, and will ultimately take place by the dark road of infernal torment, not the road of God's Mercy, the path of Divine Love and Wisdom.

According to Guénon, as you'll remember, the adoption of materialistic beliefs by the mass of mankind resulted in an actual 'solidification of the world'. But materialism has already moved past its apex, a truth which Guénon saw in 1945, and which is much more obvious today. In the late 19th century, when materialist ideology was at its strongest, both religion and 'superstition' were debunked. But today, as this ideology continues to lose power — the fall of the Soviet Union being one of the clearest signs of this — and as a belief in subtle beings and invisible worlds becomes more acceptable, such acceptance does not take the form of a return to religion and metaphysics, which continue to be eroded, but rather that of a collective fascination with mysterious and sinister possibilities, exactly as Guénon predicted. The post-modern 'transcendence' of the modernist paradigm, to which materialism was integral—Marx and Darwin being two of modernism's central pillars—has resulted not in a renaissance of traditional theology but in a nihilistic worship of fragmentation and chaos in the name of the 'celebration of diversity'. Postmodernism shows itself to be a toxic stew in which arcane science, disintegrated cultural material and 'infra-psychic' forces are mixed in relatively equal amounts. In Guénon's own words:

> the materialistic conception, once it has been formed and spread abroad in one way or another, can only serve to reinforce the very 'solidification' of the world that in the first place made it possible . . . the 'solidification' . . . can never be complete, and there are limits beyond which it cannot go . . . the farther 'solidification' goes the more precarious it becomes, for the lowest degree is also the least stable; the ever-growing rapidity of the changes taking place in the world today provides all-too-eloquent testimony to the truth of this . . . though the hold of materialism is slackening, there is no occasion to rejoice in the fact, for cyclical manifestation is not yet complete, and the 'fissures' . . . can only be produced from below; in other words, that which 'interferes' with the sensible world through those 'fissures' can be nothing but an inferior 'cosmic psychism' in its most destructive and disorganizing forms, and it is moreover clear that influences of this kind are the only ones that are really suited for action having dissolution as its objective . . . , everything that tends to favor and extend these 'interferences' merely corresponds, whether consciously or otherwise, to a fresh phase of the deviation of which materialism in reality represented a less 'advanced' stage. . . . In the Islamic tradition these 'fissures' are those by which, at the end of the cycle, the devastating hordes of Gog and Magog will force their way in, for they are unremitting in their efforts to invade this world; these 'entities' represent the inferior influences in question.
>
> ⌒ THE REIGN OF QUANTITY (pp145, 147, 202, 206)

No clearer presentation of the 'ontological agenda' of today's 'aliens' is available to us than the book entitled *Abduction: Human Encounters with Aliens*, by Pulitzer Prize-winning author and Harvard psychiatrist John E. Mack. Based on nearly one hundred cases of 'alien abduction', Dr Mack (like Jacques Vallee, whose preeminence as a UFOlogist Mack affirms) concludes that such abductions are real, and that they are carried on by entities from subtler planes of being who have the power to physically impinge upon this one. He delves more deeply than Dr Vallee into the ongoing psychological and psycho-physical 'covenant' which is often established between aliens and their abductees, but ignores, for some reason, Vallee's findings about the involvement of human groups practicing deception and mind-control.

According to Mack, alien abduction seems to run in families. Many abductees had alcoholic or emotionally frigid parents, came from broken homes, or suffered childhood sexual abuse. Mack mentions one study in which the abduction experience is related to ritual abuse by Satanic cults. Interaction with 'aliens' can begin as early as the age of 2 or 3. In childhood they often appear as relatively benign, but when the abductee reaches puberty their actions become more sinister. Abductees sometimes transfer to the aliens feelings of love which were not reciprocated in the family setting, and experience being loved in return. Many abductees, in Mack's estimation, seem particularly psychic or intuitive; many experience the development of psychic powers as a result of the abduction itself.

The 'aliens' exhibit characteristics commonly encountered in shamanism; they, or their craft, sometimes appear as animals. They also bear an obvious resemblance to traditional 'gods, spirits, angels, fairies, demons, ghouls, vampires and sea monsters'—though it appears that Mack is incapable of differentiating between the various types of subtle beings, or doesn't want to. And though UFO sightings are a world-wide occurrence, most abductions are reported from the Western hemisphere, with the United States heading the list.

(The correlation of UFO activity with emotional frigidity has an interesting sidelight: Breakaway Freudian psychoanalyst Wilhelm Reich, the father of much of today's 'bodywork', was attempting toward the end of his life—when many believe he had become mentally imbalanced—to manipulate and enhance a subtle 'life-energy' which he named 'orgone', as part of his struggle against the 'emotional plague'. This was his name for a *mass freezing of human emotion*, often expressed in terms of what he called 'character armor', as well as through social movements such as Nazism. According to Reich, UFOs, as a source of 'deadly orgone energy', were in part responsible for this plague.)

The alien abductors subject their victims to terrifying and humiliating 'medical-like' procedures. They also voyeuristically view them performing sexual intercourse, or themselves have intercourse with them. One of the major agendas of the aliens seems to be to extract human sperm and egg cells from their abductees so as to genetically engineer a 'hybrid' human/ alien race. Female abductees experience these hybrid foetuses being placed in their womb, then somehow removed a few months later, to continue their growth aboard alien 'spacecraft'.

Their 'mothers' are sometimes re-abducted, and then directed to show mother-love to these hybrid beings, who appear 'listless'. *No evidence exists of actual physical pregnancies.* After abduction, many victims experience themselves as now possessing, or as always having possessed a dual 'human/alien' identity; they sometimes see themselves as performing the same 'procedures' or 'experiments' upon new abductees as were originally performed upon them.

Dr Mack presents, in his case histories, some of the most horrifying stories of demonic attack and possession I have ever encountered, though he does not recognize them as such. He admits (p13) that 'Abductees . . . bear physical and psychological scars of their experience. These range from nightmares and anxiety to chronic nervous agitation, depression, even psychosis, to actual physical scars — puncture and incision marks, scrapes, burns and sores.' He speaks of broken marriages and alienation of affection between parents and children as among the more common after-effects, and says that negative physical and psychological effects persist even in cases where spontaneous healing of chronic or incurable diseases occurs. One would naturally assume, therefore, that his therapeutic approach would include an attempt to shield his patients from ongoing alien influence, and help them break any psychological ties which might remain. But this is not in fact the case, because Mack, appallingly, believes that the influence of the aliens, by and large, is good! He views his role as one of helping his clients to remember their abduction experiences, often via hypnosis (which, incidentally, has been proved so unreliable as a tool for accessing 'recovered memories' that the courts have recently disallowed testimony based upon it) — and then helping them to deal with the violent and horrific emotions such memories entail — *and then helping them to accept that their experience is (somehow) ultimately 'positive', 'transformative', or 'spiritual'.* He sees himself as supporting them more against skeptical therapists and family members than against the alien kidnappers themselves. 'In my work with abductees,' he says, 'I am fully involved, experiencing and reliving with them [*sic*] the world that they are calling forth from their unconscious.' One gets the distinct impression that the therapeutic session with Dr Mack is actually the missing second half of the abduction experience itself, which includes both an original deeply traumatic event or series of events, and the eventual acceptance of the experience, *in contradiction to all the patient's deepest feelings,* as a 'message' or 'mission' from the aliens, in the 'permissive', 'supportive', 'non-threatening', 'non-judgmental', 'accepting' therapeutic framework provided by Dr Mack. It would be interesting, however, to see how some of Mack's patients would react in a different environment—that of a traditional exorcism, for example. Would their deliberately suppressed feelings of being profoundly violated reassert themselves in such a context? Would the full acceptance of these feelings lead to a radically different conclusion about the aliens' true agenda? Mack himself seems to view his interaction with his clients as part of the 'composition' of the abduction experience. He describes it as a 'co-creative' process, 'the product of an intermingling of flowing-together of the consciousness of two (or more) people in the room. Something may be brought forth that was not there before in exactly the same form' (p391). Precisely.

Reading Mack is like watching, through a two-way mirror, the putterings of a confused physician who is so fascinated by the task of diagnosing a disease that he has forgotten that it is his duty to heal his patient. Perhaps he simply doesn't know how to begin to treat the disease which confronts him. But one can only conclude from his book—since he comes right out and says it—that he accepts the alien agenda reported by his tormented and traumatized patients, *because they themselves accept it*. Is this the final form of the 'client-centered therapy' of Carl Rogers? The idea that, since the patient has chosen schizophrenia, or demonic possession, the role of the psychiatrist is to support him in this choice, and help him go crazy? *Of course* the client 'accepts' the alien program: he is possessed by it, precisely as a human cell invaded by a virus, which utilizes the cell's own genetic structure to create replicas of itself, is possessed by the virus. But just because a person's immune system fails to overcome the attack of a microbe, do we therefore second it in its 'choice'? Is this good medical practice? (Not for nothing did C.S. Lewis, in *That Hideous Strength*, call the demonic space-beings and/or fallen angels battling to conquer Earth the 'macrobes'.) Mack casts about for scattered fragments of spiritual and occult lore to explain what his patients are going through, and comes up with little more than evidence that such things have always occurred, coupled with speculations based upon the statements made by the aliens themselves! But if someone kidnaps and tortures me, is that any indication that I ought to believe what he says? Is such an attitude in any way rational, not to mention sound on the level of normal human emotion? And the fact that similar things have occurred throughout history is purely elementary. The power of realities from unseen dimensions to impinge on our world has always been part of human knowledge, its suppression by reductionist materialism over the past couple of centuries notwithstanding. Mack builds his case for accepting the alien agenda on the fact that their very presence overturns the materialist paradigm. But if so, then why can't he accept the common consensus of the pre-materialist millennia, when it was well understood—as it still is by many today—that manifestations such as he reports indicate the presence of demons, and that demons are, in every case where it serves their ends—and sometimes because they simply can't help themselves—deliberate liars? He gleefully profits from materialism's denial of the validity of religion and of any sense of moral order in the universe; it is precisely what allows him to accept a purely demonic reality of a subtle nature—coupled with a sinister and self-contradictory philosophy—and then introduce it as the herald of a major paradigm-shift *because it transcends materialism*. This is exactly what Guénon meant when he said that materialism first 'solidifies' the human mindset, and then produces 'fissures' opening not on the 'celestial' but on the 'infra-psychic'.

The correct practice when confronted with such manifestations as alien abduction, for which the hard evidence continues to mount, is simply to admit the obvious, that such manifestations exist, and then proceed to ask the questions which will immediately occur to any normal, religiously-educated human being: (1) Is the manifestation in question good, neutral, or evil? (2) If it is good, what does it ask of us? (3) If it is neutral, is it useful or a waste of time? (4) If it is evil, how can we avoid and/or combat it? Someone who cannot ask even these most elementary and inevitable of questions is in no way a physician of souls. And, unfortunately, Mack falls into this category. He seems to believe that to ask moral questions about what appear to be the deliberate actions of conscious beings is somehow unscientific, and repeats the common nihilist cliché, derived from a counterfeit metaphysics, that beings from subtler planes are in some way beyond good and evil. He ignorantly attributes this counterfeit metaphysics to Tibetan Buddhism, and opposes it to that of Judeo-Christianity:

> To the polarizing perception of Christian dualism these dark-eyed beings seem to be the playmates of the Devil (Downing, 1990). Eastern religious traditions such as Tibetan Buddhism, which have always recognized the vast range of spirit entities in the cosmos, seem to have less difficulty accepting the actuality of the UFO abduction phenomenon than do the more dualistic monotheisms, which offer powerful resistance to acceptance (p 412).

In relation to the belief that higher realities are morally neutral, Frithjof Schuon's teaching on the subject is as follows: God may be 'beyond good and evil' because He transcends all relativity, but this does not mean that He is 'beyond good', or morally neutral in His relation to us, or somehow half good and half evil. He is the Sovereign Good, beyond any conceivable relationship with the fragmentary and privative manifestation we call 'evil'. His goodness transcends definition as 'the opposite of evil' not because it is in any way involved with evil, but because it is Absolute, and consequently has no opposite.

When Mack uses the word 'acceptance' in the above passage, does he mean 'acceptance as real' or 'acceptance as good and/or inevitable,' as when he helps his clients in the therapeutic setting to overcome their natural resistance and *accept* the alien agenda? He seems to be saying that Tibetan Buddhism, with its understanding of 'the vast range of spirit entities in the cosmos,' accepts them as real, whereas the Christian tradition does not. But Christianity, in seeing the aliens as 'playmates of the Devil', obviously does accept them as real, by Mack's own admission. Mack makes the word 'acceptance' deliberately ambiguous in order to imply that, while Christianity narrow-mindedly rejects the aliens as evil, broad-minded Tibetan Buddhism accepts them as a natural part of the cosmos; but all he has really been able to factually assert is that the Tibetan Buddhists believe they are real—which, of course, is also true of the Christians. His obvious intent is to drive a wedge between Christianity and Buddhism, and to imply that the Tibetans, in accepting aliens as real, necessarily accept them as good, as if Tibetan Buddhism possessed no doctrine of the demonic. Such, of course, is not the case. Both Christianity and the Vajrayana recognize the existence of demonic entities, the difference being that Christians believe they are eternally damned, while Buddhists hold that after their karmic debts are paid they can move on to relatively less infernal modes of existence, and that great saints can, on occasion, even convert them to Buddhism! But their profoundly destructive effects, and the need to vigorously combat them spiritually, are fully recognized by both traditions; to imply the contrary is either culpably ignorant or effectively slanderous to Tibetan Buddhism. And just because demons are esoterically understood in the Vajrayana as apparitions conceived in one's own mind, which symbolize obscuring attachments and passions, in no way makes them less real; after all, the human form itself is also an apparition conceived in one's own mind—which is ultimately the mind of the Buddha—symbolic in this case of the 'human state hard-to-attain', the only state from which the potential for Perfect Total Enlightenment can be realized.

Padma-sambhava, the great Vajrayana adept who brought Buddhism to Tibet, spent a lot his time combatting and subjugating demons. The following passages are from *The Tibetan Book of the Great Liberation* by W. Y. Evans-Wentz:

Then Padma thought: 'I cannot very well spread the Doctrine and aid sentient beings until I destroy evil'... he subjugated all ... demons and evil spirits, slew them, and took their hearts and blood into his mouth. Their consciousness-principles he transmuted into the syllable *Hum* and caused the *Hum* to vanish into the heaven-worlds.... Transforming himself into the King of the Wrathful Deities, Padma, while sitting in meditation, subjugated the Gnomes.... Padma performed magical dances on the surface of a boiling poisonous lake, and all the malignant and demoniacal *nagas* inhabiting the lake made submission to him ... he subjugated various kinds of demons, such as those causing epidemics, diseases, hindrances, hail, and famine.... Padma brought all the gods inhabiting the heavens presided over by Brahma under his control.... And, in other guises, Padma conquered all the most furious and fearful evil spirits, and 21,000 devils, male and female ... the goddesses Remati and Ekadzati appeared before Padma and praised him for thus having conquered all evils and all deities (pp 139–142).

In line with Mack's findings, the aliens should obviously be classed among the 'demons causing diseases and hindrances'—but if he is so respectful of Tibetan Buddhism, why doesn't he see them as forces to be subjugated? I assume it is because he is no more a Vajrayana Buddhist than he is a Christian, though he feels no shame at taking the doctrines of both traditions out of context, and using them for his own ends. 'There can be little place,' he says, 'especially within the Judeo-Christian tradition, for a variety of small but powerful homely beings who administer an odd mixture of trauma and transcendence without apparent regard for any established religious hierarchy or doctrine' (p 412). But, as we have just seen, Judeo-Christianity has a perfect place for them: the infernal regions. Their lack of 'regard' for any 'established religious hierarchy or doctrine' clearly does not represent an inability on the part of the revealed religions to make sense of them, but rather a will on the aliens' part to discredit the revealed religions—an agenda which Mack, as demonstrated in the above passage, supports. And there is no better way to undermine revealed religion than by associating the idea of 'transcendence' with the idea of 'traumatic violation', thus separating the True from the Good in the victims' minds, and associating Truth, not with Goodness, but with evil, and naked power. According to traditional metaphysics, pure Being is in itself the Sovereign Good whom we call God; consequently the more real something is the better it is, and the better something is the more real it is. It is the goal of the Antichrist to separate Truth from Goodness and Love, and unite it instead with ruthless power, so as to wipe Goodness and Love from the earth.

Mack repeatedly answers critics who attribute the abductees' acceptance of the aliens' agenda to the 'Stockholm Syndrome', the documented psychological tendency of victims to identify with their tormentors, as Patty Hearst did with the terrorists who kidnapped her. He says (p 339):

> In contrast to the narrow and self-serving purposes of human abusers and political kidnappers, the beings reveal a shared purpose, and offer the possibility of opening to an inclusive, more expansive worldview that is powerfully internalized by many abductees.

But Patty Hearst was also opened to a 'shared purpose' based on an 'inclusive, more expansive worldview,' that of global class struggle as opposed to the sheltered life of a rich and spoiled playgirl, by the Simbionese Liberation Army; and any child whose first sexual experience is with an abductor or molester has certainly had his or her worldview widened, though in a terribly destructive manner. There is no necessary contradiction between a 'self-serving purpose' and a 'more expansive worldview'. Hitler, who was not only self-serving but made the act of serving him into a pseudo-religion, opened some extremely expansive vistas to the German people. Unfortunately for them, and for the rest of the world, they were vistas of evil.

On p 407, Dr Mack attempts to *defend humiliating and dehumanizing abuse* as a positive and transformative experience. He says:

> I am often asked how experiences that are so traumatic, and even cruel at times, can also be spiritually transformative. To me there is no inconsistency here, unless one reserves spirituality for realms that are free of pain and struggle. Sometimes our most useful spiritual learning comes at the hands of rough teachers who have little respect for our conceits, psychological defenses, or established points of view.

Whatever his intent, such a sweeping statement might be construed as a defense, not only of the 'right' of aliens to abduct us, but of the 'right' of megalo-maniac gurus and unethical psychiatrists *to psychologically and sexually abuse their devotees and clients*. It is true that the Nazi death-camp experience was powerfully transformative in a spiritual sense for some Jews; Elie Wiesel and Victor Frankl come immediately to mind. But does this mean that the Nazis were a spiritual force for good in the world? Once again, I must quote the words of Jesus: 'There needs be evil, but woe to him through whom evil comes.' Whether one believes in UFOs and alien abduction or not, the grave dangers of Mack's approach should be obvious.

Incredibly, Mack sees the abduction experience as a paradigm of 'personal growth and transformation.' He presents it in terms of eight elements, or stages (pp 48–49): (1) 'Pushing through' ego-death to acceptance; (2) recognizing the aliens as intermediaries between the human state and an impersonal cosmic consciousness; (3) ecstatically experiencing a return 'Home' to this consciousness; (4) recalling past lives; (5) gaining an expanded consciousness which transcends the material level and includes great cycles of reincarnational manifestation; (6) identification of one's consciousness with a vast array of other forms of consciousness, including those of elemental spirits and dinosaurs; (7) experience of human/alien dual identity; (8) attainment of a multi-dimensional consciousness which seems to transcend the space-time matrix. Let us deal with these items one at a time.

(1) The *falsehood* here is the identification of the willing surrender of one's ego with the forcible breaking of one's will. God is not a hypnotist or a terrorist. A deep and fertile relationship with the Source of All Life cannot be the product of brainwashing and mind-control. Therefore whatever forces employ such techniques are opposed to God. As C.S. Lewis writes in *The Screwtape Letters*, speaking through the mouth of his demon Screwtape (pp 37–38):

> To us a human is primarily food; our aim is the absorption of its will into ours, the increase of our own area of selfhood at its expense. But the obedience which the Enemy demands of men is quite a different thing. ... His service [is] perfect freedom. ... We want cattle who can finally become food; He wants servants who can finally become sons.

In the words of Muhammad (upon whom be peace), 'there is no compulsion in religion.'

(2) The Jinn are, in a sense, intermediaries between the human state and higher conscious realms, simply because they inhabit a subtler plane of the Great Chain of Being—but to believe that they can be intermediaries *for us* is a *falsehood*: they are not on the 'human stem'. And if the Jinn we encounter happen to be what the Christians call 'fallen angels'—subtle-plane beings who have turned against the Source of Life through a perverted use of their free will—then they can only act as effective intermediaries between us and our own spiritual destruction. When Jesus said, 'none come to the Father but through me,' one of the things He meant was that no human being can unite with God by any other avenue than God's Humanity. As the Muslims say, human beings relate to God by virtue of our *fitrah*, our primordial, God-created human nature. Consequently, the image of God as an 'impersonal cosmic consciousness' is another *falsehood*. On the *first* level of the Great Chain of Being, God is Beyond Being, the unknowable Divine Essence, the

'Godhead' of the mystics; but we have no access to this Godhead except through the *second* level, through the personal God. And this God is not a separate Being, but is of one Essence with the Godhead. The Godhead is not impersonal, in other words, but *transpersonal*; if the Divine Personhood were not a potential within the Transpersonal Godhead, that Personhood could never appear. To believe otherwise is to identify self-transcendence and mystical Union with alienation and dehumanization. And this is an all-too-common counterfeit image of the spiritual Path in many people's minds, one which the aliens—as actual 'spirits of alienation'—are here to exploit.

(3) The ecstatic experience of a return 'Home'—a name for the aliens' point-of-origin which is taken directly from the motion picture *ET*, by the way—can only, given the horrific context, be a demonic *falsehood*. Because the aliens have access to the psychic plane, they can of course produce intense psychic experiences, as Mack repeatedly demonstrates; such experiences, as we well know, can even be initiated by chemicals. And given the hangover from materialism which still afflicts us, it is easier for them than ever before to palm off psychic experiences as Spiritual realizations, since hardly anyone nowadays is taught even the need for a 'discernment of spirits', much less the necessary criteria, and since anything of a subtler quality than the dead material level of today's ambience will likely seem 'numinous'.

According to Dr Mack, most (but not all) UFO abductions appear to be 'out-of-body experiences'. Seraphim Rose, in *The Soul After Death* (St Herman of Alaska Brotherhood, Platina, California, 1980) pp 115–116, has this to say of such experiences:

> It may be asked: What of the feelings of 'peace' and 'pleasantness' which seem to be almost universal in the 'out-of-body' state? What of the vision of 'light' which so many see? . . . These experiences are 'natural' to the soul when separated from the body. . . . In this sense the 'peace' and 'pleasantness' of the out-of-body experience may be considered real and not a deception. Deception enters in, however, the instant one begins to interpret these 'natural' feelings as something 'spiritual'—as though this peace were the true peace of reconciliation with God, and the 'pleasantness' were the true spiritual pleasure of heaven.

(4; 5) Once again, transcendence of gross bodily consciousness is no proof of Spiritual development, or even of a valid Spiritual experience. And recall of past lives, as we have already seen, is a *falsehood* if taken literally. Furthermore, since it remains on the psychic plane alone, the plane of 'metempsychosis', it is in no way Spiritual.

(6) The identification of one's consciousness with a vast array of other types of consciousness is a mark of psychic dissolution, not spiritual development. The human mandate is first to realize one's total dependence upon God, and ultimately to see oneself with God's eyes, thereby becoming identified with the eternal Archetype of Humanity within the Divine Nature, the 'primordial Adam'. Through the eyes of this Divine Humanity, we can contemplate, and gain insight into, other forms of consciousness—organic, psychic and Spiritual; this is the meaning of the myth, found in both in the Koran and the book of *Genesis*, that 'Adam named the animals': he saw into their essential natures, the Names of God which were, and are, their eternal archetypes. But to allow one's consciousness to flow horizontally into other non-human and sub-human forms via *a departure from the human form* is called 'insanity' on the psychic plane and 'damnation' on the Spiritual one. According to the Koran, after Allah created Adam, he commanded the angels to prostrate themselves to him. Every angel obeyed—except Iblis, the Muslim Satan. To open one's psyche to the endless variations of cosmic manifestation without remaining faithful to one's human form, as it exists in the mind of God, is to prostrate oneself to Iblis, and enter 'the darkness outside, where there will be weeping and gnashing of teeth.'

(7) The experience of human/alien dual identity is multiple-personality disorder on the psychic plane, and demonic possession on the Spiritual one. As the vampires of folklore turn their victims into vampires, so the alien kidnappers 'turn their victims into aliens' by 'stealing their souls'—by destroying their identification with their own humanity.

(8) The mark of true higher consciousness is Unity: 'Hear, O Israel, the Lord our God, the Lord is One.' The multidimensional kaleidoscope of the Jinn-world is destructive to Unity unless seen with the eyes of Unity: and only contemplative identification with what is higher than us on the Great Chain of Being—not with dinosaurs, who are lower than us (not to mention being extinct!), or elemental spirits, who, though subtler than us, are not *central* like we are (being something like the sparks or reverberations of the Primordial Adam on the subtle material plane)—can give us those eyes.

The aliens are liars. As Mack himself admits, on p 415, 'I would not say that aliens never resort to deceptions to hide their purposes.' And one of their lies is that the reason they deliberately suppress abductees' memories of the abduction experience is to 'protect' their victims. (The real purpose, in my opinion, is to allow the seed of psychic control to mature undisturbed.) Mack, on the other hand, claims that he has seen no evidence that recall causes any harm. Shouldn't this in itself clue him in to the presence of deception? But of course, as he admits, deception presents no problems for him, and certainly hasn't led him to question the abductors' motives. Such naivete, in any other situation, would destroy the credibility of the person exhibiting it as an objective researcher. It does so here.

Mack's desire to be deceived seems to have completely destroyed his critical faculties, which is why he can make the following absurd and contradictory statement with, presumably, a straight face:

> Through [the aliens'] interaction with the abductees they bring them (and all of us potentially) closer to our spiritual cosmic roots, return us to the divine light or 'Home', a 'place' (really a state of being) where secrets, jealousy, greed, and destructiveness have no purpose. The aliens, on the other hand, long to experience the intense emotionality that comes with our full embodiment. They are fascinated with our sensuality, our warmth, our capacity for eroticism, and deep parental affection, and they seem to respond to openhearted love. They act at times like love-starved children. They delight in watching humans in all sorts of acts of love, which they may even stage as they stand around watching and chattering as the abductees perform them (pp 415–416).

At this point it seems almost unfair to take advantage of Dr Mack's vulnerability by pointing out the dizzying inconsistencies in the above passage—but duty calls: if the aliens come from a 'Home' where secrecy has no purpose, why do they so often keep their abductions secret by wiping all memory of them from the minds of their victims? If destructiveness has no purpose there, why are they so destructive, physically, socially and psychologically, to those unfortunate enough to encounter them? If they delight in our parental affection, why is alienation of affection between parents and children often one of the after-effects of abduction (p 30)? And what does voyeuristically watching if not pornographically staging acts of human sexual intercourse have to do with love?

'The human/alien relationship itself evolves into a powerful bond' says Mack.

> Despite their resentment and terrorization, the abductees may feel deep love toward the alien beings, especially toward the leader figures, which they experience as reciprocated, despite the cold and business-like way the abductions themselves are conducted. The aliens may be perceived as true family, having protected the experiencers from human depredations, disease and loss.

But Mack, in the very same book, has documented how the aliens themselves commonly produce disease and loss! Again we are shown, with nauseating clarity, how denial is only a virtue to the true believer.

The 'powerful bond' some abductees develop with their tormenters is, of course, no proof that the relationship is healthy, because—as we all know—*evil tempts*. C.S. Lewis, in *That Hideous Strength* (pp 268–269), provides this chillingly accurate description of the demonic temptation of his hero by forces of the Antichrist:

> Suddenly, like a thing that leaped to him across infinite distances with the speed of light, desire (salt, black, ravenous, unanswerable desire) took him by the throat. The merest hint will convey to those who have felt it the quality of the emotion which now shook him, like a dog shaking a rat; for others, no description will perhaps avail. Many writers speak of it in terms of lust: a description admirably illuminating from within, totally misleading from without. . . . Everything else that Mark had ever felt—love, ambition, hunger, lust itself—appeared to have been mere milk and water, toys for children, not worth one throb of the nerves. The infinite attraction of this dark thing sucked all other passions into itself: the rest of the world appeared blenched, etiolated, insipid, a world of white marriages and white masses, dishes without salt, gambling for counters. . . . But it was like lust in another respect also. It is idle to point out to the perverted man the horror of his perversion: while the fierce fit is on, the horror is the very spice of his craving. It is ugliness itself that becomes, in the end, the goal of his lechery; beauty has long since grown too weak a stimulant. And so it was here. The creatures . . . breathed death on the human race and on all joy. Not despite but because of this the terrible gravitation sucked and tugged and fascinated him towards them.

Significantly, Mack finds that 'Virtually every abductee receives information about the destruction of the earth's ecosystem and feels compelled to do something about it' (p 413). The aliens sometimes ask the abductees why they are so destructive; for some reason the abductees usually do not think to ask the same question of them. Abductees are very often shown horrendous images of future ecological devastation, and even of the actual splitting and disintegration of the globe, and emerge more 'environmentally sensitive' than they were before.

The 'human/alien hybridization program' is presented by the aliens as a response to the state of the environment. According to Mack,

> Both men and women come to feel despite their anger [at being abducted] that they are taking part—even that they have chosen to participate—in a process that is life-creating and life-giving. Furthermore, for most abductees the hybridization has occurred simultaneously with an enlightenment

imparted by the alien beings that has brought home forcibly to them the failure of the human experiment in its present form. Abduction experiencers come to feel deeply that the death of human beings and countless other species will occur on a vast scale if we continue on our present course and that some sort of new life-form must evolve if the human biological and spiritual essence is to be preserved. *They generally do not question why the maintenance of human life must take such an odd form* (pp 414–415; italics mine).

But of course a hybridization which appears to be happening on the subtle plane is not biological, nor is the essence of the alien/human hybrids really human, any more than that of the humanized ape recently produced in Italy, in which ape and human DNA were combined. In both cases, the result is a direct betrayal of the human essence, not its preservation. (Here we have good evidence, incidentally, that the demonic forces known as 'aliens' may in fact be providing the inspiration for the science of genetic engineering, particular when it is applied to human beings. It's as if the geneticists, virtually all of whom believe that man evolved from ape-like ancestors, are somehow being forced to prove, in actual practice, the doctrines of their traditionalist opponents, who assert — as does the Mayan book the *Popol Vuh*, among other ancient texts and traditions — that apes are really degenerate men.)

And the images of the Earth splitting in two provided by the aliens are curious. No amount of humanly-produced environmental devastation could have this effect. Apart from being a possible image of the 'cracks in the downward direction' in the 'great wall' spoken of by Guénon, one logical conclusion would be that such images are being used to terrorize us to the point where we will sacrifice our sexuality, and our humanity itself, to the alien terrorists who show them to us; the self-castration of members of the Heaven's Gate cult may have the same significance. They are apparently using our legitimate fear of environmental destruction and the end of the world to confront us with a temptation which can be summarized as follows:

Nature is more important than the human form—therefore abandon your humanity, betray the human archetype which is placed directly above you in the Divine Nature, and worship instead what is below you. Do not return sexuality to its archetype in God, via normal human love and reproduction; give your erotic, emotional and reproductive energies instead to the demonic and the infra-human. If you do this you can avoid God's judgement; you can avoid the confrontation with the Divine archetype of your Humanity, and not have to see how you have fallen away from it and betrayed it; you can avoid death, or at least species death; the human form can still live (the lie goes) in sub-human form, as a demonic/human hybrid. If you want to avoid being sent to Hell, simply go to Hell on your own.

They are imposing this temptation by means of the deepest and most intense of human emotions: life-creating sexual passion, and the fear of universal death. As any good brainwasher knows, terror is one of the two most effective tools for breaking the subject's will; *relief* is the other. And when terror is intense, sometimes sexual desire is the only refuge from it. Knowing this, the aliens produce the greatest fear of which they are capable, and then offer sexual desire as a way out. By this method they appropriate the sexuality of their victims, and gain a degree of power over them which is extremely hard to counter, since if an attempt to break free is proposed, the victim fears that the terror will return.

'The aliens stress the evolutionary aspect of the species-joining process, the repopulation of the Earth subsequent to a total environmental collapse' says Mack (p 417). But then what becomes of the 'environmental sensitivity' the aliens reportedly produce in their victims? What good is environmental sensitivity in a dead world? And how can one love the earth, and wish to preserve it, if one's 'love of the earth' is the product of abduction, terror, and violation of one's human integrity? What experience could be better designed to make us *hate* the earth, and despair of doing anything to save it? What better way to make environmentalism repellent to religious believers than to associate it in their minds with demonic activity? And what better way to subvert environmentalism itself than to set up a false opposition between humanity and nature by claiming that the only way organic life — including human life — can survive is if we abandon our humanity? If the 'human experiment' has failed in its present form, if total environmental collapse is inevitable, then who's going to be motivated to preserve the natural world? And how can action to preserve the natural world be trusted to be environmentally healthy if carried on by someone with such a negative system of beliefs? Do we hire someone to reorganize our business who tells us up front that he's convinced we're going to fail? In view of this mass of deception designed to misrepresent their motives, I can only conclude that the real aim of the 'aliens' is to use our fear of the end of the world, and our guilt for destroying it, as an opportunity to lure us to our damnation.

So this is the triple demonic temptation of the latter days: (1) To worship the natural world in itself rather than worshipping God by means of it; (2) To divert our sexual powers in a sub-human direction; and (3), To directly betray the human form. And the three are intimately related, since to divert our powers of reproduction and the profound human emotions which are a natural aspect of them in a non-human direction is perhaps the most effective way of betraying our humanity; and to betray our humanity is the most effective way of destroying the earth, since our abdication of the God-given responsibility to act as His vicegerent in the material world is at the basis of our worship of sub-human ideologies, including materialism; and materialism is the worldview out of which have sprung the sub-human technologies which are destroying our planet. 'Where man is not, nature is barren,' said William Blake—to which the aliens reply, in effect, 'If dehumanization is destroying the earth, maybe *total* dehumanization can save it,' while simultaneously diverting our attention, for a moment at least, from the fact that they have already told us that it *can't* be saved: subliminal contradiction in its most terminal form. Fortunately, from all indications the alien 'visitors' are not to be believed. They are not reliable teachers—to say the very least. And sometimes the aliens themselves admit this. In an account by Jacques Vallee (*The Invisible College*, pp 17, 21), humanoid aliens told an abductee that they contact people by chance, that they 'want to puzzle people,' and ordered him 'not to speak wisely about this night.' If Dr Mack had been the abductee, I'm sure he would have been only too glad to comply with this directive.

✳ A Counterfeit Second Coming

THE myth of the UFO holds great power over the contemporary mind; it is a true sign of our times. This is due to the fact that, for all its sinister implications, there is an archetypal reality behind it. To take one example, even though UFOs appear in many different shapes—Jacques Vallee in *UFO Chronicles of the Soviet Union* [Ballantine, 1992] says that Russian UFOlogists are more willing than their Western counterparts to admit that the phenomenon is 'polyvalent'—the shining disk known as the 'flying saucer' has exercised more influence on the popular imagination than any other. Why is this?

Carl Jung, in *Flying Saucers: A Modern Myth of Things Seen in the Sky* (1959), saw in their circular shape a symbol of his 'Self Archetype', and thought that the phenomenon represented a collective longing for the Second Coming of Christ—a longing which, in my opinion, is being co-opted by the Jinn who serve Antichrist, and diverted, through collective fascination, toward a satanic counterfeit of the *parousia*.

Many UFOlogists, Erich van Däniken among them, have interpreted the vision of God's Throne in the first chapter of *Ezekiel* as a UFO manifestation, based on the brightness and swiftness of the 'four living creatures' (*hayoth*) who supported the Throne, and on the association of the creatures with 'wheels' and 'rings full of eyes' and 'a wheel within a wheel'. But Ezekiel's vision was not a sensual vision of meaningless and deliberately paradoxical aerial acrobatics produced by the Jinn, but an *intellectual* vision of God's creative power manifesting in, and as, the universe. If the Throne appeared to his physical eyes, it was only because the *meaning* of the Throne had already dawned upon his heart.

Leo Schaya, in *The Universal Meaning of the Kabbalah* (p 84), gives the symbolic meaning of Ezekiel's vision, which ought to be sufficient to allow anyone with the slightest degree of spiritual intuition see the vast difference in *level* between the UFO phenomenon and a true *theophany*:

> The 'throne', in its fullness, is the first and spiritual crystallization of all creatural possibilities before they are set in motion in the midst of the cosmos. When the 'throne' assumes its dynamic aspect and cosmic manifestation begins to move, it is called the divine 'chariot' (*merkabah*); then the four *hayoth*, or peripheral axes of creation, spring from the 'throne' become 'chariot', like 'lightning darting in all directions,' measuring all the dimensions and all the planes of manifested existence. Under the aspect of 'torches', 'brilliant lights' or spiritual 'flashes' of lightning, the *hayoth* are also called *kerubim* [cherubim], 'those who are close' to the living God, that is to say who emanate directly from God in action. While the hayothic axes are traveling in all the directions of the cosmos, out of them come 'wheels' (*ofanim*), or angelic powers, which play a part in actualizing the spherical forms and cyclical movements of the created; their spiral vibrations—as it were 'a wheel within another wheel'—are called 'whirlwinds' (*galgalim*).

As the Antichrist counterfeits Christ, so the UFOs counterfeit God's Throne, which in Muslim as well as Hebrew metaphysics represents the apex of the created order, and in Christian terms appears as the 'Throne of the Lamb' at the center of the Heavenly Jerusalem.

The aliens are here to mimic Spiritual realities on the psycho-physical level, and so prepare the way for Antichrist. As St Symeon the New Theologian says in the *Philokalia* (p 11),

> Men will not understand that the miracles of Antichrist have no good, rational purpose, no definite meaning, that they are foreign to truth, filled with lies, that they are a monstrous, malicious, meaningless play-acting, which increases in order to astonish, to reduce to perplexity and oblivion, to deceive, to seduce, to attract by the fascination of a pompous, empty, stupid effect.

As our taste in art, architecture, social forms and human relationships is jaded in these latter days, so is our taste in miracles. According to Seraphim Rose,

> Serious scientists in [the former] Soviet Union . . . speculate that Jesus Christ may have been a 'cosmonaut', and that 'we today may be on the threshold of a 'second coming' of intelligent beings from outer space.' (Sheila Ostrander and Lynn Schroeder, *Psychic Discoveries Behind the Iron Curtain*, Bantam Books, 1977. pp 98–99). . . . Perhaps never since the beginning of the Christian era have demons appeared so openly and extensively as today. The 'visitors from outer space' theory is but one of the many pretexts they are using to gain acceptance for the idea that 'higher beings' are now to take charge of the destiny of mankind . . . the 'message' of the UFOs is: prepare for Antichrist; the 'savior' of the apostate world is coming to rule it. Perhaps he himself will come in the air, in order to complete his impersonation of Christ (Matt. 24:30; Acts 1:2); perhaps only the 'visitor from outer space' will land publicly in order to offer 'cosmic' worship of their master; perhaps the 'fire from heaven' (Rev. 13:13) will be only part of the great demonic spectacles of the last times. At any rate, the message for contemporary mankind is: expect deliverance, not from the Christian revelation and faith in an unseen God, but from vehicles in the sky.
>
> ⁓ ORTHODOXY AND THE RELIGION OF THE FUTURE, pp 102, 140–42

To avoid being drawn into the camp of the Antichrist, we must overcome, with God's help, the triple temptation presented above. We must *remember* that the forms of nature are not to be worshipped, but rather that we are called upon to worship the invisible and transcendent God by means of them, recognizing them as symbolic manifestations of eternal realities hidden within the Divine Nature. As St Paul says, 'For the invisible things of Him from the creation of the world are clearly seen, being understood by the things that are made, even His eternal power and Godhead' (Rom. 1:20).

We must *remember* the sacredness and symbolic depth of our sexual powers and natures. In the words of James Cutsinger:

> [What C. S. Lewis calls] this 'real polarity' [of gender] is to be found, not only as Lewis suggests in creatures, however superhuman, but all the way up to the Divine Reality itself . . . which is the ultimate Source of everything else, and which for that reason is the source and paradigm of all distinctions. In its absoluteness and transcendence, the Divine is the archetype for everything masculine, while its infinity and capacity for immanence are displayed at every level of the feminine . . . the polar qualities revealed to us as sex are

actually and objectively on every plane of the ontological hierarchy. . . . As Seyyed Hossein Nasr has written, 'The difference between the two sexes cannot be only biological and physical, because in the traditional perspective the corporeal level of existence has its principle in the subtle state, the subtle in the spiritual, and the spiritual in the Divine Being itself.

⌒ 'Femininity, Hierarchy and God' in RELIGION OF THE HEART, ed. Seyyed Hossein Nasr and William Stoddart, p115

Gender is in fact so integral to our humanity that the way in which we live it out, or sublimate it, or dedicate it, is one of the things which determines whether or not we remain united with our human archetype. To let our sexuality fall into the power of non-human forces is to depart from the human form. To dedicate it to a fully human love, or directly to God as in the monastic vocation, is to worship God by means of the human form.

Lastly, we must *remember* what the human form really is. Allah, in the *ahadith qudsi* (the traditions in which God Himself speaks), declares that 'Heaven and earth cannot contain Me, but the heart of my believing slave can contain Me.' And in the words of St Gregory of Nyssa:

> Know to what extent the Creator has honoured you above all the rest of creation. The sky is not an image of God, nor is the moon, nor the sun, nor the beauty of the stars, nor anything of what can be seen in creation. You alone have been made the image of the Reality that transcends all understanding, the likeness of imperishable beauty, the imprint of true divinity, the recipient of beatitude, the seal of true light. When you turn to him you become that which he is himself. . . . There is nothing so great among beings that it can be compared with your greatness. God is able to measure the whole heaven with his span. *The earth and the sea are enclosed in the hollow of his hand. And although he is so great and holds all creation in the palm of his hand, you are able to hold him,* he dwells in you and moves within you without constraint. . . .'
> ⌒ SECOND HOMILY ON THE SONG OF SONGS (PG 44, 765); italics mine

According to esoteric teachings from many traditions, clearly reflected in the above passages, humanity is the 'stem' which connects the earth to God. God sustains the earth and all that is in it only through man—a doctrine which is proved negatively by the fact that man alone has the power to destroy the earth: when we no longer take God as our center, and so depart from our own humanity, the earth begins to die. It is this truth, above all, that the aliens are doing all in their power to prevent us from remembering.

Nothing happens that is not God's will. Nonetheless, according to Sufi metaphysician Ibn al-'Arabi, even though all that happens is willed by

God—because if it were possible for something contrary to His will to occur, He would not be God—not everything is part of God's *wish*. This is why He sends us sacred laws, which let us know what to do and what to avoid if we want to come nearer to Him. Evil is not good in itself; it is contrary to God's wish. But he wills it—or, in Christian terms, allows it—as part of a greater good. We don't curse the worms that devour a dead body; and from a certain perspective the 'aliens' are nothing but worms, whose job is to devour whatever is already dead in the human collective psyche. But that doesn't mean that it is a good idea to spend your time socializing with dead bodies; if you do, you will become ill. The experience of disease is a natural evil, and abduction, torture and rape are moral ones—which, to the victim, are nonetheless morally indistinguishable from natural disasters. Yet such evils, if we encounter them with a deep enough faith in our Creator, can sharpen our spiritual vigilance, and ultimately awaken us to a deeper Mercy. Just as lies testify to the Truth—not because they are true, but because the ability to recognize their falsehood is a sign of Truth's presence—so misfortune and catastrophe testify to Mercy. Even the worst sufferings can be known, God willing, as part of a Mercy which is so great that even this—even war, even cancer, even alien abduction—is swallowed up in it. As it says in the *ahadith qudsi*, 'My Mercy precedeth my Wrath'; and in the Koran: 'There is no refuge from God but in Him.'

8

Vigilance at the Eleventh Hour: A Refutation of *The Only Tradition*

THIS chapter is an example of intellectual warfare within the context of the latter days. It is characteristic of the end of the cycle that both conflicts and alliances will take ambiguous and self-contradictory forms, and that every opposition not based on the ultimate polarity which is also the ultimate decision—that between the 'sheep' and the 'goats'—will tend to change into its opposite with stunning rapidity. For the purposes of this battle I choose as my weapon the doctrines of the Traditionalist School, based on traditional metaphysics and esoterism, taking them as being closer to Absolute Truth than the doctrines presented by William W. Quinn Jr., based on academic sociology, comparative religion according to Mircea Eliade, and the teachings of the Theosophical Society, which are relatively closer to the 'absolute' falsehood of al-Dajjal, the Muslim name for Antichrist, that inevitable Shadow of Truth which is always there in potentiality, but which fully 'constellates' only at the end of the aeon. This does not mean that Mr Quinn may not emerge as a champion of truth tomorrow, or that he is not closer than I am to God at this moment, or that Traditionalist doctrines themselves may not, under certain circumstances, also prove useful to al-Dajjal. When battle is joined, however, such questions must be left for later. The doctrines of the Traditionalist School and the principles of traditional metaphysics are being seriously misrepresented; it is therefore time to draw, in Blake's words, 'the hard and wirey line of rectitude and certainty.'

The Only Tradition, by William W. Quinn, Jr. (SUNY, 1997) was to have been reviewed by Huston Smith and myself in a collaborative effort, until

Dr Smith got wind of what was in it, and decided his energies were better directed elsewhere. Quinn's book illuminated for me, like a flash of lightning on a dark night, whole areas of the Traditionalist landscape, its strengths, its weaknesses, and the specific points of potential enemy breakthrough where reinforcements are required without delay.

William Quinn is a member of the Theosophical Society, founded by Helena Petrovna Blavatsky; during the early '70s he was the publisher of one of their journals, *The American Theosophist*. The Society remains among the toughest threads running under the fabric of the New Age. Its American branch has shown some few signs of an interest in more traditional metaphysics, having published books by Frithjof Schuon, Huston Smith, and myself. And I can thank them for my first introduction to the concept of a Hierarchy of Being, and note that my editor at the Theosophical Publishing House was a student of the Vajrayana—real esoteric Buddhism, that is, not Madame Blavatsky's spurious concoction of the same name.

But, not surprisingly, the Society shows no desire to repudiate the doctrines of its founders, and therein lies the rub. Over the course of time they have spawned such spinoffs as Elizabeth Claire Prophet, whose group bought guns and holed up in Montana some years ago on a prediction by her of the end of the world (which, in my opinion, cannot be driven off with guns), and Benjamin Creme, who, in the name of his protegé the 'world-teacher Maitreya' is busy preparing the ground for the Second Coming of 'Christ' (or, as is more likely, Antichrist), much as Annie Besant and her colleagues did with Jeddu Krishnamurti in earlier years, though Krishnamurti was honorable enough to refuse to play the false Messiah according to the Society's scenario. And their name and/or mythology continue to turn up in many unexpected places. Though their books aren't very popular in New Age circles, their staying-power gives them an influence all out of proportion to their popularity, or the lack of it. A review of *The Hidden Dangers of the Rainbow* in *Gnosis* magazine some years ago scorned the evangelical Christian author, Constance Cumby, for being paranoid enough to believe that the Theosophical Society was the driving force behind the New Age movement. However, no less an author than Jocelyn Godwin (who I always considered a kind of Traditionalist, till I took a closer look at his work), in *The Theosophical Enlightenment* (SUNY 1994, p 379), states that 'The theosophists have provided almost all the underpinnings of the "New Age" movement, *their exoteric reflection. . . .*' [italics mine]; he is declaring explicitly here that the Theosophical Society is not simply the historical origin, but the *ongoing 'esoteric' center* of the New Age. Of course neither Constance Cumby nor Godwin are necessarily right about the Society; the former may be speaking out of fear and the latter out of wishful thinking, as well as in an attempt to launch a self-fulfilling prophecy. And it's clear that other groups—the Scientologists, for example, or the Unification Church—are competing with the Society for the same prize. Still, this is how the Society has tended to see itself: as a potential if not actual 'steering committee' for the New Age, the effective center of what René Guénon termed 'anti-traditional action' leading ultimately to 'counter-initiation'. As Guénon said in *The Reign of Quantity*, pp 317–318,

> Centers are likely to be established to which the organizations pertaining to the 'counter-initiation' will be attached ... there need be no cause for surprise if these centers themselves, and not merely some of the organizations that are more or less directly subordinated to them, are found to be engaged in struggles with one another, for the domain in which they are placed is nearest of all to the domain of 'chaotic' dissolution.

Godwin himself seems in many ways identified with the Society's goals. On the same page as the above quote, the last page of the book, he says: 'No previous civilization has ever had the interest, the resources, or the *inner need* ... to hold the entire world in its intellectual embrace; to take the terrifying step of *renouncing, even blaspheming its own religious tradition* in the quest for *a more open and rationalistic view*; to publish freely those secrets that were formerly under the seal of initiation; and, in short, to plunge humanity into the *spiritual alembic* in which we find ourselves today' [all italics mine]. So the destruction of Christianity—and all other traditional religions as well, of course, if they get in the way—is an 'inner need' of a society in an 'alembic' undergoing an alchemical transmutation toward a 'more open and rationalistic view'; this liquidation of the Christian tradition, conceived of as a spiritual necessity, was one of Blavatsky's life-long goals. The step is 'terrifying', yet necessary, and even heroic: in other words, it is *Promethean*. Nietzsche himself couldn't have said it better.

The succeeding paragraphs are my (unedited) review of *The Only Tradition* for *Gnosis* magazine, which can serve as an introduction to the longer review, or refutation, which follows:

✻

The 'Traditionalist' school—René Guénon, Ananda Coomaraswamy, Titus Burckhardt, Marco Pallis, Frithjof Schuon, Martin Lings, Seyyed Hossein Nasr, et. al.—is slowly but surely becoming better known, among both academics and the 'general metaphysical public'. In *The Only Tradition*, William Quinn tries to situate the school in a wider context by showing its affinities with Mircea Eliade, H. P. Blavatsky and others; both his presentation of the doctrines and history of the Traditionalists and his study of 'primitive' and 'developed' traditional cultures are interesting. But Eliade was no Traditionalist; in *No Souvenirs* he characterized them as composers of artistic 'useful myths' without 'scientific' (objective) validity. And when Quinn tries to prove that Blavatsky taught the same doctrine as Coomaraswamy and Guénon, he stumbles badly. He treats Guénon's book attacking the Theosophical Society (*Theosophiy: History of a Pseudo-Religion*) as an unaccountable lapse, though admitting Eliade praised it, and attributes Traditionalists' disagreement with Blavatsky to their ignorance of *The Secret Doctrine*. Aware that Coomaraswamy and Guénon denied human *physical* reincarnation in favor of 'transmigration' to higher (or lower) planes, he claims that

> The central point of misunderstanding concerns the perception of the Traditional writers that the . . . divine element together with surviving 'personality' (an aggregation of emotions, mind and personal memories) was thought by Theosophists to incarnate in successive corporeal forms—a notion that Blavatsky did not promulgate.

But she did:

> The atoms best impregnated with the life-principle (an independent, eternal, conscious factor) are . . . drawn once more together and become the animating principle of the new body in every new incarnation . . . as the individual Soul is ever the same, so are the atoms of the lower principles (body, its astral life-double, etc.) drawn . . . always to the same individuality in a series of various bodies.
> ⁓THE SECRET DOCTRINE [hereafter, SD] II, 671–72

Quinn laments that 'for some unknown reason' Theosophists are thought to favor Darwinism, which is anathema to Traditionalists. But Blavatsky sometimes did: 'The Brahman-pundits and the Tannaim . . . speculated on the creation of the world in a quite Darwinian way' (*SD* I, 202); 'The day *may* come . . . when the 'natural selection' as taught by Darwin . . . will form only a *part* . . . of our Eastern doctrine of Evolution' (*SD* I, 600). That she denied natural selection elsewhere in *The Secret Doctrine* only shows how confused she was. At least the Traditionalists have produced a serious body of work suitable for adults—but to learn that all prayer is black magic, or that certain primitive tribes are the product of human interbreeding with animals, or that Christ's cross is a penis, read Blavatsky.

HPB saw manifestation, cosmic and historical, as descending from higher planes (here Traditionalism agrees), 'bottoming out' (right around now), and then automatically evolving back to its Origin. The Traditionalists deny any re-ascent except that of individual consciousness; manifestation will dissolve, and a new Divine descent will inaugurate a new cycle. Quinn, following Blavatsky, substitutes evolution for apocalypse, and ignores revelation.

He accepts gnosis; possibly he believes it lets us investigate God experimentally. But God forbid that He know *us* better than we know Him, or actively intervene in human affairs, or *require* something of us. Blavatsky, too, hated revealed religion, something Quinn tries to deny. Consequently, after a telling 'Traditionalist' critique of modernity, he suddenly embraces what he has just denounced, foreseeing a post-cataclysmic 'Golden Age' repopulated by government 'breeding groups', where 'planetization' has destroyed all revealed religions in the name of a 'one world culture', a strictly hierarchical society ruled by 'scientist/metaphysicists'. But that he should envision the ideology of this hellish world (acceptable, because inevitable) as including doctrines of the Traditionalists, who admit no access to spiritual truth apart from revelation, is a travesty, especially since Traditionalists view the Golden Age of any cycle as egalitarian because 'above caste'. (Cf. Martin Lings, *Ancient Beliefs and Modern Superstitions*, p 49; see also Guénon, *The Reign of Quantity*, p 326, on 'counter-hierarchy'.) Quinn admits that his attempt to conflate Coomaraswamy, Guénon and Blavatsky will lead Traditionalists to dismiss it as 'meritless and confused.' That's not surprising, particularly in view of Madame Blavatsky's own assessment of herself as someone not worth our trust. I quote from *The Spiritualists* by Ruth Brandon, Alfred A. Knopf, 1983, p 13:

What is one to do when, in order to rule men, you must deceive them, when, in order to catch them and make them pursue whatever it may be, it is necessary to promise and show them toys? Suppose my books and *The Theosophist* were a thousand times more interesting and serious, do you think that I would have anywhere to live and any degree of success unless behind all this there stood 'phenomena'? I should have achieved absolutely nothing, and would long ago have pegged out from hunger.

✳

On p 25 of *The Only Tradition*, Quinn confuses the traditional equation of being and knowing with the nihilistic New Age doctrine that reality is created, not by objective knowledge, but simply by belief. After quoting Coomaraswamy to the effect that 'to be and to know are the same . . . recollection is life itself, and forgetfulness a lethal draught,' he comments, 'We cannot separate, in other words, what we are and what we know, any more than we can separate what we are and what we believe, since our beliefs help define our being and vice versa.' But 'recollection' here means recollection of what we *really* are, not what we think we are; recollection of what we already are in potential is the essence of 'self-actualization', of 'becoming what we are'. Beliefs do not necessarily place us in relationship to knowledge; they do so *only if they are true*. To take belief as synonymous with knowledge is to deny objectivity, and therefore worship forgetfulness. The function of revelation, along with its traditional expression, is to provide us with dogmatic beliefs which are sufficiently wise to prevent us, on the moral level, from going seriously astray, and have sufficient objective truth, on the intellectual level, to lead us on to knowledge and certainty. 'I believe that I might understand' only works within the context of revealed tradition; in other contexts—those of political propaganda or criminal fraud, for example—belief is obviously not designed to serve understanding; quite the contrary. Beliefs that are not true 'define our being' only in the sense that they distort it, while our being defines our beliefs in two different senses: insofar as our being is, in its deepest essence, Being itself, it generates all possible beliefs, according to the action of the Divine Infinity; from this perspective, the perspective of *maya-in-divinis*, 'everything possible to be believed,' in Blake's words, 'is an image of truth.' On the other hand, from the point-of-view of our human individuality, where some beliefs are 'true' because they lead to Truth, and others 'false' because they lead to perdition, our being defines our beliefs only in the sense that a darkened intellect produces only error, and a concupiscent will seeks out error in order to justify its actions.

One of Quinn's main purposes is to reconcile, somehow, the Theosophy of H. P. Blavatsky with the Traditionalism of René Guénon, Ananda Coomaraswamy, and Frithjof Schuon. But since they taught radically different doctrines, and given that the Traditionalists consider the Theosophists not only wrong but actively subversive of the truth, why would he want to? To answer this question, we need to take a look at his attempt to hide Blavatsky's life-long subversion of Tradition and hatred of revealed religion.

On p118, Quinn describes the 'first principles' he is about to present as 'a distillation . . . of all those expressed in the perspectives of Coomaraswamy, Guénon, Blavatsky. . . .' One could do the same thing with, for example, the views of Marx, Nietzsche, and Oscar Wilde, and come up with many parallels, but the exercise would be meaningless without an analysis of their differences. And given that the divergences and even violent opposition between Blavatsky and the Traditionalists are so many and so deep that Guénon wrote an entire book on them—a thankless task that I'm glad will not fall to me—a few examples will not be out of place. On p119, Quinn quotes Coomaraswamy as speaking of 'the significance of sacrifice' as one of the elements which Christianity holds in common with 'every other dialect of the primordial tradition,' having first let us know that his catalogue of principles will be a little different than Coomaraswamy's. This is not surprising, since Blavatsky (SD I, p416) asserts the following: 'Every 'sacrifice' or prayer to God is *no better than an act of black magic.*'

On p121, Quinn deals with the traditional distinction between the Formless Absolute and the personal God—the 'God' and 'Godhead' of Meister Eckhart, the *Saguna Brahman* and *Nirguna Brahman* of the Vedanta—and quotes the quintessential words of Frithjof Schuon on the subject: 'It is true that God as creator, revealer and savior is not to be identified with the Absolute as such; it is equally true that God as such, in the full depth of His Reality, is not to be reduced to his creative function.' Godhead manifests as God, but the essence of God is Godhead; God and His Essence are 'not two'. Quinn pairs this quote with one from Blavatsky: 'Parabrahman [i.e. *Nirguna Brahman*] is not "God" because it is not *a* God.' But neither Schuon, nor Eckhart, nor the Vedanta *deny* the Personal God (nor did Guénon, though perhaps he might be faulted for under-emphasizing Him, except for the fact that in concentrating on the Formless Absolute he was fulfilling his specific function). Blavatsky, however, does deny Him. In *SD II*, p194, she says: 'Nevertheless, whatever the allegory [of the separation of the sexes in *Genesis*] may mean, even its exoteric meaning necessitates a *divine* Builder of man—a 'Progenitor'. Do we then believe in such 'supernatural' beings? We say, No. Occultism has never believed in anything, whether animate or inanimate, outside nature.' And in *SD II*, p475: 'Our present quarrel is exclusively with theology. The church enforces belief in a personal God and a personal devil, while occultism shows the fallacy of such a belief.'

Finally, Quinn tries to hide Blavatsky's anti-Christian sentiments by extracting from Guénon's *Theosophy: History of a Pseudo-Relgion* a quote from Theosophist Annie Besant, stating the necessity 'above all to combat Rome and its priests, to fight wheresoever against Christianity and chase God from the skies,' and then revealing that she made this statement ten years before meeting Mme Blavatsky—as if HPB didn't hold similar views until the day she died, as the above two quotes clearly indicate: to quarrel with theology for the purpose of denying the existence of a personal God is both to 'combat Rome' and 'to chase God from the skies.' And anyone with either the stamina or the foolhardiness to read through the entire *Secret Doctrine* will find many more statements to the same purpose. For example, doctrines such as 'the Logos and Satan are one' (*SD II*, p 515) are precisely anti-Christian, since, for Christianity, the Logos is Christ; and the Theosophical denial of God (how ironic this phrase is, since 'theosophy' means literally 'God's wisdom') seems to emanate from the Society's 'entities' as well. According to Jocelyn Godwin (*The Theosophical Enlightenment*, p 329), 'Koot Hoomi', in one of the 'mahatma letters' addressed to A. O. Hume, made the following declaration: 'We deny God both as philosophers and Buddhists. We know there are planetary and other spiritual lives, and we know there is in our system no such thing as God, either personal or impersonal.' But of course Mr Hoomi is in error here, since the Buddhists have a number of names for the Absolute Principle: Nirvana; the Dharmakaya; the Adi-Buddha; Shunyata; the Buddha Nature; the Clear Light of the Void.

Godwin, in *The Theosophical Enlightenment*, characterizes Blavatsky's attitude in these terms (p 292): 'An absurd theology, supporting a corrupt priesthood and an unintelligent bibliolatry; that was what Blavatsky saw, and loathed, when she surveyed the history of Christianity.' He speaks of the 'Brothers of Luxor' (Guénon's *bête noir*), an organization with which Blavatsky was associated in her earlier years, as including in its program, unbeknownst to the rank-and-file though probably not to Blavatsky, 'the abolition of Christianity in favor of a freethinking humanism,' and on p 305 describes her *Isis Unveiled* in glowing terms as 'a clarion summons to humanity to awaken from the charmed sleep into which it had been plunged by the deceptions of Christianity and science.' And as if all this evidence were not sufficient, I can cap it with Quinn's own words. When I phoned him at his law office in Phoenix, Arizona, and confronted him with Blavatsky's stated aim of destroying Christianity, his answer was: 'Not Christianity *per se; only the Churches.*' This, of course, is like saying: 'I don't want to murder you; I only want to murder *your body.*' Nor were Blavatsky's subversive attentions directed toward Christianity alone. For her to call her stew of occultist doctrines 'esoteric Buddhism' was to subvert Buddhism; for her to reduce Judaism to phallicism and star-worship was to subvert Judaism; and for her to channel spurious 'mahatmas' was to subvert Hinduism (or Buddhism again, insofar as they were portrayed as 'Tibetans'), a job the Society tried its best to complete after her death—and usher in the reign of Antichrist in the process—by putting forth Krishnamurti as both 'Avatara' and 'Messiah'. In light of all this, the following passage by René Guénon, from *The Reign of Quantity*, pp 293–294, seems no more than a matter-of-fact description of the state of things:

> the 'counter-initiation' works with a view to introducing its agents into 'pseudo-initiatic' organizations, using the agents to 'inspire' the organizations, unperceived by the ordinary members and usually also by the ostensible heads . . . such agents are in fact introduced in a similar way and wherever possible into all the more exterior 'movements' of the contemporary world, political or otherwise, and even . . . into authentically initiatic or religious organizations, but only when their traditional spirit is so weakened that they can no longer resist so insidious a penetration . . . the last-named case . . . is the most direct application possible of dissolutionary activity.

In chapters 6 and 7, Quinn makes a muddle out of the terms 'tradition', 'philosophia perennis', and 'theosophy', deftly employing various incomplete academic definitions of 'tradition' and 'philosophia perennis' to obscure the fact that, according to the Traditionalist (or Perennialist) School, they are essentially two names for the same thing, though not without a difference in nuance having to do with the distinction-without-opposition between primordial and historical revelation. At the same time he relativizes the Traditionalist/Perennialist concept of 'Tradition', which is of course justified from a sociological standpoint, but not if this relativization is used to deny that by 'Tradition' the Traditionalists mean 'access to the Absolute via It's own Self-revelation, a revelation operating through time while in essence transcending time.' As for 'theosophy', he begins by making too wide a distinction between it and Tradition/philosophia perennis, to which it is integral, if not actually the same thing called by a different name. Next, after admitting two definitions for theosophy, one generic and traditional, the other denoting the Theosophical Society, he sets up a straw man (one of many throughout the book) by pretending to be shocked (p95) that 'even Seyyed Hossein Nasr' uses the term theosophy to denote 'traditional philosophy' (*hikmah*)—as if 'theosophy' here meant 'the Theosophical Society' which the Traditionalists hate, and not, as is obvious from the context, theosophy in the traditional and generic sense. He quotes Prof J.J. Poortman of the University of Leiden (p97) as identifying the 'older historic theosophy'—which

396 ✳ THE SYSTEM OF ANTICHRIST

Poortman expressly distinguishes from 'modern theosophy'—with such towering figures as Boehme and Plotinus, then plays upon the terms 'older' and 'modern' to portray Poortman's distinction as purely 'temporal'. Finally, since 'modern' comes after 'older', he ends by claiming Blavatsky's Theosophical Society as the direct historical successor to theosophy in the traditional and generic sense, making use of Poortman's text while directly contradicting the distinction Poortman has just made. This slight-of-hand may be useful when arguing a case at law, but it is unworthy of a 'theosopher'— unless, of course, we intend to employ this term in its modern sense! *The Secret Doctrine* is full of it.

So why is Quinn working so hard to reconcile with Tradition Blavatsky's virulent hatred of Tradition? Why can't he either simply drop her, or oppose Tradition openly in her name? The answer, in one word, is 'subversion', in Guénon's sense from *The Reign of Quantity and the Signs of the Times*. It may or may not be true that a cadre of anti-traditional occultists who identify with modern Theosophy are now deliberately moving to subvert the doctrines of the Traditionalist School, particularly in view of Guénon's 1921 attack on Theosophy in *Theosophy: History of a Pseudo-Religion*, which Quinn tries to counter in *The Only Tradition*. Perhaps, in view of certain vulnerabilities presently appearing in the Traditionalism, not the least of which is increasing public exposure, they consider that it's now payback time. As Guénon points out in *The Reign of Quantity*, pp 229–230,

> it is of first importance not to forget that, since all effective action necessarily presupposes agents, anti-traditional action is like all other kinds of action, so that it cannot be a sort of spontaneous or 'fortuitous' production, and, since it is exercised particularly in the human domain, it must of necessity involve the intervention of human agents ... initiation ... is that which really incarnates the 'spirit' of a tradition ... therefore initiation is the thing that must be opposed ... by anti-traditional action ... the term 'counter-initiation' is therefore the best for describing that to which the human agents through whom the anti-traditional action is accomplished belong.

But even though actual human groups, known and unknown, may or may not moving against the Traditionalist School in a more-or-less deliberate way, we don't need to explain every specific attack as planned and carried out by this or that specific organization. The real 'agenda' is emanating from a subtler level of things, the outer expression of which is simply the *zeitgeist*. An anti-traditional *zeitgeist*, however, is partly a strategic opportunity for, and partly the actual result of, the action of subversive spiritual forces. And most of the servants of such forces, though certainly not all, are unconscious of whom they serve. In St Paul's famous words, 'we wrestle not against flesh and blood, but against principalities, against powers, against the rulers of the darkness of this world, against spiritual wickedness in high places' (Eph. 6:12). We need to understand that Traditionalism will necessarily be under attack in a world like this, and that a great deal of this attack will be on the field of 'unseen warfare'.

Ironically, because Quinn dismisses revealed religion, in line with Blavatsky's denial of a personal God, and concentrates on intellection instead, he fails to grasp what intellection is. On p 79 he quotes Manzanedo's definition of 'the philosophia perennis' as 'the collation of truths of a natural order commonly acknowledged by man,' and claims that 'this succinct and fairly representative description would probably have few critics . . . in the sphere of Traditional philosophy.' But if Manzanedo means by 'natural order' what this phrase has meant within the context of the Abrahamic religions (rather than, say, that of certain strands of Greek philosophy) —i.e., the external, sense-based level of reality available to the 'once born', the 'natural man' — then it in no way corresponds to intellection, and would therefore not be acceptable to 'Traditional philosophy'. On p 85, Quinn correctly states that 'modern philosophy, and even its metaphysical branch, is essentially secular: accordingly, it perceives the philosophia perennis as primarily categorical and secular.' But on p 84, he has just finished saying:

> The most useful analogical symbol . . . to illustrate the difference between the conceptions of modern philosophy and the Traditional perspective . . . is Jacob's Ladder. . . . The lower rungs represent the rudimentary and relatively few principles of consensus upon which the modern philosophers would unite; the uppermost rungs represent the relatively developed and more numerous principles which the Traditional writers tend to concentrate in their discussions of the philosophia perennis. Irrespective of methodology and etiology which do indicate genuine dissimilarities between the two conceptions, one must not lose sight of the fact that the ladder itself is one, that its 'top' depends upon its 'base'.

But if the modern lower rungs of the ladder and Traditional upper rungs have a different etiology, then, in simple logic, the second cannot be derived from the first. And it is clearly untrue that the Traditional principles of the philosophia perennis depend upon 'the relatively few principles of consensus upon which the modern philosophers would unite,' since modern philosophy unanimously denies traditional principles. They depend, rather, upon

Intellection, upon the direct perception of Truth via the Intellect, which is a ray of that Truth. And since Intellection, either as inspired by the great historical revelations, or as given by the primordial Self-revelation of God which is the cosmos, is the source of all Truth, the principles held in common by modern philosophers depend upon Intellection, not it upon them, since error cannot exist without a truth to pervert—though, unfortunately, they can no longer see this, given that their conceptions are by and large self-contradictory and filled with intellectual darkness.

On p294, Quinn falsely presents, as Traditional, the mechanistic theory of cosmic and historical cycles of William I. Thompson:

> as entropy reaches its limit in chaos, there is a reversal in the cycle, a cosmic form is generated out of the only ground large enough for it, namely chaos. Chaos creates the fertile decay in which the seeds left over from the previous age of gods spring to life. . . .

But no one who believes that chaos can be the creator of form or order understands Intellection—or, for that matter, believes in God. The theory of creative chaos is the basis of the theory of 'instructional' (rather than 'descriptive') evolution, in E. F. Schumacher's terms, the idea that the lesser can give rise to the greater; it also justifies various forms of anarchistic nihilism, which operate on the belief that if a clean sweep is made of the old values and social forms, something shiny and new will automatically take their place. But the truth is, entropy never reverses 'on its own'; as a description of the essential nature of all material manifestation, the Second Law of Thermodynamics is right. The dissolution of cosmos at the end of the cycle does result in a potentially 'fertile chaos' where the seeds—or to be strictly accurate, the *eggs*—of the new cycle lie in latency. But it is fertile only in potential; in order for the new cycle to emerge into actuality, *it must be fertilized*. The 'spirit of God' must 'move on the face of those waters'. The formless *prima materia* must be impregnated with form by the Logos. And that impregnation is a sovereign act of God. It is not dependent upon historical and cosmic cycles because it comes from outside them. It is the cycles, rather, which are dependent upon It. And the fact that God's creative Act is eternal in relation to all temporal cycles does not mean that it is mechanistically inevitable on the plane of those cycles. It is a free gift of Form to that which can only long for Form; darkness, no matter how potentially fertile, cannot say 'let there be light'. And the receptivity of the purified human soul bears the same relationship to Intellection, in the microcosm, as the cosmic *prima materia* does to the Logos, in the macrocosm. Intellectual vision 'informs' us, it 'forms us within'—but it cannot do so until we stop struggling to define and maintain our own identity, and 'die before we die.'

According to the law of entropy, whatever has come into cosmic manifestation has already begun to die. This is what the Buddha was referring to in his 'Fire Sermon', when he declared that the universe, the senses, the mind—all that has entered the realm of name and form—is on fire. God's creative Act, however, is eternal. And so, at the moment when manifestation loses its ability to draw more life from the Divine Act of Self-revelation which created it, it dissolves, it returns to the 'waters'—at which point its struggle to maintain its separate existence no longer obscures that eternal, radiant, revelatory Act, which strikes, again, the still mirror of those waters, and draws the potentials hidden in their depths up into formal manifestation, out of chaos and into cosmos. 'He who seeks to keep his life shall lose it, but he who loses his life, for My sake, shall find it.'

The denial of revelation leads to a false image of intellection as a kind of 'higher empiricism'. Those 'esoterists' who are looking for a metaphysics without religion, an esoterism without the fullness of Tradition, will be tempted to see 'the deep things of God' as their private preserve, as arcane mysteries to be delved into, quasi-scientifically, by the 'intellect' transformed into a slave of mental passion, but not as the wisdom and power of the Living God, Who has a will and exercises it, Who actively intervenes in human affairs, and Who, far from being a mere specimen for their occult researches, requires something of *them*. What C.S. Lewis says of the God of Pantheism, in *Miracles* (the Macmillan paperback, pp 93–94), is equally true of the God of false intellection:

> The Pantheist's God does nothing, demands nothing. He is there if you wish for Him, like a book on a shelf. He will not pursue you. There is no danger that at any time heaven and earth should flee away at his glance. If He were the truth, then we could really say that all the Christian images of kingship were a historical accident of which our religion ought to be cleansed. It is with a shock that we discover them to be indispensable. You have had that shock before, in connection with smaller matters—when the line pulls at your hand, when something breathes beside you in the darkness. So here; the shock comes at the precise moment when the thrill of *life* is communicated to us along the clue we have been following. It is always shocking to meet life where we thought we were alone. 'Look out!' we cry, 'it's *alive*.'

But since Quinn's God is not 'living' in this sense, he habitually speaks of intellection in Promethean and voluntaristic terms: of '*using* the "intellectual intuition'" (p 22), of 'The *conscription* of intellectual intuition . . . to *pierce* the higher and subtler principles of the doctrine' (p 88), and of the 'barrier . . . which prevents modern philosophers from piercing . . . the perennial truths which await resolution by each individual' (p 75). He implicitly denies that we can *receive* truths through revelation and Tradition (though of course we must realize them on our own), and identifies intellection with a Promethean individualism in the philosophical realm. Frithjof Schuon's doctrine is worth repeating here:

> A cult of intelligence and mental passion take man further from truth. Intelligence withdraws as soon as man puts his trust in it alone. Mental passion pursuing intellectual intuition is like the wind which blows out the light of a candle.

Such identification with intellection coupled with the conscious or implicit denial of revelation is one of the things which define the self-interested esoterics in conflict with the exoteric authorities. As I read Ibn al-'Arabi's position in his *Futuhat al-makkiyya*, the ability to accept exoteric norms *after* coming to an understanding of the meaning of inner realities, of states, stations, witnessings and unveilings, is the mark of the finished esoterics, 'the People of Blame', as opposed to the one-sided esoterics or *batinis* (the 'Sufis'), and the simple exoteric believers. Seyyed Hossein Nasr, in *Islamic Spirituality II*, defines 'the People of Blame' as the self-identified esoterics who stand out from the crowd, the ones blamed by the exoteric *ulema* for thinking, or acting as if, they are not bound by the *shari'at*—in other words, Ibn al-'Arabi's 'Sufis'—whereas for Ibn al-'Arabi, 'the People of Blame' are the ones who have transcended the esoteric/exoteric dichotomy, and are consequently blamed by the *Sufis* for, as far as they can see, abandoning the inner path and becoming normal, uninteresting, exoteric believers again. (Kierkegaard, in his figure of the 'Knight of Faith', defines the identical station.) The metaphysical principle upon which this tripartite division is based is, in the language of the Vedanta, 'Brahman is beyond both form and formlessness,' and, in the words of Ibn al-'Arabi (in my paraphrase), 'God is non-delimited in the absolute sense, i.e., He is not delimited by his own non-delimitation.' Those who conceive of God as delimited, as possessing form, are the simple believers; those who conceive of Him as formless and non-delimited are the one-sided esoterics, the *batinis*, the 'Sufis'; those who conceive of Him as beyond formlessness as well as form, as not delimited by His own non-delimitation, are the finished esoterics, the People of Blame. If God is beyond both form and formlessness, then the exoteric forms of the revealed religions are theophanies, not veils—the same being true of any particular form whatsoever. In the words of Ibn al-'Arabi (William C. Chittick, *The Sufi Path of Knowledge*, p 260),

> The Reality is the actual situation of Being. . . . The Shari'at is identical with the Reality. . . . When the Sufis saw that both the elect and the common people practiced the Shari'at and that only the elect knew the Reality, they distinguished between the Shari'at and the Reality. They made the Shari'at pertain to the properties and rulings of the Reality which were manifest, and they made the Reality pertain to its properties and rulings which are non-manifest.

Furthermore, if each revealed religion is, in essence if not in its contingent manifestations, a complete theophany, then there is no need to add one to the other, any more than I would need to add someone else to myself, or two others, or five others, in order to stand as a manifestation of the Self within every self. As soon as I realize that 'what is here is elsewhere, and what is not here is nowhere,' my spiritual greed is at an end.

Quinn's denial of the traditional doctrine of apocalypse, which for Christians necessarily includes the second coming of Christ, for Muslims the 'second coming' of the Prophet Jesus (whose advent, according to some, will be announced by the Mahdi), for Jews the advent of the Messiah, for Buddhists the coming Maitreya Buddha, and for Hindus the appearance of the Kalki Avatara, is intimately related to his denial of revelation: if God cannot actively intervene in human affairs—or if it would inconvenient for us if He did—then He can no more end a cycle of human manifestation and inaugurate a new one than He can found a revealed religion; the cycle of manifestation is consequently mechanistic, inevitable, an expression of 'scientific' law like the orbit of the Earth around the Sun, not the form taken in space and time by God's eternal act of Self-revelation. And so Quinn believes (p 293), more or less in line with Blavatsky, that

> spiritual evolution moves in a cyclical, helical spiral through the interplay of opposite polarities, and this Traditional view is the perspective of temporal (historical) dynamic of which Hegelian historical dialectic is a rough approximation. Indissolubly fused with this helical-cyclical approach to evolution are the two processes of *enantiodromia* and the compensation theory (which Guénon calls 'reinstatement'), which operate in tandem; that is, the germ or seed of the 'thesis' dyad is present in the 'antithesis' dyad, to borrow Hegel's terms, and that while one dyad is in manifestation, its partner begins to grow after the nadir of its cyclic spin is reached and will eventually equal and then

supersede it until it reaches its zenith (at which point its partner is at its nadir), and so on . . . ; in light of this we can say that the Traditional view of periodicity probably precludes the *total* annihilation of humanity on earth.

But leaving aside the fact that 'enantiodromia and the compensation theory' are not Traditional, but Jungian, Quinn misrepresents Guénon's theory of 'reinstatement', which does not *replace* the dissolution of manifestation at the end of the cycle, but happens immediately before it (see *The Reign of Quantity*, pp 328–329). And he ought to know that the version of the cycle-of-manifestation he presents is in no way the Traditionalist one, as he claims, and that 'the total annihilation of humanity on earth' is indeed a distinct possibility, depending upon the magnitude of the cycle presently ending, since he himself quotes Coomaraswamy (p 130) to the effect that, after the *mahapralaya* or great dissolution, 'the seeds, ideas, or images of the future manifestation persist during the interval of inter-Time of resolution on a higher plane of existence, unaffected by the destruction of manifested forms,' not in 'special repositories' of human breeding-stock, or small, remote enclaves of esoteric survivalists. That having been said, I want to make it clear that I do not necessarily believe that every human being will perish from the earth in the fairly near future, nor do I place any hope in the continuity of human history and human life. My faith in God and my sense of the significance of earthly life depend neither upon one nor the other. Eschatological hope is vertical hope; it requires neither the destruction of the earth nor its preservation to be realized, since it has to do with 'a new heaven and a new earth'. And yet this new heaven and earth are intimately related to this heaven and this earth, an apparent paradox which explains Guénon's oracular statements in *The Reign of Quantity*: that the end of the cycle is the end of 'a' humanity; that it is the end of time but not the end of space; that it is the complete dissolution of manifestation but not the end of terrestrial existence. To pin one's hopes on the destruction of the earth is despair: 'there needs be evil, but woe to him through whom evil comes.' But to pin them on the future continuity of human history is a false hope: true hope cannot be based on a projection of our present fears and desires into a future time when, by some uncertain means, what we hope for will triumph over what we fear. The true hope is vertical—in other words, contemplative and eschatological. Just as contemplation detaches us from hope and fear relating to future events by replacing temporal hope with hope in God's present Mercy, and temporal fear with fear of God's present Grandeur—the height and depth of the *axis mundi*—so eschatological hope is vertical in exactly the same sense, and vertical hope is beyond the question of whether or not all life, or all human life, will perish from the earth in the foreseeable future—though to pretend that the destruction of the earth is a matter of indifference to us is another extreme, since love of God's earth is part of the love of God, and we would be insanely arrogant, and emotionally dead, if we were to claim that the end of all earthly life simply could not touch us: even Christ wept over Jerusalem. What we do know is that this cycle, this 'humanity', is about to end, and that this end will be—or rather is—the occasion for a radical breakthrough of eternity into time. In this is our hope. In the words of Thomas Merton, from 'The Time of the End is the Time of No Room' (*Raids on the Unspeakable*, pp 65–75):

> In the Biblical sense, the expression 'the End' does not necessarily mean only 'the violent, sudden, and bad end.' Biblical eschatology must not be confused with the vague and anxious eschatology of human foreboding. We live in an age of two superimposed eschatologies: that of secular anxieties and hopes, and that of revealed fulfillment. Sometimes the first is merely mistaken for the second, sometimes it results from complete denial and despair of the second. In point of fact the pathological *fear of the violent end* which, when sufficiently aroused, actually becomes a thinly-disguised *hope for the violent end*, provides something of the climate of confusion and despair in which the more profound hopes of Biblical eschatology are realized. . . . For eschatology is not *finis* and punishment, the winding up of accounts and the closing of books: it is the final beginning, the definitive birth into a new creation. It is not the last gasp of exhausted possibilities but the first taste of all that is beyond conceiving as actual.

This seemingly inescapable but actually illusory alternative between historical despair and historical hope, which is in reality only another form of despair—between, that is, the fear of death and the desire to die, which are intimately related in so many ways—is in reality the projection of a false metaphysical dichotomy. In a sense it has to do with our belief in evolution and our worship of progress, which have been for so many (including myself until fairly recently) not only the basic assumptions which give meaning to our life-struggles, but also the philosophical basis for our solidarity with humanity and the earth, fundamental concepts which widen our horizons, give our actions a significance beyond our petty personal interests, and move us toward compassion and self-transcendence. In other words, they are those modernist dogmas which have specifically replaced Christian charity and hope in Divine Providence. But now that the myths of biological and social progress are so profoundly threatened by the devolution and regress we see all around us, many of us have lost our *raison d'être*, our rationale for leading any life beyond our narrow selfish desires. What is it all for? we ask. History and evolution must be going somewhere; they must have a goal. If they aren't going somewhere, if they 'fail', then the whole human struggle is meaningless. And if we can't see how evolution and progress could 'triumph' in the material world, then we will be tempted to posit a higher, subtler evolution which can triumph, somehow, in higher worlds. And this triumph of the human *spiritual* struggle must have a meaning beyond our simple extrication of ourselves from the bondage of incarnate life. Incarnate life, its bondage, and our escape from this bondage must mean something. And what else could they logically mean, we ask—and in so doing place ourselves in the company of H.P. Blavatsky, Rudolf Steiner and Teilhard de Chardin—but that the manifestation and re-integration of the Universe must actually *add something new to the nature of God?* Because otherwise, we say to ourselves, the Gnostics are right: the universe, including human incarnate existence, is a mistake, either on our part or on the part of the Godhead Itself; all we can do in the face of it is to about-face, admit the whole thing was a bad proposition, and return to, and thus restore, the wounded Godhead. So the false metaphysical dichotomy is this: Either God too is evolving, or he has devolved and must be restored. But from the standpoint of *gnosis*, which is the only field upon which this false dichotomy can be resolved, we see that the sense that evolution and human history have an ultimate significance *within time*, as with Chardin's 'Omega Point', or, as with the Gnostics, the sense that evolution and history are meaningless because time itself is a mistake, *both* depend on a denial that God is Absolute, Infinite, Perfect, and sufficient unto Himself. Once this truth of God is understood, however, we then come to the vision of time as an aspect of God's Infinity, just as the unchanging principles are aspects of His Absoluteness, and of time as not going anywhere but back to God—a motion which cannot take place in the future, lest we fall into a kind of 'post-eternal Deism', the complement and opposite of the more familiar pre-eternal brand, but is actually taking place Now, in Eternity. The eternal past, the past as Now, *sub specie aeternitatis*, is Creation; the eternal future, the future as Now, *sub specie aeternitatis*, is Apocatastasis. And the meaning of time is: that it is encompassed by, and exists as a manifestation of, Eternity, where all meaning resides.

On p 269, Quinn asserts, correctly, that 'In the Traditional view . . . the cosmos does not find meaning in the individual; the individual finds his or her meaning in the cosmos, just as the part finds its meaning in the whole.'

But on p 272–73, he claims that Carl Jung was 'in some ways close to the Traditional perspective,' and supports it with the assertion that 'To Jung, the neurosis of modernity is in seeking mass, external, quantitative answers to a problem whose only solution is to be found through individual, internal, and qualitative or depth-psychological means.' Perhaps these positions can be reconciled — apart from the implied identification of metaphysics and depth psychology, which is as wrong as it can be — by asserting that it is the individual's sole responsibility to find his or her meaning in the cosmos, and thereby in the Principle of which the cosmos is a manifestation, though he or she can only accomplish this with the 'aid' of the cosmos itself, conceived of as a God-given support for the contemplation of the Divine Nature, something which can take place (in most cases) only within the context of revealed doctrine. But it is not immediately apparent that Quinn understands this.

If Carl Jung is in some ways 'close' to the Traditionalist perspective, it is this situation of being 'so near yet so far' which has, more than any other single factor, prevented the Traditionalist School from resurrecting a fully traditional and principial psychology — not to mention Jung's profoundly subversive effect upon Christianity, especially Roman Catholicism. It's as if modern rationalism separated doctrinal proficiency from an understanding of the efficacy and symbolic meaning of images within the Catholic world, the result being that Catholics, having a deep responsiveness to symbolic images at it were 'in their blood', sensed that they needed to regain such an understanding, but sought it in Jungianism instead of in the fullness of their own tradition, with disastrous results. If only Titus Burckhardt and others with a Traditional perspective had gotten to alchemy long enough before Jung did to have allowed them to explicate its full range of psychological meaning and application, not simply its metaphysical symbology, without having to worry about being identified with Jungianism!

Jung and his school are not without penetrating and useful psychological insights, and some of his doctrines are as if shadows cast by a valid metaphysical perspective. The 'Self archetype', for example, is close to what Sufis mean by the Heart — i.e., the 'central point' of the psyche where it is intersected by a ray of the Spirit — and Jung's 'descending hierarchy' of psychic layers, the Shadow, the Syzygy ('anima'-and-'animus') and the Self *could* be seen as the psychic reflections of the body, the psyche *per se* (based, as it is, on a subject/object mode of perception) and the Spirit, according to the principle that 'what is highest in principle is lowest in manifestation.' But, as Burckhardt points out in his chapter on 'Modern Psychology' from *Mirror of the Intellect*, Jung's unwillingness to posit an objective metaphysical dimension, and his explicit derivation of the 'collective unconscious' from the structure of the human brain, which he sees as connecting us with our animal past via evolution, renders his doctrine not merely insufficient, but actively subversive of traditional metaphysics.

Jung's role in modernity, and his affinity with the new anti-traditional global elites, is brought out by Christopher Lasch in his *The Revolt of the Elites and the Betrayal of Democracy* (New York & London, W. W. Norton & Company, 1995, pp 236–239):

> The beauty of Jung's system, for those threatened with 'meaninglessness' as he liked to call it, was that it offered 'meaning' without turning its back on modernity. Jung assured his followers, in effect, that they could remain thoroughly modern without sacrificing the emotional solace formerly provided by orthodox religion. . . . It was the gifted individual, the one who accepted the burden of maturity, that Jung addressed in the essays collected in 1933 under the inevitable title of *Modern Man in Search of a Soul*. By outgrowing tradition, the fully modern individual gained a wider perspective but unavoidably cut himself off from his more conservative fellows. A 'fuller consciousness of the present removes him . . . from submersion in common consciousness,' from the 'mass of men who live entirely within the bounds of tradition.' This is why the solution of the 'modern spiritual problem,' as Jung called it, could not possibly lie in a return to 'obsolete forms of religion,' any more than it could lie in a purely secular worldview. . . . Modern man, having 'heard enough about guilt and sin,' was rightly suspicious of 'fixed ideas as to what is right,' suspicious of spiritual counselors who 'pretended to know what is right and what is not.' Moral judgement, in any case, 'took something away from the richness of experience.'

> [Jung's version of psychoanalysis was] the means by which to liberate the religious imagination from its enslavement to dying creeds. By providing access not only to the unconscious life of individuals but to the 'collective unconscious' of the human race, Jungian psychoanalysis excavated the permanent structure of religious mythology, the raw material out of which the modern world might construct new forms of religious life appropriate to its needs. Jung invited his patients and readers to range through the whole array of mythologies and spiritual techniques—all of them equally available for inspection, thanks to the expansion of historical consciousness in the modern world—and to experiment with a variety of combinations until they found the one best suited to their individual requirements. . . . The educated classes, unable to escape the burden of sophistication, might envy the naïve

faiths of the past; they might even envy the classes that continued unthinkingly to observe traditional faiths in the twentieth century, not yet having been exposed to the wintry blasts of modern critical thinking. They could not trade places with the unenlightened masses, however, any more than they could return to the past. Once the critical habit of mind had been assimilated, no one who understood its implications could find any refuge or resting place in premodern systems of thought and belief. It was this experience of disillusionment, more than anything else, that was held to distinguish the artist and the intellectual from the unreflecting creatures of convention, who distrusted artists and intellectuals precisely because they could not bear to hear the bad news.

[NOTE: For a revealing exposé of Jung's overt Anti-Christianity and Neo-Paganism, see *The Jung Cult* (Princeton University Press, 1994) and *The Aryan Christ* (Random House, 1997), both by Richard Noll.]

Every group centered around a set of beliefs and values—in other words, every group—possesses a view of society. And this is certainly true of the Traditionalists, whose 'critique of the modern world' is an integral, though not quintessential, aspect of their teaching. But the very habit of contemplating eternal principles may make some of them (or rather us) slow to recognize sweeping social changes. Traditionalist writers are still warning us against egalitarianism and socialism, whereas the real sign of our times, on the socio-economic level, is the fall of Communism, and the vast and growing global disparity between the rich and the poor. Nor is the United States exempt from these trends, as anyone who is willing to look can see. Lester Thurlow, in his blurb for *The Winner-Take-All Society* (1995) by Robert H. Frank and Philip J. Cook, writes: 'History will look back and see the shift in the American distribution of earnings since the 1970s as the largest that any society has ever had without a revolution or a military defeat and subsequent occupation.' And on p 229 of that book, the authors quote journalist Mickey Kraus:

> We've always had rich and poor. But money is increasingly something that enables the rich, or even the merely prosperous, to live a life apart from the poor. And the rich and semi-rich increasingly seem to *want* to live a life apart. . . .

Or, in the words of Christopher Lasch from *The Revolt of the Elites* (p 29):

> The general course of recent history no longer favors the leveling of social distinctions but runs more and more in the direction of a two-class society in

which the favored few monopolize the advantages of money, education, and power.

In many ways 'Traditionalist sociology' is similar to that of Ortega y Gasset in *The Revolt of the Masses* (except for certain progressivist assumptions which the Traditionalists deny), who lamented the rise of the rootless, secularized masses with no sense of tradition, and the disappearances of the older aristocracies who had been the repositories of cultural and spiritual values. But it is Christopher Lasch's thesis in *The Revolt of the Elites* that the shoe is now on the other foot, that it is the new global 'elites' who represent progressivism and secularism, while the 'masses' of today are comparatively conservative and traditional. As sociologist of religion Peter Berger puts it, in a line often quoted by Huston Smith: If East Indians are the most religious people on earth, and Swedes the least religious, then America (and, I would add, the New World Order) is like a nation of Indians ruled by Swedes.

According to Lasch (p 215),

Among elites [religion] is held in low esteem—something useful for weddings and funerals but otherwise dispensable. A skeptical, iconoclastic state of mind is one of the distinguishing characteristics of the knowledge classes. Their commitment to the culture of criticism is understood to rule out religious commitments. The elites' attitude to religion ranges from indifference to active hostility. It rests on a caricature of religious fundamentalism as a reactionary movement bent on reversing all the progressive measures achieved over the last three decades.

Lasch's distinction between Ortega y Gasset's 'revolt of the masses' and today's 'revolt of the elites' is worth quoting at length:

Ortega and other critics described mass culture as a combination of 'radical ingratitude' with an unquestioned belief in limitless possibility. The mass man, according to Ortega, took for granted the benefits conferred by civilization and demanded them 'peremptorily, as if they were natural rights.' Heir of all the ages, he was blissfully unconscious of his debt to the past. Though he enjoyed advantages brought about by the general 'rise in the historical level,' he felt no obligation either to his progenitors or to his progeny. He recognized no authority outside himself, conducting himself as if he were 'lord of his own existence'. His 'incredible ignorance of history' made it possible for him to think of the present moment as far superior to the civilizations of the past and to forget, moreover, that contemporary civilization was itself the product of centuries of historical development, not the unique achievement of an age that had discovered the secret of progress by turning its back on the past.

These habits of mind, it would seem, are more accurately associated with the rise of meritocracy than with 'the revolt of the masses'. Ortega himself admitted that the 'prototype of the mass man' was 'the man of science' — the 'technician', the specialist, the 'learned ignoramus' whose mastery of his own 'tiny corner of the universe' was matched only by his ignorance of the rest. But the process in question does not derive simply from the replacement of the old-fashioned man of letters by the specialist, as Ortega's analysis implies; it derives from the intrinsic structure of meritocracy itself. Meritocracy is a parody of democracy [and here Quinn is more honest than some, having no use for democracy]. It offers opportunities for advancement, in theory at least, to anyone with the talent to seize them, but 'opportunities to rise,' as R. H. Tawney points out in *Equality*, 'are no substitute for the general diffusion of the means of civilization,' of the 'dignity and culture' that are needed by all 'whether they rise or not.' Social mobility does not undermine the influence of the elites; if anything, it helps solidify their influence by supporting the illusion that it rests solely on merit. (pp 40–41)

The market in which the new elites operate is now international in scope. Their fortunes are tied to enterprises that operate across national boundaries. They are more concerned with the smooth functioning of the system as a whole than with any of its parts. Their loyalties — if the term is not itself anachronistic in this context — are international rather than regional, national, or local. They have more in common with their counterparts in Brussels or Hong Kong than with the masses of Americans not yet plugged into the network of global communications. (p 34)

Curiously enough, it is Robert Reich, notwithstanding his admiration for the new class of 'symbolic analysts', who provides one of the most penetrating accounts of the 'darker side of cosmopolitanism'. Without national attachments, he reminds us, people have little inclination to make sacrifices or to accept responsibility for their actions. 'We learn to feel responsible for others because we share with them a common history, ... a common culture, ... a common fate.' The denationalization of business enterprise tends to produce a class of cosmopolitans who see themselves as 'world citizens, but without accepting ... any of the obligations which citizenship in a polity normally implies.' But the cosmopolitanism of the favored few, because it is uninformed by the practice of citizenship, turns out to be a higher form of parochialism. Instead of supporting public services, the new elites put their money into the improvement of their own self-enclosed enclaves. (pp 46–47)

The 'zones' and 'networks' admired by Reich bear little resemblance to communities in any traditional sense of the term. Populated by transients, they lack the continuity that derives from a sense of place and from standards of conduct self-consciously cultivated and handed down from generation to generation. (p 40)

Quinn sometimes gives the impression that he would agree with the above critique, though from a specifically Traditionalist perspective. On pp 284–285, liberally quoting Guénon and Coomaraswamy, Quinn convincingly laments

'cultural' pollution (and/or culturocide), wherein by military conquest, economic domination, or any other form of imposed hegemony or imperialism, the quantitative industrial cultures of the modern West have corrupted or destroyed Traditional cultures. This is more than a passing of traditional society, but more actually an active campaign that proceeds 'by subjugating a people; by taking from them what is most precious, namely their own culture; by coercing them to adopt mores and institutions of a foreign people; for forcing them into the most odious work in order that they should acquire things which for them are perfectly useless' [citation from Guénon's *Crisis of the Modern World*].

First by a process of forced colonization and domination, then by a process of attrition, one by one the various indigenous cultures with which the modern West has come into contact since the Renaissance have gradually disintegrated, in the strict sense of the word. Time and again, 'the fact that we have destroyed the vocational and artistic foundations of whatever traditional cultures our touch has infected,' as Coomaraswamy once wrote, has left the planet with fewer and fewer pristine and coherent Traditional cultures. They have either been forced to relinquish or have gradually abandoned their Traditional ways, based on a qualitative mythological or metaphysical worldview, and literally 'bought in' to the illusion of material progress. . . .

For these countries, these cultures, the pollution is twofold and nearly instantaneous. The visible pollution from the new motorways and factories built respectively to expedite the high-entropy transit crucial to industrialism and to exploit cheap local labor is the outer signal of pollution of a more devastating kind in the Traditional view: the trade of meaning, value, wholeness, sacrality, and quality of life for meaninglessness, relativism, fragmentation, secularism, and quantity.

I agree with this assessment completely. But in the next chapter, in what is probably the most sinister moment in all of Quinn's book, via a stunning manifestation of what George Orwell called 'doublethink', he does a complete about-face, and takes as his hope and his ideal what he has just lamented as an unmitigated disaster. On p301, he speaks in glowing terms of the new globalization: '. . . when in world history has there ever been such an effort expended in planetization of thought; in international cooperation as exemplified by the United Nations; in unanimity and conformity brought about by world trade, science, technology; in networks of satellite data-gathering and telecommunications; and in educational and artistic exchanges as there is now? International organizations whose *sole* purpose is the promulgation of planetary consciousness now exist, and internationally constituted spiritual communities now proliferate.' But what is a 'planetization of thought' based on a 'unanimity and conformity brought about by world trade, science, technology' but an 'imposed hegemony' originating in 'the quantitative industrial cultures of the modern West,' which continues to destroy Traditional societies by 'taking from them what is most precious, namely their own culture'?

So Quinn is not a critic of Lasch's rebellious elites, but at many points a member of them, though he is smarter than most in that he openly admits that things cannot go on as they are, that the present world is headed for cataclysm. And as is common among the new global elites, he speaks highly of primitive cultures as repositories of traditional metaphysics (Chapter 9), while admitting the existence of 'pandemic ethnocentrism and xenophobia, parochialism, tribalism and group solipsism' (p300), though he attributes an excessive worry about these trends only to the nay-sayers skeptical of planetization, whereas planetization is alive, well, and right on track. But up to a certain point, both attitudes are justified. And is not this 'ethnocentrism, xenophobia, parochialism and tribalism' often the very expression of the struggle for survival of the more Traditional cultures, whose disappearance Quinn pretends to lament? It is often characteristic of members of the global elite to appreciate primitive cultures as if they were a kind of wildlife — thus the otherwise justified use of the term 'endangered cultures' — while looking at ethnic separatists, whether Basque, Tamil, Serbian, or (as is becoming increasingly appropriate to mention) locally or nationally-identified North American Anglo-Saxon, as breaks on progress to be swept aside. In other words, a non-globally-identified cultural or ethnic group with no political power is considered to represent a pristine primitivism worth preserving, while the same group with a degree of such power is an enemy of 'planetization'; (this, parenthetically, is why Quinn quotes from *The Reign of Quantity* (p 217) to the effect that 'shamanism will be found to include rites comparable to certain others of the highest order,' and ignores Guénon's statement on the next page that 'a very real degeneration must be suspected' in shamanism, 'such as may sometimes amount to a real deviation.') And, in point of fact, even as planetization moves to destroy all pre-industrial cultures, the bookshelves of at least the American sector of the global elites are filled with books on the spiritualities of such cultures, as their walls are covered with their artifacts, ranging from African tribal carvings purchased from native craft collectives to Mayan statuettes smuggled across the Mexican border by 'collectives' of art thieves. And while the elites' patronage of primitive artists may be of some help to those struggling cultures—or those struggling bandits—the money used to purchase the objects in question is derived from the global economy which is systematically destroying the cultures which produce them, and which also includes the global craft import trade, legal or otherwise. It is here that Lasch's largely-justified characterization of the global elites as essentially secular needs to be modified.

Secular they may be, when seen from a traditional perspective, but that doesn't mean that some of them aren't extremely interested in religions; all they reject is *religious faith*. They consider the world's religious traditions, including the esoterisms of these traditions, as a cultural resource which is there for them to exploit—just as they exploit natural resources and cheap labor—in order to fill the void left in their souls by their unrepentant secularism. The characteristic 'religion' of some (but not all) sectors of the global elite is a kind of 'world fusion spirituality'—which, however, is essentially psychic, not spiritual—made up of texts, music, ritual objects, yogic and magical practices, and even shamanic initiations collected from around the world. This may be easier to grasp if we remember that certain members of the business community have always played with the idea of membership in secret societies. The Masons, the Elks, the Oddfellows, the Shriners, and the Druids represent a long tradition of bourgeois involvement in pseudo-initiatic organizations, some of which—particularly the Masons—show signs of possible descent from true initiatic societies in the distant past. Guénon believed the Masons to be the degenerate offspring of a valid initiatic lineage, whose esoteric symbolism, if not its 'barakah', has retained real traditional elements. And the initiatic pretentions of Freemasonry, as well as its connections to the business community, survive to this day. Many such 'men's clubs' are international in scope, and certain of their symbols and practices—whether strictly for entertainment or possibly for much more serious reasons—remain secret; this has undoubtedly made some of them useful to multinational corporations in the process of expanding their reach. If we couple this with the strand of 'motivational mysticism' represented by Dale Carnegie and Norman Vincent Peale, as well as the mass of magical and quasi-magical ideas and techniques brought into the business world by the ex-hippies of the Baby Boom, the 'esoteric religiousity' of the globalist elites no longer seems so far-fetched. Internationally known Vatican diplomat, author, and exorcist Fr. Malachi Martin maintained that the leadership of the Masons, which according to him has successfully subverted the Catholic church, is drawn from these elites, and that most of the 'Luciferians' he encountered in his work were high-ranking members of the business, professional, and church communities—though I hasten to add that New Age practices one might encounter in the business world are certainly not all Satanist in origin or intent. But given that the bourgeoisie has always had its secret societies—as the aristocracy its 'esoteric' order of knighthood—the popular idea that all psychic or magical ideas are 'fringe' phenomena is simply not accurate. And if there is one characteristic 'spiritual' paradigm in this corporate-consultant world, or at least the sector of it I have experienced directly, it is shamanism—either that or something else which goes by the same name. According to New Age and/or New Class mythology, shamanism, because it can be defined as or reduced to a set of 'archaic techniques of ecstasy' (to quote the subtitle of Mircea Eliade's famous work on the subject) is the most transportable of all spiritualities, perfectly suited to the class of 'elite transients' described by Lasch.

Since it is technically rather than culturally-based, it is not so deeply tied to local cultures as is Russian Orthodoxy, for example, or Islam—or so the story goes; and as a set of 'techniques' rather than 'dogmas', it is highly appealing to a class which values 'skill'—particularly mental or psychic skill—over loyalty to traditional values, or faith in God. Supposedly the most individualistic of all spiritualities, it is also the most potentially Promethean, since—at least according to the New Age mythology in question—it is based upon magical exploits rather than the sacrifice of ego, and upon insight considered not as a product of contemplative ascesis, or a gift of God, but as the result of a sort of 'raid on the mysteries', according to a paradigm that is closer to espionage than it is to religion. Quinn's 'internationally constituted spiritual communities' are, in part, psychic and 'neo-shamanic' networks for the elites.

On p 303, Quinn admits that

> though their emphases differed, Coomaraswamy and Guénon each
> insisted on participation and regular initiation in a *living* Tradition in order

to understand and assimilate the first principles and the concomitant esoteric teachings. Similarly, they each rejected the notion of an eclectic 'religious Esperanto' borrowed from . . . the various Traditional systems.

'However,' he goes on to say,

> they both died before it could be stated unequivocally that upon the face of the earth one can no longer find any thoroughly Traditional cultures, that all that remains of the former survive in isolated pockets of remote, rural areas.

But what is true of Traditional cultures is not true of Traditions, which can and do survive. My Islamic Sufism, with its traditional teachings and practices, its living masters, its spiritual states and stations, and my wife's Eastern Orthodoxy, with its traditional liturgy, its patristic teachings, its communion of the saints and its miracles, are more alive than Quinn will ever know—and that in the heartland of 'planetization' and 'religious Esperanto', the San Francisco Bay Area.

And then, apparently without any qualms of conscience, Quinn subverts the entire life-work of Guénon and Coomaraswamy, right before our eyes—men he claims to respect. On p302, referring to the objections of Guénon and Coomaraswamy to 'a single universally acceptable syncretic faith embodying all this is "best in every faith"', he says:

> But because the basis of a planetary culture if it is to be a new Traditional culture must be a spiritually oriented planetary consciousness, and because this latter must contain sacred principles inherent in, common to, and representative of the world's major religions, the unavoidable conclusion is that the first principles of natural metaphysics that alone satisfy these prerequisites must play a primary role that at first sight may appear to be such a 'universally acceptable syncretic faith.'

And on pp303–304, he claims that if

> the unprecedented outpouring of the philosophia perennis or theosophia—the Tradition—in the late nineteenth and twentieth centuries was the progenitor of a new, orthodox planetary living Tradition . . . then based on their lives' work, Guénon and Coomaraswamy would have been key contributors to any future planetary Traditional culture—a subtle irony in light of their position on 'religious Esperanto'.

And then:

> Planetization has already begun—both technologic and conceptual—as we have seen. But the vision of a planetary culture based on the precepts of

Traditional culture as outlined by Guénon and Coomaraswamy is a new entry into the field of futurism.

It is also a new entry into the field of mendacity: Tradition without Traditions would be like humanity without human beings. How right Walter Benjamin was when he said: 'The dead are not safe'!
   On pp304–305, Quinn unveils his true object of worship:

> By definition, the social structure of the Traditional planetary culture must be hierarchical, and of this Tradition refers only to a spiritual elite determined solely by virtue of ability, whose function it will be to relay, as it were, the higher metaphysical principles and the doctrine that unfolds from them.... Presumably this will be the role of advanced scientists/metaphysicists ... and/or religionists and students of philosophy—like Guénon, for example—who concentrate on these subjects.

But a traditional caste hierarchy and a meritocracy such as Quinn envisions, and falsely equates with Tradition, and two very different things. Brahmins and Kshatriyas are the product of meritorious birth, not meritorious cut-throat competition. On p39 of *The Revolt of the Elites*, Christopher Lasch speaks of the 'arrogance of power' to which the 'best and the brightest' are congenitally addicted, and says,

> This arrogance should not be confused with the pride characteristic of the aristocratic classes, which rests on the inheritance of an ancient lineage and on the obligation to defend its honor. Neither valor and chivalry nor the code of courtly, romantic love, with which these values are closely allied [i.e., the values of Western 'Kshatriyas'], has any place in the world view of the best and the brightest. A meritocracy has no more use for chivalry than a heredity aristocracy has for brains. Although heredity advantages play an important part in the attainment of professional or managerial status, the new class has to maintain the fiction that its power rests on intelligence alone. Hence it has little sense of ancestral gratitude or of an obligation to live up to responsibilities inherited from the past. It thinks of itself as a self-made elite owing its privileges exclusively to its own efforts.

And, on p44:

> An aristocracy of talent—superficially attractive ideal, which appears to distinguish democracies from societies based on heredity privilege—turns out to be a contradiction in terms: The talented retain many of the vices of aristocracy without its virtues. Their snobbery lacks any acknowledgement of reciprocal obligations between the favored few and the multitude. Although

they are full of 'compassion' for the poor, they cannot be said to subscribe to the theory of noblesse oblige, which would imply a willingness to make a direct and personal contribution to the public good.

When Quinn says that 'the social structure of the Traditional planetary culture must be hierarchical,' he is necessarily referring either to a future development in the present cycle, or to the Golden Age of the next cycle; on pp 303–304 he says he isn't sure whether the signs of planetization point to the advent of a new *avatara* (i.e., a new cycle), or to the development of the doctrines of Blavatsky and the Traditionalists into a new Traditional planetary culture. But according to the Traditionalists, the Golden Age of any new cycle is *non-hierarchical*. In the words of Martin Lings (*Ancient Beliefs and Modern Superstitions*, p 49), 'The Golden Age is by definition the age when all men are "above caste".' So Quinn is wrong there. And if he is talking about a future development of a Traditional, hierarchical planetary culture within this cycle, then he is universally contradicted by Tradition, which sees the caste system as a way of prolonging the glory of the Golden Age into later periods, but recognizes that Traditional caste hierarchy must become increasingly impossible as the Kali-yuga progresses, since the majority of men have now fallen 'below caste' as in the Golden Age they were 'above' it. And the 'reinstatement' predicted by Guénon to take place directly before the dissolution of the cycle is a brief announcement of the cycle to come, not an earthly 'millennium' of the latter days—the belief in which, according to Orthodox Christian authorities, constitutes the heresy of 'chiliasm'. So Quinn is wrong there too. Therefore the only thing he can possibly be referring to is what René Guénon calls the 'counter-hierarchy': the reign of the Antichrist. On pp 325–326 of *The Reign of Quantity and the Signs of the Times*, Guénon writes:

> one can already see sketched out, in various productions of indubitably 'counter-initiatic' origin or inspiration, the idea of an organization which would be like the counterpart, but by the same token also the counterfeit, of a traditional conception such as that of the 'Holy Empire', and some such organization must become the expression of the 'counter-tradition' in the social order; and for similar reasons the Antichrist must appear like something that could be called, using the language of the Hindu tradition, an inverted *Chaktavarti*.... His time will certainly no longer be the 'reign of quantity' ... it will on the contrary be marked, under the pretext of a false 'spiritual restoration', by a sort of reintroduction of quality in all things, but of quality inverted with respect to its normal and legitimate significance.

After the 'egalitarianism' of our times there will again be a visibly established hierarchy, but an inverted hierarchy, indeed a real 'counter-hierarchy', the summit of which will be occupied by the being who will in reality be situated nearer than any other being to the very bottom of the 'pit of Hell'.

The chilling implication of this passage, given that Quinn is a well-informed student of Guénon, is that he seems to actually cast himself in the role of a servant of the Antichrist, at least in the eyes of Guénonistes, and other Traditionalists. Why would he do this? A clue to the answer appears on p 303 of *The Only Tradition*: 'If planetization is an inevitable fact, then eventually . . . there will only be one culture remaining on earth. *How we value this future occurrence is not at issue here*' [my italics]. So he is saying that if something is inevitable, we cannot call it good or bad. If it was inevitable that the Jews perish in the holocaust—which clearly it was, since it actually happened— then we cannot deplore it. We must accept it. In other words, he is in a state of spiritual despair. Here we can see how worship of blind fate, which is one form of nihilism, is a denial of Divine Providence. Fate-worship is the satanic counterfeit of the faith—which leads to the knowledge—that everything that happens is God's Will, and everything God wills is good; whereas, according to fate-worship, everything that happens would have happened anyway, so that everything is meaningless—but we can *confer* meaning upon it by worshipping it, even if we hate it, and empower ourselves by becoming the priests of it. After all, who wants to back a loser? But to say that we can make no moral judgements on events, or even on our own actions (which is part of the same belief-system) since they are all God's will, is to deny that it is also God's will that there be divinely-instituted moral laws, and that every human being should possess, at least virtually, a divinely-implanted moral sense, which leads us to be delighted by manifestations of good and appalled at manifestations of evil, even though all manifestations of good and evil are indeed God's will, and thus part of a greater Good. If good and evil did not exist, this moral law and this moral sense would have no field of operation, and it is God's will that they operate, since they are indeed in operation. As Rumi puts it, God is like a doctor: the doctor wants there to be illness, otherwise he could not make a living, but he is also opposed to illness, otherwise he would not heal it. Or God is like a baker: he wants people to be hungry, otherwise he could not find a market for his bread, but he is also opposed to hunger, otherwise he would not feed them.

In Appendix A, Quinn's Theosophical hatred for revelation becomes more explicit. In line with this hatred, he does his best (pp 324–325) to

erode the full meaning of Tradition as the word is used by Guénon and
Coomaraswamy. In terms of Christianity, he defines as part of 'tradition' the
gospels, the deutero-Pauline epistles, the pseudepigrapha and the apocrypha, and *excludes* from 'tradition', for no apparent reason but pure subversion, the 'genuine apostolic letters' and the later theological commentaries,
brutally splitting the Christian tradition like you'd split a log. Next he turns
his attentions to Judaism and Islam. He asserts that 'we know Moses probably did not write the Pentateuch containing the direct revelation of the Dec-
alogue, nor did Muhammad write down his visions and communications
with Gabriel; both were recorded decades and even centuries later.' Thus by
confusing the Pentateuch, which only reached its final form in the post-
exilic period, with the Koran, which was written down verbatim from the
recollections of actual contemporaries of the Prophet (upon whom be
peace) who committed it to memory—the mnemonic prowess of nomadic
cultures like that of the Arabs being undeniable—he is able to portray the
Koran not as the revelation of God to His Prophet, but, implicitly, as a tex-
tual pastiche thrown together by later generations. Then he attacks revelation directly:

> Despite questions about the historicity of these revelations, they are *regarded*
> as revelations, so the relevant point to this discussion in terms of the distinc-
> tion between tradition and revelation is that in the case of Moses, Muham-
> mad, and for that matter, Joseph Smith [*sic*!], a *claim of revelation* is made that
> includes the communication between mortal man and a deity or deific figure.
> Once revealed, however, the content, irrespective of its etiology, is 'handed
> over' from ancestors to posterity.

So the crux for Quinn is not whether the revelation in question is *true*
because it comes from God, but only whether it is *believed*; a plausible fabri-
cation, or a smart lie, is as good as a valid theophany. A phrase of the poet
Paul Valéry springs immediately to mind in this context: 'If you don't believe
in God, don't quote Him.'

In Appendices C and D, Quinn attempts to confuse traditional esoteric
spirituality with occultism and parapsychology. He posits two basic ontological belief-systems, the 'scientific' (empirical, materialistic, rational) and
the 'supernormal' (non-empirical, non-materialistic, supra-rational), and
shows, correctly, how the first view is reductionist in that it denies the second, and the second view is synthetic, in that it includes the first, while limiting it to its own proper field of study, the material world. But 'rationality'
cannot be strictly identified with the empirical pole, since the rational mind

reaches its highest and most consistent mode of operation in conforming itself to the supra-rational, i.e. when it is applied to revelation, or acts under the guidance of intellection. The first application produces theology, the second, theosophy (as a mode of expression, that is, not as *gnosis per se*, which is how Schuon sometimes uses the word). Quinn, understandably, places the 'occult arts' and 'paranormal phenomena' on the supra-rational side, and reminds us (as if we needed reminding) that those on the empirical, materialistic side regularly debunk these phenomena, along with the higher reaches of intellection and metaphysics. But in doing so he ignores the fact that one of the 'signs of the times' is an unholy alliance between rationalistic, empirical thinking, including arcane technology, and the occult sciences. As Guénon prophesied in *The Reign of Quantity*, 'classical' materialism is now splitting apart under its own dead weight, and flooding the world with energies from the 'infra-psychic' realm; an attraction to psychic powers, and a belief, for example, in UFOs and alien entities that bear all the marks of classical demons, have become pandemic in our society, *without calling the materialistic paradigm into question* in any essential way, a questioning which could only bear fruit if the dimensions of true, traditional spirituality were collectively understood. (As C. S. Lewis' demon Screwtape says in *The Screwtape Letters*, p 33: 'If once we can produce our perfect work—the Materialist Magician, the man, not using, but veritably worshipping, what he vaguely calls 'Forces' while denying the existence of 'spirits'—then the end of the war will be in sight.') Quinn ignores this glaring development. He goes on to point out (Appendix D) the inevitable shortcomings of a social science approach to integral cultures and esoteric spiritualities, making the cogent and highly-quotable point (p 339) that 'it is both a semantic and a metaphysical inversion to attempt a phenomenology of noumena'—but then he includes *parapsychology* along with theosophy and esoterism as an element of the ontological view loosely shared by Coomaraswamy and Guénon—and if the discipline of parapsychology is not an attempt to create 'a phenomenology of noumena', then what is?

Finally, in Appendix D, Quinn employs the approach of 'ethnomethodology' (à-la Harold Garfinkel, Trent Elgin, and Carlos Castaneda) to justify an infiltration of traditional cultures and esoteric spiritualities on the part of those who have realized that their scholarly curiosity about such subjects can in the end only be satisfied by investigating them 'from within'. The sympathetic anthropologist who seeks to understand unfamiliar traditions 'on their own place of reference' (Eliade), and the mystical-secret-hunting, esoteric-initiation-collecting spiritual adventurer (Castaneda)—who, like any good post-modern, has jettisoned the sense of objective truth so he can 'buy' the traditions he needs to devour with the *total* yet *provisional* acceptance of the nihilist, or double agent — are confused with the legitimate exemplars of the traditions themselves. True, the parasite desires to become 'one' with its host, but the job of the physician — or in this case, metaphysician — is not to unite but to separate them.

Trying to put the contemporary flow of social forces into one sentence, I came up with: 'The globalization of the elite leads to the balkanization of the masses.' In Christopher Lasch's words (pp 47–48),

> The world of the late twentieth century presents a curious spectacle. On the one hand, it is now united, through the agency of the market, as it never was before. Capital and labor flow freely across political boundaries that seem increasingly artificial and unenforceable. Popular culture follows in their wake. On the other hand, tribal loyalties have seldom been so aggressively promoted. Religious and ethnic warfare breaks out in one country after another: In India and Sri Lanka; in large parts of Africa; in the former Soviet Union and the former Yugoslavia.

And, I would add, in Oklahoma City, where the secessionist militias of the plains and mountain states, largely Christian and white supremacist, flexed their muscles. What Quinn characterizes as 'pandemic ethnocentrism and xenophobia, parochialism, tribalism, and group solipsism,' which can so easily be portrayed as a purely negative and reactionary resistance to the wonders of planetization, is actually inseparable from it. Given the metaphysical truth that manifestation, considered in its form rather than its essence, is not Principle, it must reveal the Divine Unity in multiple mode; a multiplicity of cultures and religious revelations, like a multiplicity of human individuals, is metaphysically necessary. Therefore any attempt to artificially homogenize world culture and religion must be compensated for by fragmentation and conflict; when an organic multiplicity is suppressed, the principle on which it is based must re-assert itself, but in a negative form. In other words, it is impossible for planetization to triumph on its own terms. At the moment it seems to have triumphed, its instability will have reached critical mass, and it will simply dissolve. So when Quinn, on p 305, says

> a future planetary Traditional culture ... must be *unanimous* — accepted and participated in by all — for without this unanimity it could not be considered Traditional,

he is not only completely inverting the meaning of the word 'Traditional', and giving the lie to his expansive lamentation, on p 284, over 'cultural' pollution (and/or culturocide) . . . by military conquest, economic domination, ('neocolonialism'), or any other form of imposed hegemony or imperialism,

but is placing his faith in something which, fortunately, will not come to pass. Furthermore, on the same page, he bases the ability of each individual in such a 'planetary Traditional culture' to 'see the unity, the sacrality, the oneness of life' on 'its universal acceptance as a *scientific fact*' [italics mine]. This, of course, is a direct inversion of the meaning of Tradition. The vision of the unity and sacrality of life can only be established by Intellection and Revelation, not by scientific experiment. We've known for generations that the oxygen we breathe is produced by the earth's forests; has that prevented us from cutting them down?

When I first read William Quinn Jr.'s extremely plausible version of the future, even though I was appalled, I felt tempted. I was tempted, first, to despair, since according to Quinn, everything that I love is barren, and will die, while everything that I hate is all-too-fertile, and will inevitably triumph. My Islam, my Sufism, will die out, as will my wife's Russian Orthodoxy and Hesychasm. The future belongs to planetization, to the global elites, to a generic, world-fusion 'spirituality' of psychic technicians, to our *intelligent, competent* New Age masters, not the poor imbalanced superstitious cranks whose only function was to destroy all sacred traditions so those Higher Men could take over. And then—for an instant—I felt the second temptation: if you can't beat them, join them. If you do, maybe your writings will have some small influence on the gray, terrible future ahead. You may not be saved, but at least you will be—*remembered*.

By the grace of God, I overcame that temptation. Let me and my worldly hopes be crushed, I said; at least I will have remained faithful to the Truth as God has given me the light to see it, because that Truth is eternal. Whatever happens on the ground of human history, That One will remain inviolate, Lord of the worlds, owner of the Day of Judgement. All is perishing except His Face.

And then an interesting thing happened. As soon as I resigned myself, and my traditions, to inevitable destruction, I saw that this destruction is far from inevitable. If Christianity could survive the Roman Empire; if Judaism could survive the Pharaoh, the Babylonian captivity, the Nazi terror; if the religion of the Lakota could survive the 'manifest destiny' of the Anglo-Saxon race, then Islam and Sufism can also survive. And Orthodox Christianity. And maybe even Tibetan Buddhism. Not, perhaps, as ruling principles of entire civilizations, but as the hidden 'stems' which connect the world of manifestation to its Principle. *Of course* revealed Truth and the Traditions which transmit it will last until the end of time, for the same reason that the breath of life must last until the death of the body—because without it, life cannot go on. If, according to Sufism and Hasidism, the world is maintained in existence by its hidden saints, perhaps the same can be said of its hidden traditions. If Christianity must return to the catacombs; if, as the Prophet said (upon whom be peace) 'Islam began in exile and will end in exile: blessed are those who are in exile!' then so be it. And if the battle known as Armageddon is destined to be fought on the field of history, as it most certainly is being fought right now on the dividing line that passes straight through every human soul, then, when the call comes—not the call of this or that socio-political agenda, but the lightning that comes forth from the East and shines even to the West—and if I live to see it, then I will be ready. Ya Mahdi! Ya Issa!

✳ On Unseen Warfare

The Traditionalist School, and its surrounding field of influence where an interest in 'the perennial philosophy' is steadily growing, are not exempt from the pressure of the forces presently acting to destroy and/or pervert all expressions of true spirituality. Rather, if it is accurate to say that Traditionalism, whether or not we exclusively identify it with the Traditionalist School as presently constituted, represents the fullness of metaphysical truth, it is to be expected that the forces tending to pervert the doctrine will be more active in the Traditionalist world than anywhere else. The 'unseen warfare' the traditional spiritualities are presently engaged in is not only against the passions of the lower soul, but also against objective psychic forces—the Jinn, let us say, or at least those among them who are actively opposed to God—which exploit these passions. This, of course, has always been true. But the concerted, global effort of what Guénon called the 'infra-psychic' to pervert all valid religious and spiritual organizations by *inverting* religious symbolism has had to wait until 'the eleventh hour' to appear in its true, undeniable, and terminal form.

St Paul said it best: 'we wrestle not against flesh and blood, but against principalities, against powers, against the rulers of the darkness of this world, against spiritual wickedness in high places' (Eph. 6:12). We need to understand that Traditionalism will necessarily be under attack in a world like this, and that a great deal of this attack will occur in the subtle realm.

But to admit the reality of this level of things requires a great deal of balance. Paranoia, and the resulting fanaticism, are the result of, (1) placing the perceived 'agenda' on the wrong ontological level, and (2) forgetting that all this is a lawful manifestation of the latter days, and that in the last analysis nothing happens that is not God's will. If we attribute to human beings what are really the actions of the *kafir* Jinn, and to the Jinn what are better understood as the actions of God, then we are paranoid. However, if we use the truth that all events are God's will to deny the actions of the Jinn, and the truth that some of the Jinn are at war with religion to deny the actions of actual human groups—Guénon's 'agents of the counter-initiation'—then we are dangerously complacent. Such complacency may be nothing but a way of denying the *fear* we feel in the face of the psychic forces abroad in the world in these latter days, forces which will tempt us either to seek the blessing of the 'principalities and powers', whether material, social or psychic—since life outside the terms in which they define it will be made to seem hopeless, unproductive or foolish, if not completely impossible—or to defy 'the rulers of the darkness of this world' in a simplistic, naive and/or prideful manner, thus unwittingly becoming their agents in the very act of opposing them. It is important to remember here that we are called upon to be 'wise as serpents' as well as 'harmless as doves', and that to oppose diabolical cunning with innocence, nobility and courage alone is to court destruction.

In times like these, a critical analysis of social and collective psychological forces, as well as (insofar as is possible) the 'agendas' emanating from the subtle psychic realm, may simply be another form of examination-of-conscience. Where has the evil of the world, where has the coming regime of the Antichrist, established its foothold in me? The expression of principial Truth is not and never can be a case of propaganda; it is not a socio-political act, but a liturgical one. The 'cash value' of this work is laid up in another world—mysteriously present in the Center of this one—where moth and rust do not corrupt, nor thieves break in and steal.

9

Comparative Eschatology

ESCHATOLOGY is the science of four 'last things': individual
death; individual destiny in the afterlife; the end of this world or cycle of
manifestation; the renewal of life and existence after that end. This essay
deals with the latter two—with apocalypse, the re-absorption of forms by
their celestial archetypes, and the re-manifestation of those forms in the
'Golden Age' of the cycle to come. In this chapter I compare the eschatological lore of eight traditions: Zoroastrianism, Hinduism, Buddhism, Judaism, Christianity, Islam, the Hopi, and the Lakota. When viewed syn-
optically, the prophecies of these eight traditions appear as rays, or facets, of
a single Form.

According to a hadith of Muslim, as paraphrased by William Chittick,

> God will appear at the resurrection in a multitude of forms, but His crea-
> tures will deny Him until He appears in a form that corresponds to their
> own belief. It is only the perfect men, whose hearts encompass all the Divine
> Names in perfect equilibrium, who will recognize God in whatever form He
> displays.

✳ Saoshyant vs. Angra Mainyu: Zoroastrian Eschatology

The prophecies of the 'end times' from many traditions predict a degeneration of spirituality, civilization and the environment leading to an apocalyptic conflict. But it seems likely that Zarathushtra (Zoroaster) was the first
to sum up all the forces opposed to religion and human life in a single figure:
Angra Mainyu (later called Ahriman). Many ancient gods had their dark

antagonists; Set, for example, was the brother and enemy of the Egyptian Osiris. But most of these antagonisms were seen in terms of the yearly cycle of the seasons, or the heroic exploits of a world-sustaining savior, like the demon-subduing Krishna. Zarathushtra, however, conceived of the struggle of light against darkness in terms of the entire cycle of manifestation, envisioning a definitive victory of the forces of light at the end of time, during the apocalyptic event called in ancient Persian *Frashegird*. Thus many scholars see Zoroastrianism as the original ancestor of Judeo-Christian eschatology, and Angra Mainyu as the prototype of both Satan and the Antichrist. The coming eschatological savior, Saoshyant, is the Zoroastrian equivalent of the Hindu Kalki Avatara, the Jewish Messiah, the Christ of the second coming, the Muslim Mahdi, and similar in many ways to the future Buddha, Maitreya.

The central theophany in Zoroastrianism is fire, which is also the prime agent of the Last Judgement. In the account of Frashegird from the *Bundahish*, a great meteor will strike the earth [cf. Rev. 8:10–11; 9:1ff.] and kindle the eschatological fire. Rivers of molten metal will flow. To the righteous they will seem like warm milk; to the unrighteous, like molten metal. The wise experience the flame of Ahura Mazda ('Lord of Wisdom') as light — in other words, enlightenment; the deceitful, as punishing fire. According to the Zoroastrian scriptures called the *Yashts*, some of which are believed to go back to c. 2000 BC,

> in order that the dead shall rise up, that Living One, the Indestructible, shall come, the world be made wonderful at his wish. . . . When Astvaterets [Saoshyant] comes out from Lake Kansaoya, messenger of Mazda Ahura, son of Vispa-tauvairi [his virgin mother], brandishing the victorious weapon . . . then he will drive the Drug ['Deception', an epithet of Angra Mainyu] from the world of Asha [Divine Law]. He will gaze with wisdom, he will behold all creation . . . he will gaze with eyes of sacrifice on the whole material world, and heedfully will he make the whole material world undying. . . . An[g]ra Mainyu of evil works will flee, bereft of power.
> ⌢ YASHT 19

One wonders if the Pahlevi *drug* or *druj* is related to the Syriac word *daggal* which also denotes 'deception', and from which *dajjal*, the Arabic name for Antichrist, is derived.

To prophesy that Saoshyant will immortalize the material world through *heedfulness*, and by *gazing on it with wisdom* and *with eyes of sacrifice* is to say that the world will transformed, via the sacrifice of the human ego, from a literal material object into a theophany, a vision of the eternal Names of God; it will once again be seen as Adam saw it in Eden. In Blake's words, from *The Marriage of Heaven and Hell*,

> The ancient tradition that the world will be consumed in fire at the end of six thousand years is true.... For the cherub with his flaming sword is hereby commanded to leave his guard at the tree of life, and when he does, the whole creation will be consumed, and appear infinite and holy, whereas now it appears finite & corrupt. This will come to pass by an improvement of sensual enjoyment.

The function of Man is to act as God's eye on the created world, to unite it with its Archetype through divine contemplation, and only secondarily to work, in line with this contemplative vision, with natural forces and conditions. As human consciousness is purified in the spiritual and eschatological fire, the world will lose its literalistic 'materiality' (which, as pure negation, is not itself capable of being saved) and become what it always was, an immortal paradise. This apocalyptic restoration of the natural world is very close to the idea of the redemption of the cosmos in Eastern Orthodox Christianity, where the sacrament of the Eucharist, by which Christ's Incarnation and Redemption are propagated throughout space and time, is sometimes identified with the transfiguration of the universe. In the words of Orthodox theologian Olivier Clement,

> The world was created as an act of celebration, so that it might share in grace and become Eucharist through the offerings of human beings. And that is precisely what Christ, the last Adam, has accomplished. By his death and resurrection he has brought glory to the universe. It is this transfigured creation that is offered to us in the Eucharist....
> ⌒THE ROOTS OF CHRISTIAN MYSTICISM, p110

According to most scholars, Zarathushtra lived around 660 BC. Yet linguistic evidence indicates that the 17 *Gathas*, those parts of the Zoroastrian scriptures (the *Avesta*) which were composed directly by him, may be as much as 4,000 years old. Whether another Zarathushtra actually lived in 2000 BC, or whether the historical Zarathushtra acted as the prophetic renewer of an older tradition, composing his *Gathas* in an archaic sacerdotal language, the Zoroastrian religion is of great antiquity; even if it was not the direct ancestor of the Abrahamic faiths, it profoundly influence all three of them. We must always remember, however, that no authentic religious tradition is patched together out of historical influences. If one tradition contributes material to another, it is only because they share the same essential

Truth—and because the host tradition, in terms of the place and time in which it is destined to appear, is the privileged receptacle of that Truth.

✳ Messiah: Jewish Eschatology

(This section is largely based on Gershom Scholem's The Messianic Idea in Juda-ism, *Schocken Books, New York, 1971)*

The shadowy figure of the Messiah appears in many places throughout Jewish scripture: in the major and minor prophets; in the *Psalms*; in *Genesis*; also in many apocryphal books such as *Fourth Ezra*, *First* and *Second Enoch*, the *Baruch* apocalypses and the *Testament of the Twelve Patriarchs*. Many conceptions of his nature coalesce: he will be a king of the house of David; a priest of the line of Levi, or Aaron; he will vanquish Israel's enemies and establish a kingdom of peace. As a king, he is like David come back; as a renewer of the law, he is like Moses. The concept of the 'suffering servant' from Isaiah 53, who through his death brings redemption to others, also became attached to the figure of the Messiah. According to Scholem, pp 50–51,

> Only after the Bible did . . . varying conceptions as that of an ideal state of the world, of a catastrophic collapse of history, of the restoration of the Davidic kingdom, and of the 'Suffering Servant' merge with the prophetic view of the 'Day of the Lord' and a 'Last Judgement.'

Messianic Judaism tends to downplay individual redemption in favor of the redemption of the nation, and ultimately the world. The Messianic Age is viewed as a total renovation, or restoration, of earthly life as God meant it to be. (Scholem sees the tendency of Christianity to emphasize individual redemption, in this world or the world to come, as one of the places where it diverges from the Jewish idea. Yet Jesus, in his crucifixion, rejected individual salvation in his own case, taking upon himself the sins of the nation and the race, just as the Zaddik in Hasidism may suffer personally to gather the scattered 'sparks' of the Divine Immanence, the *Shekinah*.)

Jewish Messianism is traditionally revolutionary and catastrophic. Through the Messianic breakthrough may be either gradual or instantaneous, it is not a product of historical development. Rather, the Light of God breaks through from a transcendent Source, destroys history and totally transforms it. Scholem characterizes the atmosphere preceding the coming of the Messiah as a time of

428 * THE SYSTEM OF ANTICHRIST

world wars and revolutions ... epidemics, famine, and economic
catastrophe ... apostasy and the desecration of God's name ..., the upset-
ting of all moral order to the point of dissolving the laws of nature (p12).

According to the *Mishnah*,

> In the footsteps of the Messiah presumption will increase and respect disap-
> pear. The empire will turn to heresy and there will be no moral reproof. The
> house of assembly will become a brothel galilee will be laid waste, and the
> people of the frontiers will wander from city to city and none will pity them.
> The wisdom of the scribes will become odious and those who shun sin will
> be despised; truth will nowhere be found. Boys will shame old men and old
> men will show deference to boys. 'The son reviles the father, the daughter
> rises up against the mother' (Micah 7:6). The face of the generation is like
> the face of a dog. On whom shall we then rely? Our father in heaven.

Moses Maimonides (who rejects the miraculous and apocalyptic conception
of the Messiah, the resurrection of the dead, etc.) has this to say about his
advent:

> The Messiah will arise and restore the kingdom of David to its former
> might. He will rebuild the sanctuary and gather the dispersed of Israel. All
> the laws will be reinstituted in his days as of old. Sacrifices will be offered
> and Sabbatical and Jubilee years will be observed exactly in accordance with
> the commandments of the Torah. But whoever does not believe in him or
> does not await his coming denies not only the rest of the prophets, but also
> the Torah and our teacher Moses.

Maimonides repeats the tradition that the war between Gog and Magog
and the return of the prophet Elijah will take place before the Messiah's
coming, maintaining however that 'no one knows how they will come about
until they actually happen.'

The messianic *tikkun* or restoration as presented in the kabbalism of Isaac
Luria is utopian and post-millennialist rather than apocalyptic; it will happen when, through human spiritual labor, all the scattered sparks of the
Shekinah are gathered together again and the 'vessels' restored, which burst
at the moment of the creation because they could not withstand the out-
pouring of God's power. Yet it gave rise to the basically pre-millennialist
messianic movement of Sabbetai Zevi, which ended in apparent disaster
when the 'false Messiah' converted to Islam under threat by the Sultan of
Turkey, whom he had attempted to convert to his brand of Judaism, in 1666.
Sabbatianism, though not politically militant, was a true mass movement.

Its shameful and shocking failure, according to Scholem, set the stage for the post-millennialist and spiritualizing movement of Hasidism under Israel Baal Shem Tov, which re-interpreted messianism, at least initially, in radically interior terms.

According to traditional Judaism, the Jews are cautioned not to 'press for the End', since the coming of the Messiah is in the hands of God alone. Yet the fervent belief in that coming, not surprisingly, sometimes resulted in religious and political activism based on chiliastic ideas, which routinely ended in disaster. And, partly in response to the failure of such Messianic utopianism, there developed within the stream of the Kabbalah another more introverted way of 'pressing for the End'. It was believed that the great Kabbalist or Zaddik has the power to bring the Messiah through inner spiritual struggle, theurgy, or magic. He can descend into the realm of darkness, the world of the *kelipot*, the 'shells' or 'husks' (the root principles of materialism?), which he has the power to 'sweeten', thereby transmuting the wrath of God, gathering the scattered sparks of the Shekinah and reuniting them with the Creator. In so doing, he prepares the way for the Messiah. The great spiritual master, in other words, has the power to harrow Hell, like Christ did; *but this work is forbidden.* A legend is told of a great kabbalistic magician who captured Sammael, the Devil, and could therefore have brought about the redemption of Israel—if only he had not been seduced by his captive. (That the magical attempt to overcome evil on the macrocosmic level is forbidden to the Zaddik or Kabbalist is paralleled by the legend that Jesus was one of 30 saints of his time who had the power to bring back the dead; they were forbidden to do this, but Jesus broke the rules!)

According to some authorities, when the Messiah comes he will bring a new Torah; in the Biblical account, however, he will simply reveal the Torah in its fullness. The *Talmud* says that in the Messianic age the Torah will either be obeyed more strictly and perfectly than is possible now, or mostly abrogated. (According to the extremist and antinomian followers of Sabbetai Zevi, it will be entirely abrogated; whatever is now prohibited, in the Messianic age will be allowed, if not required.) A stricter and more complete Torah and a largely or totally abrogated one appear as extreme opposites. But could there be, by any chance, a hidden identity between them?

The *Zohar*, the central classic of kabbalistic literature attributed to Moses Cordovero, may provide the answer. According to the more recent parts of the *Zohar*, and their exegesis by the Sabbetians, there are two Torahs: the Torah of the Tree of Life and the Torah of the Tree of Knowledge of Good and Evil. The Torah of the Tree of Life is the Law as it was in Paradise before

Adam sinned, the pure expression of God's creative power and wisdom, with no admixture of privation or evil. The Torah of the Tree of Knowledge is the Torah as we know it now in this fallen world.

Since both trees, according to the tradition, sprout from the same root, it could be said that the Tree of the Knowledge is an edited version, or darkened vision, of the Tree of Life. The first set of the tablets of the Law brought by Moses from Sinai, which he destroyed when he saw the people worshipping the Golden Calf, held the Torah of the Tree of Life. The second set contained the Torah of the Tree of the Knowledge of Good and Evil.

The meaning of this tradition is fairly clear: this fallen world is Paradise as seen through the veils of the ego. As long as the consequences of Adam's sin have not been suffered through and expiated under the influence of God's grace, the ego is still in force, the world still effectively (if not essentially) fallen. And the ego of this fallen world cannot withstand, or understand, the Torah of the Tree of Life, where everything is lawful because everything is a manifestation or an act of God. It interprets the primal power and innocence of God's Self-manifestation not as a fullness of Divine Life into which no evil can come, but as a Divine validation of chaos, and thus a as license to harm oneself and others. What on a higher level of interpretation is Paradise (the summit of Sinai being the symbol of this higher level), on a lower one is a worship of the unredeemed passions, the Golden Calf—in Sufi terms, the 'commanding self'. Moses brought the higher Law by which man is reunited to his Creator; the people could only see this as a reinstitution of Paganism. (In the same way, St Paul's doctrine that Christians were no longer under 'the curse of the law' led in some instances to libertinism, as in the excesses of the *agape* feasts railed against in the epistle of Jude.) Therefore a second, edited version of the Torah, tailored to this fallen order of perception, had to be substituted, a Torah based on commands and prohibitions, on 'the Knowledge of Good and Evil'. (The Torah of the Tree of Life is strictly analogous to the Islamic *Rahman*, God's universal and all-creating mercy, and to Ibn al-'Arabi's concept of the Divine Will, which is the cause of everything that actually occurs, thus in a sense making everything lawful—to God, that is. And the Torah of the Tree of the Knowledge of Good and Evil corresponds to the Islamic *Rahim*, God's particular and saving mercy, and to Ibn al-'Arabi's Divine Wish, the basis of the Muslim *shari'at* which is incumbent on all believers—because human beings are not God. The Torah of the Tree of Knowledge would also correspond to the figure of Moses in the Koran, and the Torah of the Tree of Life to the immortal prophet Khidr, whom the Sufis identify with the unnamed master, shocking and incomprehensible in his actions, encountered by Moses in the Koran, Surah of *The Cave*.)

In the Messianic age, the Torah of the Tree of Knowledge is replaced by the Torah of the Tree of Life. In a sense this is a 'new' Torah—though in reality it is simply the old one, understood now in its fullness. This Torah is more strictly and perfectly obeyed than was possible in the past because now that the fullness of God's Life has been unveiled to all men, it is virtually impossible to disobey it. Torah has risen from the level of the will, which can choose to obey or disobey, and come to rest on the level of the Intellect, where all is Truth. Truth commands obedience not through specific commands and prohibitions, but simply by being what It is. Truth is obeyed not through the struggle to remain faithful to behavioral norms, but simply by being recognized. And where commands and prohibitions are transcended, the Law is abrogated—not through being broken, however, but through being perfectly fulfilled. (In the words of Jesus, 'I come not to destroy the Law, but to fulfill it.') In Taoist terms, the Tao, the Way—perfectly analogous, on one level, to the Torah of the Tree of Life—is followed by means of *wu wei*, 'not doing', or 'acting without acting'. In *wu wei*, the dichotomy between assuming active responsibility and simply letting things take their course is entirely transcended; this is how it will be in the Messianic age.

According to the Aggadah, the Messiah was born on the day the second Temple was destroyed, and is now in occultation, like the Shiite Twelfth Imam. In 2nd century legend, well before the establishment of the Roman papacy, he is pictured as residing secretly in Rome. It is as if the Jews said to the Romans, 'You destroy our Temple? Very well: the very spirit and principle of our Temple will then become the hidden ruler of your own Empire.' In later years this legend gave Jews a traditional basis for seeing the Pope as a counterfeit or anti-messiah, a kind of usurper of the secret messianic rule. The *Tractate Sanhedrin* of the Talmud says that 'The Son of David will not come until the kingdom is subverted to heresy.' It is difficult not to see in this tradition a prediction that the tremendous genius of the Jewish people will be diverted in psychic and materialistic directions—as represented by Freud and Marx, for example, as well as by the present secularism of the State of Israel.

Sometimes the figure of the Messiah is doubled: there will be a Messiah son of Joseph as well as a Messiah son of David. The Messiah son of Joseph—although he is not, as Scholem points out, to be identified with the 'suffering servant of Isaiah—perishes in the eschatological combat, defeated by Antichrist. After this the Messiah son of David comes, kills the

Antichrist, and establishes the Kingdom. (The figure of Antichrist in Judaism, though based in part on the Gog of *Ezekiel* and the Fourth Beast in *Daniel*, only makes his fully developed appearance in the Jewish apocrypha.) This tradition is closely paralleled by the Shïite Muslim story that when the Mahdi comes he will be defeated and killed by the Antichrist, after which the Antichrist himself will be slain by the prophet Jesus.

According to the commentary on *Habakkuk* in the *Dead Sea Scrolls*, the priestly Messiah of the End of Days, like Adam, will encompass past present and future, and so be able to interpret the visions of the ancient prophets regarding the total course of the history of Israel. Like the Kalki Avatara, and the Word of God in the Christian *Apocalypse*, he is 'the beginning and the end'.

In the 10th chapter of the *Tractate Sanhedrin* from the Talmud, it is said that 'The Son of David will come only in a generation wholly guilty or a generation wholly innocent.' The messianic breakthrough into a totally corrupt world is necessarily pre-millennialist, since the Messiah must then establish righteousness by means of a revolutionary and apocalyptic cataclysm, just as his appearance in an already-purified world must be post-millennialist. Isaac Luria's messianic *tikkun*, for example, is post-millennialist; in Lurianic Kabbalah, the Messiah comes when we have sufficiently purified ourselves through our own actions; he is an automatic reflection of this purity. On the other hand, the Messianic movements of Bar Kochba and Sabbatai Zevi, the one political and military, the other mystical and spiritual, were necessarily pre-millennialist. These conceptions, like those of the abrogation vs. the perfect observance of the Torah, would seem to be totally opposed. Once again, however, it is the *Zohar* which points out, though in a veiled way, their hidden identity.

Following the Aggadah, the *Zohar* sees the Messianic breakthrough as gradual, though not thereby as the product of a historical development. The coming of the Messiah is not a human achievement, but a divine miracle. According to the *Zohar*, the gentiles (called 'Esau' or 'Edom') received their illumination at a single stroke, after which they slowly began to lose it. Israel, on the other hand, received its illumination gradually. As the loss of strength and illumination among the gentiles continues, Israel will slowly grow in power and knowledge, to the point where they will be able to overcome them and destroy them. After this the divine light will grow in Israel to the point where all things will be restored. The separation between creature and Creator will be transcended. The world will return to the state of Eden, and every man and woman will behold the Shekinah 'eye to eye'.

My exegesis of this doctrine is as follows: The gentiles or 'Esau' are the outer world of creation; they are history itself. 'Israel', on the other hand, is the inner world of the soul. According to Hindu and Greco-Roman doctrine, the cosmic cycle of manifestation begins with a God-given Golden Age, and then degenerates; the 'nations' receive their illumination all at once, then progressively lose it.

This 'historical entropy' is related to the net entropy of all physical processes. The very existence of a sensual world 'outside' the perceiving subject is in fact an expression of this entropy: if the Sun and the stars were not burning themselves away, we would not see anything; if matter were not crumbling, vaporizing, eroding and dissolving, we would not hear or smell or feel or taste anything. Matter *is* entropy. The expanding universe represents the dissipation inherent in everything material, as well as the ultimate fate of all those to whom matter is the central reality.

In the inner dimension of the soul, however, the opposite motion takes place. To the degree that one's sense of reality is withdrawn from the sensual world and placed on the ascending ladder of Being which is 'inner' in relation to that world, the pull of the senses and the heavy literalism of historical reality lose force, till the contemplation of spiritual realities conquers and overcomes the oppressive force of material contingencies; this is the return from 'captivity' and 'exile' and the entry into 'the Promised Land'. First we rise to an understanding of the sensual, material world as a subjective, psychic experience; secondly, the ultimate spiritual Witness of this psychic experience of the material world is progressively unveiled. As the outer world is always expanding and dissipating, so the inner world, to the degree that we place our attention upon it, is always being 'recollected', always coming to a point. (In Sufi terms, the outer world is the realm of *tafraqa*, dispersion, and the inner one the realm of *jam'*, gathering or concentration.) This simultaneous and double motion can be represented by two superimposed triangles, where the apex of the lower triangle (the manifestation of YHVH by means of creation) is the central point of the base of the upper triangle (the return to YHVH through spiritual contemplation), and vice versa. This diagram is a form of the Shield or Star of David (the Seal of Solomon), which is one emblem of the Adam Kadmon (another being the kabbalistic Tree of Life of the ten *sephiroth*) who in the eschatological dimension is the Messiah as well: the 'Human Form Divine', created in the 'image and likeness of God', being the secret form of YHVH, which transcends and thereby encompasses both His creation of the cosmos and the universal *tikkun* of the cosmos to its root in Him.

When the 'generation' of the outer world is wholly guilty and corrupt—when it is completely dead to us, since we have died to it—then the 'generation' of the inner world will be wholly innocent, since it knows only God, Who is 'of too pure eyes to behold iniquity.' It is precisely in this sense that the Messiah will come in a 'generation' which is totally innocent in one sense and totally corrupt in another.

But the Messiah, like Adam, does not exclusively represent the triumph of inner recollection over outer manifestation, material and historical, but encompasses both dimensions. The Jewish hope for a restored terrestrial kingdom is not simply abandoned or superseded therefore, but rather totally transformed. As in the Christian *Apocalypse*, the messianic kingdom—the New Jerusalem, bride of the Messiah—represents both a new heaven and a new earth.

According to the *Zohar*, the Messiah will not come until the tears of Esau are exhausted. This is the same story told in a different way. Jacob is 'Israel', the name he received after his struggle with the angel at Peniel, in the course of which he overcame the 'descending' current of manifestation and entered the 'ascending' current of *tikkun*, these being the two directions in which the angels moved in his dream of the Ladder, which is a type of the kabbalistic Tree of Life. In the context of this world, he came out of the struggle lame; in the context of the next world, he won the blessing of God. Jacob's brother Esau, then, represents the attachment to the descending current of creation—so fresh and childlike in Eden—which ultimately leads to dissipation in the materialistic vision of things that will always sell its invisible birthright, its share in the world to come, for 'a mess of pottage', the visible material goods of this world. (That Jacob could only get the patriarchal blessing from his blind father Isaac through deceit represents the fact that the path of *tikkun* is inner and esoteric. That one aspect of this deceit required Jacob to dress in an animal skin so that Isaac would believe he was blessing his hairy son Esau represents the transfiguration of the materialistic or animalistic lower nature of man on the Path of its return to the Creator.) The color of Esau, Isaac's first-born, and also of the pottage for which he sold his birthright, is red. Red symbolizes creation, primal life-energy; Esau shares this color-symbolism with Adam, the first-created man, whose name means 'red clay'. But the redness of this primal vitality is also the redness of violence, the fall from the pole of *forma* toward the pole of *materia* which ends as a descent into materialism; this is one reason why it was adopted by the 'reds', the Marxists. And it is not Isaac's first-born son Esau—God's original creative impulse—who receives the blessing, but his younger son Jacob, symbol of *tikkun*, the reversal of the cosmogonic process, otherwise knows as the spiritual Path. The exhaustion of the tears of Esau represents the exhaustion of materialism, the termination of the impulse to run after the lost Paradise into the wilderness of matter, energy, space and time. In metaphysical terms, it is the exhaustion of the current of creative manifestation for this cycle.

Rabbi Israel of Rizhin said: In the days of the Messiah man will no longer quarrel with his fellow but with himself. The struggle with the outer world will be superseded by the struggle to conquer the inner world; in Muslim terms, the Lesser Jihad will give way to the Greater. (W.B. Yeats also, in *A Vision*, predicted that the coming age would be 'antithetical' as the one passing away was 'primary'. The primary character, or humanity in primary ages, battles with conditions, while the antithetical character, or man in antithetical ages, battles with himself.) Rabbi Israel also said that the Messianic world will be a world without images, 'in which the image and its object can no longer be related.' In negative terms, in terms of the 'generation totally corrupt,' this indicates the solipsistic nadir of postmodernism, where all experiences are considered to be without objective referent — mere images. In the positive terms of 'a generation wholly innocent,' it refers to the *tikkun* or reabsorption of all things into their invisible and transcendent principles. If image and object, or *phenomenon* and *noumenon*, or cosmic manifestation and its Divine Source, can no longer be 'related' as two separate terms, it means that they are either totally divorced or totally united. The former state is Hell; the latter is Paradise; the final separation between the divorced condition and the married condition is the Last Judgement.

✱ Maitreya: Buddhist Eschatology

In most schools of Buddhism, the future Buddha — either the last Buddha of this cycle of manifestation, or simply the next Buddha to appear — will be named Maitreya, a word which means 'moonlight' (It may or may not be significant that the Prophet Muhammad, considered as perfectly receptive to the light of Allah, is also compared to the moon.) In *Maitreya, The Future Buddha* [ed. Alan Sponberg and Helen Hardacre, Cambridge University Press, 1988], my main authority for this exposition, contributor Jan Nattier calls Maitreya the 'anointed' heir of Shakyamuni, the historical figure we know as 'the Buddha'. He would therefore be, at least in the narrow etymological sense, a *messiah* or *christ*, which in Hebrew and Greek respectively mean 'anointed one'—though Nattier may simply be using the word 'anointed' in a loose, generic sense. His name may well relate him to the Zoroastrian savior Mithra; Joseph M. Kitagawa, in the same book, draws parallels between Maitreya and the Zoroastrian Saoshyant.

The Buddhist doctrine of cyclical time is notoriously a-historical, generating predictions like 'a few thousand years from now the human life-span will have increased to 80,000 years,' a statement which clearly can only have a symbolic or mythological meaning. And where the Hindu doctrine of cycles usually accepted by the Traditionalists, via Coomaraswamy and Guénon, begins with a Golden Age, descends through Silver, Bronze, and Iron ages, then ends with an apocalyptic dissolution, after which a new Golden Age descends fully-formed from the heavenly worlds, the Buddhists view cyclical time more horizontally, as a rising and falling of vast aeonic waves; the cosmic environment gradually sinks in its ability to receive the truth, and then gradually rises. The Hindu doctrine of cycles is substantially the same as that of the classical Greeks, and roughly in line with Christian and Muslim eschatology; the Buddhist doctrine is shared by the Jains, and was more-or-less the one adopted by the Theosophical Society, except for the fact that the Buddhist place the next Golden Age thousands of years in the future (roughly 2,500 years according to some schools, though certain teachers now tend to shorten this to 500 years, given the degeneracy of the times), whereas H. P. Blavatsky in *The Secret Doctrine* saw it as imminent.

Be that as it may, most Buddhists agree with traditional Christians, Muslims and Hindus that our present age is on a downward course. We are in the 'last 500 years of the dharma,' the final period of the cycle at the end of which Buddhism will die out, or live on only as a empty shadow of its former self. The age itself will end in war before the appearance of Maitreya, just as, in Christian eschatology, Armageddon will precede the Second Coming of Christ. Many, such as Martin Lings, identify Maitreya with the Hindu Kalki, the 10th and last avatar of Vishnu, who will come at the end of the degenerate Kali-yuga to end this cycle and inaugurate a new one, particularly in view of the fact that the Hindu scripture the *Bhavagata Purana* identifies the ninth avatar of Vishnu with the historical Buddha. The Theravadins view Maitreya as the last of the five Buddhas of the present time-period, which, though it will end with the degeneration of Buddhism, is seen as 'the good eon', as opposed to the Hindu understanding of our time as the Kali-yuga, and Age of Iron. The Mahayana Buddhists, on the other hand, usually assign Maitreya to the far distant Golden Age of the next cycle, when the world will have finally recovered from the degeneration and apocalyptic end of this one; he does not inaugurate this cycle but only enters it when the time is ripe. This Mahayana version of Maitreya could therefore be called 'post-millennialist', though not in the progressivist or reformist sense, since Buddhism sees its cycles of spiritual flowering and degeneration more as the seasons of a pre-established pattern than as the product of human action or its abdication. The fruits of karma ripen more to the spiritual advancement or retardation of the individual than to the worsening or betterment of the world. Some Mahayana Buddhists however, particularly in China and Southeast Asia, have envisioned Maitreya as destined to appear in this very 'final 500 years of the dharma,' perhaps even within the present generation, seeing him as a revolutionary/apocalyptic figure similar to Christ or the Mahdi or the Jewish Messiah—a system of beliefs which, as in the case of analogous doctrines within the Abrahamic religions, has tended to produce dynastic struggles or popular liberation movements headed by quasi-religious 'pretenders' claiming to be the expected Buddhist Savior.

Maitreya will appear during the reign of a world monarch, a *chakravartin* ('turner of the wheel'). Jan Nattier repeats the prophecy that he will be announced by Kashyapa, a disciple of Shakyamuni who has remained in suspended animation through the ages until the time when he will emerge as herald of Maitreya. (Nattier hears in 'Kashyapa' the Persian name of 'Keresaspa', the designated herald of the Zoroastrian savior Saoshyant. Keresaspa will also emerge from 'occultation' or suspended animation to play his role.) According to the Tendai School, he will be a Singhalese king by the name of Dhutta-Gamani, brother to Maitreya and also his first disciple. Others give the king's name as Shanka. According to one story, he will renounce his throne in order to follow Maitreya. Since Shanka will necessarily be of the kingly-warrior caste, a *kshatriya*, Maitreya—unlike Gautama, who was also a *kshatriya*—will be of the highest priestly caste, a *brahmin*. Such a conjunction between a Buddha and a *chakravartin* takes place very rarely; according to the Mahayana lore recounted by Padmanabh S. Jaini, in his chapter 'The Stages in the Bodhisattva Career of Tathagata Maitreya', it only occurs 'at the start of each new ascension within an intermediate eon (*antarkalpa*) in a given time cycle (*mahakalpa*).' We are now 'at the tail end of an *antarkalpa*, which is moving rapidly toward a minor apocalypse.' Thus Maitreya will incarnate in the far distant future, in a new civilization supported by 'two wheels of the law', the wheel of merit leading to Paradise, turned by a *chakravartin*, and the wheel of renunciation leading to Nirvana, turned by himself as Buddha. This would appear to be the Buddhist version of the Hindu *satyayuga* or Golden Age, when worldly abundance and other-worldly bliss are not the opponents of final Liberation, as they often must be for us in this Age of Iron, but rather the disciples of it.

✳ The Parousia: Christian Eschatology

There is so much contemporary Christian literature relating to the latter days and the apocalypse, especially from the Evangelical wing of the church, that instead of trying to make sense of that profusion I will simply draw on what has fallen effortlessly into my hands. My wife's conversion to Russian Orthodoxy has added many new books to our shelves, among which are *The Apocalypse of St John: An Orthodox Commentary* by Archbishop Averky of Jordanville, based on many patristic sources (notably the *Commentary on the Apocalypse* by St Andrew, Archbishop of Caesaria, c. 5th century) and *Ultimate Things: An Orthodox Christian Perspective on the End Times*, by Dennis E. Engleman, which was recommended to us by Rama Coomaraswamy. Both books have the advantage of being largely based on the earliest Christian sources, and both walk the fine line between an over-literal and an over-allegorical interpretation of scripture. They are perfectly timely, but not so tied to the daily news that they run the risk of being trampled by the course of events. Much of this section is based on the above two books, supplemented by Guénon's *The Reign of Quantity and the Signs of the Times*.

The Orthodox interpretation of the *Apocalypse* and its doctrine of eschatology in general departs from many Evangelical interpretations in two major ways. First, it is firmly a-millennial. Christ will not come to establish a thousand-year earthly reign after the tribulation, as in pre-millennialism, nor will he descend to crown a thousand-year rule of Christendom established by his followers, as in post-millennialism. Such millennialism was condemned, as the heresy of 'chiliasm', by the Second Ecumenical Council. For most Orthodox, as well as for St Augustine and most traditional Catholics, the 'millennium' described in Rev. 20:1–10, when Satan shall be bound, is the church age itself, and is largely past.

In my own opinion, the placing of the millennium after the eschatological combat, which has led many into interpreting it as a worldly Christian empire of the future, has to do with the secret correspondence between the Church Militant and the Church Triumphant. If Christ's kingdom is 'not of this world', and if membership in it is based on one's dying with Christ and so participating in His resurrection, then Christians are in one sense beyond the Apocalypse already, dwelling in a heavenly 'millennium' which will have no end.

The second main departure from Evangelical eschatology has to do with the materialistic interpretation of 'the rapture', a notion based, according to Engleman, on the visions of a Scotswoman, Margaret Macdonald, in 1830. The supporters of this doctrine cite Rev. 3:10, 'I also will keep you from the hour of trial which shall come upon the whole world,' as well as 1 Thess. 4:15–17, according to which the living in Christ shall be 'caught up . . . in the clouds to meet the Lord in the air,' and Matt. 24:29–31, when the angels shall gather together the elect 'from the four winds, from one end of heaven to the other.' According to Engleman, this has nothing to do with a levitation or dematerialization of Christians so they can escape the tribulation, but with an 'instantaneous spiritual transformation.' In support of this he cites John 17:15: 'I do not pray that You should take them out of the world, but that You should keep them from the evil one.'

In my own opinion, since in I Thessalonians the living are to be caught up *after* the resurrection of the dead, to meet them in the air, this may also simply refer to the entry of the saved into heaven after death. In any case, it has nothing to do with a special dispensation to Christians allowing them to escape the great tribulation, since it will happen after the tribulation has ended. Engleman and other Orthodox Christians believe that the Evangelical expectation of an earthly millennium, and the belief that Christians will escape the tribulation, are precisely the erroneous doctrines which will lead many of them to mistake Antichrist and his earthly rule for Christ and his Kingdom. And, I would add, the doctrine of the rapture is in part responsible for the contemporary fascination with 'alien abductions'. (The hippy version of the rapture was that all the good hippies would be taken away to a new world in the alien 'mothership'.)

Engleman quotes St Augustine's summary of Christian eschatology from *The City of God*:

> Elias the Tishbite shall come; the Jews shall believe; Antichrist shall persecute; Christ shall judge; the dead shall rise; the good and the wicked shall be separated; the world shall be burned and renewed.

And while he accepts the Apocalypse as both a spiritual and a future historical event, Augustine cautions against taking its symbols too literally, and especially against setting dates, since 'of that day and hour no one knows, not even the angels in heaven, but my Father only' (Matt. 24:36).

The four beasts in the Book of Daniel which come up out of the sea Engleman interprets as four world empires. The last beast, with ten horns, three of which are torn out to make room for a little horn 'speaking pompous words' is interpreted as Rome, which is extended to cover the several world empires which arose out of Western Christendom, including the coming New World Order. According to St Hippolytus, the 'little horn' is Antichrist. The fourth beast is analogous to the Beast of the *Apocalypse*, having seven heads and ten horns, which many see as seven successive kingdoms and ten contemporary kings. The sea from which the four beasts in *Daniel* and the Beast of the *Apocalypse* emerge is interpreted as the tempestuous sea of collective humanity. (I tend to see it more as the 'collective unconscious', the mass psychological condition of the fallen human soul, which comes to essentially the same thing. As the 'sea' is mass psychology, so the 'air' is the psychic plane *per se*, inhabited by those subtle beings called in the Bible 'the powers of the air', who are generally considered demonic.)

The global empire of the fourth beast in *Daniel* will be the base of operations for Antichrist. The Jews will return to their homeland. The Temple will be restored. In it the Antichrist will be acknowledged by the Jews as their Messiah, and later as God. Most of Christendom will abandon its doctrines to follow him.

The end times will be times of mass apostasy and demonic deception. Such apostasy cannot be stopped; the best one can do is avoid being influenced by it, which in itself will be a kind of life-or-death struggle. When the Antichrist arises, it is time to return to the catacomb church, since the 'above-ground' church, even Orthodoxy itself, will for the most part worship him.

If Satan is the ape of God, Antichrist can be called the ape of Christ. He will counterfeit the life experiences and miracles of Christ, even, as far as possible, the resurrection. Like Christ, he will be a teacher. He will be a king of this world, as Christ is a monarch of a kingdom not of this world; he will be a high priest of all religions, requiring that all men worship him as God. He will begin his reign with a show of mildness, which will quickly become a reign of terror. He will deceive many — including himself, according to some, since he will not know that he is really Antichrist.

The symbol for both Christ and Antichrist, according to St Hippolytus, is the lion. (It's an interesting fact that the god *Legba*, the 'Christ' of the Voudoo religion, is also symbolized by the lion.) As Guénon says in *The Reign of Quantity*, the Antichrist can adopt the very symbols of the Messiah, using them of course in an inverted sense. . . . In the same way there can and must be a strange resemblance between the designations of the Messiah (*El-Mesiha* in Arabic) and of the Antichrist (*El-Mesikh*). . . . *Mesikh* can be taken as a deformation of *Mesiha*, by a mere addition of a dot to the final letter; but at the same time the first word means 'deformed', which correctly expresses the character of the Antichrist' (pp326–327; n173).

In the early 1800s, St Nilus revealed that Antichrist would be born 'without man's sowing'—by artificial insemination or genetic manipulation, presumably—from the womb of an evil woman; his emergence will thus be a satanic counterfeit of the virgin birth of Jesus. In Guénon's words (*The Reign of Quantity*, p328),

> the false is necessarily also the 'artificial', and in this respect the 'counter-tradition' cannot fail, despite its other characteristics, to retain the 'mechanical' character appertaining to all the productions of the modern world, of which it itself will be the last.

According to St Hippolytus, the mother of Antichrist will come from the Tribe of Dan, the only tribe of Israel not mentioned in the *Apocalypse*, and which is called (in Gen. 49:17) 'a serpent by the way, a viper by the path.' (The serpent-god of Voudoo, *Danbhala*, is perhaps related to the Tribe of Dan, especially since one of the many tributaries to the magical syncretism of Voudoo was a heterodox form of Ethiopian Judaism. The place of Dan, among the regions in Palestine assigned to the tribes of Israel, is in the North, which may indicate that he, like the serpent in Eden, has something to do with the fall of the Hyperborean Paradise.)

The number of the Beast, 666 (Rev. 13:18), is interpreted (*Ultimate Things*, p140) as follows: While 7 is the number of God, Who transcends manifestation, 6 is the number of complete manifestation. Therefore 666 refers to 'the kingdom of man and nature without God' extended into the realms of body, mind and soul. (Guénon, in *The Reign of Quantity*, [chap. 39, n7] says that 'the number of the Beast' is also a solar number—another example of the 'ape of Christ' principle, since Christ is 'the Sun of Righteousness'.) The Image of the Beast in Rev. 13, which the second beast who is the False Prophet causes to be set up and worshipped by all men, is identified with the image with gold head, silver chest, bronze belly, iron legs, and feet of iron mixed with clay dreamt of by King Nebuchadnezzar (Dan. 2:31–44), which falls after having its feet broken by 'the stone not cut by hands'—the Kingdom of God—and further identified with the idol of gold set up by the king to be worshipped by all men in *Daniel* 3. The different metals represent four world empires from Babylon to Rome; the Image of the Beast is thus the totality of the kingdom of man set up against the kingdom of God. (The Traditionalist writers identify the image in *Daniel* with the four world ages in Greco-Roman and Hindu traditions. The fact that the feet of the image are partially of clay refers to the ontological instability of the end times. The final destiny of materialism, symbolized by iron which seems so strong and permanent, is dissolution, since matter is the most instable and ephemeral of all things. The abandonment of the concept of solid matter by modern physics, and the fragmentation of our image of the material world by the electronic media, are clear signs of this dissolution.)

The Antichrist, according to the *Apocalypse*, will rule for 'seven days' which are really seven years, though even this period of time should not be taken too literally.

According to Engleman, he will rise to power in a politically unified world. His capital will be Jerusalem, his seat a renewed Jewish Temple. (Conservative Jews in Israel are prepared even now to rebuild the Temple, and believe that the one who leads them to rebuild it will be the Messiah.)

The Prophets Enoch and Elias, the 'two witnesses' of Rev. 11:3–5, will then return and denounce the Antichrist. (According to the Old Testament, neither Enoch nor Elias experienced death, which is why the Sufis identify Elias with Khidr the 'immortal prophet'.) They will be martyred by Antichrist, rise again after three and one-half days, and ascend into heaven. Because of their ministry, a remnant of the Jews will be converted to Christ.

After the martyrdom of the witnesses, the Tribulation will begin. The Beast will place his mark upon all who submit to him, without which none can buy or sell. The world will be enslaved. The great end-time plagues will come. The Temple will be desolated. And Christians everywhere will be persecuted.

According to the *Apocalypse* and *Zechariah*, the final battle will be fought in the valley of Armageddon near Jerusalem. Satan will deceive the nations, Gog and Magog (Rev. 20:7–9) and gather them together for battle, where they will be destroyed by fire from heaven. The greatest earthquake in the history of the earth will take place. The Euphrates river will dry up. The Archangel Michael will go to war with the dragon (Satan) 'in heaven', defeat him, and cast him out (Rev. 12:7–9).

Then Christ, the Word of God, will come down from heaven. With his angelic armies he will go to war against the Beast, the False Prophet and their armies, triumph over them, and cast them into the lake of fire (Rev.

19:11–21). The Heavenly Jerusalem will descend. The dead will rise and be judged. There will be a new heaven and a new earth.

The *Apocalypse* contains one fascinating episode which I've never heard anyone comment upon. Rev. 17:16–17 reads as follows:

> And the ten horns which thou sawest upon the beast, these shall hate the whore, and shall make her desolate and naked, and shall eat of her flesh, and burn her with fire.

> For God hath put it into their hearts to fulfill his will, and to agree, and give their kingdoms unto the beast, until the words of God shall be fulfilled.

On the face of it, this seems to say that the Antichrist himself, or the ten horns upon his head, who are his servants the ten kings, will destroy the Whore of Babylon. First the Whore is seen riding on the beast (Rev. 17:3); but then the ten kings slay her, after which—according to God's will—they turn their kingdoms over to the beast. What are we to make of this?

Perhaps it refers to a time of luxury and over-indulgence which gives way to a time of harshness, and which seems by its very degeneracy to justify that harshness, as the decadence of the Weimar Republic lent credibility to Hitler's draconian measures. It may also picture a unified world economy whose breakup, due to internal contradictions, resurgent nationalism or other factors, ushers in the reign of Antichrist, who alone seems capable of restoring order.

✳ The Imam Mahdi and the Prophet Jesus: Muslim Eschatology

(My main source for this section is Islamic Messianism: The Idea of the Mahdi in Twelver Shi'ism, *by Abdulaziz Abdulhussein Sachedina, State University of New York Press, 1981. Sachedina's primary sources are Muhammad ibn Ali al-Baqir and Jafar al-Sadiq, the 5th and 6th Shiite Imams.)*

The signs of the Hour of Judgement in Islamic tradition are many. The moon will be split in two, symbolizing the breaching of the psychic isthmus between this material 'sublunary' world and the next world, the barrier between time and eternity. (The disappearance of the sea at the coming of the new heaven and the new earth in Rev. 21:1 undoubtedly has the same meaning; the sea is unstable and ever-shifting like the psyche, and the moon rules the sea.) According to a *hadith* of the Prophet, buildings will reach the sky as the end approaches, and men will dress like women. (Interestingly, St Nilus of Mount Athos, in the 19th century, also mentioned cross-dressing as an apocalyptic sign; and I would add that since polarity is the principle of all cosmic manifestation, the erosion of sexual differences is a clear sign of the dissolution of earthly humanity.) Among other signs, the Koran predicts a great earthquake (Surah 'The Earthquake'), like the one described in Rev. 16:18. Surah (96), 'The Prophets', speaks of a time when 'Gog and Magog are unloosed, and they slide down out of every slope, and nigh has drawn the true promise'; the same Surah makes reference to a 'beast' which will come 'out of the earth' in the latter days and speak to men 'when the Word falls on them.' According to one *hadith*, which sounds like a version of the modern Evangelical Christian idea of the Rapture, 'God will send a cold wind from the direction of Syria'—the North—'and no one who has in his heart as much as a single grain of good shall remain in the earth without being taken.' (Compare Matt. 24:40–4 and 1 Thess. 4:17; also *The Siege of Shambhala*, below.)

Islamic eschatology shares with Christianity the belief that Jesus will return at the end of time. Muslims, however, who call Jesus 'the Spirit of God' and even accept the doctrine of the virgin birth, still see him as a great prophet but not the Son of God since, according to the Koran, God 'neither begets nor is He begotten.'

Along with the second coming of Jesus, Muslims also expect the advent of the Mahdi, the 'rightly-guided one', whom the Shiïtes identify with Muhammad al-Mahdi, the occulted Twelfth Imam. The doctrine of the Mahdi is much more highly developed in Shiïsm, where it has achieved dogmatic status, than in Sunni Islam; some Sunnis, in reaction against the Shiïte conception, even repeat the tradition that 'There is no Mahdi save Jesus, the Son of Mary.' Nonetheless, according to the great Muslim historian, Ibn Khaldun, from his *Muqaddima*,

> It has been well known (and generally accepted) by all Muslims in every epoch, that at the end of time a man from the family (of the Prophet) will without fail make his appearance, one who will strengthen Islam and make justice triumph. Muslims will follow him, and he will gain domination over the Muslim realm. He will be called the Mahdi. Following him, the Antichrist will appear, together with all the subsequent signs of the Hour.
> ⌒'ISLAMIC MESSIANISM, p14)

The Mahdi will appear 'after hearts become hard and the earth is filled with wickedness' (cf. Matt. 24:10–12). According to the *hadith* of Muhammad, 'no one will more resemble me than al-Mahdi.' He will 'fill the earth with equity and justice, even as it has been filled with inequity, injustice and tyranny.' He will appear in the end times, when the sun rises in the West. Another sign of his advent will be an eclipse of the sun in the middle of Ramadan and of the moon at the end—an astronomical impossibility. He will come during the *fitan* ('trials'), sedition and civil strife, the tribulation of the latter days. The descent of Jesus during the rule of al-Mahdi will be the sign of the Hour.

According to Sunni sources, Jesus will slay the Antichrist:

> He will descend to the Holy Land at a place called Afiq with a spear in his hand; he will kill with it al-Dajjal and go to Jerusalem at the time of the morning prayer. The Imam will seek to yield his place to him, but Jesus will refuse and will worship behind him according to the Shari'a of Muhammad. Thereafter he will kill the swine, break the cross, and kill all the Christians who do not believe in him. Once al-Dajjal is killed, the Peoples of the Book will believe in him and will form one single *umma* of those who submit to the will of God. Jesus will establish the rule of justice and will remain for forty years, after which he will die. His funeral will take place in Medina, where he will be buried beside Muhammad, in a place between Abu Bakr and 'Umar'.
>
> ⁓Islamic Messianism, pp171–172)

Like the Christ of the *Apocalypse*, al-Qaim al-Mahdi ('he who rises up, the rightly-guided') will embody the principle of inflexible justice, rather than the quality of severity tempered with diplomacy and mercy exhibited by the Prophet Muhammad (upon whom be peace). According to Shiite sources, he will inherit the Prophet's coat of mail, his short spear, and his sword, *Dhu al-Fiqar* (meaning either 'two-pointed' or 'doubly piercing'), which he gave to Ali ibn abi-Talib. In the Shiite version, al-Mahdi, not Jesus, will slay the Antichrist.

According to a tradition of Ali, the emergence of Antichrist or *al-Dajjal* will be preceded by a time of great hardship, a 'tribulation'. On his forehead will be written 'This is the *kafir* ('non-believer'), which everyone, literate or illiterate, will be able to read. Like Jesus, he will ride on a donkey. He will sound a call which will be heard from one end of the earth to the other. He will claim to be God. On the day of his emergence, his followers will be wearing something green on their heads. In a place named Afiq (just as in the Sunni account) in Syria, on a Friday, three hours before sunset, God will cause him and his followers to be killed by 'the one behind whom Jesus shall worship'—the Twelfth Imam, the Mahdi. This will be the beginning of the great revolution of the Imam—the one counterfeited in 1979 by the Ayatollah Khomeini—after which no repentance will be accepted (pp 172–173).

According to a *hadith* of Jafar al-Sadiq, the Mahdi will enter Mecca with a yellow turban on his head and driving a herd of goats. He will be wearing the Prophet's patched sandals and carrying his staff. He will appear as a youth. He will proceed to the Kaaba, where he will be met during the night by Michael, Gabriel and a host of angels. He will stand between the hills Rukn and Maqam, announce himself, and demand allegiance. The people will assemble. Then God will cause four pillars of light to rise into the heavens; everyone on earth will see them, and know that al-Qaim has emerged. Imam al-Hussein (the Prophet's grandson, the Second Imam), wearing a black turban, and 12,000 *shi'a* of Ali will rise from the dead; (anyone who makes obeisance to al-Hussein before the rise of al-Qaim is an infidel). Al-Qaim al-Mahdi will lean his back against the wall of the Kaaba and extend his hand, from which a light will shine out. The first of many to make obeisance to him will be Gabriel, followed by the faithful among the *jinn*, the nobles of Mecca and others.

All this will happen at sunrise. After the sun has climbed higher, a voice from the East will announce that the Mahdi has come. The whole earth will hear it. But at sundown, a second voice will cry from the West, announcing the coming of an Ummayad 'anti-Mahdi'. Many will be led astray by this call.

The Mahdi will reveal the true text of the scriptures of Adam and Seth, Noah and Abraham, as well as the Torah, the Psalms and the Gospel. The followers of these scriptures will acknowledge that he has restored them to their true form, as they were before the texts were distorted. Then he will read the Koran, and its followers will acknowledge that nothing whatever had been distorted in the text of the Book. He will tear down the Kaaba and rebuild it as it was in Adam's time. He will fight against the unbelievers and slay them. He will kill al-Sufyan, the Ummayad false messiah (who may or may not be the same figure as the earlier one I have called the 'anti-Mahdi'.) Ali will return from the dead to dwell in a huge tent, as big as a whole country, supported on four pillars. Heaven and earth will be illuminated. All secrets will be revealed (pp 161–166).

William C. Chittick, in *Islamic Spirituality I*, gives an esoteric commentary by the Sufi Al-Jili from his *Al-Insan al-kamil*, dealing with some of the scripture passages and traditions relating to the Hour of Judgement:

> Al-Jili interprets the events that take place at the end of time in terms of the voluntary death or Greatest resurrection experienced by the spiritual

traveler. According to a *hadith*, Gog and Magog will appear on earth, eating its fruits and drinking its seas; once they are slain, the earth will revive. In the same way the ego's agitation and corrupt thoughts take possession of the earth of a man's heart, eat its fruits and drink its seas, so that no trace of spiritual knowledge can appear. Then God's angels annihilate these satanic whisperings with sciences from God: the earth is revived and it gives abundant harvest. This is a mark of man's gaining proximity to God. As for the beast of the earth, it will come to tell the earth's inhabitants about the truths of the promises concerning the resurrection. In the same way, the traveler reaches a stage of unveiling where he comes to understand the inward mysteries of religion; this is a favor from God, so that 'the troops of his faith will not retreat before the armies of the continuing veil.' Just as the people will not be convinced of the coming of the Hour until the appearance of the beast, so the gnostic will not understand all the requisites of Divinity until the spirit appears from out of the earth of his bodily nature. The conflict between al-Dajjal and Jesus refers to the battle between the ego and the spirit, while the appearance of the Mahdi alludes to man's becoming 'the Possessor of Equilibrium at the pinnacle of every perfection.' Finally, the rising of the sun from the West marks the realization of the ultimate human perfection (p 401).

Several Surahs of the Koran deal with the Hour of Judgement, among them 'The Overthrowing' (81), 'The Cleaving' (82), 'The Sundering' (84), 'The Earthquake' (99), and 'The Calamity' (101). Here are some relevant passages which, like most of the Koran, can be interpreted both in terms of outward events and of inward spiritual transformation:

From 'The Cleaving':

In the name of Allah, the Beneficent, the Merciful.
When the heaven is cleft asunder,
When the planets are dispersed,
When the sea is poured forth,
And the sepulchres are overturned,
A soul will know what it hath sent before (it) and what
left behind . . .

From 'The Overthrowing':

When the Sun is overthrown,
And when the stars fall,
And when the hills are moved,
And when the camels big with young are abandoned,

And when the wild beasts are herded together,
And when the seas rise,
And when the souls are reunited,
And when the girl-child that was buried alive is asked
For what sin she was slain,
And when the pages are laid open,
And when the sky is torn away,
And when hell is lighted,
And when the garden is brought nigh,
(Then) every soul will know what it hath made ready . . .

From 'The Sundering':

When the heaven is split asunder,
And attentive to her Lord in fear,
When the earth is spread out
And hath cast out all that was in her, and is empty,
And attentive to her Lord in fear!
Thou, verily, O man, art working toward thy Lord a
work which thou shalt meet (in His presence). . . .
. . . . I swear by the afterglow of sunset
And by the night and all that it enshroudeth,
And by the moon when she is at the full,
That ye shall journey on from plane to plane.
What aileth them, then, that they believe not?

✳ Christian and Muslim Eschatology Compared

As we have already seen, there are many parallels between Muslim and Christian eschatological lore. Martin Lings, in *The Eleventh Hour*, quotes the Sunni tradition of the Prophet, that

A body of my people will not cease to fight for the truth until the coming forth of the Antichrist. . . . When they are pressing on to fight, even while they straighten their lines for the prayer when it is called, Jesus the son of Mary will descend and will lead them in prayer. And the enemy of God, when he seeth Jesus, will melt even as salt melteth in water. If he were let be, he would melt into perishing: but God will slay him at the hand of Jesus, who will show them his blood upon his lance.

Given the undeniable difference in levels, the slaying of Antichrist by Jesus obviously parallels the story told in many Orthodox icons of St Michael, where the archangel is shown in the act of slaying the Antichrist—with a lance. Furthermore, when the Mahdi manifests himself at the Kaaba, according to the Shiite tradition of Jafar al-Sadiq, the Sixth Imam (see above), he receives obeisance not only from the faithful, but from the angels and the Jinn; thus al-Mahdi, like St Michael, is also the leader of the 'heavenly host'. (Jafar recounts another tradition that the false Ummayad messiah will also be slain by an archangel, not by Michael, however, but by Gabriel.) In the Shiite traditions, as we have seen, it is not Jesus' role but the Mahdi's to kill the Antichrist, also with a lance. The title of the Mahdi, *sahib al-sayf,* 'master of the sword', connects him with the Kalki Avatara (see below) in the *Bhagavata Purana* and also with the Christ of Rev. 19:12; 21, and who says of himself in the Gospels that 'I come not to bring peace, but a sword.' Is the 'two-edged sword' of Jesus Christ in the *Apocalypse* related to *Dhu'l Fiqar,* the two-pointed sword wielded by both the Prophet Muhammad and the Imam Ali, upon whom be peace?

The Orthodox icons of St George and St Michael seem to present Michael as the angelic archetype of George, who is his active agent in this world. Both employ the lance. As Michael kills the Antichrist, so George kills the Dragon, which, in the Apocalypse, symbolizes Satan, whom the Antichrist serves. Muslims venerate St George as identical with the Sufi immortal prophet Khidr, whom Sufis also identify with Elias. According to the book of Malachi, as well as the Gospels, Elias is supposed to come to restore all things before the great and terrible Day of the Lord. Leo Schaya identifies Elias with the Mahdi.

Lings recounts the *hadith* that the Antichrist will be 'a man blind in his right eye, in which all light is extinguished, even as it were a grape.' In a tradition of Ali, the Antichrist's single eye is 'in the center of his forehead, shining like a star'—which is paralleled by an apocalyptic vision of St John of Kronstadt, where he was conducted in the spirit by St Seraphim of Sarov through scenes of the coming of the Antichrist. In one scene, Antichrist sits enthroned on the altar in Jerusalem, presumably in the Church of the Holy Sepulchre—though the Dome of the Rock or a restored Jewish Temple are also possible interpretations—wearing 'a golden crown with a star'. (*Divine Ascent, A Journal of Orthodox Faith,* vol. 1, no. 1.)

The fact that Antichrist only has sight in the left eye signifies, according to the Sufi Najmo-d Din Razi, that he is a materialist, aware of this world but blind to the next. His perception is cut off from the higher spiritual worlds; he recognizes nothing beyond the world of the senses. (A similar truth is expressed in Eastern Orthodox icons, where Satan is always shown in profile, with only one eye visible: sin involves a lack of perspective.) But the tradition that the single eye of Antichrist is in the center of his forehead, shining like a star, has a different significance. The star in the forehead is a representation of the *ajña-chakra*, the 'third eye', which is the organ of subtle or spiritual insight. This means that the Antichrist will be capable up to a point of co-opting and perverting the faculties of higher perception, possibly only on the subtle level of 'remote viewing' and the like, but possibly also on the level of a mental understanding of metaphysical truth, or even that of a frigid indifference playing the part of a high spiritual detachment—a cold, heartless contemplation of the 'existential nakedness' of things masquerading as a deep contemplation of pure Being. It may ultimately be true that the only level of consciousness totally immune from perversion will be the 'cardiac' consciousness which the Sufis, and the Hindus, and the Eastern Orthodox Christians call the 'Heart', the level of the Image of God within us, whose inner core—the 'eye of the Heart'—is the Divine Witness, the *atman*. The 'rapture' which protects God's elect from the tribulation brought on by the Antichrist may, on one level of meaning, be an absorption into the 'paradise of the Heart' when all else in society and the human soul has been invaded by darkness. St Augustine, in *The City of God*, defines demonic evil as *knowledge without love*—which can never be the highest form of knowledge, the knowledge of the *logoi*, the prototypes of all things as they exist in the mind of God; this degree of knowledge, he implies, cannot exist without love. When demonic lovelessness invades the head, the only refuge is the Heart—which does *not* mean that the only protection from perverted thinking is intense emotion. The Antichrist is equally capable of perverting emotion, which is perhaps one of the symbolic meanings of the Whore of Babylon. The strategy is not to abandon the head and hide in the Heart, but to 'sever the head'—which is a Sufi symbol for overcoming the 'headstrong' ego—and place it, as it were, within the Heart. In other words, knowledge must deepen, until it is no longer my little individual attempt to understand the world and the God Who made it, but God's eternal creative act of Self-witnessing within me, and, through me, within the mirror of the world, since it is ultimately this Divine Act of Self-witnessing which creates both self and world.

The star-crowned Antichrist is a counterfeit of Christ, whose birth was announced by a star; this is another example of the parallel symbology between Christ and Antichrist. Rev. 2:28 says, 'And I will give [him who overcomes] the morning star.' According to Archbishop Averky in *The Apoc-alypse of St John: An Orthodox Commentary*, this means either that he will receive Christ, who in 2 Peter 1:19 is called 'the morning star' that shines in the hearts of men, or that he will receive dominion over Satan, who in Isaiah 14:12 is identified with Lucifer, the morning star.

The one-eyed nature of Antichrist represents a counterfeit of the Divine Unity. When Jesus said, 'If your eye become single, your whole body shall be filled with light,' he was referring to the Eye of the Heart which witnesses the Unity of God, and transmits the light of that Unity to the individual psyche, from the psyche to the body, and from the body to the universe, which is thereby restored to its Edenic state, where the world presented to us by our senses is experienced as the primordial mirror of the Names or Energies of God. But the single eye of the Antichrist can only see and wor-ship the universe as if it literally *were* God, mystifying and glamorizing mat-ter for the purpose of denying the Divine Transcendence, in the manner of anti-religious materialists like Carl Sagan. Those who seek unity and stabil-ity through the worship of matter will, however, find themselves worship-ping chaos instead. In the words of the Gospels, they are those whose 'house is founded on sand,' on a swarm of sub-atomic particles ruled by random indeterminacy, as well as on the chaos of mass 'atomic individualism' which is the social expression of this vision of things. The only source of stability, the only 'rock', is the Divine Nature, where the radiant eternal forms or *logoi* of all things rest in the mind of God.

According to Shïite tradition, the Twelfth Imam Muhammad al-Mahdi was 'occulted' (hidden away) in childhood to prevent his assassination, reminding one of Rev. 12:1–5, where the 'woman clothed with the sun' gives birth to a 'man child', who was to 'rule all nations with a rod of iron,' but who was 'caught up to God, and to His throne' to avoid being devoured by 'a great red dragon having seven heads and ten horns.' World chaos will be among the signs of his imminent return. When he does, the mothers nursing their infants will abandon them in fear; cf. Matt. 24:19, 'And woe to those that are with child, and to them that give suck in those days!' It is unlawful to men-tion (or reveal) the name of al-Mahdi, or ask his whereabouts, of fix the time of his advent, though many traditions say it will be in the 'near future'. Compare Rev. 19:11–12, where the rider on the white horse, called Faithful and True 'had a name written that no man knew, but He Himself,' and Matt. 24:26, 'if they shall say unto you, Behold, he is in the desert; go not forth: behold, he is in the secret chambers; believe it not,' as well as Matt. 24:36, 'But of that day and hour knoweth no man, no, not the angels of heaven, but my Father only.' Compare also Rev. 22:7: 'Behold, I come quickly,' and Rev. 3:12–13, 'I will write upon [him that overcometh] my new name.'

The Mahdi will also bring a new Book; compare Rev. 5:1–2, 'And I saw in the right hand of him that sat on the throne a book written within and on the backside, sealed with seven seals. And I saw a strong angel proclaiming with a loud voice, Who is worthy to open the book, and to loose the seals thereof?'; compare also the *Sepher ha-Yasher* or Book of Justice which, according to Jewish tradition, will be brought by Elias in the latter days (see below). And just as we are warned in Matt. 24:24–27 not to run after false Christs and false prophets on hearsay, 'For as the lightning cometh out of the East, and shineth even to the West; so shall the coming of the Son of Man be,' so the greatest authority in Shiite Islam, the Sixth Imam Jafar al-Sadiq, declares 'Beware, those who claim [that the Mahdi has come] before the rise of al-Sufyani [the Ummayad false messiah, similar to Antichrist] and the voice from the sky are liars.'

An interesting parallel, which is also a clear divergence, between the Koran and the *Apocalypse*, has to do with a beast which shall rise out of the earth in the latter days. In Islamic tradition, Antichrist emerges from the earth; in Christian tradition, from the sea. (Certain Islamic versions, however, also speak of Antichrist as a sea-demon.) In the Christian version, just as the Beast who is Antichrist rises out of the sea, so a second beast (Rev. 13:11), identified with the False Prophet, comes out of the earth, and causes men to receive the mark of the Beast (presumably the first) on their foreheads or their right hands. Likewise, according to Surah 27:82, 'When the Word falls on them, we shall bring forth for them out of the earth a beast that shall speak unto them.' According to commentary of Ali ibn abi-Talib on this passage, when the beast appears,

> He will carry Solomon's seal and Moses' staff. He will place the seal on the face of every believer, leaving the words 'This is a believer in truth'; and on the face of infidel, leaving the words 'This is an infidel in truth'. . . . Then the beast will raise its head, and everyone from East to West will see it, after the sun has risen from the West. When it lifts its head, repentance will no longer be accepted.

The beast of the Koran is clearly neither the Antichrist nor the False Prophet of the *Apocalypse*. Yet both the beast of the Koran and the False Prophet rise from beneath the earth, from the abode of the dead, which in many traditions stands for all that has been repressed and forgotten in the individual or collective human soul. The False Prophet perhaps symbolizes the human evil hidden in that soul, just as the first beast, the Antichrist, who rises not from the earth of the human world but from the sea of the 'collective unconscious', symbolizes the part of that soul which is open to, and controlled by, a trans-human, satanic evil, the Dragon. But the beast of the Koran would seem to stand for the totality of the collective human soul, the hidden good as well as the hidden evil—the *nafs* on every level, whether commanding, accusing, or at peace, now speaking the full truth of its nature under the compulsion of the Spirit. As also happens on the spiritual Path, where travelers 'die before they are made to die,' the descent of the Word or Spirit causes all that has been concealed in the soul to rise into plain view; and when this process is complete, the possibility of individual action, and thus of individual repentance, is ended, either by physical death or by annihilation in God. In the light of the Word it is men's deeds, as measured against the staff of Moses (representing the law), and their psychic dispositions, as divined by Solomon's seal (representing his power over the Jinn, i.e., the realm of the psyche) which testify definitively as to who is destined for the Garden and who for the Fire. The faces of both groups are sealed by the seal-ring of Solomon because, according to Islamic doctrine, 'acts are judged by their intent.'

✳ Hindu Eschatology: Kalki and Christ Compared

The Hindu scriptures known as the *Puranas* are thought by some to have been composed between the 4th and the 16th centuries AD. Traditional Hindu authorities, however, attribute them to the ancient sage Vyasa, who is also believed to have composed the *Mahabarata*, and see them as written versions of much older oral traditions, since they are in fact mentioned in the *Upanishads* (c. 600–300 BC) and even the *Brahmanas* (c. 800–600 BC). The word 'purana' itself means 'ancient', or perhaps 'ancient-new', in order to express the perennial freshness and timeliness of the primordial wisdom. There are eighteen major puranas: six dedicated to Brahma, six to Vishnu, and six to Shiva. The Vaishnava puranas contain the Hindu doctrine of cosmic cycles, as well the history of the avatars of Vishnu, of whom Krishna is probably the best-known.

The parallels between certain sections of the Puranas and the Book of *Apocalypse*, particularly parts of the *Vishnu Purana* (dated 6th century by

Joseph Campbell) and the *Bhavagata Purana* (dated 10th century), are numerous and striking. These scriptures, as well as the *Bhasa Bharata* and the *Agni Purana* (which is not Vaishnava but Shaivite) contain predictions of the advent of the Kalki avatara, the 10th avatar of Vishnu in the last period of the cycle, the first nine having already come and gone. Some scholars explain this similarity on the basis of an early Christian influence within Hinduism. But it is equally likely that both renditions of the Savior destined to appear in the end-times are variations of a single tradition, related to the doctrine of the cosmic cycle or Great Year common to the ancient Mesopotamians, the Hindus, the Greeks, the Norse, and even the Lakota, and probably based on the astronomical precession of the equinoxes. Joseph Campbell traces this tradition to at least c. 300 BC in Mesopotamia, though the lists of antediluvian kings numerologically related to the Great Year go back to much earlier times, while the number-system they employ, based on the number 60, is found as far back as c. 3200 BC. Sumerian and Babylonian king-lists usually name ten kings, which is also the number of patriarchs from Adam to Noah inclusively—a fact that leads one to wonder whether the Hindu doctrine of the ten major avatars of Vishnu, of which Kalki will be the last in this cycle, is a later version of the same constellation of ideas, particularly since Noah came at the end of one world-age and went on to inaugurate the next. The number ten is related to the Hindu cosmic cycle, the *manvantara*, through its division into the four *yugas*: the Satya-yuga, the Treta-yuga, the Dvapara-yuga and the Kali-yuga. The Treta-yuga is three-fourths as long as the Satya-yuga, the Dvapara-yuga one half as long, and the Kali-yuga one-fourth as long, yielding the numbers 4, 3, 2, and 1, whose sum is ten.

According to the *Vishnu Purana*,

> When the practices taught by the Vedas and the institutes of the law shall have ceased, and the close of the Kali age shall be nigh, a portion of that divine being who exists of his own spiritual nature in the character of Brahma, and who is the beginning and end, and who comprehends all things, shall descend upon earth: he will be born in the family of Vishnuya-sas, an eminent Brahman of Shambhala village as Kalki, endowed with the eight superhuman faculties. By his superhuman might he shall destroy all the Mlechchas [foreign barbarians] and thieves, and all whose minds are devoted to iniquity. He will then re-establish righteousness on earth; and the minds of those who live at the end of the Kali age shall be pellucid as crystal. The men who are thus changed by virtue of that particular time shall be as

the seed of human beings, and shall give birth to a race who shall follow the laws of the Krita age, or age of purity [another name for the Satya-yuga].

Kalki, as 'a portion of that divine being who exists . . . as Brahma [the Creator]' is obviously analogous, though not theologically equivalent, to Christ, the Son of God the Father. He is called 'the beginning and the end', which is precisely how Christ describes himself in Rev. 1:8. His re-establishment of righteousness on earth is like the new heaven and the new earth of chapter 21 of that book, and the minds 'pellucid as crystal' of those who live to see him suggest the Heavenly Jerusalem, whose 'light was like a stone most precious, even like a jasper stone, clear as crystal' (Rev. 21:11).

The height of the wall surrounding the Heavenly Jerusalem, measured by the angel in Rev. 21:17, is given as 'an hundred forty-four cubits, the measure of a man, that is, of the angel.' This is a direct reference to the '144,000 redeemed from the earth' (Rev. 14:3), and indicates that the Heavenly Jerusalem is a projection of the 'angelic' essence of human form within the mind of God; the 144,000 redeemed are, as it were, the living bricks of that City. The 144,000, as well as the '24 elders' of Rev. 4:4,10, suggest not so much a numerical collection of individuals as a deployment, on different planes of manifestation, of the human archetype, the *seed of Man*. (In Mark 4:16, human individuals themselves are compared to seeds.) 'The men who are thus changed by virtue of that particular time' who 'shall be the seed of human beings' are thus roughly analogous to the 24 elders and the 144,000 redeemed, as long as we understand 'seed' to refer to the subtle-plane prototype of the humanity of the next aeon, the new heaven and the new earth, not to the scattered survivors of a material catastrophe. And the idea that men shall be 'changed' clearly echoes 1 Cor. 15:51–52, where St Paul says 'we shall all be changed, in a moment, in the twinkling of an eye, at the last trump.'

The following is account of Kalki from the *Bhagavata Purana*:

When the Kali age, whose career is so severe to the people, is well-nigh past, the Lord will appear in his divine form (consisting of Sattva alone). . . . Lord Vishnu, the adored of the whole animate and inanimate creation, and the Soul of the universe, appears (in this world of matter) for protecting the virtue of the righteous and wiping out (the entire stock of) their Karma (and thereby liberating them). The Lord will appear under the name of Kalki in the house of the high-souled Vishnuyasa—the foremost Brahman of the village of Shambhala. Riding a fleet horse named Devadutta . . . and capable of subduing the wicked, the Lord of the universe, wielding . . . the eight divine powers ... and possessed of [endless] virtues and matchless splendour, will traverse the globe on that swift horse and exterminate with His sword in tens of millions robbers wearing the insignia of royalty. Now when all the robbers are thus exterminated, the minds of the people of the cities and the country- side will become pure indeed because of their enjoying the breezes wafting the most sacred fragrance of pigments on the person of the Lord Vasudeva [Kalki]. With Lord Vasudeva, the embodiment of strength, in their heart their progeny will grow exceedingly strong. ... When the Lord Sri Hari, the Protector of Dharma, appears as Kalki, Satyayuga [the Golden Age] will prevail (once more). ...

Martin Lings, in *The Eleventh Hour*, identifies Kalki with both Maitreya Buddha and the Christ:

Like Christianity, [Hinduism] depends on the *Avatara*, that is, the descent of Divinity into this world; and for the maintenance of the tradition there is a succession of no less than ten Avataras. As far as historic times are con- cerned, the seventh and eighth of these, Rama and Krishna, are the most important for Hinduism itself. The ninth, specifically non-Hindu (literally 'foreign') is generally considered to be the Buddha; and the tenth, Kalki, 'the rider on the white horse', will have the universal function of closing this cycle of time and inaugurating the next, which identified his descent with the sec- ond advent of Christ.

The 'rider on the white horse' appears in the same role as Kalki in the 19th chapter of Revelation:

And I saw heaven opened, and behold a white horse; and he that sat upon him was called Faithful and True, and in righteousness he doth judge and make war.
And his eyes were as a flame of fire, and on his head were many crowns; and he had a name written, that no man knew, but he himself. (19:11–12)
And out of his mouth goeth a sharp sword, that with it he should smite the nations: and he shall rule them with a rod of iron: and he treadeth the wine- press of the fierceness and wrath of Almighty God. (19:15)
And I saw the beast, and the kings of the earth, and their armies (i.e., the 'tens of millions [of] robbers wearing the insignia of royalty) gathered together to make war against him that sat on the horse, and against his army. And the beast was taken, and with him the false prophet that wrought mira- cles before him, with which he deceived them that had received the mark of the beast, and them that worshipped his image. These both were cast alive into a lake of fire burning with brimstone.

And the remnant were slain with the sword of him that sat upon the horse, which proceeded out of his mouth: and all the fowls were filled with their flesh. (19:19–21)

In Eastern Orthodox icons, both St Michael and St George are shown riding on white horses, doing battle with the Antichrist and the Dragon respectively. The striking similarities between Hindu and Christian eschatology can be explained, I suppose, by a diffusion of motifs. Yet as a friend of mine pointed out, no integral tradition accepts myths or doctrines from outside its borders unless they are intrinsically compatible with its central vision. Hinduism and Christianity, when they look toward the end of the Aeon, gaze deeply upon the same objective reality. Nor is this visionary disclosure of the spiritual archetypes incompatible with any particular stream of historical influence, because history is providential; the eternal, spiritual world is the ultimate source of the historical one: 'time is the moving image of Eternity.'

✳ Hindu, Judeo-Christian, Lakota, and Hopi Eschatology Compared

As I have already pointed out, one of the greatest errors of the New Age, which has infiltrated liberal Christianity as well, is to identify the primal religions with their own anti-transcendentalism, to implicitly deny nature as a theophany of the Great Spirit and take it instead as a material object—'Spaceship Earth'—to be worshipped in and for itself. However, those of the primal religions which have preserved the Primordial Tradition relatively intact have a much greater affinity with the great revealed religions than with contemporary Neo-Paganism or New Age ideology. Evidence of this affinity can be seen in many areas of myth and doctrine, and one of these is eschatology. Both Lakota and Hindu traditions, for example, share the doctrine of a continuous cycle-of-manifestation, each cycle divided into four ages. I quote from Traditionalist author Joseph Epes Brown, from his book *The Sacred Pipe: Black Elk's Account of the Seven Rites of the Oglala Sioux*, p9, n15:

Accounting to Siouan [Lakota] mythology, it is believed that at the beginning of the cycle a buffalo was placed at the West in order to hold back the waters. Every year this buffalo loses one hair, and every age he loses one leg. When all his hair and all four legs are gone, then the waters rush in again, and the cycle comes to an end.

A striking parallel to this myth is found in the Hindu tradition, where it is the bull Dharma (the divine law) who has four legs, each of which represents an age of the total cycle. During the course of these four ages (*yugas*), true spirituality becomes increasingly obscured, until the cycle (*manvantara*) closes with a catastrophe, after which the primordial spirituality is restored, and the cycle begins once again.

It is believed by both the American Indian and the Hindu that at the present time the buffalo or bull is on his last leg, and he is very nearly bald. Corresponding beliefs could be cited from many other traditions. See René Guénon, *The Crisis of the Modern World*. [See also Frithjof Schuon, *The Feathered Sun*: Bloomington, World Wisdom Books, 1990. pp 113–114.]

As for parallels with Judeo-Christian eschatology, perhaps the clearest is the Lakota doctrine of the sacred 'red and blue days'. 'These,' according to Joseph Epes Brown, 'are the days at the end of the world when the moon will turn red and the sun will turn blue. But, since for the traditional man everything in the macrocosm has its counterpart in the microcosm, there may be an end of the world for the individual here and now, whenever he receives illumination from *Wakan-Tanka*, so that his ego or ignorance dies, and then he lives continually in the Spirit.'

According to the prophet Joel (chapter 2 verse 31, echoed in Matt. 24:29 and Mark 13:24), 'The sun shall be turned into darkness, and the moon into blood, before the great and terrible day of the Lord.' Both traditions state that the moon will turn red, and the sun is certainly 'darkened' if it turns blue. Furthermore, dark blue is identified with or substituted for black in the color symbolism of many nations. Blue-skinned Krishna is sometimes called *Kala*, 'the black one', and in Richard Wilhelm's commentary on his translation of the I *Ching* it is stated that 'Black, or rather dark blue, is the color of heaven.' According to Epes Brown, blue (not surprisingly) is also 'the color of the heavens' in Lakota symbolism.

The darkened sun and red moon obviously relate to solar and lunar eclipses; a moon in eclipse will often show a dull red color. But few seem to know that the actual color of the midday sun to the naked eye, as I proved to myself during childhood by staring into it for short periods, is a shimmering blue-black. As for the symbolic meanings of these colors as attributed to sun and moon, they can be taken on at least two levels. From the point of view of the 'ego or ignorance' as it dies, the darkening of the sun represents the veiling of the Intellect, as when Jesus on the cross cried out, 'My God, my God, why have you forsaken me?' and the reddening of the moon the outbreak of the passions. When the Intellect is veiled, the passions run riot; such are the conditions universally predicted for the end of the Kali-yuga. The moon is a universal symbol for the world of the psyche, which is turned both toward the 'sublunar' cycles of nature as their proximate cause, and toward the Sun of the Intellect, its ultimate Source. The second orientation is the symbolic meaning of the moon in Islam, representing not so much the psyche in itself as the transcendent center of the psyche, the 'Heart'—the level of being the Virgin Mary was speaking from in Mark 1:46 when she said 'My soul doth magnify the Lord.' The first orientation is represented by the various pagan moon-goddesses who rule the cycles of fertility.

From the point of view of the eternal archetypes, however, blue sun and red moon have a different meaning. As we have seen, René Guénon in *The Reign of Quantity* presents the course of any cycle of manifestation as a descent from the pole of Essence, whose symbol is the sun, to the pole of Substance, symbolized by the moon. But Essence and Substance, as archetypes, never themselves enter into manifestation, the first because of its exaltation, the second because of its simplicity. Just as Essence is above form, and therefore inconceivable, so Substance is below form, and consequently incapable of being discovered or possessed (this, incidentally, is why the quest of physics for an 'ultimate particle', or its equivalent, will never end).

Insofar as Essence and Substance are echoed in the manifest world, Essence appears (in Aristotelian terms) as *forma* or prototype, that which confers form, and Substance as matrix or *materia*, that which receives form. As the cycle descends, however, *forma* gradually becomes obscured behind the veils of *materia*, while *materia* progressively adopts the prerogatives of *forma*, though only in an illusory sense; as the eternal forms through which God creates the material world become hidden, it begins to seem as if matter somehow had the power to create itself. The celestial blue of *forma* is darkened, while *materia* takes on the angry red hue of self-assertive materialism; in the words of Charles Peguy (which epitomize, in a sense, the doctrine of world-ages from Plato's *Republic*): 'everything begins in mysticism and ends in politics.' *Forma* and *materia* ultimately become so confused with one another that the world-sustaining polarity between them breaks down, and the cycle ends in chaos. But when the sun turns blue and the moon turns red, this indicates a purifying re-polarization of forma and *materia*, which returns them to their original archetypes. The blue sun is a symbol of Essence or pure quality manifesting as the celestial order, the Father principle; the red moon is a symbol of Substance or pure receptivity manifesting as life energy, the power to draw essences or qualities into manifestation, the Mother principle. *Forma* is no longer encumbered now by the dark shells of *materia*, but directly reveals Essence, while *materia* no longer arrogates to itself the power to confer form, but directly manifests the receptive virginity of Substance. So the stage is set for the reunion of Divine Father and Divine Mother, the 'wedding feast of the Lamb', the procreation of 'a new heaven and a new earth'.

Joseph Epes Brown presents the Lakota doctrine of *forma* vs. Essence and *materia* vs. Substance as follows:

> As the distinction is made within Wakan-Tanka between Father and Grandfather, so the Earth is considered under two aspects, that of Mother and Grandmother. The former is the earth considered as the producer of all growing forms, in act; whereas Grandmother refers to the ground or substance of all growing things—potentiality. This distinction is the same as that made by the Christian Scholastics between *natura naturans* and *natura naturata*. (p6, n7)

Mother Earth, then, is *materia*, and Grandmother Earth is Substance; Father and Grandfather Spirit are *forma* and Essence; or, on a higher octave, Being and Beyond-being. According to Epes Brown,

> *Wakan-Tanka* as Grandfather is the Great Spirit independent of manifestation, unqualified, unlimited, identical to the Christian Godhead, or to the Hindu *Brahma-Nirguna*. *Wakan-Tanka* as Father is the Great Spirit considered in relation to His manifestation, either as Creator, Preserver, or Destroyer, identical to the Christian God, or the Hindu *Brahma-Saguna*. (p5, n6)

The Hopi, too, have a tradition of four successive worlds, which are both temporal ages and ontological levels. According to *The Book of the Hopi* by Frank Waters, the first world is Tokpela, Endless Space. On one level, Tokpela is the world of Beyond Being, where Tiowa, the Formless Absolute, exists in solitude, before creation; on another, it is the world of the first creation. (As the four ages progress, they become less like ontological levels and more like historical periods; we are moving from the pole of qualitative *forma* to that of quantitative *materia*). In this guise, since it is associated with the mineral *sikyasvu*, gold, it is obviously the Golden Age. In Tokpela—perhaps to be identified with the paleolithic—the people live in peace with the animals and with each other. It is destroyed partly through the deceptions of Kato'ya, the handsome one, who is described as 'a snake with a big head', clearly analogous to the serpent in *Genesis*. (This is interesting, given that the Hopi are among the tribes least influenced by Christianity.) As the first world begins to degenerate, the chosen from among the people begin their migration; they follow a cloud by day and a star by night, just as the chosen people in *Exodus* follow a pillar of cloud and a pillar of fire. As Tokpela is destroyed by fire, they take refuge underground with the Ant People, who are analogous to the primordial earth-born ant-men of Greek myth, the *myrmidons*.

Next the people emerge from the underground world of the ants and enter the second world, Tokpa, Dark Midnight, whose mineral is *qochasiva*, silver. This is the Silver Age, apparently the neolithic, when handicrafts and village life are developed. The second world is destroyed by water and ice when the twins Poqanghoya and Palongawhoya, guardians of the poles, leave their stations and the earth flips over twice. The people again take refuge underground with the ants, and then emerge into the third world.

The third world, Kuskurza, is related to the mineral *palasiva*, copper—a major constituent of bronze. So we are now in the Bronze Age. In Kuskurza the people overpopulate and use their reproductive power for evil—copper being identified, in traditional symbolism, with Venus, the erotic principle. They develop a high technology, live in cities, and fly on shields covered with hide called *patuwvotas*—strikingly similar to the flying *vimanas* described in the Hindu *puranas*—which they use as engines of war. Kuskurza, like Atlantis, is destroyed by water; whole continents sink beneath the waves.

As the third world is about to end, Spider Woman—a figure who is something like the *shekhinah* of Sotuknang, the demiurge, the first created being, who in turn is the active energy of Tiowa, the Creator—tells the people to get inside of hollow reeds to escape from the flood. She later directs them to make these reeds into boats. She leads them in a migration over water, searching for the fourth world. (The boats made of reeds remind one of the Egyptian reed boat that Thor Heyerdahl used to cross the Atlantic in his Ra Expedition, thus proving that the Egyptians—or Atlanteans— could have populated the New World, though the direction of their journey, East and a little North, suggests a Southwest Asian origin.) During this migration, they send out birds for land, just as Noah did in *Genesis*, but no land is to be found.

After stopping at a continent which was not their true destination, they arrive at the fourth world, called Tuwaqachi, the World Complete, where life is hard. This is the world we presently occupy. The mineral associated with the fourth world is the 'mixed mineral' *sikyapala*, analogous to the iron mixed with clay which composes the feet of the statue dreamt of by King Nebuchadnezzar in the Book of Daniel; so Tuwaqachi would seem to be the

462 ✳ THE SYSTEM OF ANTICHRIST

Iron Age. The spiritual guardian of Tuwaqachi is Masaw, who was also the ruler of Kuskurza, the third world, and who brought it to an end through his corruption. He is here because Tiowa decided to give him a second chance—a chance he seems to have wasted. The Hopi myth clearly implies that this world too will be destroyed by the abuse of reproductive power and high technology. Here we can see again, through the convergence of Hinduism, Judeo-Christianity, Aristotle and the teachings of the Hopi and the Lakota, how traditional metaphysics, the science of eternal principles, is both primordial and universal.

✳ The Siege of Shambhala: Tibetan Buddhist Eschatology

Tibetan Buddhist eschatology, notably the lore which appears in the Kalachakra Tantra, differs in important respects from that of other forms of Buddhism. In *Tibet* by Thubten Jigme Norbu (Simon & Schuster, 1968), a tulku of the Gelugpa Lineage and elder brother of the Dalai Lama, the following account is given, which has clear affinities with the eschatologies of many other traditions. The *Shambhala Smonlam* says:

> Fearless, in the midst of your army of gods,
> Among your twelve divisions,
> You ride on horseback.
> You thrust your spear toward the chest of Hanumanda,
> Minister of the evil forces drawn up
> Against Shambhala.
> So shall evil be destroyed.

Shambhala is the name of a city and country 'to the North' where some of the original teachings of Tibetan Tantra are believed to have originated. In the final period of the cycle, when religion and morality will have degenerated and the earth grown colder, the city of Shambhala will be the only place on earth where the teachings of Buddha are preserved. As soon as the encroaching corruption of the surrounding world reaches the city walls, the god-king of Shambhala will ride out against the leader of the evil forces and slay him.

Lhasa will be covered with water during that time. After evil is destroyed, Tsong Khapa will arise from his tomb at the Ganden Monastery and Buddhism will be renewed for a thousand years. Then will come the end of the world, which will be accomplished first by fire, then by wind, then by water. A very few human beings will survive, in treetops and caves (esoterically speaking, by virtue of intellectual height and spiritual depth). The gods will come from Ganden Paradise and take these people back with them, who will receive spiritual teachings and become immortal. Finally, when the wind again churns the milky ocean and the world is re-created, those enlightened ones of the final days, saved from the former cycle of manifestation, will be the stars in the sky. (Compare Dan. 12:3, according to which, at the end of time, 'they that be wise shall shine as the brightness of the firmament; and they that turn many to righteousness as the stars for ever and ever.')

Hanumanda would appear to be something like a Tibetan Antichrist. (Elsewhere his name is given as Krinmati, a barbarian overlord.) The twelve divisions of his opponent the god-king are paralleled by the '[more than] twelve legions of angels' ready to defend Jesus in Matt. 26:53, as well as the 12,000 followers of Ali who rise from the dead at the coming of the Mahdi in Muslim eschatology, and the 12,000 sealed elect from each of the 12 tribes of Israel in Rev. 7:4–8. (The number 12 obviously suggests the Zodiac, which would identify the various eschatological armies with what are called in the Old Testament 'the host of heaven'—the stars: 'The stars in their courses are fighting on the side of the just.') The siege of Shambhala itself clearly suggests the battle of Armageddon, when Jerusalem will be encompassed by armies. 'I will gather all nations against Jerusalem to battle; and the city shall be taken. . . . Then shall the Lord go forth, and fight against those nations. . . .' (Zech. 14:2–3). The motif of the 'rapture' also appears, as found in both Christian and Islamic tradition, along with the myth of the millennium—Tibetan Buddhist eschatology, according to the present rendition, is 'pre-millennialist'—as well as the prophecy that the mounted eschatological hero will slay an Antichrist-like figure with a spear or lance.

According to the account given by John Newman, co-author of *The Wheel of Time: Kalachakra in Context* (Madison: Deer Park Books, 1985), the 'messiah' figure and king of Shambhala who defeats the forces of evil is Raudra Charki—who, interestingly enough, is named as the last of the 'Kalkis', a lineage of the rulers of Shambhala founded by the first Kalki, the great Yashas, whose queen was Tara. So he would seem to be at least partly identifiable with the Kalki Avatara of the Hindu *Puranas*. Raudra Charki's grandson, future ruler of Shambhala, will be Kashyapa, the name given to Maitreya's herald in the Mahayana prophecy recounted above.

The fact that the earth will be colder during the Siege of Shambhala suggests the Norse *Fimbulwinter*, as well as elements in the Zoroastrian myth of the Var of Yima (see below), of which the legend of Shambhala appears to be a Tibetan rendition. Both Shambhala and the Var of Yima are situated 'in the North', making them variations on the theme of the Hyperborean Paradise.

According to some Tibetan accounts, the city of Shambhala is near the Oxus river in Central Asia. This would seem to confirm the tradition repeated by Gurdjieff follower J. G. Bennett that the word Shambhala, according to folk-etymology at least, is really the Arabic Shams-i-Balkh, 'Sun of Balkh', the name of the Zoroastrian Fire-temple in the ancient city of Balkh in the valley of the Oxus. In an alternate and possibly more reliable account given by John Newman, however, Shambhala is located in the Tarim basin, directly to the north of Tibet, east and slightly to the north of Balkh. Newman identifies the Sita river mentioned in the Kalachakra scriptures with the Tarim. In the *Vishnu Purana* on the other hand, Shambhala is the small village in India where the Kalki Avatara will be born. But wherever the quasi-geographical Shambhala may or may not be located, the true site of this miraculous city-state is in the 'Eighth Clime', the *'alam al-mithal*, the Imaginal Plane. Its god-king, the Kalki, is—like King Arthur, the immortal prophets Khidr and Elijah, the Zoroastrian Yima, and the occulted Twelfth Imam—one more rendition of Guénon's 'King of the World', the archetype of Man for the present aeon, enthroned on the subtle plane, and surrounded by the Terrestrial Paradise, which is his emanation, his *shakti*.

The eschatological lore of many traditions is reflected in the mirror of this Tibetan 'legend of the end'.

✳ Benjamin Creme, Prophet of the Theosophical Antichrist

(*All quotes are taken from* The Emergence Quarterly, *background information issue, a free publication of the Maitreya Movement*)

As a counterpoint to these traditional eschatologies, we should take some time to look at one of the clearest of the contemporary inverted eschatologies, that of Benjamin Creme, whose teachings are based on the doctrines of the Theosophical Society, particularly those of Alice Bailey, author of *The Reappearance of Christ* (1948). Creme is so obviously playing the role of False Prophet to his occulted 'Maitreya' figure as Antichrist, that one suspects he may be doing it deliberately. His 'Antichrist' is probably too literal a false

Messiah to be the real Antichrist; still, Creme's ministry demonstrates how the roles of 'Antichrist' and 'False Prophet' are in the air right now.

Creme claims to be in constant telepathic contact with the 'Master Maitreya', who is the one expected by Christians as Jesus, by Jews as the Messiah, by Muslims as the Mahdi, etc. 'Maitreya' descended from his mountain retreat in the Himalayas in 1977 to become an Indian or Pakistani living in London. He comes not as a religious leader but as a guide to those of all religions, as well as atheists. 'A real disciple', he says, 'is one who will respect the traditions. Respect your own religions, your own ideologies — in brief, your own thought-form, and you will experience the Master.' Clearly the truth of religion, or of the secular ideologies, does not concern him. It doesn't even matter whether or not you believe in God. 'Maitreya' gives lip service to the transcendent unity of traditional religious doctrines; his teachings, however, repeatedly contradict these doctrines. The Master is apparently 'above' questions of truth, and it is for this reason that I do not believe what he says. Under the influence of his energy, says Creme, 'more and more people will revolt, because old habits, centuries-old codes imposed on the mind, must be broken. People will not accept imposed solutions.' This does not sound, to me, much like respect for all traditions and ideologies.

Commercialization and the reign of market forces are a scourge, says 'Maitreya'. I agree. 'The new politics will no longer be molded by the 'isms' of capitalism or socialism, but created from self-respect in individuals and nations. Liberty, freedom and salvation will be the objectives of everyone', Creme writes, 'and they are all the same. The reality of global interdependence will become an established fact in our awareness.' Well, it has. But today's new sense of global interdependence, which is becoming increasingly burdensome and anxiety-ridden, is precisely a product of commercialization and market forces. And if both the hard lessons of history and an elemental understanding of psychology haven't yet taught us that freedom and salvation are not always the same thing, then there's little I can add. External freedom sometimes serves salvation and sometimes undermines it, but no one who is not willing, if need be, to sacrifice self-determined action in order to save his soul, has yet learned the difference between the bondage of libertinism and the Liberation which can only come from strict obedience to the Source of love and truth. Such obedience is, however, foreign to Creme. 'The politicians alone, Maitreya says, are to blame for the desperation of those addicted to drugs. 'If people are so straitened in life that they cannot even eat properly ... they will lead desperate lives.' This is a half-truth, obviously: are there no such things as rich drug addicts?

•

Creme banks on a world economic crash starting in Japan to bring us to our senses, awaken us to higher values, and give 'Maitreya' a chance to take over. He apparently hopes for a Theosophical world revolution of the 2000s on the order of the Communist upsurgence during the Great Depression of the 1930s.

It was 'Maitreya' who decreed the fall of the Soviet Union and ended Apartheid in South Africa. It is he who is presently producing, from somewhere in the London suburbs, all the apparitions of angels, the Virgin Mary, the Buddha and Christ throughout the world, miraculous healing wells, milk-drinking statues in India, vanishing hitchhikers predicting the Second Coming, and mysterious crosses of light appearing in windows all over the world, starting in southern California. His 'platform' is simple: The unity of humanity; a new civilization based on sharing, economic and social justice and global cooperation; adequate food, clothing, housing, and medical care; the regeneration of the environment; and an end to world hunger, along with mass spiritual enlightenment: a Buddha in every pot. As Dennis Engleman writes in *Ultimate Things* (pp 179–180),

> Antichrist will develop a reputation as a phenomenal problem-solver. His uncanny ability to anticipate outcomes and to propose solutions will seem prophetic and visionary to a world unaware of his secret manipulations. War, economic disturbance, social injustice, political instability, religious intolerance—no difficulty will escape his soothing touch.

Who can disagree with these lofty goals? Who but the superstitious, the hide-bound, the corrupt or the insane could oppose them? Who but degenerates, said Hitler, could oppose full employment, a more spiritual culture which gives hope and direction to the young, and an end to the shameful and oppressive provisions of the Treaty of Versailles? Who but bourgeois reactionaries, said Marx, could oppose a classless society, based on the principle of 'from each according to his abilities, to each according to his needs', where no one over-indulges and no one starves? What 'Maitreya' proposes is good—but good, of course, can be co-opted. And what can be expected from someone who claims to be engineering massive world changes, as well as a global manifestation of vanishing hitchhikers, from somewhere in the London suburbs? Or from people imbalanced enough to believe in him?

A recurrent theme in 'Maitreya's' teachings, like those of the founder of EST, the late Werner Erhardt, is the ending of world hunger. What could be more compassionate, more blameless? However, according to Sachedina in *Islamic Messianism*, p 173,

Al-Dajjal's [the Antichrist's] role at the End of Time is almost identical to that of Satan, as explained in traditional sources, because he will tempt people by bringing food and water, which will be scarce at that time.

Creme looks forward to the day when 'Maitreya' will manifest himself to the world:

At the earliest possible moment, Maitreya will demonstrate His true identity. On the Day of Declaration, the international television networks will be linked together. By invitation of the media, we will see Maitreya's face on television, but He will not speak. Instead, each of us will hear his words telepathically in our own language as he simultaneously impresses the minds of all humanity. Even those who are not watching Him on television will have this experience. At the same time, hundreds of thousands of spontaneous healings will take place throughout the world. In this way we will know that this man is truly the World Teacher for all humanity.

So Creme and his Theosophical friends are hoping to stage a global mass-suggestion event. According to *Ultimate Things* (pp 134–135),

A mankind accustomed to laser shows, high-definition television and other spectacles will be thrilled by Antichrist. The media will love him; public figures of all types will turn out in his support. Yet the enthusiasm will have sinister origins. Saint Ignatius Brianchaninov warns, 'The false spirits, sent throughout the world, will incite in men a generally high opinion of the antichrist, universal ecstasy, irresistible attraction to him.' As John the Baptist, 'the Forerunner', prepared the way for Jesus' public ministry, a uniquely cunning man will set the stage for Antichrist's advent. This person, referred to in Scripture as 'the false prophet', will enthrall the world by means of cunningly staged spectacles.... A humanity taught by science that whatever they want they can have, and by Hollywood to believe that whatever they see is true, will be enchanted and mystified by the wonders of the false prophet. His magical presentations will pique, and at the same time deaden, the longing in their souls for true heavenly visions. (pp 182–183)

In the words of Martin Lings (*The Eleventh Hour*, pp 97–98), 'As in Christianity, it is believed in Islam that [the Antichrist] will cause corruption, and that by his power to work marvels he will win many to his side.'

According to Creme, 'Maitreya' has been emerging *gradually* into the public view so as not to infringe humanity's free will.' But according to Engleman (p 254),

Unlike Antichrist, who will have had to deceive mankind, and use all the modern technology available to advance his cause, Christ's Second Advent will cause an immediate spiritual shock throughout the world. 'It will not be necessary or possible for persons to communicate news of the coming of the Son of God', wrote Saint Ignatius Brianchaninov. 'He will appear suddenly . . . to all men and to all the earth at the same time.'

I won't go into Creme's 'esoteric philosophy' in detail, since it is basically that of the Theosophical Society. I will, however, quote three passages. The first is attributed to the master Djwhal Khul, as channeled by Alice Bailey: 'All activity which drives the human being forward toward some form of development—physical, emotional, intuitional, social—if it is in advance of his present state, is essentially spiritual in nature.' But 'in advance' toward what? The thug working out so as to be a stronger thug, the thief sharpening his senses and manual dexterity so as to be a better thief, the spy developing his intuition so as to be a better spy—these are spiritual pursuits? (According to the way my own intuition has developed, I hear in the name 'Djwhal Khul' the Arabic words *Dajjal*, 'Antichrist', and *Qul*, 'recite'.)

The second passage attempts to define the nature of God: 'Esotericism postulates that *God* is the sum total of all the laws, and all the energies governed by these laws, which make up everything in the manifested and unmanifested universe—all that we see and cannot see.' This is not esotericism, however, but scientism, the familiar superstitious worship of natural laws and invisible energies which always crops up when theology is influenced by science, or when popularized science is turned into a religion. True esoterism, on the other hand, knows God as an Absolute, Perfect and Infinite Essence Who is equally a Person, a Reality which in Itself cannot be grasped or encompassed in terms of any conceivable form. God is inconceivable not because He is devoid of personhood, but because, rather than being this or that person, He is Personhood Itself—not as an abstract category, however, but as a unique Essence. For the vulgar and muddled 'esotericism' of Benjamin Creme, on the other hand, God is nothing but a heap of everything, an infinite conglomeration of every this and every that.

The third passage is of more immediate interest:

> According to the Ageless Wisdom, the *anti-Christ* is not one individual who lives at a certain point in time, but an *energy* released before the advent of the Christ. It comes to pave the way for the building-forces of the Christ by destroying the old crystallized ways that block growth for society. While the anti-Christ is an energy, it does manifest through individuals and has done so at different times throughout history, most notably through the Emperor Nero in Roman times, and more recently through Hitler and some of his closest associates. With the defeat of the Axis powers during World War II,

the work of the anti-Christ energy was completed for this age and will not manifest again for over 3,000 years.

So if Benjamin Creme is to be believed—as clearly he wants to be, and with very good reason—'Master Maitreya' cannot be the Antichrist! But *Hitler*, pave the way for the Christ? Hitler as John the Baptist, as Elijah? I don't think so. In the words of Orthodox Archbishop Averky of Jordanville, as recounted in *Ultimate Things*,

> The fundamental task of the servants of the coming Antichrist is to destroy the old world with all its former concepts and 'prejudices' in order to build in its place a new world suitable for receiving its approaching 'new owner' who will take the place of Christ for people and give them on earth that which Christ did not give them.

We must never forget that what appears as ridiculous on the surface may be profoundly sinister in its depths; as 'Master Maitreya' himself tells us, complacency is among the worst of vices. Dr Rama Coomaraswamy, in his essay 'The Desacralization of Hinduism for Western Consumption', has this to say regarding Alice Bailey, who succeeded Annie Besant as head of the Theosophical Society, and her plans for a new world religion:

> It is interesting to look at Bailey's instructions about the orthodox religions of the world. Initially the New Agers are to argue for religious liberty in their public releases. Only later will they insist on the new mandatory world religion that their books call for, a religion completely breaking with the concept of Jesus Christ and God the Father. Those who do not go along with this are to be eliminated by means of violence—called by her 'a cleansing action'. We are clearly on the way to point Omega and the reign of antichrist.

✳ Motif of the Herald: the Will and the Intellect

In most eschatological traditions, the coming Messiah or Avatar is heralded by a forerunner, as Jesus by John the Baptist. In Jewish eschatology, the Messiah is to be announced by Elias, one of the two prophets of the Old Testament who never suffered death, which is why the contemporaries of Jesus wondered if John the Baptist might be Elias come back. The second coming of Jesus is to be announced by the 'two witnesses' of the Apocalypse, who are identified with Elias and Enoch, the second of the two immortal prophets of the Old Testament. The advent of the Buddha Maitreya will be heralded by Shakyamuni's disciple Kashyapa, who has also remained in some form of 'occultation' or suspended animation, and that of Saoshyant by Keresaspa, who will likewise remain immortal on the plane of subtle manifestation until his time arrives. The descent of the Prophet Jesus in Islamic eschatology will be announced by the Mahdi, who has survived through the ages in suspended animation or 'occultation', just as the Mahdi himself, in the Shiite account, is heralded by the 'voice from the east after sunrise.' And though the Kalki Avatara is not announced by a specific figure, he is 'hosted' by Vishnuyasa the Brahmin, in whose household he is born, just as Maitreya is born in the same household as King Dhutta-Gamani, his brother, or during the reign of King Shanka. (The resurrection of the great Tibetan teacher Tsong Khapa, whose name certainly sounds like 'Kashyapa' and 'Keresaspa', is a similar motif, though Tsong Khapa is not a herald.)

So the eschatological Savior almost always has a partner, who usually arrives before him to announce his coming. The announcer has remained in suspended animation over the long ages, while the Savior, though in a sense representing the re-appearance of an earlier Savior, also carries the flavor of an entirely new advent, a descent of Eternity into time, a re-manifestation of saving Truth, fresh from the celestial worlds. (In the Zoroastrian account it is Yima the first prophet who remains in suspended animation, to return at the advent of Saoshyant.)

The relationship between the Savior and his herald is also that between a partial and a complete manifestation of the same reality. John the Baptist was a militant prophet, Jesus a priest and king. The same is true of Elias vis-à-vis the Messiah, or the defeated Messiah son of Joseph vs. the triumphant Messiah son of David. In Islam the Mahdi is the herald of the prophet Jesus, since he comes before him. However, Jesus will worship behind al-Mahdi, who will act as Imam (in the sense of prayer-leader), though this is perhaps best understood as an act of supreme courtesy, since al-Mahdi will initially seek to yield his place to Jesus. And according to al-Jili's account, Jesus is the militant one, since he slays Antichrist, while the Mahdi who dawns after the battle is done personifies equilibrium restored. The Buddha Maitreya, who is a *brahmin*, in some accounts is announced by his brother and first disciple, King Dhutta-Gamani, rather than by Kashyapa, just as the herald and first disciple of Jesus was his cousin, John the Baptist; according to other versions, Maitreya is destined to appear and work with the universal monarch Shanka. In Hindu eschatological tradition, the militant Kalki Avatara is born in the household of the *brahmin* Vishnuyasa.

In every case, then, we have an eschatological partnership between a militant figure and a 'spiritual' or pneumatic one. The polarization of the Jewish Messiah into priestly and kingly versions (to take only one example) is thus a universal motif. This can be explained historically as a product of the tension between the repeated failure of Messianic hopes in their political expression and the eternal hope for spiritual renewal; political defeat always forces the defeated to ask how their intent might have been purer and their dedication deeper, and such questioning often leads to the idea that only after the people have spiritually purified themselves will salvation come. This is why revolutionary messianism is often pre-millennialist, and spiritual messianism (insofar as it grows out of revolutionary defeat) post-millennialist. But since history itself is the fluid expression in time of eternal metaphysical principles, the roots of the polarization between militant and pneumatic eschatological figures must be sought on higher planes of being.

In some cases the militant is the herald and the pneumatic the Savior; in others the reverse is true. The Christ of the first advent (announced by John), the Buddhist Maitreya (announced by Dhutta-Gamani) and the Mahdi vis-à-vis Jesus (at least in al-Jili's account) are spirituals announced or preceded by militants. On the other hand, the Jewish Messiah (heralded by Elias), the Kalki Avatara of Hinduism (paired with Vishnuyasa) and the Word of God in the *Apocalypse*, the Christ of the Second Coming (heralded by Enoch and Elias) are militants announced or hosted by spirituals. This characterization is far from perfect, obviously, since the Elias who announces the Messiah was certainly a prophetic militant during his earthly life, which is why many of the Jews recognized the same quality in the militant Baptist. And in the various Muslim accounts, Jesus is sometimes the militant slayer of Antichrist and al-Mahdi the restorer of equilibrium after the battle, while sometimes he is the one who, after the Mahdi himself is overcome by Antichrist, overcomes him in turn and so restores order. But the polarization between militancy and transcendence, however it is worked out in a particular tradition or account, remains in clear relief.

In my opinion, the significance of this pairing is as follows: The militant figures represent the will, the spiritual ones the Intellect. Will asserted, will defeated, and Intellect unveiled are thesis, antithesis and synthesis; the will, at least on the human level, must both do its best work and admit its ultimate powerlessness before the Intellect can dawn. At the beginning of the spiritual Path, the traveler wills to follow God, he takes full personal responsibility. Then commanding *nafs* constellates, showing the individual will its ultimate powerlessness; finally God (if He so wills) takes the field and slays the *nafs*. Moses kills the overseer, flees to the wilderness, and sees God in the burning bush. Christ ministers, is crucified, and rises. Muhammad receives his mission, is exiled to Medina, returns to Mecca in triumph. The Messiah son of Joseph is defeated by Antichrist, who in turn is overcome Messiah son of David. The Twelfth Imam appears, is occulted, returns on the Last Day.

As on the spiritual Path so in the eschatological scenario: from one perspective, a person's individual effort to grow in the Spirit precedes the full dawning of that Spirit; from another, it is the initial free gift of that Spirit which alone makes such effort possible. That Moses kills the Egyptian overseer and flees into the wilderness, after which God speaks to him, indicates in esoteric terms that the struggle of the human will against the lower self—even though that will cannot triumph in its own terms (Moses did not gain personal power through killing the overseer but became a homeless fugitive)—must still precede the dawning of the Transcendent Intellect, to which it finally makes obeisance. The same truth is symbolized in Islam by the conquest of the Antichrist by the Prophet Jesus (i.e., the overcoming of the will of the lower self by the will obedient to, and empowered by, God), and the subsequent restoration of equilibrium by the Mahdi (the dawning of the Divine Intellect after the will, in victory and defeat, is pacified), and in the Jewish one by the Messiah son of Joseph who goes to battle with the Antichrist and is killed, only to be followed by the Messiah son of David who defeats and kills the Antichrist. In Buddhist tradition, the fact that the King Shanka of the *kshatriya* or warrior caste renounces his throne to follow the *brahmin* Maitreya reflects the identical doctrine. In Schuon's words (*Stations of Wisdom*, p157),

> What separates man from the Divine Reality is the slightest of barriers. God is infinitely close to man, but man is infinitely far from God. This barrier, for man, is a mountain . . . which he must remove with his own hands. He digs away the earth, but in vain, the mountain remains; man however goes on digging in the Name of God. And the mountain vanishes. It was never there.

In another sense, however, the Divine Truth, which the Intellect both sees and is, cannot be realized unless the will makes obeisance to it. So while the Intellect remains on a higher plane than the will, the full activation of the will in service of the Intellect represents the complete incarnation, or realization, of what on the plane of the Intellect is only virtual in relation to man, though complete and fully realized in relation to God. Furthermore, there is nothing more militant and rigorous in its effects than the dawning of objective Truth. Absolute objectivity, the sword of the discriminating Intellect, is both perfect judgement and perfect forgiveness, without the slightest distinction between them. God witnesses nothing but Himself—this is His rigor—and knows all things *as* Himself—this is His mercy.

When the immortal and occulted herald is a militant figure, this possibly represents the maintenance of a spiritual tradition on the legalistic level alone, paired with a suspension of the full power of human obedience until the direct knowledge of God is again unveiled. When the hidden herald is a pneumatic figure, this may symbolize a guardianship of esoteric lore by marginalized or clandestine schools, or such lore as preserved, unbeknownst to its preservers, in the forms of exoteric religion, until such time as inner spiritual potentials can again be manifested outwardly in the fullness of human life.

✳ The 'Brief Millennium'

Those writers of the Traditionalist school who deal most directly with eschatology—René Guénon, Martin Lings, and Leo Schaya—do not anticipate an earthly millennium of the latter days. They are not chiliasts. They do, however, see a brief 'restoration' before the end of the cycle. In *Perspectives on Initiation* (p 254), René Guénon has this to say about the advent of the Mahdi:

> Moreover, this [total Messianic] rectification will have to be prepared, even visibly, before the end of the present cycle; but this can only be done by one who, by uniting in himself the powers of Heaven and Earth, of East and West, will manifest outwardly, both in the domain of knowledge and in that of action, the twin sacerdotal and royal power that has been preserved across the ages in the integrity of its unique principle by the hidden keepers of the primordial tradition.

And Martin Lings, in *The Eleventh Hour*, says the following about the 'restoration' or 'brief millennium':

> After 'an imminent world-wide devastation, not total, but nonetheless of cataclysmic proportions, and not final, because it is 'before the end', though there are grounds for conviction that 'the end' itself cannot be far off, there is reason to anticipate a 'redress before the close of the cycle,' based in part on the prophecy in Matt. 24 referring to the 'great tribulation such as was not since the beginning of the world,' especially in view of verse 22: 'And except

those days should be shortened, there should be no flesh saved: but for the elect's sake those days shall be shortened.'

One would think that the Shiïte Muslim account of the advent, battles, final triumph and just rule of the Mahdi would be purely chiliastic, since Shiïsm, perhaps more than any other tradition except the Judaic one, conceives of the eschatological event as a revolution against tyranny (though such a revolution is also a clear subtext in the Christian *Apocalypse*). And in many ways the attribution of chiliasm to Shiïte Islam is justified. According to one account, for example, the Mahdi, or his successor, will rule for 309 years. 309, however, is also the number of years the legendary Seven Sleepers of Ephesus remained in their cave in a state of suspended animation, which would lead me to suspect that this time-period may be a veiled reference to a posthumous state. Another account gives his rule as 19 years; a Sunni account says 5, 7, or 9 years. He will die 40 days prior to the resurrection of the dead and the Day of Judgement. (A related tradition of the 'brief millennium' states that upon his second advent, Jesus will reign for 40 years after slaying Antichrist, and then die.)

It is also possible to interpret the Shiïte 'millennium', as well as the Christian one (Rev. 20:1–10), as a 'kingdom' not of this world. Jafar al-Sadiq is reported as saying, according to one source, that the Mahdi will rule for 7 years, and according to another that the rule of al-Mahdi will be as long as heaven and earth endure, and all his subjects will be in either heaven or hell—a fairly clear though veiled reference to a posthumous state. The same source quotes him to the effect that after the rule of the Mahdi will come the day of resurrection. If his rule is a posthumous one, however, this 'resurrection' must refer to the *mahapralaya*, the re-absorption of even the highest formal paradises into their Absolute Principle.

The concept of a brief millennium can perhaps also be discerned in the Old Testament book of Joel:

The floors shall be full of wheat, and the vats shall overflow with wine and oil. And I will restore to you the years that the locust hath eaten.... (2:24–25) And it shall come to pass afterward that I will pour out my spirit upon all flesh; and your sons and your daughters shall prophesy, your old men shall dream dreams, your young men shall see visions:
And also upon the servants and upon the handmaids in those days will I pour out my spirit.
And I will show wonders in the heavens and in the earth, blood, and fire, and pillars of smoke.

The sun shall be turned into darkness, and the moon into blood, before the great and terrible day of the Lord come.
And it shall come to pass that whosoever shall call on the name of the Lord shall be delivered. . . . (2:28–32)

But what, if any, is the organic relationship between the idea of a brief millennial flowering immediately before the end of the cycle, suggesting the brief, terminal rally that a dying person will often exhibit, and a posthumous 'kingdom' which will have no end? The answer will be obvious to anyone who has experienced the atmosphere of joyous liberation and infinite possibility accompanying a cultural renaissance which has finally arrived after a long period of imaginative repression, or the rising portents and opening shots of a truly just social revolution, no matter how destructive the effects of these developments may ultimately be, several decades or centuries down the line. The experience is precisely that of a breakthrough of Eternity into passing time. The days of the Round Table are always short, but the Throne of Arthur, in Avalon, remains. In this world, a moment is over in an instant; in the next world, which is within this world in Essence as well as ahead of it in time, this moment has no end.

✳ End and Beginning are in God's Hands

People in the New Age movement, as well as many who are simply secularists, often believe that anyone holding the doctrine that this world must end actually wants it to end. They think of traditional eschatology as a negative self-fulfilling prophecy that prevents humanity from facing and solving global problems, and look at religious believers as spiteful maniacs who want everything to be destroyed just so they can be proved right. In some cases this may be true. But still, all that has a beginning in time also has an end. Is it a sign of mental illness to admit this? Is every person who admits, for example, that all who are born must die, necessarily depressed or suicidal?

In Chapter Ten of *Ultimate Things*, 'Why the Devil Hates a Crowd', Dennis Engleman debunks the overpopulation problem as 'bloated-earth propaganda,' and maintains that 'euphemisms like "birth control" and "reproductive services" primarily mean abortion.' He repeats the tradition, common though not dogmatic, that 'only when there are enough believers to fill the places in Heaven vacated by the fallen angels, will Christ return.'

Though his book is wonderful—I would recommend it to anyone interested in the lore of the latter days—I can't entirely agree with him here. The overpopulation problem is very real. And while the same general mindset seems to be behind both birth control and abortion, in another way they are diametrically opposed: the less available and effective birth control is, the more unwanted pregnancies there will be, and the more unwanted pregnancies, the more abortions. Abortion is clearly a great evil, which Engleman rightly compares to human sacrifice. While in my opinion it is justified in some cases, such as incestuous rape, massive deformation of the fetus or virtual certainty of the mother's death—though even here I'm uneasy—it should never be undertaken lightly. Even Ken Kesey of the LSD-scattering Merry Pranksters, in one of the *Whole Earth Catalogues* around 1970, said that the major fly in the ointment of the whole Liberal/Counterculture program was abortion.

As for the legend that Christ will return when the number of believers equals the number of fallen angels, this to me represents a subtle spiritual truth which has been dragged down to the literal level. It could be used, for example, to justify Christian polygamy, since this would increase the Christian birthrate. And if Christ will only return when there are enough Christians born, then why did St Paul teach that 'It is better not to marry'?

According to Orthodox Christian and Muslim eschatology, Antichrist will co-opt the doing of good works. Does this mean that to perform good works under the regime of Antichrist is ultimately to do evil?

Antichrist, or his system, will attempt to set up the following double bind, which in many ways is already in evidence: 'Whoever does good necessarily serves me, because all good is my property; whoever would oppose me, therefore, has no choice but to do, or allow, evil.' Preventing overpopulation is a clear good. But if the macro-solution to the population problem results in massive human rights abuses, as it apparently has in China, then this good becomes a tributary to evil. Protecting the environment is a clear good. Humanity, in Genesis, is commanded by God to 'replenish' the earth, and according to Rev. 11:18, God in the latter days will reward His 'servants the prophets' but will 'destroy them which destroy the earth.' But if protecting the environment is done according to an oppressive, materialistic or scientistic paradigm which denies the theomorphic nature of man, then this good also serves an evil end. So not every way of doing good ultimately serves the Good. If a good end does not justify evil means, neither do good proximate ends or means justify an end which is ultimately evil. Death is clearly an evil, but the loss of one's immortal soul is a fate worse than death.

Any large collective effort, such as protection of the environment or the prevention of overpopulation, will necessarily generate profiteers, and attract those who are looking for political power and economic advantage. And the final parasite on all good efforts for this cycle will be the system of Antichrist. But it will always be possible to do material good in such a way that it serves spiritual good. Any effort aimed at improving material conditions, if it is based on true compassion, and on a spiritual appreciation of the human form and the natural world as signs of God's presence and symbolic manifestations of His Nature, is a form or worship. We need not, and must not, allow the system of Antichrist to co-opt all good, to the point where, in reaction against it, we become examples of cruelty or indifference which that system can use to prove its own necessity and legitimacy. All concrete good that can be done an a basis other than that of Antichrist will undercut his power and delay his advent, giving more souls time to reject error, to discern and choose the Truth. The perennial question is: When do such efforts stop being direct expressions of the good, and start becoming attempts to seize power for the abstract purpose of establishing the good, with the result that good is dethroned and power idolized? And how far can a given group or individual, in a given place and time, take power in the name of good without starting to suppress good in the name of power? Only deep spiritual discernment, based on radical submission to God's will, can answer this question.

Perhaps the greatest area of conflict and polarization between secular and the traditional eschatologies is environmentalism. Many traditional Christians see a Neo-Pagan 'Green Socialism' which worships the material cosmos in place of the Transcendent God, and denies the theomorphic nature of man, as the price of saving the environment, and they are not willing to pay it. And many environmentalists, especially those with Neo-Pagan tendencies, believe that the very idea of Transcendence, as held by the traditional religions, is at the basis of environmental destruction. They forget that it is science and technology, not religion, which are destroying the environment, and that the roots of the present regime of science and technology are in the Neo-Pagan revival of classical learning during the Renaissance, not in the transcendentalism of the Christian Middle Ages. It is precisely the belief that this world is all there is which inflames our desire to 'have it all now', and forces us to devastate the earth in the process of getting it.

It is possible, however, to work to protect the environment, in a small way, without opting for de-humanizing and anti-spiritual macro-solutions. According to Evagrius of Pontus:

As for those who are far from God.... God has made it possible to come near to the knowledge of him and his love for them through the medium of creatures. These he has produced, as the letters of the alphabet, so to speak, by his power and his wisdom.

Likewise the Koran teaches that

In your creation and in all the beasts scattered on the earth there are signs for people of true faith. In the alternation of night and day, and in the provision which Allah sendeth down from the heavens whereby he quickeneth the earth after its death, and in the distribution of the winds, are signs for people who are intelligent.

⟶ KORAN 45:4–6

On the basis of doctrines like these, it is possible to perform environmental service as a liturgical or contemplative act, without exalting collective material survival above the salvation of the human soul.

But if the earth is doomed, many say, then why care for the environment? This is like saying, 'why maintain your health if you're going to die anyway? Why continue to care for an elderly mother if she doesn't have long to live?' If something or someone needs care, and we have the power to give that care, then we give it. As in the path of *karma-yoga* from the *Bhavagad-Gita*, we perform the action for its own sake—that is, for God's sake—and dedicate the fruits of the action to Him.

In Rev. 19:17–18, on the day of the eschatological combat the 'fowls that fly in the midst of heaven' are invited to feast on 'the flesh of kings, and the flesh of captains, and the flesh of mighty men ... and the flesh of all men.' And according to 2 Pet. 3:10, 'the heavens shall pass away with a great noise, and the elements shall melt with fervent heat, the earth also and the works that are therein shall be burnt up.' But Dennis Engleman (*Ultimate Things*, p 258) repeats the doctrine that

The 'end of this world' does not produce obliteration (except of evil) but rather restoration and renewal. 'For this world shall pass away by transmutation, not by absolute destruction,' wrote Blessed Augustine, 'and therefore the apostle says, "For the figure of this world passeth away" (1 Cor. 7:31). The figure, therefore, passes away, not the nature.

According to St Irenaeus, as quoted by St Andrew of Caesarea, 'Neither the essence nor the being of the creation will perish.' As René Guénon says in *The Reign of Quantity* (pp 330–331, 336):

The end now under consideration is undeniably of considerably greater importance than many others, for it is the end of a whole *Manvantara*, and so of the temporal existence of what may rightly be called a humanity, but this, it must be said once more, in no way implies the end of the terrestrial world itself, because, through the 'reinstatement' that takes place at the final instant, this end will immediately become the beginning of another *Manvantara* . . . it can be said in all truth that 'the end of a humanity' never is and never can be anything but the end of an illusion.

It does not appear to be strictly doctrinal, then, that all life, or even all human life, must necessarily be destroyed—or necessarily preserved—at the end of this cycle.

From the material standpoint, a few species or a number of human individuals may survive, through which life could begin again. From the spiritual standpoint, all will be destroyed and burnt up, after which the Creator will renew all things. But in order to save our souls—which is the only reason we're here on earth in the first place—we must adopt the spiritual standpoint and let the material level (which is a subset of, and subordinate to, the spiritual) take care of itself according to God's design. To be willing to face the eschatological event as the end of this cycle of manifestation, to stand ready to allow oneself and all living things to die and be reborn at the touch of the Almighty, is the door to the New Heaven and the New Earth. But to plan for one's own physical survival beyond Apocalypse, or to imagine how the race could survive in material terms, through the stockpiling of computer-tended human genetic material in secret underground caves, or whatever other dehumanizing high-tech survivalist fantasies may presently be hatching in the brains of those who don't know what a human being is because they don't believe in God, is to become a servant of the Antichrist. God will save, destroy, and re-create life as He will; whoever places his hopes in something other than that Will has reserved his place in the Fire.

10

Facing Apocalypse

And I saw a new heaven and a new earth: for the first heaven and the first earth were passed away; and there was no more sea.

And I John saw the holy city, new Jerusalem, coming down from God out of heaven, prepared like a bride adorned for her husband.

And I heard a great voice out of heaven saying, Behold, the tabernacle of God is with men, and they shall be his people, and God himself shall be with them and be their God.

And God shall wipe away all tears from their eyes; and there shall be no more death, neither sorrow, nor crying, neither shall there be any more pain: for the former things are passed away.

Rev. 21:1–4

If we subscribe to a spirituality that would be invalidated by an end to the world, then our spirituality is not true. The same can be said, however, for a spirituality which requires the end of the world in order to validate it. The purpose of meditation upon the end of things is twofold. First, since the possibility of the end of human existence on the material plane is an inescapable part of the quality of our time, we need to have doctrinally orthodox and spiritually fruitful ways of relating to it. Secondly, the end of things is always there, no matter what period of history we live in. All things are impermanent; death comes to all. The end of things remains a reminder that we must put our hands to the plough and accomplish our salvation while we still can, since time is always short. It is also a perennial metaphor for the true death, which is the death of the ego, and the true immortality, which is the eternity of the Rock of Ages, impervious to the waves of time, the cycles of creation, and dissolution which break against it.

According to the Traditionalists, the latter days are not without their own particular blessings and spiritual opportunities, which could exist at no other point in the cycle. The first is the comparative ease of spiritual detachment, to those who are at all inclined in that direction. In Martin Lings' words, 'Detachment is an essential feature of the sage, and this virtue, which in better times could only be acquired through great spiritual efforts, can be made more spontaneous by the sight of one's world in chaotic ruins.'

The second blessing is that of encyclopedic knowledge. 'If human societies degenerate on the one hand with the passage of time,' says Schuon, 'they accumulate on the other hand experiences in virtue of old age, however intermingled with errors these may be.' Knowledge of the great spiritual traditions of the world, such as made possible the writing of this book, was much more difficult to access even a few decades ago.

The third blessing, in this extreme old age of the macrocosm, is the enhanced possibility of spiritual serenity and insight. In *The Eleventh Hour*, Martin Lings writes:

> There is . . . a feature of normal old age, the most positive of all . . . in virtue of which our times are unique. It is sometimes said of spiritual men and women at the end of their lives that they have 'one foot already in Paradise.' This is not meant to deny that death is a sudden break, a rupture of continuity. It cannot but be so, for it has to transform mortal old age into immortal youth. None the less, hagiography teaches that the last days of sanctified souls can be remarkably luminous and transparent. Nor is it unusual that the imminence of death should bring with it special graces, such as visions, in foretaste of what is to come. The mellowing of spirituality, which is the highest aspect of old age itself, is thus crowned with an illumination which belongs more to youth than to age . . . in the macrocosm, the nearness of the new Golden Age cannot fail to make itself mysteriously felt before the end of the old cycle. . . . (p66)

✳ The Transcendent Unity of Religions as Spiritual Practice

The Transcendent Unity of Religions is not simply a doctrine; it is also a practice. It is important to understand this, since if our relationship to it remains limited to doctrine, it will sink to the level of abstraction, and lose its transcendent dimension. It will become mere exoteric ecumenism, or comparative religion, or a purely mental search for the metaphysical principles common to all traditions.

Frithjof Schuon and other Traditionalists usually explain the Transcendent Unity of Religions by means of what I call 'the Traditionalist Spiderweb'—a symbol which is also found, for example, in Plotinus. As a young man, Schuon encountered, in his home town of Basle, Switzerland, a venerable Black marabout who was visiting from Senegal. During their talk, the old man drew a circle on the ground with radii connecting the circumference with the center. 'God is the center,' he said; 'all paths lead to Him.' This may have been the genesis of the Spiderweb in Schuon's mind; the full symbol, however—in both Schuon and Plotinus—includes a number of concentric circles which represent different planes of reality, what I have called elsewhere in this book 'the Great Chain of Being'. The circles, like those in the *Divine Comedy*, indicate the relative nearness or distance of a plane of Being from its central Principle, whereas the radii indicate incomparable quiddities ('whatnesses') which are precisely themselves and nothing else, irrespective of the level of Being on which they appear, just as the scent of a rose is precisely that scent and no other, whether we are catching only the faintest hint of it on the wind, or bathing in a pool full of rosewater. In Aristotelian terms, the radii symbolize *essence* and the concentric circles *existence*; the points where circle and radius intersect represent actual existing things, where essence ('whatness') and existence ('isness') are concretely united. A rock, for example, cannot be a rock if it lacks either the quality of rocklikeness, or the quality of actually being there. In actual existing things—rocks, galaxies, human beings, spirits, angels—essence and existence are united only relatively, since it is possible to distinguish one radius or one concentric circle from another. Only in the Center, only in God Himself are essence and existence absolutely united: 'I Am That I Am.'

In terms of the Transcendent Unity of Religions, each radius is a single integral and revealed religious tradition. The fact that it radiates from the Center indicates that it has been revealed by God; the fact that all radii meet *only at the center* indicates that the unity of religions is not ecumenical ('worldly'), but transcendent.

Religions come together, in other words, not by virtue of their relative comparability, but on the ground of their incomparable uniqueness. The field of comparative religion, the level on which we can say 'Islam is like Christianity in this way but unlike in that; Hinduism is like Buddhism, or Islam, or Christianity, in these ways but unlike in those' is not that of the Transcendent Unity of Religions.

The Traditionalist Spiderweb can also be seen as a kind of 'Traditionalist Stonehenge', a circle of separate and discrete doorways, each of which gives a unique view of the same Center, where, let us say, a great Light shines. It is only possible to look through one doorway at a single time. I can look sideways from my Muslim doorway, and see my wife Jenny kneeling in the light streaming through her Christian doorway, but that light will always be, for me, a reflected light. For her, Jesus is the Christ, the only-begotten Son of God. For me, as a Muslim, he is a great prophet, the Spirit and Word or God, born of a virgin and destined to return at the end of the age to slay the Antichrist; but he is not the Son of God, since according to the Koran, 'He [Allah] neither begets nor is He begotten.' So do we then disagree about the nature of Jesus? If we spent our time looking 'sideways' in religion, we would have to disagree. Jesus would have to be either a great prophet, or the Son of God; he could not be both. But the essence of religion, which is the spiritual Path, does not move sideways. It travels only from whatever place on the circumference of our circle we happen to find ourselves, according to the imponderabilities of race, culture, religion, place of birth, individual psychology and personal destiny, and straight toward the Center, toward the One God. And that God is so great, so embracing of all conceptions of Him, and at the same time so fundamentally independent of all conceptions of Him, that every view of Him, if it is indeed directed toward the Center along an unbroken ray emanating from that Center, produces a unique and incomparable vision of God's Reality which, far from being relative to other views, is blessed and confirmed by the Absolute, and partakes of its nature; this is Schuon's doctrine of the 'relatively Absolute'. Each view of God—whether it be that of a revealed religion, or of an individual within that religion, or of a moment within the life of that individual—is unique and incomparable, since it is a vision of God the Incomparable, God the Unique. While I am contemplating that God, I have neither the time nor the perspective to compare my doctrine with that of another; while I am comparing and contrasting doctrine, I am not contemplating God.

God, however, is not only incomparable, for which read 'transcendent'; He is also comparable, for which read 'immanent'. If God were not absolutely beyond all conception, He would not be Unique. He would be comparable, relative, able to be defined by something other or less than Him, and therefore not God. But if God were not also in a sense comparable to created things, we could form no conception of Him, and thus have no way to know Him. And since created things, in essence, are nothing else than conceptions of Him, symbolic manifestations of His Attributes, or Energies, or Names, then if God were incomparable while not at the same time having an aspect of comparability, there would be no universe. So once we understand God's

Uniqueness, we can also understand how all created things are unique in themselves precisely because they reflect that Uniqueness. Furthermore, if we have the power to see things as they are in themselves, we also have the secondary power to compare them not with their common Source, but with each other, to see how they are alike in some ways and different in others. Here, however, is where we must heed Shakespeare's warning that 'comparisons are odious.' The power to compare existing things with each other rather than with their transcendent Source is the origin of abstraction, and the danger of abstraction, immensely convenient though it is, and even necessary to our lives according to the way the human mind works, is that we may begin to think that the abstract category is the origin of the unique particulars which comprise it, rather than the other way around. The nation, in a sense, produces the citizen; but it is much truer to say, and in line with a higher order of reality, that the citizen—or rather the human being, who is much more than his or her mere citizenship—produces the nation.

As we move away from the center of the Spiderweb, the tendency toward abstraction increases. Essences, symbolized by the radii, are still absolutely unique; but this truth becomes obscured as we move down through the concentric circles, toward lower levels of being. Higher levels of being reveal the uniqueness of the essences; lower levels obscure it. Consequently, on the material or socio-historical level, abstraction begins to confuse individuals, and cultures, and religions. A religion, on this level, is primarily defined by how it is like others or different from them. A culture becomes a set of quantitative parameters, a population, a mass of resources, a collection of laws and institutions, a gross national product. An individual becomes a statistical monad, fodder for the actuarial tables of an insurance company, a cipher. In Guénon's terms, motion toward the Center is toward Essence, or quality; motion toward the periphery is toward Substance, or quantity. (Substance as opposed to Essence, that is, not as opposed to the 'accidents'; the philosophical term 'Substance'—*ousia*—vis-à-vis its accidents, itself begins to take on the meaning of 'Essence', whereas Guénon is using 'Substance' more as synonymous with the Aristotelian/Thomistic *materia*, as opposed to *forma* which is nearly synonymous with 'Essence'.)

The Platonic Ideas or Names of God are often thought of as abstract categories, partly due to the fact that, on the plane of language, the most particular images are necessarily the most sensual. Language anchors our sense of the particular to the sensual level; the words we must use for higher-than-sensual realities become more and more abstract as we ascend the Great Chain of Being. This, however, is not true of the realities themselves:

A Platonic Idea is not an abstract category, in other words, but *a higher level of particularity*. Many men may be the origin of the abstract category 'man', but the *concrete Idea* 'Man' is the origin and creator of many men. A Platonic Idea is not the abstract lowest common denominator of many particulars, but the concrete 'highest common denominator' of the individuals which compose it, who, in relation to it, are relative abstractions. The Platonic Idea 'Man' does not contain only whatever is common to all human beings — which, because there are two sexes, would have to exclude genital organs, as it would exclude arms, legs and eyes as well because there are also amputees and eyeless persons, and so on — but rather everything that 'Man' in all his variations could ever manifest, and all this in a single form. This is why the original human form in Plato's *Timaeus* is an androgyne, and also a sphere: the spherical form represents in this case the simultaneous and synthetic realization of all human possibilities. And because Ideas are not pale abstractions but higher orders of particularity, realities which are *more concrete* than matter, the Persian mystical philosophers, such as Suhrawardi — in line with their Jewish, Christian, and Zoroastrian brethren — were led to a vision of the Platonic Ideas as vast, powerful and *conscious* beings: in other words, as angels. According to Judeo-Christian angelology, for example, the archangel Michael is not an abstract symbol of spiritual warfare; he is a individual, conscious being of vast wisdom and power who is the commanding general of this warfare — not because of *what* he is but because of *who* he is. Nonetheless, he remains the very essence and Idea of spiritual warfare, 'incarnate' on the archangelic plane. There is ultimately no contradiction between the personal and the archetypal orders of reality, since both are attempts to express the quality of essences, and essences are incomparable; they are incapable of being fully defined in terms other than themselves.

(I said above that the words we use to describe higher-than-sensual realities — realities more concrete than sense experience — must become increasingly abstract to the degree that their objects become more concrete. The exception to this is when we use words not as *descriptions* but as *names*. 'Spiritual warfare' is an abstract concept; 'Holy Michael' is a concrete person. Consequently, the most concrete and reality-charged words in existence are the Names of God, which are used in various traditions to invoke — in other words, to recognize — His presence. His Names are not primarily our descriptions of Him, but rather His acts of self manifestation to us.)

Abstraction, however, has an 'ascending' function as well, by which it too can serve the vision of the Transcendent Unity of Religions. Comparative religion, if pursued thoroughly and in depth, reveals two things: (1) That the doctrines of the different religions all draw closer to each other as the mystical centers of these religions are approached, and (2) that perfect unanimity, on the level of doctrine, is never in fact achieved. The Muslim Sufi Ibn al-'Arabi and the Christian sage Meister Eckhart are much closer to one another than, say, the doctrines of the Church Councils within Christianity and the *ulema* within Islam; nonetheless, Eckhart remains thoroughly Christian, Ibn al-'Arabi quintessentially Muslim. Comparative religion serves the vision of religions in their Transcendent Unity not by positing a 'horizontal' universalism by which the doctrines of the various revealed religions are mixed together until they lose all character, but by 'triangulating', so to speak, a common point of Origin—an act which requires, geometrically, at least two entirely unique and separate points-of-view. The fact that the doctrines of all religions become more and more alike as their respective mystical centers are approached proves that this Origin is really there, and has a real character. The fact that the doctrines of the religions, while they draw ever closer together, never actually meet this side of the Absolute, proves that this Origin is truly transcendent, and entirely beyond conception. The Word, the Divine Logos, is One; it is nonetheless the first principle of creation and division. The Paths only meet in the virginal and maternal Silence before, and out of whom, the Word is spoken.

The Transcendent Unity of Religions is not simply a doctrine, as I have said; it is also a practice. And if the practice is not kept fresh, the doctrine degenerates. I have heard Martin Lings, in a taped lecture, floundering before an audience of religious exoterists, unable to counter the assertion that 'According to the logical principle of non-contradiction, Jesus Christ cannot both be and not be the unique incarnation of God; if Christianity, based on this belief, is true, then other religions, which deny it, must be false.' Lings attempted to answer this objection to the Transcendent Unity of Religions by comparing Christ to the avatars of Vishnu, like Krishna, who made the same claim to Divinity as he did. But Christ is not one among the ten avatars of Vishnu; he is, from the Christian perspective, the sole avatar, the only-begotten Son of God. Only the understanding that every view of the Absolute has a dimension of incomparability, that it is blessed by the Absolute with God's own Absoluteness, and is thus 'relatively Absolute', could have answered the questioner's objection—perhaps not to his satisfaction, but nonetheless to the full satisfaction of the Truth.

The doctrine of the Transcendent Unity of Religions calls up immense social and psychological forces, which act to drive a wedge between the term 'transcendent' and the term 'unity'. Those who unconsciously begin to err in the direction of unity as opposed to transcendence will be impelled toward a horizontal universalism; this is Schuon's analysis, in his book *Spiritual Perspectives and Human Facts*, of the fate of the Ramakrishna Order under Vivekananda and his successors. Ramakrishna, as a saint of the highest degree, was able to see and embody the unity of religions from a transcendent perspective, one which did not destroy but rather fulfilled his quintessential Hinduism. The Ramakrishna Order, on the other hand—at least according to Schuon—began to depart from Orthodox Hinduism in the direction of a shallow universalism, a charge which has been leveled, ironically, at Schuon himself in terms of Islam. At the other extreme, those who, without realizing it, begin to err in the direction of transcendence as opposed to unity will come into the field where the inexpressible and Transcendent Absolute demands a form in the relative world through which it can be expressed, and will consequently be tempted to absolutize the essentially relative aspects of their religious tradition, seeing its absoluteness through the distorting lens of its relativity rather than through the open door of its transcendence; this is the idolatrous and literalistic shadow of Schuon's doctrine of the 'relatively Absolute'. Thus the Transcendent Unity of Religions, given the lateness of the times as well as the simple limitations of human nature, will inevitably generate its two 'guardian beasts' rising up on both sides of its temple doorway to divert the course of all who cannot really understand it: To the left, the Gog of universalism; to the right, the Magog of exclusivism, whose socio-historical expressions are modernism or post-modernism on the one hand (the principle behind political and economic globalism) and reactionary fundamentalism on the other (the principle behind the 'tribalist' reactions against globalist hegemony).

To practice the Transcendent Unity of Religions is to walk a razor's edge which passes through one of the most formidable of the metaphysical 'pairs-of-opposites'. It is immensely demanding, psychologically, philosophically and contemplatively, because the doctrine of Transcendent Unity ultimately emanates from what is perhaps the highest intelligible level of metaphysical principle. According to Schuon, God is both Absolute and Infinite. The absoluteness of God is the source of His transcendence, and the origin of the uniqueness of each God-given religious form. The infinity of God is the source of His immanence, the origin of the underlying unity of all true religions. These are the Shiva and Shakti of His Self-revelation in the religious sphere. To hold to God's absoluteness alone and reject His infinity is to fall into religious authoritarianism; to hold to His infinity and reject His absoluteness is to drift into religious promiscuity.

In concrete terms, the practice of the Transcendent Unity of Religions comes down to six different kinds of hard work: First, to accept one of the revealed religions and remain faithful to it, both in terms of outer practice and of inner truth. Second, to view from the vantage point of one's inherited or adopted religion the vistas of Truth provided by the other religions, and intuit their intrinsic unity. Third, whenever one finds oneself strictly identifying one's religious form with God in such a way as one is actually worshipping the form instead of the Deity, to stop, and remember God. Fourth, whenever one finds oneself looking sideways at other religions, pridefully or anxiously wondering whether those forms are better or worse than one's own, to stop, and remember God. Fifth, whenever one's 'monkey-mind' begins to stitch together a patchwork idol made up from fragments of many religious traditions, to stop, and remember God. Sixth, whenever one finds oneself taking spiritual pride in one's understanding of abstract metaphysical principles, looking down from this false elevation on the revealed traditions as backwaters of literal-mindedness, provincial superstition and mere humanity, to stop, and remember God.

Loyalty to a single religion, *after* one has already realized that other religions are God-given and efficacious, is like loyalty to one's spouse. My wife is my beloved, my one and only, not because she is better than all other women according to this or that set of criteria, but because she is incomparable. And I don't have to denigrate other women to prove it: 'comparisons are odious'. She is my 'best' not because she is better than other women, but because, freely chosen, she is God's gift to me alone. If other men love their wives, should this lead me to question whether I should love my own? If she is insulted I will defend her, but I will not insult other men's wives out of some misguided sense that I am thereby doing her honor.

It is the same with religion. A person's religion is the spouse of that person's Spirit, just as someone's husband or wife is the spouse of that person's body and soul. Where true love is, comparison cannot enter. In the words of the Bengali poet Vidyapati (from *In Praise of Krishna: Songs from the Bengali*, tr. by E. C. Dinock and D. Leverton), speaking as Radha, Krishna's beloved:

as wing to bird
water to fish,
life to the living — so you to me.
But tell me,
Madhava, beloved
who are you?
Who are you really?
Vidyapati says, they are one another.

✳ The Transcendent Unity of Religions vs. The System of Antichrist

According to Rev. 20:7–8,

> When the thousand years are expired [the millennium during which the devil is bound, identified by Orthodox theologians as the church age], Satan shall be loosed out of his prison, and shall go out to deceive the nations which are in the four quarters of the earth, Gog and Magog, to gather them together to battle: the number of whom is as the sand of the sea.'

According to *The Apocalypse of St John: An Orthodox Commentary* by Archbishop Averky of Jordanville, the meaning of *Gog* in Hebrew is 'a gathering' or 'one who gathers', and of *Magog* 'an exaltation' or 'one who exalts'. 'Exaltation' suggests to me the idea of transcendence as *opposed* to unity, 'gathering' the idea of unity as *opposed* to transcendence. The implication, here, is that one of the deepest deceptions of Antichrist in the last days of the cycle will be to set these two integral aspects of the Absolute in opposition to each other in the collective mind, and on a global scale, in 'the four quarters of the earth'. As for the economic and political expression of this barren satanic polarity, the false cohesion of left-wing tyranny, as well as today's global capitalism, would fall under Gog, while both the false hierarchicalism of right-wing tyranny and the violent absolutism of the various 'tribal' separatist movements opposed to globalism, both ethnic and religious, would come under Magog. In terms of religion, those liberal, historicist, evolutionist, quasi-materialist and crypto-Pagan theologies which emphasize God's immanence as opposed to His transcendence are part of Gog, while those reactionary theologies which exalt transcendence over immanence, look on the material world as a vale of tears, denigrate the human body, and view the destruction of nature with indifference if not secret approval, since the best we can hope for is to get it all over with, are part of Magog. The conflict between the two is precisely the satanic counterfeit of the true eschatological conflict described in Rev. 19:11–20, between the King of Kings and Lord of Lords, and the Beast with his false prophet. Those who can be lured to fight in a counterfeit war between elements which ought to be reconciled, because they are essentially parts of the same reality as seen in a distorting mirror, will miss their call to fight in the true war between forces which neither should nor can be reconciled: those of the Truth and those of the Lie. (NOTE: Globalism, insofar as it sets the stage for the emergence of Guénon's 'inverted hierarchy', also contains the seed of Magog, while tribalism, as the common inheritance of all who are excluded from the global elite, holds the seed of Gog; in the latter days, no party or class or sector can long retain its ideological stability; the 'rate of contradiction' approaches the speed of light.)

In a world profoundly polarized between the Gog of syncretist globalism and the Magog of exclusivist 'tribalism'—a word which is beginning to denote what used to be called 'nationalism' or 'patriotism' or 'loyalty to one's religion'—the Transcendent Unity of Religions clearly represents a middle path, or third force, at least in the religious field. It is equally opposed to the universalism of the global elites and the violent self-assertion of the funda-mentalist 'tribes' oppressed and marginalized by these elites. Perhaps this is one reason why groups and individuals who hold to this doctrine have been subjected to the immense degree of psychic pressure which observers on the outskirts of the Traditionalist School, such as myself, cannot fail to note. It is reasonable to conjecture that Antichrist would like nothing better than to subvert and discredit the Traditionalists, since the Transcendent Unity of Religions is one of the few worldviews that could possibly stand in the way of the barren and terminal conflict between globalism and tribalism which is the keynote of his 'system' in the social arena.

If all possible alternatives to the struggle between globalism and tribalism disappear from the collective mind, then Antichrist has won. He can use economic and political globalism and the universalism of a 'world fusion spirituality' to subvert and oppress all integral religions and religious cul-tures, forcing them to narrow their focus and violate the fullness of their own traditions in reaction against it. He can drive them to bigoted and ter-roristic excesses which will make them seem barbaric and outdated in the eyes of those wavering between a global and a tribal identification, and set them at each other's throats at the same time. Unite to oppress; divide and conquer.

In this light, we can see that the exclusivism of conservative and/or tradi-tional Christianity is both its greatest strength and its greatest weakness; the same could be said, with certain reservations, of Judaism and Islam. The exclusivism of these Abrahamic religions allows them to consciously fortify themselves against the System of Antichrist—Christianity by its 'catacomb spirit', its ability, ultimately derived from monasticism, to build spiritual for-tresses against the world, and Islam by the fact that dar al-Islam remains the largest bloc of humanity which, in part, is still socially and politically orga-nized around a Divine Revelation, although to greatly varying degrees, as were Medieval Europe and the Byzantine Empire. On the other hand, their very exclusivism has prevented these religions, in all but a few instances, from making common cause against globalist universalism and secularism. They remain vulnerable to the 'divide and conquer' tactics of the system of Antichrist, a phase which could well be the prelude, if traditional eschatological speculations such as those found in Dennis E. Engleman's *Ultimate Things* are to be believed, to a later 'unite to oppress' phase — a capitulation by the exhausted exclusivists, longing for the end of endless conflict, to the satanic universalism of Antichrist himself.

According to *Ultimate Things*, Antichrist will reveal himself in Jerusalem and proclaim himself King of the Jews; the Jewish nation, as well as many Christians, will accept him. From the Islamic perspective, however, any world ruler who begins as a King of the Jews and is later submitted to by the Christians would be immediately and universally recognized as Antichrist himself. It is inconceivable, unless traditional and even fundamentalist Islam were to virtually disappear, that such a figure could tempt Muslims to accept him as the Mahdi or the eschatological Jesus. So if the predictions Engleman recounts are in any way accurate, he is in fact presenting, as the most likely eschatological scenario, a mass apostasy of Jews and Christians which would leave only the Muslims aware of who Antichrist really is, and ready to do battle with him. How then could Antichrist emerge as a true global monarch, albeit a satanic one? Perhaps the militant opposition of an Islam discredited in the eyes of the rest of the world to an almost universally admired 'savior' is the very thing which will ultimately consolidate his power. I hasten to say that this is in no way a prediction; God forbid. I am simply allowing myself to imagine various scenarios based on the quality of ultimate irony and self-contradiction which is the keynote of all historical forces in these latter days. And one of the twists of this irony is the fact that many semi-secularized Muslims — Dodi al-Fayed, for example — seem much more in tune with the mores of postmodern globalist culture than any Christian I could name.

If the greatest strength and greatest weakness of traditional Christianity is in its exclusivism, the comparable strength and weakness of Buddhism, especially in the West), is in its ability to 'fit in'. (The same goes for heterodox Westernized Hinduism and various influences, such as Feng Shui, Taoist meditation, and Sino-Japanese martial arts, originating in the Far East.) At its best, this represents a radical detachment from the norms of 'the world', allowing it to avoid all forms of dogmatic literalism and fundamentalism, and the marginalization such a stance often entails. At its worst, it indicates a capitulation to the collective egotism of this very 'world'. In the

United States at least, Buddhism is an acceptable part of the general Neo-Pagan cultural drift, which, while it may not identify with globalism, nonetheless often ends by serving it. (The same is true of certain strands of American Sufism, especially those which attempt to separate the Sufi tradition from Islam.) As a religion which recognizes a fall (into ignorance) and posits a goal of salvation (via enlightenment), it 'naturally' has a much greater affinity with the Abrahamic religions than with a Paganism which accepts the ontological status quo and seeks only to profit from it. But that's not how things have worked out sociologically. American Buddhism, as a non-theistic religion (though certainly not an atheism, since it possesses a doctrine of the Absolute), has been attractive to many people—especially, as it turns out, many American Jews—who are in flight from their own narrow-minded and superstitious ideas of God. An acquaintance of mine, a traditional Catholic who studied for years under the Hopi elders, tells the story of a 'Buddhist Halloween party' where a well-known American Buddhist teacher, dressed as a 'Sufi', made the statement that Buddhism is better than the Abrahamic religions because, just like the Native Americans, the Buddhists don't believe in God—a statement which my friend knew, from long personal experience with Native American spirituality, to be totally false. It was nonetheless an idea which would 'play well' to the general liberal, New Age and Neo-Pagan culture from which this teacher draws his students, the kind of people whose appreciation for the American Indians is even more destructive to Native American spirituality than their attraction to Buddhism is to Buddhism.

The false ecumenism of Neo-Pagan, New Age culture is the seed-bed for that 'world fusion spirituality' in which fragments of every spiritual tradition are promiscuously thrown together, to their mutual corruption. True ecumenism on the other hand—the outer expression of the 'esoteric ecumenism' of the Transcendent Unity of Religions, which understands the very uniqueness and particularity of the authentic religious traditions as the transcendent basis for their unity—is not a syncretistic amalgam or a diplomatic glossing-over of doctrinal differences, but a united front against a common enemy: that unholy alliance of scientism, magical materialism, idolatry of the psyche and postmodern nihilism which is headed, with all deliberate speed, toward the system of Antichrist.

Leo Schaya, writing primarily from the standpoint of Jewish esoterism, sees the eschatological mission of Elias as a re-establishment of the 'unanimous tradition' in preparation for the advent of the Messiah. Before the event known in *Genesis* as the 'confusion of tongues' which followed the fall of the Tower of Babel, humanity spoke a single religious language. After that time, however, God's Self-revelation to Man took the form of discrete religious traditions, each one self-enclosed and self-sufficient. The Tree of Life, which had been a single trunk, now divided into several branches. According to Schaya, however, the primordial unanimity is destined to be re-established before the end of the cycle:

> According to Jewish tradition, the entire Torah of Moses amounts to no more than a single line of the *Sepher ha-Yasher* [the 'Book of Justice' which Elias must bring with him], which means that this Book, by virtue of not being 'scriptural' but 'operative' in nature, will be the veritable final accomplishment of Scripture, the 'realization' which by definition goes immeasurably beyond the 'letter'. At the same time, Judaism tacitly places the remaining 'lines' of this 'Book' at the disposal of all the Divine revelations, whatever they may be, each one formulating or announcing in its fashion the same Eternal Truth and the same Destiny of man and the world. The 'Book' of Elias is the integral Wisdom of the unanimous Tradition and the eschatological Manifestation of the one and only Principle. For the Jews, Elias represents the transition from traditional exclusiveness to the universality which they too possess, since they affirm that the Tishbite will raise his voice so loud to announce the spiritual peace that it will be heard from one end of the earth to the other; and the Doctors of the Law teach that 'the righteous of all nations have a portion in the life to come' or, again, that 'all men who are not idolaters can be considered Israelites.'

Elias must re-establish all things in the name of, and for the sake of, that spiritual 'peace' which the Messiah will bring once and for all: it will be crystallized forever in the New Jerusalem 'founded by — or for — peace', according to the etymology of *Yerushalem* or *Yerushalaim*. Elias came down, and has come down for centuries, to the world below to prepare, with the concurrence of those he inspires, this final state of humanity. He reveals, little by little and more intensively and generally toward the end, the spiritual and universal essence, the transcendent unity of all authentic religions. It is as if the radiant city were being patiently built by putting one luminous stone after another into place. The motivating power of this task can be called the 'Eliatic flow', at least in the orbit of the Judeo-Christian tradition, whereas other traditions will each use their own terms to describe this same universal flow. According to the terminology of Jewish esoterism, this flow belongs to the 'river of highest Eden', the 'river of Yobel' or 'great Jubilee' which is final

Deliverance. Apocalypse calls it 'the river of the water of life, clear as crystal' Rev. 22:1); it will be crystallized in the 'precious stones', the unquenchable lights of the New Jerusalem.

⌐'The Mission of Elias', STUDIES IN COMPARATIVE RELIGION, vol. 14, nrs 3 and 4, pp 165–166

The doctrine of 'the Book of Elias' is strictly paralleled by the Shiïte Muslim doctrine that when al-Mahdi emerges from his occultation he will bring a new Book. That this Book represents the Primordial Tradition itself, which transcends the revealed traditions without negating them, is indicated by the tradition that the Mahdi will 'rule the people of the Torah according to the Torah, and the people of the Gospel according to the Gospel, and the people of the Koran according to the Koran.' (Nasir al-Din Tusi, *Ghayba*). That the Mahdi will restore the scriptures of Adam and Seth, and tear down the Kaaba so as to rebuild it as it was in Adam's time, also refers to the Primordial Tradition. The same order of truth is perhaps symbolized in Rev. 7:4–8 by the '144,000 sealed' who are drawn (12,000 at a time, like the 12,000 followers of Ali who will rise from the dead to follow the Mahdi) from each of the twelve tribes of Israel, and who in this context cannot be strictly identified with the Jews, but must represent twelve separate facets of the human form, and also by the fact that the Heavenly Jerusalem will contain no temple, 'for the Lord God Almighty and the Lamb are the temple of it' (Rev. 21:22–23). In the words of Jesus, 'other sheep have I.'

The prophecy that the primordial unity of religious truth will be re-established before the end can also be found in the Zoroastrian tradition. According to the *Vendidad* (2), Yima, the first man, the Zoroastrian Adam, was the human being to whom Ahura Mazda first preached the Ahuric or Zoroastrian religion; likewise Jews and Muslims, on the same plane of understanding, see Adam not only as the first man but also the first prophet. After expanding, cultivating and ruling the world of manifestation for (as I read it) 1800 years, Yima was summoned by Ahura Mazda, who predicted that bad winters would come to the material world, one of which would be especially destructive. (This is substantially the same doctrine as the eschatological *Fimbulwinter* of Norse mythology; the name *Yima* is also related to the Norse *Ymir*, the original giant who was slaughtered to create the material world, whose bones became the mountains, whose blood the rivers, etc.). Ahura Mazda then commanded Yima to build a *var* ('enclosure') with a square floorplan, stock it with golden hay, and gather into it the seed of the best plants, the best animals, the best human beings, 1800 persons in all, as well as the sun, moon and stars, which, in the var, can be seen setting and rising only once a year. However, to the inhabitants of the var, each day will be as a year. (1800 x 80 = 144,000, the number of the elect in the New Jerusalem.) There is to be a river watering the var, which will also contain meadows, houses—the whole manifest world in microcosm.

The Var of Yima, then, is the Zoroastrian equivalent of Noah's ark, though the world-destroying catastrophe is seen as a freeze rather than a flood. It is also similar in some ways to the New Jerusalem, which is likewise four-square and watered by a river. Yima's Var, however, seems to be underground; it is an enclosure, a cave, and also an ancient subterranean kingdom, like the Celtic realm of 'faerie', whose denizens reside in 'fairy hills'—the barrow tombs which dot the Western European landscape; as such, it is analogous to the *kiva* of the Ant People of Hopi myth. (The birthplace of Christ in a stable or cave surrounded by animals, his crib a manger filled with hay, and his visitation by three 'wise men' who are usually considered to have been Zoroastrian Magi, would tend to identify him with Yima, at least in the eyes of Zoroastrians, but also perhaps to those Jews, such as the Essenes, who may have maintained ongoing Zoroastrian connections.)

According to the story, Yima's Var was designed to help humanity and nature survive a series of hard winters; yet it is also said that the Var of Yima will only be opened at Frashegird, the end of time. So it becomes clear that the 'hard winters' actually represent the freezing and contraction of the cosmic environment, including human perception, which must worsen as the cycle unfolds. As Blake identified Noah's flood as an overwhelming of the Atlantean Golden Age by 'the Sea of Space and Time', so the 'bad winters' of Zoroastrian myth represent in some ways the increasing materialism of human society, and the consequent relegation of the vision of Eternity to a mythological underground kingdom. 'Underground' equals 'repressed'; what was once an immediate sensual vision of the natural world *sub specie aeternitatis* is now hidden away, for safekeeping, in 'the cave of the Heart'.

In 1927, Guénon published a book entitled *Le Roi du Monde*, 'The King of the World'. It dealt with the myth of the sacred Center in various religions (Mecca, Jerusalem, Olympus, etc.) and posited the existence of a Primordial Center, an original Hyperborean Paradise, from which all others derive, an assertion which has led some to criticize him for indulging, like Gurdjieff and Idries Shah, in occultist geographical romanticism of the 'Shangri-La' variety—Shangri-La itself, of course, being a late literary rendition of the same myth of Hyperborea, the land of eternal spring which lies in the extreme North, 'behind the North Wind'. This original Center is the source of the Primordial Tradition, whose representative, in terms of the Abrahamic religions, is Melchizedek. In the book of *Genesis*, Melchizedek, King of Salem and Priest of the most high God, blesses Abraham, in what Guénon identifies as a ceremony of initiation. Melchizedek is also mentioned in Ps. 110:4: 'The Lord swore and will not repent: thou art a priest forever after the order of Melchizedek.' Jesus comments upon this psalm in *Mark* and *Luke*, as does Peter in his Pentecost sermon as recounted in *Acts*. Guénon compares Melchizedek with the Hindu Manu, and other original priests and lawgivers.

It is fairly clear that the Zoroastrian Yima is another version of this 'King of the World'. The Sufis too have a concept of 'The Pole of the Age' — obviously a Hyperborean symbol — which is similar in many ways to the Shiïte doctrine of the Mahdi, the occulted Twelfth Imam; Shiïte esoterism in fact identifies the Mahdi with Melchizedek. The lineage of this unknown Pole, or *Qutub*, would therefore appear to be the Sufi version of the primordial priesthood of Melchizedek, who, since he had no father or mother, is in a certain sense immortal: unborn, thus never to die. This places him in the same category as the 'immortal prophets' Enoch, Elias and the Sufi Khidr, 'the Green One', identified by Muslims with both Elias and St George. As Melchizedek was Abraham's master in the Old Testament, so Khidr is the name given by Sufis to the master encountered by Moses in the Koran. The King of the World also has obvious affinities with figures such as Arthur, and all the other 'once and future kings' of world mythology. Arthur's knight Owain, in the romance of 'Owain and the Countess of the Fountain' becomes master of the Fountain of Life; the same is true of many of the sacred kings mentioned in Frazer's *The Golden Bough*, and of Khidr as well, who guards the Fountain of Life which is placed 'between the two seas', on the *barzakh* (isthmus) between this world and the next — in one sense the subtle or *faerie* realm, in another sense the Heart, situated between the bitter waters material multiplicity and the sweet waters of spiritual Unity. The Heavenly Jerusalem also encloses the Fountain of Life.

The Var of Yima is identified as the Hyperborean Paradise by the fact that it contains sun, moon and stars, which once a year (or once a day) can be seen setting and rising. Facing south in the Northern Hemisphere (i.e., looking out from the North), one is in a position to view the points where the sun and moon rise and set; facing north, one can view the stars rising and setting simultaneously. The celestial aspect of the Var of Yima is thus revealed in the constellations of the Great and Little Bear, the Revolving Castle or *caer sidi* of the Byrthonic Celts where departed kings consort with the White Goddess, in endless motion about the Pole Star (the *Qutub*), that 'still point of the turning world' which is the visible pivot of Eternity in the created order, the door which leads beyond the cycles of birth and death. (Guénon, in *Science of Sacred Symbols*, claims that *var* and *bear* are the same word.) The fact that the Var contains the seeds of all living things, including the circling heavens, indicates that it is not only a Temple but also an Aeon: an entire cycle of manifestation witnessed simultaneously as a single form. The Tree of Life in the New Jerusalem, which bears twelve kinds of fruit, one each month—an obvious reference to the zodiac—has the same meaning: a complete cycle of time conceived in a single moment.

The Lakota call south 'the direction we always face', and in so doing identify themselves as Hyperboreans, whose seat is in the North, beyond the cycles of time, from which point they look South into this material world. They further identify the north-south axis as 'the good red road' and the east-west line of the Sun's track as 'the black (or blue) road of difficulty.' Shamanism in general can be described as a Hyperborean spirituality. Not only is its home in the far North (Siberia), but the 'axial' structure of Siberian shamanism, according to which the shaman ascends and/or descends the World Tree, up through many paradises or down through many underworlds, like the angels ascending and descending the ladder in Jacob's dream, reveals it as a Polar manifestation. (Sometimes the shaman will use an actual ladder during his trance.) A poem from the Altaic tradition, adapted from Mircea Eliade's *Shamanism: Archaic Techniques of Ecstasy*, speaks of a shamanic journey to a 'Prince Ulgan' who lives in the sky, and who is described as the one 'for whom the stars & sky /are turning a thousand times /turning a thousand times over'—a Siberian version of the transcendent God as 'the King of the World' in his celestial 'var'. In the same poem the shaman is shown climbing the sky in the shape of a goose. Migrating geese, who in Celtic mythology are identified with the souls of the dead (and, undoubtedly, the unborn), follow the north-south Hyperborean path, the Good Red Road, which is a projection onto the horizontal plane of the *axis mundi*, the vertical path uniting Heaven and Earth. This path is identified with, among other things, the human spinal column: in Yoga terminology, the *sushumna nadi* with its seven *chakras*. *Paramhamsa* or 'exalted gander' is also an epithet of Hindu yogis.

This North-South orientation places Hyperborean spirituality on a higher ontological plane than those religions whose sacred point of 'orientation' is the East. Facing East we witness all forms and events as they enter the cycle of manifestation from the Unseen; facing West, we watch as they leave it. But if we face North, we are oriented to that Eternal Center which is beyond manifestation entirely; it is as if, instead of turning within the cycles of birth and death, those cycles were to turn within us. Hyperborean religion is thus Edenic and Primordial. When Adam and Eve were cast out of Paradise, they traveled to 'the East of Eden'; this, in my opinion, represents a fall from an aeonian and Hyperborean North-facing spirituality to a cyclical and Solar East-facing one—in Lakota terms, a departure from the Good Red Road to walk the Black Road of Difficulty (cf. Gen. 3:19: 'In the sweat of thy face thou shall eat bread'). And the fact that, in so many ancient traditions, demonic forces are pictured as coming out of the North indicates both the rigor of Transcendence, and the fact that the way back to Hyperborea, in this cycle, is closed; the gates of Eden are blocked by the Cherubim and the flaming sword which turns every way (Gen. 3:24). The seat of the Tribe of Dan, for example, from whom the Antichrist is supposed to emerge, is in the extreme north of Israel. In other words, we can't ignore time; we must conform our spirituality to the needs of the particular point in the cycle where we find ourselves, or risk invoking demonic energies. And this means, among other things, that shamanism is not what it used to be. To practice it this late in the cycle, especially if one is not born into one of the primal religions, is to encounter spiritual dangers which did not exist when the cycle was young. Undoubtedly some of the primal traditions are still host to powerful, balanced shamans dedicated to spiritual enlightenment and human service—and God knows best.

According to Guénon, Melchizedek represents the Primordial Tradition for the Abrahamic religions; but it is probably simpler and more enlightening to say that the King of the World is *Adam*, in line with the Muslim doctrine that man is not only God's *abd* or slave, but also His *khalifa* or vicegerent. The metaphysical principle, here, is that since every fall is from a relatively more real and more eternal plane of being to a relatively less real and more temporal one, there is always a sense in which the fall in question never took place; a fall into illusion is always, in *one* sense, illusory. (Herman Hesse's novel *Journey to the East* is all about this.) As the Buddhists say, 'all beings are enlightened from the beginning.' So the Adam who never fell, the archetype of Man in the subtle material plane, who is Yima, the Hindu Manu, and Melchizedek, is, in a way, still ruling us. If he were not still there on the subtle plane we would not still be here on the material plane, since he is part of our 'stem', our living and ongoing connection with our Creator via the Unseen World. The question is, can we turn to him as a 'Pole' in any real and spiritually effective sense? Much water has flowed under the bridge since the Golden Age, and it keeps flowing faster and faster. Primordial spiritualities can still look to that one who is called by the Mandaeans of Iraq 'the Secret Adam', but historical man is not primordial now, except in essence. The cycle has moved on; we have entered the world of fall and redemption, and so must turn to saviors instead, prophets like Abraham, Moses and Muhammad, avatars like Rama, or Krishna, or Jesus. Certainly religions still exist which look back to the Primordial Ancestor rather than to the Savior, already come or yet-to-come, as their spiritual focus; this is true of many African religions and of totemism in general, as it was of the ancient Chinese worship of the Yellow Emperor. But virtually all these religions show signs of serious degeneration. And the lateness of the hour is further reflected, in a way I take to be normative, by the fact that the cult of Brahma the Creator has essentially died out in Hinduism; Hindu devotees now look either to Vishnu the Preserver or Shiva the Destroyer. Furthermore, history has proceeded so far toward the end of the aeon that the expected advent of Kalki, or Maitreya, or al-Mahdi, or the eschatological Christ begins to exert its magnetic attraction, and become our new spiritual Center. Cyclically speaking, this leaves the primordial Adam far behind.

And yet eternity is never 'behind'. The truth that Adam, in a specific sense, never really fell, will always be there in the background of this fallen world. It is in some ways closer in Islam than in Christianity, at least Western Christianity, since Muslims do not recognize a total fall of man, a corruption of the human substance itself, but only *ghaflah*, 'heedlessness', the Platonic *amnesia*—though the consequences of this heedlessness are as dire as those of any original sin. In Islam, a human being can still stand as Adam before God, in his original unfallen nature, his *fitrah*. But as Blake shows through his figure of Albion the Ancient Man, the King of the World is, in a very real sense, fallen or deposed. Within the Christian universe, he needs Christ to redeem him; this is what is meant by 'the harrowing of hell' which follows the crucifixion and precedes the resurrection. (Yima, too, is fallen in one way, unfallen and eternal in another.) As in Blake's *Jerusalem*, Jesus must awaken Albion/Adam from his death-like sleep upon the Rock of Ages, where he lies submerged, like the lost Atlantis, beneath the Sea of Space and Time.

Guénon in *The Reign of Quantity* says that Antichrist will be a kind of inverted *Chakravartin*, a false World King. So the question inevitably arises: What does this false King have to do with the true King of the World supposedly still reigning in Shambhala/Belovodia/Avalon? Are they at war in that other world? If the King of the World is in one sense unfallen and still reigning, and in another sense deposed, and if the Antichrist is destined to appear as a false World King, then exactly what is the eschatological role of *le Roi du Monde?*

In C. S. Lewis' *That Hideous Strength* a war is fought between the powers of Light and Darkness to see if the ancient Pagan magic represented by Merlin—who himself had no human father, and who never died (like Elias, Enoch, Khidr, and the Twelfth Imam) but was 'occulted'—will fall under the power of the forces of Truth, or those of Antichrist. If we take Merlin as representing the Primordial Tradition, at least to Lewis (who furthermore relates Merlin to the priesthood of Melchizedek), we can support him in his intuition that the remnants of certain archaic spiritualities can and will support the forces of Light in the eschatological combat: According to the relevant Zoroastrian doctrine, during Frashegird the Var of Yima will be opened; its inhabitants will emerge and join the cosmic struggle until the final triumph of the good. So primordiality joins forces with eschatology, just as one's original nature as created by God joins forces with redemption and divine Grace; Yima supports Saoshyant; the first 'savior' fights by the side of the last. In the same way, Shiïte eschatology envisions a return of the most righteous as well as the most unrighteous of the dead before the general resurrection, giving the righteous an opportunity to triumph at last over their oppressors. The most common epithet of the Shiïte Mahdi, *al-Qaim,* 'he who rises', denotes both the resurrection of the dead and to a 'rising up' against tyranny. When John the Baptist, dressed in animal skins and eating gathered rather than cultivated food, announced the advent of Jesus Christ, I believe he was consciously enacting the part of the Primordial Adam (possibly in his Essene/Mandean rendition) as herald and ally of the Savior.

Since the eschatological event is a breakthrough of Eternity into time, it has to include all the manifestations of Divine Truth comprised within the cycle which is coming to a close; it must be a summing up as well as a death and rebirth. The emphasis of the Traditionalist writers on the Primordial Tradition and the Transcendent Unity of Religions is therefore a necessary and providential expression of spiritual truth for these latter days.

The ever-present shadow of primordiality, however, is atavism. The return of the archaic spiritualities, in degenerate form, toward the end of the cycle inevitably has a destructive effect on the revealed religions. Only the messianic theophany itself has the power to shake primordiality free from its atavistic husk. And the distinction between the Transcendent Unity of Religions on the one hand, and that syncretistic 'world fusion spirituality' which is the hallmark of Antichrist on the other, a collection of fragments entirely postmodern in its nihilism, is simply too subtle to be understood by everyone attracted even to traditional metaphysics. (Schuon himself seems to have suspected as much in *The Transcendent Unity of Religions*, his second book, when he characterized his open revelation of esoteric doctrines as an abnormal response required by an abnormal situation, and expressed his belief that 'the harm which might in principle befall certain people from contact with the truths in question is compensated by the advantages others will derive from the self-same truths.') The satanic shadow of the Transcendent Unity of Religions, in other words, is precisely the pseudo-esoterism of the Antichrist. If the symbolic patron of the primordial spirituality is Adam, then we can say, using Christian terminology, that although he has been redeemed through Christ's sacrifice, the consequences of his sin have not thereby been erased. Since the Redemption, he, and the human race, have been in a purgatorial state. His soul is in Paradise, but his descendants—who are, in one sense, his body—though virtually redeemed ('it is finished') are not fully sanctified ('take up your cross and follow Me'). Only in apocalypse, only at the resurrection of the body, when the dead rise and the living are changed, are the consequences of human action, both virtuous and sinful, finally harvested on the macrocosmic level. Only then is the good grain stored away and the weeds consigned to the fire. Therefore to invoke primordial spirituality in the latter days of the cycle, before the second coming of Christ invokes it definitively, is to further the agenda of both good and evil, both Christ and Antichrist. It is to make virtually present, along with the primordiality of the Edenic state, the entirety of the human *karma* for this cycle, and in so doing serve the final polarization, that separation of sheep from goats which will climax at the battle of Armageddon.

In *Logic and Transcendence*, Frithjof Schuon clearly articulates what he hopes (though hardly expects) to accomplish by promulgating his doctrine of Transcendent Unity of Religions:

> In the cyclic period in which we live, the situation of the world is such that exclusive dogmatism (though not dogmatism in itself, since dogmas are necessary as immutable foundations and have inward and inclusive dimensions) is hard put to hold its own, and whether it likes it or not, has need of certain esoteric elements, without which it runs the risk of exposing itself to errors of a much more questionable kind than gnosis [which, to Schuon, is not an error, though it certainly is to some dogmatists]. Unhappily the wrong choice is made; the way out of certain deadlocks is sought, not with the help of esoterism, but by resorting to the falsest and most pernicious of

philosophical and scientific ideologies, and for the universality of spirit, the reality of which is confusedly noted, there is substituted a so-called 'ecumenism' which consists of nothing but platitudes and sentimentality and accepts everything without discrimination.

The obverse attitude, of narrowly literal belief, is still spiritually feasible within a closed system knowing nothing of other traditional worlds, but in the long run it is untenable and dangerous in a universe where everything meets and interpenetrates. . . . It has become impossible effectively to defend a single religion against all others by declaring the rest anathema without exception; to persist in so doing (unless living in a still medieval society in which case the question does not arise) is a little like attempting to maintain the Ptolemaic system against the evidence of verified and verifiable astronomical facts. All the same, we do not believe that the spiritual solidarity thus imposed on us can or must imply complete mutual understanding; it can stop half way, at least for the average person, particularly as it is always possible to put in parentheses those questions which one cannot or does not wish to resolve. What we have in mind, let us stress once more, is not the idea—self-defeating in practice—of a generalized metaphysical and quintessential understanding, but simply the possibility of an adequate understanding which will serve, on the one hand, to safeguard the religious heritage against the advances of the ubiquitous scientistic mentality, and, on the other, to bring about a perfectly logical and unsentimental solidarity between those who traditionally take cognizance of transcendence and immortality. (pp 4–5)

Schuon seems to have foreseen possible harm to individuals from the open revelation of esoteric truths, as well as the inevitable tendency to mistake the Transcendent Unity of Religions for syncretism. But when he dismisses 'a generalized metaphysical and quintessential understanding,' what I would call an extra-traditional, generic metaphysics, as merely 'self-defeating in practice,' he seems not to have fully grasped the danger of this development, a danger which, with the clarity of hindsight, I have demonstrated in *Chapter Nine*, and elsewhere in this book. Self-defeating it may be, in spiritual terms; in social and psychological terms it is self-propagating. As Guénon says in *The Reign of Quantity*, pp 293–294:

The 'counter-initiation' works with a view to introducing its agents . . . even . . . into authentically initiatic . . . organizations, but only when their traditional spirit is so weakened that they can no longer resist so insidious a penetration . . . the last-named case . . . is the most direct application possible of dissolutionary activity.

And, I would add, these 'agents' are not necessarily individuals; they can just as easily be unconscious beliefs and assumptions with a high degree of collective psychic energy behind them.

The danger of a primordial approach to spirituality is that it may lead its devotees to imagine that the Golden Age has actually returned. But even if the boundaries of the present cycle grow so translucent, due to its extreme old age, that the outlines of the cycle to come can be clearly seen through the skin of it, still, we cannot get there from here. And to believe that we can get there from here, without the inconvenience of apocalyptic judgement, or simply one's own personal death, is perhaps the central error of the New Age. The shape of the primordial tradition *must* shine through the thinning walls of material reality at the end of the cycle; the light it gives has the crucial function of preparing us as nothing else could for the wrath to come, and the greater Mercy by which that wrath is destined to be overwhelmed, when death is swallowed up in victory. But those who follow that light in a literal fashion, as if they could possess it, are being led into deep temptation: what could be more spiritually deluding than to believe that a primal Edenic innocence can be openly manifested in this most degenerate of human times, without casting our most precious pearls before the worst pigs of the cycle? We hippies tried that, and learned the hard way that it doesn't work. If we want to be harmless as doves, we had better also be wise as serpents.

It was Frithjof Schuon's mission (though not his alone) to unfold the Maya of the Transcendent Intellect for the final period of this cycle, and project his incomparable doctrinal formulations on the vast screen of it. Maya, however, is boundless, uncontrollable, ruthlessly scattering the seeds of all things, good and evil, stale and fresh, wise and deluded. As an aspect of the Divine Infinity, it cannot be kept within either moral or doctrinal bounds. In the face of this Maya, all one can do is submit to God's will and implore His grace, sacrificing all self-willed attempts to reach pragmatic or conceptual closure. This is the path to Paradise—just as persistence in the struggle to derive strategic imperatives or make systematic sense out of the mystery of God's Infinite Self-disclosure is the path to Hell. It is for just this purpose, apparently, that the Maya of the Transcendent Intellect is unfolded in eschatological times: to separate the sheep from the goats.

✳ Struggling with Tradition

I said above that the first thing required if a person wants to practice the Transcendent Unity of Religions is simply to accept one of the revealed religious traditions and remain faithful to it, in terms both of outer practice and of inner truth. But how simple is this, really? The truth is that it is not simple at all, especially today. So many aspects of life that in more stable times used to be the birthright of nearly everyone—a family, a community, a marriage, a craft or profession, a religion—now have to be achieved by the kind of extravagant *tour-de-force*. Not everyone with the normal degree of human talent and development is necessarily capable of finding, or constructing, that matrix of meaning and value which used to be given—or, as progressivists like to call it, 'imposed'—by traditional social standards and institutions. And not the least among the 'wars of orientation' we must fight in these times is the struggle to come to terms with a traditional religious universe.

This struggle has several aspects. The first is to overcome one's own modernist or postmodernist or materialist or occultist assumptions honestly, without simply suppressing or denying them—by means of the Intellect, that is, not simply by means of the will. Each assumption has to be clearly identified, confronted with the traditional doctrine it was invented to hide, and defeated in conscious intellectual combat, a combat which takes into account the whole range of our feelings as well as our ideas, since feelings are often simply ideas we aren't clear on yet, just as ideas, when fully realized, do not contradict our truest feelings, but are in one sense the objective or 'crystallized' forms taken by those feelings. To merely adopt a set of traditional values in the same way that one acquired one's modernist values—by unconscious ego-identification—will never be enough. It may turn one into a reactionary or a 'purist', but never into a traditionalist. On the other hand, to wait until all one's emotional and intellectual objections are answered before making a traditional commitment is, in most cases, to wait too long. As soon as one's Intellect, one's spiritual center, is attracted to a traditional form—an attraction which will manifest in terms of both thought and feeling, though depending on our psychological type we will tend to be more aware of one than the other—then the will must respond. If it does not, if we try to hold our will to commit ourselves in abeyance until our intellectual understanding is perfect, then we may have already missed the boat. Each deepening of the understanding must be matched by a motion of the will, otherwise we will fritter our lives away building academic air-castles, and fail to take even the first real step. As the Roman centurion said to Jesus, 'I believe, Lord; help thou mine unbelief.'

When one experiences one's spiritual life as a chaos of uncertainties and conflicting attractions, a traditional religious form may look like a point of absolute stability, a safe harbor against the storms of both the outer world and the fragmented soul. Unfortunately, this is not always the case. Stability is really there, but it is often paired with a level of instability and conflict greater than the outer world alone can produce. Churches and synagogues and ashrams and zawiyas and mosques and zendos are human institutions, filled with their share of human foibles. And the very fact that their purpose for existing is to put us in touch with the Absolute, the 'rock of ages', will often magnify these foibles out of all proportion. Ethical lapses which seem hardly worth mentioning in, say, a lawyer, will appear shockingly blasphemous in a minister or spiritual teacher. And, in a way, this reaction is justified; the closer we get to the Light, the sharper and darker the Shadow becomes. The instability of one's 'commanding self' and the attacks of the World and the Devil are nowhere so intensified as in close proximity to that absolute stability which is Divine Truth. And the burns to the soul inflicted by the shortcomings of a spiritual leader will in many cases be even deeper than those produced by an unethical lawyer or doctor, especially if one's sincerity is greater than one's wisdom; this goes double, of course, for the esoteric spiritual Path. At this point it is necessary to apply the metaphysical truth everything that happens, whether it appears good or evil to us, is a manifestation of the Divine. All things are not wise or good as choices, but all things are *true* as acts and words of God. The human ego, still practicing its cunning and asserting its agendas in close proximity to God's wisdom and power is as good a definition of Satan as any you could name. And when Satan has apparently taken over a church or spiritual group, often the only thing one can do, in view of the fact that one is not a saint, is to get the hell out before one's soul is permanently damaged. As they say in Jamaica, 'sometimes absence of body is better than presence of mind.' But the fact remains that the acrobatics of the individual or group ego in the face of the Absolute constitute not only the most dangerous form of spiritual delusion, but also the most powerful form of spiritual purgation. The deeper the delusion, the deeper the lesson—for those who have eyes to see, and the stamina to endure, and God's permission to take the risk.

Another aspect of the struggle with tradition is the fact that all traditions are under fire in these latter days, by the forces of postmodern globalism on the one hand, and reactionary or separatist reactions to globalism on the other. The perennial difficulties of the spiritual life, the ascetic struggle with the impulses of the commanding self, taking place in the context of the normal drama of human relationships heightened by proximity to the Spirit, is compounded in these times by uncertainty as to the doctrines and practices themselves. What constitutes a heretical break with tradition, and what is simply a wise adaptation to the conditions of the time? What is in reality a heroic defense of Tradition, of a unique and irreplaceable vehicle of relationship between the Absolute and our earthly life, and what is really nothing but a violently fanatical or stupidly petrified defense of accidental matters, albeit of ancient pedigree, which have no necessary bearing on the spiritual life?

The struggle to come to terms with Tradition coupled with the parallel struggle to evaluate the health or illness of the traditional form one is attracted to can place an overwhelming burden on one's relationship with God. Many people today, awakening to this burden, simply throw it off, concluding—with the eager help of the contemporary world—that it's not worth the trouble. It's so much easier, confronted with a world increasingly divided between postmodern cultural pluralism and fundamentalist reaction to simply say 'a pox on both your houses,' opt for a self-directed 'individualist' spirituality, or simply sink into a numb, cynical isolation. And we must also remember that the struggle to get one's religious affiliation into a more or less stable form, while necessary, is not sufficient to define one's spiritual path. We are not here to identify with religious forms, but to remember God. Our quest for forms which possess depth, stability and orthodoxy must be seen in light of that higher and more central Goal.

✳ To Fight or Not to Fight

The looming One World Government shows many signs of being the predicted regime of Antichrist. But as I have already pointed out, it's not quite that simple, since the 'tribal' forces reacting against globalism are ultimately part of the same system. According to one of many possible scenarios, the satanic forces operating at the end of the Aeon would be quite capable of establishing a One World Government only to set the stage for the emergence of Antichrist as the great leader of a world revolution *against* this government, which, if it triumphed, would be the *real* One World Government. Or the martyrdom of Antichrist at the hands of such a government might be a deliberate or even staged self-sacrifice, counterfeiting the death of Christ and leading to a counterfeit resurrection. I am not saying that this will happen; I am not prognosticating. I only wish to point out that Antichrist, as a counterfeit manifestation of the Divine universality, will have the capacity to use all sides in any conflict, including a global one, to build his power—except the ultimate Messianic Conflict, called Armageddon in the *Apocalypse*, which is initiated and concluded by God Himself.

The 'discernment of spirits' in apocalyptic times can perhaps be reduced to the ability to answer, in many different circumstances, a single question: *what is the real war?* If the Antichrist can tempt us to fight prematurely, or on too restricted a field—or, conversely, if he can influence us to delay too long before choosing sides—then he has won. Here, however, is the danger of the approach I have taken, that of multiplying the criteria by which the coming Avatara can be distinguished from Antichrist. The danger is that we may become stuck in a kind of paranoid infinite regression, as in the world of espionage where every double agent is really a triple agent and things are never what they seem. Because, in another sense, things are always what they seem—to the pure in heart. If you know your own ego, you know the Antichrist; if you know the God within you, you know God. The criteria by which we can recognize the Antichrist are the same as those by which we can recognize sin: If we understand what Divine Wisdom is, we will recognize what is contrary to that Wisdom; if we know what Divine Love is, we will be sensitive to what violates that Love. The signs of the end in the various traditional eschatologies cannot be applied directly to history, without first being applied to the state of one's soul. Only after 'the discernment of spirits' is established within our own intellect, will, and affections can we turn and see the forces operating in these latter days of world history in the light of objective truth. If we know how the ego operates, especially when it attempts to appropriate our struggle against temptation in order to claim holiness for itself, or break its way into the mysteries of God in order to claim wisdom, then we will not be fooled by the analogous moves of the Antichrist on the field of history.

Antichrist's ability to fight simultaneously on all sides in a war in order to spread delusion, paranoia and self-perpetuating conflict, which is a satanic parody of God's hidden presence behind every human mask, is perhaps nowhere better illustrated than in contemporary Israel. Every act of oppression and/or legitimate self-defense by the Israeli government, every act of terrorism and/or legitimate self-protection by the Palestinian 'extremists', every act of self-contradictory 'moderation' by the PLO, and every act of intervention and/or neglect by Iran, Russia, Egypt, Syria, Lebanon, Jordan, the United States, Western Europe, or the U.N., produces—after a certain point—the identical effect: the hardening of lines, the escalation of conflict. This is not to say that some lines of action are not better than others, only that the situation has a life of its own, and possesses the power to impose its tax upon all conceivable ways of relating to it.

It is quite astounding to realize that, according to one view of the situation, the same socio-political 'slots' exist in Palestine today as in the time of Jesus, two thousand years ago, though they are occupied by profoundly different forces. The Israeli Government stands where the Scribes and Pharisees then stood. The militant Palestinians occupy the niche of the Zealots. The United States and/or the U.N. can stand-in for the Roman Empire. And the unique position of Jesus, at the crux or *cross* where all contemporary social forces converged, is now occupied by Yasser Arafat, crucified as he is on the horns of every contradiction... but clearly Arafat is no Jesus; he in no way transcends the conditions he occupies; he is merely the puppet of them.

Jesus of Nazareth was deeply aware of contemporary political forces. On the human level, he had to be. This did not mean, of course, that he was some kind of political revolutionary; he may in fact have needed a certain political savvy simply to avoid being forced to take sides—for or against the party of the Temple in its accommodation with Rome, for or against the Zealots—in a world where everyone apparently had to take sides, where everything was moving inexorably toward the Jewish Revolt of 66 AD. For example, when his opponents challenged him to answer, in public, whether or not it was lawful to pay the Roman tax, they thought they had him. If he had said 'yes', he would lose his following in the Zealot sector, who, because they interpreted the tax an act of emperor-worship, which had been officially established in some Roman provinces, considered it a blasphemy against Yahweh, especially since the Roman denarius in which the tax was to be paid bore an image of the emperor, seen by the Zealots as an idol, a 'graven image'. He would also have lost his moral authority to criticize the Scribes and Pharisees, who had made an accommodation with the Roman colonial government. He would have been drawn into the party of the temple authorities, at least in the eyes of the people, which would have alienated him from both the Zealots and the Essenes. On the other hand, if he said 'no', he would have been simply identified with the Zealots, and would have lost touch with his wider public. He would also have been liable to premature arrest on a provable charge of sedition; consequently his death would have meant no more than the death of, say, someone like Barabbas. Like thousands of other, he would have died as a 'one-dimensional' rebel against Rome, and been forgotten.

His way of passing through the 'symplegades' of this socio-political contradiction represented a masterpiece of 'sublimation', and may give us a clue as to how to avoid being drawn into false or narrowly-defined conflicts, and travel instead the path which leads to the true war. First, he asked someone in the crowd to hand him the coin of tribute, thus demonstrating, first, that he had no money himself, that he was of the 'poor' to whom he came to preach the 'good news' — in Arabic, *fuqara*, the plural of *fakir* which is synonymous with 'Sufi' — and secondly that the 'idolatrous' coin in question was in free circulation. Secondly, when he asked 'whose image is this?' and was answered 'Caesar's,' he was distancing himself from the Zealots by clearly demonstrating that the coin could not be an idol for the simple reason that Caesar was not God, which is why one could render to Caesar what was Caesar's without committing blasphemy. At the same time he was saying, in effect, that to send the image of the little false god back to him was in no way to worship him, but could even be seen as an act of condescension on the part of the Jews, who knew and worshipped the Living God; their self-respect, their privileged position as the chosen people could in no way be violated by humoring the petty narcissism of these little self-appointed Caesars. So without a marvelous degree of political and psychological savvy, Jesus would inevitably have been drawn into political conflict, and his mission would have failed. (This, of course, is the situation seen from the standpoint of Jesus' humanity; from the point-of-view of His Divinity, His mission was ordained by God; it could not fail.) And this object-lesson on how to avoid being drawn too far into premature and narrowly-defined political conflicts which compromise one's spiritual perception and one's readiness to heed God's true call also has its esoteric side, as a 'parable-in-action' of how to pass beyond the pairs-of-opposites and realize the Absolute. The Eastern Orthodox Christians interpret 'what is Caesar's' as the coin's weight in gold, and 'what is God's' as the shape of a human being stamped upon it, made in the image and likeness of God. The matter of our lives will always belong to this world; our wealth will pass to others, as our bodies to the earth. But our form belongs to God in eternity, unto ages of ages. This is why, in the resurrection, it is capable of being newly 'incarnated' in a glorious and incorruptible substance. The lesson is: that it is not the *matter* of our lives we must protect from the Antichrist — as certain survivalists clearly believe — but our *form*. In the latter days, as always, the real struggle is not to retain our possessions, or even our lives, but to avoid losing our souls. Ultimately, this is all that is required of us.

In a world defined by false conflicts of every kind, what is the true war? The Muslim answer is: 'The Greater Jihad, the war against everything in oneself that is opposed to God.' But the Greater and the Lesser Holy Wars—the Lesser Jihad in this case being the struggle in the outer world against all that would attack or subvert religion—are not unrelated. All we can hope for in the end times—and it is really the greatest hope humanity can ever be blessed with—is that we ourselves will remain faithful to the Truth. But sometimes, in order not to be driven away from that Truth by fear, or lured away by satanic seduction, it must be actively defended in the outer world, either by word or by deed. If we are not willing to risk our reputations, our livelihoods or our lives when circumstances demand it, how can we be sure that our inner faithfulness to God is anything more than lip service, or spiritual pride? On the other hand, if we had truly defeated the Beast within, the 'commanding self', the world's terror and seduction would have no power over us. So the Lesser Jihad, no matter how necessary in certain circumstances, is always in one sense a 'projection' of the Greater Jihad on the world stage; it is the war against the commanding self fought in allegory, and by proxy.

Perhaps the best answer to the question 'to fight or not to fight?' is: Learn to deal only with the single enemy, inner or outer, who is directly in your path. If you try to fight somebody else's battle, God will not support you. And if you depart from your own true path because you are hungry for conflict, or just impatient to get it all over with, then you have already been defeated. This is why it is so important to know your path as it really is, so you can tell the difference between God-given talents which must not be buried, and self-imposed agendas which need to be sacrificed.

The least that can be said in concrete terms is that a denunciation of the regime of Antichrist, such as that by the 'two witnesses' in the *Apocalypse*, will be appropriate in many circumstances—though clearly not in all, since concealment for self-protection, or protection of others, will sometimes be called for. But we must always remember that the war against Antichrist in the outer world—and even more so the inner world—is also fertile ground for the growth of spiritual pride. What could be more heady than the belief that one is part of an elect remnant called on by God to defy the Beast? We have seen plenty of heartless political and religious fanatics possessed by this idea, and we are destined to see many more. Luckily, triumph in worldly terms is ultimately not possible to the faithful in the latter days, though small victories can still be won. The best we can hope for is that we all—from whatever true and God-given religion we may arise—will some day find ourselves with our backs against the same wall. O fortunate wall! Every hope will be realized there, by those who, through God's grace, have been left with no other hope but Him.

According to some Sufis, Antichrist is precisely the *nafs al-ammara*, the commanding self or 'demanding ego'; the conflict between globalism and tribalism is a reflection of the *apparent* conflict, in the *nafs*, between complacent pride and violent rebelliousness. The following passage is from *Marmuzat-e asadi* of Najmo 'd'Din Razi; citations are from the Koran:

Now, in exposition of the truth about Jesus and the Antichrist and the respective contrast and similarity between them, it may be said that the similarity is superficial and the contrast fundamental. From the point of view of appearance they are both called the 'Messiah', and both have a donkey, and they are both alive, and they both bring the dead to life.

Now, Jesus is called the 'Messiah' through traveling the heavens, while the Antichrist is called the 'Messiah' by traveling the earth from east to west. Jesus is heavenly and the Antichrist is earthly. Jesus has vision and confers vision on others; visionary because in his infancy he said, 'Indeed I am the devotee of God' ('Mary', 30), and conferring vision by virtue of healing 'the blind and the leper' ('The Family of Imran', 49; 'The Table Spread', 110), while the Antichrist is blind and a blinder of others, for he presents the Truth as falsehood and falsehood as the Truth. Now, Jesus brings the dead to life as a miracle to provide grounds for faith, while the Antichrist quickens the dead as a demonstration of powers to lure one into denying faith. And the emergence of Antichrist out of the earth serves to bring about a reign of oppression and corruption on earth, while the descent of Jesus from heaven is to bring about a reign of equity and justice.

Be aware that all in the realm of form is a reflection of that which is in the realm of spirit, and all that is in the realms of form and spirit is represented in man. Hence the 'Jesus-ness' in you is your spirit, as of Jesus it is said: 'We breathed of Our Spirit into it [Mary's womb] ('The Banning', 12), while of you it is said: 'I breathed My Spirit into him [Adam] ('Al-Hijr', 29). Jesus brings the dead to life, as the spirit brings life to the lifeless frame. Jesus had a mother, whereas the Divine Breath served in place of a father for him; likewise the spirit (of each person) is mothered by the elements and fathered by the Breath. Jesus is sublime and the spirit is sublime; Jesus is the Word and the spirit is the Word, as indicated by the expression that the 'spirit is by command of my Lord' ('The Night Ascension', 85). Jesus rode a donkey, as the spirit rides the body.

And the Antichrist is represented in you by your 'demanding ego'. The Antichrist is one-eyed, just like your ego, seeing only the world and being blind to the hereafter. Whatever the Antichrist presents as heaven is actually hell, and what he presents as hell is really heaven; by the same token, the ego presents carnal passions and pleasures as paradisical, though they are actually infernal, and it presents one's spiritual devotion and worship as hellish, though they are really heavenly in nature.

The Antichrist mounts a donkey, and your ego possesses bestial qualities. The mystery of it all is that, though Jesus was in the world, as was the Antichrist, Jesus was carried up to heaven for a while, while the Antichrist was locked up in the bowels of the earth. Then, Antichrist will first be brought out to rampage over the earth and create havoc and wreak corruption, claiming divinity. Next, Jesus will be brought down and given dominion, claiming to be the devotee of God. He will succeed in slaying the Antichrist, then set about establishing a reign of prosperity, justice and equity. After a time, he will pass from this world, and the Day of Judgement will be at hand.

In the same way, spirit and ego are brought together in the world of humanity. However, the spirit is taken up into the heaven of the heart, while the Antichrist of the ego is confined in the earth of the human state. It takes several years for humanity to develop its full potential and for the constituents of the body to properly mature. First, the Antichrist of the ego emerges from the confines of infancy, mounted on the ass of animal qualities, launching forth on its program of wreaking havoc in the world, claiming divinity in the manner of 'Have you seen the one who makes desire his god. . . ?' ('Kneeling', 23), and exhorting one toward the hell of greed and lust as the heavenly goal, while decrying the heaven of devotion and worship as hell. He slays the believers of praiseworthy, angelic qualities with the unbelievers' hands of satanic and condemnable qualities, raising the dead powers in human nature, until, all of a sudden, the grace unimaginable bears from on high the Jesus of spirituality, mounted on the regal wings of the Gabriel of the Law, taking flight from the lofty heaven of the heart to descend into the world of humanity.

Reason, left behind, gazes as his departing stirrup,
While Love surges ahead, mounted by his side.

Jesus slays the Antichrist of the ego, by severing his head of material nature, and establishes the dominion of the justice and equity of spirituality in the

world of humanity, destroying the swine of greed, shattering the cross of
fleshly nature, and slashing the bonds of passion.

⌒JESUS IN THE EYES OF THE SUFIS, Dr Javad Nurbakhsh, pp 61–64

When the Antichrist rises, Christ is near. When the ego comes into plain
view, the spiritual Intellect, since it sees the whole system of it, is no longer
veiled by it; the Eye of the Heart is open. When what we thought was a
solid object is seen to be a shadow, then, like all shadows, it bears witness to
the Light.

Evil, like everything else, is here to teach us. In the beginning it teaches us
its own massive reality as a wall which separates us from God, a power to be
combatted without quarter. In the end, it teaches us its own emptiness, its
fundamental unreality. But until we know its reality, we can never know its
emptiness. Until we know that the struggle against evil is entirely up to us,
and that the battle will never end, we will never know that, in reality, the
struggle against it is God's business alone, and the battle is ended already. It
was never necessary. It never began. When, as is predicted in the Hindu
scriptures for the end of the cycle, 'a hundred suns arise at once in the sky,' no
nothingness can be located; no shadow appears. When God Himself takes
the field of battle, He encounters no resistance: because only God is.

We must begin the war against the passional soul, whether seen on the
world stage or recognized within, in a state of holy seriousness, fully cogni-
zant of the formidable nature of the evil to be combatted, which initially
seems to cover all things. But how can we know evil *as* evil, if evil is all there
is? What are we comparing it to in order to make that judgement? What
and where is the Light by which we can say 'this is light, and this is darkness?' To ask this question is the first stage of the journey from self-involved
illusion to Divine Reality. This journey can be mapped in 7 stages:

(1) We accept conditions with our ego, by identification. Evil is not real,
or is at most identified with my experience of suffering, which is a meaningless misfortune to be avoided, even if I must become unreal to do so—as if
unreality were a kind of security rather than a name for hell.

(2) Evil is real and external, though basically material. It is not simply my
suffering, but the suffering of others too. We must combat it.

(3) Evil is real, internal, and psychological. It is an expression of the 'herd
instinct', the mass subjectivity which controls our feelings, thoughts, and
actions by means of the 'collective unconscious'. It is combatted through a
psychological understanding of our beliefs and motivations, leading to a de-
identification with the unconscious mores collective of society, Jung's process of 'individuation'.

(4) Evil is real, external, and spiritual. We must witness against it in order not to be seduced by it, but we can't overcome it; only God's representative on the field of history, only the Messiah, can defeat the Antichrist.

(5) Evil is real, spiritual, and transpersonal. It is a product of conscious spiritual entities in rebellion against God. It is combatted through the spiritual power of prayer and exorcism.

(6) Evil is real, internal, spiritual, and a concern of myself alone; it is the activity of the commanding self. It is overcome through the act of forgetting self and remembering God.

(7) Since all the evil of the world is merely my own, it is ultimately unreal. Only God is real; there is no god but God, no reality but the Reality. The Buddha sees only Buddhas. What on lower levels we must still call evil is revealed as necessary to God's manifestation, an expression of His Majesty and His Justice.

But the fact that all events are ultimately acts of God, Who is the Sovereign Good, does not absolve us of personal moral responsibility; we have no right to say 'God made me do it.' 'There needs be evil,' said Jesus, 'but woe to those through whom evil comes.' Nor should taking personal moral responsibility be used as a pretext to deny the reality of demonic influence, any more than we should use our recognition of such influence to conceal the ways in which we are affected by the emotions and belief-systems of collective society. Our concentration on these emotions and belief-systems should not blind us to the apocalyptic events in the world around us, nor should the recognition of apocalyptic signs prevent us from doing what little we can in concrete terms when the opportunity for service arises.

Each higher level of our understanding of evil does not negate those below it, but embraces them. The higher level is the true 'informing context' of the lower, which reveals both its necessary limitations, and its precise role in the scheme of things. Therefore the ultimate context, even for concrete service and political action, is the understanding that all events are acts of God; the 'liturgical' way of action in light of this knowledge is simply to play one's role as God has assigned it, assuming He has also given us the light required to recognize it.

✳ The Esoteric Apocalypse

When consciousness is centered on the plane of the psyche, experiences arising on the material plane are interpreted according to whether they support or threaten our sense of identity, which is psychic. When consciousness begins to be withdrawn from the psychic plane to the plane of Spirit—which, as pure Witness and pure Knowledge, necessarily transcends experience—then all experiences, including sense experiences, are understood as emanating from the psychic level, and known, simultaneously, both as possible temptations and as actual manifestations of God. Insofar as these experiences have the potential of seducing consciousness into a re-identification with the psychic level, thus reinforcing the sense of a limited, subjective experiencer, they are temptations. Insofar as these temptations are resisted, the events in question can no longer be called experiences, but are revealed as aspects, or instances, of the Self-manifestation of the Absolute.

On the psychic level, the world we experience is necessarily interpreted in terms of good and evil. And since consciousness fixed on the psychic level cannot witness that level, the contents of the psyche must appear in 'projected' form as the events of our lives. (For all his metaphysical errors, Carl Jung knew this, teaching that 'whatever is repressed is necessarily projected.') But when consciousness begins its pilgrimage from the level of psyche to the level of Spirit, the psyche emerges from that unconsciousness; it is unveiled before the face of the Spiritual Witness. And when, by virtue of that Witness, all events, including material events, are known as emanating from the psychic plane—just as the psychic plane as a whole is known as a dramatization of those *truths* which reside eternally on the Spiritual plane—then the psychic projections upon the material plane are withdrawn. The world ceases to be an object experienced by an individual subject, and is transformed into a visionary apparition contemplated by the Divine Witness—or, in Buddhist terms, by no one.

As consciousness continues to move from psyche to Spirit, events begin to be seen not as good or evil influences, but as forces which either in fact do, or in fact do not, pull our consciousness to identify them, causing it to abandon the Spiritual level and return to the psychic. This is what Sufis mean when they say that 'the sin of the believer is concupiscence; the sin of the gnostic is heedlessness.' Events apparently good can tempt to heedlessness, just as events apparently evil can support mindfulness and spiritual vigilance.

In terms of intellectual warfare, of the struggle to overcome error and embrace Truth, the shift from psyche to Spirit causes the errors we recognize, in ourselves or others, to manifest themselves directly. As we begin to witness them instead of simply criticizing them or struggling against them, they appear before us; they are concretely embodied and fully enacted. In other words, they become lessons—if, that is, we resist the temptation to identify with them—and an error that is really a lesson is no longer a form of falsehood, but a form of Truth. When error is fully embodied as Truth through our own actions, the result is deep and spontaneous remorse. When error is fully embodied as Truth through the actions of others, the result is deep and spontaneous gratitude.

The motion of consciousness from psyche to Spirit, during which latent errors arise, fully-formed and fully-enacted, until they are revealed as forms of Truth, is the esoteric significance of apocalypse, which means 'revelation'. Physical death is a *symbol* of the death of the ego—of the belief that the human psyche is autonomous and self-created. The end of the world is a *symbol* of the 'recollection' produced by the death of the ego—the gathering together of the scattered fragments of the psyche through withdrawal of the projections of that psyche into the abstract wilderness of matter, energy, space and time.

Experience is inseparable from the sense that someone exists who is capable of having experiences. At the ultimate end of the cycle of manifestation, which is the world—at the ultimate end of the cycle of experience, which is the ego—this 'someone' is confronted by *Kali*, the Black One. She is *Maya*, she is Mahashakti—at once both the unknowable Divine Essence, and every veil that simultaneously hides and reveals this Essence, with absolutely no distinction between them. To the degree that we try to hold on to our life in the face of *Kali*, she takes that life. To the degree that we let go of our life in the face of *Kali*, she *is* that life.

Experience is *Maya*, it is *Shakti*. If we identify with it, it becomes part of *Avidya-maya*, of the stream of God's cosmic manifestation, the ultimate end of which is 'the death of God'. If we break identification with it, it becomes part of *Vidya-maya*, of the stream of God's redeeming and re-integrating mercy, the ultimate end of which is final Liberation from the bonds of contingent existence.

✳ The Apocalyptic Function of Antichrist

Antichrist is the great scapegoat, who extracts from the soul all that is sub-human, abortive and exhausted, leaving the human substance purely receptive to the light of God. He is not the compassionate scapegoat as Christ is, who bears our impurities willingly, thereby demonstrating that even our deepest flight from God actually takes place *in* God, if we only knew it. As foreshadowed in the figure of Judas, he is nothing but the vehicle which transports all that has failed to attain integral form into the fires of annihilation, because it has refused to submit to God's will, refused to be fully *created* by Him, and has therefore never known Him. And here is perhaps the deepest counterfeit the Antichrist is capable of: to portray the sullen, meaningless, barren suffering of the ego unwilling to let go of itself as the self-sacrificial suffering of that divine Love which 'bears all things, believes all things, hopes all things, endures all things.' In the face of Antichrist, his fascination and his horror, his despair and his blindness, and his unutterable boredom, all one need do is choose the Real and reject what never could be real: simply, at whatever cost, like Christ when he overcame Satan in the desert, like the Buddha when he withstood Mara the Tempter, under the tree of Enlightenment, on the adamantine spot.

The Tibetan Buddhists say: 'roll all blames into one.' In the process, the crimes of a cruel and mysterious fate become the fruits of karma, the consequences of the deliberate actions of sentient beings. The karma of all sentient beings becomes my own karma, the structure of my ego. And finally the crimes and sufferings of my ego become the inevitable shape of THE ego, void of all substance in the face of the Absolute. All are forgiven because no one is to blame but him — and 'he' is no one.

The esoteric meaning of the Antichrist is: that there is only one ego. My ego is THE ego; the God Who dwells in my Heart is THE God. When my ego is annihilated, all ego is annihilated, because there is no other ego. When the God in my Heart is unveiled, He is unveiled for everyone, for all beings, because there is only one Heart. When a saint cries out, 'I am the worst of sinners!' the inner meaning is: I am the ONLY sinner. I am Adam eating the forbidden fruit; by the same token, I am Christ suffering the consequences of this act, triumphing over them, and rising up out of the ruins of them. I am the Buddha gaining enlightenment for himself, and thereby for all sentient beings, because in the eyes of the enlightened Buddha there are no such things as 'numberless sentient beings to be enlightened' nor 'the Buddha who vows to enlighten them.' Enlightenment is One. God is One. There is no god but God.

When I first saw the Antichrist, my response was: 'This means that I no longer have a single enemy on this earth. May all beings be well; may all beings be happy.' When Antichrist lived with me in my own house, he perverted my view of God's universe, he whispered accusations against this person or that person, this group or that group; he claimed they were followers of the Antichrist. But when he left my house to go out into the world and spread devastation, when I saw him rising like a shadow over all the earth, not a shred of hatred was left in my heart. He had nothing more to teach me, except his own emptiness, his shadow-nature. By revealing himself as pure shadow he bore witness to the Light, the great penetrating, searching, unveiling, unmanifesting, and healing light of God now breaking over the world. The breaking of that Light is eternal. It is at the core of every moment. The end of the world lies hidden in every moment. The termination of the cycle, the dissolution of all things, the passing away of heaven and earth, the dawning of the new heaven and the new earth, is always there, in time present pregnant with time future, where the whole creation groans to be delivered—until *now*. 'When a man rejects error and embraces truth,' said William Blake, 'a final Judgement passes upon that man.'

The proper use, the specific spiritual practice of apocalyptic times is: To let everything be taken away from us, except the Truth. When Blake cried, 'Whatever can be destroyed must be destroyed!' this is what he meant. Whoever can—with the aid of Heaven—not reverse, but simply *resist* the tremendous centrifugal, scattering, attenuating and sinking forces active at the end of the Aeon, will find that all the dross in his soul, all the sin, all the spiritual heaviness and intellectual darkness of the latter days, has been stolen from him by the Antichrist. He is welcome to it. By a radical catharsis analogous to the one attempted by the Greek playwrights, enacted not on the Athenian but the world stage, and that of the human soul, Almighty God, through the agency of Antichrist—if, that is, we recognize that Deceiver and inwardly resist him—will literally scare the hell out of us. He will burn out sorrow with sorrow and fear with fear, since only in the presence of God's Mercy can we face the full depth of the sorrow and fear all of us feel at the end of the cycle, and witness their essential emptiness. If we can resist despair in all its forms, including violent panic, cold-heartedness, and false luciferian hope, then, after all the karmic residues of the entire cycle have been torn away from us, there we will stand, naked, in utter simplicity, before the face of God. This is the meaning of 'for the sake of the elect those days shall be shortened,' and 'the meek shall inherit the earth.' Whatever in us 'crystallizes', to use one of Schuon's favorite terms, in the presence of Absolute Truth, will be 'gathered into the barns' where the fertile potentials, the 'seed corn' for the next Aeon, are stored. 'He that shall endure to the end, the same shall be saved': he shall be *saved up*. Whatever withstands the end of time stands at the beginning of time. Whatever is beyond time withstands its end. If 'time is the moving image of eternity,' then that in us which remains untouched by time is part of That of which the image is made. The 'New Age' believes that certain 'highly evolved' human beings can survive on earth to become the spiritual and even temporal leaders of the next Golden Age; but this is merely the literalistic counterfeit of the true doctrine. The truth is simply that whatever in us resists the temptation to flee from God by taking refuge in chaotic dissolution—to hide from the destruction of matter, or the fear of this destruction, in matter itself, which is one meaning of 'they shall pray for the mountains to fall and cover them'— but dies instead a vigilant and obedient death before the face of the One Reality, will enter the feast of the Pirs, the Shaikhs, the Tzaddiks, the deified Ancestors who are the fathers and prototypes of all cycles of manifestation, they who are called in the book of *Apocalypse* 'the twenty-four Elders before the Throne of the Lamb.' As it *was* in the end. As it *is* in the beginning.

✲ The Practice of Apocalypse

In my humble opinion, the central spiritual 'gesture' for apocalyptic times is the following:

When you find yourself in a state of fear or grief over the evil of the world, the degeneration of humanity and the ruin of the earth, know that this evil, ruin and degeneration are nothing but the mass resistance of the world to the impending advent of the Mahdi, the Tenth Avatar, the Messiah—and that the fear or grief you are presently experiencing are *your way of participating in that resistance.* Knowing this, simply stop resisting Him, and let the Messiah come. Stop trying to maintain the world in existence by the power of your ego; let it go. Let it end. Let your ego end. You've been fighting off the Messiah: cease hostilities now, 'resist not evil' (which is how your ego experiences Him), lay down your weapons, and let Him break through 'the clouds of heaven', the clouds of individual and collective egotism which have separated earth from its divine Source ever since the fall of man.

I asked my spiritual advisor to comment on the above paragraph, since advising an unknown public on questions of spiritual practice is not something I have either the right or the capacity to do on my own slim authority. His response was, 'Remember, though: the world is perfect.'

In other words: the Messiah is already here. He has always been here. In each spiritual moment, the world comes fresh from the hand of the Creator. As God is perfect, so His expression is perfect—if, that is, we can witness it, with all its wonders and horrors, as His immediate manifestation. This is the real *Revelation*: 'Behold, I make all things new' (Rev. 21:5). May God, through the grace of my Master, grant me the capacity, and the humility, to know this not only with the mind, but with the whole Heart.

I will end this book, as is appropriate, with the words of Frithjof Schuon, from *Light on the Ancient Worlds*, p 49:

> Even believers themselves are for the most part too indifferent to feel concretely that God is not only 'above' us, in 'Heaven', but also 'ahead' of us, at the end of the world, or even simply at the end of our own lives; that we are drawn through life by an inexorable force and that at the end of the course God awaits us; that the world will be submerged and swallowed up one day by an unimaginable irruption of the purely miraculous—unimaginable because surpassing all human experience and standards of measurement. Man cannot possibly draw on his past to bear witness to anything of the kind, any more than a may-fly can expatiate on the alternation of the seasons; the rising of the sun can in no way enter into the habitual sensations of a creature born at midnight whose life will last but a day; the sudden appearance of the orb of the sun, unforeseeable by reference to any analogous phenomenon that had occurred during the long hours of darkness, would seem like an unheard of apocalyptic prodigy. And it is thus that God will come. There will be nothing but this one advent, this one presence, and by it the world of experiences will be shattered.

INDEX

Lightning Source UK Ltd.
Milton Keynes UK
UKOW03f0606190417
299439UK00001B/80/P